The Day's Recipe

Each day when you awaken
Just offer God the day.
Each task that's undertaken
Whether work or play
Offer Him your happiness,
Your cares and troubles, too.
Just tell Him that you don't forget
All He's done for you.
Now, if you follow this recipe
You surely soon will find
Your life will be without a care
and full of bright sunshine.

Marie Arnold, Medford

**5th Printing
November, 2000**

About our cover...

This design depicts what is unique to Minnesota so the pine trees stand majestically over calm lake waters. The trees provide shade and protection to all of God's creatures. Water, baptism's symbol, a sign of rebirth and in our state, it is in abundance for recreation, cool and clean refreshment. The waters branch out and flow in many directions, like the members of the Catholic Daughters of the Americas. The dove of peace rises over the land, trees and waters creating the spirit of love, unity and charity.

ISBN 0-9653975-0-5

POTLUCK

The dictionary defines "potluck" as the regular meal available to a guest for whom no special preparations have been made - whatever the family meal happens to be.

Perhaps the definition of a "Minnesota POTLUCK" might more accurately be described as a group of people of common interest coming together to share a meal to which each has made a contribution in the form of a "dish to pass".

The concept of this POTLUCK follows rather closely - Catholic Daughter members sharing their favorite recipes, which when compiled into a book, constitute a "balanced meal"...making friends and strangers alike welcome and at ease in our homes and communities sharing the true Christian meaning of hospitality.

Zonda Befort, Mazeppa

Potluck for Habitat

Each year the National Officers of the Catholic Daughters of the Americas choose a state or country to "blitz build" a home for Habitat for Humanity. The Catholic Daughters of the state or country in which the home is built provide the "seed" money (minimally one-half of the cost) to build the home, with the National Catholic Daughters providing the rest of the funds.

The first home was built in Oklahoma City, Oklahoma shortly after the disastrous bombing of their Federal Building. Since then, homes have been built in New York, California, Louisiana, and New Jersey.

The Catholic Daughters of Minnesota would very much like to build a Catholic Daughter Habitat House in Minnesota and have been raising funds for that purpose. Approximately one-half of the amount needed has been realized.

With the fifth reprinting of POTLUCK, the Minnesota Catholic Daughters have made a decision to designate the proceeds realized by the state court from that reprinting to the Habitat House in Minnesota Fund. We thank you for purchasing this cookbook and being a special part of helping us realize our dream of building a Habitat House in Minnesota.

Shirley Seyfried, State Regent
Minnesota Catholic Daughters of the Americas

POTLUCK continues

Nearly 20,000 cookbooks have been distributed since our initial printing in 1994. Each edition has included updates relating to our evolving organization. Our hope is that you recognize the good cooks that we are and have learned more about the Catholic Daughters of the Americas in reading through these pages.

God bless and may your kitchens always be warm...
Lois M. Nelson, POTLUCK Project Chair

Minnesota State Officers
2000-2002

State Regent	**Shirley Seyfried** Fergus Falls
First Vice State Regent	**Lois Nelson** Medford
Second Vice State Regent	**Kathy Kennedy** Moorhead
State Secretary	**Zonda Befort** Mazeppa
State Treasurer	**Vicki Boeckman** Elmore
Immediate Past State Regent	**Donna Farrell** Marshall
State Chaplain	**Fr. Rick Lambert** Mahnomen
National Director	**Shirley Ettestad** International Falls

Following are the thirty-one courts that are active in the state of Minnesota with their organizational date and current Court Regents identified:

Organized	Cout Name & City	2000-2002 Regent
1939	Santa Maria #247 Adrian	Mary Ellen Kellen
1974	Our Lady of the Fields #2107 Argyle	Alana Kuznia
1921	Joan of Arc #691 Blue Earth	Shirley Maher

1920	Caledonia #555 Caledonia	Mildred Schmitt
1970	Bishop Schenk #2010 Crookston	Sr. Joyce Selander
1925	Theresa #973 Currie	Delores Schmitt
1964	Holy Rosary #1916 Detroit Lakes	Marg Riordan
1962	St. Margaret #1888 Eveleth	Barbara Turk
1921	St. Mary #615 Fairmont	Virginia Maday
1948	St. Cabrini #1466 Fergus Falls	Phyllis Novak
1921	St. Margaret Mary #605 International Falls	Judy Potter
1924	Little Flower #854 Iona	Joanne Halbur
1924	St. Bernard #866 Lismore	Deborah Lutmer
1970	St. Justin #2020 Mahnomen	Priscilla Staska
1920	St. Rose of Lima #546 Mankato	Joan Landis
1938	St. Joan of Arc #1291 Marshall	Sharon Kinker
1961	St. Mary Peter #1864 Mazeppa-Bellchester	Ellen Huneke
1960	St. Anne #1840 Medford	Cathy Hackett

Year	Parish	Name
1920	St. Mary #509 Moorhead	Rosemary Zurn
1931	Owatonna #1180 Owatonna	Nancy Janke
1920	St. Rita #409 Perham	Dorothy Doll
1945	St. John #1371 Pipestone	Eulialia Koll
1920	Plainview #497 Plainview	Catherine Taubel
1971	St. Cecilia #2025 Red Lake Falls	Gaylene Schmitz
1951	Queen of Peace #1588 Slayton	Glenna Miller
1959	St. Charles #1791 St. Charles	Denise Sackreiter
1959	St. James #1820 St. James	Janet Ziebarth
1952	St. Peter #1601 St. Peter	Audrey Schmitz
1946	Sacred Heart #1424 Waseca	Margaret Zimmerman
1923	Madonna #839 Wilmont	Barbara Springman
1914	Winona #191 Winona	Irene Mulyck

~APPLE DARLINGS~

Take 1 women: Any variety with lots of pulp
any age...
any shape...
any color

Spice with: enthusiasm, concern, love, patience, knowledge, talents, prayer, spirit, faith, ability, action, involvement.

Sweeten with the "JOY" of belonging to C D A

Simmer gently until the aroma of our "Apple Darling" is delicately scented with an "A-peeling" sense of:
caring
sharing
knowing
doing and being.

This "Apple Darling" can be served immediately, but is best when baked in a slow oven until done to perfection; giving a feeling of accomplishment and fulfillment.

HOW SWEET IT IS TO SERVE THE LORD

Lu Heer, Winona

✟ ✟ ✟ ✟ ✟

LIFE'S RECIPE

1 cup of Good Thoughts
1 cup of Kind Deeds
1 cup of Consideration For Others

3 cups of Sacrifice For Others
3 cups of Forgiveness
2 cups of Well Beaten Faults

Mix these thoroughly and add tears of joy and sorrow and sympathy for others. Flavor with little gifts of love. Fold in 4 cups of prayer and faith to lighten other ingredients and raise the texture to great height of Christian living. After pouring all this into your daily life, bake well with the heart of human kindness. Serve with a smile!

Court Saint Margaret Mary, International Falls

TABLE OF CONTENTS

*** Signify quick and easy recipes throughout POTLUCK.
Enjoy!*

~COFFEE IN HEAVEN~

I'm sure there'll be coffee in heaven-
It has such a heavenly smell,
that tickles my sensitive nostrils
With delight that mere words cannot tell.

Wholesome is milk's connotation,
And tea as a drink holds its own,
Water's all right when you're thirsty
But coffee's a class all alone.

Coffee that's strong, aromatic,
Amber-colored and clear as a bell,
That needs no creaming or sugar
A bitter taste to dispel.

Pitkin says life starts at forty
And discernment of tastes for most men,
So I'm sure there'll be coffee in heaven,
For our tastes will be keenest by then.

-by Sister Anne Marie Weinreis

✠ MEMBERSHIP ✠

Are you a Catholic woman and *at least* 18 years of age?
If so, Catholic Daughters is looking for you!! We want you
to be a member of the largest organization of Catholic women
in the Americas!!

The world we live in today is exciting and ever changing.
We have many challenges ahead of us. Catholic Daughters
has motivated thousands of women to meet new challenges
and respond to the teachings of the faith. Our motto, *"Unity
and Charity"* inspires us to work together for those less fortunate.

What do Catholic Daughters do??

We   * feed the hungry
     * clothe the naked
     * care for abused children and battered women
     * combat the evils of abortion and euthanasia
     * help the homeless
     * get involved with our legislators to bring change where
       needed
     * support priests and seminarians
     * provide aid to disaster stricken areas
     * care for the aged and disabled
     * help alcohol and drug abuse victims
     * provide care for AID patients
     * support youth and pro life programs...

AND SO MUCH MORE!!

Right now, someone you know would be delighted if you
extended a Catholic Daughter invitation to them. Encourage
your friend (co-worker, neighbor, mother or daughter-in-law,
sister, etc.) to attend a meeting with you. Let them see first
hand what joy there is in serving Jesus through Catholic
Daughters!!

One Step

One step won't take us very far;
We've got to <u>keep on walking</u>.

One word won't tell folks who we are:
We've got to <u>keep on talking</u>.

One inch won't make us very tall:
We've got to <u>keep on growing</u>.

One little deed won't do it all:
We've got to <u>keep on going</u>!!

For additional information about joining Catholic Daughters, please contact a member or officer of your area court, or contact a member of the State Membership Committee:

Cindy Bullerman
25751 State Hwy 91
Adrian, MN 56110

Cheryl Holzer
Rt #2, Box 69
Perham, MN 56573

Jane Killian
217 Chandler Ave.
Eveleth, MN 55734

Deb Rowekamp
Rt #2, Box 69A
St. Charles, MN 55972

Lois Nelson
Box 161
Medford, MN 55049

APPLE OR FRUIT DIP**

1 (8 oz.) pkg. cream cheese   ¾ cup brown sugar
¼ cup powdered sugar   1 tsp. vanilla

Have cream cheese at room temperature. Beat until creamy. Add sugars and vanilla. Blend well. Refrigerate at least 2 hours. Use with any cut up fruit. Apple slices are especially good.

Anita Bartholome, Bellechester
Wilma Gustaf, Slayton
Teresa Lynch Droogsma, Circle Pines

FRUIT DIP

1 jar marshmallow creme   1 lg. can crushed pineapple,
1 carton Cool Whip   drained

Mix marshmallow creme, Cool Whip and a little bit of pineapple juice. Serve with cut up fruits of your choice (chunks and slices of fruit, such as fresh pineapple, cantaloupe, honeydew, watermelon, grapes, etc.) Nice served with sweet breads.

Viola Maday, Fairmont

ARTICHOKE SPREAD

2 (8 oz.) cans artichoke hearts   1 cup Parmesan cheese
1 cup mayonnaise   1 tsp. garlic salt

Mix and put in lightly greased casserole dish. Top with more Parmesan cheese. Bake at 325° for 25 to 30 minutes. Serve with crackers.

Rozie Ochry, Detroit Lakes
District Deputy, 1988-1992
Donna Armstrong, Fergus Falls

HOMEMADE BARBECUE SAUCE

½ cup brown sugar   ½ cup vinegar, dark or white
½ cup ketchup   1 Tbsp. mustard, salad type
1 Tbsp. onion, finely chopped   Salt and pepper

Mix together. Pour onto ribs, pork chops or on top of meat loaf. Recipe can be doubled and balance can be kept in refrigerator.

Margaret Kochmann, Mahnomen

BACON AND SWISS APPETIZERS

1 pkg. refrigerated crescent rolls
1½ cups (6 oz.) shredded Swiss
  cheese
3 eggs, slightly beaten
¾ cup milk
1 Tbsp. chopped onion
8 slices bacon, cooked and
  crumbled
1 Tbsp. parsley flakes

Separate rolls and pat into bottom of a 9x13 inch pan. Overlap edges and come up slightly on the sides of the pan. Sprinkle cheese over top of dough. Combine eggs, milk and onion. Pour over cheese. Sprinkle with bacon and parsley. Bake at 425° for 15 minutes. Cut into 2 inch squares. Serve warm.

Karen Riopelle, Argyle

FROZEN BANANAS

2 Tbsp. peanut butter
½ cup evaporated skim milk
2 bananas, cut in half
Chopped nuts or crunchy bran
  cereal

Mix peanut butter with milk until it is the consistency of egg whites. Roll bananas in peanut butter mixture, then roll in nuts and/or cereal. Place in freezer until frozen. Serves 4.

Jane Rowe, Owatonna

FLAT BREAD APPETIZERS

1 stick butter or margarine,
  softened
½ cup grated Parmesan cheese
2 tsp. Beau Monde seasoning
Dash of pepper
1 rounded tsp. parsley flakes
Crisp flat bread (Kavli Crisp)

Mix first 5 ingredients and spread on flat bread. Bake at 350° for 3 to 4 minutes or until lightly browned.

Carol Haubrich, Pipestone

BREAD CUPS

12 slices bread
1 can tuna or ham
1 can mushroom soup
½ cup Cheddar cheese
1 egg
1 Tbsp. Worcestershire sauce
1½ tsp. lemon juice
½ cup soft bread crumbs
1 sm. onion, chopped fine
Salt and pepper to taste

Trim crust from bread and cut in 4 pieces. Butter both sides. Mix all the other ingredients together. Put buttered bread squares in small muffin pan. Add 1 tablespoon mixture on top of bread. Bake at 350° for 30 minutes. Can be frozen after baking.

Lil Robertson, Argyle

HOT BROCCOLI DIP

1 (8 oz.) pkg. cream cheese
1 (10 oz.) can mushroom soup
1 (8 oz.) pkg. shredded Cheddar
cheese
1 (10 oz.) pkg. frozen chopped
broccoli, thawed

Combine all ingredients in a casserole dish. Microwave at 70% power setting for 8 minutes. For a double recipe, microwave for 12 minutes. Serve with crackers. May combine all ingredients in a saucepan. Cook over medium-low heat, stirring constantly until all ingredients are combined.

Lucretia Heer, Winona
District Deputy, 1990-1994

COTTAGE CHEESE DILL DIP

²/₃ cup cottage cheese
Lemon juice to taste
2 Tbsp. dill weed
Pepper and paprika to taste

Blend until smooth. 150 calories.
Variations: Experiment with different herbs.

Mary Steinbach, Blue Earth

CREAM CHEESE BALL

2 (8 oz.) pkgs. cream cheese
1 stick butter or margarine
4 cloves garlic, crushed
1 bunch green onions, finely
chopped (approx. 1 cup,
tops and all)
2 Tbsp. parsley, chopped*
1 cup chopped pecans

*If fresh parsley is not available, substitute with dry parsley.
Mix all ingredients. Shape into a ball. Chill several hours or overnight. Garnish with parsley and serve with Ritz crackers or melba rounds.

Eunice R. Riles, Baton Rouge, LA
First Vice National Regent, 1994-present
Served on National Board since 1982, a total of 12 years

FAVORITE DIP

1 (3 oz.) pkg. cream cheese
½ cup chopped pecans
¹/₈ cup chopped green pepper
1 Tbsp. chopped onion
½ cup crushed pineapple

Blend together well; serve with crackers or chips. If it seems too solid for dipping, add a little pineapple juice or sour cream.

Marian Schloegel, Winona

CHEESE BALL

1 (8 oz.) pkg. cream cheese, softened	Black olives
1 stick margarine or butter	Onion flakes
Green olives	Assorted crackers

Mix cream cheese and margarine or butter. Add remaining ingredients. Can be shaped into a ball or served from a suitable bowl. Delicious on crackers!

Suzanne Lonneman, Adrian

MEXICAN DIP

1 (8 oz.) pkg. cream cheese	1 (8 oz.) carton sour cream
1 tsp. Lawry's seasoned salt	1 pkg. taco seasoning
1 (8 oz.) jar mild taco sauce	1 lb. browned ground beef

Mix cheese, sour cream and salt together and spread on 12 to 14 inch platter. Next, spread on layer of taco sauce, then add the taco-seasoned beef, following instructions on seasoning packet for meat. Top with chopped lettuce, tomatoes, cheese, onions, black olives (whatever you like). Serve with tortilla chips.

Jane Kemper, Waubun

BAKED SLO BALL DIP

1 lg. French round bread	2 Tbsp. beer
2 (8 oz.) pkgs. cream cheese, softened	2 tsp. Worcestershire sauce
3 (6½ oz.) cans chopped clams, drained (save ¼ cup liquid)	2 tsp. lemon juice
	1 tsp. Tabasco sauce
2 Tbsp. grated onion	½ tsp. salt

*Hollow out bread and save cubes. Crust should be 1½ to 2 inches thick. Blend all other ingredients well and put in bread bowl. Wrap in foil and bake at 250° for 3 hours. Heat bread cubes about 3 minutes and serve with dip.

Kathy Kennedy, Moorhead
State Secretary, 1992-1996

CRAB DIP**

Cover plate or tray with **softened cream cheese**. Cover cheese with **Heinz cocktail sauce**. Top with cut up **crab**. Serve with crackers. Ritz or Hi-Ho work well.

Jane Kemper, Waubun

CRAB DIP

1 (8 oz.) pkg. cream cheese
¼ cup mayonnaise
¼ tsp. garlic powder
½ tsp. onion powder
2 tsp. sugar
2 tsp. prepared mustard
1 lb. sea legs, chopped
½ cup celery, chopped fine

Mix cream cheese, mayonnaise, garlic powder, onion powder, sugar and mustard. Mix until well blended. Add sea legs and celery. Serve with crackers or croissants. Delicious.

Leone M. Brule, Crookston

BAR-B-Q-CHICKEN WINGS

2 lbs. chicken wings
2 Tbsp. soy sauce
2 Tbsp. sugar
Dash of garlic powder
2 Tbsp. ketchup

Cut wings into 3 sections, discard tips. Mix remaining ingredients and pour over chicken in glass container. Marinate overnight in refrigerator. Spread on baking pan. Bake at 350° for 1 hour, brushing with marinade if wings appear to be drying.

Clari Miller, International Falls

CHICKEN TIDBITS**

10 chicken breasts
½ to 1 cup butter, melted
24 Ritz crackers, crushed
¾ cup Parmesan cheese
¾ cup chopped pecans
½ tsp. salt
2 tsp. sweet basil

Cut chicken into 1½ inch chunks. Dip in melted butter. Combine crackers, cheese, pecans, salt and basil. Roll chicken into mixture, coating well. Place on cookie sheet. Bake at 325° for 25 minutes or until browned. These can be prepared ahead of time, placed on cookie sheet, and frozen. When frozen, place in plastic bag to conserve moisture. Thaw before baking.

Imelda Millard, International Falls

CHICKEN WINGS

3 lbs. chicken wings
⅓ cup soy sauce
3 Tbsp. white vinegar
3 Tbsp. white sugar
3 Tbsp. brown sugar
1 tsp. ground ginger
1 clove garlic

Remove tips from wings and separate into two pieces. Marinate in the remaining ingredients overnight or for a few hours. Line a baking pan with foil. Spread chicken wings in pan and bake at 350° for 1 hour.

Irene Streit, Fairmont

SHANGHAI CHICKEN WINGS

10 to 20 chicken wings	1 tsp. garlic powder
1 cup water	1 tsp. ginger
1 cup soy sauce	¼ cup unsweetened pineapple
1 cup sugar	juice
¼ cup cooking oil	

Set chicken wings aside. Mix rest of ingredients in a bowl. Add chicken wings and marinate overnight, at least 8 hours. Bake at 350° for 1½ hours. Chicken wings are now ready to be served; however, they can be put into a slow cooker on low heat until ready to be served.

Beverly Pawloski, Argyle
Judy Potter, International Falls

SEASONED OYSTER CRACKERS**

2 (12 oz.) pkgs. oyster crackers	½ tsp. dill weed seasoning
1 pkg. Hidden Valley dry dressing	½ tsp. garlic salt
½ tsp. lemon pepper seasoning	1 cup corn oil

Put all ingredients, except corn oil, in a brown paper bag. Pour warm corn oil, a little at a time, in the bag and shake well. Put in the microwave for 2 minutes on low.

Marie Pelzel, Caledonia
Elaine Gilmore, Fairmont

GRANDMA'S NEWEST SNACK (CHEX MIX)

3 cups rice, corn, or wheat squares	1 tsp. cinnamon
	¼ tsp. nutmeg
1 cup dry roasted peanuts or mixed nuts	½ cup chocolate candy-coated pieces
3 Tbsp. margarine or butter, melted	½ cup unsalted popcorn, popped

Combine cereal and nuts in an ungreased 9x13 inch baking pan. Combine margarine, cinnamon and nutmeg; mix well. Drizzle evenly over cereal mixture. Toss well. Bake in preheated 350° oven for 14 to 16 minutes or until browned and crisp, tossing once. Let cool completely. Stir in candy and popcorn. Makes 4½ cups snack mix.

Ann Rademaker, Blue Earth

WORLD FAMOUS CHEX MIX

2 cups butter
½ box Cheerios (12 to 16 oz.)
½ box Rice Chex (12 to 16 oz.)
½ box Corn Chex (12 to 16 oz.)
½ box Wheat Chex (12 to 16 oz.)
1 (12 oz.) box Pretzel sticks

¼ cup Worcestershire sauce
1 Tbsp. garlic powder
1 Tbsp. onion powder
1 Tbsp. celery salt
1 can mixed nuts

Mix all ingredients and bake at 200° for 2 hours, stirring every 15 minutes. Adjust amounts of cereals per family tastes.
Variation: Mary adds 5 oz. Cheerios, 16 oz. peanuts, and 16 oz. cashews or pecans.

Kathryn Gillis, Faribault
Mary Burmeister, Winona

CAJUN PARTY MIX

2½ cups Corn Chex cereal
2 cups Rice Chex cereal
2 cups Crispix cereal
1 cup mixed nuts
1 cup mini pretzels
1 Tbsp. dried parsley

½ cup melted butter
1 tsp. celery salt
1 tsp. garlic powder
¼ to ½ tsp. cayenne pepper
¼ tsp. hot pepper sauce

Combine cereals, nuts and pretzels. Pour into a 15x10x1 inch pan. Mix remaining ingredients and pour over cereals; mix. Bake at 250° for 40 to 60 minutes, stirring every 15 minutes. Yields 8 cups.

Veronica Knoll, Argyle

PUPPY CHOW

1 cup peanut butter
1 cup butter or margarine
1 (12 oz.) pkg. chocolate chips

1 cup dry roasted peanuts
12 oz. Wheat or Rice Chex
1 Tbsp. vanilla

Melt peanut butter, butter or margarine and chocolate chips together. Pour over peanuts and Chex. Put gradually into brown paper bag with powdered sugar and shake to coat.

Barbara Kahle, New Ulm

* * * * * * * *

Apart from me you can do nothing. John 15:5
Carol Rupp, Adrain

MINIATURE CREAM PUFFS

Cream Puffs:

1 cup water

½ cup butter or margarine

1 cup flour

4 eggs

Heat water and butter to rolling boil in saucepan. Stir in flour. Stir vigorously over low heat until mixture forms a ball, about 1 minute. Remove from heat. Beat eggs thoroughly, one at a time. Beat until smooth. Drop dough by slightly rounded teaspoonfuls onto ungreased baking sheet. Bake at 400° for 25 minutes or until golden brown and dry. Remove from baking sheet and cool. Makes 70 puffs. Fill with one of the following fillings.

Chicken Filling:

3 cups cooked chicken or turkey, minced

½ cup celery, finely chopped

¼ cup green olives, chopped

¾ cup mayonnaise

Hawaiian Filling For Cream Puffs:

2 cups ground cooked ham

1 (8¾ oz.) can crushed pineapple

½ cup celery, chopped fine

½ cup sour cream

¼ tsp. paprika

⅛ tsp. pepper

⅛ tsp. cloves

Salt to taste

Mix all ingredients for the filling you choose. This is a big favorite at our Spring Salad Bar Luncheon every year. Fill each cream puff by slitting partially crosswise and place a heaping spoonful of mixture in each.

Rose Stoltman, Argyle

Mary Ann Deschene, Argyle

CUCUMBER SANDWICHES (OPEN FACE)

1 cup sour cream or plain yogurt

2 (8 oz.) pkgs. cream cheese

½ cup chopped dill pickle

Cocktail rye bread

Cucumber sliced very thin

Dill weed

Mix the cream cheese, sour cream and dill pickles. Spread mixture on rye slices. Top with cucumber slice and sprinkle with dill weed. Stack in container with freezer waxed paper in between. Make up 2 days ahead.

Mary Bundy, Winona

* * * * * * * *

Lord, at the start of this new year help me to live it boldly and, by the power of God, to be a sign of hope to those around me.

Lucille Taylor, Adrian

DILL DIP FOR VEGETABLES

2 cups sour cream
1 cup mayonnaise
½ Tbsp. dill weed
2 Tbsp. onion, minced
1 tsp. seasoning salt
½ Tbsp. parsley flakes, minced

Mix all ingredients and store in a covered container in refrigerator. Good with carrots, celery, cauliflower, broccoli, or any fresh vegetables.

Bunny Janovsky, St. James

DILL DIP

⅔ cup mayonnaise
(not Miracle Whip)
⅔ cup sour cream
1 Tbsp. instant minced onion
1 Tbsp. parsley
1 Tbsp. dill weed
1 tsp. Beau Monde seasoning

Blend all ingredients; set aside for several hours. Flavors blend, so do not use fresh onion or parsley. Serve with vegetables. Very good.

Ottilia Winter, Iron

DRIED BEEF DIP

1 (8 oz.) pkg. cream cheese
2 Tbsp. Miracle Whip
¼ cup stuffed olives, chopped if desired
1 (3 oz.) jar dried beef, chopped
Onion salt to taste

Use with vegetables or chips. Also with crackers.

Loretta Chisholm, Ada

CHAMPAGNE FRUIT COMPOTE

1 qt. strawberries
2 oranges, peeled and sectioned
2 kiwi fruit
1½ cups red or green grapes
2 to 3 Tbsp. sugar
1½ cups champagne (½ bottle)

In a bowl, combine fruit and sugar. Cover and chill. Just before serving, pour champagne over fruit. You may use any other fruit also. Use 7-Up if you prefer instead of the champagne.

Myrna Murphy Ventrucci, Eveleth

* * * * * * * *

All things bright and beautiful,
All creatures great and small
All things wise and wonderful,
The Lord God made them all.
Alice Reiners, St. Louis Park

FRUIT PIZZA

Crust:

2 cups flour   ½ cup powdered sugar
1 cup butter

Blend ingredients and press in pizza pan. Bake at 350° for 15 minutes.

Filling:

1 (8 oz.) pkg. cream cheese,   1 cup Cool Whip
  softened   1 tsp. vanilla
½ cup powdered sugar   1 tsp. almond flavoring

Mix ingredients and spread on cooled crust. Top with your favorite **fruits** (grapes, pears, apples, kiwi, blueberries, strawberries, raspberries, peaches, bananas, etc.)

Jackie Svenby, Medford

FRUIT CUP

2 Tbsp. sugar   1 (14½ oz.) can apricot halves,
3 Tbsp. minute tapioca   undrained
2½ cups water   1 (11 oz.) can mandarin oranges,
1 (6 oz.) can concentrated   drained
  frozen orange juice   1 (20 oz.) can crushed pineapple,
1 Tbsp. lemon juice   undrained
1 (16 oz.) pkg. frozen peaches   3 bananas, sliced
1 (16 oz.) pkg. frozen strawberries

Combine sugar, tapioca and water in medium saucepan. Bring to boil and cook until slightly thickened. Cool. Pour into very large mixing bowl. Add undiluted orange juice concentrate and lemon juice. Add the fruit. Spoon into plastic cups. Freeze. Remove from freezer about 1½ hours before serving. Makes about 16 (8 oz.) servings. Just about any fruit, fresh or frozen, can be substituted for the above. Gingerale can also be added just before serving.

Jane Armon, Blue Earth

GARLIC STICKS

10 day old hot dog buns,   1 stick butter or margarine
  cut in half lengthwise   ¼ tsp. garlic powder

Melt butter and add garlic powder. Roll bun sticks in butter and place on cookie sheet. Bake at 200° for 2 hours, one hour on each side.

Carol Haubrich, Pipestone

HAM BALLS

1 lb. ground ham	2 eggs, well beaten
1½ lbs. ground pork	1 cup milk
2 cups bread crumbs	

Combine and form into about 36 medium size balls. Arrange in baking dish and pour the following mixture over meat balls.

1 cup brown sugar	½ cup vinegar
1 Tbsp. dry mustard	½ cup water

Bake at 325° for 1 hour, turning balls after 30 minutes.

Cecelia Spartz, Slayton

CLOVER HONEY

10 cups sugar	1 tsp. alum
2½ cups water	

Bring to a boil; turn down heat and simmer for 10 minutes. Remove from heat and add **30 white clover blossoms** and **18 purple clover blossoms**. Let clover soak in sugar mix for 10 minutes. Strain through cheese cloth; pour in jars and seal. Makes about 4 pints. DO NOT WASH CLOVER. Pick blossoms right after a rain.

Renie Bzdok Hall, Baudette

RHUBARB-BLUEBERRY JAM

7 cups diced rhubarb	2 (3 oz.) boxes strawberry or
4 cups sugar	raspberry jello
1 can blueberry pie filling	

Place rhubarb in a large kettle. Turn on low until it is really juicy, then add the sugar; mix well and bring to a boil for 8 minutes. Add the pie filling and boil for 2 minutes. Add the 2 boxes of jello. Stir well and remove from the stove immediately. Pour into jars. Store in the refrigerator after cooled.

Variation: Helen suggests substituting apricot pie filling with apricot jello.

Dorothea A. Hadlick, Delavan
State Treasurer, 1980-1984
District Deputy, 1972-1978
Agnes Pfaffinger, Blue Earth
Helen McCabe, Caledonia

BLUEBERRY JAM

4 cups blueberries, washed and cleaned	2 cups sugar
	1 (3 oz.) pkg. lemon gelatin

Crush cleaned berries in a large 3 quart pot. Add sugar and gelatin. Bring to a full boil. Boil hard for 2 minutes, stirring constantly. Pour into sterilized jars and seal or freeze after 24 hours.

Margaret Tri, Mazeppa

21

STRAWBERRY JELLY

3 cups fresh, clean strawberries   3 cups sugar

Combine strawberries and 1 cup sugar. Bring slowly to a boil and boil for 3 minutes, then add 1 cup sugar and boil another 3 minutes. Add 1 cup sugar and boil for another 3 minutes. Turn fire off and stir to dissolve. Pour into a 9x13 inch pan and let stand for 8 hours. Stir frequently. Pour into clean jars and freeze.

Beverly Schreier, Currie

ZUCCHINI JAM

6 cups zucchini, peeled and grated
¼ cup water
6 cups sugar
1 cup crushed pineapple and juice
1 (6 oz.) box apricot jello

Cook zucchini in water until transparent. Add sugar and pineapple. Boil 6 minutes and add jello. Put in jars. This can also be frozen.

Shirley Sundby, Argyle

JEZZABELL SAUCE

1 (16 oz.) jar apple jelly
1 (16 oz.) jar pineapple preserve (ice cream topping)
1 sm. whole can dry mustard
1 sm. (8 oz.) jar horseradish
1 Tbsp. cracked ground pepper

Blend ingredients until well blended. Enough to use over 3 blocks of cream cheese (8 oz.) It also keeps well in the refrigerator. Good to have on hand during the holidays.

Olive Hastad, Tempe, AZ
Vice State Regent, 1962-1966
State Regent, 1966-1970
National Director, 1970-1974

MEATBALLS IN SAUCE

2 lbs. ground beef
1 pkg. dry Lipton onion soup mix
3 eggs
1 cup bread crumbs or croutons, crushed

Combine beef, soup, eggs, and crumbs and make into meatballs. Bake at 325° for 30 minutes.

Sauce:
1 (12 oz.) bottle chili sauce
1 (12 oz.) bottle water
1 can whole cranberry sauce
1 cup brown sugar

Combine in saucepan and bring to a boil. Pour over meatballs in a crockpot or roaster. Heat at 250° for 4 hours.

Lila McGill, Winona

SWEET AND SOUR MEATBALLS

2 lbs. ground beef	½ tsp. pepper
2 eggs	½ tsp. garlic powder
½ cup cracker crumbs	1 bottle chili sauce
½ cup water	½ cup grape jelly
½ tsp. salt	2 Tbsp. lemon juice

Combine beef, eggs, cracker crumbs and water. Mix and add spices. Form into small balls. Brown on cookie sheet at 400° for approximately 15 minutes. Heat chili sauce, grape jelly and lemon juice. Put meatballs in crockpot. Pour sauce over. Heat until good and hot. Makes approximately 48 small meatballs. Sauce is also delicious with cocktail weiners.

Mary Johoda, Moorhead
Jo Elijah, New Ulm

HOT PECAN DIP

½ cup chopped pecans	½ tsp. garlic salt
2 tsp. butter	¼ tsp. pepper
½ tsp. salt	½ cup sour cream
1 (3 oz.) pkg. chopped dried beef	¼ cup chopped green pepper
2 tsp. milk	1 (8 oz.) pkg. cream cheese
1 sm. onion, chopped	

Toast pecans in butter and salt. Whip remaining ingredients together. Put in an 8 inch square pan or pie plate. Sprinkle pecans on top. Bake at 350° for 20 minutes. Serve with crackers and vegetables.

Variation: Use ½ cup macadamia nuts instead of pecans.

Rozie Ochry, Detroit Lakes
District Deputy, 1988-1992

MUSTARD SAUCE FOR HAM

½ cup light brown sugar, firmly packed	2 eggs
¼ cup prepared mustard	2 Tbsp. butter or margarine
	¼ cup cider vinegar

In small saucepan, beat first 4 ingredients with rotary beater, then add the cider vinegar. Cook on low heat, stirring constantly until slightly thickened, about 10 minutes. Cool at room temperature or refrigerate before serving. Will keep for weeks in refrigerator.

Phyllis Sheridan, Crookston

CALIFORNIA NACHOS

1 can refried beans	4 or 5 green onions, sliced
Tortilla chips	1 tomato, chopped
1 (4 oz.) pkg. Cheddar cheese, shredded	Black olives, sliced
	Sour cream
1 (4 oz.) pkg. Monterey Jack cheese, shredded	Guacamole

Heat refried beans until spreadable. Meanwhile, spread tortilla chips on large cookie sheet. Spread heated beans over chips. Layer cheese, onions and tomatoes over chips. Bake at 250° for 20 minutes. Top with black olives and serve with sour cream and guacamole.

Guacamole:

2 or 3 ripe avocados	1 tsp. lemon juice
¼ cup chopped onion	Salt and pepper to taste
1 chopped tomato	

Put avocado pit in guacamole to keep it from turning brown. Refrigerate.

Note: This dish can be served as a meal by adding 1 pound browned ground beef.

Colleen Bents, Rushmore

SUPER SUPPER NACHO DIP

1 lb. hamburger	1 (10 oz.) pkg. Cheddar cheese, shredded
1 med. onion, chopped	
1 can refried beans	Ripe olives, as desired
1 (16 oz.) jar mild to medium salsa	Diced green chilies, as desired
	Sour cream, as desired

Brown hamburger with onions. Spread refried beans on bottom of a 9x13 inch pan. Alternate layers with hamburger, salsa, and shredded cheese. Bake at 350° until cheese melts. Top with ripe olives, diced green chilies, and sour cream. Serve with Tostitos, Doritos, or crackers.

Joanne Halbur, Iona

RANDY'S NACHO DIP

1 lb. hamburger	1 lb. mild Mexican Velveeta cheese, sliced
1 pkg. taco seasoning	
1 can Hormel chili without beans	1 bottle medium Ortega taco sauce

Brown hamburger. Add taco seasoning and put in crockpot. Add rest of ingredients and let cook until all cheese is melted and mixture is hot.

Lilianna St. Aubin, Marshall

24

ORANGE CREAM FRUIT DIP

1 (16 oz.) carton light sour cream 1 Tbsp. orange juice
2 Tbsp. brown sugar, firmly 1 Tbsp. grated orange peel
   packed Fresh fruit, cut up
Stir all ingredients except fruit. Cover, refrigerate at least 2 hours.
Serve with fresh fruit. Yield: 2 cups.

Anita Bartholome, Bellechester

ORANGE FUN POPS

1 (6 oz.) can orange juice 1 cup plain low-fat yogurt
   concentrate 1 tsp. yogurt
1 (6 oz.) can water
Blend all ingredients and pour into ice cube trays. Put a drink-
ing straw (cut) into each cube. Freeze several hours.

Veronica Tramel, Morristown

PICKLED PIKE

1 qt. cut up fish fillets ½ cup iodized salt
Cover with **vinegar** and let stand in refrigerator for 5 days. Stir
everyday. Last day, drain and wash in cold clear water. Let stand
in cold water for 45 minutes. Boil 212°, **1 quart white vinegar** and **2
cups sugar** when cool to 106°. Add **2 tablespoons mixed pickling
spices** (no cinnamon bark); when cold, add **2 tablespoons sweet
wine** (Boone's strawberry wine). Slice **onions** as much as you like.
Add to fish and pour the COLD syrup over fish. Keep in refrigerator. Cut fish into ½ inch wide strips.

Dolores Zammert, Euclid

EASY BEET PICKLES

2 cans whole tiny beets 1 cup beet juice
½ cup white vinegar 1 stick cinnamon
1 cup sugar
Drain beets and save juice. Place beets in quart jar. Combine
remaining ingredients, bring to boil, pour over beets and refrigerate. Add water to beet juice to make one cup, if necessary.
Note: This is an economical, easy way to make beet pickles
when garden-produced beets are unavailable.

Ann Coulombe, International Falls

BEET PICKLES

Beets
3 cups sugar
3 cups vinegar
3 cups water

1 Tbsp. salt
1 Tbsp. mixed spices (I tie this
    with the salt)

Cook beets and leave standing until cold. Peel them and cut any size you wish. Fill the jars, then pour on juice and seal. Very good.

Esther Echternach, New Richland

BOHEMIAN DILL PICKLES

Onion
Fresh dill
Garlic
Celery
Cucumbers
Sugar

Alum
10 cups water
6 cups vinegar (Heinz apple
    cider ONLY)
¾ cup salt

Put 1 slice of onion in bottom of jar, 1 head of dill, garlic, and 2 pieces of celery. Pack jar with small cucumbers. Add 1 tablespoon sugar and ⅛ teaspoon alum. Heat the water, vinegar and salt to a boil. Pour over cucumbers and seal.

Ione Gonsorowski, Thief River Falls

SWEET DILL PICKLES

1 qt. dill pickles
3 cups sugar

⅔ cup vinegar
2 Tbsp. mixed pickling spice

Combine sugar, vinegar and spice. Bring to a boil and boil for 1 minute. Cool slightly. Drain pickles (slice if necessary). Repack in jar. Strain warm syrup and pour over pickles. Refrigerate for 1 week before using.

Margaret Carr Guerber, Blue Earth

MOM'S SWEET DILLS

1 cup sugar
1 cup water
1 cup vinegar

1½ tsp. salt
Cucumbers, fairly large
Sterilized jars/covers

Boil first 4 ingredients up good. Split cucumbers in sections lengthwise and put in jars with sprig of dill on top. Pour boiling hot liquid of cucumbers in jars. Seal jars and leave in cooker until water comes to a boil, then take out.

Michele Maher Ritter, Winnebago

ICE BOX PICKLES

1 gal. pickles, cut thin	¼ cup salt
2 onions	1 tsp. tumeric
3 cups white sugar	1 Tbsp. celery seed
3 cups white vinegar	1 Tbsp. mustard seed

Mix all ingredients and store in refrigerator. Enjoy.

Betty Schaffer, Currie

REFRIGERATOR PICKLES

7 cups cucumbers or zucchini, unpeeled and thinly sliced	1 cup sugar
	2 Tbsp. salt
½ to 1 cup chopped onions	1 tsp. celery seed
1 cup vinegar	1 tsp. dill weed

No cooking. Mix ingredients in large jar and keep in refrigerator, loosely covered. Will keep indefinitely.

Clarise Miller, Winona

POPCORN CAKE

6 qts. popped popcorn	½ cup margarine
6 oz. Spanish peanuts	½ cup oil
1 lb. gumdrops	1 lb. marshmallows

Combine popcorn, peanuts and gumdrops in a large pan. Melt margarine, oil and marshmallows. Pour over dry mixture and stir. Pack hard into a greased bundt pan or angel food cake pan. Cool. Slice with a bread knife.

Bonnie Bartlett, St. Peter

REUBEN APPETIZERS

30 slices party rye	¼ cup Thousand Island dressing
½ lb. corned beef	Swiss cheese
1 (8 oz.) can sauerkraut, well drained	

Put rye on cookie sheet. Top with corned beef, sauerkraut, dressing and cheese. Place in oven under broiler, 6 inches from heat. Heat 2 to 3 minutes until cheese melts.

Vivian (Vi) Larson, Argyle

27

REUBEN DIP

1 cup mayonnaise
1 sm. chopped onion
1 (13 oz.) can sauerkraut, drained

2 (2½ oz.) pkgs. chipped or corned beef
2 cups shredded Swiss cheese
Rye bread or rye crackers

Mix all ingredients in casserole dish. Bake, uncovered, at 350° for 30 to 40 minutes (until brown). Serve with snack size rye bread or rye crackers.

Jan Herda, Medford

SALMON CHEESE BALL

1 (8 oz.) pkg. cream cheese
1 (7 oz.) can salmon
1 Tbsp. lemon juice
1 tsp. Liquid Smoke

1 chopped onion
1 tsp. horseradish
Chopped walnuts
Parsley Flakes

Soften cheese and add ingredients and roll into a ball. Roll cheeseball in chopped walnuts and parsley flakes.

Roberta Tissek, St. Paul
Ruth Dornack, Wabasha

SAUSAGE BALLS**

1 lb. hot Italian sausage
1 lb. sharp Cheddar cheese

3 cups Bisquick

Remove casing from sausage and mix with shredded cheese and Bisquick until well blended. Shape into marble-sized balls and bake on ungreased sheet at 350° for 20 minutes. Makes about 120 to 130 balls. Can be frozen. Reheat about 10 minutes in preheated oven.

Beulah Scheurer, Mankato

FRESH SALSA**

6 to 8 garden fresh tomatoes
2 to 3 (4 oz.) cans diced green chilies
½ cup minced onion
2 to 4 cloves garlic, crushed

Salt to taste
1½ tsp. sugar
1 Tbsp. vinegar
1 tsp. Cilantro, optional

Peel tomatoes by placing in boiling water for 1 minute; plunge into cold water. Slip off skin with knife point. Seed and dice tomatoes after cool. Add all ingredients and mix well. Let stand for at least 30 minutes for the flavors to blend. Serve with chips. Refrigerate leftovers.

Pam Wolter, St. Charles
State Youth Chair, 1994-1996

SALSA

30 tomatoes, unpeeled	3 Tbsp. Accent
6 green peppers	4 Tbsp. vinegar
1 med. zucchini	4 Tbsp. salt
4 lg. onions	1 tsp. pepper
6 hot peppers	3 sm. cans tomato paste
12 toes garlic	

Grind first 6 ingredients. Add other ingredients and cook 10 to 15 minutes. Put in jars and seal. Hot water bath for 5 minutes. Yield is about 9 pints.

Sandy Schneider, International Falls

CLUB SAUCE

12 lg. tomatoes	2 cups sugar
6 lg. bell peppers, chopped	1 cup vinegar
2 Tbsp. salt	3 onions, chopped fine

Combine ingredients in pot; bring to a boil, then simmer for 2½ hours, uncovered, stirring occasionally. Seal in while hot in hot sterilized jars.

Judy Schultz, St. James

MAKE YOUR OWN SEASONING SALT

1 cup salt	1 tsp. onion powder
1 tsp. thyme	1 tsp. curry powder
1 tsp. oregano	2 tsp. dry mustard
1 tsp. garlic powder	2 tsp. paprika

Combine all ingredients and blend well. Store in jar with airtight closure.

Pat Rivard, Argyle

SEA LEGS OR LOBSTER DIP

1 (8 oz.) pkg. cream cheese	1 tsp. sugar
¼ cup mayonnaise	Dash of salt
1 tsp. grated onion	5 oz. crab (sea legs) or fresh
Dash of garlic salt	lobster, cubed
1 tsp. prepared mustard	3 Tbsp. dry white wine, optional

In microwave, melt cream cheese. Blend in all ingredients, except lobster and wine. Blend well. Add lobster and gradually stir in wine. Keep warm in chafing dish or fondue pot. Serve with crackers or bread sticks.

Clarice Vik, Crookston

SHRIMP SPREAD

1 can tomato soup
1 (8 oz.) pkg. cream cheese
1 pkg. Knox gelatin
½ cup chopped celery
½ cup chopped onion
½ cup chopped green pepper
1 cup mayonnaise
2 cans deveined shrimp

Heat soup and cream cheese over low heat. Dissolve gelatin in ¼ cup cold water, then add to soup mixture. Add vegetables and mayonnaise. Fold in shrimp and pour into mold. Very good with crackers for an appetizer.

Rosie McGinty, Holland

SHRIMP APPETIZER PLATTER

1 (8 oz.) pkg. cream cheese
½ cup dairy sour cream
¼ cup mayonnaise
2 cans broken shrimp, rinsed and drained
1 cup seafood sauce
2 cups shredded Mozzarella cheese
1 green pepper, chopped
3 green onions, chopped
1 lg. tomato, diced

Combine cream cheese, sour cream and mayonnaise. Spread on platter or pizza pan. Scatter shrimp over cream cheese mixture. Pour seafood sauce over shrimp, layer with shredded cheese and green pepper, green onions and tomatoes. Serve with crackers or chips.

Rosalie Peterson, Argyle

SOY SAUCE MARINADE

½ cup soy sauce
½ cup water
2 Tbsp. vegetable oil
2 Tbsp. lemon juice
4 Tbsp. brown sugar
¼ tsp. liquid hot pepper sauce, optional
1 garlic

Combine ingredients. Use to marinate beef, pork, or chicken before grilling or broiling. Makes 1¼ cups. Marinate overnight. Serve leftovers as au jus.

Natalie McCleary, Crookston

SMOKED SALMON DIP**

1 (1 lb.) can red salmon
1 (8 oz.) pkg. cream cheese
1 Tbsp. instant onion
3 drops Liquid Smoke
3 Tbsp. lemon juice
1 Tbsp. horseradish

Mix salmon and cheese; add remaining ingredients. Chill. Mold or firm into log. Roll in chopped nuts and parsley flakes.

Margaret Carr Guerber, Blue Earth

SPINACH SPREAD

1 cup sour cream
1 cup water chestnuts, cut up
1 env. vegetable soup mix

1 cup mayonnaise
1 box frozen spinach, thawed
and drained

Mix well. Serve with cubed garlic bread or on crackers.

Sandy Amberg, Waubun

SPINACH DIP

1 cup mayonnaise
1 pkg. frozen spinach, thawed
and squeezed dry and
chopped fine

2 sm. scallions or 1 sm. onion,
chopped fine
1 pkg. Hidden Valley Ranch
dressing (original recipe with
buttermilk)

Mix all ingredients. Chill and serve with crackers or vegetables.

Madelyn Tauer, Plainview

CHOCOLATE COVERED STRAWBERRIES

1 (12 oz.) pkg. semi-sweet
chocolate bits
6 Tbsp. butter or margarine

½ tsp. vanilla
Washed strawberries with stems

In a microwave safe bowl, zap chocolate bits on high 2 to 3 minutes. Stir well. Continue zapping until melted. Stir in butter or margarine and vanilla. Zap another 30 seconds or so if needed to melt butter. Stir until smooth. Dip strawberries in chocolate, swirling to coat evenly. Place on waxed paper and set in a cool dry place to set. Other fruits and vegetables can be used for dipping.

Fran Timmers, St. Paul

TACO AVOCADO DIP

1 (8 oz.) pkg. cream cheese,
room temperature
1 (6 oz.) carton frozen avocado
dip, thawed
1 (4 oz.) carton sour cream
1 tsp. lemon juice
Pinch of salt

Green onion, diced or chopped
Tomatoes, diced
Lettuce, chopped
Green or black olives
Cheddar cheese, grated
Taco sauce

Blend cream cheese, avocado dip, sour cream, lemon juice and salt. Spread ¼ inch thick on a large platter or 3 or 4 plates. Sprinkle on top the following green onions (top and all), diced lettuce, diced tomatoes, olives (chopped), Cheddar cheese and sprinkle with taco sauce over all. Serve with taco flavored chips. May add some green peppers, if desired.

Sylvia Diedrick, Crookston

APPETIZERS & BEVERAGES

TACO DIP

1 (8 oz.) pkg. cream cheese   1 pkg. taco seasoning mix
1 (16 oz.) carton sour cream   Dash of Tabasco sauce
Soften cream cheese. Add ingredients. Spread in shallow pan.
For toppings, put **tomatoes, green peppers, black olives, onions, lettuce** and **shredded cheese** on top and chill. Dip with taco chips.

Lori Nelson, Wilmont
Joan Hannasch, Bellechester

LAYERED TOSTADO DIP

1 (16 oz.) can refried beans   Dash of hot pepper sauce
½ tsp. chili powder   1 cup ripe olives, chopped
2 avocados, peeled and chopped   1 or 2 tomatoes, chopped
½ cup Miracle Whip   1 (4 oz.) can chopped green
4 bacon slices, cooked crisp   chilies, drained
and crumbled   1 cup (4 oz.) natural Monterey
¼ cup chopped onion   Jack cheese
½ tsp. salt
Combine beans and chili powder; mix well. Combine avocados, Miracle Whip, bacon, onion and seasonings; mix well. Layer bean mixture, avocado mixture, olives, tomato, chilies, and cheese in a shallow bowl (such as pie plate). Serve with tortilla chips.

Jill Adolphson, Argyle

VEGETABLE DIP

1 cup sour cream   1 Tbsp. dill weed
1 cup salad dressing   1 Tbsp. parsley flakes
1 tsp. Beaumont   Onion, cut up fine
Mix all ingredients. Makes 2 cups.

Esther Echternach, New Richland
Rosie Kelly, Waseca

WILD RICE STUFFED MUSHROOMS

½ cup uncooked wild rice   2 Tbsp. butter, mixed with
1 lb. lg. fresh mushrooms   1 tsp. parsley, 1 tsp. oregano
1 med. onion, chopped fine   and a dash of garlic
    5 slices bacon, fried crisp and
    crumbled
Cook rice and drain well. Remove mushroom stems and chop. Saute with onion and butter. Stir in rice and bacon. Sprinkle with fresh Parmesan cheese on top. Bake at 350° for about 20 to 25 minutes. Serve hot.

Le Johnson, Owatonna

32

* * BEVERAGES * *

APPLE JUICE

1 gal. apples
1 gal. boiling water

1 gal. juice (from apples)
1 cup sugar

Cut apples in half to make 1 gallon apples. Place in plastic container. Pour 1 gallon of boiling water over apples. Let stand 30 hours. Drain off juice in 6 quart pan. Boil well the juice and sugar. Place in sterilized jars and seal. Serve as apple juice, blend with iced tea for a delightful flavor.

Sr. Mary Ann Welsch OSB, Moorhead
Joan Schmitz, Moorhead

CHOCOLATE MEXICANO

6 cups milk
½ cup sugar
3 sq. chocolate
1 tsp. ground cinnamon

¼ tsp. salt*
2 eggs, beaten
2 tsp. vanilla
Stick Cinnamon

*I don't use salt and it tastes wonderful.

In saucepan, combine milk, sugar, chocolate, cinnamon, and salt (if desired). Heat and stir until chocolate melts and milk is very hot. Gradually stir one cup of hot mixture into eggs. Return to saucepan. Cook 2 to 3 minutes over low heat. Remove from heat. Add vanilla, beat with rotary beater until very frothy. Pour into mugs, garnish with cinnamon stick.

Patt Thorpe, International Falls

FRUIT 'N JUICE BREAKFAST SHAKE

1 very ripe banana
¾ cup pineapple juice
½ cup low-fat vanilla yogurt

½ cup strawberries, stemmed
and rinsed

Break banana into small pieces and put in the blender with pineapple juice, yogurt and strawberries. Secure lid and blend until smooth. Divide the shake between glasses and serve immediately. Per serving: 168 calories, 1 g fat.

Laurie Sazama, Perham

GRASSHOPPERS

5 qts. vanilla ice cream
1 pt. creme De Cocoa (clear)

½ pt. creme De Menthe
½ pt. whipping cream

Mix above with hand mixer and freeze. Can be served as dessert in a dish or thawed as a drink.

Frances Kunz, Waseca

33

IRISH CREAM LIQUOR

1¼ cup Irish whiskey, brandy, rum or bourbon
1 (14 oz.) can sweetened condensed milk
1½ cups whipping cream
2 cracked eggs
2 Tbsp. chocolate syrup
2 tsp. instant coffee
1 tsp. vanilla
½ tsp. almond extract
2 uncracked eggs (clean)

Combine all ingredients in blender, except for the uncracked eggs. Blend until smooth. Add the uncracked eggs, one at a time and blend well. The shells will dissolve after a couple days. May be stored tightly covered in refrigerator up to one month. Stir or shake well before serving. (We prefer it with brandy and you may add a little vanilla ice cream in it before serving.) Wonderful after dinner drink!

Claudia R. Bosch, Dickinson, ND
National Director, 1992-1996

CHAMPAGNE PUNCH

2 bottles domestic champagne
1 bottle ginger ale
2 pts. pineapple sherbet

Chill champagne and ginger ale. Pour pineapple sherbet in large punch bowl. Sherbet will get foamy. Serves 20 to 24 single servings.

Mary Lynn Bissonette, Blue Earth

TOO EASY PUNCH

2 (2 liter) bottles 7-Up or Sprite, diet or regular
½ gal. sherbet (the flavor is your choice and will be the color of your punch

Chill pop well. Empty 1 (2 liter) bottle into punch bowl. Using a small scoop or spoon, add sherbet to pop. Pop will fizz and foam. Use about ½ of the sherbet. Stir well until punch is creamy and only small bits of sherbet remain. Serve. If your bowl is large enough, you may use all of pop and all of sherbet at once. You may add to this as the party goes on by maintaining the ratio of 2 liters of pop and 1 quart of sherbet. This recipe serves about 35. (Depending on how hot out it is.) Rainbow flavored sherbet makes a gray punch - great for Halloween parties - not great for the bridal shower!

Jane Killian, Eveleth
Sherryl Holzer, Perham

34

HOLIDAY FRUIT PUNCH

8 cups cold water
4 cups sugar
1 lg. can orange juice
1 lg. can unsweetened pineapple juice

1 cup lemon juice
1 cup lime juice
1 (28 oz.) bottle ginger ale

Stir together the cold water and sugar. Bring to a boil and boil for 5 minutes. Remove from heat. Add the orange juice, pineapple juice, lemon juice and lime juice. Chill. Just before serving, stir in 1 bottle ginger ale to one half of the above recipe. Freeze the balance for future use. (Unless you are serving a large crowd.) Instead of the ginger ale, any uncola beverage can be used.

Lila Ballman, New Ulm

STRAWBERRY CHAMPAGNE PUNCH

1 (12 oz.) can frozen Hawaiian punch
1 (10 oz.) pkg. frozen strawberries

$^2/_3$ cup orange juice
3 Tbsp. lemon juice
1 (12 oz.) bottle champagne
1 (12 oz.) bottle ginger ale

Mix the first 4 ingredients. Just before serving, add champagne and ginger ale.

Cecilia Spartz, Slayton

EASY FRUIT PUNCH

2 (32 oz.) cans Hawaiian fruit punch

1 (1 qt.) bottle ginger ale
1 qt. raspberry sherbet

Combine all ingredients and add ice cubes to chill. Add whiskey or Vodka (optional). Fills one punch bowl.

Mary Lynn Bissonette, Blue Earth

7-7-PUNCH

1 (12 oz.) can frozen orange juice
1 (12 oz.) can frozen lemonade
1 lg. can pineapple juice
1 (20 oz.) can diced pineapple and juice

1 liter 7-Up
1 liter ginger ale
Fruit on top (sliced oranges, lemons, cherries, strawberries)

Mix in order given. Float 1 or 2 fruits on top of your choice.

Alice Lynch, Winona
District Deputy

35

PUNCH (TO SERVE 125 PEOPLE)

4 pkgs. cherry Kool Aid
4 cups sugar
1 lg. can frozen lemon juice
2 lg. cans Hawaiian punch
2 lg. cans pineapple juice
1 qt. ginger ale
1 qt. 7-Up

Mix all ingredients. (Important: don't add ginger ale and 7-Up until just before serving.)

Mildred Schmitt, Caledonia

RUSSIAN TEA

2 cups Tang
½ cup instant tea
½ cup sugar
1 tsp. cinnamon
½ tsp. cloves

Use 2 rounded teaspoons per cup of hot water.

Martha Erickson, St. Peter

BANANA SLUSH

3 lg. bananas   1 lg. can crushed pineapple
Blend these in a blender. Add:
1 cup sugar   3 cups orange juice
½ cup real lemon juice

Blend these again and freeze. Add ginger ale or 7-Up.

Lori Hebig, Medford

CAMPAIGN SLUSH

½ lg. (23 oz.) can pineapple juice
1 (12 oz.) can frozen lemonade concentrate
3 oz. lemon juice
1½ pkg. Kool Aid (flavor to compliment selected fruit)
1 cup sugar
1 pkg. frozen fruit*

*Fresh can be used - strawberries, raspberries, and peaches are especially tasty.

Stir all into a 5 quart ice cream pail. Add water to fill within 1 inch of rim. Put in freezer and stir as it sets to distribute fruit evenly.

Variation: 1 cup of fruit flavored brandy or schnapps can be added to "spice up" your campaign or party.

Lois Nelson, Medford
Youth Chair, 1988-1994
State Second Vice Regent, 1994-present

36

LEMONADE SLUSH PUNCH

4 pkgs. Kool Aid lemonade,   4 qts. water
    unsweetened   1 (12 oz.) can frozen lemonade
4 cups sugar   1 (2 liter) bottle of Squirt

Mix the Kool Aid, sugar and the water. Add the frozen lemonade and freeze. When ready to use, take out of freezer and thaw until thick slush. Add the Squirt and enjoy!

Sue Herder, Fergus Falls

PINA COLADA SLUSH

1 (16 oz.) can cream of coconut   1 pt. white rum
1 (46 oz.) can pineapple juice

Combine all ingredients and freeze. Mixture will get slushy. To serve, combine $^2/_3$ cup slush and $^1/_3$ cup 7-Up in a glass.

Irene McNea, Fairmont

RHUBARB SLUSH

8 cups rhubarb   ½ cup lemon juice
2 qts. water   1 pkg. strawberry jello
3 cups sugar

Cook the rhubarb in the water and strain. Add the sugar, lemon juice and strawberry jello to the strained juice. Dissolve and cool. Freeze in ice cream pail, stirring occasionally. To serve, put in glass and add **7-Up** or **strawberry pop**.

Catherine Hauch, St. Peter
Second Vice Regent, 1978-1980
State Regent, 1980-1984
District Deputy for 7 years

SLUSH PUNCH

3 (3 oz.) pkgs. jello (your choice)   2 cups lemon juice (Real
3 cups sugar   Lemon brand)
6 cups boiling water   14 cups cold water
    3 lg. cans pineapple juice

Dissolve jello and sugar in boiling water. Add rest of ingredients. Freeze in 5 quart ice cream pails (or equivalent size containers). Remove from freezer about 4 hours before using. Put in punch bowl and pour **gingerale** over all.

Zonda Befort, Mazeppa
State Education Chair, 1988-present

PUNCH

1 (6 oz.) pkg. strawberry jello	1 (64 oz.) can unsweetened
1 cup sugar	pineapple juice
2 cups boiling water	1 (12 oz.) can frozen lemonade
5 cups cold water	concentrate

Mix jello and sugar and dissolve in boiling water. Add cold water, pineapple juice and lemon juice to the jello and sugar mixture. Freeze until needed.

Mae Machulda, St. Paul

MAKE AHEAD LEMONADE BASE

2½ cups water	½ tsp. lemon peel, finely
1¼ cups sugar	shredded
1¼ cups lemon juice	

In a medium saucepan, heat and stir water and sugar over medium heat until sugar is dissolved. Cool. Add lemon juice and peel to sugar syrup. Store up to 3 days in refrigerator (mix with water to taste).

Evelyn Brady, Medford

~ON THE OUTSIDE~

Inside - no matter how bad we think it is
It's always worse for someone outside.

While we complain about "Hotdish Again!"
Someone outside is digging for a scrap of meat.

While we're disgusted because all that's playing are reruns
Someone outside roams the lonely streets.

While we whine that our car is a heap of junk
Someone outside lies in a doorway and watches us go by.

While we complain about having to go to school or work
Someone outside sits on the corner and begs
barely knowing how to read.

While we think we're cold when the thermostat drops
to a chilling 68 degrees
Someone outside shivers against a building
with wind chills reaching 10 below.

Next time you think you have it bad
Think of the someone outside who would love to be you!

Betty Hager, Owatonna

✠ OUR HISTORY ✠

Catholic Daughter courts were originally started and sponsored in 1903 by the Knights of Columbus. Today, the Catholic Daughters of the Americas is the largest Catholic women's organization in the world.

The first Catholic Daughters court in Minnesota was started in Winona on February 2, 1913.

On February 20, 1923, Catherience Fleming of Moorhead got a letter from the National Office appointing her to call a state convention.

This was done on March 4, 1923, in Mankato. Catherine Fleming was elected the first State Regent; Rose English, Mankato, State Secretary; Susan Boquet, Caledonia, State Treasurer; Mary Tucker, State Advocate; Agnes Schroeder, Perham, State Monitor and Fr. Louis O'Day, State Chaplain. There were a total of twelve courts in the state.

The second state convention was held May, 1925, in Winona. There were then fifteen courts and 1,189 members. The per capita tax was set at $.50. In those two years, $4,733.86 was given to charity.

Also, in 1926, the first Junior Catholic Daughters Court in Minnesota was established on December 19th in Fairmont. At one time, five courts with over 115 junior members were active.

In 1965, the state newspaper started by Olive Hastad, Moorhead, was named the *Go-Pher News* with four issues per year.

In 1966, *Everybody's Favorite*, was released as a statewide fund-raiser. 10,000 books were sold in eight months! This cookbook was reprinted seven times during the next ten-year period, netting the state and local courts around $60,000 for their many charitable projects.

Thirty-nine courts with 4,431 members were active in 1978. Today we have thirty-three courts and a membership of 3,600.

State and National conventions are held every two years with state/national officers elected at that time. Also, bylaws and resolutions are voted upon at each convention. Some actions taken: 1975-Heart Speaks to Heart program with four involvements was instituted; 1976-eliminated the offices of lector and trustees; 1978-the name of the organization was changed to CATHOLIC DAUGHTERS OF THE AMERICAS; 1985-deletion of the wearing of hats with the robes during formal ceremonies.

Over the years, we Catholic Daughters have donated many hours and dollars to various charities. At each state convention, a project is selected for the next biennium with members supporting it at the rate of $1.00 per year. At present, this is the Total Life Care Centers, Dorothy Day Houses, and Caring and Sharing in Minneapolis.

Minnesota Catholic Daughters continue to support many charities at all levels of this organization and throughout their communities.

Kathryn Kennedy, Past State Secretary

MINNESOTA STATE COURT
State Regents

Catherine Flemming	1923-1927	Moorhead
Helen Hoeppner	1927-1931	Winona
Adeline Schnaus	1931-1939	Mankato
Angelus LeGros	1939-1946	Adrian
Mary Haynes	1946-1948	New Ulm
Catherine Tierney	1948-1952	St. Paul
Virginia Roerkohl	1952-1958	Caldonia
Adele Wolfe	1958-1962	Minneapolis
Evelyn Koppi	1962-1966	Currie
Olive Hastad	1966-1970	Moorhead
Dorothy Willette	1970-1974	Easton
Rose Nixon	1974-1978	Winona
Ester Palubicki	1978-1980	Perham
Catherine Hauch	1980-1984	St. Peter
Rose Guillemette	1984-1986	Mankato
Joyce Stock	1986-1990	Mahnomen
Shirley Ettestad	1990-1994	International Falls
Donna Farrell	1994-1998	Marshall
Shirley Seyfried	1998-present	Fergus Falls

* * YEAST BREADS * *

ANADAMA BREAD

2 cups water	2 pkgs. dry yeast
2 tsp. salt	½ cup lukewarm water
½ cup yellow cornmeal	2 tsp. sugar
2 Tbsp. Crisco	5 cups white flour
½ cup dark molasses	

Cook water, salt and cornmeal until quite thick, stirring constantly. Add Crisco and molasses; let cool. In a small bowl, warm water, sugar and yeast; let stand. Combine both mixtures. Add 2½ cups flour and mix well. Add another 2½ cups flour and knead well. Put in a greased bowl; cover and let rise until doubled. Turn out on floured board. Let stand 15 minutes. Make into two loaves (or biscuits). Let rise until doubled. Bake at 375° for 20 to 25 minutes for biscuits or 45 to 50 minutes for loaves.

Helen Lynch, Plainview

BROWN BREAD

¼ cup warm water mixed with	½ cup oil
1 tsp. sugar	½ cup wheat bran
2 pkgs. dry yeast	½ cup oat bran
1½ cup liquid (warm water)	3 Tbsp. wheat germ
1 cup coffee (need not be fresh)	1 cup whole wheat flour
1 tsp. salt	6 cups flour
½ cup molasses	Raisins, optional
½ cup brown sugar	

To water/sugar mixture, add yeast and let stand a few minutes. In a large bowl, put liquids, salt, molasses, brown sugar and oil. Add yeast mixture, then add brans, wheat germ, whole wheat flour and white flour. Mix well. Let raise. Put in 3 loaf pans. Let rise until double. Bake at 350° for 35 to 40 minutes.

Helen Bye, Crookston

CEREAL BREAD

1 qt. milk	2 tsp. salt
1 cake yeast	3 Tbsp. shortening
2 cups corn flakes	7 plus cups flour
1 cup oatmeal	

Heat milk, use ½ cup for yeast. Pour milk over cereal, salt and shortening. Cool to lukewarm. Stir in 2 cups flour. Add yeast and mix well. Add flour. Knead 10 minutes. Rise 1½ hours. Punch down. Put in 3 loaf pans. Raise 1 hour. Bake at 375° for 40 minutes.

Marguerite Langenberg, Winona

BREADS

39

HALF-BROWN BREAD

4 cups warm water	1 cup water
2 heaping Tbsp. yeast	1 cup brown sugar
6 Tbsp. sugar or honey	6 Tbsp. lard
5 tsp. salt	6 cups whole wheat flour
6 cups white flour	

Place warm water in mixing bowl; add yeast. Mix until dissolved with electric mixer. Add sugar, salt and white flour. Blend. Cover bowl with Saran Wrap and towel. Let rise. Meanwhile, boil water, then add sugar and lard. Cool. Add to above mixture, stirring by hand. Add wheat flour. Turn out on floured board. Let rest 20 minutes, covered with towel. Knead 10 minutes. Place in greased bowl; let rise. Punch down, let rise again, and punch down. When dough rises again, form into 5 loaves. Place in greased pans. Bake at 375° for 35 minutes. Cool slightly, remove from pans.

Eileen L. Harguth, Waseca

COTTAGE CHEESE ROLLS

3 cups flour	1 pkg. dry yeast
¼ cup sugar	¼ cup warm water
½ cup butter	1 egg, beaten
1 cup large curd cottage cheese	

Combine flour, sugar, butter and cottage cheese. Mix as for pie crust dough. To this mixture, add dry yeast which has been dissolved in warm water. Add beaten egg. After mixing thoroughly, roll out on floured board. Roll fairly thin.

Filling:

1 cup ground walnuts	½ tsp. almond extract
½ tsp. vanilla	3 Tbsp. melted butter
1 cup brown sugar	

Spread filling on dough. Roll up and cut into 20 pieces. Place in a greased 9x13 inch pan. Let raise 2½ hours. Bake at 375° for 30 minutes. When warm, spread with frosting, made to your liking using **butter, powdered sugar** and **cream.**

Lillian Bundich, Eveleth

* * * * * * * *

Do not be saddened this day, for rejoicing in the Lord must be your strength. Nehemiah 8:10
Pam Luettel, Adrian

BREADS

BUBBLE BREAD

1 cake yeast
1 cup milk, scalded
1¼ cups sugar, divided
¼ cup shortening
1 tsp. salt

2 eggs
Flour
1 tsp. cinnamon
Melted butter

Sprinkle yeast on cooled milk. Cream ¼ cup sugar, shortening, and salt. Add eggs and combine with milk mixture. Add enough flour to make soft dough. Place in a greased bowl and let rise until doubled in bulk. Pour onto floured board and pat out thin. Cut dough in rounds (I use a canning jar lid). Mix cinnamon with remaining 1 cup sugar in bowl. Melt butter in separate bowl. Dip rounds in melted butter, then cinnamon and sugar and place on end in angel food cake pan. Let rise 1½ hours. Bake at 350° for 25 minutes.

Denise Gathje, St. Charles

HOMEMADE BUNS

½ cup lukewarm water
3 Tbsp. sugar

2 pkgs. dry yeast or household
    yeast

Mix in a small bowl. Combine:

2½ cups lukewarm milk or water
1 tsp. salt
½ cup shortening

½ cup sugar
2 eggs
7 cups flour

Mix mixtures together, only using about 3 cups flour; add flour slowly and beat between additions. Add eggs and yeast mixture and mix well; add rest of flour. Knead well, then cover and let rise double bulk. Knead down again and in 10 minutes shape into biscuits, buns, or rolls. Bake at 400° until golden brown. Brush with butter.

Mary Burg, Caledonia

HERB BREAD (PANASONIC BREAD MACHINE)

2 cups bread flour
2 Tbsp. sugar
1 Tbsp. dry milk
1 tsp. salt
⅞ cup water
1 Tbsp. butter

2 Tbsp. parsley
1 Tbsp. caraway seed
1 Tbsp. dill
1½ tsp. dry yeast (Use 1 tsp. if
    using quick rising type)

Lil Robertson, Argyle

MOTHER'S ICE BOX BISCUITS

1/3 cup lard	2 eggs
1/2 cup sugar	Flour to make soft dough
1 tsp. salt	2 lbs. prunes
1 cup boiling water	1 can apricot solo
2 pkgs. dry yeast	Sugar and cinnamon to taste
2 cups warm water	

Mix the first 4 ingredients and cool to lukewarm, stirring occasionally. Soak the dry yeast in the lukewarm water. Add the yeast and eggs and just enough flour to mix nicely with electric beater. By hand, add enough flour to make a soft non-sticky dough. Let rise until double. Knead down and let rise again. You may use the same day or put it in the refrigerator. Punch down. Will keep 3 to 4 days in refrigerator. May also roll out as wanted by keeping refrigerated. Soak the prunes overnight and cook 40 minutes. Pit and mash with potato masher. Add the apricots, sugar and cinnamon. Roll dough thin and cut in 3 inch squares. Fill, seal and let rise. Bake at 350° for 20 to 25 minutes.

Rose Manderfeld, Medford

BUNS

3 pkgs. dry yeast	1 egg, beaten
2 cups warm water	1/2 cup sugar
1/2 tsp. sugar	2 tsp. salt
1/4 cup shortening	6 to 7 cups flour

Dissolve yeast in warm water with 1/2 teaspoon sugar. Melt shortening and add to water. Add 1/2 cup sugar and salt. Let cool until lukewarm. Add 2 cups of the flour, mixing well. Add beaten egg and yeast and beat well. Add another 2 cups flour. Beat well. Add another 2 cups flour and mix well. Use the last cup of flour to knead only a few minutes. Put in a greased bowl, cover, and let rise until double in size. Put in greased pans, let rise until double in bulk. Bake at 350° for 15 to 25 minutes, depending on size of the buns.

Eleanore Askew, Eveleth

* * * * * * * *

If God can paint a rainbow from the weeping skies above, just think what he can do with human tear drops and His Love.

Author Unkown
Colleen Bents, Rushmore

BUNS OR ROLLS

5 cups warm water
½ cup margarine (1 stick)
2 pkgs. dry yeast
¾ cup sugar
1 Tbsp. salt
2 cups whole wheat flour
White flour to make a soft dough

Put 4 cups warm water in large bowl. Cut up margarine and put into the water. Stir until melted. Put dry yeast and 1 cup water in small bowl. Add sugar and salt to water and margarine. Stir; add whole wheat flour. Stir well; add yeast. Stir. Add white flour, 1 cup at a time, until the dough can be handled. Place dough on a floured surface. Knead and place into a greased bowl. Let rise at least an hour, until doubled. Shape into buns on cookie sheet, which has been sprayed with Pam. Let rise until doubled. Bake at 400° for 8 minutes. Makes about 4 dozen, depending on size.

Margaret Kochmann, Mahnomen

ENGLISH MUFFIN BREAD

2 pkgs. active dry yeast
3 cups unsifted white flour
1 Tbsp. sugar
¼ tsp. baking soda
2 cups milk
½ cup water
3 cups unsifted white flour

Combine first 4 ingredients. Heat milk and water until very warm (120°-130°); add to dry ingredients and beat well. Add 3 cups flour and stir to stiff batter. Spoon into 2 loaf pans which have been greased and sprinkled with cornmeal. Sprinkle tops with cornmeal. Let rise in warm place for 45 minutes. Bake at 400° for 25 minutes. Remove from pans immediately.

Grace M. Rinaldi, Hawthorne, CA
National Regent, 1994-present (served 16 years on National Board)
Vivian Fick, Slayton

QUICK YEAST BUNS

2 pkgs. yeast
½ cup warm water
1 Tbsp. sugar
6½ cups flour
1 cup warm water
1 cup milk, scalded
3 eggs
6 Tbsp. shortening, melted
1 tsp. salt
⅓ cup sugar

Dissolve yeast in ½ cup warm water. Add 1 tablespoon sugar and set aside. Mix 3 cups flour, 1 cup warm water and milk. Add the yeast mixture, then the beaten eggs, shortening, salt, ⅓ cup sugar and remaining flour. Set aside until double in bulk. Shape into buns and let rise again. Bake at 350° for about 20 minutes.

Amy O'Brien, Plainview

KROFI (SLOVENIAN DOUGHNUTS)

1 oz. yeast	1 tsp. salt
6 Tbsp. warm milk	Heaping ½ cup sugar
Sugar	Lemon peel from ½ lemon
1½ lbs. flour (5 cups)	1 tsp. rum
1 stick butter	6 egg yolks
1 cup milk	

Dissolve yeast in 6 tablespoons warm milk and a little sugar. Set aside and let rise. Meanwhile, sift flour into bowl. Melt butter; add milk, salt, sugar and flavoring. To the warm mixture, add egg yolks and beat with mixer until foamy. Now, add risen yeast and the milk mixture to the flour in bowl. Mix and beat with a wooden spoon and later with hand, until blisters form and dough no longer sticks to hand and bowl. Dough should be soft. You may have to add more milk if necessary. Let rise in warm place away from drafts, until double in bulk. Punch down and let rise again. Prepare a board or tablecloth and dust with flour. Put dough on it and pat with hand to finger thickness. Cut out with doughnut cutter without the center hole. Let rise, covered, in warm place until double. Fry in hot fat or Crisco shortening, which is about 2 to 3 inches deep. I cover pan for the first side, then uncover pan and fry on other side.

Remember: to assure a light krof, the dough should be soft and NOT kneaded on a board like bread, but beaten with a wooden spoon or hand (yours). Also a good flour is important. I use GOLD MEDAL. Keep everything that comes in contact with krof, WARM. It takes a lot of practice, so don't despair the first time.

Gisela Babich, Eveleth

OVERNIGHT BUNS

Step One:

3 eggs	2 tsp. salt
½ cup Mazola oil	2½ cups warm water
¾ cup white sugar	10½ cups flour

Beat eggs, then add remaining ingredients.

Step Two:

Dissolve **1 teaspoon sugar** in **1 cup lukewarm water**. Add **1 package dry yeast**; let stand 1 minute. Mix both mixtures together at 5:00 p.m. Punch down every hour for 3 hours. On fourth hour, shape into buns. Grease pans very well. Set on table, cover, and let rise overnight. Bake first thing in the morning. Makes large batch. Bake at 400° for 15 to 20 minutes.

Note: If you want them to be crusty on all sides, place on greased baking sheet about ½ to 1 inch apart.

Helen Kraus, Kellogg
Mary Lou Schouweiler, Kellogg

CINNAMON TWISTS

1 cup milk	2 pkgs. active dry yeast (4 tsp.)
2/3 cup sugar	2 eggs
1 tsp. salt	7 cups flour
1/2 cup butter or margarine	1 cup sugar
1 cup warm water (not hot)	1 Tbsp. cinnamon

Scald milk. Stir in sugar, salt and butter or margarine. Cool to lukewarm. Measure into bowl the 1 cup warm water. Sprinkle in yeast. Stir until dissolved, then stir in milk mixture. Add beaten eggs and 4 cups flour. Beat until smooth. Stir in about 3 cups flour. Turn dough out on lightly floured board. Knead. Place in greased bowl. Cover and let rise in warm place until doubled, about 1 hour. Divide dough in thirds. Roll each part into a square about 12x12 inches. Brush very lightly with melted butter. Mix sugar and cinnamon. Sprinkle center third of each square with this mixture. Fold 1/3 of dough over center third; sprinkle with some sugar-cinnamon mixture. Fold remaining third of dough over the two layers. Cut into strips 3/4 inches wide. Take hold of each end of strip and twist tightly in opposite directions. Seal ends. Place on greased baking sheets about 1 1/2 inches apart. Let rise until double. Bake at 350° for about 25 minutes. While warm, frost tops with icing made of **1 cup confectioner's sugar, 1 tablespoons milk** and **1/4 teaspoon vanilla**. Makes 1 1/2 dozen.

Joan Jones, Wilmont

NO KNEAD CHEESE BREAD

1 cup milk	2 Tbsp. shortening
1 cup water	2 pkgs. yeast
1 tsp. salt	1 cup grated Cheddar cheese
3 Tbsp. sugar	4 1/2 cups flour

Heat milk to boiling point, then cool to lukewarm. Add water, salt, sugar, shortening and dry yeast. When yeast is dissolved, add grated cheese and flour. Stir until well blended. Cover and let rise until doubled in bulk. Stir and beat batter for 1/2 minute. Bake in a well greased angel food cake pan or 2 medium size loaf pans. Bake at 350° for 1 hour. Lower heat if too brown.

Lorraine Halbersma, Pipestone
District Deputy, 1996-present

* * * * * * * *

There never was a greater love nor will there ever be, when Jesus said I've chosen you, you have not chosen me. John 15:16
Margaret Roetzel, Adrian

STROLLEN CHRISTMAS BREAD

½ cup sugar
½ tsp. salt
¾ cup milk, scalded
2 pkgs. quick dry yeast
½ cup lukewarm water
6 cups flour

2 eggs, beaten
¾ cup soft butter
¼ tsp. nutmeg
½ cup currants, diced citron,
   candied lemon peel,
   candied cherries
½ cup almonds, chopped

Add sugar and salt to scalded milk and cool. Dissolve yeast in lukewarm water; add cooled milk mixture with 1 cup flour. Cover and let rise double. To sponge, add the beaten eggs, soft butter, 5 cups flour and nutmeg. Add fruit and nuts dredged in flour. Knead on a floured board until elastic. Place in butter bowl. Let rise until double bulk. Punch down; let rest 10 minutes. Divide into 2 pieces. Roll into rectangle ½ inch thick. Spread with soft butter and fold lengthwise. Place on cookie sheet, let rise until double. Bake at 350° for 50 minutes. You can frost if desired. (Be sure to add flour slowly.)

Lorraine Schmitt, Caledonia

DINNER ROLLS

2 pkgs. yeast
¼ cup warm water
1½ cups warm milk
¾ cup melted butter
2 eggs, lightly beaten
⅓ cup sugar

1 tsp. salt
1 tsp. powdered cardamom
4 to 5 cups flour
Melted butter
1 egg yolk mixed with 1 tsp.
   water

Sprinkle yeast over warm water, stirring to dissolve. In a mixing bowl, combine milk, butter, eggs, sugar, salt, and cardamom. Stir until thoroughly blended. Add yeast mixture. Gradually beat in enough flour to make a soft dough. Cover with plastic wrap and towel. Refrigerate overnight. This may also be stared early in the morning, refrigerated, and prepared for evening meal. Turn dough out on floured board and knead lightly, adding flour if dough is too sticky. Roll out and form into desired shapes. Place rolls on greased baking sheets or muffin tins. Cover and let rise about 1 to 1½ hours or until doubled in size. Brush rolls with either the melted butter or egg glaze. Bake in preheated 350° oven for 10 to 15 minutes or until golden.

Idella Miller, Tulsa, OK
National Director, 1992-1996

CARAMEL CINNAMON ROLLS

Caramel:

¹/₃ cup butter	1 Tbsp. water
½ cup brown sugar	1 Tbsp. corn syrup

Bring to a boil; pour in bottom of roll pan. Add nuts if desired. Place rolls on top and bake.

Rolls:

1 cup milk	1 Tbsp. salt
1 cup water	1 stick oleo
½ cup sugar	

Put all in saucepan and heat until oleo is melted. Dissolve **2 packages yeast** in ½ **cup warm water**; add **1 beaten egg** and enough **flour** so dough is not sticky (approximately 5½ to 6 cups). Knead well; let rise; work down once and let rise again. Shape into cinnamon rolls or plain rolls. Let rise and bake at 375° for 15 to 20 minutes.

Agnes Herrig, Iona
District Deputy, 1996-present

FRENCH BREAD

1 pkg. Fleishmann's active dry yeast	3 Tbsp. soft shortening
	1½ tsp. salt
1¼ cups very warm water	4 cups flour

In mixing bowl, dissolve yeast in very warm water. Stir in shortening and salt. Mix in flour in two additions, with spoon, then hand, until easy to handle. Turn onto lightly floured board; cover. Let rest 10 minutes. Knead until smooth and elastic. Round up; place in a greased bowl and cover with cloth. Let rise in warm place (85°) until doubled, 1½ to 2 hours. Punch down; let rise again until double, 45 minutes. Punch down; cover and let rise 15 minutes. Roll into an oblong 15x10 inch. Roll up tightly, seal edge. With hands, roll to taper ends. Place on a lightly greased baking sheet. Make slashes 2 inches apart on top. Let rise uncovered about 1 hour. Heat oven to 375° (quick mod.) Put pan of water in oven on top shelf 30 minutes before baking. Brush with water. Bake 20 minutes. Brush with mixture of 1 egg white and 2 tablespoons water. Return to oven and bake 25 minutes longer.

Sister Mary John, Argyle

* * * * * * * *

We should not live to make a living, but rather live to make a life that is worth living. —Rex Shoaf

Michele Hoffer, Adrian

GRANOLA BREAD

2 pkgs. active dry yeast
2 cups warm water
2 tsp. salt
2 Tbsp. honey or molasses

4 Tbsp. oil
4 to 4½ cups unsifted flour
2½ cups granola

In a large bowl, soften yeast in warm water. Stir in salt, honey, oil and 2½ cups flour; beat well. Stir in granola and the remaining flour to form a stiff dough. Knead on floured surface until smooth, about 8 minutes. Cover and let rise in warm place until double in size. Punch down dough and let rise again. After dough has risen again, divide and make 2 loaves of bread or make 1 loaf and cinnamon rolls. Use a 9x5 inch loaf pan which had been greased. Cover and let rise about 45 minutes. Bake at 350° for 40 to 45 minutes or until golden brown and loaf sounds hollow when tapped. Remove from pan and cool. Very good.

Agnes Herrig, Iona
District Deputy, 1996-present

HOT CROSS BUNS

⅔ cup sugar
1 tsp. salt
2 pkgs. dry yeast
5 cups flour

1½ cups milk
½ cup butter
2 eggs
1 cup dark raisins

Combine sugar, salt, yeast and 1½ cups flour. Heat milk and butter or oleo, until very warm (120° to 130°); add to flour mixture. Beat in 1 egg and 1 cup flour to make a thick batter. Beat 2 to 3 minutes. Stir in raisins and additional flour (about 2 to 2½ cups) to make soft dough. Turn dough on floured surface and knead until smooth, about 10 minutes. Add more flour while kneading. Shape dough into ball and place in greased bowl. Cover and let rise about 1 hour. Punch down dough on floured surface. Divide into 15 equal pieces. Cover and let rest in bowl for 15 minutes. Grease a 9x13 inch pan. Shape dough into balls and place in pan. Cover, let rise until doubled, about 1 hour. Preheat oven to 350°. Beat remaining egg. Cut a cross on each bun and brush with the egg. Bake 25 minutes or until buns are golden. Cool for 15 minutes. Fill cross with icing made of ¾ cup powdered sugar and 1 tablespoon milk.

Addy Bastianelli, Eveleth

BREADS

48

ITALIAN BREAD WITH CHIVES

4½ to 5½ cups unsifted flour	2 to 3 cups chopped chives
1 Tbsp. sugar	Cornmeal
1 Tbsp. salt	Oil
2 pkgs. Fleischmann's dry yeast	1 egg white
1 Tbsp. softened margarine	1 Tbsp. cold water
1¾ cups very warm tap water (120° to 130°)	

In large bowl of mixer, mix 1½ cups flour, sugar, salt and dry yeast. Add softened margarine. Gradually add tap water. Beat 2 minutes at medium speed, scraping bowl occasionally. Add ¾ cup flour and beat at high speed 2 minutes. Add chives. Stir in enough additional flour to make a stiff dough. Knead until smooth and elastic, 8 to 10 minutes. Cover and let rise 20 minutes. Divide dough in half (makes 2 loaves). Roll each half into 15x10 inch shape. Roll up tightly and pinch to seal. Taper ends by gently rolling back and forth. Place on greased baking sheet sprinkle with cornmeal. Brush dough with oil. Cover loosely with plastic wrap and let rise until double. Make 3 to 4 diagonal cuts with sharp knife across top of each loaf. Bake at 425° for 20 minutes. Remove and brush with egg white mixed with water. Bake 10 minutes more until golden brown.

Lillian Bundich, Eveleth

JULEKAKE (CHRISTMAS BREAD)

2 cups milk	½ cup lukewarm milk
1 cup butter	2 eggs, slightly beaten
1 cup sugar	1 cup mixed fruit (like for fruit cake)
8 cups flour	
1 tsp. salt	2 cups raisins
2 tsp. ground cardamom	1 cup chopped almonds
2 cakes of yeast	

Heat 1 cup of the milk enough to melt butter, then add sugar and other 1 cup lukewarm milk. Sift together flour, salt and cardamom. Add to milk mixture. Dissolve yeast in lukewarm ½ cup milk; add eggs and add to flour mixture. Add fruit dredged with flour and knead well. Add flour slowly to all mixture. Let rise double and cut into three 2 pound loaves or you can make any size and let rise until double. Bake at 400° for 7 minutes; reduce heat to 375° and bake 40 minutes. You may shape in round loaves and bake on pie tin or in a bread pan.

Mildred Schmitt, Caledonia
State Publicity Chair, 1996-present

KOLATCY

½ cup scalded milk
3 Tbsp. shortening
3 Tbsp. sugar
1½ tsp. salt
½ cup water

1 pkg. or cake yeast, active dry
or compressed
1 egg
3¼ cups sifted flour

Combine the scalded milk, shortening, sugar and salt. Cool to lukewarm by adding ½ cup water. (The water used to dissolved dry yeast should be subtracted from the water in the recipe.) Add yeast and blend in egg. Gradually add the flour and mix until well blended. Cover and let stand for 15 minutes. Cook chopped prunes, ⅓ cup water and ⅓ cup sugar until soft. Cool and add walnuts. Pat out dough and cut in squares 1½ to 2 inches. Roll each square in a round and place in greased pan. Let rise until double in bulk, about 45 minutes to 1 hour.

Filling:

1½ cups chopped prunes
⅓ cup water

⅓ cup sugar
¾ cup chopped walnuts

Make a dent with back of spoon in each roll and fill with prune filling. Bake at 375° for 15 to 20 minutes. When cool, frost with powdered sugar icing.

Evelyn Rountree, International Falls

MICROWAVE ENGLISH MUFFIN BREAD

5 cups flour
1 Tbsp. sugar
2 tsp. salt
¼ tsp. baking soda

1 pkg. rapid rise yeast
2 cups milk
½ cup water
Cornmeal

Mix 4 cups flour, sugar, salt, baking soda and yeast. Heat liquids to 125° to 130°. Add to dry ingredients. Beat well. Add last cup of flour to make stiff batter. Spoon into two 8 or 9 inch loaf pans that have been sprayed with Pam and coated with cornmeal. Sprinkle tops with cornmeal. Cover and microwave on 50% heat for 1 minute. Let rest 10 minutes. Repeat cooking and resting until doubled in size. Bake each loaf separately on 100% high heat for 6½ minutes. Top of loaf will be flat and pale in color. Let rest for 5 minutes, then remove from pan. Or, let raise for 30 minutes in warm place and bake in 400° oven for 25 minutes. Remove from pan immediately.

Jeanne Heer, Winona

OATMEAL BREAD

1½ cups boiling water
1 Tbsp. shortening
1 tsp. salt
1 cup quick cooking oatmeal
1 pkg. dry yeast

¾ cup warm water
¼ cup molasses
½ cup brown sugar
5 cups flour

Combine boiling water, shortening, and salt. Stir in oatmeal and cool. Soften yeast in warm water. Add molasses, brown sugar and 1 cup flour and beat until smooth. Add oatmeal mixture and enough flour to make a stiff dough. Mix thoroughly and knead smooth. Put dough in greased bowl, cover and let rise until doubled. Punch down and divide in two. Let rest for 10 minutes. Place in pan and rise for 1 hour. Bake at 375° for 45 to 50 minutes.

Mary LaBine, Argyle

REFRIGERATED PANCAKES

1 qt. buttermilk
2 tsp. sugar
2 tsp. soda
1 pkg. dry yeast
4 cups flour

2 Tbsp. baking powder
1 tsp. salt
½ cup cooking oil
6 eggs, well beaten

Mix buttermilk, sugar, soda and yeast. Add flour, baking powder, salt and oil. Lastly, add well beaten eggs. Store in refrigerator up to three weeks. Stir well before using. Thin with cream if too thick.

Fern Bergeron, Argyle

HERMITS PANCAKES

⅓ cup sugar
2 pkgs. yeast
4 cups lukewarm water
3 eggs

3 cups flour
¼ cup oil
1 tsp. salt

Add sugar and yeast to warm water; dissolve. Add eggs and beat. Add flour, oil and salt. Stir and cover. Let rise until light and foamy, 30 to 40 minutes. Fry. It smells like homemade bread. It is a large recipe, but you can freeze them and reheat.

Margaret A. Filipovich, Eveleth

* * * * * * * *

God has granted us this new day to do with as we will...Let's fill it with kindness, happiness, love, joy and good will.

Author Unkown
Joyce Eickhoff, Adrian

BUCKWHEAT PANCAKES

1¼ cups warm water   ⅓ pkg. dry yeast
1 cup buckwheat flour   ¼ tsp. salt
⅓ cup whole wheat flour   1 tsp. molasses

Mix all ingredients and let stand until morning. Keep covered and warm as with bread. In morning, add ⅓ **teaspoon soda** and bake. Makes about 12 to 14 small pancakes. Serve with warm brown sugar syrup.

Brown Sugar Syrup:
1 cup dark brown sugar, packed   ¾ cup water

Mix brown sugar and water in kettle and bring to boil. Boil about 1 minute. If too sweet, add more water.

Celestine Neeser, Lewiston

MOM'S POLISH COFFEE CAKE

¾ cup sugar   ⅔ cup raisins
5 eggs   5 to 6 cups flour
½ cup lard or vegetable oil   1 tsp. salt
2 cups warm water   1 tsp. nutmeg
1 pkg. yeast in ½ cup warm water

Beat sugar and eggs together. When shortening is melted in the warm water, add to egg mixture. Add dissolved yeast. Add raisins. Stir in flour to make a stiff dough. Let raise until double in size. Knead and let rise again. Pour into 2 large or 3 small greased loaf pans.

Topping:
½ cup flour   1 to 2 Tbsp. butter
⅔ cup sugar

Mix ingredients and sprinkle over top of loaves. Let rise and bake at 350° for 30 to 40 minutes.

Gertrude Schroeder, Fairmont

BUTTERMILK ROLLS

1 pkg. dry yeast   ⅓ cup shortening
¼ cup warm water   1 tsp. salt
¼ cup sugar   1 cup lukewarm buttermilk
1 egg   3½ to 3¾ cups flour

Dissolve yeast in warm water. Add rest of ingredients. Let rise until double in bulk. Make into rolls. Let rise. Bake at 350° for 15 to 20 minutes or more.

Margaret Gaul, Iona

ELEPHANT EARS

1 pkg. dry yeast
¼ cup lukewarm water
2 cups sifted flour
1½ Tbsp. sugar
½ tsp. salt
½ cup butter

½ cup milk, scalded and cooled
1 egg yolk
2 Tbsp. soft butter
2½ cups sugar
3½ tsp. cinnamon
Chopped nuts, optional

Dissolve yeast in water. Mix flour, 1½ tablespoons sugar, and salt. Cut in butter as for pastry. Combine milk and egg yolk with yeast; add to flour mixture and mix well. Chill 2 hours. Turn dough onto lightly floured board. Punch down; cover with cloth and let rise 10 minutes. Roll into rectangle; spread with soft butter. Mix ½ cup sugar and 2 teaspoons cinnamon. Sprinkle evenly over dough. Roll as for jelly roll; cut into 1 inch slices. Mix remaining sugar and cinnamon. Coat slices in mixture, then flatten into 5 inch rounds. Sprinkle with nuts. Place on ungreased cookie sheet and drizzle with melted butter and sprinkle with sugar mixture. Bake at 400° for 12 minutes. Makes 1½ dozen.

Mary Babich, Eveleth

NO KNEAD ROLLS

4 cups lukewarm water
3 tsp. salt
1 cup sugar
4 pkgs. dry yeast

2 eggs, beaten
½ cup lard
13 to 15 cups flour

Add salt, sugar and dry yeast to warm water. Add beaten eggs and lard. Mix flour in with wooden spoon. Finish mixing with hands. Grease bowl and let double, about 2 hours. Roll or pat out about ½ inch thick. Good for crescent rolls, buns, or cinnamon rolls. Let rise another 1½ to 2 hours and bake at 400° until pinkish brown.

Carole Schumacher, Waseca

RYE BREAD

½ cup brown sugar
4 Tbsp. shortening
1 cup molasses
2 cups rye flour

4 cups hot water
2 cakes yeast
½ cup warm water
1 Tbsp. salt

Mix brown sugar, shortening, molasses and rye flour. Pour hot water over and stir until shortening dissolves. Dissolve yeast in warm water. When the first mixture has cooled, add the yeast. Knead in enough white flour to make a stiff dough. Put in a greased bowl to rise. When doubled, punch down and let rise again. Divide into flour loafs and place in loaf pans, greased. Let rise and bake at 350° for 45 to 60 minutes.

Rosalie Peterson, Argyle

BREADS

FOUNDATION ROLL RECIPE

1 cup milk	2/3 cup sugar
1 cup lukewarm water	1/2 cup shortening
2 pkgs. yeast	1 tsp. salt
7 cups flour	Nutmeg
2 eggs	

Scald the milk and cool. In lukewarm water, add the yeast. Mix and combine with milk. Add this mixture to 3½ cups flour and mix well. Beat the eggs and add sugar, soft shortening, salt and a pinch of nutmeg. Mix well. Add this to the flour mixture, mix and add the remaining 3½ cups flour. Knead for 10 minutes. Let dough rise to double. Divide dough and make buns in greased pans. Let rise and bake at 375° until brown. Makes about 50 medium sized buns. You can use this recipe for making filled biscuits also.

Martha Pete, Medford

SWEET ROLLS

2 pkgs. active dry yeast	2 tsp. salt
1/2 cup warm water (not hot, 110° to 115°)	1/2 cup soft shortening
	2 eggs
1½ cups lukewarm milk	7 to 7½ cups flour
1/2 cup sugar	

In bowl, dissolve yeast in water. Add milk, sugar, salt, shortening and eggs and half of flour. Beat with a mixer, about 10 minutes. Add remaining flour to handle easily. Knead until smooth. Put in a greased bowl, turning once; cover and let rise. Punch down and let rise again. Make into cinnamon rolls. Put in a 9x13 inch pan with **1 cup brown sugar** and ½ **cup cream**, mixed on the bottom. Bake at 350° for 25 minutes.

Marilyn LeBlanc, Crookston
Mary Huesmann, Caledonia

SHREDDED WHEAT BREAD

2 cups boiling water	3 Tbsp. shortening
3 shredded wheat biscuits	2 pkgs. yeast
1/2 cup sugar	1/3 cup warm water
1 tsp. salt	5 to 6 cups flour
1/3 cup molasses	

Pour boiling water over shredded wheat biscuits; add sugar, salt, molasses and shortening. Let cool. Dissolve yeast in warm water. Mix with shredded wheat mixture; add flour and knead. Let rise to double in bulk. Put in loaf pans or make some into buns. Let rise again. Bake at 375° for 25 to 30 minutes.

Marie Karsnia, International Falls

FAVORITE ROLLS

1/3 cup warm water
1 tsp. sugar
1 env. yeast
1½ cups milk
½ cup water

5 Tbsp. sugar
2 tsp. salt
¼ cup melted shortening
6 cups flour, approximately

Combine 1/3 cup warm water and 1 teaspoon sugar. Sprinkle yeast on top of water and let stand. Combine milk, ½ cup water, 5 tablespoons sugar and salt and heat until lukewarm. Stir the yeast mixture and combine with the milk mixture. Add 3 cups of flour and stir until perfectly smooth. Add shortening and stir. Gradually add rest of the flour, stirring as it is added. When dough is easily handled, knead well. Place in a large bowl and cover. Let rise until doubled in bulk. Knead again, then let rise once more. Form into buns or biscuits. Let rise. Bake at 350° or 375° (depending on your oven) for 20 minutes.

Catherine Taubel, Theilman
District Deputy, 1992-1994

RAISED WAFFLES

1 pkg. dry yeast
½ cup warm water
2 cups warm milk
½ cup melted butter
1 tsp. salt

1 tsp. sugar
2 cups flour
2 eggs
¼ tsp. baking soda

Dissolve the yeast in warm water. Let stand 5 minutes. Add the milk, butter, salt, sugar and flour, then beat until smooth and blended. Cover with plastic wrap. Let stand overnight at room temperature. Just before cooking the waffles, beat in the eggs and add the baking soda. Mix well. The batter will be very thin. Cook according to waffle maker, about 3 minutes. Makes 8 to 10 waffles. Make sure you have the batter in a large enough bowl as the batter rises overnight. These are very light waffles. Serve with syrup or fresh fruits.

Joan Parries, Moorhead

* * * * * * * *

*Commit to the Lord whatever you do and
your plans will succeed. Proverbs 16:3*
Ginny McKeown, Adrian

SWEDISH RYE BREAD

1 pkg. yeast	1½ cups hot water
¼ cup lukewarm water	2½ cups sifted medium rye flour
¼ cup medium brown sugar	3 Tbsp. caraway seed, or 2 Tbsp.
¼ cup light molasses	orange peel, grated
1 tsp. salt	3½ to 4 cups sifted white flour
2 Tbsp. shortening	

Soften yeast in ¼ cup lukewarm water. In large bowl, combine brown sugar, molasses, salt and shortening. Add hot water and stir until sugar is dissolved. Cool. Stir in rye flour. Beat well. Add yeast and caraway seed or orange peel, grated. Mix well and stir in sifted white flour. Cover and let rest 10 minutes. Knead on well floured surface until smooth, about 10 minutes. Place dough in lightly greased bowl. Cover and let rise in warm place until double in bulk, about 1½ hours. Punch down and make into 2 balls. Place on cookie sheet and let rise until double in size. Bake at 375° for 25 to 35 minutes.

Loretta Keahey, Owatonna

EASY SWEET ROLLS

2 pkgs. dry yeast	½ cup melted shortening
2 cups warm water	2 eggs
1 tsp. salt	¼ cup brown sugar
1/3 cup sugar	¼ cup melted butter
6½ cups flour	¼ cup nutmeats

Dissolve yeast in warm water; add salt, sugar and 2 cups flour. Beat with electric mixer for 2 minutes. Add shortening and eggs. Beat for 2 minutes and add 4½ cups sifted flour. Mix well and let stand for 20 minutes. Make into any desired rolls. For cinnamon rolls, roll out an oblong piece of dough, spread with butter, cinnamon and brown sugar. Roll up and slice. Place cut slices in a pan which has been spread with the brown sugar, melted butter and nutmeats. Let rolls rise for about 1 hour or until light. Bake in moderate oven for 20 minutes. Makes approximately 3 dozen.

Note: Recipe is submitted from original Catholic Daughters Cookbook "Everybody's Favorite!"

Mrs. Earl Erdman, Lismore

* * * * * * * *

Except a grain of wheat fall into the ground and die, it abideth alone: But if it die, it bringeth forth much fruit. John 12:24
Alana Kuzina, Argyle

WILD RICE YEAST BREAD

1 pkg. dry yeast	1 tsp. salt (small dashes)
1/4 cup warm water	1/4 cup melted butter
2 1/2 cups warm water	1/2 cup mashed potatoes
1/4 cup brown sugar	8 cups flour
1/2 cup molasses	1 cup cooked wild rice

Combine yeast in 1/4 cup warm water and mix well. Add 2 1/2 cups more warm water; add sugar, molasses, salt, butter, mashed potatoes and 2 cups of flour. Mix well and beat until smooth. Add wild rice and 5 to 6 cups of flour to make a soft dough. Place on floured board and knead for about 5 minutes. Place in buttered bowl and let rise in warm place until dough doubles in size. Punch down and let rise again. Shape into 3 loaves and place in greased 9x5 inch loaf pans. Let rise again until double. Bake at 375° for 45 minutes.

Dorothy Bolin, International Falls

BREADS

* * QUICK BREADS * *

SOUR CREAM ALMOND COFFEE CAKE

1 1/2 cups sugar	3 cups flour
3/4 cup butter	1 1/2 tsp. baking powder
3 eggs	1 1/2 tsp. soda
1 1/2 tsp. vanilla	3/4 tsp. salt
1/2 tsp. almond extract	1 1/2 cups sour cream

Grease a 12 cup bundt pan, or two 9x5x3 inch loaf pans. Beat sugar and butter; add eggs, vanilla and almond extract in large bowl for 2 minutes. In another bowl, combine flour, baking powder, soda and salt. Gradually add dry ingredients alternately with sour cream to the first mixture. Spread in prepared pan, then sprinkle with topping.

Crumb Topping:

1/2 cup flour	1/2 tsp. almond extract
1/4 cup sugar	1/2 cup slivered almonds
1/4 cup cold butter, cut in small pieces	

Sprinkle on cake and bake at 350° in bundt pan for 1 hour. About 45 minutes for smaller pans, or until toothpick inserted in center comes out clean. Cool slightly on wire rack, then remove from pan.

Helen Cahill, Moorhead

FRESH APPLE BREAD WITH CINNAMON BUTTER

2 cups flour	1¼ cups sugar
2 tsp. baking powder	2 eggs
½ tsp. salt	1½ cups apples, peeled and
½ tsp. cinnamon	finely grated
¼ tsp. nutmeg	½ cup chopped pecans
½ cup butter	

Sift flour, baking powder, salt, cinnamon and nutmeg. Cream butter and sugar until light and fluffy. Beat eggs, one at a time, beating hard after each addition. Stir in dry ingredients and apples, half at a time. Fold in pecans. Grease and flour a 9x5x3 inch loaf pan. Pour batter into prepared pan and bake at 350° for 1 hour or until done. Cool 10 minutes in pan. Serve with cinnamon butter.

Cinnamon Butter:

3 Tbsp. butter	¼ tsp. cinnamon
½ cup sifted confectioners sugar	

Cream butter with sugar. Add cinnamon. Chill before serving.

Fern Bergeron, Argyle

APPLE BREAD

¼ cup shortening	1 tsp. baking powder
⅔ cup sugar	1 tsp. salt
2 eggs	2 cups raw apple, coarsely
2 cups flour	grated
1 tsp. soda	

Cream shortening and sugar until light and fluffy. Beat in eggs. Sift dry ingredients and add to other mixture. Add coarsely grated raw apple. Pour in greased loaf pan. Bake at 350° for 50 to 60 minutes. Do not cut until cold. (Spray nonstick on the pan first.)

Bernadine Hildebrandt, Waterville

APPLE BREAD

½ cup vegetable oil	2 eggs
2 cups sugar	½ tsp. vanilla

Mix, then add **2 cups chopped, peeled apples** and ½ **cup chopped nuts**.

3 cups flour	½ tsp. baking powder
2 tsp. cinnamon	½ tsp. salt
1 tsp. baking soda	

Mix and add dry ingredients with **2 tablespoons milk**. Put batter into 2 greased and floured 8x4 inch bread pans. Bake at 350° for 50 to 60 minutes. Cool 1 hour before removing from pan. (I use 2 medium sized tinfoil pans and 2 small ones and bake 40 minutes.)

Marilyn Ellenz, Caledonia

SPICY APPLE MUFFINS

1 egg, beaten
1 cup milk
¼ cup shortening
1 cup finely chopped apples,
 sweetened with ¼ cup sugar

2 cups flour
¼ cup sugar
½ tsp. salt
4 tsp. baking powder
½ tsp. cinnamon

Combine egg, milk, shortening and apples. Add dry ingredients and mix only until moistened. Fill greased muffin tins ⅔ full. Bake at 400° for 20 to 25 minutes. Serve warm.

Cristel Schumacher, Waseca

DANISH ALMOND CREAM ROLLS

Rolls:

2 (3 oz.) pkgs. cream cheese,
 softened
½ to 1 tsp. almond extract
½ cup powdered sugar
½ cup finely chopped almonds

2 (8 oz.) cans Pillsbury crescent
 dinner rolls
1 egg white
1 tsp. water
¼ cup sliced almonds

Heat oven to 350°. In small bowl, beat cream cheese, almond extract and powdered sugar until fluffy. Stir in ½ cup chopped almonds. Separate 1 can of dough into 4 rectangles; firmly press perforations to seal. Press or roll each to form a 7x4 inch rectangle; spread each with about 2 tablespoons of the cream cheese filling to within ¼ inch of edges. Starting at longer side, roll up each rectangle, firmly pinching edges and ends to seal. Gently stretch each roll to 10 inches. Coil each roll into a spiral with the seam on the inside, tucking end under. Place on ungreased cookie sheets. Repeat with remaining can of dough and cream cheese filling. In a small bowl, combine egg white and water; brush over rolls. Sprinkle with ¼ cup sliced almonds. Bake at 350° for 17 to 23 minutes or until deep golden brown.

Glaze:

⅔ cup powdered sugar
¼ to ½ tsp. almond extract

3 to 4 tsp. milk

In small bowl, blend all ingredients, adding enough milk for desired drizzling consistency; drizzle over warm rolls. Makes 8 rolls.

Florence Cupkie, Owatonna

* * * * * * * *

Praise ye the Lord. Praise O ye servants of the Lord, praise the name of the Lord. Blessed be the name of the Lord from this time forth and for evermore. From the rising of the sun unto the going down of the same, the Lord's name is to be praised. Psalm 113:1-3
Mary Armstrong, Adrian

APRICOT BREAD

1 cup dry apricots, cut in ¼ inch pieces
1 cup sugar
2 Tbsp. soft butter
1 egg
¼ cup hot water
½ cup orange juice
2 cups flour
2 tsp. baking powder
1 tsp. salt
¼ tsp. soda
½ cup nuts, cut up

Soak apricots 30 minutes. Mix sugar and butter and stir in egg, hot water and orange juice. Stir in flour, baking powder, salt, soda and nuts. Let stand 20 minutes, then bake in 5x10x3 inch loaf pan at 350° for 55 to 65 minutes.

Pat Depuydt, St. Peter

BANANA NUT BREAD

½ cup butter or margarine
1 cup sugar
2 eggs
3 ripe bananas
2 cups flour
1 tsp. baking soda
½ cup nutmeats

Cream butter and sugar; beat eggs and fold into the butter mixture. Mash the bananas; stir into other ingredients. Beat mixture with flour and soda. Add nutmeats if desired. Turn into greased and lightly floured loaf pan. Bake at 350° for about 1 hour.

Mary Weidert, Lismore
Genivieve Jajn, Caledonia
Monica Thompson, Plainview
Sister Janet Derner Clements, SSND

CHERRY BANANA NUT BREAD

½ cup shortening
1 cup sugar
2 eggs, beaten
2 cups flour
1 tsp. soda
3 med. bananas
1 (10 oz.) bottle red maraschino cherries
½ cup chopped nuts

Cream shortening and sugar. Add beaten eggs. Sift flour and soda together and add. Mash the bananas and add. Drain the cherries good and leave whole. Add chopped nuts. (If dough is too stiff, can add about 2 teaspoons milk.) Bake at 350° for 45 to 50 minutes in a loaf pan. Cool good before cutting and serving.

Bea Hawkins, Waseca
Mary Senst, Plainview

BREADS

60

BEST BANANA BREAD

½ cup margarine
½ cup granulated sugar
½ cup brown sugar
2 lg. eggs
2 tsp. soda
¼ tsp. salt

1¾ cups flour
½ cup sour cream or half and
  half
3 med. sized bananas
½ tsp. vanilla
½ cup chopped nuts

Cream margarine and sugars. Beat in the eggs. Mix in the dry ingredients which have been sifted together, alternately with sour cream. Add bananas and vanilla. Add nuts. Place in greased and floured loaf pans. Bake at 350° for 45 minutes. Cool in pans. Freezes well.

Martha Manderfeld, Medford
Ottilia Winter, Iron

NEVER-FAIL BANANA BREAD

1 cup mashed banana
1½ Tbsp. sour milk
1 tsp. lemon juice
½ cup shortening
1 cup sugar
2 eggs

2 cups sifted flour
1½ tsp. baking powder
¼ tsp. salt
½ tsp. soda
1 cup nuts

Mix banana, sour milk and lemon juice. Add rest of ingredients. Pour into a greased pan. Let stand at room temperature for 20 minutes before baking. Bake at 350° for 45 to 60 minutes.

Eileen Harguth, Waseca
Rita Yetzer, Medford

BANANA BREAD

1½ cups sugar
¾ cup shortening
3 egg yolks
1½ cups mashed bananas
¾ cups cold water

3 cups flour
1½ tsp. baking powder
1½ tsp. soda
3/8 tsp. salt
3 beaten egg whites

Mix sugar and shortening. Beat in egg yolks. Add mashed bananas and cold water. Mix the dry ingredients and add to the above mixture. Fold in beaten egg whites. Bake at 325° to 350° for about 1 hour. This is a very moist bread and freezes well.

Gwen Johannes, Blue Earth

BLACK BOTTOM CUPS

2 (3 oz.) pkgs. cream cheese, softened
1/3 cup sugar
1 egg
1 (6 oz.) pkg. semi-sweet chocolate chips
1½ cups flour
1 cup sugar
¼ cup unsweetened cocoa

1 tsp. baking soda
½ tsp. salt
1 cup water
1/3 cup oil
1 Tbsp. vinegar
1 tsp. vanilla
½ cup chopped nuts
2 Tbsp. sugar

Combine cream cheese, 1/3 cup sugar, and egg in a small bowl and mix well. Stir in chocolate chips and set aside. Combine flour, 1 cup sugar, cocoa, soda, and salt. Add water, oil, vinegar, and vanilla. Beat 2 minutes at medium speed. Fill muffin cups half full. Top each with 1 tablespoon cream cheese mixture. Sprinkle with sugar and nuts. Bake at 350° for 20 to 30 minutes. Remove from pan and cool. Refrigerate leftovers. Makes 18 muffin cups.

Jean Strelow, Winona

QUICK BLUEBERRY MUFFINS

1 cup vanilla ice cream, softened
1 cup self-rising flour
1 cup fresh blueberries

1 Tbsp. butter or margarine, melted
2 Tbsp. sugar

In a medium bowl, mix ice cream and flour. Fold in blueberries; spoon into six greased muffin cups. Bake at 375° for 20 to 25 minutes or until muffins test done. While hot, brush muffin tops with butter and sprinkle with sugars. Serve warm. Yield: 6 servings.

Charlotte Morgan, Morristown

BLUEBERRY MUFFINS

1 cup uncooked oatmeal
1 cup orange juice
3 cups flour
4 tsp. baking powder
1 tsp. salt

½ tsp. baking soda
1 cup sugar
1 cup salad oil
2 to 3 beaten eggs
3 to 4 cups fresh blueberries

Mix oatmeal and orange juice. Combine rest ingredients, adding berries last. Fill muffin papers quite full. May sprinkle top with cinnamon, sugar and chopped nuts. Bake at 400° for 15 minutes.

Eulalia Koll, Pipestone
State Treasurer, 1990-1994
State Community Chair, 1994-1996
State Quality of Life Co-Chair, 1996-present

BLUEBERRY COFFEE CAKE

¼ cup margarine
¾ cup sugar
1 egg
½ cup milk
½ tsp. almond extract

2 cups flour
2 Tbsp. baking powder
½ tsp. salt
2 cups blueberries

Cream margarine with sugar; add egg and milk and extract. Mix flour, baking powder and salt; add to first mixture. Carefully fold in blueberries. Spread in greased 9x13 inch cake pan.

Topping:

¼ cup sugar
⅓ cup flour
¼ cup margarine

¼ cup brown sugar
½ tsp. cinnamon

Mix ingredients and sprinkle over coffee cake. Bake at 350° for 45 minutes.

Mary Ann Sullivan, Fairmont

BLUEBERRY MUFFINS

¼ cup safflower or corn oil
½ cup brown sugar
1 cup white flour
1 tsp. baking soda
2 tsp. baking powder
¼ tsp. salt

1 cup 1% buttermilk or skim milk
1 egg or 2 egg whites
⅓ cup oat bran
⅓ cup wheat germ
⅓ cup oatmeal
1⅓ cups blueberries (no sugar)

Combine oil, brown sugar, flour, soda, baking powder and salt. Add buttermilk, egg, oat bran, oatmeal and wheat germ and moisten. Stir in blueberries. Fill paper lined or greased muffin pans ¾ full with batter. Bake at 400° for 20 minutes or until toothpick inserted into center comes out dry. Cool on wire racks. Makes 16.

Note: can substitute raisins for blueberries.

Gertrude Miller, Caledonia

BLUEBERRY MUFFINS

2 cups flour
1 cup sugar
1 Tbsp. melted butter
2 tsp. baking powder
1 tsp. baking soda

1 cup milk
1 egg
⅓ cup oil
½ tsp. salt

Combine the above ingredients by hand, then add **2 cups fresh blueberries**. Put in greased tins. Bake at 350° for 20 minutes.

Teresa Kerkvliet, Marshall
Donna Polacec, Eveleth

AUNT DOROTHY'S MOLASSES BLUEBERRY MUFFINS

1/3 cup margarine
1 cup sugar
1 egg
1/4 cup molasses
2 1/2 cups flour
1 tsp. baking soda
1 tsp. ginger
1 cup sour milk
1 cup blueberries

Cream margarine; add sugar and mix. Add egg and mix. Add molasses and mix. Sift flour, baking soda and ginger together. Add 1/3 of flour and stir. Add the rest of the milk and stir. Add the rest of the flour and stir. Stir in the blueberries.

Pat Rivard, Argyle

MAPLE BRAN MUFFINS

1 cup sour cream
1 cup maple syrup
2 eggs
1 cup flour
1 tsp. soda
1 cup bran flakes (I use fruitful bran)
1/3 cup raisins
1/3 cup chopped walnuts

Combine sour cream, syrup and eggs. Mix flour and soda; add bran, raisins and nuts. Combine with sour cream mixture. May use wire whip for all mixing. Spoon into greased muffin tins or baking cups half full. Bake at 375° for 20 to 25 minutes. Makes about 18 muffins.

Mary Bartly, Blue Earth

ALL BRAN MUFFINS

1 1/4 cups flour
1/2 cup sugar
1 Tbsp. baking powder
1/4 tsp. salt
2 cups Kellogg's All-Bran
1 1/4 cups milk
2 bananas, mashed
1 egg
1/4 cup vegetable oil

Stir together flour, sugar, baking powder and salt. Set aside. In large mixing bowl, combine All Bran cereal and milk. Let stand about 5 minutes or until cereal softens. Add egg and oil and beat well. Add mashed bananas. Add flour mixture, stirring only until combined. Portion batter evenly into twelve 2 1/2 inch muffin tins, coated with cooking spray. Bake at 400° for about 20 minutes or until lightly browned. Serve warm. Yield: 12 muffins.

Marjorie Ness, Faribault

SPICE-BRAN MUFFIN
(LOW CHOLESTEROL AND LOW FAT)

¼ cup non-fat plain yogurt   1½ tsp. baking powder
¼ cup skim milk   1 Tbsp. ginger
Whites from 2 lg. eggs   1 tsp. cloves
¼ cup molasses   Raisins, optional
¼ cup honey or maple syrup   Nutmeats, optional
½ cup wheat bran

Whisk the yogurt, skim milk, and egg whites together. Add the mixture of molasses and honey and stir with a wooden spoon. Add the wheat bran, baking powder, ginger and cloves. Mix and pour into greased muffin tins. Bake at 350° for 25 to 30 minutes.

La Vonne Amberg, Medford

BANANA OR APPLE RAISIN BRAN MUFFINS

1½ cups wheat bran shreds   2 egg whites or ¼ cup egg
1 cup skim milk   beaters
¼ cup oil   1 tsp. cinnamon
½ cup honey   1¼ cups flour
1½ cups either peeled and   2 tsp. baking powder
   grated apple, or 1½ cups   ½ tsp. baking soda
   mashed banana   ½ tsp. salt
¾ cup raisins

Heat oven to 400°. Lightly spray 12 count muffin tin. In a large bowl, soak cereal in milk for 5 minutes. Stir in "wet" ingredients and then "dry" ingredients. Fold in just until dry ingredients are moistened. Makes 12 large muffins. Bake 20 minutes. This is a low cholesterol recipe.

Marge Olson, Eveleth

REFRIGERATOR BRAN MUFFIN READY MIX

5 cups flour   2 cups sugar
5 tsp. baking soda   1 cup shortening
1 to 2 tsp. salt   4 eggs, beaten
2 cups boiling water   1 qt. buttermilk
2 cups All-Bran   4 cups Bran Buds

Sift together flour, soda and salt. Pour boiling water over All Bran; set aside. Cream sugar and shortening in a 6 quart bowl until fluffy. Add eggs; beat well. Add dry ingredients and All Bran. It is recommended to use an ice cream pail with cover. Grease tins or paper line. Fill muffin tins ⅔ to ¾ full. Bake at 375° to 400° for 20 minutes. Do not stir. Once the batter is put in the refrigerator, do not stir the batter, just dip it out to fill tins. Keep in refrigerator up to six weeks.

Rebecca Storey, St. Charles

6 WEEK BRAN MUFFINS

5 cups flour	1 (15 oz.) box bran flakes with
5 tsp. baking soda	raisins
2 tsp. salt	4 eggs
2 tsp. ground allspice	1 cup vegetable oil
3 cups sugar	1 qt. buttermilk
	2 tsp. vanilla

Combine first 4 ingredients in large bowl; add sugar and bran flakes. Mix well. In mixer bowl, beat eggs; add and blend oil, buttermilk and vanilla. Pour egg mixture over flour mixture and stir well. Place used batter in airtight container in refrigerator, will keep for 6 weeks. When ready to use, do not stir batter when dipping it out. Bake in muffin tins at 375° for 20 minutes.

Margaret Zimmerman, Waseca
State Secretary, 1978-1982
State Vice Regent, 1982-1986
Marian Lager, Caledonia

MOLASSES BRAN MUFFINS

2 cups All Bran cereal	1½ cups flour
1½ cups milk	½ cup sugar
¼ cup molasses	1½ tsp. baking soda
¼ cup shortening	½ tsp. salt
1 egg	½ cup raisins

Combine cereal, milk and molasses. Let stand 1 to 2 minutes until cereal is softened. Add shortening and egg; beat well. Combine flour, sugar, soda and salt. Mix well. Stir in raisins. Add cereal mixture; stir just until moistened. Bake at 400° for 14 to 18 minutes or until toothpick inserted in center comes out clean. Makes 18 muffins.

Lillian Walske, Winona

CARAMEL ROLLS

2 loaves frozen bread dough	½ cup butter
½ tsp. cinnamon	¾ cup ice cream
½ cup white sugar	1 cup brown sugar

Thaw and cut each loaf into 16 pieces. Roll each cube of dough in the cinnamon and white sugar, mixed. Place in a 9x13 inch pan. Melt butter, ice cream and brown sugar. Mix and pour over bread cubes. Cover and place in refrigerator. Let rise in refrigerator overnight. Bake at 350° for 40 minutes.

Debra McNamee, Mahnomen

SPICED COCONUT-CARROT MUFFINS

2 cups flour
1 Tbsp. baking powder
1 Tbsp. ground cinnamon
¼ tsp. cloves
¼ tsp. ginger
¼ tsp. nutmeg
1 cup brown sugar
¾ cup white sugar
1 cup shredded coconut
1 cup shredded peeled carrots
1 cup raisins
1 apple, peeled and coarsely chopped
½ cup chopped walnuts
¼ cup oil
½ cup applesauce
½ cup buttermilk
3 lg. eggs
1 Tbsp. vanilla

Line muffin tins with liners. Sift first 6 ingredients into large bowl. Mix in both sugars, then coconut, carrots, raisins, apple and nuts. Whisk in rest of ingredients gradually. Bake at 375° for about 25 minutes.

Karen Riopelle, Argyle

BOHEMIAN COFFEE CAKE

3 cups flour
1 cup white sugar
1 cup brown sugar
1 cup butter or margarine
2 eggs, well beaten
1 cup sour milk or buttermilk
1 tsp. soda
¼ tsp. salt
1 cup chopped dates
1 cup chopped nuts

Sift the flour and mix with the sugars and the butter or margarine until it is as fine as cornmeal. Take out 1 cup of this mixture and save for topping. To the remainder, add the well beaten eggs, sour milk or buttermilk, soda, and salt. Mix well and pour into two 8x10 inch pans or one 9x13 inch pan. Cover with chopped dates and nuts, then sprinkle the rest of the flour and sugar mixture over all. Bake at 350° for 20 to 25 minutes. Serve warm or cold.

Pat Schiefelbein, Waseca

COFFEE CAKE

4 eggs
1 cup sugar
1 cup oil
2 cups flour
1 tsp. baking powder
1 can fruit pie filling

Beat eggs and add sugar and oil; mix well. Add flour and baking powder and stir until blended. Put batter into a 9x13 inch pan. Drop pie filling on top by spoon. Bake at 350° for 30 minutes.

Joyce Kadlec, Pipestone

BUTTER COFFEE CAKE

1 yellow cake mix	4 eggs
1 pkg. instant vanilla pudding	1 tsp. vanilla
¾ cup oil	1 tsp. butter flavoring
¾ cup water	

Beat all ingredients for 8 minutes at high speed. Grease tube pan or bundt pan. Sprinkle ¼ cup chopped nuts in bottom of pan.

Topping:

¼ cup sugar	¼ cup nuts
2 tsp. cinnamon	

Add batter to pan, then topping, alternately in 3 parts. Bake at 350° for 45 to 55 minutes. Cool 8 minutes and turn out. Leave cake wrong side up (if tube pan).

Glaze:

1 cup powdered sugar	½ tsp. butter flavoring
½ tsp. vanilla	Enough milk to mix

Drizzle glaze over cake.

Anna Koski, Moose Lake

PRUNE NUT COFFEE CAKE

3 Tbsp. water	¼ tsp. cloves
1 Tbsp. lemon juice	1/16 tsp. salt
½ cup chopped pitted prunes	1 loaf frozen sweet roll dough,
¼ cup sugar	thawed (or favorite sweet roll
¾ tsp. grated lemon rind	dough)
½ tsp. vanilla	¼ cup walnuts

Mix water, lemon juice and prunes over medium heat. Bring to a boil and reduce to simmer or until prunes are very soft. Stir in sugar, lemon rind, vanilla, cloves and salt. Cool to room temperature. Roll dough to 18x10 inch rectangle. Spread filling to ½ inch of edges. Sprinkle walnuts on, and from long side, roll as for jelly roll, sealing edge well. Place sealed side down on large baking sheet, forming a ring. (Seal ends.) With scissors, cut form outer edge to within ¾ inch of center at 1 inch intervals. Twist each section slightly to show filling. Let rise until double. Bake at 350° for 30 minutes. Can be glazed.

Glaze:

1½ cups powdered sugar	¾ tsp. vanilla
3 Tbsp. milk	

Kris Maas, Owatonna

GOOD COFFEE CAKE

1 Duncan Hines yellow cake mix 1 cup sour milk
4 eggs 1 cup chopped nuts
²/₃ cup oil

Mix all ingredients in order given. Mix topping of ¼ **cup brown sugar** and ¾ **teaspoon cinnamon**. Put half of batter in bundt pan, sprinkle with half of topping. Add rest of batter and sprinkle with rest of topping. Bake at 350° for 1 hour.

Agnes Fuchs, Marshall

RHUBARB COFFEE CAKE

½ cup margarine 1 tsp. soda
1½ cups sugar ½ tsp. salt
1 egg 1 cup buttermilk
1 tsp. vanilla 3 cups rhubarb, cut up
2½ cups flour

Cream margarine and sugar; add eggs and vanilla. In separate bowl, mix flour, soda and salt. Add to creamed mixture alternately with buttermilk. Stir in rhubarb. Put in 3 greased pie pans or a 9x13 inch pan. Sprinkle **1 cup brown sugar** over pan (pans.) Bake at 350° for 45 to 50 minutes. In small pan, heat ½ **cup oleo, 1 cup sugar,** and ½ **cup half and half** or **evaporated milk**, stirring until sugar dissolves. Pour over coffee cake when done.

Donna Harguth, Waseca

SOUR CREAM COFFEE CAKE

1 stick margarine 1 tsp. soda
1 cup sugar 1 tsp. baking powder
2 eggs ½ pt. sour cream
2 cups flour ½ tsp. almond extract
½ tsp. salt ½ cup nuts

Cream margarine and sugar. Add eggs, one at a time. Add dry ingredients alternately with sour cream, then add almond extract and nuts. Sprinkle with ¼ **cup sugar** and **1 teaspoon cinnamon** (mixed) over mixture and then bake at 350° for 45 minutes.

Bea O'Brien, Waseca

BROCCOLI CORNBREAD

2 boxes Jiffy cornbread mix 1 (12 oz.) carton cottage cheese
4 eggs 1 (10 oz.) box frozen broccoli
2 stick butter or margarine 1 med. onion, chopped

Mix all ingredients. Bake in a greased 9x13 inch pan at 350° for 45 minutes.

Marge Eiden, Fairmont

HOMEMADE SYRUP

1 cup white sugar
1 cup brown sugar
1 cup Karo syrup
1 cup water
1 tsp. maple flavor

Bring to a boil and add maple flavor.

Martha Schoenborn, Mahnomen

COLONIAL CORN BREAD

1½ cups yellow cornmeal
2 cups flour
2 Tbsp. sugar
4 tsp. baking powder
1 tsp. salt
2 eggs
2 cups milk
4 Tbsp. bacon drippings or
shortening of your choice

Combine cornmeal, flour, sugar, baking powder and salt in large bowl. Add eggs and milk. Stir to make smooth batter. Stir in bacon drippings. Pour into two greased 8x8x2 inch pans. Bake at 450° for 25 minutes or until crusty and golden brown. Cool slightly in pans on wire racks. Serve warm. May be served with soft butter or homemade jelly. 16 servings.

Florence Dotterwick, Winona

MEXICAN CORN BREAD

1 cup yellow cornmeal
⅓ cup flour
2 Tbsp. sugar
1 tsp. salt
2 tsp. baking powder
½ tsp. soda
2 eggs, beaten
1 cup buttermilk
½ cup vegetable oil
1 (16 oz.) can cream style corn
⅓ cup onion, chopped
2 tsp. chopped pepper
½ cup shredded Cheddar
cheese

In a mixing bowl, combine first 6 ingredients. Combine remaining ingredients and add to dry ingredients; stir only until moistened. Pour into greased 9 inch square baking pan or 10 inch heavy skillet. Bake at 350° for 35 to 40 minutes or until bread is golden brown and tests done. Serves 8 to 10.

Eleanor Simon, Owatonna

INDIAN (CORN MEAL) PUDDING

5 cups skim milk
½ cup cornmeal
⅓ cup dark molasses
2 Tbsp. sugar
½ tsp. salt
¼ tsp. ginger

Scald milk and stir in cornmeal very gradually to avoid lumping. Add the remaining ingredients after milk has thickened. Pour into a buttered baking dish and bake at 300° for 2 hours.

Dorothy Zinda, Owatonna

AMISH FRIENDSHIP BREAD

Starter:

2 cups flour	1 env. yeast
2 cups warm water	1 tsp. salt
¼ cup sugar	

Mix all ingredients in an ice cream pail and let stand overnight in a warm place with a lid; do not cover tightly.

Day 1:
Receive starter, cover loosely; do not refrigerate.

Day 2, 3, 4:
Stir.

Day 5:
Add **1 cup sugar, 1 cup flour** and **1 cup milk**. Stir until well mixed.

Day 6, 7, 8:
Stir.

Day 9:
Pour 1 cup each into 3 containers. Keep one and give two to friends. To remaining batter, add:

3 eggs	**2 tsp. cinnamon**
⅔ cup oil	**½ tsp. baking powder**
2 cups flour	**¼ tsp. salt**
1 cup sugar	**1 apple, peeled and chopped**
1¼ tsp. soda	**Nuts and raisins, optional**

Beat all ingredients and pour into 2 regular bread pans that have been well greased and floured. Bake at 350° for 40 to 50 minutes or until done.

Leone Buchmayer, Caledonia

CRANBERRY BREAD

2 cups flour	Rind and juice from 1 orange
1 cup sugar	2 Tbsp. shortening
1½ tsp. baking powder	1 egg
½ tsp. soda	1 cup cranberries, cut into halves
½ tsp. salt	Nutmeats, optional

Measure flour and blend dry ingredients. Add **water** to orange juice to make ¾ cup. Mix shortening, orange juice mixture and egg. Add to flour mixture. Fold in cranberries, carefully, not to make bread red. Grease a loaf bread pan and bake at 350° for 1 hour. Cool well before cutting; use a very sharp knife.

Margaret Johnson, Texas
Bernice Collins, Iona
Cyrilla Esch, Caledonia
Nina Smith, Plainview

CRANBERRY MUFFINS

1 cup sugar
½ cup shortening
2 eggs
¾ cup orange juice
2 cups flour
½ tsp. soda
1½ tsp. baking powder

1½ tsp. nutmeg
½ tsp. ginger
1 tsp. cinnamon
1 tsp. vanilla
1½ cups chopped cranberries
½ cup nuts

Cream sugar and shortening. Add eggs and orange juice. Sift flour, soda, baking powder and spices. Add to rest of ingredients with vanilla. Fold in cranberries and nuts. Bake at 350° for 25 minutes. Makes 18 muffins.

Marie Reisdorf, St. Charles
Lil Beaumont, St. Peter

EASY CARAMEL ROLLS

¼ cup butter or margarine
½ cup brown sugar
½ cup light corn syrup
1 tsp. maple flavoring

2 loaves frozen white bread
    dough, thawed
More butter, brown sugar and
    cinnamon
Raisins, optional

Melt the ¼ cup butter in a 9x13 inch pan; add the brown sugar, corn syrup and maple flavoring. Stir to blend. Roll out thawed bread, spread with butter, brown sugar, cinnamon and raisins if desired. Roll up and slice. Put slices in pan (lightly grease sides of pan) and let raise until triple in size. Bake at 350° for 20 to 25 minutes. Turn out of pan immediately. Makes about 1½ dozen rolls.

Pauline Kochevar, Eveleth

EASY CARAMEL ROLLS

2 Tbsp. margarine
1 Tbsp. water
½ cup brown sugar firmly
    packed

½ tsp. cinnamon
Nuts, optional
9 frozen cinnamon rolls or other

In an 8 inch square pan, melt margarine; add water, brown sugar and cinnamon. Cook over low heat until caramel texture. Remove from heat; sprinkle nuts over. Let cool. Place frozen cinnamon rolls over caramel mixture and let raise. Bake at 350° until browned, approximately 15 to 17 minutes.

Alice M. Hutchens, Waseca

BUNDT CARAMEL ROLLS

Pecans

Cinnamon

2 dozen rhodes frozen rolls

1 sm. pkg. butterscotch pudding (not instant)

Butter completely bundt pan. Sprinkle pecans on bottom. Layer frozen rolls and sprinkle with cinnamon. Sprinkle dry butterscotch pudding on top.

Caramel Mixture:

½ cup butter

½ cup brown sugar

Pour over top of rolls. Let rise. Bake at 325° for 40 minutes. Remove from oven and let cool slightly. Turn upside down on a large cookie sheet.

Betty Ruths, Waterville

SHORT 'N' SWEET CARAMEL BUBBLE RING

⅓ cup chopped pecans

¾ cup sugar

4 tsp. ground cinnamon

2 (11 oz.) refrigerated bread sticks (16)

⅓ cup margarine or butter, melted

½ cup caramel ice cream topping

2 Tbsp. maple flavored syrup

Generously grease a 10 inch fluted tube pan. Sprinkle about half of the pecans in the bottom of the pan. Set aside. Stir together sugar and cinnamon; set aside. Separate each package of dough into 8 pieces, making a total of 16 pieces. DO NOT unroll. Cut the pieces in half crosswise. Dip each piece of dough into melted margarine or butter, then roll in sugar mixture. Arrange dough pieces, spiral side down, in the prepared pan. Sprinkle with remaining pecans. In a measuring cup, stir together caramel topping and maple flavored syrup, drizzle over dough in pan. Bake at 350° for approximately 35 minutes or until dough is light brown, covering with foil the last 10 minutes to prevent over browning. Let stand for 1 minute only (if it stands for more than 1 minute, the ring will be difficult to remove from pan.) Invert onto a serving platter. Spoon any topping and nuts remaining in the pan onto rolls. Serve warm. Makes 10 to 12 servings.

Romana Posch, St. James

* * * * * * * *

Every word is true from the beginning and every one of thy righteous judgments endureth forever. Psalm 119:160

Mary Christianson, Argyle

BREADS

CARROT BREAD

1 cup brown sugar
¾ cup oil
2 eggs
1½ cups flour
1 tsp. cinnamon

½ tsp. salt
½ tsp. soda
1 tsp. baking powder
1 cup grated carrots
½ cup nuts

Beat the first 3 ingredients well. Combine rest of ingredients and add to creamed mixture. Bake in greased loaf at 350° for 1 hour. Cut time for smaller loaves.

Agnes Post, Thief River Falls

CHRISTMAS MORNING CRANBERRY MUFFINS

¼ cup sugar
1 cup fresh cranberries, coarsely chopped
1½ cups flour
¼ cup sugar
2 tsp. baking powder
1 tsp. salt

½ tsp. cinnamon
¼ tsp. ground allspice
1 egg, beaten
¼ tsp. grated orange peel
¾ cup orange juice
⅓ cup melted butter
¼ cup chopped walnuts

Sprinkle sugar over chopped cranberries and set aside. In a bowl, stir flour, sugar, baking powder, salt, cinnamon and allspice. Make a well in the center of dry ingredients. Combine egg, peel, juice and butter. Add all at once to flour mixture; stir to moisten. Fold in cranberry mixture and nuts. Fill greased or paper lined cups and bake at 350° for 15 to 20 minutes or until golden.

Lorraine Halbersma, Pipestone
District Deputy, 1996-present

CHOCOLATE CHIP FRUIT BREAD

½ cup margarine or butter
1 cup sugar
2 eggs
1 cup mashed bananas
2 cups flour

1 tsp. baking soda
¼ cup nutmeats
¼ cup chocolate chips
½ cup chopped maraschino cherries

Cream margarine, sugar and eggs. Add mashed bananas and mix well. Stir in sifted flour and soda. Add nutmeats, chocolate chips and berries. Mix and pour in loaf pan lined with foil. Bake at 350° for 45 to 60 minutes.

Carole Schumacher, Waseca

SOUR CREAM COFFEE CAKE

½ cup sugar
1½ tsp. cinnamon
½ cup walnuts, chopped
1 yellow cake mix
1 pkg. instant vanilla pudding mix

4 eggs
¾ cup water
1 tsp. vanilla
1 cup sour cream
¼ cup cooking oil

Grease bundt pan heavily. Mix first 3 ingredients. Use part of the mixture to cover all sides of pan. Use remainder for layering. Blend all other ingredients for batter. Alternate layers of batter and sugar mixture. Bake at 350° for 1 hour. Cool well before removing from pan.

Geri Dobie, International Falls

SAVORY CHEESE BREAD

2 cups flour
4 tsp. baking powder
1 Tbsp. sugar
½ tsp. onion salt
½ tsp. oregano
¼ tsp. dry mustard

1¼ cups shredded sharp
Cheddar cheese
1 egg, well beaten
1 cup milk
1 Tbsp. melted butter

Combine flour, baking powder, sugar, salt, oregano, mustard and cheese. Set aside. Combine egg, milk and melted butter. Add this to dry ingredients. Stir just until moistened. Spread batter in greased loaf pan. Bake at 350° for 45 minutes.

Sandy Schneider, International Falls

COFFEE CAKE**

1 cup sugar
4 eggs
1 cup cooking oil

2 cups flour
1 tsp. baking powder
1 can pie mix of your choice

Mix all ingredients, except pie mix. Spread half of batter in a lightly greased and floured 9x13 inch pan. Spread pie mix over this. (May use cherry, blueberry or apricot or whatever you like best.) Top with remaining batter. Sprinkle cinnamon and sugar mix on top. Bake at 350° for 30 minutes. Very good and easy to do.

Anita Ackerman, Slayton

CHEESE BLINTZ COFFEE CAKE**

2 (3 oz.) pkgs. Philadelphia
cream cheese
2 (10 oz.) pkgs. refrigerator
biscuits

½ cup sugar, mixed with 1 tsp.
cinnamon
4 Tbsp. melted butter

Cut cream cheese into 20 pieces. Flatten the biscuits and roll the cheese into balls. Place 1 teaspoon sugar/cinnamon inside the biscuit with the cheese ball and close it up. Put melted butter in bundt pan. Sprinkle sugar and nuts. Place biscuits into bundt pan and bake for 25 minutes. Let cool 5 minutes before serving on plate top with sour cream and preserves.

Cecelia Raleigh, St. Paul

SPECIAL EASY COFFEE CAKE**

1 pkg. yellow cake mix
3 eggs

1 can pie filling (apple, cherry,
or blueberry)

Combine all ingredients and mix until moist. Divide between 2 greased and floured bread pans or a 9x13 inch cake pan.
Topping:

½ cup butter or oleo
½ cup powdered sugar

1 cup flour

Combine the above and sprinkle over the 2 loaves or cake pan and bake at 350° for about 50 minutes. Check to see if toothpick inserted comes out dry (in the cake part).

Reda A. Goemer, St. Paul

OH BOY COFFEE CAKE

1 cup shortening
2 cups sugar
4 eggs
3 cups flour, sifted
3 tsp. baking powder

½ tsp. salt
1 cup milk
Cinnamon and sugar mixture
½ tsp. vanilla

Cream shortening and sugar. Add eggs and beat very well. Sift dry ingredients, except the cinnamon and sugar mixture. Add with milk to egg mixture. Beat very well. The more you beat the lighter it gets. Grease an angel food cake pan and dust with cinnamon and sugar mixture. Put batter in pan in 3 layers; sprinkle each layer with the cinnamon and sugar mixture and on top. Bake at 325° for 1 hour and 10 minutes. Cool ½ hour before removing. Do not invert pan.

Rosemary Kramer, Winona

DANISH PUFF

½ cup butter
1 cup flour

2 tsp. water

Mix like pie crust. Divide into parts. Press on cookie sheet in a 12x3 inch rectangle. Set aside.

½ cup butter

1 cup water

Bring to a boil; add **1 cup flour** and beat very well. Remove from the stove; add **3 eggs**, one at a time and beat until creamy. Spread mixture evenly over the two crusts. Bake at 350° for 1 hour. Frost with light powdered sugar icing and add sliced almonds on top.

Donna Farrell, Marshall
State Regent, 1994-present
First Vice State Regent, 1990-1994

DATE NUT LOAF

1 cup dates, cut up	1 egg
1 tsp. soda, sprinkled over dates	1½ cups flour
1 cup boiling water	¾ cup brown sugar
1 Tbsp. Crisco	¼ tsp. salt
½ cup nuts	1 tsp. vanilla

Pour boiling water over dates; let stand. Mix the rest of the ingredients; add the date mixture. Bake in loaf pan at 350° for 1 hour.

Lorraine Klaseus, Mankato

DATE NUT BREAD

2 cups chopped dates	2 eggs
2 tsp. soda	1 tsp. vanilla
2 cups boiling water	3 cups flour
2 Tbsp. butter or margarine	½ tsp. salt
1½ cups sugar	¾ cup nuts

Put dates in bowl; add soda. Pour boiling water over and let set. Cream butter, sugar, eggs and vanilla; beat well. Add flour, salt, date mixture and nuts. Bake at 325° for 45 minutes.

Helen Houselog, Holland

DONUTS

2¼ cups flour	1 Tbsp. shortening
2 tsp. baking powder	2 eggs
1 cup sugar	1 tsp. vanilla
1 tsp. salt	¾ cup milk or buttermilk
¼ tsp. nutmeg	

Sift dry ingredients; add softened shortening. Add eggs, vanilla and milk. Fry at 365° in 2 inches of shortening.

Frances Kunz, Waseca

MA GIESLEIS DONUTS

3 Tbsp. lard
1 cup sugar
3 eggs
1 cup milk
3½ cups flour

4½ tsp. baking powder
1 scant tsp. salt
½ tsp. nutmeg
1 tsp. vanilla

Mix lard, sugar and eggs. Gradually add milk with the flour, baking powder and salt sifted together. Add nutmeg and vanilla and chill overnight. Roll out about ⅓ inch thick. Put in greased 400°, turn immediately. Do not roll too many ahead of time; they get soft when warm.

Margaret Stadtler, Caledonia

DOUGHNUTS

3 eggs, beaten light
1 cup sugar
3 Tbsp. shortening, melted
   Mix and set aside.
2 tsp. baking powder
4 cups flour or enough to roll
   only

1 cup sour cream
½ tsp. soda

1 tsp. salt
½ tsp. nutmeg
¼ tsp. cinnamon

Sift together and add to above mixture. Turn on floured cloth and knead. Chill overnight. Roll out ⅓ inch thick and fry in grease at 400° until brown. Turn as soon as it comes to top of grease.

Lorraine Schmitt, Caledonia

BAKED CAKE DOUGHNUTS

1½ cups flour
½ cup sugar
2 tsp. baking powder
¼ tsp. salt
¼ tsp. nutmeg

1 lg. egg
½ cup milk
⅓ cup melted butter
½ tsp. vanilla
Jelly or marmalade

In a bowl, mix flour, sugar, baking powder, salt and nutmeg. In a small bowl, mix egg. Blend with milk, melted butter and vanilla. Add to flour mixture and stir just to moisten. Spoon half of batter into 12 buttered muffin tins. Add ½ teaspoon jelly to each, top equally with remaining batter. Bake at 400° until golden brown, 18 to 20 minutes.

Topping:
⅓ cup sugar
½ tsp. cinnamon

⅔ cup melted butter

Mix sugar and cinnamon. Brush baked doughnuts with melted butter and roll in sugar. Serve warm. Makes 12. Store in airtight container for future use.

Margaret Liebrenz, Owatonna

FRUIT BREAD

¼ cup dates, cut up
½ cup raisins
1 cup prunes, cut up
1 cup water
½ cup margarine

1 tsp. vanilla
½ tsp. salt
1 tsp. soda
1 cup flour
½ cup chopped nuts

Boil dates, raisins, and prunes in water for 5 minutes. Add margarine and cool. Add remaining ingredients and mix well. Bake in greased loaf pan at 350° for 25 to 30 minutes. Cool. Makes about 12 slices.

Alice Ditsch, International Falls

SUNDAY FRENCH TOAST

8 slices French bread, ¾ inches thick
4 eggs
1 cup milk
2 Tbsp. grand mariner or orange juice

1 Tbsp. sugar
½ tsp. vanilla
¼ tsp. salt
2 Tbsp. butter or margarine
Powdered sugar

Arrange bread in single layer in a 12x8x2 inch baking dish. In medium bowl, with rotary beater, beat eggs with milk, grand mariner (or orange juice), sugar, vanilla and salt until well blended. Pour over bread. Turn slices to coat evenly. Refrigerate, covered, overnight. In hot butter in skillet, saute bread until golden, about 4 minutes on each side. Sprinkle with powdered sugar. Serves 4.

Alice Boucher, Crookston

GOOD COMPANY FRENCH TOAST

French bread, cut in thick slices (10 to 12 to loaf)
About 1 egg for each 2 slices

¼ cup milk for each egg
Add little salt

Soak each slice (10 minutes each side or less time). Melt ½ **stick oleo or butter** in cake pan. Put egg bread in oleo and turn over. Bake at 450° for 20 minutes. Serve with bacon, sausage, or ham.

June Ankeny, Blue Earth

GARLIC TOAST

1 loaf French bread, sliced
1 lb. butter

1 lb. margarine
2 Tbsp. garlic powder

Melt butter, margarine and garlic powder together. Dip the slices of French bread into the butter mixture. Bake at 300° on both sides until light brown on a cookie sheet. After all toast is done, turn off oven and let toast cool in oven; it will dry out that way.

Jan McDonald, Owatonna

GARLIC BUBBLE LOAF

1 loaf frozen bread dough	½ tsp. garlic powder
¼ cup melted margarine	1 tsp. parsley flakes
1 egg, beaten	¼ tsp. salt

Thaw and cut bread dough into 1½ inch squares. Mix together melted margarine, egg, garlic powder, parsley flakes and salt. Dip each dough piece into mixture and place in greased loaf pan. Pour unused portion of mixture over top of dough. Let rise until it doubles in size. Bake at 375° for 30 minutes.

Arleen Borden, International Falls

GINGER MUFFINS

1 beaten egg	½ tsp. baking soda
½ cup sugar	½ tsp. ginger
¼ cup molasses	¼ tsp. nutmeg
¼ cup salad oil	¼ tsp. cinnamon
1 cup flour	½ cup boiling water
⅛ tsp. salt	

Combine all ingredients, adding water last. Fill muffin cups ⅔ full. Bake at 350° for 25 to 30 minutes. Makes 1 dozen.

Lorraine Klaseus, Mankato

GINGERBREAD

2 eggs, beaten	1½ tsp. cinnamon
¾ cup brown sugar	½ tsp. cloves
¾ cup dark molasses	½ tsp. nutmeg
¾ cup melted shortening	1 tsp. soda
2½ cups flour	½ tsp. salt
2 tsp. baking powder	1 cup boiling water
2 tsp. ginger	

Add beaten eggs to the sugar, molasses and melted shortening. Add the dry ingredients which have been mixed together and sifted. Last, add the boiling water all at once and stir quickly and pour in floured tins or a cake pan. Small loaf tins work well. Bake at 350° for 30 to 40 minutes. Glaze top if you like or slice like banana bread and spread with butter.

Lorraine Olson, Crookston
District Deputy, 1978-1982
State Community Chair, 1982-1984

GLORIFIED GINGERBREAD

2 cups flour
1 cup sugar
½ tsp. cinnamon
½ tsp. ginger
½ cup shortening

1 egg
2 Tbsp. molasses
1 cup sour milk
½ tsp. soda
1½ tsp. baking powder

Sift flour, then measure and sift with sugar, cinnamon and ginger. Cut shortening in until mixture is of crumb-like consistency. Take out ½ cup of this for topping. Beat egg, molasses and ¾ cup sour milk. Add to first mixture. Combine soda and baking powder with remaining ¼ cup sour milk. Mix quickly and add to other ingredients. Pour into well buttered 8x8 inch pan. Sprinkle the ½ cup of topping on. Bake at 350° for 40 to 45 minutes.

Sally Lubinski, Plainview

GOLDEN HARVEST MUFFINS

2 cups all-purpose flour
2 cups whole wheat flour
4 tsp. baking soda
2 cups sugar
1 tsp. salt
2 tsp. cinnamon
½ tsp. cloves
4 cups shredded peeled apples

1 cup shredded carrots
1 cup coconut
1 cup raisins
1 cup chopped walnuts
1½ cups oil
½ cup milk
2 tsp. vanilla
3 beaten eggs

Combine dry ingredients. Add apples, carrots, coconut, raisins and walnuts. Mix well. Add oil, milk, vanilla and eggs. Stir until moistened. Fill greased muffin tins and bake at 350° for 20 to 25 minutes.

Agnes Prairie, Russell

HERB BREAD

2 loaves French bread, cut
    in 1 inch slices
2 sticks soft butter
1 tsp. parsley flakes

¼ tsp. oregano
¼ tsp. dill weed
¼ tsp. garlic powder

Spread the above mixture on both sides of the sliced bread. Lay slice back together and wrap in foil. Spread any left over mixture on top, sprinkle with Parmesan cheese and little more parsley flakes. Bake at 400° for 10 minutes.

Mary Ann Schmitz, Caledonia

LEMON BREAD

1 lemon cake mix
4 eggs
⅓ cup oil

1 pkg. instant lemon pudding
½ cup powdered sugar
4 Tbsp. lemon juice

Mix cake, eggs, oil and lemon pudding. Bake in 2 loaf pans at 350° for 35 minutes. Prick holes in loaves while warm and pour the mixed lemon juice and powdered sugar on loaf. Cool in pan.

Ianilla Koob, Iona

MORNING GLORY MUFFINS

2 cups flour
1¼ cups sugar
2 tsp. baking soda
2 tsp. cinnamon
½ tsp. salt
1 cup coconut
3 eggs

1 cup salad oil
2 tsp. vanilla
½ cup raisins
1 apple, peeled, cored and
  grated
2 cups grated carrots
½ cup chopped nuts

Mix flour, sugar, soda, cinnamon, salt and coconut. Add eggs, oil and vanilla. Mix in remaining ingredients. Bake in muffin tins at 350° for 20 minutes. Freezes well.

Gladys Boucher, Crookston
Angie Wosick, Moorhead
Josephine Kochmann, Mahnomen

MUFFINS

1½ cups flour
1½ tsp. baking powder
½ tsp. salt
¼ tsp. mace
½ cup sugar

⅓ cup oil
1 egg
1 tsp. vanilla
½ cup milk

Mix flour, baking powder, salt and mace. Beat together sugar, oil, egg and vanilla at medium speed for 30 seconds. Add flour and milk alternately to egg mixture on low speed. Put ⅔ cup into 10 greased muffin tins. Bake at 350° for 15 to 20 minutes or until firm. Mix **½ cup sugar, 6 tablespoons melted butter,** and **1 teaspoon cinnamon.** Remove muffins while hot and roll in sugar, cinnamon mixture.

Dorothy Steinbauer, Medford

NUT BREAD

1 cup brown sugar	1 tsp. soda
2 eggs	2 cups flour
1 cup sour cream	1 cup nutmeats

Beat hard the brown sugar and eggs. Add sour cream, soda, flour and nutmeats. Bake in loaf pan at 350° for 45 minutes or until toothpick comes out clean.

Monica Galvin, Currie
Doris Desrosier, Crookston

NUT BREAD

2 cups brown sugar	2 cups flour
3 egg yolks with little water added	1 tsp. soda in a little vinegar
	½ tsp. salt
1 cup sour milk	1 cup chopped nuts

Bake in two small bread pans or one ordinary bread pan at 350° for 1 hour.

Cordula Brady, Caledonia

NUT BREAD

1 cup brown sugar	1 tsp. soda, dissolved in warm water
1 egg	
1 cup sour milk or buttermilk	1¾ cups flour
	½ cup nuts, chopped

Mix ingredients in order given and bake at 375° for 1 hour. Makes 1 loaf.

Rita Krzebietke, New Albin, IA

OATMEAL MUFFINS

1 cup quick cooking oats	1 Tbsp. melted shortening
1 cup sour milk or 1 cup sweet milk and 1 Tbsp. vinegar	1 cup flour
	1 tsp. baking powder
1 egg	½ tsp. soda
½ cup brown sugar	½ cup walnuts or raisins, optional

Soak oatmeal in sour milk for 15 minutes. Add egg and beat well. Add sugar and mix. Add cooled shortening. Mix, then add the sifted flour with baking powder and soda. Bake in greased muffin pans ²/₃ full at 400° for 15 to 20 minutes or until brown. Makes 1 dozen muffins.

Clarice Schmitz, Mankato
Margaret Tri, Mazeppa

PINEAPPLE NUT BREAD

1 egg
¼ cup milk
¼ cup melted shortening
1 (8 oz.) can crushed pineapple
1 cup white raisins
½ cup chopped pecans

2 cups flour
½ cup sugar
1 tsp. baking powder
½ tsp. soda
½ tsp. salt

Combine beaten egg, milk, shortening, pineapple, raisins and pecans. Combine flour, sugar, baking powder, soda, and salt. Pour above mixture over flour mixture. Mix just until all is moistened. Bake in greased and floured 9x5x3 inch bread pan at 350° for 1 hour. Let rise 10 minutes before putting in oven.

Mary Huesmann, Caledonia

HE MAN HOT CAKES

1 egg
2 Tbsp. melted shortening
¾ cup plus 3 Tbsp. milk
1 cup flour
2 Tbsp. sugar

½ tsp. salt
2 Tbsp. baking powder or 1 Tbsp.
baking powder and 1 tsp.
soda

Beat egg and add melted shortening and milk. Add dry ingredients and stir. Never stir later on, just cut batter from sides of bowl. Bake on heated griddle or in fry pan.

Dee Alt, St. Peter

COUNTRY PANCAKES

1½ cups sifted flour
1 Tbsp. baking powder
2½ Tbsp. sugar
½ tsp. salt

1½ cups milk
1 egg, beaten
3 Tbsp. melted margarine or
cooking oil

Mix dry ingredients in bowl. Blend in milk, egg and margarine or oil. Stir only until moistened yet bumpy. Bake on hot griddle.

Angeline DeWitte, Holland

PANCAKES

5 eggs, beaten
1 qt. buttermilk
1 tsp. salt
1 tsp. baking powder

1½ tsp. soda
2 Tbsp. white sugar
3 cups flour

Beat eggs; add buttermilk, salt, baking powder, soda and sugar. Stir in flour. Don't over-mix.

Martha Schoenborn, Mahnomen

POLISH APPLE PANCAKES

1 cup flour
1 Tbsp. sugar
½ tsp. salt
1 egg
1 cup milk

1 Tbsp. vegetable oil
3 to 5 med. apples, peeled and thinly sliced or shredded coarsely
Confectioner's sugar, optional

In a bowl, combine flour, sugar and salt. In another bowl, lightly beat egg; add milk and oil. Add dry ingredients and stir until smooth. Fold in apples. Pour batter by half cupfuls onto a lightly greased hot griddle and spread to form 5 inch circles. Turn when bubbles form. Cook the second side until golden brown and apples are tender. Sprinkle with confectioner's sugar if desired or you can use maple syrup. Yield: 14 to 16 pancakes. Very Good!

Mary Jane Conroy, St. Peter

BUTTERMILK PANCAKES

2 cups buttermilk
2 eggs
1 tsp. salt
3 Tbsp. corn oil

1 tsp. soda
¼ cup sugar
2 cups flour

In mixing bowl, combine buttermilk, eggs, salt, oil, soda and sugar. Beat well and add the flour. If batter is too thin, add a little more flour. Drop batter on heated griddle. Serve with maple syrup or favorite topping.

Angie Bork, Fountain City, WI
Gladys Doris, International Falls

BLUEBERRY YOGURT PANCAKES

1 cup all-purpose flour
1 Tbsp. sugar
1 tsp. baking powder
½ tsp. baking soda
¼ tsp. salt
⅛ tsp. ground nutmeg

1 egg
½ cup plain yogurt
½ cup milk
2 Tbsp. salad oil
¾ cup fresh or unsweetened frozen blueberries

Stir together flour, sugar, baking powder, soda, salt and nutmeg. Beat egg with yogurt and milk in a large bowl. Beat in oil, then add flour mixture. Stir just until combined. (Batter can be a little lumpy.) Grease seasoned pancake griddle. Use a scant ¼ cup batter for each pancake. Serve at once with butter and syrup. Makes about twelve 4 inch pancakes. Makes 3 to 4 servings.

Isabelle Rahm, International Falls

BLENDER OATMEAL PANCAKES

1 cup dry quick cooking oatmeal	1 tsp. soda
1½ cups buttermilk	1 tsp. sugar
½ cup flour	2 eggs
	¾ tsp. salt

Mix oatmeal and buttermilk. Add flour, soda and sugar. Add eggs and salt. Put in blender and blend briefly. Serves 2 to 4.

Bernadine Flynn, Windom

POTATO PANCAKES

5 potatoes	1 Tbsp. parsley, chopped
2 eggs, beaten	½ tsp. salt
1 Tbsp. flour	Pinch of pepper
1 med. onion, chopped	

Pare potatoes and grate into cold water to keep from discoloring. Drain well. Add eggs and flour to potatoes. Blend in onion, parsley, salt and pepper. Heat ½ inch hot oil in frying pan. When oil is hot, pour spoonfuls of batter in for each pancake. Cook until browned and crisp. Drain on paper towel. Serve with favorite fixings.

Rosalie Grams, Janesville

GERMAN OVEN PANCAKE

½ cup sifted flour	2 Tbsp. butter or margarine, melted
3 slightly beaten eggs	
½ cup milk	¼ tsp. salt

Gradually add flour to eggs, beating with rotary beater. Stir in milk, melted butter and salt. Thoroughly grease a 9 or 10 inch oven proof skillet. Pour batter into cold skillet; bake in very hot oven (450°) for about 20 minutes. It will puff up in an irregular manner. Loosen pancake from skillet with wide spatula. Cut into wedges with sharp knife. Serve with confectioner's sugar, fresh lemon sprinkle over that, and more melted butter. Or, cover half of whole pancake with apple pie filling (canned or homemade) or thick applesauce (1½ to 2 cups) and fold over. Serve in wedges with whipped topping or ice cream, or drizzle with melted butter and powdered sugar, or serve plain.

Kathy Dibble, Chicago
Joan Parries, Moorhead
Theresa Kubicek, Owatonna

PINEAPPLE CARROT BREAD

3 cups all-purpose flour
2 cups sugar
1 tsp. baking soda
1 tsp. cinnamon
¾ tsp. salt
3 eggs
2 cups shredded carrots
1 cup vegetable oil
1 (8 oz.) can crushed pineapple
1 cup chopped pecans or walnuts
2 tsp. vanilla
¾ cup powdered sugar, optional
1 to 1½ tsp. milk, optional

In large bowl, combine flour, sugar, baking soda, cinnamon and salt. In another bowl, beat eggs. Add carrots, oil, pineapple, nuts and vanilla. Stir in dry ingredients until moistened. Spoon into two greased and floured 8½x4½x2½ inch loaf pans. Bake at 350° for 65 to 75 minutes. Cool 10 minutes in pan before removing to wire rack. Frost if you wish.

Geneva Fessel, Waterville

QUICK PECAN ROLLS**

Pecan halves, as much as you want
1½ to 2 cups pecan rolls (18 frozen Rhodes rolls)
¾ cup brown sugar
2 Tbsp. water
2 tsp. cinnamon
1 stick butter
1 pkg. butterscotch pudding (not instant)

Butter a 9x13 inch pan heavily; sprinkle pecan halves over bottom of pan. Place rolls in pan on top of pecans. Melt together in sauce the brown sugar, water, cinnamon and stick of butter. Spoon syrup mixture over top of rolls. Sprinkle package of dry butterscotch pudding mix over top. Prepare the night before; cover with foil and put in cold oven overnight. In morning, remove foil and bake at 350° for 20 minutes. Let cool 5 to 10 minutes, then turn over onto tray. Scrape extra syrup from pan and drizzle over rolls.

Doris Halvorson, International Falls

POPPY SEED LOAF**

1 pkg. white or yellow cake mix
½ cup Wesson oil
¼ cup poppy seed
4 eggs
1 tsp. vanilla
1 (3 oz.) pkg. vanilla pudding
1 cup warm water

Beat for 4 minutes. Bake in 2 loaf pans at 325° for 45 minutes.

Anita Orzechowski, Winona

PUMPKIN BREAD

3⅓ cups flour
2 tsp. soda
1½ tsp. salt
1 tsp. cinnamon
1 tsp. nutmeg
1 tsp. cloves

3 cups sugar
1 cup oil
4 eggs
⅔ cup water
2 cups pumpkin
1 cup chopped walnuts

Sift dry ingredients together in a large mixing bowl. Mix well, adding remaining ingredients. Mix all until smooth. Place in 3 greased bread pans. Bake at 350° for 1 hour or until tested done with a toothpick. Cool, wrap and refrigerate one day before serving.

Nancy Andert, Currie

PUMP-CAN BREAD

3 cups flour
1 Tbsp. baking powder
1 tsp. salt
1 tsp. cinnamon
½ tsp. nutmeg
¼ tsp. ground cloves
½ cup pecans, chopped

2 eggs, beaten
1 cup milk
1 cup canned pumpkin
¾ cup light brown sugar
¼ cup oil
1 tsp. baking soda

Mix flour, baking powder, salt and spices. Add pecans. In separate bowl, blend eggs, milk, pumpkin, brown sugar, oil and soda. Add all at once to dry ingredients. Stir only until the flour is moistened. Pour batter into two greased 1 pound coffee cans. Bake at 350° for 1 hour and 15 minutes, or until done. Cool 15 minutes before removing from cans. Cool thoroughly before cutting.

Rosalie Grams, Janesville

RANCH BREAD

2 eggs
1 cup mashed bananas
½ cup melted shortening, cooled
¼ cup chopped nuts

¼ cup maraschino cherries, cut up
¼ cup chocolate chips
2 cups flour
1 cup sugar
2½ tsp. baking powder
½ tsp. salt

Beat eggs until thick. Blend in bananas, melted shortening, nuts, cherries and chocolate chips. Sift dry ingredients into a bowl, make a well in the center and add liquids all at once. Stir until moistened. Put into well-greased bread pan and bake at 350° for 45 minutes.

Anita McNulty, Eveleth

RAISED DOUGHNUTS

3 to 3½ cups flour
2 pkgs. yeast
¾ cup milk
⅓ cup sugar

¼ cup corn oil
2 tsp. salt
2 eggs

In mixing bowl, combine 1½ cups flour and yeast. In saucepan, heat milk, sugar, oil and salt until warm, stirring constantly. Add eggs. Add to dry mixture. Beat thoroughly. Stir in enough remaining flour to make a soft dough. Turn onto lightly floured surface. Knead until smooth and elastic. Put in lightly greased bowl. Cover and let rise 30 to 45 minutes. Punch down. Divide dough in half. Roll to ½ inch thickness. Cut with doughnut cutter. Let rise until very light 30 to 40 minutes. Fry in deep fat at 375° until golden. Drain on paper toweling. Roll in sugar while warm or frost with glaze.

Glaze:
2 cups powdered sugar
¼ cup milk

1 tsp. vanilla

Angie Bork, Fountain City, WI

RAISIN GEM MUFFINS

1 cup raisins
¾ cup water
¾ cup sugar
1 egg
½ cup oleo

½ tsp. cinnamon or nutmeg
Pinch of salt
1½ cups flour
1 tsp. baking soda
½ tsp. baking powder

Bring to boil and simmer for 5 minutes the raisins and the water. Drain, saving the water. Bring volume of water to ½ cup by adding water as necessary. Cream sugar, egg, oleo, cinnamon or nutmeg and salt. Add flour, soda and baking powder; mix well. Add raisins and raisin water; blend. Fill lined (or use baking non-stick spray) muffin tins about ²/₃ full. Sprinkle with sugar. Bake at 350° for 25 minutes.

Kathryn Aldrich, Eveleth

* * * * * * * *

But the Lord is faithful and he shall strengthen you and keep you from the evil one. And the Lord direct your hearts into the love of God, and into the patient waiting for Christ. II Thessalonians 3:3,4
Vi Larson, Argyle

RHUBARB BREAD

1½ cups brown sugar
⅔ cup salad oil
1 egg
1 tsp. vanilla
1 cup sour milk

1 tsp. salt
1 tsp. soda
2½ cups flour
1½ cups diced fresh rhubarb
½ cup chopped nuts

Cream first 3 ingredients. Add vanilla and mix. Add milk alternately with dry ingredients, then add rhubarb and nuts. Pour into two greased loaf pans. Sprinkle over the batter a mixture of **½ cup sugar** and **1 tablespoon butter or margarine**. Bake at 325° for 60 minutes. Do not overbake. "Ambrosia from the garden!" My family looks forward to this each spring and anyone who has tasted it asks for the recipe. I found this in the Minneapolis paper many years ago.

Lorraine Kantor, International Falls
Helen Griffen Waldorf, Perham
Leona Buchmayer, Caledonia
Gen Bleess, Blue Earth

RHUBARB MUFFINS

½ cup brown sugar
¼ cup sugar
⅓ cup salad oil
½ cup sour milk
1¼ cups flour
½ tsp. cinnamon

½ tsp. salt
1 cup rhubarb, cut fine
1 egg
½ tsp. soda
½ tsp. vanilla
½ cup chopped nuts

Mix and pour into muffin tins.
Topping:
¼ cup sugar
¼ tsp. cinnamon

2 tsp. butter

Mix and sprinkle over muffins. Bake at 325° for 25 minutes. Makes 12 large muffins.

Bubbles Cunningham, Waseca

* * * * * * * * *

*Pleasant words are as honeycomb, sweet to the soul,
and health to the bones. Proverbs 16:24*
Irene Nowacki, Argyle

90

NUTTY RHUBARB MUFFINS

¾ cup packed brown sugar	2 cups all-purpose flour
½ cup buttermilk or sour milk	½ tsp. salt
⅓ cup vegetable oil	½ tsp. baking soda
1 egg, beaten	1 cup diced rhubarb
1 tsp. vanilla	½ cup chopped nuts

In a small mixing bowl, combine brown sugar, buttermilk, oil, egg and vanilla; mix well and set aside. In a medium mixing bowl, combine flour, baking soda and salt. Add egg mixture; stir just until combined. Add rhubarb and nuts. Spoon the batter into 12 greased muffin cups.

Topping:

¼ cup packed brown sugar	½ tsp. ground cinnamon
¼ cup chopped nuts	

Mix ingredients and sprinkle over tops of muffins. Bake at 375° for 20 minutes or until muffins test done. Yield: 1 dozen.

Leona Buchmayer, Caledonia
Patty Durand, Argyle
Luella Andert, Slayton

RAISIN OAT MUFFINS

1½ cups low-fat buttermilk	½ cup egg substitute
1½ cups rolled oats	½ cup brown sugar
1½ cups all-purpose flour	⅓ cup oil
1 Tbsp. baking powder	1 tsp. maple flavoring
½ tsp. baking soda	1 cup raisins
2 tsp. ground cinnamon	

Preheat oven to 400°. Use muffin cups or spray with vegetable cooking spray. Pour buttermilk over oats. In another bowl, mix flour with baking powder, soda and cinnamon. Add to soaked oats. Combine egg, brown sugar, oil and flavoring. Add to flour mixture. Add raisins. Gently fold together until moistened. Spoon into muffin cups. Bake 20 to 25 minutes; cool 5 minutes.

Armella Willaert, North Mankato

IRISH SODA BREAD

¾ cup wheat germ	1 tsp. salt
1½ cups white flour	1 tsp. soda
1½ cups whole wheat flour	2½ cups buttermilk
2 Tbsp. sugar, optional	

Mix dry ingredients; gradually add milk to make soft moist dough. Pour into greased, floured bread pan (loaf). Bake at 350° for 1 hour. Makes 1 loaf.

Betty Burg, Caledonia
Lorraine McMahon, National Executive Secretary, New York, NY

STRAWBERRY BREAD

3 cups all-purpose flour
2 cups sugar
1½ tsp. cinnamon
1 tsp. baking soda
1 tsp. salt

1 cup cooking oil
4 beaten eggs
2 cups crushed strawberries
1¼ cups chopped pecans or
walnuts

Combine flour, sugar, cinnamon, soda and salt in one bowl and set aside. Combine oil, eggs and strawberries. Stir into flour mixture just until moistened. Add chopped nuts. Pour into two greased 8x4x2 inch loaf pans. Bake bread at 350° for 1 hour. Makes 2 loaves.

Grace Kaveney, St. Peter
Bea Hawkins, Waseca
Paulette Hansen, Red Lake Falls

STRAWBERRY BREAD

½ cup butter or margarine
1 cup sugar
2 eggs, separated
2 cups flour
1 tsp. baking powder
1 tsp. soda

½ tsp. salt
1 cup crushed fresh strawberries
(slightly sweetened), or
1 (10 oz.) pkg. frozen berries,
thawed and drained

Cream butter and sugar. Add egg yolks. Combine dry ingredients; add alternately with strawberries and beat well. Lastly, fold in well beaten egg whites. Bake in greased large loaf pan or 2 small tins at 350° for 50 to 60 minutes. Mix filling ingredients and spread on cooled crust. Top with your favorite fruits (grapes, pears, apples, kiwi, blueberries, strawberries, raspberries, peaches, bananas, etc.)

Luella Heim, Medford

SUNSHINE MUFFINS

1½ cups flour
1 cup whole wheat flour
1⅔ cups sugar
2 tsp. baking powder
½ tsp. salt
¾ cup butter or margarine,
melted

3 eggs, beaten
⅔ cup fresh orange juice
1 tsp. vanilla
1 tsp. orange extract
1 Tbsp. orange marmalade
½ cup chopped walnuts

In a large bowl, combine flours, sugar, baking powder and salt. Add remaining ingredients. Stir just until moistened (batter may be lumpy). Fill greased or papered muffin cups ⅔ full. Bake at 350° for 15 to 20 minutes or until top of muffin springs back when lightly touched. Yield: 15 to 18 muffins.

JoAnn Zelesnikar, Eveleth

STRAWBERRY MUFFINS

Muffins:

2 cups flour
1 Tbsp. baking powder
½ tsp. salt
1 cup strawberries, hulled and chopped

⅓ cup sugar
½ cup heavy or whipping cream
1 egg, lightly beaten
½ tsp. vanilla
¼ cup melted butter

Combine flour, baking powder and salt. In a separate bowl, combine strawberries and sugar. Let stand 5 minutes. Stir in cream, egg and vanilla until well blended. Add strawberry mixture. Add melted butter. Stir with fork just until blended. Put in muffin cups and sprinkle with topping. Bake at 400° for 12 to 15 minutes.

Topping:

⅓ cup flour
¼ cup sugar
¼ cup finely chopped pecans

2 Tbsp. butter, room temperature
½ tsp. cinnamon

Sue Stangler, Waseca

SWISS BREAD

1 long loaf French bread
1 (8 oz.) pkg. sliced Swiss cheese
¾ cup butter

1 med. onion, diced
2 Tbsp. poppy seeds

Put bread on heavy foil. Cut into thick slices (don't cut quite through the bottom). Put 1 slice of cheese on each slice of bread. Melt the butter with the diced onion. Add the poppy seeds. Pour over the bread. Sprinkle with paprika. Wrap well and bake at 350° for 20 minutes.

Anne Varner, Zumbrota

WHIPPED CREAM WAFFLES

For each person, allow:

½ cup whipping cream
1 egg

2 heaping Tbsp. flour
¼ tsp. baking powder

Whip the cream. Add beaten egg or eggs, then sifted dry ingredients. (One recipe makes two regular waffles.)

Marie Palmer, New Ulm

YELLOW BREAD

1 yellow cake mix
1 pkg. instant vanilla pudding
¾ cups water
¾ cup oil

1 tsp. vanilla
1 tsp. butter extract
4 eggs

Beat ingredients for 8 minutes. Pour half of batter in 2 loaf pans. Mix ¼ **cup sugar** and **1 teaspoon cinnamon**. Spread over loaf mixture. Top with remaining butter. Bake until golden brown.

Note: 1 package raspberry jello may be used instead of cinnamon mixture.

Marcia Peterson, Mahnomen

SPICY PINEAPPLE ZUCCHINI BREAD

3 eggs
1 cup salad oil
2 cups sugar
2 tsp. vanilla
2 cups shredded zucchini
1 cup crushed pineapple, well
drained
3 cups flour

2 tsp. soda
1 tsp. salt
½ tsp. baking powder
1½ tsp. cinnamon
¾ tsp. nutmeg
1 cup chopped nuts
1 cup raisins or currants

Mix all ingredients. Bake at 350°. Test for doneness with toothpick.

Lillian Patterson, Wabasha
Jean Schindler, Red Lake Falls

ZUCCHINI BREAD

3 eggs
1 cup cooking oil
¾ cup white sugar
¾ cup brown sugar
3 cups flour
1 tsp. baking soda

1 tsp. salt
2 tsp. cinnamon
¼ tsp. baking powder
2 cups zucchini, grated
1 cup nuts or raisins, optional

Mix the eggs, oil and sugars. Sift the flour, soda, salt, cinnamon and baking powder. Add it to the egg mixture. Add the zucchini and nuts or raisins. Pour into two greased bread pans. Bake at 350° for 45 minutes.

Zita Mittelstaedt, Waseca
District Deputy, 1996-present
Jeanne Schuetzle, Cary, IL

ZUCCHINI NUT BREAD

1 cup melted butter	½ tsp. soda
1 cup sugar	½ tsp. nutmeg
1¾ cups flour	1 cup grated zucchini
2 eggs	½ cup nuts
½ tsp. salt	1 tsp. vanilla

Combine all ingredients and put in a 9x5x3 inch pan. Bake at 350° for 50 to 60 minutes or until toothpick comes out clean.

Roberta Tissek, St. Paul

ORANGE ZUCCHINI BANANA BREAD

6 eggs	1½ cups grated zucchini
4 cups sugar	1½ cups mashed bananas
2 cups oil	1 cup orange juice concentrate
6 cups flour	2 tsp. lemon extract
2 tsp. baking soda	

Beat eggs with sugar and oil. Add dry ingredients. Add zucchini, bananas, orange juice and lemon extract. Pour into 4 greased and floured loaf pans. Bake at 350° for 1 hour.

Kate Huneke, Bellechester

ZUCCHINI MUFFINS

2 cups whole wheat flour	2 egg whites, slightly beaten
1 Tbsp. baking powder	¼ cup oil
½ tsp. salt	¼ cup honey
1 tsp. cinnamon	1 cup zucchini, shredded
¾ cup skim milk	

Heat oven to 375°. Grease muffin tins lightly with oil. Mix dry ingredients thoroughly. Mix remaining ingredients. Add to dry ingredients. Stir until dry ingredients are barely moistened. Batter will be lumpy. Fill muffin tins ⅔ full. Bake 20 minutes.

Catherine Shikonya, Winona

* * * * * * * *

For the eyes of the Lord are over the righteous,
and his ears are open unto their prayers. I Peter 3:12

Lord, help me to put away my selfish pride and
show my Christian witness by being friendly to others.
Lil Robertson, Argyle

PRETZELS

At certain times long, long ago
In countries far away,
The people made a bread that would
Remind them they should pray.

Some water, salt and flour
Were mixed with greatest care,
then the dough was shaped like arms
That cross the heart in prayer.

We too can have this twisted bread
At any time of day,
The little pretzel still is here
Reminding us to pray.

✞ MINNESOTA LIFE CARE CENTERS ✞

The Minnesota Life Care Centers were incorporated in February, 1974 in response to the U.S. Supreme Court decision legalizing abortion on January 22, 1973. These Centers are based on the belief that every person, including the unborn, has an inalienable right to life "from conception to natural death". The focus of the Life-Care Centers is women with crisis pregnancies. The Centers provide an alternative to abortion by helping women bring their babies to term at a difficult time in their lives. The Centers offer free, confidential pregnancy testing, counseling, and referrals for adoption, shelter, financial aid, support groups, and other social services. Some of the larger centers are actually clinics offering low-cost basic medical care. Most of the Centers supply maternity clothes, and baby clothes, diapers, and furniture. Some even provide a food shelf. The Life-Care Centers depend on individual and group donations in order to carry out their very important mission.

✞ DOROTHY DAY HOUSES ✞

The Dorothy Day Houses are houses which provide temporary shelter for those people who find themselves in need of the basic requirements of food, clothing, and housing. All persons are welcome regardless of race, sex, or creed. Families with children are also taken.

The houses are run by a "live in" volunteer who makes decisions, and oversees activities. A back up group of concerned community volunteers meet with the "live in" volunteer once a week to help with decision and policy making.

People can stay at the Dorothy Day House for a period of two weeks during which time they are assisted in finding employment, housing, and whatever they need from various community services. The amount of time a person can stay can be altered under personal crisis needs.

✞ SHARING AND CARING HANDS ✞

Sharing and Caring Hands is a non profit organization which is dedicated to helping the poor and destitute. Operating from a storefront in Minneapolis, it helps to provide food, clothing, dental and medical care, social services and support to more than 5,000 people who come there each week. Caring and Sharing Hands was founded 11 years ago by 53 year old Mary Jo Copeland, a married mother of 12. She works ten hours a day, four days a week to provide help for the homeless in what is now the most successful private organization for the homeless in Minneapolis. More than 1,000 volunteers help run the organization. Donations from private groups and churches provide the operational funds.

Shirley Seyfried, State Regent

He asks us to be His hands and His feet,
to go out and find those sheep;
He asks us to think of them with His mind
and love them with His heart.
He sends us His own Holy Spirit
to fill us with his thoughts and desires.

* * CAKES * *

MOCK ANGEL FOOD CAKE

2¼ cups sifted cake flour	3 tsp. baking powder
2 cups sugar	1 tsp. cream of tartar
1 tsp. salt	1 tsp. vanilla
1 cup boiling water	½ tsp. almond extract
8 egg whites	

Sift flour, sugar and salt together three times. Add boiling water; beat well with hand whipper or slotted spoon until sugar is dissolved. Cool to room temperature. Let separated egg whites warm to room temperature. When flour mixture is cool, beat in the baking powder. Whip egg whites with cream of tartar and flavorings until whites will hold very stiff peaks. Gently fold in flour mixture. Spread in ungreased 9x13 inch pan. Bake at 350° for 30 minutes or use touch test. Invert pan with props under corners until cool.

Irene Streit, Fairmont

MOCK ANGEL FOOD CAKE

1 cup milk	6 or 7 egg whites
2 cups cake flour	1 scant tsp. cream of tartar
2 cups white sugar	1 tsp. vanilla
2 tsp. baking powder	Pinch of salt

Boil milk; let cool to lukewarm. Sift flour, sugar and baking powder three times. Add milk to dry ingredients and mix. Beat egg whites and cream of tartar until soft peaks form. Add vanilla. Fold into flour and milk mixture. Bake in a 9x13 inch pan at 325° for 25 minutes or until it tests done with a toothpick.

Lucy Burke, St. James

APPLE KUCHEN

½ cup butter or margarine, softened	2½ cups thinly sliced apples
	1 cup dairy sour cream
1 (18 oz.) pkg. plain yellow cake mix	2 egg yolks, slightly beaten
	½ cup sugar
1 cup coconut	1 tsp. cinnamon

Cut butter into dry cake mix until crumbly. Mix in coconut. Pat mixture lightly into ungreased 9x13 inch cake pan, building up edges slightly. Bake at 350° for 10 minutes; arrange apple slices on the warm crust. Mix sour cream and eggs; put sugar and cinnamon on apples and then drizzle cream and egg mixture over. Bake at 350° for 30 minutes or until apples are done.

Jean Demmer, Caledonia

CHOCOLATE APPLE CAKE OR CUPCAKES

½ cup shortening
1 cup sugar
2 eggs
1½ cups flour
1 tsp. soda
1 tsp. cinnamon
½ tsp. cloves

1 Tbsp. cocoa
½ tsp. salt
½ cup coffee
2 cups raw apples
Raisins and nuts, if desired
1 tsp. vanilla

Mix shortening, sugar and eggs. Add flour and dry ingredients alternately with coffee. Add apples, raisins and nuts. Put in a 9 inch pan or in cupcake tins, greased or named cupcake papers. Bake at 350° for 20 to 25 minutes.

Gladys C. Wimmer, Littlefork

APPLESAUCE CAKE

½ cup soft shortening
2 cups sugar
1 lg. egg
1½ cups thick applesauce
2½ cups sifted flour
1½ tsp. soda
1½ tsp. salt

½ tsp. allspice
1 tsp. cinnamon
½ tsp. cloves
½ cup water
½ cup nuts, chopped
½ cup raisins, optional

Cream shortening and sugar. Add egg and applesauce; beat well. Sift flour, soda, salt and spices and add to creamed mixture, alternately with water. Blend in nutmeats and raisins. Pour into a 9x13 inch greased and floured pan. Bake at 350° for 30 to 35 minutes. Top with caramel sauce and whipped cream.

Marie Deschene, Argyle

MOM'S CHOPPED APPLE CAKE

4 med. apples
2 cups sugar
2 beaten eggs
¾ cup oil
1 tsp. vanilla

2 cups flour
1½ tsp. soda
2 tsp. cinnamon
¾ cup chopped nuts

Peel and chop apples; add to sugar and let stand 1 hour. Mix eggs, oil and vanilla; add to apple mixture. Add dry ingredients to first mixture. Bake in a 9x13 inch pan at 350° for 40 minutes. Top with powdered sugar frosting.

Leona Kremer, Iona
Eulalia Koll, Pipestone
Fran Murphy, Mankato

APPLE CAKE

2 cups sugar	4 cups diced apples
1½ cups Crisco or oleo	2 eggs
1 tsp. vanilla	2½ cups flour
1 tsp. salt	2 tsp. soda
3 tsp. cinnamon	1 cup nuts, chopped

Mix all ingredients and bake in a 9x13 inch pan at 350° for 40 to 45 minutes. Let cool and serve with the topping.

Topping:

1 cup brown sugar	4 Tbsp. butter
2 eggs	1 (9 oz.) carton Cool Whip

Boil brown sugar, eggs and butter very carefully as it burns easy. Cook until thick. Cool well, then add Cool Whip. Mix with mixer. For a 9x13 inch cake, I cut the frosting recipe in half. I use about ¾ of Cool Whip.

Fran Frodl, Owatonna
District Deputy, 1962-1968
State Secretary, 1968-1972
State Ecumenical Involvement Chair, 1974-1976
State Cookbook Chair, 1965-1979

RAW APPLE SPICE CAKE

4 cups apples, peeled and sliced	2 cups flour
3 eggs	2 tsp. cinnamon
1 cup salad oil	1 tsp. soda
2 cups sugar	½ tsp. salt
1 tsp. vanilla	1 cup chopped nuts

Slice apples and spread on bottom of a 9x13 inch pan. Does not have to be greased. Beat eggs and salad oil until thick. Add sugar, vanilla, flour, cinnamon, soda, salt and chopped nuts. Spread or drop batter over the apples. Bake at 350° for 45 minutes to 1 hour. After cake is cool, frost with Cream Cheese Icing.

Cream Cheese Icing:

1 (8 oz.) pkg. cream cheese	1 Tbsp. lemon juice
1 Tbsp. melted margarine	2 cups powdered sugar
2 tsp. vanilla	

Combine all ingredients and cream well. Put frosting on a cooled cake.

Cecilia Spartz, Slayton

MOIST APPLE CAKE

2 cups sugar
1½ cups salad oil
3 eggs
2 cups flour
1 tsp. salt
1 tsp. baking powder

1 tsp. soda
1 tsp. nutmeg
1 cup cut up dates
1 cup nuts
3 cups sliced raw apples
2 tsp. vanilla

Mix the sugar and oil in a large bowl; cream well and add eggs one at a time. Beat 1 minute. Mix dry ingredients and add to creamed mixture. Dredge (or dust) dates and nuts in flour before adding the mixture. Add apples and vanilla. Bake in a 9x13 inch greased and floured pan at 325° for 1 hour or until done.

Arneta Middendorf, Owatonna

EGG FREE APPLESAUCE CAKE

2 med. apples
½ cup oleo
1 cup sugar
1 tsp. cinnamon
¼ tsp. cloves
¼ tsp. nutmeg
½ tsp. salt

1 tsp. soda
2½ cups flour
1 tsp. baking powder
1 tsp. vanilla
Raisins, nuts or any fruit you
    prefer

Peel and slice apples; cover with water and cook until done. Set aside. In mixing bowl, add oleo, sugar, cinnamon, cloves, nutmeg and salt; cream. Put soda in a cup and add the hot apples with some of the water and add to the shortening mixture. Mix well and add flour and baking powder. Mix well and add vanilla, fruit and nuts. Bake in a well greased and floured loaf pan at 350° for approximately 1 hour or until an inserted toothpick comes out clean.

Imogene Williams, Mankato

FRESH APPLE CAKE

2 cups flour
2 tsp. soda
1 tsp. salt
4 cups diced, peeled apples
2 eggs

2 cups sugar
2 tsp. cinnamon
½ cup salad oil
1 cup nutmeats

Mix dry ingredients. Place apples in bowl and break eggs over them. Stir and add sugar, cinnamon, oil and nuts. Add dry mixture and beat together well. Bake in a greased and floured 9x13 inch pan at 350° for approximately 45 minutes. Test for doneness.

Harriet Violette, Red Lake Falls

RAW APPLE CAKE

2 cups sugar	2 cups flour
½ cup butter	1 tsp. cinnamon
2 eggs	1 tsp. nutmeg
4 Tbsp. hot water	1 tsp. soda
2 tsp. vanilla	1 cup nuts
½ tsp. salt	5 cups peeled raw apples, diced

Cream sugar and butter. Add eggs, water and vanilla. Add dry ingredients, nuts and apples. Bake in a 9x13 inch pan at 350° for 45 minutes.

Butterscotch Sauce:

½ cup butter	½ cup cream
1 tsp. maple flavoring	½ cup white sugar
½ cup brown sugar	

Boil until dissolved. Pour on cake. Top with whipped cream.

Eileen Harguth, Waseca

APPLE CAKE

2 cups sugar	1 tsp. salt
½ cup butter	½ tsp. cinnamon
2 eggs	3 cups chopped apples
2 cups flour	1 cup chopped nuts
2 tsp. soda	

Cream sugar and butter; add eggs and beat well. Sift remaining ingredients; add, beating well. Add apples and nuts. Put in a 9x13 inch pan and bake at 300° for 1 hour. Serve with caramel sauce.

Caramel Sauce:

1¼ cups brown sugar	1 cup cream
1 cup white sugar	1 tsp. vanilla
¼ cup butter	

Boil sugars and butter for 5 minutes, stirring constantly. Add cream while hot. Bring back to boil, remove and add vanilla.

Florine Driscoll, Moorhead

* * * * * * * *

The Lord also will be a refuge for the oppressed.
A refuge in times of trouble. Psalm 9:9

Thank you, God, for your protecting love. Make
us able to face those times when we must suffer.
Karen Riopelle, Argyle

RAW APPLE CAKE

2½ cups flour
1 tsp. soda
1 tsp. baking powder
1 tsp. salt
2 cups raw chopped apples

½ cup nuts, optional
1 cup white sugar
1 cup brown sugar
2 eggs
½ cup milk

Mix flour, soda, baking powder, and salt. Fold apples and nuts if desired. Mix brown and white sugars, eggs, and milk alternately with flour mixture. Fold in nuts and apples.

Topping:

3 Tbsp. white sugar
1 tsp. cinnamon

½ cup nuts

Spread topping over batter. Bake at 350° for 35 minutes or until done.

Alvina May, La Crescent

500 CAKE (BANANA)

½ cup butter or margarine
¾ cup white sugar
¾ cup brown sugar
2 eggs
½ cup sour milk
1 cup mashed bananas

1 tsp. vanilla
2 cups all-purpose flour
1 tsp. soda
⅓ tsp. baking powder
½ cup chopped nuts or ½ cup chopped dates

Beat the butter, sugars and eggs until fluffy. Add sour milk, bananas and vanilla. Sift flour and soda and baking powder and add to banana mixture. Beat until well combined. Bake in a 8x12 inch pan at 350° for 25 minutes. Especially good with a caramel or cream cheese frosting. Why they call this a 500 cake, I don't know. I got it from my mother and remember baking it as a girl. I've been married 49 years and still make it. It is an easy from scratch recipe that I use when I need to take a cake some place. There is never any left to bring home.

Bernice Groh, Waterville

* * * * * * * *

*God is able to make all grace abound toward you; that ye...
may abound in every good work. II Corinthians 9:8*

*I place this day in your care, O God, thanking you for the
blessed assurance that Jesus is mine.*
Florence Yutrzenka, Argyle

BANANA CAKE

½ cup shortening	2 cups sifted flour
1½ cups sugar	⅛ tsp. salt
2 eggs, separated	1 tsp. baking powder
1 cup mashed bananas	1 tsp. soda
⅔ cup sour milk	

Combine shortening, sugar, egg yolks, bananas, and sour milk. Sift flour, salt, and baking powder. Add soda to egg whites that have been beaten and add to other ingredients. Add **1 teaspoon vanilla**. Bake at 350° for 35 to 40 minutes.

Florence Maas, Medford

BANANA CAKE

1⅓ cups sugar	1 tsp. soda
½ cup shortening	¾ tsp. salt
2 eggs, unbeaten	2 cups flour
½ cup milk	1 tsp. vanilla
1 tsp. baking powder	1 cup mashed bananas

Cream sugar, shortening and eggs. Add milk alternately with dry ingredients (mixed together); add vanilla. Bake at 375° for 30 minutes or until done.

Frosting:

¾ cup white sugar	1 tsp. white syrup
¾ cup brown sugar	1½ cups half and half cream

Boil until it forms a soft ball in water. Beat until cool and bubbly. Add ¼ **cup butternut** or **nuts** and **vanilla**. Beat until spreading consistency.

Wanda Bauer, Caledonia

BANANA CAKE

1⅔ cups sugar	1¼ tsp. baking powder
⅔ cup shortening	1¼ tsp. soda
2 lg. eggs	1 tsp. salt
1¼ cup mashed banana	2¼ cups flour
⅔ cup milk	

Cream sugar and shortening; add eggs and bananas. Stir in remaining ingredients. Bake in a greased 9x13 inch cake pan at 350° for 40 to 45 minutes.

Frosting:

Cook ¾ **cup milk** with **3 tablespoons flour** until thick. Cool. Cream ¾ **cup butter** with **1 cup sugar, a pinch of salt,** and 1½ **teaspoons vanilla**. Beat in cooked mixture for 10 to 15 minutes.

Lucy Pansier, Faribault

BANANA CAKE**

1 pkg. yellow cake mix	Pinch of salt
2 eggs	1 cup water
1 tsp. baking soda	3 ripe mashed bananas

Beat all ingredients for 2 minutes. Pour into a 9x13 inch greased pan. Bake at 350° for 30 to 40 minutes. Cool and frost.

Frosting:

1 sm. pkg. vanilla instant pudding	1½ cups cold milk
	4 oz. Cool Whip

Agnes Prairie, Russell
Rita Cook, Adrian

BANANA AND CREAM BUNDT CAKE

⅓ cup shortening	2 cups flour
1¼ cups sugar	1¼ tsp. baking powder
2 eggs	1 tsp. baking soda
1 tsp. vanilla	1 cup sour cream
1¼ cups mashed bananas	¾ cup walnuts, optional

Cream shortening and sugar; add eggs one at a time, beating well after each addition. Blend in vanilla; add bananas. Mix well. Combine flour, baking powder and baking soda; add alternately to creamed mixture with sour cream, stirring until just combined. Stir in walnuts. Pour into greased and floured bundt pan. Bake at 350° for 50 minutes. Cool 10 minutes before moving from pan to a wire rack. When cool, dust with powdered sugar.

Beverly Thraen, Slayton

BEETNIK CAKE

1½ cups cooked beets	1¾ cups sugar
½ cup cocoa	½ tsp. salt
1 tsp. vanilla	½ Tbsp. soda
1¼ cups salad oil	3 beaten eggs
2¼ cups flour	

Prepare cooked beets (cool slip skins, grind fine before measuring). Combine cocoa, vanilla, and salad oil; mix thoroughly. Add the sifted dry ingredients. Add the eggs and beet mixture to the batter. Pour into a 9x13 inch greased and floured pan and bake at 350° until toothpick inserted in middle comes out clean. Frost with your favorite icing.

Teresa Ford, Iona

CARROT CAKE

2 cups sugar
1½ cups oil
3 eggs, beaten
2 tsp. soda
1 tsp. salt
1 cup coconut
2¼ cups flour

2 tsp. cinnamon
2 tsp. vanilla
1 cup chopped nuts
2 cups grated carrots
1 lg. can crushed pineapple
  and juice

Cream sugar, oil and eggs; add remaining ingredients and mix well. Pour into a 9x13 inch greased pan and bake at 350° for 1 hour. Frost with cream cheese frosting.

Sharon Everett, International Falls

CARROT CAKE

2¼ cups all-purpose flour
2 cups sugar
2 tsp. soda
1 tsp. cinnamon
½ tsp. salt

2 cups shredded carrots
1½ cups oil
4 eggs
1 cup chopped nuts

In a large bowl, blend all ingredients, except nuts, at low speed until moistened. Beat 3 minutes on high speed. Stir in nuts. Pour in a 9x13 inch pan which has been greased on bottom only. Bake at 350° for 40 to 45 minutes.

Frosting:

3 cups powdered sugar
2 Tbsp. butter or margarine,
  melted

1 (8 oz.) pkg. cream cheese,
  softened
1 tsp. vanilla

Blend all ingredients and beat until smooth. Frost cake.

Jean Landsteiner, St. James

COOKED CARROT CAKE

1½ cups sugar
1¼ cups oil
4 eggs, well beaten
2½ cups flour
1 tsp. salt
2 tsp. soda
2 tsp. cinnamon

1½ cups pureed carrots, or
  3 jars baby food
1 tsp. vanilla
1 cup raisins
1 cup crushed pineapple,
  drained
1 cup nuts

Cream sugar and oil; add eggs. Combine dry ingredients. Add alternately with carrots. Add vanilla, raisins, pineapple and nuts. Blend well. Bake at 350° for 45 to 50 minutes in a 9x15 inch pan, or it will make 40 cupcakes. It is very tasty without frosting.

Albina Kajer, Owatonna

"BEST-EVER" CARROT CAKE

1½ cups corn oil
2 cups sugar
3 eggs
2 cups flour
2 tsp. soda
½ tsp. salt

2 tsp. cinnamon
2 tsp. vanilla
2 cups shredded raw carrots
2 cups nuts
¼ cup crushed pineapple

Combine oil, sugar and eggs and beat well. Sift the dry ingredients and add to egg mixture. Stir in vanilla, shredded carrots, nuts and pineapple. Pour into greased and floured 9x13 inch pan and bake at 350° for 1 hour. Cool and frost.

Frosting:

1 (3 or 4 oz.) pkg. cream cheese
¼ cup margarine
1¼ cups powdered sugar

⅛ to ¼ cup crushed pineapple
¼ cup nuts, chopped
1 cup coconut, optional

Combine all ingredients and cream well; spread over cooled cake.

Lorraine Grass, Owatonna
Sue Herder, Fergus Falls
Beverly Schreier, Currie

EXPLORER CARROT CAKE

3 eggs
¾ cup salad oil
¾ cup buttermilk
2 cups sugar
2 tsp. vanilla
2 cups flour
2 tsp. soda
2 tsp. cinnamon

½ tsp. salt
2 cups grated raw carrots
½ cup crushed pineapple,
    drained
1 cup nuts
1 cup Rice Krispies
1 cup coconut

Combine eggs, oil, buttermilk, sugar and vanilla; mix and then add flour, soda, cinnamon and salt. Mix and add rest of ingredients. Bake in a 9x13 inch pan at 350° for 40 to 45 minutes. Frost with cream cheese frosting.

Rosella Sogge, Fairmont

· · · · · · · ·

Blessed are the merciful: for they shall obtain mercy. Matthew 5:7

Father, help me be as gentle and kind
to others as I want you to be to me.
Lorrayne Yutrzenka, Argyle

CHERRY CAKE

½ cup butter
1½ cups sugar
1 cup cherry juice or sweet milk
3 cups cake flour
3 tsp. baking powder
½ tsp. salt
1 sm. bottle maraschino cherries
4 egg whites

Cream shortening and sugar; add cherry juice (take juice of small bottle cherries and add milk to make 1 cup). Sift flour, baking powder and salt; add to above mixture. Gradually add cherries just before the stiffly beaten egg whites folded in last.

Rosie Frank, Caledonia

BIT O'WALNUT CHIFFON CAKE

1 cup plus 2 Tbsp. sifted cake flour (spoon lightly into cup, don't pack)
¾ cup sugar
1½ tsp. baking powder
½ tsp. salt
¼ cup cooking (salad) oil
2 med. unbeaten egg yolks
¼ cup plus 2 Tbsp. cold water
1 tsp. vanilla
4 egg whites
¼ tsp. cream of tartar

Measure first 4 ingredients and sift together into mixing bowl. Make a well and add in order oil, egg yolks, cold water and vanilla. Beat with spoon until smooth. Measure egg whites and cream of tartar into large mixing bowl. Whip until whites form very stiff peaks. They should be much stiffer than for angel food or meringue. DO NOT UNDERBEAT. Pour egg yolk mixture gradually over whipped egg whites gently folding with rubber scraper just until blended. DO NOT STIR. Sprinkle over top of batter ½ **cup finely chopped walnuts**, gently folding in with a few strokes. Pour into ungreased pan immediately. Bake in a 5x10x3 inch loaf pan or a 9x3½ inch tube pan at 325° for 50 to 55 minutes; or 8x8x2 inch or 9x9x2 inch square pan at 350° for 30 to 35 minutes. Or until top springs back when lightly touched. Immediately turn pan upside down, placing tube part over neck of funnel or bottle, or resting edges of square or loaf pans on two other pans. Let hang, free of table, until cold. Loosen from sides and tube with spatula. Turn pan over and hit edge sharply on table to loosen.

Rita Krzebietke, New Albin, IA

* * * * * * * *

If you were arrested today for being a Christian, would there be enough evidence to convict you?
Gloria Bradley, Zumbrota

CAKES, CANDIES & FROSTINGS

CHOCOLATE CAKE

2 eggs
Pinch of salt
2 cups sugar
4 Tbsp. cocoa

1 cup sour cream
2 cups flour
1 cup boiling water
2 tsp. baking soda

Add eggs and salt; beat well. Add sugar to mixture; beat well. Add cocoa and a little hot water mixed together; add this to above. Add sour cream, then flour. Lastly, add the boiling water and soda mixture to the batter. Pour batter into a greased and floured 9x13 inch pan. Bake at 350° for 30 to 35 minutes until done.

Emma Reiter, Slayton

EASY DESSERT**

1 chocolate cake mix (or any flavor desired)
1 can sweetened condensed milk

1 can chocolate fudge topping
1 (8 oz.) carton Cool Whip
1 pkg. Bit-o-Brickle

Make cake according to directions on box. When done, immediately poke holes all over in cake. Mix sweetened condensed milk and chocolate fudge topping and pour over cake. When cool, spread with Cool Whip and sprinkle with Bit-o-Brickle.

Variation: use 1 jar caramel topping instead of fudge topping.

Marie Chaput, Crookston
Helen Bzdok, Holmestad

SAVE THE DAY CHOCOLATE CAKE

1 pkg. white cake mix
1 pkg. instant chocolate pudding
2 cups milk

3 egg whites
1 tsp. vanilla

Beat all ingredients very well with an electric mixer. Bake at 350° for 40 minutes (batter must be poured into a 9x13 inch pan).

Topping:

3 egg yolks
1 cup evaporated milk
1 cup sugar

1 stick margarine
1 tsp. vanilla
1 cup coconut

Combine all ingredients in a heavy saucepan. Cook over low heat, stirring until thick. Spread on cooled cake. Keep chilled if it must stand out a long time.

Beulah Reed, Slayton

ZUCCHINI CHOCOLATE CAKE

½ cup margarine	1 tsp. baking soda
¼ cup oil	½ tsp. baking powder
1¾ cups white sugar	1 tsp. cinnamon
2 eggs, beaten	½ cup sour milk
2½ cups flour	2 cups zucchini, peeled and
4 Tbsp. cocoa	grated
	1 tsp. vanilla

Preheat oven to 325°. Cream margarine, oil and white sugar. Beat in eggs and set aside. Sift dry ingredients and add alternately with sour milk to creamed mixture. Add zucchini and vanilla. Beat everything in large bowl well. Grease a 9x13 inch pan or use Pam on bottom. Pour batter into greased pan. Spread evenly.

Topping:

1 cup chopped walnuts	1 cup chocolate chips
½ cup brown sugar, packed	

Mix ingredients well and spread evenly on the cake batter before baking. Bake at 325° for 40 to 45 minutes or until done.

Corrine Zenk, Slayton

MOCK GERMAN CHOCOLATE CAKE

1 pkg. white cake mix	1 tsp. red food coloring
1 pkg. instant chocolate pudding	⅛ cup butter, melted
2 cups milk	3 egg whites, beaten
1 tsp. vanilla	

Mix cake mix, pudding mix and 1 cup milk; beat well. Add vanilla and food coloring. Add 1 cup milk and the butter. Fold in beaten egg whites. Bake at 350° for 35 to 45 minutes. Test with toothpick.

Frosting:

1 cup sugar	½ cup butter
1 cup evaporated milk	1 tsp. vanilla
3 egg yolks, beaten	

Mix all ingredients, except vanilla, and cook, stirring constantly. Add vanilla and spread over cake. Melt **6 candy bars** over hot water; put over butter frosting and swirl around.

Monica Thompson, Plainview

CAKES, CANDIES & FROSTINGS

FLOURLESS CHOCOLATE CAKE

7 eggs, separated	2 sqs. melted chocolate
¾ cup sugar	½ cup broken pecans
Pinch of salt	½ tsp. cream of tartar

Beat the egg yolks well; add the sugar, salt, chocolate and nuts. Beat egg whites stiffly and add cream of tartar. Fold the first mixture very carefully into egg whites. Put in two 8 inch springform pans (wax paper or greased and floured).

Icing:

1¼ cups powdered sugar	1 egg
1 sq. melted chocolate	1 tsp. vanilla
1 stick softened margarine	

Dorothy Bliss, Omaha, NE

BLACK CHOCOLATE CAKE

2 cups flour	²/₃ cup salad oil
1¾ cups sugar	1 egg
½ cup cocoa	1 cup sour milk
½ tsp. salt	1 tsp. vanilla
2 rounding tsp. soda	1 cup black coffee

Mix dry ingredients. Make hole in center and add oil, egg, milk and vanilla. (Note: make your sour milk, by adding a tablespoon of vinegar to a cup of milk). Mix well and last, add boiling hot coffee (strong). Bake at 350° for 40 minutes in a 9x13 inch pan.

Fran Frodl, Owatonna
District Deputy, 1962-1968
State Secretary, 1968-1972
State Ecumenical Involvement Chair, 1974-1976
State Cookbook Chair, 1965-1979

CHERRY CHOCOLATE CAKE

1 pkg. Devil's Food cake mix	1 (21 oz.) can cherry pie filling
1 tsp. almond extract	2 eggs, beaten

Stir all ingredients by hand until well mixed. Pour in a 9x13 inch pan. Bake at 350° for 20 minutes or until toothpick comes out clean.

Frosting:

1 cup sugar	5 Tbsp. butter
¹/₃ cup milk	

Boil all ingredients for 1 minute. Stir constantly; remove from heat and add **1 cup chocolate chips**. Stir until smooth. Frost warm cake. Cool before cutting.

Father Gerald Meidl, Marshall
State Chaplain, 1994-present

ONE-EGG CHOCOLATE CAKE

2 sqs. chocolate, cut up
½ cup boiling water
1 cup sifted flour
1 cup sugar
½ tsp. soda
½ tsp. salt

¼ tsp. double acting baking
powder
¼ cup butter or margarine
¼ cup buttermilk
½ tsp. vanilla
1 egg

Have all ingredients at room temperature. Melt chocolate in boiling water, then cool mixture. Sift dry ingredients and add to cooled chocolate mixture. Add shortening and beat. Add buttermilk, vanilla and egg. Beat 1 more minute. Bake at 350° for 35 to 40 minutes in an 8x8x2 inch pan.

Variation: Myrtle suggests ½ cup cocoa for bar chocolate.

Patt Thorpe, International Falls
Myrtle Bahr, International Falls

SOUR CREAM CHOCOLATE CAKE

1 stick oleo or butter
3 sqs. unsweetened chocolate
1 cup water
2 cups flour
Dash of salt

2 cups sugar
1½ tsp. baking soda
½ cup sour cream
3 eggs

Melt oleo and chocolate in 1 cup water. Add flour, salt, sugar and soda; mix well. Add sour cream and eggs. Mix well for 2 minutes. Pour into a 9x13 inch pan. Bake at 350° for 45 minutes.

Variation: Rosie suggests 1 less egg and using 3 tablespoons cocoa for bar chocolate.

Kathryn Aldrich, Eveleth
Rosie Kelly, Waseca

PRIZE WINNING CHOCOLATE CAKE

½ cup butter
2 cups sugar
2 eggs
2 sqs. chocolate, melted
2 tsp. soda

2½ cups flour
½ tsp. salt
1 cup buttermilk or sour cream
¾ cup warm water
1 tsp. vanilla

Cream butter and sugar. Add eggs and melted chocolate. Add dry ingredients alternately with sour milk. Last, add warm water and vanilla a little at a time, beating well after each addition. Bake at 350° for approximately 40 minutes. Test with toothpick. Use a loaf pan or 3 round layer pans.

Jean Beyer (Emma Huot's recipe, Jean's mother), Red Lake Falls

CHOCOLATE CHIP DATE CAKE

½ lb. dates, chopped	1½ cups sugar
1½ tsp. soda, sprinkled over dates	½ cup butter or margarine
	2 eggs
1½ cups boiling water	2 cups flour

Chop dates. Sprinkle with soda. Pour boiling water over dates and soda. Cool. Combine rest of ingredients and add to date mixture. Pour into a 9x13 inch pan.

Topping:

1 tsp. cinnamon	½ cup sugar
1 (6 oz.) pkg. chocolate chips	½ cup chopped nuts

Mix ingredients and spread over cake mixture in pan. Bake at 350° for 40 minutes.

Norma Frank, Mazeppa

CINNAMON STRUESSEL CAKE

½ cup packed brown sugar	1 cup water
½ cup chopped nuts	½ cup oleo or butter, softened
1½ tsp. ground cinnamon	4 eggs
1 pkg. Betty Crocker super moist butter brickle cake mix	

Grease and flour bundt pan. Preheat oven to 350°. Mix brown sugar, nuts and cinnamon; set aside. Beat cake mix, water, oleo and eggs in large bowl according to directions. Sprinkle brown sugar mixture over batter and fold in for marbled effect. Bake from 40 to 45 minutes. Cool 10 minutes; remove from pan and cool completely. Spread top of cake with glaze:

Cinnamon Glaze:

Heat **½ cup ready to spread frosting** (vanilla), **1 teaspoon oleo or butter** and **½ teaspoon cinnamon** in a 1 quart saucepan over medium heat, stirring constantly, until of desired consistency.

Corine Deeny, Waterville

EASY BAKE COFFEE CAKE

1 cup sugar	2 cups flour
4 eggs	1 tsp. baking powder
1 cup cooking oil	

Mix all ingredients. Spread half of mixture in a greased 9x13 inch pan. Spread **1 can pie filling** (cherry or other) over. Spread the remaining batter over the pie filling. Sprinkle with a little **cinnamon and sugar** mixture. Bake for 40 minutes. Drizzle a little **frosting** on top.

Gladys Bruns, Lismore

COOKIES AND CREAM CAKE

1 pkg. Pillsbury Plus white
    cake mix
1/3 cup oil
1 1/4 cups water

3 egg whites
1 cup Oreo cookies, coarsely
    crushed

Heat oven to 350°. Grease and flour a 9x13 inch cake pan. Mix all ingredients in large bowl, except crushed cookies, at low speed until blended, then at high speed for 2 minutes. Gently stir in the crushed cookies. Bake for 25 to 35 minutes. Cool and frost with cream cheese frosting. Garnish with some of the crushed cookies.

Ann Rothschadl, Waubun

CRAZY CHOCOLATE CAKE**

3 cups flour
2 tsp. soda
1 tsp. salt
2 cup sugar
1/3 cup cocoa

1 tsp. vanilla
3/4 cup salad oil
3 Tbsp. vinegar
2 cups water

Using a 9x13 inch pan, sift flour, soda and salt. Add sugar and cocoa. Make 3 holes in the mixture. In one, put vanilla; put salad oil in the second, and vinegar in the third. Pour the water on top and stir with a fork. Bake at 350° for 30 minutes.

Variation: Helen suggests this frosting:

Frosting:
1 cup sugar
4 Tbsp. milk

4 Tbsp. butter
2/3 cup chocolate chips

In a pan, bring to a boil and cook 30 seconds, no more; remove from stove and add chocolate chips.

Gertrude Grubish, Waterville
Sharon Klinkhammer, Mahnomen
Helen Felber, Waseca

DEVIL'S FOOD CAKE

1 cup sugar
1/4 cup shortening
1 cup warm coffee
1 1/4 cups flour

1 tsp. soda
1/2 tsp. cream of tartar
2 Tbsp. cocoa
1/2 tsp. salt

Mix first 3 ingredients. Sift the remaining ingredients. Add **1 teaspoon vanilla**. Mix well and pour into a 9x9 inch greased and floured pan. Bake at 350° for about 30 minutes. Cool and frost with boiled fudge frosting.

Agnes Herzog, Owatonna

DIRT CAKE**

2 Tbsp. butter
1 (8 oz.) pkg. cream cheese
2 pkgs. instant French vanilla
   pudding
3 cups milk

1 (16 oz.) carton nondairy
   whipped topping
1 pkg. Oreo cookies
1 pkg. Gummi worms

Beat butter and cream cheese. Mix pudding and milk. Mix this with cream cheese mixture. Fold in whipped topping. Crush Oreos. Layer in pail; serve with shovel. A big hit with kids!

Stephanie Stamarski, International Falls

DUMP CAKE**

1 (No. 2) can apricot pie filling
1 (No. 2) can crushed pineapple
   with juice
1 yellow cake mix

1 cup coconut
1 cup walnuts or almonds
1 cup margarine, melted

In a 9x13 inch greased cake pan, put the ingredients in the pan in the order given. The cake mix is spread over the pie filling and pineapple, then add the other 2 ingredients. Spread the melted butter over all. Bake at 350° for 1 hour.

Frances Maas, Grand Rapids

ECLAIR CAKE

1 (1 lb.) box graham crackers
2 (2¾ oz.) box French vanilla
   instant pudding

3½ cups milk
1 (8 oz.) carton whipped
   topping such as Cool Whip

Butter bottom of a 9x13 inch pan and line with one layer of graham crackers. Mix pudding and milk in mixer bowl at medium speed for 2 minutes. Blend in whipped topping. Alternate layers of pudding and crackers (2 pudding and 3 cracker layers).

Frosting:

2 pkgs. pre-melted unsweetened
   chocolate
2 Tbsp. corn syrup
2 tsp. vanilla

3 Tbsp. soft butter
1½ cups powdered sugar
3 Tbsp. milk to make mixture
   smooth

Mix ingredients well. Frost cake and refrigerate overnight or for 24 hours before serving.

Romana Posch, St. James

GINGER CAKE

½ cup vegetable oil
½ cup sugar
1 cup molasses
2 eggs
2½ cups flour
1 tsp. cinnamon
1 tsp. cloves
1 tsp. ginger
½ tsp. salt
2 tsp. soda
1 cup boiling water

Put all ingredients, except soda and water, in a bowl. Add soda to boiling water, then add to mixture. Mix and put in a 9x13 inch pan. Bake at 325° for 30 minutes. Top with icing.

Lemon Icing:
1 cup butter
1½ cups powdered sugar
1 tsp. lemon flavoring

Mix and spread on cooled cake.

Sandra Stafki, Perham

GRAHAM STREUSEL CAKE

2 cups graham cracker crumbs
   (28 squares)
¾ cup chopped nuts
¾ cup brown sugar
1½ tsp. cinnamon
¾ cup margarine, melted
1 pkg. white cake mix
1 cup water
⅓ cup vegetable oil
3 eggs

Preheat oven to 350°. Grease a 9x13 inch pan. Mix cracker crumbs, nuts, brown sugar, cinnamon and margarine. Beat cake mix, water, oil and eggs in large bowl until moist. Beat at medium speed for 2 minutes. Pour 2⅓ cups batter into pan. Sprinkle 2 cups crumb mixture over batter. Pour remaining cake into pan. Sprinkle remaining crumbs over cake. Bake 45 minutes. Cool. Drizzle with powdered sugar glaze made of **1 cup powdered sugar** and **1 or 2 tablespoons water**.

Diane Pawlowski, Argyle

SUPER LEMON CAKE**

1 box lemon cake mix
1 (3 oz.) pkg. lemon jello
4 eggs
¾ cup oil
¾ cup water

Beat cake mix, jello, eggs, oil and water for 4 minutes. Put in a 9x13 inch pan and bake at 350° for 35 minutes or until done. Remove cake from oven. Prick entire surface with a fork. Pour on glaze. Cool and enjoy!

Variation: May use yellow cake mix with 1 tsp. lemon extract.

Elaine Schlichte, Currie
Jeanne Schuetzle, Cary, IL

HAWAIIAN DELIGHT CAKE

1 yellow cake mix
3 sm. pkgs. instant vanilla
   pudding
3 cups milk

1 (8 oz.) pkg. cream cheese
2 lg. cans crushed pineapple,
   well drained
1 (12 oz.) carton Cool Whip

Mix and bake cake mix in jelly roll pan or divide into one 9x13 inch pan and one 8 inch square pan. Bake at 350° for 15 minutes; let cool. Mix pudding, milk and cream cheese and spread on cooled cake. Spread or sprinkle crushed pineapple over pudding mixture. Cover with Cool Whip. Cover all with saran wrap and chill thoroughly (overnight is best). Chopped nuts or toasted coconut can be sprinkled on top.

Mary Frederick, Faribault

LEMON CAKE

1 lemon cake mix
1 (6 oz.) pkg. lemon jello
2 cups boiling water
1 cup 7-Up

1 pkg. instant lemon pudding
1 cup milk
1 (8 oz.) carton Cool Whip

Prepare and bake cake according to directions on package. Combine jello and water (this is less water than when making regular jello). When liquid has cooled, add 7-Up. After cake is baked, and still warm, pierce with fork all over and pour liquid over to let seep in. Refrigerate 4 hours. Prepare instant pudding with 1 cup milk; add Cool Whip. Keeps up to 10 days in refrigerator.

Marie Arnold, Medford

MANDARIN ORANGE CAKE

2 cups flour
2 cups sugar
2 tsp. soda
2 eggs

2 tsp. vanilla
1 tsp. salt
2 cans mandarin oranges,
   drained

Beat all ingredients 3 minutes. Bake in a 9x13 inch greased pan at 350° for 30 to 35 minutes. Bring ¼ **cup brown sugar, 3 tablespoons butter** and **3 tablespoons milk** to a boil and dribble over the cake while warm.

Aurore Bedard, Argyle

MANDARIN ORANGE CAKE

1½ cups sugar
2 eggs
2 cups flour

2 tsp. soda
2 cans mandarin oranges with juice

Mix all ingredients and bake at 350° for 35 to 40 minutes.

Frosting:
3 egg yolks
1 scant cup sugar

1 stick margarine or butter
1 cup evaporated milk or cream

Cook eggs, sugar, butter and milk until thick, then add **1 cup coconut** and **½ cup nuts**.

Caroline Berg, Plainview

MILE-A-MINUTE MOCHO CUPCAKES

½ cup shortening
1 cup sugar
1 egg
1⅓ cups flour
¼ tsp. salt
1 Tbsp. baking powder

½ tsp. soda
½ tsp. cocoa
½ cup milk
1 tsp. vanilla
½ cup hot coffee

Cream shortening and sugar; add egg and beat well. Add flour sifted with salt, baking powder, soda and cocoa, alternating with the milk and vanilla. Add coffee. Fill cupcake holders ⅔ full. Bake at 375° for 20 minutes. Cool, then frost with favorite frosting.

Doris Desrosier, Crookston

OATMEAL CAKE

1¼ cups boiling water
1 cup quick oatmeal
½ cup butter
2 eggs
1 cup brown sugar
1 cup white sugar
1⅓ cups flour

1 tsp. salt
½ tsp. cinnamon
½ tsp. nutmeg
1 tsp. baking powder
1 tsp. soda
1 tsp. vanilla

Pour boiling water over oatmeal and butter. Beat eggs with brown and white sugars; add oatmeal mixture and beat well. Add dry ingredients and vanilla. Bake in a 9x13 inch pan that has been greased and floured, at 350° for 40 minutes.

Topping:
¼ cup butter
½ cup brown sugar
1 cup coconut

½ cup nuts
1 cup chocolate chips
1 tsp. vanilla

Mix ingredients. Put on cake when it comes out of oven, put back in oven for 10 minutes or until coconut is browned.

Dorothy McCormick, Caledonia
Joan Shipe, Fergus Falls
Jeanette Rolfes, Iona

ORANGE CAKE

1 orange
1¼ cups sugar
½ cup butter or shortening
2 eggs, beaten
2 cups flour

½ tsp. baking powder
½ tsp. soda
½ tsp. salt
1 cup sour milk
1 cup ground raisins or dates

Squeeze juice from orange. Combine with ¼ cup sugar. Stir until sugar is dissolved and set aside. Cream 1 cup sugar and shortening. Add eggs. Sift flour; measure and sift with baking powder, soda and salt. Add alternately with sour milk to first mixture. Add dates or raisins which have been ground with squeezed orange. Mix until well blended. Pour into a well oiled 9x13 inch pan. Bake at 375° for 40 minutes. Pour orange juice over cake before removing from pan.

Adeline Timmer, Lakeville

AURORE'S ORANGE CAKE

1 cup raisins
Juice and rind of 1 orange
1 cup nuts
1 cup white sugar
½ cup shortening
1 egg, beaten

1 cup sour milk or buttermilk
1 tsp. soda, dissolved in 2 Tbsp.
    warm water
½ tsp. salt
2 cups flour

Grind raisins, orange rind and nuts and set aside. Mix sugar and shortening; add beaten eggs, milk, soda and salt. Mix in flour and ⅔ of the raisin mixture. Pour into a greased and floured 9x13 inch pan. Bake at 350° for 45 minutes. Pour the orange juice over top while cake is still hot. Use the rest of the raisin mixture in powdered sugar or cream cheese frosting. Can also add raisin mixture to 8 ounce carton of whipped topping and spread over cake. Sprinkle chopped nuts on top. This can be done 3 or 4 hours before serving and put in refrigerator. It slices nicely.

Edith St. Germain, Argyle

• • • • • • • • •

*You are able to feel very rich when you look
at all the things you have that money cannot buy.*
Lorraine Liffrig, Mazeppa

ORANGE SLICE CAKE

3½ cups sifted flour   1 cup butter or margarine
½ tsp. salt   2 cups sugar
½ lb. orange slices, cut up   4 eggs
1 (8 oz.) pkg. dates, chopped   1 tsp. soda
1 cup nuts   ½ cup buttermilk
1 can (3¼ cups) flaked coconut

Mix 3 cups flour and salt together. Combine orange slices, dates, nuts, and coconut. Mix well with ½ cup flour and set aside. Cream butter, sugar, gradually adding eggs. Beat until light. Combine soda and buttermilk; add alternately with flour mixture, then fold in candy mixed with the ½ cup flour. Spoon in 10 inch tube pan. Bake for 1 hour and 45 minutes. When cake comes out of the oven, pour over **1 cup orange juice** mixed with **2 cups confectioner's sugar**. Pour over cake while still in tube pan, leave to next day to take out of tube pan. Wrap in saran wrap to keep well. This could serve as fruit cake at Christmas for those who do not like citron fruits.

Joan Petzel, Caledonia

PEPSI-COLA CAKE

3 Tbsp. cocoa   ¼ tsp. salt
1 cup Pepsi-Cola   2 eggs
2 sticks margarine   1 tsp. vanilla
2 cups sugar   ½ cup buttermilk
2 cups unsifted flour   1 tsp. soda

Boil cocoa, Pepsi, and margarine. Put sugar, flour and salt into large bowl. Pour boiling Pepsi mixture over and beat until smooth. Beat in eggs and vanilla. By hand, stir in buttermilk and baking soda. Pour into greased 9x13 inch pan and bake at 350° for 35 to 45 minutes.

Icing:
1 stick margarine   1 lb. confectioner's sugar
3 Tbsp. cocoa   1 tsp. vanilla
6 Tbsp. Pepsi   ½ cup nuts

Boil margarine, cocoa, and Pepsi for 5 minutes. Beat in sugar until smooth. Add vanilla and nuts. When done, pour on hot Pepsi icing.

Doris Eisbrener, Thief River Falls

ORANGE CAKE

½ cup margarine
1 cup sugar
2 eggs, beaten
1 cup raisins
1 orange peel with pulp

1 cup nuts
1 tsp. soda to 1 cup sour milk
2 cups flour
1 tsp. vanilla

Cream shortening, sugar and beaten eggs. Add raisins, orange peel and nuts (that have been put through grinder; save juice from orange). Add sour milk with flour and vanilla. Bake at 350° for 40 minutes. Mix the juice of orange with ½ cup sugar and put on cake after it is taken from oven (while still hot).

RoseAnn Morin, International Falls

POPCORN CAKE

½ cup oil
½ cup butter
1 lb. marshmallows

8 qts. popped corn
1 cup nuts
1 lb. small or cut up gum drops

Cook oil, butter and marshmallows. Pour over the popped corn, nuts, and gumdrop mixture. Press firmly into an angel food tin. Let stand until firm. Slice and serve.

S. Mary Ann Welsch, Moorhead

BEST EVER PINEAPPLE CAKE

2 eggs
2 cups sugar
2 cups flour
1 lg. can crushed pineapple, undrained

2 tsp. soda
1 tsp. salt
1 tsp. vanilla
¾ cup nuts

Beat eggs; add remaining ingredients and mix well. Bake in a well greased and floured pan at 350° for 30 to 35 minutes.

Frosting:

1 stick margarine
1 (8 oz.) pkg. cream cheese

1½ cups powdered sugar
1 tsp. vanilla

Mix all ingredients well. Frost as soon as you take it out of the oven. May sprinkle chopped nuts or 1 cup coconut over top of frosting if desired. Refrigerate for 2 days before serving.

Mary Haley, North Mankato
Leona Kremer, Iona

PINEAPPLE CAKE

2 cups sugar
2 cups flour
2 eggs
2 tsp. baking soda
1 lg. can crushed pineapple, undrained

1 cup coconut
1 cup chopped nutmeats
1 tsp. vanilla
½ cup vegetable oil

Mix the first 4 ingredients well. Add remaining ingredients and mix. Put in a 9x13 inch greased cake pan. Bake at 350° for 45 minutes or until done. Pour the following frosting over cake while the cake is warm.

Frosting:
½ cup brown sugar
¼ cup margarine

½ cup milk

Cook in a saucepan until syrupy. Add nuts if desired after removing from heat. Pour over cake.

Marion Kruger, Adrian

POPPY SEED CAKE

3 eggs
2 cups sugar
2 cups Mazola oil
1 lg. can evaporated milk

3 cups flour
1 cup poppy seed
3 tsp. baking powder

Mix the first 4 ingredients. Add the remaining ingredients and mix well. Divide between 2 well greased 9x9x2 inch square pans. Bake at 350° for 45 to 50 minutes.

Eva Balaski, International Falls

POPPY SEED CAKE

Bake 1 **white cake mix** with **2 tablespoons poppy seeds** in a 9x13 inch pan or two 8 inch layer tins at 350° for 30 minutes.

Filling:
1 cup sugar
2 Tbsp. cornstarch

1½ cups milk
4 egg yolks

Cook until thick. Add 1 **teaspoon vanilla** and **chopped nuts**. Cool filling and spread over cooled cake.

7-Minute Frosting:
2 egg whites
1½ cups sugar
⅛ tsp. salt

⅓ cup water
1 Tbsp. white corn syrup
1 tsp. vanilla

Beat all ingredients for 1 minute before putting on water; place in a double boiler over boiling water and beat 7 minutes. Take off boiling water and beat until cool and thick enough to hold firm swirls before spreading on cake.

Marilyn Ellenz, Caledonia

POPPY SEED CAKE

¼ cup poppy seeds
1 pkg. white cake mix
½ cup oil
4 eggs

Amount of water called for in
cake mix
1 pkg. vanilla instant pudding
1 (8 oz.) carton Cool Whip

Mix all ingredients except Cool Whip. Bake at 350° for about 35 minutes or until toothpick comes out clean. Cool cake. When cool, spread with Cool Whip.

Topping:

1 cup brown sugar
¼ cup orange juice
½ cup oleo

¼ cup water
1 Tbsp. flour
2 eggs, beaten

Mix ingredients and cook until thick. Cool topping. Spread cooled topping on top of Cool Whip. Refrigerate cake.

Geraldine Holzer, St. Charles

POTICA CAKE

1 yellow Duncan Hines cake mix
1 box instant coconut pudding
4 eggs

½ cup sour cream
½ cup milk
½ cup Crisco oil

Preheat oven to 350°. Grease a 10 inch tube pan and flour. Mix cake mix and coconut pudding together in mixing bowl. After mixing well, make a well and add eggs, sour cream, milk and oil. Mix and scrape bowl; beat 2 minutes.

Filling:

½ lb. ground walnuts
½ tsp. cinnamon

2 Tbsp. brown sugar

Mix ingredients well and add to cake mixture. Pour into greased and floured tube pan. Bake at 350° for 1 hour. This is excellent served with Cool Whip or whipped cream.

Mayme Rozinka, Eveleth

POUND CAKE

1 Duncan Hines butter cake mix
4 eggs, room temperature
½ cup Crisco oil (no other)
1 (8 oz.) carton sour cream

1 tsp. vanilla
1 tsp. almond flavoring
1 cup sugar
2 tsp. milk

Preheat oven to 350°. Mix cake mix, eggs, oil and sour cream in large mixing bowl. Add vanilla and almond flavoring. Mix all together and beat 10 minutes (yes ladies, 10 minutes). Pour into greased and floured bundt pan. Bake at 350° for 1 hour and 5 minutes. Cool and drizzle with sugar and milk mixed together. This is a lovely cake, soft and elegant. It can be served any way.

Mayme Rozinka, Eveleth

WONDERFUL POUND CAKE

²/₃ cup shortening	2¼ cups sifted cake flour
1¼ cups sugar	1¼ tsp. salt
1 Tbsp. lemon juice	1 tsp. baking powder
1 tsp. grated lemon peel	3 eggs
²/₃ cup milk	

Stir the shortening until softened. Gradually and sugar. Cream until light and fluffy. (Beat about 3 minutes on medium speed of mixer.) Add lemon juice to peel. Add milk and mix enough to break up creamed mixture. Sift flour, salt and baking powder and add to creamed mixture; mix until smooth (about 2 minutes) on low speed of mixer. Scrape bowl often. Add eggs one at a time, beating 1 minute after each (low speed of mixer). Beat additional 1 minute at end. Pour into greased 9½x5x3 inch loaf pan. Bake at 300° for about 1 hour and 20 minutes. When thoroughly cool, sift confectioner's sugar over top of cake, cut into thin slices.

Mary Christianson, Argyle

PRUNE CAKE

2 cups sugar	½ tsp. nutmeg
3 eggs	½ tsp. cinnamon
1 cup oil	½ tsp. mace
2 cups flour	1 cup chopped nuts
½ tsp. baking powder	1 cup chopped cooked prunes
1 tsp. soda	1 cup buttermilk
1 tsp. salt	

Cream sugar, eggs and oil. Add remaining ingredients and mix gently. Bake at 350° for 45 minutes or until done. While cake is warm, punch holes with fork. Heat ½ **cup orange juice** with **1 cup sugar** until dissolved. Pour hot topping over cake.

Lita Schreier, Currie

OUR FAVORITE RAISIN SPICE CAKE

1 cup sugar	¹/₈ tsp. salt
½ cup shortening	1¾ cups flour
1 cup raisins	2 eggs
1 cup water	1 tsp. soda
½ tsp. cinnamon	1 tsp. vanilla
¼ tsp. nutmeg	½ cup nuts
¼ tsp. cloves	

Bring the sugar, shortening, raisins, water and spices to a boil for 1 minute. Cool, then add the flour, eggs, soda, vanilla and nuts. Mix well. Put cake batter in a 9x13 inch pan. Bake at 350° for about 25 minutes. Frost with your favorite frosting.

Susan Ruether, Perham

CAKES, CANDIES & FROSTINGS

ROCKY ROAD NUT CAKE

1¾ cups sugar	1 tsp. vanilla
1½ cups flour	4 eggs
¼ tsp. salt	1 cup chopped walnuts
1 cup margarine, melted	4 cups miniature marshmallows

Sift dry ingredients. Add margarine, vanilla and eggs; mix well. Fold in walnuts. Pour into a 9x13 inch cake pan. Will not get too thick. Bake at 350° for 15 minutes. Top immediately with marshmallows.

Butterscotch Icing:

1 cup brown sugar, packed	½ cup milk
½ cup margarine	¼ tsp. salt

Boil for 3 minutes. Add **1 cup confectioner's sugar** and beat until smooth. Drizzle on top of marshmallows. Let set until firm before cutting.

Marcella Toulouse, Red Lake Falls

RHUBARB CAKE

4 cups cut up rhubarb	3 cups miniature marshmallows
1 pkg. red jello	1 white or yellow dry cake mix
1 cup sugar	

Place the first 4 ingredients in a 9x13 inch cake pan. Sprinkle dry cake mix on top and bake at 350° for 30 minutes or test for doneness. Rhubarb can be quite juicy.

Magdalene Kirschman, Red Lake Falls

HELEN'S SUPER RHUBARB COFFEE CAKE

1 stick margarine	1 tsp. salt
1½ cups sugar	1 tsp. soda
1 lg. or 2 sm. eggs	2 cups flour
1 cup sour milk	2 cups rhubarb
1 tsp. vanilla	

Mix in order given. (Mix rhubarb with a portion of flour.) Spray a 9x13 inch pan with Pam; add cake mixture.

Topping:

½ cup brown sugar	1 tsp. cinnamon
½ cup nuts	

Mix topping and add to top. Bake at 350° for 50 minutes to 1 hour.

Shirl Maher, Blue Earth
Cordula Brady, Caledonia
Elaine Salentiny, Euclid

RHUBARB CAKE

1½ cups brown sugar
½ cup shortening
1 egg
1 cup buttermilk or sour milk
2 cups sifted flour

1¼ tsp. soda
1 tsp. vanilla
½ tsp. salt
Cut in 2 cups rhubarb

Mix in order given. Pour in a greased 9x13 inch pan.

Topping:

⅓ cup white sugar
1 tsp. vanilla

1 tsp. cinnamon

Mix and sprinkle on top of cake. Bake at 350° for 50 minutes.

Mary Kuchenbecker, Elmore
Rita Arendt, Mazeppa
Alvina May, La Crescent
Anna Koski, Moose Lake

RHUBARB PUDDING CAKE

1 cup sugar
1 egg
2 Tbsp. melted butter or oleo
1 cup buttermilk or sour milk
½ tsp. salt

½ tsp. baking soda
1 tsp. baking powder
2 cups flour
1 cup diced fresh rhubarb

Blend sugar, egg and butter together. Beat in buttermilk until smooth. Stir salt, baking soda, baking powder and flour. Stir dry ingredients into buttermilk mixture; mix well. Stir in rhubarb. Pour into greased 9 inch square baking pan.

Topping:

2 Tbsp. melted oleo

½ cup sugar

Combine and sprinkle on top of batter. Bake at 350° for 45 minutes or until cake tests done.

Vanilla Sauce:

½ to 1 cup sugar
½ cup oleo

½ cup evaporated milk
1 tsp. vanilla

Mix sugar, oleo and milk and bring to boil. Cook 1 minute, stirring constantly. Remove from heat and stir in vanilla. Serve sauce over cake. Yields 12 servings.

Marge Kingsley, St. Charles

* * * * * * * *

People need love the most when they deserve it the least.
Margaret Wagner, Mazeppa

RHUBARB CAKE WITH CARAMEL SAUCE

1 ½ cups sugar
1 egg
2 cups flour
½ tsp. salt
2 cups rhubarb, cut fine

½ cup shortening
1 cup sour milk
1 tsp. soda
½ cup nuts

Mix in order given. Sprinkle with **brown sugar** and **cinnamon**. Bake at 350° for 40 to 45 minutes.

Caramel Sauce:
½ cup butter
½ cup sugar
½ cup brown sugar

1 Tbsp. flour
1 tsp. vanilla

Cook all ingredients except vanilla until thick. Add vanilla and serve hot over cake.

Mary Senst, Plainview

BEST EVER RUM CAKE

1 or 2 qts. rum
1 cup butter
1 tsp. sugar
2 lg. eggs
1 cup dried fruit

Lemon juice
Nuts
Brown sugar
1 tsp. soda
Baking powder

Before starting, sample rum to check quality. Good, isn't it? Now proceed. Select large mixing bowl, measuring cup, etc. Check rum again. It must be just right. To be sure rum is of proper quality, pour one level cup of rum into a glass and drink it as fast as you can. Repeat. With electric mixer, beat 1 cup of butter in a large fluffy bowl. Add 1 teaspoon of sugar and beat again. Meanwhile, make sure rum is alright. Try another cup. Open second if necessary. Add leggs, 2 cups of fried druit and beat till high. If druit gets stuck in beaters, pry loose with drewscriber. Sample rum again, checking for tonscisticity. Next, sift 3 cups pepper or salt, (really doesn't matter). Sample rum. Sift ½ pint lemon juice. Fold in chopped butter and strained nuts. Add 1 bablespoon of brown thugar, or whatever color you can find. Mix well. Grease oven. Turn cake pan to 360°. Pour mess into boven and ake. Check rum again and bo to ged.

Florence Yutrzenka, Argyle

SAUERKRAUT CAKE

⅔ cup sauerkraut, chopped 1 tsp. baking powder
1½ cups sugar 2¼ cups sifted flour
⅔ cup margarine ¼ tsp. salt
3 eggs 1 tsp. soda
1 tsp. vanilla 1 cup water
½ cup cocoa

Drain liquid from sauerkraut. Cream sugar and margarine. Beat eggs well and add to creamed mixture. Add vanilla. Sift dry ingredients together and add to first mixture, alternately with 1 cup water. Stir thoroughly then stir in sauerkraut. Pour into greased and floured 9x13 inch cake pan. Bake at 350° for 30 minutes.

Frosting:
1 stick margarine 1 lb. powdered sugar
1 (8 oz.) pkg. cream cheese ¼ cup cocoa

Cream margarine and cheese. Add sugar and cocoa. Mix thoroughly and spread on cake. The sauerkraut tastes like coconut or chopped nuts in this cake. It stays moist.

Margaret Domeier, New Ulm

SHEET CAKE

½ cup butter 2 tsp. cinnamon
¼ cup cocoa ⅛ tsp. salt
½ cup cooking oil 1 tsp. soda
1 cup water ½ cup buttermilk
2 cups sugar 1 tsp. vanilla
2 cups flour 2 eggs

Bring the butter, cocoa, cooking oil and water to a boil. Add sugar, flour, cinnamon and salt and beat well. Dissolve soda in buttermilk. Add buttermilk, vanilla and eggs to preceding mixture. Bake in a 12x18 inch pan at 375° for 20 minutes.

Frosting:
¼ cup butter ½ lb. powdered sugar
2 Tbsp. cocoa ½ tsp. vanilla
3 Tbsp. milk ½ cup nuts, optional

Mix butter, cocoa and milk and heat until butter is melted and pour over powdered sugar. Beat well and add vanilla and nuts. Spread over cake while still warm. Buttermilk can be made by adding 1 teaspoon vinegar to ½ cup milk.

Janet Fuerstenberg, Wilmont

EASY PICNIC SPICE CAKE

2 cups flour
1¹/₃ cups sugar
3½ tsp. baking powder
1 tsp. salt
1 tsp. cinnamon
½ tsp. nutmeg

¼ tsp. cloves
²/₃ cup shortening
1 cup milk
1 tsp. vanilla
2 eggs, unbeaten

Sift the first 7 ingredients into a medium size bowl. Add shortening and mix into dry ingredients as you would pie crust. Add milk, vanilla and the eggs. Beat well with electric mixer until smooth. Bake at 350° for 35 minutes.

Maxine Lynn, Adrian

WATERGATE CAKE

1 pkg. white cake mix
1 cup club soda
¾ cup cooking oil

3 eggs
1 box pistachio instant pudding
½ cup chopped pecans

Mix cake mix, club soda, cooking oil, eggs and instant pudding. Mix thoroughly for about 2½ minutes. Fold in nuts. Pour into a greased 9x13 inch pan. Bake at 350° for 40 minutes.

Topping:
1 box pistachio pudding
1 cup milk

1 (9 oz.) carton Cool Whip

Beat pudding and milk for 2 minutes. Fold in Cool Whip and spread on cake.

Grace Kaveney, St. Peter

ZUCCHINI CAKE

½ cup margarine
½ cup oil
1¾ cups sugar
2 eggs
1 tsp. vanilla
2½ cups flour
4 Tbsp. cocoa

1 tsp. baking soda
½ tsp. salt
½ tsp. cinnamon
½ tsp. baking powder
½ cup sour milk
2 cups shredded zucchini

Beat margarine, oil, sugar, eggs and vanilla. Add dry ingredients, milk and zucchini. Beat well. Pour into a greased and floured 9x13 inch pan. Combine ¼ **cup chocolate chips,** ¼ **cup chopped nuts** and ¼ **cup brown sugar** in small bowl, then sprinkle over batter. Bake at 325° for 30 to 40 minutes.

Delores Vlaisavljevich, Eveleth

QUICK ZUCCHINI CAKE

1 box yellow cake mix
4 eggs
½ cup vegetable oil
1 tsp. cinnamon
1 Tbsp. vanilla

2 cups zucchini, unpeeled and grated
½ cup raisins
½ cup chopped walnuts

Beat cake, eggs, oil, cinnamon and vanilla in large bowl for 6 to 7 minutes. Fold in zucchini raisins and nuts. Grease and flour 10 minutes bundt pan. Spoon in batter. Bake at 350° for 40 to 50 minutes. Test with toothpick. Cook longer and test at 5 minute intervals. Remove from pan and cool. Sprinkle with powdered sugar if desired. Yields 16 to 20 servings.

Helen Schmitz, Red Lake Falls

* * CANDIES * *

ALMOND BARK

2 pkgs. almond bark, melted
2 cups crunchy peanut butter
4 cups Rice Krispies

2 cups miniature marshmallows
1 cup nuts
½ cup red cherries, cut up

Mix all ingredients and spread in large pan or drop by spoonfuls on waxed paper.

Harriet Violette, Red Lake Falls

MICROWAVE CARAMELS

1 cup butter
2¼ cups brown sugar, packed
Dash of salt

1 can sweetened condensed milk
1 tsp. vanilla
1 cup white corn syrup

Melt butter for 2 minutes; stir in sugar, salt, milk and corn syrup. Cook to soft ball stage (236° to 238°) on candy thermometer. This usually takes 15 minutes. Stir and take temperature check. Cook 5 minutes more. Pour into a 9x13 inch pan or 2 loaf pans. Cool. Cut into 1 inch squares. Wrap each piece in wax paper. Makes at least 50 pieces.

Helen Chesney, Owatonna

CARAMELS

2 cups brown sugar
1 cup corn syrup
2 cups cream
Dash of salt

2 tsp. butter
2 cups nuts
1 tsp. vanilla
2 Tbsp. butter

Boil sugar, syrup, cream, salt and butter until real thick, just about hard boil. Add nuts, vanilla and butter. Place in buttered pan. When cool, cut in squares and wrap in wax paper.

Lorraine Klaseus, North Mankato

BEST EVER CARAMELS

2 cups sugar
1 cup firmly packed brown sugar
1 cup butter, softened
1 cup milk

1 cup whipping cream
1 cup light corn syrup
1¼ tsp. vanilla

In a 4 quart saucepan, combine all ingredients except vanilla. Cook over low heat, stirring occasionally, until sugar is dissolved and butter is melted, 20 to 25 minutes. Continue cooking, without stirring, until candy thermometer reaches 248° or small amount of mixture dropped into ice water forms a firm ball, about 2 hours. Remove from heat; stir in vanilla. Pour into buttered 9x13 inch pan. Cool completely; cut into 1x1½ inch pieces. Yield: 6 dozen.

Irma Vroman, Marshall
District Deputy, 1992-1996
State Scrapbook Chair, 1994-present

CREAMY BUTTER FUDGE

3 cups sugar
⅓ cup cocoa
⅛ tsp. salt
1 Tbsp. unflavored gelatin
1 cup whipping cream
½ cup milk

¼ cup light corn syrup
½ cup butter
½ cup margarine
1½ tsp. vanilla
1½ cups chopped walnuts or
    pecans

Combine all ingredients except vanilla and nuts in a heavy 4 quart saucepan; blend well. Bring to a rolling boil, stirring constantly. Continue to cook until mixture registers 234° (soft ball stage) on candy thermometer, gradually lower heat and stir gently. Remove from heat; pour into bowl. Cool 20 minutes; add vanilla and beat with mixer on low speed until creamy. Stir in nuts, spread into a 9 inch square pan. Cool and cut into squares. Makes approximately 50 pieces.

Rosie Deutz, Marshall

MICROWAVE CARAMELS

1 cup butter
2¼ cups brown sugar
Dash of salt

1 cup light corn syrup
1 can sweetened condensed
  milk

Melt butter in large glass bowl. Add rest of ingredients. Stir well. Cover with plastic wrap. Microwave on high, full power, for 10 minutes. Uncover, stir well. Microwave on 50% power for 16 to 18 minutes until soft ball stage. Add **1 teaspoon vanilla**. Pour into a 12x7 inch pan that has been buttered. When cool, cut and wrap in wax paper. (Makes very creamy tasting caramels.)

Leone Brule, Crookston

CHOCO NUT CARAMEL BARS

1 (11½ oz.) pkg. milk chocolate
  morsels (2 cups)
2 Tbsp. shortening
1 (14 oz.) pkg. caramels

5 Tbsp. butter
2 Tbsp. water
1 cup peanuts, coarsely
  chopped

Melt chocolate morsels over hot water. Stir until smooth with shortening. Pour half into an 8x8 inch pan lined with foil. Refrigerate until firm. Return remaining chocolate mixture to low heat. Combine caramels, butter and water over boiling water. Stir until smooth. Stir in nuts until well blended. Pour in chocolate lined pan. Spread even. Refrigerate about 15 minutes. Top with remaining chocolate. Return to refrigerator. Chill until firm.

Marilyn LeBlanc, Crookston

VELVEETA CHEESE FUDGE

1 lb. Velveeta cheese
1 lb. butter
4 lbs. powdered sugar

1 cup Hershey's cocoa
1 tsp. vanilla
Nuts, optional

Melt cheese and butter; sift powdered sugar and cocoa together and mix well. Add vanilla. Add nuts if desired. Put into a greased 9x13 inch pan. Makes 6 pounds and freezes great.

Amy Tammaro, Eveleth

COCOA DROPS

4 cups sugar
1 cup milk
¼ cup butter

½ cup cocoa
1 tsp. vanilla
6 cups oatmeal

Combine the first 4 ingredients and boil 1 minute. Add vanilla and oatmeal; mix well. Drop by tablespoon on wax paper. Let set until hardened.

RoseAnn Morin, International Falls

CAKES, CANDIES & FROSTINGS

DIVINITY

3 egg whites (large size)
3 cups sugar
¾ cup water
2 tsp. vanilla

1 cup white Karo syrup
1 cup crushed nuts (black walnuts are best)

Beat egg whites well. Cook remaining ingredients together. Boil to hard crack stage. Pour immediately into whipped egg whites. Beat until it begins to cool and hold shape. Add vanilla and nuts. Continue beating until it holds shape. If it doesn't hold shape, let it stand and stir occasionally. Seldom fails to hold shape. If placed in a covered container it may become soft. If so, place in dish ahead of time and it will harden. Also, if it becomes too hard, place in a covered container. Freezes well.

Marilyn Hawkins, St. Peter

NEVER-FAIL DIVINITY

½ cup water
2 cups sugar
Pinch of salt

¼ cup walnuts
1 (7 oz.) jar marshmallow creme

Boil water, sugar and salt for 2 minutes. Pour in thin stream over marshmallow creme and beat until glossy. Fold in nutmeats. Spoon into drops or spread in a pan.

Jean Schindler, Red Lake Falls

FAMOUS CANDY BARS

½ cup white sugar
½ cup brown sugar
1 cup syrup
1 cup peanut butter
6 cups corn flakes

1 cup salted peanuts
1 cup semi-sweet chocolate chips
1 cup milk chocolate chips

In saucepan, mix sugars and syrup and bring to a boil over low heat. Boil for ½ minute. Remove from heat and add the peanut butter and stir well. In a large bowl, stir corn flakes and peanuts and add the syrup mixture. Firmly press mixture in a greased 9x13 inch pan. Melt both cups of chips together. Spread over mixture. Cut into squares when cool.

Monica Stoderl, Iona

FOUR LAYER BARS

⅓ cup melted margarine
1 cup graham cracker crumbs
1 cup coconut
1 cup semi-sweet chocolate chips

1 cup chopped walnuts
1 can sweetened condensed milk

Place all ingredients in an 8x8 inch pan in the order listed. Bake at 350° for 25 minutes or until set.

Lucille Makynew, Eveleth

GINGERED PECANS

½ cup champagne
4 egg whites, lightly beaten
2 cups sugar
2 tsp. salt
2 tsp. cinnamon
1 tsp. ginger
8 cups pecans

Preheat oven to 250°. Spray cookie sheet with nonstick spray. Combine champagne, egg whites, sugar and salt. Add spices and nuts, toss to coat. Spread on cookie sheet and bake for 1 hour, stirring occasionally to prevent sticking.

Variation: Almonds - use 3 teaspoons cinnamon and no ginger. Walnuts - use 1 teaspoon cinnamon, 1 teaspoon nutmeg, ¼ teaspoon cloves, ¼ teaspoon allspice and ¼ teaspoon ginger.

JoAnne McCarthy, Eveleth

OPERA NUT CREAMS

2 cups sugar
¾ cup heavy cream
½ cup milk
1 Tbsp. light corn syrup
⅛ tsp. salt
1 tsp. vanilla
¾ cup chopped walnuts
1 (6 oz.) pkg. semi-sweet
  chocolate chips

Combine sugar, cream, milk, corn syrup and salt in a 4 quart saucepan. Mix well. Bring to a boil on medium heat. Place thermometer in mixture; cook to 236° (soft ball stage). Remove from heat; cool to 110° (lukewarm) without stirring. Beat in vanilla until mixture loses its gloss. Add nuts; spoon into buttered 8 inch square pan. Cool to firm. Spread melted chips on top. Cut into squares.

Helen Olson, Winona

FUDGE

3 cups chocolate chips
1 can Eagle Brand sweetened
  condensed milk
1 tsp. vanilla
Chopped nuts, optional

Melt all ingredients and pour into an 8x8 inch buttered pan. Cool and cut into squares. Enjoy.

Sallie Raleigh, Belle Plain

FABULOUS FUDGE

1 cup butter
5 cups sugar
1 can evaporated milk
1 (12 oz.) can chocolate chips
1 (12 oz.) pkg. German
  chocolate
1 (7 oz.) jar marshmallow creme
1 cup nuts, optional

Bring butter, sugar and evaporated milk to a boil. Boil 5 minutes, stirring constantly. Add remaining ingredients and stir until melted and well mixed. Pour into large, buttered jelly roll pan.

Mary Lou Schouweiler, Kellogg

CAKES, CANDIES & FROSTINGS

FUDGE

1 (8 sq.) pkg. bakers semi-sweet
   chocolate
²/₃ cup sweetened condensed
   milk
1 tsp. vanilla
¼ tsp. salt
½ cup chopped nuts

Heat chocolate; add milk in saucepan over low heat until chocolate is melted. Remove from heat. Add vanilla and salt. Stir in nuts. Spread in an 8x8 inch loaf pan. Chill until firm. Cut in small squares (18 pieces). Recipe can be doubled.

Roberta Tissek, St. Paul

EASY FUDGE

¼ cup butter
²/₃ cup evaporated milk
1²/₃ cups sugar
½ tsp. salt
1 pkg. chocolate chips
1 (10 oz.) pkg. miniature
   marshmallows
1 tsp. vanilla

Melt butter slowly in a large saucepan. Mix in evaporated milk, sugar and salt. Stir over medium heat. Bring to a full rolling boil for 5 minutes, stirring constantly. (Time when the mixture starts to bubble.) Remove from heat. Immediately add the chocolate chips and marshmallows; stir until melted. May add walnuts if desired.

Diane Green, Fulda

GOURMET NO-FAIL FUDGE

1 (12 oz.) can Carnation's
   evaporated milk
3¾ cups sugar
1½ (12 oz.) pkgs. Nestle's semi-
   sweet Toll House chocolate
   chips
1 lb. butter (not margarine)
4 tsp. vanilla

(NO SUBSTITUTE BRANDS ARE TO BE USED.) Needed is 1 large kettle or thicker pan (5 qt. size). Butter the sides of the kettle or pan. Pour in evaporated milk. Add the sugar and stir well. Bring to boil on medium heat, then begin timer set for 6 minutes. Stir ingredients only once. Remove from the heat, (burner) immediately. Add chocolate chips and butter (cut into small pieces for easy blending). Stir until chocolate chips and butter are well blended. Add the vanilla. With electric mixer, setting high speed, beat for 15 to 20 minutes. (Stir sides occasionally.) The ingredients will become smooth, creamy and satiny. Pour fudge into a buttered 9x13 inch pan. Walnuts and cherries may be added after beating the fudge if desired. Refrigerate to set up for 3 hours. Cut into squares the size of your preference. Fudge may be placed in containers and frozen. Allow fudge to thaw out for 20 minutes before serving, for a creamier taste. Yield: 5 pounds.

Bobbi Whitney, Fergus Falls

NO FAIL FANNY FARMER FUDGE

4 cups sugar	1 (16 oz.) pkg. chocolate chips
1 can Carnation milk	1 Tbsp. vanilla
1 cup butter	2 cups walnuts

Cook sugar and milk to a rolling boil for 6 minutes. Add butter and chocolate chips. Mix well and add vanilla and walnuts. Pour into buttered cake pan and cut when cool. This is a never fail fudge and makes a large batch.

Virginia Stamps, St. Peter

FANNY FARMER FUDGE

1 sm. can condensed milk	2 plain Hershey candy bars
2 cups sugar	1 Tbsp. butter
3 sqs. chocolate	1 tsp. vanilla

Put milk in saucepan; add sugar and chocolate and stir. Put on very slow heat until it begins to boil. Boil slowly for 5 minutes. Remove from heat and add the Hershey bars, the butter and vanilla. Stir until Hershey bars are dissolved. Pour into a buttered pan. Cut in squares when cooled. Can add chopped nuts to this too, before pouring into buttered pan.

Mardelle Harguth, Waseca

MINIATURE MAPLE NUT CUPS

1 cup flour	1 egg
¼ cup sugar	¼ tsp. maple extract
6 Tbsp. butter	1 Tbsp. sugar
1 Tbsp. butter	Pecans
¼ cup dark corn syrup	

Mix flour, sugar and 6 tablespoons butter. Divide into 16 balls. Press into 16 miniature muffin cups. Melt 1 tablespoon butter; stir in rest of ingredients and mix well. Spoon into pastry lined cups. Top with one whole pecan or pecan pieces. Bake at 350° for 20 to 25 minutes.

Norma Frank, Mazeppa

PEANUT BRITTLE

1 lb. butter (must be butter)	1 bag Spanish peanuts
2 cups white sugar	

Cook butter and sugar over medium heat, stirring constantly, until nice and brown. Remove from heat and stir in peanuts. Pour in a jelly roll pan and let cool. No soda.

Rose Przybylski, Argyle

PEANUT BRITTLE

2 cups white sugar
1 cup corn syrup
1 lb. raw peanuts
2 tsp. soda

1 tsp. butter
1 tsp. vanilla
1 tsp. salt

Boil the sugar and corn syrup for 5 minutes, then add peanuts and boil 8 minutes more. Add soda, butter, vanilla and salt. Pour on a buttered pan and cool.

Elsie Walz, Mahnomen

MICROWAVE PEANUT BRITTLE

1 cup sugar
½ cup light corn syrup
1 cup raw unsalted peanuts
¹/₈ tsp. salt

1 tsp. butter
1 tsp. vanilla
1 tsp. baking soda

Combine sugar, corn syrup, peanuts and salt in 2 quart microwave bowl. Microwave, uncovered, on high for 7 to 8 minutes, stirring well after 4 minutes. Add butter and vanilla and blend well. Microwave on high for 1 minute. Peanuts will be lightly browned and syrup will be very hot. Add baking soda and stir until light and foamy. Pour mixture onto a lightly greased cookie sheet. When brittle is cool, break into small pieces and store in airtight container. Makes 16 servings. Per serving: 133 calories, 2 g protein, 5 g fat, 22 g carbohydrate, .6 mg cholesterol, 79 mg sodium.

Lee Mikolai, Blue Earth

PEANUT BUTTER CUPS

2 cups peanut butter
½ cup margarine

2½ cups powdered sugar
½ tsp. vanilla

Mix and press into a 9x13 inch buttered pan. Mix **2 tablespoons melted butter** and **1 cup chocolate chips**. Melt together and spread on top of peanut butter mixture and let cool. Cut into pieces.

Sandra Stafki, Perham

PEANUT BUTTER FUDGE

2 cups white sugar
½ cup milk

2 Tbsp. peanut butter
½ tsp. vanilla

Cook sugar, peanut butter, and milk over low heat until it reaches soft ball stage (238°). Add vanilla. Cool and beat until creamy. Pour into buttered pan or dish and cut into squares.

Mardelle Harguth, Waseca

PEANUT BUTTER FUDGE

1 pt. marshmallow creme	2 cups sugar
1 cup peanut butter	2/3 cup milk
1 tsp. vanilla	

Combine marshmallow creme, peanut butter, and vanilla in large bowl. Set aside. Combine sugar and milk in saucepan. Cook on medium heat to soft ball stage. Pour over ingredients in bowl and hand beat until cool and pour into square pan that has been lightly sprayed.

Carole Schroeder, Medford

PEANUT BUTTER FUDGE

1 cup brown sugar, packed	5 lg. marshmallows
1 cup white sugar	1 (12 oz.) jar creamy peanut
½ cup milk	butter

In a heavy 2 quart saucepan, combine sugars, milk and marshmallows. Bring to a boil over medium heat, stirring until the sugar dissolves and marshmallows melt. Remove from heat and stir in peanut butter. Pour into a buttered 8 inch square pan. Cool and when firm, cut into squares. Yield: 3 dozen pieces. Fudge will keep for several weeks if wrapped and stored in an airtight container in the refrigerator.

Mary Pavik, Fairmont

BEST PEANUT BUTTER FUDGE

1 lb. white almond bark	1 cup peanut butter (creamy or chunky)

Melt almond bark in top of double boiler over hot water; stir in peanut butter. Pour into buttered pan. Cool; cut into squares.

Frances Majerle, Eveleth

TRIPLE CHOCOLATE PEANUT CLUSTERS

1 (16 oz.) pkg. white chocolate	1 (6 oz.) pkg. milk chocolate
1 (6 oz.) pkg. semi-sweet chocolate chips	chips
	1 (16 or 24 oz.) jar unsalted dry roasted peanuts

Place chocolate in 2 quart microwave casserole. Melt in microwave on high for 1 minute at a time, stirring frequently (about 3 minutes total time). Stir in peanuts, drop by tablespoonfuls onto wax paper and refrigerate. Makes 3½ to 4 dozen.

Betty Ericson, International Falls

ANNIE'S CARAMEL CORN

1 cup Parkay	½ tsp. soda
½ cup dark syrup	6 cups popped corn
2 cups brown sugar, or 1 cup white and 1 cup brown sugar	

Cook Parkay, syrup and sugar. Bring to boil and boil 5 minutes. Remove from heat. Add soda; mix well. Pour over popped corn. Bake at 250° for 1 hour. Stir every 15 minutes. Spread to dry.
Variation: Jean adds 1 to 2 cups peanuts.

Marge Sehnert, Owatonna
Marietta Johanneck, Red Lake Falls
Jean Demmer, Caledonia

CRAZY POPCORN

2 qts. popped corn	1 cup margarine
1⅓ cups pecans	½ cup Karo syrup
⅔ cup almonds	1 tsp. vanilla
1⅓ cups sugar	

Mix popped corn and nuts on cookie sheet. In saucepan, combine sugar, margarine and syrup. Bring to a boil over medium heat. Boil 10 to 15 minutes, stirring occasionally. Remove from heat and add vanilla. Pour over popped corn and nuts. Mix to coat, spread to dry. Break in pieces and store in tight container.
Note: Recipe submitted from original Catholic Daughters Cookbook "Everybody's Favorite!"

Mrs. Art Loosbrock, Lismore

STRAWBERRY PARTY COOKIES

2 Tbsp. sugar	1 (15 oz.) can sweetened condensed milk
2 pkgs. strawberry jello	
1 tsp. vanilla	2 (7 oz.) pkgs. fine flaked coconut
½ tsp. almond extract	

Mix sugar, jello and flavorings with sweetened condensed milk. Add coconut and mix well. Chill in refrigerator. (Red Christmas sugar.) Roll into balls and shape like strawberries; then roll in red sugar. Make leaves (regular butter frosting colored green) and top berries with leaves.

Diane Green, Fulda

TURTLE PRETZELS

1 (14 oz.) pkg. caramels
1 Tbsp. water
1 (10 oz.) pkg. pretzel rods

1 (8 oz.) bar German sweet
   chocolate or semi-sweet
   chocolate
2 tsp. shortening
1 cup finely chopped pecans

In a double boiler, melt caramels in water. Dip half of each pretzel into the hot caramel. Place on a greased sheet of foil to cool. In a saucepan, melt the chocolate and shortening over low heat. Dip the caramel-coated end of the pretzels into the chocolate; sprinkle with nuts. Return to foil.

Kris Sellner, New Ulm

* * FROSTINGS * *

HIGH HUMIDITY BUTTERCREAM FROSTING

1½ cups oleo or Crisco
⅛ cup dry Dream Whip

1 tsp. vanilla or almond extract

Mix and whip in mixer for 3 to 4 minutes, then add the following:

¼ cup flour
⅔ to ¾ cup milk (less in hot
   weather)

2 lbs. powdered sugar

Mix with electric mixer until it is light and fluffy. Good for decorating and will keep for several weeks in refrigerator.

Mary Klug, Waseca

CARAMEL FROSTING

2 cups brown sugar
½ cup butter or margarine
5 Tbsp. evaporated milk

Dash of salt
1 tsp. vanilla
½ tsp. baking powder

Put sugar, butter, milk and salt in a pan. Cook over medium heat. Boil 2 minutes, stirring constantly. Remove from heat. Add vanilla and baking powder. Beat with electric beater 5 minutes. Add hot water while icing cake, if necessary.

Helen Cahill, Moorhead

CARAMEL POWDERED SUGAR FROSTING

6 Tbsp. butter or oleo
6 Tbsp. cream or milk
½ cup brown sugar

1 tsp. vanilla
Enough powdered sugar
to make thin frosting

Bring butter, milk and brown sugar to a boil. Boil for 1 minute or so. Add vanilla and enough powdered sugar to make a thin frosting. If too thick, will get hard. Beat until ready to spread on cake.

Marianne Kerr, Slayton

EASY FUDGE FROSTING

6 Tbsp. margarine   1 Tbsp. milk
1⅓ cups white or brown sugar   ½ cup chocolate chips

Combine margarine, sugar and milk. Boil for 1 minute. Remove from heat; add chocolate chips. Beat until spreading consistency and put on cake or bars.

Tyeresa Ford, Iona

GOOD FROSTING

1½ cups granulated sugar   ½ cup chocolate chips
6 Tbsp. milk   1 tsp. vanilla
4 Tbsp. margarine

In a saucepan, stir the sugar, milk and margarine. Bring to full boil and boil for 30 seconds. Remove from heat and add chocolate chips and vanilla. Stir until smooth and creamy.

Geneva Fessel, Waterville

NO-FAIL FROSTING

½ cup white sugar   ½ cup Crisco
2 Tbsp. flour   1½ cups powdered sugar
½ cup milk

Mix white sugar and flour in small saucepan. Add milk and cook until thick. Cool. Add Crisco and beat well, then add powdered sugar. Beat very well with electric mixer.

Joan Guck, Perham

WHIPPED CREAM FROSTING

1 cup milk   ½ cup oleo
4 Tbsp. flour   ½ cup butter
1 cup granulated sugar   ½ tsp. vanilla or almond
                                       flavoring

Stir the milk and flour in a small, heavy saucepan over low heat until thick. Set aside and let cool thoroughly. Beat well until fluffy; sugar, butter and oleo. Add the flour/milk paste and beat at high speed for 5 to 10 minutes. Clean sides of bowl frequently so all of ingredients blend well. Add flavoring of your choice. This frosting tastes like whipped cream and takes food colors very well. Excellent for special occasion cakes.

Jane Killian, Eveleth

Our Program Symbol

By definition, a circle is a curved line with every point equal distance from the center and bound together by a common interest. The seven point program of the CIRCLE OF LOVE is bound together by the common interest – LOVE.

The small heart in the center is taken from the logo of the HEART SPEAKS TO HEART program. By utilizing this portion of the logo and part of the Heart Speaks to Heart program that is compatible with the Circle of Love, a smooth transition occurs.

The Cross and Crown in the center of the heart is the national symbol of the Order – the Catholic Daughters of the Americas.

The Seven points selected indicate the needs of the Church and community best served by the Catholic Daughters. The program itemizes these needs with suggestions on how Catholic Daughters can effectively serve.

✝ LEADERSHIP ✝

A leader should be an individual who knows the way, goes the way, and shows the way. Did you know that communication occurs in four main forms – speaking, listening, reading and writing? The average American spends the following percent of time as follows: Listening 43%, Speaking 32%, Reading 15%, Writing 11%.

An effective leader knows the elements of good planning. She agrees and understands the goals of her organization. She gathers information on current situations, prospective resources, and future requirements. She involves as many persons as possible. She will diagnose the needs of persons she proposes to serve, and she will be responsible for the actions and implementation of plans.

A motivating leader is a person who treats others with respect; recognizes good work; helps develop skills; listens to ideas; and allows others to think for themselves.

A good leader does problem solving. She will choose a problem to solve. She will discuss the apparent issue. She will define and analyze the issue. She will develop alternative solutions. She will make a decision, and finally she will implement her solution.

Meg Schmidt, State Leadership Chair

✝ YOUTH ✝

Tomorrow's promise lives in today's youth.

The youth of today will be the national, world and church leaders of the future. Catholic Daughters of the Americas have made a deep commitment to help and encourage the youth of today and support all family life issues.

We do this through involvement in World Youth Day, Prayer Partners for First Communion/Confirmation, the Living Rosay, Ronald McDonald House, Birthright and much more.

Along with these involvements, our courts sponsor scholarships and education contests to promote learning. We also sponsor spiritual growth for our youth through Net Retreats and Youth Rallies.

As Catholic Daughters we are committed to helping our youth grow both physically and spiritually.

past **State Youth Co-chairs**
Betty & Lucie Thompson

* * COOKIES * *

ADVENTURES

1 cup butter	2 eggs
1½ cups white sugar	1 tsp. vanilla
2 cups chopped dates	4 cups Rice Krispies
2 tsp. milk	1 cup chopped nuts

Melt butter and sugar over low heat. Add dates and cook until it boils, stirring constantly. Remove from heat. Add milk and beaten eggs. Stir and return to heat and cook 2 minutes. Remove from heat and add vanilla. Pour over Rice Krispies and nuts. Mix and cool a little. Roll into balls, then in coconut. Cool on wax paper in refrigerator. Makes 60 balls.

Pernilla Ernster, Caledonia

ALMOND CRUNCH COOKIES

1 cup sugar	2 eggs
1 cup powdered sugar	4½ cups flour
1 stick margarine	1 tsp. salt
½ cup butter flavored Crisco	1 tsp. soda
1 cup oil	1 tsp. cream of tartar
1 tsp. almond extract	1 pkg. almond brickle chips

Blend sugars, margarine, Crisco and oil well. Add extract and eggs and mix well. Gradually add flour, salt, soda, cream of tartar and chips. Chill 30 minutes. Roll in balls, dip in sugar and flatten. Bake at 350° for 12 to 15 minutes.

Marian Schloegel, Winona

TOASTED ALMOND SNOWBALLS

1 cup soft butter or margarine	¾ cup toasted almonds, chopped
2 cups flour	
½ tsp. salt	1½ tsp. vanilla
½ tsp. baking powder	½ cup powdered sugar

Mix and bake at 350° for 10 to 12 minutes. Roll in powdered sugar while warm. Roll again after cookies are cool so they stay nice and white. Delicious and crunchy.

Marianne Berger, New Ulm

* * * * * * * *

*May you be in heaven a half hour
before the devil knows you're dead.*
Rita Huneke, Mazeppa

ANGEL KISSES

1 cup butter or margarine
¾ cup confectioner's sugar, sifted
2 cups flour
1 tsp. vanilla
1 (12 oz.) pkg. mint chocolate chips

Cream butter or margarine and sifted sugar. Add flour and vanilla and mix well. Stir in mint chocolate chips. Shape dough by small rounded teaspoonfuls into balls. Place balls on ungreased cookie sheet and bake at 350° for 8 to 10 minutes. Makes several dozen.

Margaret Gall, St. Charles

RAW APPLE COOKIES

½ cup shortening
1 cup sugar
1 cup apples, peeled and chopped
1 tsp. vanilla
1 tsp. salt
1 tsp. soda
1 tsp. baking powder
2 cups flour
Walnut pieces or halves

Mix shortening, sugar, apples and vanilla. Separately sift salt, soda, baking powder and flour. Combine dry ingredients with the apple mixture. Shape dough into golf ball sized balls. Roll in a sugar, cinnamon, nutmeg mixture. Place on a greased cookie sheet. Before baking, press a walnut meat into each cookie. Bake at 350° for about 13 minutes or until lightly browned.

Carol Dalton, International Falls

AUNT SALLY COOKIES

1 cup sugar
1 cup shortening
2 well beaten eggs
½ cup molasses
1 cup sour milk
5 cups flour
2 tsp. cream of tartar
4 tsp. soda
1 tsp. ginger
1 tsp. cinnamon

Mix in order given. Roll out thin and cut with a Spam can. Bake in moderate oven but do not overbake.

Frosting:
½ cup sugar
½ cup water
1 tsp. vinegar

Boil to a medium ball stage. Pour this over **2 well beaten egg whites** and beat. While still hot, add **12 cut marshmallows**. Beat until consistency to stay on cookies. (Very good!)

Mary Ann Simon, Mahnomen

COOKIES & BARS

142

APPLESAUCE DROP COOKIES

1 cup margarine	½ tsp. nutmeg
2 cups sugar	2 tsp. soda
2 eggs	4 cups flour
2 cups mushy applesauce	1 tsp. vanilla
½ tsp. salt	1 cup raisins
1 tsp. cinnamon	1 cup nuts
¼ tsp. cloves	

Mix margarine, sugar and eggs thoroughly. Stir in applesauce. Mix all dry ingredients and stir into applesauce mixture. Add vanilla, raisins and nuts. Chill at least 2 hour. Heat oven to 400°. Drop rounded tablespoonfuls of dough about 2 inches apart, on a lightly greased baking sheet. Bake 9 to 12 minutes or until almost no imprint remains when touched lightly. Frost when cool.

Frosting:

1 (3 oz.) pkg. cream cheese, softened	1 tsp. vanilla
1 Tbsp. butter	2 cups powdered sugar

Loretta Koob, Slayton

BANANA OATMEAL COOKIES

2 cups flour	1 cup sugar
1 tsp. cinnamon	1 cup shortening
¼ tsp. nutmeg	2 eggs
½ tsp. salt	1 cup mashed bananas
1 tsp. baking powder	2 cups rolled oats
¼ tsp. baking soda	½ cup nuts, optional

Sift first 7 ingredients. Add shortening, eggs and banana. Beat until smooth, about 2 minutes. Fold in rolled oats and nutmeats. Drop from spoon onto greased cookie sheet. Bake at 375° for 12 to 15 minutes.

Corrine Thompson, Waseca

BUTTERSCOTCH COOKIES

3½ cups flour	2 cups brown sugar
½ Tbsp. soda	2 eggs, beaten lightly
½ Tbsp. cream of tartar	½ Tbsp. vanilla
½ cup butter or other shortening	

Sift flour, soda and cream of tartar. Cream butter, sugar and eggs, then the sifted ingredients along with the vanilla; mix well. Shape in round or square loaf. Wrap in wax paper and let stand in a cool place. Cut in thin slices. Bake in hot oven 8 to 10 minutes. May add chopped fruit such as cherries.

Jeanette Rolfes, Iona
Lorraine Schmitt, Caledonia

BUTTERSCOTCH DELIGHT

2½ cups white sugar	5 cups flour
2½ cups brown sugar	2½ tsp. baking powder
2½ cups shortening	2½ tsp. baking soda
5 eggs	2½ tsp. salt
2 Tbsp. vanilla	5 cups oatmeal
½ cup milk	

Combine the first 6 ingredients and mix until smooth. Add the flour, baking powder, soda and salt and beat until smooth. Add the oatmeal and mix well. Drop by spoonfuls onto greased cookie sheet. Bake at 350° until done, about 10 to 12 minutes. Makes 12 to 15 dozen cookies.

Lydia Maxwell, International Falls

BOX OF CAKE MIX COOKIES

1 box white cake mix	¼ cup water
½ cup oil	1½ cups angel flake coconut
1 egg	1 tsp. almond extract

Always mix in order given. Drop batter by spoonfuls to lightly greased sheet. Bake at 350° for 14 minutes. Makes 4 dozen.

Variation: Some other combinations of cake mixes and flavorings are: Lemon cake mix and lemon flavoring; strawberry cake mix and almond flavoring; chocolate chip cake mix and walnut flavoring; cherry chip cake mix and almond flavoring; butter pecan cake mix and butter flavoring; caramel flavor cake mix and maple or butter flavoring; or you can use your own combinations. Just keep the basic recipe intact.

Pat Schmidt, Slayton
District Deputy, 1988-1992

CAROL'S FAVORITE COOKIES

½ cup shortening	1 tsp. baking powder
1½ cups brown sugar	1 tsp. soda
2 eggs	1 cup sour cream
1 tsp. vanilla	1 cup chopped dates
2¾ cups flour	1 cup chopped nuts

Mix all ingredients and bake at 350° until done. Cool and frost.

Frosting:

½ cup butter	1 tsp. vanilla
2 cups powdered sugar	Cream or milk

Carol Eischens, Plainview

CEREAL COOKIES

1 cup white sugar
1 cup brown sugar
1 cup butter
1 egg
1 tsp. vanilla
1 cup cooking oil
1 cup Rice Krispies

1 cup coconut
3½ cups flour
1 tsp. salt
1 tsp. cream of tartar
1 tsp. baking soda
1 cup quick oatmeal
½ cup nuts

Blend sugars and butter. Add egg, vanilla and cooking oil. Add Rice Krispies and coconut. Add flour, salt, cream of tartar and baking soda. Add quick oatmeal and nuts. (Special note: All ingredients should be mixed in the order given.) Drop by spoon or press with fork onto a baking sheet. Bake at 350° for 12 minutes.

Irene Raboin, Slayton

CHERRY DATE SKILLET COOKIES

1 cup butter
1 cup brown sugar
1 (8 oz.) pkg. chopped dates
1 egg
1 cup flakes coconut

1 Tbsp. vanilla
3 cups Rice Krispies
½ cup chopped maraschino cherries
2½ cups flaked coconut

In a 10 inch skillet, melt butter over medium heat. Stir in sugar and dates; remove from heat. Add egg; return to heat. Continue cooking over medium heat, stirring constantly, until mixture boils all over the top, 4 to 6 minutes. Boil for 1 minute, stirring constantly; remove from heat. Add remaining ingredients, except 2½ cups coconut; stir until all ingredients are moistened, 1 to 2 minutes. Let stand 10 minutes; shape rounded teaspoons of dough into 1 inch balls. Roll in coconut. Yield: 5 dozen.

Pernilla Ernster, Caledonia

CHOCOLATE CHIP BANANA OATMEAL COOKIES

¾ cup margarine
1 cup sugar
2 eggs
1 cup mashed bananas
¾ tsp. soda
¾ cup walnuts, if desired

½ tsp. cinnamon
1¾ cups rolled oats
1½ tsp. salt
2 cups flour
1 pkg. semi-sweet chocolate chips

Cream margarine, sugar and eggs; add bananas and beat well. Add remaining ingredients and blend well. Drop by rounded teaspoons onto ungreased cookie sheet. Bake at 350° for 10 to 12 minute. Makes about 5½ dozen.

Marie Kolb, Mentor
Alice Walker, Moorhead

COOKIES & BARS

145

CHOCOLATE OATIES

2 cups white sugar
¼ cup cocoa
½ tsp. salt
½ cup milk

¼ lb. margarine
½ cup peanut butter
3 cups oatmeal
1 tsp. vanilla

Cook sugar, cocoa, salt, milk and margarine until it comes to a boil and boil 1 minute. Remove from heat and quickly add peanut butter, oatmeal, and vanilla. Spread in a 9x13 inch pan or drop by teaspoon on wax paper.

Gloria VanOverbeke, Marshall

SUPER-DUPER CHOCOLATE COOKIES

4 oz. unsweetened chocolate
½ cup shortening
2 cups sugar
2 tsp. vanilla
4 eggs

2 cups flour
2 tsp. baking powder
⅛ tsp. salt
½ cup nuts, chopped

Melt chocolate and shortening. Add sugar and vanilla and beat. Add eggs one at a time. Sift the flour with baking powder and salt. Add this mixture. Fold in nuts. Chill dough. Form dough into balls. Roll in powdered sugar. Bake at 350° for 12 to 15 minutes. They will crinkle like ginger snaps.

Lucile Tyrrell, Eveleth

ALMOST HOME CHOCOLATE CHIP COOKIES

2 cups brown sugar
1 cup shortening (½ butter and
    ½ Crisco)
2 eggs
2 tsp. vanilla

3 cups flour
2 tsp. cream of tartar
2 tsp. baking soda
1 tsp. salt
1 (12 oz.) pkg. chocolate chips

Cream brown sugar and shortening; add eggs and vanilla and beat well. Sift dry ingredients; add slowly. Stir in chocolate chips. Roll into balls. Bake at 350° for about 15 minutes. If you like soft cookies bake until light brown. For a crisp cookie, bake a little longer.

Edythe Short, Slayton

DELUXE CHOCOLATE CHIP COOKIES

1 cup brown sugar
1 cup white sugar
1 cup oil
2 eggs
1 tsp. salt
2 tsp. soda

1 cup butter
2 tsp. vanilla
4 tsp. cream of tartar
4 cups flour (¼ cup more may
    be added)
1 (20 oz.) pkg. chocolate chips

Mix and bake at 350° until done.

Mary Welscher, Caledonia

CHOCOLATE CHIP

1½ cups brown sugar
¾ cup Crisco
2 Tbsp. milk
1 Tbsp. vanilla
1 egg

1¾ cup flour
1 tsp. salt
¾ tsp. soda
1 cup chocolate chips

Heat oven to 375°. Cream sugar, Crisco, milk and vanilla. Beat egg and add, then sift dry ingredients. Add remaining ingredients. Drop by teaspoon and bake 8 to 10 minutes. Don't overbake.

Ann Sturm, St. Peter

GOOD CHOCOLATE CHIP COOKIES

½ cup butter
½ cup shortening
¾ cup white sugar
¾ cup brown sugar
3 med. eggs

1 tsp. vanilla
2⅔ cups flour
½ tsp. baking soda
½ tsp. salt
1 (12 oz.) pkg. chocolate chips

Preheat oven to 350°. Cream butter, shortening and the sugars. Add eggs and vanilla and beat until light and fluffy. Add dry ingredients gradually. Add chocolate chips. Drop batter by rounded teaspoon onto a baking sheet. Bake 8 to 10 minutes.

Jane Dick, St. Charles

CHOCOLATE CHIP COOKIES

¾ cup sugar
¾ cup brown sugar
1 cup margarine
2 eggs
1 tsp. vanilla

1 tsp. baking soda
2½ cups flour
½ tsp. salt
2 cups chocolate chips

Combine sugars and margarine and mix well. Add eggs, vanilla, baking soda, flour and salt. Mix well. Add chocolate chips. Spoon on cookie sheet and bake at 350° for approximately 10 minutes.

Amy Hellevik, Medford

GREAT CHOCOLATE CHIP COOKIES

1 cup Crisco shortening
1 cup brown sugar
½ cup white sugar
1 tsp. vanilla
2 lg. eggs

2¼ cups flour
1 tsp. baking soda
1 (12 oz.) pkg. real chocolate chips (2 cups)

Cream first 5 ingredients, then add remaining ingredients and mix well. Drop by spoon on baking sheet. Bake at 350° for 12 to 15 minutes, or until light brown. Do not overbake. Makes 2½ dozen.

Emilee Schultz, International Falls

"COWBOY" CHOCOLATE CHIP COOKIES

1 cup white sugar
1 cup firmly packed brown sugar
1 cup shortening
2 eggs, beaten
2 cups flour
1 tsp. soda
1 tsp. baking powder
½ tsp. salt
2 cups oatmeal
1 tsp. vanilla
1 cup chocolate chips
½ cup chopped walnuts

Cream the sugars and shortening. Add eggs and beat until fluffy. Add flour, soda, baking powder and salt that has been sifted together. Add the oatmeal and vanilla, then add the chocolate chips and the chopped nuts. Mix up real good and drop from spoon on cookie sheet. Bake at 350° for 15 minutes. These can be kept in freezer for a long time.

Vicki Andrejewski, Waseca

CHOCOLATE CHIP CORNFLAKE COOKIES

1 cup brown sugar
1 cup white sugar
½ cup margarine
½ cup butter
1 egg
2 tsp. vanilla
1 Tbsp. milk
3½ cups flour
1 tsp. salt
3 tsp. soda
1 cup oil
2 cups cornflakes
1 cup quick oatmeal
1 (12 oz.) pkg. chocolate chips

Mix sugars, margarine, butter, egg, vanilla and milk. Stir in dry ingredient mixture and oil alternately into sugar mixture. Stir in flakes, oatmeal and chocolate chips by hand. Bake at 350° for about 10 to 12 minutes.

Mary LaBine, Argyle

CHOCOLATE CHIP PUDDING COOKIES

1 cup margarine
¾ cup brown sugar
½ cup white sugar
2 eggs
1 tsp. vanilla
1 (3.8 oz.) pkg. instant
   chocolate pudding
1¼ cups flour
1 tsp. soda
1 (12 oz.) pkg. chocolate chips
½ cup nuts

Cream margarine and sugars. Add eggs, vanilla and instant chocolate pudding. Add flour, soda, chocolate chips and nuts. Makes a stiff batter. Drop by teaspoon on cookie sheet. Bake at 350° for 8 to 10 minutes.

Kathleen Riopelle, Argyle

COOKIES & BARS

CINNAMON ALMOND COOKIES

1¾ cups sliced almonds (6 oz.) 1 cup sugar
2 sticks butter or margarine 1 egg, separated
   (1 cup) 2 cups flour
2 tsp. cinnamon

Butter a 10½x15½ inch jelly roll pan. Preheat oven to 350°. Break the almonds into pieces by pressing and squeezing in a bag. Cream butter, cinnamon and sugar with mixer. Beat in egg yolk and gradually add flour just until mixed. Place dough by large mounds in pan and spread to cover pan using large spoon. Cover dough with waxed paper and press smooth with hands. Remove paper. Beat egg white until foamy and brush evenly over dough. Sprinkle crushed almonds on top. Cover with waxed paper and roll with straight sided glass. Remove paper. Bake 45 minutes until golden brown.

Glaze:

1 cup powdered sugar 1 Tbsp. lemon juice or 1½ tsp.
1 Tbsp. melted butter   almond flavoring with 1½ tsp.
1 Tbsp. boiling water water

Drizzle glaze over hot cookies right after taking out of oven. Allow to cool 10 minutes. Cut while warm; remove to cool. Makes 32 bars.

Jessie Laurion, International Falls

1927 CHOCOLATE DROP COOKIES

1½ cups flour ½ cup milk
½ tsp. salt 1 tsp. vanilla
1 tsp. baking powder 2 sqs. chocolate, melted
½ cup butter 1 cup nutmeats, chopped
1 cup brown sugar

Mix flour, salt and baking powder. Cream butter and sugar. Add milk and vanilla. Add to flour mixture. Stir in melted chocolate, then add nuts. Drop by heaping teaspoons onto ungreased baking sheets about 2 inches apart. Bake at 350° for 15 minutes.

Imogene Williams, Mankato

COCONUT COOKIES

½ cup butter ¾ cup coconut
2 cups sugar 3 cups flour
2 eggs 1 tsp. soda
2 Tbsp. milk 1 tsp. salt
1 tsp. cream of tartar 1 tsp. vanilla

Cream butter with sugar; add eggs. Beat well, then add the other ingredients. Drop by teaspoons onto cookie sheet. Bake at 350° for 10 to 12 minutes but do not over bake.

Mary Strand, Waseca

COCONUT COOKIES

½ cup butter
¼ cup Crisco
1 (14 oz.) bag shredded coconut
2¼ cups sugar
6 eggs, beaten

3 tsp. vanilla
1¾ cups flour
1½ tsp. baking powder
¾ tsp. salt

Melt butter and Crisco and add coconut and cook over low heat until coconut is golden brown. Stir constantly. Remove from heat and add sugar and mix well. Cool. When cool, add eggs and vanilla and beat. Add dry ingredients. Drop from teaspoon on greased cookie sheet making 4 at one time. Bake at 350° for 10 minutes. Remove at once onto waxed paper turning cookie over. Roll around wooden spoon handle forming cornucopia shape. This recipe makes 50. This is a family recipe I make every Christmas filling them with whip cream. Delicious.

Dianne Rohde, Fergus Falls

CHRISTMAS RIBBON COOKIES

2½ cups flour
1½ tsp. baking powder
½ tsp. salt
1 cup butter
1½ cups sugar
1 egg
1 tsp. vanilla

Red food coloring
¼ cup chopped red candied
    cherries
Green food coloring
¼ cup chopped almonds or
    other nuts
1 sq. chocolate, melted

Sift flour, baking powder and salt. Cream butter and sugar; add egg. Add to flour mixture, then add vanilla. Divide the dough into 3 equal parts. Color 1 part pink with red food coloring and add the red cherries. Color another part light green with food coloring and add the nuts. Add chocolate to the third part. Line a loaf pan with waxed paper. Place chocolate layer first, patting into place, then add green layer next, and finally the pink one. Chill in refrigerator overnight. Slice and bake at 350° for 12 minutes. Do not slice too thin because the colors will fade and then they aren't so pretty. Do not overbake.

Note: One could add red cherries to pink part, green cherries to green part, and nuts to chocolate part.

Ann Maas, Waseca

* * * * * * * *

Be kind, loving and understanding to the homeless and lonely.
Margaret Seipel, Mazeppa

STUFFED-DATE DROPS

1 lb. pitted dates (about 70)	1¼ cups sifted flour
1 (3 oz.) pkg. pecans	½ tsp. baking powder
¼ cup shortening	½ tsp. soda
¾ cup brown sugar	¼ tsp. salt
1 egg	½ cup sour cream

Stuff dates with half of pecan nut. Cream shortening and sugar until light. Beat in egg. Sift dry ingredients and add alternately with sour cream to creamed mixture. Stir in dates, a few at a time, works best. Drop on greased cookie sheet. A date for each cookie, or take a small amount of dough and put around the date. Bake at 400° for 8 to 10 minutes.

Golden Frosting:

½ cup butter	¾ tsp. vanilla
3 cups powdered sugar	3 Tbsp. water

Lightly brown butter; remove from heat. Beat in powdered sugar; add vanilla. Slowly add water until spreading consistency. Ice cookies.

Mary Powers, Moorhead

"OUR FAVORITE CRISPIES"

1 cup white sugar	1 tsp. cream of tartar
1 cup brown sugar	1 tsp. soda
1 cup margarine	1 tsp. salt
1 cup salad oil	½ cup chopped nuts
2 eggs	1 cup flaked coconut
1 tsp. vanilla	1 cup quick oatmeal
3¾ cups flour	1½ cups Rice Krispies

Cream sugars, margarine and oil. Add eggs and beat until fluffy. Add vanilla, 2 cups of the flour sifted with cream of tartar, soda and salt. Mix well and add the rest of the flour and other ingredients. Chill dough several hours. From balls of dough and press down with flat bottom glass that has been dipped in sugar. Bake at 375° for 10 to 12 minutes.

Esther Palubicki, Perham
State Treasurer, 1970-1974
State First Vice Regent, 1974-1978
State Regent, 1978-1980

* * * * * * * *

*Humility is that strange possession that you lose
the moment you find that you've got it.*
Ann Varmer, Zumbrota

DELICIOUS COOKIES

1 cup brown sugar
1 cup white sugar
1 cup margarine
1 cup oil
1 egg
2 tsp. vanilla
3½ cups flour
1 tsp. salt

1 tsp. cream of tartar
1 tsp. soda
1 cup coconut
1 cup rolled oats
1 cup Rice Krispies
1 cup chocolate chips
Walnuts, optional

Mix as listed and drop by spoonful onto cookie sheet. Bake at 350° for 10 to 12 minutes.

Jean Beyer, Red Lake Falls

DATE-FILLED DROP COOKIES

1 cup shortening
2 cups brown sugar
2 eggs
⅓ cup milk

1 tsp. vanilla
3¼ cups flour
1 tsp. baking powder

Cream shortening; add brown sugar, then eggs. Stir in milk and flavoring. Add dry ingredients. Drop by teaspoon on baking sheet, about 2 inches apart.

Filling:

1½ to 2 cups or ½ lb. dates, chopped
⅔ cup sugar

⅔ cup water
1 Tbsp. lemon juice
½ cup chopped nuts

Combine dates, sugar and water. Cook and stir until thick. Remove from heat and add lemon juice and nuts. Cook before filling cookies. Center ½ teaspoon filling on dough. Put a small amount of dough on top of filling. Bake at 375° for about 10 minutes or until light brown.

Lois Manka, International Falls

DISHPAN COOKIES

1 cup sugar
1 cup brown sugar
1 cup oil
1 tsp. vanilla
2 eggs

2 cups flour
1 tsp. soda
¾ cup oatmeal
½ tsp. salt
2 cups corn flakes or Special K

Mix first 5 ingredients well. Add remaining ingredients and mix well by hand in large bowl. Drop by teaspoons on baking sheet. Bake at 350° for 8 to 10 minutes.

Shirl Maher, Blue Earth

EASY DAY COOKIES

1 cup white sugar
1 cup brown sugar
1 cup shortening
1 cup Crisco oil
1 cup oatmeal
1 cup Rice Krispies
½ cup grapenuts

1 cup coconut
2 eggs
1 tsp. vanilla
1 tsp. soda
1 tsp. cream of tartar
3½ cups flour

Mix all ingredients and refrigerate overnight. Roll in balls, dip in white sugar, and flatten with glass. Bake at 350° for 10 to 15 minutes.

Florence Klonecki, Winona
Helen Bye, Crookston

MOM'S OLD FASHIONED FILLED COOKIES

2 cups sugar
1 cup shortening, part butter
2 eggs
1 cup milk
Filling:
1 pkg. dates (½ lb.), cut up
2 cups raisins

3 tsp. baking powder
1 tsp. vanilla
1 tsp. salt
Enough flour to roll, about 3 cups

1 cup water

Cook filling ingredients. Roll out a cookie and place teaspoon of filling on it and cover with another cookie. Fork down the outside to seal. Bake at 375° until light brown. (Roll cookie thin.)

Helen Fisch, Caledonia

FILLED ICE BOX COOKIES

Filling:
1 lb. dates, chopped
½ cup water

½ cup sugar
2 tsp. freshly grated orange rind

Cook ingredients until thick and let cool.

Dough:
1 cup white sugar
1 cup brown sugar
3 beaten eggs

1 rounded tsp. soda
1 cup margarine
1 tsp. vanilla

Mix ingredients and chill. Divide dough into 2 parts and roll to ¼ inch thickness, spread with cold filling, roll up like a jelly roll. Cover and place in refrigerator. Slice and bake as needed. Will keep several days in the refrigerator.

Gwen Johannes, Blue Earth

COOKIES & BARS

153

FORK COOKIES

1 cup brown sugar
1 cup white sugar
1 cup butter or lard
2 tsp. soda
2 tsp. cream of tartar

3 eggs
1 tsp. vanilla
3½ cups flour
1 tsp. salt

Mix all ingredients. Roll in balls and press down with a fork. Bake at 375° for 10 to 12 minutes.

Variation: You can add a bag of chocolate chips or peanut butter (1 cup), if desired.

Teresa Ford, Iona

GARBAGE COOKIES

¾ cup shortening
1 cup packed brown sugar
½ cup sugar or ⅓ cup honey
1 egg
¼ cup water
1 tsp. vanilla
3 cups oats
1 cup wheat flour

1 tsp. salt
½ tsp. soda
2 tsp. cinnamon, mixed with
   2 tsp. nutmeg
2 cups chocolate chips
2 cups raisins
1 cup slightly crushed peanuts

Bake at 350° for 12 to 15 minutes. Beat shortening, sugars, egg, water and vanilla. Slowly add all other ingredients (sometimes its easier to mix with you fingers). Let mixture stand for 1 hour. Roll into cookie balls, about 1 inch; flattened on greased cookie sheet.

Carol Vande, St. Peter

GINGER BALL COOKIES

1½ cups shortening
2 cups white sugar
2 eggs
3 Tbsp. molasses

4 cups flour
4 tsp. soda
1 tsp. cloves
2 tsp. ginger

Cream shortening and sugar. Add eggs and molasses. Add sifted dry ingredients. Let cool in refrigerator for a while. Roll in balls and then sugar. Bake at 375° for 10 minutes. Makes 4 dozen.

Genevieve Fairbanks, Mahnomen

FROSTED GINGER COOKIES

¼ cup shortening
½ cup sugar
1 egg
⅓ cup light molasses
2 cups flour, unsifted
1 tsp. soda
½ tsp. salt
1¼ tsp. ginger
½ tsp. cinnamon
½ tsp. cloves
½ cup water

Preheat oven to 350°. Mix shortening and sugar until creamy. Add egg and beat well. Stir in molasses. Mix flour, baking soda, salt and spices thoroughly. Add to molasses mixture alternately with water. Drop by teaspoonfuls onto greased baking sheet about 2 inches apart. Bake 10 minutes or until lightly browned. Remove from baking sheet while warm. Cool on rack. Mix powdered sugar with enough water to make a stiff but spreadable frosting. Makes 5 dozen cookies.

Margaret Hilleshiem, Kellogg

GINGER SNAPS

3¾ cups flour
¾ cup Crisco
1½ cups sugar
2 eggs
4 level tsp. soda
½ tsp. cinnamon
½ tsp. ginger
¾ cup molasses

Mix and roll in balls the size of a walnut. Press down a little and bake at 350° for about 13 minutes. Frost when cool.

Susan Ruether, Perham

GUMDROP JEWEL COOKIES

3½ oz. flaked coconut
½ cup milk
2 cups sifted flour
½ tsp. soda
½ tsp. salt
½ cup shortening
¾ cup brown sugar, packed
2 eggs
1 tsp. vanilla
½ tsp. almond extract
1 cup small spice gumdrops, halved

Combine coconut and milk; let stand 15 minutes. Sift flour, soda and salt. Cream shortening and sugar until light and fluffy. Stir in eggs, vanilla and almond extract and beat well. Stir in coconut mixture. Add flour mixture all at once, stirring to blend. Stir in gumdrops. Drop by rounded teaspoonfuls 3 inches apart onto lightly greased sheets. Bake at 350° for 12 to 15 minutes until lightly browned. Cool on wire racks. Store in tightly covered container. Makes 5 dozen.

Clarice Vik, Crookston

HALFWAY COOKIES OR BARS

1 cup shortening	1 tsp. baking powder
½ cup brown sugar	1 tsp. baking soda
½ cup white sugar	1 tsp. vanilla
2 egg yolks	1 pkg. chocolate chips
4 tsp. water	1 pkg. nuts
2 cups flour	

Mix and spread into greased pan. Sprinkle with chocolate chips and nuts. Beat **egg whites** until stiff and add **1 cup brown sugar**. Frost and bake at 350° until done.

Mrs. Edwin Reddemann, New Ulm

HAYSTACKS

4 cups sugar	1 cup peanut butter
1 cup milk	9 cups oatmeal
1 cup butter	2 tsp. vanilla
½ cup cocoa	

Combine first 4 ingredients and bring to boil. Remove from heat and add remaining ingredients. Stir and drop by tablespoons on cookie sheet. Chill.

Bev Bragg, Ranier

SLICED ICE BOX FROZEN COOKIES

1 cup white sugar	1 tsp. salt
1 cup brown sugar	1 tsp. cream of tartar
1 cup shortening	1 tsp. vanilla
2 eggs	½ cup nutmeats
3½ scant cups flour	½ cup raisins, optional
1 tsp. soda	

Mix sugar, shortening and eggs. Sift dry ingredients; add vanilla and nuts slowly. Roll into long roll on wax paper and wrap tightly. Freeze and slice off and bake at 375° for 10 to 12 minutes.

Betty Fitzpatrick, Brownsville

THREE INGREDIENTS MACAROONS

2⅔ cups coconut	⅓ cup sweetened condensed
1 tsp. vanilla	milk

Mix all ingredients and drop by teaspoonfuls 1 inch apart on greased cookie sheet. Bake at 350° for 8 to 10 minutes. Remove from pan immediately. Makes 2½ dozen. Nice for Christmas.

Viola Maday, Fairmont

M&M COOKIES

½ cup Crisco	¼ tsp. water
½ cup brown sugar	½ tsp. soda
¼ cup white sugar	⅓ tsp. salt
½ tsp. vanilla	¾ cup M&M's
1 egg	1 cup plus 2 Tbsp. sifted flour

Mix Crisco, sugars, vanilla, egg, water, soda and salt. Add the M&M's and then the flour. Bake at 375° for 10 to 12 minutes.

Elsie Walz, Mahnomen

MELTING COOKIES

¾ cup cornstarch	Pinch of salt
⅓ cup icing sugar	1 cup flour
1 tsp. vanilla	½ lb. (or 1 cup) margarine

Mix ingredients and shape into balls. Place on ungreased cookie sheet and flatten with floured fork. Bake at 375° for 10 minutes.

Lemon Frosting:

1 tsp. softened margarine	Rind and juice of ½ lemon
1 cup icing sugar	

Combine ingredients. If too thin, add more sugar. Frost when cookies are cooled. If cookies dough is too soft of handle, chill for 1 hour.

Sharon Everett, International Falls

MILLION DOLLAR COOKIES

½ cup white sugar	1 tsp. vanilla
½ cup brown sugar	2 cups flour
1 cup margarine	¼ tsp. soda
1 egg	½ tsp. salt

Cream sugar, margarine, egg and vanilla. Add flour, soda and salt. Roll into balls and roll in additional sugar. Flatten with glass. Bake at 350° until brown.

Myrtle Bahr, International Falls
Laurette Welter, Crookston

MOLASSES COOKIES

1½ cups margarine	4 cups flour
2 cups sugar	2 tsp. soda
2 eggs	1 tsp. cinnamon
½ cup molasses	

Cream margarine and sugar. Add eggs; mix rest of ingredients in order given. Bake at 350° for 10 to 12 minutes.

Helen Houselog, Holland

COOKIES & BARS

SOFT MOLASSES COOKIES

¾ cup white sugar
½ cup margarine, melted
1 egg, beaten
½ cup molasses
½ tsp. ginger

½ tsp. cinnamon
½ tsp. nutmeg
1 tsp. soda
3 cups flour

Mix sugar and shortening well, then add the remaining ingredients. Stir until everything is well mixed. Chill dough 1 hour. Roll out and cut with large circle cookie cutter. Bake on greased cookie sheet at 350° for 8 minutes.

Marilyn Petit, Plainview

MOLASSES CRISP'S COOKIES

2 cups sugar
1½ cups shortening
2 eggs
½ cup molasses
4 cups flour

1 tsp. salt
4 tsp. soda
1 tsp. cloves
1 tsp. ginger
2 tsp. cinnamon

Mix sugar, 2 tablespoons at a time, into shortening until light and fluffy. Add unbeaten eggs and beat well. Stir in molasses. Stir remaining ingredients and add ⅓ at a time to sugar mixture and mix well. Bake at 350° for 10 minutes.

Florence (Fuzz) Hammers, Perham
State Secretary, 1984-1988
State 2nd Vice Regent, 1988-1990

AUNT LILLIAN'S MOLASSES CRINKLES

¾ cup soft shortening
1 cup brown sugar, packed
1 egg
¼ cup molasses
2½ cups flour

2 tsp. baking soda
¼ tsp. salt
1 tsp. cinnamon
1 tsp. ginger
½ tsp. cloves

Roll into balls the size of large walnuts. Dip top in sugar; place on baking sheet sugar side up. Bake at 375° until set but no hard. (Hint: add ¼ teaspoon water to make a softer cookie.) Yield: 3 dozen.

Barbara Kleinschmidt, Winona
State Publicity Chair, 1995-1996

COOKIES & BARS

158

MONSTER COOKIES

6 eggs	½ lb. butter
1 lb. brown sugar	1½ lb. peanut butter
2 cups white sugar	9 cups oatmeal
1 Tbsp. vanilla	½ lb. chocolate chips
1 Tbsp. light Karo syrup	½ lb. M&M's
4 tsp. soda	½ lb. butterscotch chips

Mix all ingredients. Roll into walnut size balls and smash down on cookie sheet sprayed with nonstick. Bake at 375° for 12 to 15 minutes.

Bernadine Hildebrant, Waterville

NO BAKE CHOCOLATE COOKIES

2 cups sugar	½ cup milk
3 Tbsp. cocoa	½ tsp. salt
⅔ cup butter	1 tsp. vanilla

Boil all ingredients for 1 minute. Add:

3 cups oatmeal	1 cup coconut
½ cup chopped nuts	½ cup peanut butter

Roll into small balls and chill.

Variation: Joyce substitutes 2 cups oatmeal, 1 cup nuts and 2 cups Cheerios for the oatmeal, nuts, coconut and peanut butter.

Joyce Kerrigan, Winona

MOM'S OATMEAL COOKIES

1 cup shortening	1 tsp. vanilla
½ cup white sugar	Pinch of salt
½ cup brown sugar	1 tsp. cinnamon
2 eggs, beaten	2 cups flour
1 scant tsp. soda, mixed in	1 cup raisins
¼ cup milk	Nuts, optional
2 cups oatmeal	

Mix shortening and sugar. Add eggs and soda in milk, then add the oatmeal and vanilla. Mix salt and cinnamon in flour then add flour and raisins. Drop by spoonfuls on cookie sheet and bake at 350° until done. May frost with powdered sugar frosting if desired.

Catherine Persing, Wilmont
Myrtle Traun, Moorhead

OVERNIGHT OATMEAL COOKIES

1 cup shortening
1 cup brown sugar
1 cup white sugar
2 eggs, beaten
1 tsp. soda
1½ cups flour
3½ cups oatmeal
1 tsp. vanilla

Cream shortening and sugar. Add beaten eggs. Sift and add dry ingredients. Add oatmeal and vanilla. May add 1 teaspoon nutmeg and ½ cup walnuts if desired. Form into a loaf. Let stand in refrigerator overnight. Slice and bake at 350° for 10 to 12 minutes.

Beverly Pawloski, Argyle
Pat Schmidt, Slayton
lanilla Koob, Iona

OATMEAL PUDDING COOKIES

1¼ cups unsifted all-purpose
flour
1 tsp. baking soda
1 cup butter or margarine,
softened
¾ cup light brown sugar, firmly
packed
¼ cup granulated sugar
1 (3¾ oz.) pkg. vanilla instant
pudding
2 eggs
3½ cups quick cooking rolled
oats
1 cup raisins

Mix flour with baking soda. Combine butter, sugars and pudding mix in large mixing bowl; beat until smooth and creamy. Beat in eggs. Gradually add flour mixture, then stir in oats and raisins. (Batter will be stiff.) Drop from teaspoon onto ungreased baking sheets, about 2 inches apart. Bake at 375° for 10 to 12 minutes. Makes about 5 dozen.

Mary Burns, Janesville

FRUITED OATMEAL COOKIES

4½ cups flour
2 tsp. soda
1 tsp. cinnamon
1 cup shortening
1¼ cups brown sugar
1 cup white sugar
4 eggs
1 cup water
4 cups oatmeal
1 tsp. almond extract

Drop by rounded teaspoons 3 inches apart. With back of spoon, make dent in center, fill with ½ **teaspoon preserve** (any kind) and top with ½ teaspoon dough. Bake at 400° for 10 minutes.

Fran Fehrenbach, Perham

OATMEAL CHIP COOKIES

½ cup oleo
½ cup Crisco
1 cup white sugar
1 cup brown sugar
2 eggs
1 tsp. salt
1 tsp. baking soda
2 cups flour
1½ cups oatmeal
1 cup chocolate chips

Cream oleo, Crisco and sugars well. Stir in eggs, salt and baking soda. Add flour, oatmeal and chocolate chips. Bake at 350° for 15 minutes.

Barbara Schreier, Currie

CHOCOLATE OATMEAL COOKIES

1 cup shortening
2 cups sugar
2 eggs
3 sqs. chocolate
2 tsp. vanilla
1½ cups flour
2 tsp. baking powder
1 tsp. salt
3 cups oatmeal
1 cup nutmeats

Cream shortening and sugar. Add eggs and beat well. Add the melted chocolate and vanilla and blend. Add flour, baking powder and salt. Add oatmeal and nuts. Drop by spoonfuls on cookie sheet. Bake at 350° for about 10 minutes.

Dorothy Osborne, New Ulm

OATMEAL, MOLASSES, RAISIN COOKIES
(Health Food Cookies)

2 cups melted vegetable
   shortening
2 cups light molasses or honey,
   or 1 cup of each
4 eggs, beaten
¼ cup hot water
4 cups white flour
4 cups whole wheat flour
8 cups quick oatmeal
2 cups sugar
2 Tbsp. soda
1 tsp. salt
2 cups chopped walnuts
3 cups raisins, or any combination of your favorite dried fruit

Combine shortening, molasses, eggs and hot water; mix well. Add remaining ingredients and mix well. Drop by spoonfuls onto greased sheet pan. Flatten with the bottom of glass that has been greased and dipped in sugar. Bake at 350° for 8 to 10 minutes. Makes 10 to 12 dozen cookies. These can be kept very well in the freezer, or dough can be kept in sealed container in the refrigerator for 6 to 8 weeks so you can bake a fresh pan of cookies anytime. Great snack for hungry children!

Cathy Doll, Perham

COOKIES & BARS

OATMEAL-PEANUT BUTTER COOKIES

¾ cup butter or margarine
½ cup peanut butter
1 cup sugar
1 cup brown sugar
2 eggs
¼ cup milk
1 tsp. vanilla

2 cups flour
1 tsp. baking soda
1 tsp. salt
1 tsp. cinnamon
½ cup quick cook oatmeal
1 cup raisins

Cream butter, peanut butter and sugars. Add eggs, milk and vanilla; blend. Add flour, soda, salt and cinnamon. Stir in oatmeal and raisins. Drop by spoonfuls and bake at 350° for 12 minutes.

Altha Spaeth, Mahnomen

ORANGE COOKIES

1 cup Crisco shortening
1 cup brown sugar, packed
2 eggs, beaten
1 cup milk
3½ cups sifted flour
1 tsp. salt

1 tsp. soda
2 tsp. baking powder
Grated rind of 1 orange
½ cup pecans or walnuts,
    chopped
1 tsp. vanilla

Cream shortening; add brown sugar and eggs. Add milk alternately with flour, salt, soda and baking powder, to the shortening. Blend well. Mix in orange rind, nuts and vanilla. Drop by rounded teaspoons on greased baking sheet. Bake at 375° for about 10 minutes; cool and glaze.

Frosting:

1 Tbsp. butter or margarine
1 cup powdered sugar

Juice of small orange

Cream butter or margarine; add sugar and enough orange juice to make frosting of spreading consistency. Makes about 7 dozen.

Ann Reef, International Falls

PEANUT BUTTER COOKIE CUPS

1 roll peanut butter cookie
    dough

1 pkg. miniature Reese's peanut
    butter cups

Cut a slice of cookie dough, then quarter that slice. Place one of the quarters into a miniature muffin tin. Put a peanut butter cup on top of dough (do not press hard). Bake at 375° for 7 to 10 minutes or until dough forms around peanut butter cup.

Nell Cook, Plainview

PEANUT BLOSSOMS

1/3 cup peanut butter	1 egg
1/2 cup butter	1¾ cups flour
1/2 cup white sugar	1 tsp. baking soda
1/2 cup brown sugar	1/2 tsp. salt
1 tsp. vanilla	1 pkg. chocolate stars

Cream first 4 ingredients. Add vanilla and then egg. Sift flour, soda and salt. Combine dry mixture with batter and shape dough into balls. Flatten with glass. Bake at 375° for 8 minutes. Press stars in cookie and bake an additional 2 to 5 minutes.

Bernadine Kremer, Iona

PEANUT BUTTER COOKIES

1 cup butter or margarine	2 eggs
¾ cup brown sugar	1¾ cups flour
¾ cup granulated sugar	1 cup All Bran
1 tsp. vanilla	¾ cup rolled oats
1 cup peanut butter	2 tsp. soda

Melt butter; beat with the sugars, vanilla, peanut butter and eggs. Add dry ingredients. Drop by teaspoons onto ungreased cookie sheet. Bake at 350° for 15 to 18 minutes. Remove to rack to cool. Makes 7 dozen cookies.

Mary Lou Schouweiler, Kellogg

PEANUT-BUTTER COOKIES

¾ cup peanut butter	1 egg
1/2 cup Crisco	1¾ cups flour
1¼ cups brown sugar	¾ tsp. salt
3 Tbsp. milk	¾ tsp. baking soda
1 Tbsp. vanilla	

Combine peanut butter, Crisco, brown sugar, milk and vanilla; mix. Add eggs. Combine flour, salt and baking soda. Add to creamed mixture. Mix and drop by teaspoonfuls. Bake at 375° for 6 to 8 minutes.

Fun Variation: Shape into balls. Roll in chopped peanuts. Press center with a teaspoon. Bake 6 to 8 minutes. Press miniature peanut butter cup into depression.

Sue Stangler, Waseca

PEANUT BUTTER COOKIES

1 cup butter or margarine	1 tsp. vanilla
1 cup peanut butter	2½ cups flour
1 cup white sugar	1½ tsp. soda
1 cup brown sugar	½ tsp. salt
2 eggs	

Cream the butter or margarine with the peanut butter and sugars until smooth. Add the eggs and vanilla. Sift the flour, soda and salt in a bowl and add to the creamed mixture; mix well. Roll into 1 inch balls and put on ungreased cookie sheet. Press down with either a fork or the bottom of a glass dipped in sugar for each cookie. Bake at 375° for 10 to 12 minutes. Makes about 7 dozen cookies.

Marva Taylor, Adrian

PEANUT BUTTER COOKIES

2 cups brown sugar	4¾ cups cake flour
2 cups granulated sugar	1½ tsp. soda
1½ cups (3 sticks) margarine	1 tsp. salt
1½ tsp. vanilla	1½ cups peanut butter
3 eggs	

Preheat oven to 350°. Cream sugars, margarine and vanilla until mixture is light and fluffy. Add eggs and blend well. Add flour, soda and salt. Mix well. Stir in peanut butter. Drop by teaspoons onto greased cookie sheet. Bake 10 to 12 minutes.

Note: Cookies will appear half done, they firm up as they cool.

Alice M. Hutchens, Waseca

PINEAPPLE COOKIES

1 cup brown sugar	1 (No. 2) can crushed pineapple
1 cup white sugar	with juice
1 cup shortening	4 cups flour
3 eggs	1 tsp. baking soda
1 tsp. vanilla	½ tsp. salt

Mix sugars, shortening, eggs, vanilla and pineapple. Add dry ingredients to the above mixture. Stir well. Chill at least 1 hour. Heat oven to 350°. Drop rounded teaspoonfuls of dough about 2 inches apart, on a lightly greased baking sheet. Bake about 10 minutes or until no imprint remains when touched lightly.

Marianne Kerr, Slayton

COOKIES & BARS

POWDERED SUGAR COOKIES

1 cup white sugar	4 cups plus 4 rounded Tbsp. flour
1 cup powdered sugar	1 tsp. soda
1 cup butter or margarine	¼ tsp. salt
1 cup vegetable oil	1 tsp. cream of tartar
2 eggs	1 tsp. vanilla

Cream sugars, butter or margarine, and oil; beat in eggs. Add dry ingredients. Stir in vanilla. Mix all ingredients well. Chill dough and roll into balls. Dip cookie balls into sugar and press down. Bake at 375° for 12 minutes or until light brown.

Dena I. Zamani, Fergus Falls

GREAT PUMPKIN COOKIES

2 cups flour	1 cup white sugar
1 cup quick oatmeal	1 egg
1 tsp. soda	1 tsp. vanilla
1 tsp. cinnamon	1 cup pumpkin
½ tsp. salt	1 cup chocolate chips, nuts or
1 cup butter or margarine	raisins, optional
1 cup brown sugar	

Mix dry ingredients. Cream butter and sugars until fluffy. Add egg and vanilla. Add pumpkin. Add flour mixture. Bake at 350° for 20 to 25 minutes or until firm and lightly browned. Frost with icing. Can add peanut butter to icing.

Angie Wosick, Moorhead

RAISIN OATMEAL COOKIES

2 cups flour	1 cup sugar
1 tsp. salt	2 eggs
1 tsp. baking powder	1 tsp. vanilla
1 tsp. baking soda	2 cups shredded coconut
1 cup soft shortening	1 cup raisins
1 cup packed brown sugar	1 cup quick oatmeal

Sift flour, salt, baking powder and soda. Cream shortening; add sugars and cream until fluffy. Add eggs and vanilla. Add flour mixture with coconut, raisins and oatmeal. Drop on ungreased sheet and bake at 375° for 8 to 12 minutes. Makes 5 dozen.

Lorraine Kraft, Blue Earth

COOKIES & BARS

OATMEAL RAISIN COOKIES

1½ cups raisins	2½ cups flour
½ cup water	1 tsp. soda
1 cup butter	½ tsp. salt
1 cup sugar	1½ cups oatmeal
1 cup brown sugar	½ cup nuts
2 eggs	1 tsp. vanilla

Boil raisins with water. Mix in order. Drop from teaspoon onto cookie sheet. Bake at 350° for about 10 minutes.
Variation: Dorothy adds 1 teaspoon cinnamon.

Rosie Kelly, Waseca
Dorothy Doll, Perham

RAISIN COOKIES

2 cups raisins	½ tsp. allspice
1 cup water	3 eggs
1½ tsp. soda	1 tsp. vanilla
1 cup soft shortening	1 tsp. baking powder, mixed
2 scant tsp. salt	with 4 cups flour
½ tsp. cinnamon	1 cup nuts
½ tsp. nutmeg	1 cup sugar

Boil raisins and water for 5 minutes; drain and leave ½ cup water on raisins and cool. Add soda, shortening, salt, cinnamon, nutmeg, allspice, eggs and vanilla. Add flour mixture. Fold in nuts. Chill the dough (makes it easier to handle). Drop by teaspoons on an ungreased cookie sheet at 400° for 10 to 12 minutes.

Cyrilla Esch, Caledonia

RAISIN DROP COOKIES

1½ cups raisins	3 cups flour
1 cup water	1 tsp. soda
1 cup shortening	1 tsp. salt
1 cup sugar	1 tsp. nutmeg
2 eggs	1 tsp. cinnamon

Boil raisins and water for 1 minute. Set aside to cool. Cream shortening; add sugar and eggs. Combine all ingredients and sift in alternately with cooled raisins and water. Bake at 350° for 15 to 20 minutes. These cookies stay soft and moist.

Marguerite Larson, Owatonna

RHUBARB COOKIES

1½ cups diced rhubarb	1 tsp. soda
1 cup light raisins or cut up dates	1 tsp. cinnamon
¼ cup water	½ tsp. salt
1 stick oleo	1 cup cut up nuts
1½ cups white sugar	2 eggs
2½ cups flour	

Use a large saucepan to cook and mix the whole recipe. Grease cookie sheets. Cook rhubarb, raisins and water until rhubarb is soft and most of water is absorbed, about 10 minutes. In the same pan, add oleo and white sugar. Stir until blended. Add flour, soda, cinnamon, salt and nuts. Stir well and add eggs. Stir until well mixed. Drop by heaping teaspoonfuls onto the greased cookie sheet. Bake 13 to 15 minutes. Let stand a few minutes on sheet before removing. These are moist cookies that keep well in the refrigerator and have a great taste!

Mrs. Clement Pestka, Waseca

RICE KRISPIE COOKIES

1 cup white sugar	½ tsp. salt
1 cup brown sugar	1 cup quick cooking oatmeal
1 cup cooking oil	1 cup Rice Krispies
1 cup margarine or butter	3½ cups flour
1 egg	1 tsp. soda
1 tsp. vanilla	1 tsp. cream of tartar

With electric mixer, mix sugars, oil, margarine, egg, vanilla and salt. Stir in oatmeal, Rice Krispies, flour, soda and cream of tartar. Roll into balls and press down with a fork. Bake at 400° for 9 minutes.

Margaret Jeffrey, Winona

ROCKS

1 cup brown sugar	2 cakes chocolate
1 egg	1½ cups Jersey Lily flour
½ cup melted butter	1 cup nuts
½ cup sweet milk	½ tsp. soda

Drop from a spoon into a buttered dish and bake until desired doneness.

Note: This recipe was submitted by a Miss Hattie Comstock to the 'Jersey Lily Cookbook' and Jersey Lily Flour was produced by a mill in Janesville, Minnesota at one time. Judging from the names of those submitting recipes, I would estimate the book was printed in the early 1900's.

Ceclia McBride, Janesville

ROSETTES

2 eggs
2 Tbsp. sugar
¼ tsp. salt

1 cup milk
1 cup flour

Beat eggs slightly; add sugar, salt and milk. Stir in flour gradually and beat until smooth. Use a rosette iron and slip into hot grease (lard or oil) then into batter, not allowing batter to come over top of the iron. Fry for at least 20 seconds. Remove from iron with clean piece cheese cloth and allow to cool. Should the batter fail to adhere to the mold, the iron is overheated. If the rosettes blister, undoubtedly, the eggs are beaten too much. To insure crisp rosettes they should be fried somewhat moderately heat. Rosettes sufficiently fried will come from the irons freely.

Agusta Kunst, Clear Lake

RUM BALLS

1 cup butter or margarine
2 cups sugar
2 eggs
1 lb. chopped dates

1 tsp. rum extract
6 cups Rice Krispies
Coconut

Cook first 4 ingredients for about 15 minutes; cool. Add rum extract; mix. Stir in Rice Krispies. Shape into small balls; roll in coconut.

Garnet Ames, International Falls

RUSSIAN TEA BALLS

1 cup butter
½ cup powdered sugar
2 cups flour

1 cup chopped walnuts
1 tsp. vanilla

Blend all ingredients. Roll into small balls. Place on ungreased cookie sheet and bake at 375° until lightly brown, about 15 minutes. When cool, roll in powdered sugar.

Rose Nixon, Winona
State Regent, 1974-1978

SALTED PEANUT COOKIES

2 cups brown sugar
1 cup shortening
2 eggs
1 tsp. vanilla
1½ cups flour

1 tsp. baking powder
1½ tsp. soda
2 cups oatmeal
1½ cups salted peanuts, crushed
1 cup corn flakes, crushed

Cream the sugar and shortening; add eggs and vanilla; mix well. Add sifted dry ingredients; mix. Add oatmeal, nuts and corn flakes. Drop by spoonfuls on cookie sheet and bake at 375° for 10 to 12 minutes.

Lucille Rassier, Littlefork

COOKIES & BARS

SPRITS

1 cup shortening (½ butter or margarine)
¾ cup sugar
1 egg
½ tsp. baking powder
1 tsp. almond flavoring
Dash of salt
2¼ cups flour

Cream shortening and sugar. Beat well. Add egg; beat well. Add remaining ingredients. Mix well. Put in cookie press. Bake at 350° until light brown.

Eileen Ryan, St. Peter

STARLIGHT MINT SURPRISE COOKIES

3 cups flour
1 tsp. soda
½ tsp. salt
1 cup butter (½ shortening may be used)
1 cup white sugar
½ cup brown sugar
2 unbeaten eggs
1 Tbsp. water
1 tsp. vanilla
1 (9 oz.) pkg. solid chocolate mint candy wafers
Walnut halves

Sift flour, soda and salt. Cream butter and the sugars well. Add the unbeaten eggs, water, and vanilla and beat well. Blend in dry ingredients gradually; mix thoroughly. Cover and chill at least 2 hours. Enclose a wafer in about 1 tablespoon of chilled dough. Place on greased baking sheet about 2 inches apart. Top each cookie with a walnut half. Bake at 350° for 10 to 12 minutes.

Marcella Conway, Waseca

STRUL

1 cup sugar
1 cup shortening (should be at least part butter)
2 eggs, beaten
1 cup rich milk
2 cups flour
½ tsp. baking powder
Vanilla and salt

Cream sugar and shortening, adding milk alternately with flour mixture. Add vanilla and salt. Drop by a teaspoonful on the hot iron. When brown, roll up on the wooden stick. Lay on paper towel.

Augusta Knust, Clear Lake, IA

SUGAR COOKIES

3 cups flour
1 tsp. salt
1 tsp. soda
1 cup butter
2 eggs
1 cup sugar
3 Tbsp. milk
1 tsp. vanilla

Sift flour, salt, soda and mix with butter like pie crust. Beat eggs well; add sugar, milk, and vanilla; beat a little more. Add dry ingredients. Put in refrigerator overnight. Bake the next morning at 350°.

Frances Goodrich, St. Charles

WINTER SUGAR COOKIES

2 eggs	2 tsp. baking powder
3 Tbsp. milk	1 tsp. soda
1 tsp. vanilla	¾ tsp. salt
1 cup sugar	1 cup Crisco shortening
3 cups flour	

Mix eggs, milk, vanilla and sugar. Sift flour, baking powder, soda and salt. Work in shortening, then add egg mixture. Roll out and cut with cookie cutters. Bake at 350° for 5 to 6 minutes. Ice with powdered sugar frosting. Decorate.

Helen Shaw, Winona

SUGAR COOKIES

1 cup white sugar	3 cups flour
1 cup butter	1 tsp. cream of tartar
1 egg	1 tsp. soda
1 tsp. vanilla	

Mix and roll. Wrap in waxed paper; put in refrigerator or freezer. Slice; place on greased cookie sheet. Bake at 350° for 10 minutes.

Beulah Scheurer, Mankato

ROLL OUT CHRISTMAS COOKIES

3 eggs, beaten	2 tsp. vanilla
1 cup sugar	2 tsp. cream of tartar
1 cup shortening	1 tsp. soda
3 cups flour	1 tsp. salt

Mix well in order given. Roll out on floured board; cut in desired shapes. Bake on cookie sheets at 325° until lightly brown. Cool and frost with powdered sugar icing in various colors; sprinkle with small colored sugars, etc. Double the recipe to make twice the cookies.

Rose Nixon, Winona
State Regent, 1974-1978
Margaret Tri, Mazeppa

GRANDMA TYRRELL'S SUGAR COOKIES

2 cups sugar	1 tsp. nutmeg
1 cup shortening	4 cups flour
3 eggs	1 heaping tsp. baking powder
2 level tsp. baking soda, mixed	1 tsp. salt
in 1 cup sour cream	

Cream sugar and shortening. Add eggs cream well. Add sour cream and soda, then the rest of the ingredients. Chill dough. Roll out and cut with shape. Sprinkle with sugar. May use colored sugar at holiday time. Bake at 425° for 10 to 12 minutes.

Helen Basile, Eveleth

PLAIN WHITE SUGAR COOKIES

1 cup powdered sugar	1 tsp. soda
1 cup white sugar	1 tsp. cream of tartar
1 cup oil, shortening, or butter	1 tsp. salt
1 cup margarine, softened	4½ cups flour
2 eggs	1 tsp. almond extract, optional
1 tsp. vanilla	

Cream together first 4 ingredients; stir in eggs and vanilla. Add dry ingredients and mix until well blended. Roll dough into balls; flatten with sugar coated glass (may use sugar and nutmeg when flattening cookies). Bake at 375° for 10 to 12 minutes.

Cyrilla Frodl, Waterville
Myrtle Traun, Moorhead
Monica Galvin, Currie
Carole Gardner, Winona
Doris Labine, Argyle

MAE'S SUGAR COOKIES

1 cup shortening, softened (½ butter)	1 egg yolk
	Vanilla
1 (3 oz.) pkg. cream cheese, softened	2½ cups flour
	¼ tsp. baking soda
1 cup white sugar	

Cream softened shortening, cream cheese and sugar until smooth and creamy. Add egg yolk and vanilla; stir until blended. Add dry ingredients and mix. Shape dough into two rolls. Chill overnight. Slice thin. Bake at 325° for 13 to 15 minutes.

Rose Sommerstad, Waseca

SUGAR COOKIES

1 cup shortening	5 cups flour
2 cups sugar	1 Tbsp. baking powder
3 eggs, beaten	1 tsp. salt
3 Tbsp. milk	½ to 1 tsp. nutmeg

Cream shortening; add sugar and beat. Add beaten eggs and milk; mix well. Add dry ingredients and additional flour to make a stiff dough. Roll on floured cloth to about ⅛ inch thickness. Cut with floured cookie cutter. Sprinkle with sugar, if desired. Bake at 425° for about 8 to 10 minutes. Makes about 5 dozen. You can frost with a butter icing if desired.

Mary Anderson, Plainview

SUNFLOWER DROP COOKIES

1 cup shortening	2 cups oatmeal
2/3 cup sugar	2 cups flour
2/3 cup brown sugar	1 tsp. salt
2 eggs	1 tsp. baking soda
2 tsp. hot water	1 1/2 cups sunflower nuts
1 tsp. vanilla	

Cream shortening and sugars; add eggs. Add hot water and vanilla. Add dry ingredients and mix. Drop on greased cookie sheet. Bake at 375° for 10 to 12 minutes.

Corrine Thompson, Waseca

SWEDISH CHRISTMAS COOKIES

6 egg yolks, separated	1/2 tsp. lemon extract
3/4 cup shortening	2 cups flour
3/4 cup sugar	1/2 tsp. salt
3 Tbsp. cream	

Separate eggs; drop yolks in hot water. Cook slowly until solid; cool. Press yolks through sieve; mix shortening, sugar, cream and extract. Add dry ingredients; mix well. Chill. Roll out, cut with cookie cutter. These handle well and hold shape when baked.

Easy Icing:

1 Tbsp. evaporated milk	2 drops food coloring

Mix and paint unbaked cookies. Paint with child's paint brush; make color as bright as desired, it will hold that color and cookies are decorated when they are baked. Bake at 350° for 10 to 12 minutes.

Eleanor Christofferson, Owatonna

WALNUT COOKIES

2 cups quick oatmeal	1 tsp. vanilla
1 cup brown sugar	2 eggs
1/2 cup oil	3/4 cup chopped walnuts
1/2 tsp. salt	1 cup flaked coconut

Mix oatmeal, sugar and oil in large bowl. Let stand for 3 hours. Add salt, vanilla, eggs, walnuts and coconut; mix. Drop from teaspoon onto a greased cookie sheet. Bake at 350° for 8 to 10 minutes.

Adelia Sondag, New Ulm

WHEATIES COOKIES

1 cup sugar	1 tsp. baking powder
1 cup brown sugar	1 tsp. baking soda
1 cup margarine or Crisco	2 cups coconut
2 eggs	2 cups Wheaties
2 cups flour	1 tsp. vanilla

Cream sugars and shortening. Add eggs and beat well. Add dry ingredients and flavoring; mix well. Stir in coconut and wheaties. Drop by teaspoonfuls on baking sheet. Bake at 350° for 15 minutes.

Agnes Kotewa, Fairmont

WHEEL COOKIES

¾ cup butter	¾ tsp. soda
1½ cups sugar	¾ tsp. salt
1 egg and vanilla	3 Tbsp. water
3 cups flour	2 (1 oz.) sqs. chocolate

Cream butter, sugar, egg, vanilla, dry ingredients and water. Cut dough into 2 parts, one white and add chocolate to other half. Roll on wax paper like a jelly roll and chill. Cut each roll lengthwise in 4 parts, brushing the open side with hot milk; place alternately and chill. Make like refrigerator cookies. Bake at 325° for 10 minutes.

Mary Burg, Caledonia

* * BARS * *

ALMOND BARS

First Layer:

1 cup butter	½ cup powdered sugar
2 cups flour	

Mix and pat in a 9x13 inch pan. Sprinkle a small package of slivered almonds on top. Bake at 350° for 15 to 20 minutes.

Second Layer:

1 (8 oz.) pkg. cream cheese	½ cup sugar
2 eggs	1 tsp. almond flavoring

Beat cream cheese until creamy. Add eggs, sugar and almond flavoring. Beat and spread over first layer. Bake at 350° for 15 to 20 minutes.

Frosting:

½ cup melted butter	Scant 1½ Tbsp. milk
1½ cups powdered sugar	1 tsp. almond flavoring

Mix and spread over top when cool.

Marcella Jeno, Owatonna
District Deputy, 1992-1996

ALMOND CRISP BARS

Graham crackers
¾ cup brown sugar
1 cup butter
1 (4 oz.) pkg. sliced almonds

Line a buttered jelly roll pan with graham crackers. Boil brown sugar and butter for 2 minutes. Pour boiled mixture over graham crackers. Sprinkle sliced almonds on top. Bake at 350° for 8 minutes. Cool slightly before cutting. Delicious!

Bernita Seitzer, St. Peter

ANGEL FOOD BARS

1 pkg. angel food cake mix
1 can lemon pie filling
1 cup flaked coconut

Mix all ingredients well and place in a greased and floured cookie sheet pan. Bake at 350° for 25 minutes. Can be frosted or just sprinkled with powdered sugar.

Phyllis Guzek, Red Lake Falls

APPLE BARS

2½ cups flour
1 tsp. salt
1 cup shortening
2 egg yolks, mixed with milk
   to make ⅔ cup
1½ cups corn flakes, crushed
15 to 20 raw apples, peeled,
   cored and sliced
1¼ tsp. cinnamon
1½ cups sugar

Mix flour, salt and shortening as for pie crust. Work egg yolk/milk mixture into crust. Roll out half crust and place on cookie sheet, building up sides. Sprinkle cereal on top of crust; add apples, cinnamon and sugar. Roll out remaining dough and place over apple mixture. Bake at 350° for 1 hour. May spread powdered sugar mixed with water on top after bars are cooled.

Maureen Mittelstadt, Blue Earth

PLAIN APPLE BARS

2½ cups flour
1 Tbsp. sugar
1 tsp. salt
1 cup butter flavor Crisco
1 egg yolk and enough milk to
   make ⅔ cup
5 cups sliced apples
½ cup sugar
1 tsp. cinnamon

Mix flour, sugar and salt; cut in Crisco. Spread half of dough in a 9x13 inch cake pan. Mix apples, sugar and cinnamon and spread over crust. Top with remaining rolled out dough and glaze with beaten egg white. Bake at 400° for 40 minutes.

Mary Bulfer, Fairmont

APPLE DATE BARS

1 cup dates, cut small	1 egg
1 cup raw apples, cut small	1 tsp. vanilla
1 tsp. soda	½ tsp. salt
1 cup boiling water	1½ cups flour
½ cup margarine	1 cup chopped nuts
1 cup white sugar	

Chop the dates and apples into small pieces. Mix with soda and boiling water. Let stand until cool. Cream margarine and sugar; add egg and vanilla; beat until fluffy. Add dry ingredients alternately with apple and date mixture. Bake at 350° for 30 minutes.

Topping:

4 Tbsp. margarine	3 Tbsp. cream
½ cup brown sugar	1 cup coconut

Mix margarine, brown sugar, cream and coconut. Spread on top of baked bars. Brown under broiler but watch carefully.

Irene Yutrzenka, Argyle

APPLESAUCE BROWNIES

½ cup butter or shortening	1 tsp. vanilla
2 sqs. baking chocolate	1 cup flour
1 cup sugar	½ tsp. baking powder
2 eggs	¼ tsp. baking soda
½ cup applesauce	½ cup chopped nuts

Melt butter and chocolate. Add the sugar; mix well. Add beaten eggs, applesauce, vanilla and dry ingredients (which have been sifted together). Add nutmeats. Bake in a 9x13 inch pan at 350° for 25 minutes. Cut in pan while warm; frost with fudge frosting.

Veronica Judd, Faribault

APPLESAUCE BROWNIES

½ cup oil	2 cups flour
2 Tbsp. cocoa	1½ tsp. soda
1½ cups sugar	½ tsp. salt
1 can unsweetened applesauce	2 unbeaten eggs

Combine ingredients. Beat 1 minute; pour in a greased 9x13 pan.

Topping:

½ cup chopped nuts	1 sm. pkg. chocolate chips
2 Tbsp. sugar	

Mix and sprinkle on brownies. Bake at 350° for 35 minutes or until toothpick comes out clean.

Teresa Kerkvliet, Marshall

APPLESAUCE BARS

1½ cups sugar
1 tsp. cinnamon
2 tsp. soda
¼ tsp. nutmeg

⅛ tsp. cloves
½ cup oleo
1½ cups unsweetened applesauce
2½ cups flour

Mix sugar, cinnamon, soda, nutmeg and cloves, then add oleo, applesauce and flour. Bake in jelly roll pan at 350° for 30 minutes.

Frosting:

4 Tbsp. oleo
1½ cups powdered sugar

½ tsp. vanilla
2 Tbsp. milk

Mix and frost bars while warm.

Malaine Majeres, Wilmont

APPLESAUCE CAKE BARS

½ cup butter
1 cup sugar
1 egg
1 tsp. vanilla
1 cup dates, sliced fine
2 tsp. soda

1 cup nuts, coarsely chopped
1½ cups applesauce
½ tsp. cinnamon
¼ tsp. cloves
2 cups cake flour
Confectioner's sugar

Cream butter and sugar; add egg and vanilla and beat, then add rest of ingredients, except confectioner's sugar. Turn out in well buttered bread pans. Bake at 350° for 15 minutes. Cut into squares and dust with confectioner's sugar. These keep well. Yield: 3 dozen.

Cecilia Headlee, St. Peter

LUSCIOUS APRICOT BARS

⅔ cup dried apricots
½ cup soft butter
¼ cup granulated sugar
1⅓ cups sifted regular flour
½ tsp. baking powder

¼ tsp. salt
1 cup packed brown sugar
2 eggs, well beaten
1 tsp. vanilla
½ cup chopped nuts

Rinse apricots, cover with water and boil 10 minutes. Drain, cool and chop. Heat at 350°. Grease an 8x8x2 inch pan. Mix butter, sugar and 1 cup flour until crumbly. Pack into pan. Bake 25 minutes. Sift ⅓ cup flour, baking powder and salt. Beat brown sugar into eggs. Mix in flour mixture, then vanilla, nutmeats and apricots. Spread over baked layer. Bake 30 minutes, or until done. Cool in pan. Cut into 32 bars. Roll in powdered sugar.

Leona Welsh, New Albin, IA

COOKIES & BARS

DELICIOUS BROWNIES

1 cup water	2 cups flour
¼ cup cocoa	½ cup sour milk with 1 tsp. soda
½ cup oil	(sour with 1 tsp. vinegar)
2 cup white sugar	2 eggs

Put water, cocoa and oil in bowl. Bring to a boil (I boil in microwave). Stir at least once to mix. Add sugar and flour to cocoa mixture, and mix with electric mixer. Add soda to milk, then add milk/soda mixture and eggs to batter and mix. Pour batter into lightly greased and floured large bar pan. Bake at 375° for about 25 minutes.

Frosting:

1 cup white sugar	⅓ cup oleo or butter
¼ cup milk	½ cup chocolate chips

Bring sugar, milk, and butter to a good boil. Remove from stove. Beat in chocolate chips. Let stand a bit. Beat more to desired thickness. Spread on cooled brownies. Cut as desired.

Jacqueline Dulas, Medford

BUTTERMILK BROWNIES AND FROSTING

1 stick oleo	½ tsp. salt
1 cup water	½ cup buttermilk
¼ cup cocoa	2 eggs, beaten
½ cup Crisco	1 tsp. soda
2 cups flour	1 tsp. vanilla
2 cups sugar	

Combine oleo, water, cocoa and Crisco in a saucepan and bring to a boil. Mix flour, sugar and salt in large bowl. Add the cocoa mixture; mix well. Stir in the buttermilk, eggs, soda and vanilla; mix well. Pour into a greased and floured jelly roll pan. Bake at 400° for 15 minutes.

Frosting:

1 stick oleo	3½ cups powdered sugar
¼ cup cocoa	Dash of salt
⅓ cup buttermilk	1 tsp. vanilla

Combine oleo, cocoa and buttermilk in a saucepan and bring to a boil. Pour over the powdered sugar, salt and vanilla. Beat well. Spread on brownies while hot. Chopped nuts may be sprinkled over top.

Marilyn Malmgren, St. James
Florence Walker, Red Lake Falls

BROWNIES

1 cup sugar	1 (16 oz.) can Hershey's syrup
½ cup margarine or 1 stick butter	1 cup flour
4 eggs	Pinch of salt

Mix all ingredients at once. Bake at 350° for 20 to 25 minutes. I use regular brownie pan.

Frosting:

¼ cup margarine	1 cup sugar
¼ cup milk	¼ cup chocolate chips

Melt margarine and mix in milk and sugar. Bring to a boil; remove from heat and add chocolate chips. Stir until chips melt and mixture thickens. Spread on cooled brownies.

Variation: Frosting is optional.

Florence Maas, Medford
Joyce Kadlec, Pipestone
Elaine Gilmore, Fairmont
Kay Cox, Adrian

CAKE MIX BROWNIES

1 pkg. chocolate cake mix	2 eggs
1 pkg. instant vanilla pudding mix	2 cups milk

Mix all ingredients and put in a jelly roll pan. Bake at 350° for 30 minutes.

Frosting:

1 cup sugar	¾ cup miniature marshmallows
¼ cup milk	½ cup chocolate chips
¼ cup butter	

Let sugar, milk and butter come to a rolling boil. Remove from heat; add marshmallows and chocolate chips. Stir until melted and spread on bars.

Alice Walker, Moorhead

BUTTERSCOTCH BROWNIES

¼ cup shortening	1 tsp. baking powder
1 cup light brown sugar, packed	½ tsp. salt
1 egg	½ tsp. vanilla
¾ cup sifted flour	½ cup broken nutmeats

Melt shortening over low heat and blend in brown sugar. Cool. Stir in egg; sift flour, baking powder and salt together. Add to shortening-sugar mixture. Add vanilla and nuts. Spread in well greased and floured 8x8x2 inch square pan. Bake 20 to 25 minutes until light touch with finger leaves slight imprint. Cut into bars while warm. Makes 18 (1x2½) bars. Double recipe for a 9x13 inch pan.

Helen Shaw, Winona

MY FAVORITE BROWNIES

½ cup oleo	2 cups sugar
½ cup salad oil	⅛ tsp. salt
¼ cup cocoa	1 tsp. soda, dissolved in
1 cup water	½ cup buttermilk
2 cups flour	2 eggs
2 tsp. cinnamon	1 tsp. vanilla

Beat all ingredients well and put in cookie sheet pan. Bake at 400° for 20 minutes.

Frosting:

3 Tbsp. milk	¼ cup oleo
2 tsp. cocoa	

Bring to a boil; add **2½ cups powdered sugar, 1 teaspoon vanilla** and **½ cup chopped walnuts.** Stir well. Pour over bars while still hot.

Sharon Lynn, Adrian
Loretta Nemanick, Eveleth

FUDGE BROWNIES

4 sqs. unsweetened chocolate	2 cups sugar
1 cup butter or margarine	4 eggs
1½ cups sifted flour	1½ tsp. vanilla
1 tsp. baking powder	2 cups walnuts or pecans,
½ tsp. salt	coarsely chopped

Preheat oven to 350°. Lightly grease a 15½x10½x1 inch pan. Place chocolate and butter in saucepan; melt. Remove from heat; let cool. Sift flour with baking powder and salt; set aside. In large bowl, beat sugar and eggs until light. Beat in chocolate mix and vanilla. Spread evenly in pan and bake 25 to 30 minutes. Makes 2 dozen.

Iris Rivers, Winona
Margaret Gall, St. Charles

BUTTER PECAN TURTLE BARS

Crust:

2 cups flour	½ cup butter, softened
¾ cup light brown sugar	

Combine and blend until crumbly and pat firmly in bottom of a 9x13 inch ungreased pan. Sprinkle **1½ cups pecan halves** on top and set aside. In small saucepan, combine **1½ cups light brown sugar** and **⅔ cup butter.** Cook over medium heat, stirring constantly, until mixture comes to a boil. Boil 60 seconds, stirring constantly. Drizzle mixture over pecans and crust. Bake at 350° for 18 to 20 minutes until caramel layer is bubbly and crust is a light brown. Remove from heat and immediately sprinkle with **1½ cups chocolate chips**. Spread chips evenly as they melt. Cool. You might want to put them in the refrigerator until topping sets, then cut.

Adeline Mracek, Owatonna

BUTTERSCOTCH BARS

1 ¼ cups flour
½ cup margarine or butter
¼ cup white sugar
2 eggs, beaten
1 ½ cups brown sugar
1 tsp. vanilla

¼ cup butter or margarine, melted
2 Tbsp. vinegar
½ cup raisins
½ cup nuts

Mix first 3 ingredients for crust and pat evenly in an 8x11 inch pan. Beat eggs until thick; add sugar, vanilla, melted margarine, vinegar, washed and drained raisins, and chopped nuts. Pour filling over crust (unbaked). Bake at 350° for 25 to 30 minutes.

Note: For a 9x13 inch pan, use 1⅓ cups flour plus a rounded teaspoon more of margarine for crust. Use 3 eggs for filling plus ¾ to 1 cup raisins. A quick and easy bar that tastes like butter brickle.

Les Raymond, International Falls

CARAMEL BARS

Crust:
1 cup oatmeal
1 cup flour
¾ cup brown sugar

¾ cup melted butter
1 tsp. salt
½ tsp. soda

Mix; press in a 9x13 inch pan. Bake at 350° for 10 to 15 minutes.

First Layer:
1 cup dark Karo syrup
¾ cup white sugar

1 cup crunchy peanut butter

Boil syrup and sugar; add peanut butter. Put over cooled crust.

Topping:
6 Tbsp. milk
6 Tbsp. margarine

1 ½ cups white sugar
1 (6 oz.) pkg. chocolate chips

Boil milk, margarine and sugar for ½ minute. Add chocolate chips; let melt. Spread over caramel layer.

Rose Stoltman, Argyle

CARAMEL BARS

32 Kraft caramels
1 (14 oz.) can sweetened condensed milk
1 cup oatmeal
1 cup flour

¾ cup brown sugar
¾ cup oleo
½ tsp. soda
¼ tsp. salt
1 cup chocolate chips

Melt caramels and milk; set aside. Mix oatmeal, flour, brown sugar, oleo, soda and salt. Put ⅔ of mixture in a 9x13 inch pan and bake at 350° for 10 minutes. Cover with chocolate chips. Put the caramel mix on top of chips. Sprinkle rest of the oatmeal mix on top and bake for 15 minutes more.

Kathleen Phipps, Blue Earth

COOKIES & BARS

CARAMEL BARS

32 caramels (may use whole bag)
6 Tbsp. cream
3 Tbsp. margarine
¾ cup margarine, melted
1 cup flour
1 cup oatmeal
¾ cup brown sugar
1 tsp. baking soda
½ tsp. salt

Melt caramels, cream and 3 tablespoons margarine in double boiler. Mix remaining ingredients. Reserve 1 cup of mixture for top. To remainder, add **4 tablespoons cream** and pat into a 9x13 inch pan with fork or floured hands. Bake at 350° for 10 minutes. Remove and sprinkle with ½ **to 1 cup chocolate chips.** Pour on caramel sauce. Sprinkle ½ **cup chopped walnuts or cashews** and reserved crumbs on top. Bake at 350° for 15 minutes.

Carol Marti, New Ulm
Mary Heppelmann, Bellechester

CARAMEL LAYER BARS

50 caramels
⅓ cup evaporated milk
1 box German chocolate cake mix
¾ cup melted butter
⅓ cup Carnation milk
1 cup chopped nuts
1 cup chocolate chips

Melt caramels and evaporated milk over hot water, stirring constantly (or in the microwave); set aside. Combine cake mix, melted butter, Carnation milk and nuts; mix by hand. Press half of mixture into a 9x13 inch cake pan and bake at 350° for 6 minutes. Sprinkle with chocolate chips; spread caramel mixture over the chocolate chips. Crumble the reserved dough over caramel mixture. Bake 15 to 18 minutes. Cool about 30 minutes and cut into squares.
Variation: Use butter pecan cake mix and butterscotch chips.

Cyrilla Lande, Waseca
Anna Akemann, Waseca

CARAMEL RICE KRISPIE BARS

2 pkgs. miniature marshmallows
¾ cup butter
8 cups Rice Krispies
1 (14 oz.) pkg. caramels
1 can sweetened condensed milk

Melt 1½ packages marshmallows with ½ cup butter. Remove from heat and mix in cereal. Pat ⅔ of mixture into a greased 10x15 inch pan. Sprinkle remaining marshmallows on top. Unwrap caramels; melt with condensed milk and remaining ¼ cup butter. Pour over mixture in pan. Pat remaining ⅓ cereal mixture on top of caramel layer. (Hint: dampen fingers with water before patting cereal on top of caramel mixture.) Refrigerate. Cut into bars.

Gen Roessler, Elysian

CARAMEL SPARKLE BARS

32 individually wrapped
caramels, unwrapped
1 (5½ oz.) can evaporated milk
(⅔ cup)
½ to ¾ tsp. grated orange rind
1 cup flour
1 cup quick cooking oats,
uncooked
1 cup chopped nuts

½ cup brown sugar, firmly
packed
½ cup wheat germ
½ tsp. baking soda
¼ tsp. salt
½ cup butter or margarine,
melted
1½ cups M&M's plain chocolate
candies

Combine caramels and milk in a 1½ quart saucepan. Cook over low heat, stirring occasionally until smooth and blended. Stir in orange rind; reserve. Combine flour, oats, nuts, brown sugar, wheat germ, baking soda and salt in a bowl; stir in butter, mixing until crumbly. Reserve 1 cup mixture. Press remaining crumb mixture onto bottom of greased 9x13 inch baking pan. Bake at 375° for 10 minutes. Top with 1 cup candies; pour in caramel mixture, spreading evenly. Top with reserved crumb mixture and remaining ½ cup candies; press in lightly. Continue baking 25 minutes or until golden brown. Cool slightly. Chill 30 minutes. Cool completely at room temperature. Cut in desired size when cool.

Ruth Huebl, Waseca

PEANUTTY CARAMEL SQUARES (SNICKERS)

⅓ cup butter
½ cup sugar
1 cup flour
¼ tsp. salt
¼ tsp. baking soda

4 Snicker bars (or 10 fun size)
1 Tbsp. butter
2 Tbsp. milk
½ cup shredded coconut
Few drops almond extract

Cream butter with sugar. Sift flour, salt and soda together. Add to creamed mixture; mix until crumbly. Reserve ½ cup crumbs for topping. Spread remaining crumb mixture on bottom of an 8x8 inch pan. Bake at 350° for 12 minutes. Meanwhile, melt Snicker bars with butter and milk in a saucepan, mixing until creamy. Stir in coconut and almond extract. Spread chocolate mixture over baked crumb mixture. Top with reserved crumbs. Bake at 350° for 12 to 15 minutes.

Ann Kuhn, Mahnomen

* * * * * * * *

We must have courage. Courage is fear that has said its prayers.
Mary Jo Luhman, Goodhue

COOKIES & BARS

CARROT BARS

2 cups white sugar	2 tsp. soda
2 cups flour	1¼ cups oil
2 tsp. cinnamon	4 eggs, beaten
1 tsp. salt	3 (4½ oz.) jars carrot baby food

Mix all ingredients. Put in large cookie sheet pan (jelly roll pan). Bake at 350° for 35 to 40 minutes.

Frosting:

1 (8 oz.) pkg. Philadelphia cream cheese	1 lb. powdered sugar (2²/₃ cups)
¼ lb. margarine	1 tsp. vanilla

Beat with mixer and spread on bars. Sprinkle chopped nuts on top if desired.

Mary Garry, Euclid
District Deputy, 1982-1986

CEREAL SNACK SQUARES

¼ cup margarine	5 cups corn flakes
1 (10 oz.) pkg. marshmallows	1 cup bran cereal
¼ cup peanut butter	

Butter a 9x13 inch pan. Melt margarine and stir in marshmallows and cook on medium heat for 1½ to 2 minutes. Add remaining ingredients. Press into pan.

Marilyn Pepit, Plainview

CHERRY BARS

Base:

½ cup flour	½ cup brown sugar
¼ tsp. soda	1 cup quick oatmeal
⅛ tsp. salt	⅓ cup melted butter

Mix and press into a 9x9 inch ungreased pan. Bake at 350° for 10 minutes.

Topping:

¼ cup flour	2 eggs, beaten
¾ cup sugar	¾ cup cut up maraschino cherries
½ tsp. baking powder	
¼ tsp. salt	½ cup flaked coconut
	½ cup nuts

Pour topping on crust and bake 30 minutes more; cool and cut into bars.

Leone Frank, Caledonia

183

CHERRY BARS

1 cup shortening	3 cups flour
1¾ cups sugar	1½ tsp. baking powder
4 eggs	½ tsp. salt
1 tsp. vanilla	1 can pie cherries

Cream the shortening and sugar. Add eggs one at a time, stirring after each addition. Stir in vanilla. Mix all dry ingredients. Spread ²/₃ of dough in a 10x15 inch pan. Pour canned cherries on top of dough. Drop remaining dough by spoonfuls on top of the cherries. Bake at 350° for approximately 45 minutes. Frost with powdered sugar frosting.

Dorothy Gannon, Waseca

HOLIDAY CHERRY CHEESE BARS

Crust:

1¼ cups flour	½ cup coconut
½ cup brown sugar	1 cup chopped walnuts
½ cup Crisco	

Mix crust ingredients, except nuts; reserve ½ cup crust mixture. Press remaining in a 9x12 inch pan and bake at 350° for 12 to 15 minutes until lightly browned.

Filling:

2 (8 oz.) pkgs. cream cheese, softened	2 eggs
	2 tsp. vanilla
²/₃ cup sugar	1 (21 oz.) can cherry pie filling

Beat cream cheese, sugar, eggs and vanilla; spread over crust (while hot); return to oven for 15 minutes longer. Spread pie filling on top (while hot). Mix reserved ½ cup crumbs with nuts and sprinkle over cherry mix. Bake 15 minutes. Cool and refrigerate.

Eleanor Christofferson, Owatonna

CHOCOLATE CARAMEL BARS

1 (14 oz.) pkg. caramels	¾ cup butter
²/₃ cup evaporated milk	1 cup chopped walnuts
1 pkg. German chocolate cake mix	1 (6 oz.) pkg. chocolate chips

Melt the caramel with ¹/₃ cup evaporated milk in microwave. Mix the cake mix, butter, ¹/₃ cup evaporated milk and nuts. Spread half of the batter in a greased 9x13 inch pan and bake at 350° for 5 to 10 minutes. Spread caramel mixture and chocolate chips on top and crumble remaining half of cake mixture on top of caramel/chocolate chips. Bake 15 to 20 minutes.

Audrey Schmitz, St. Peter

COOKIES & BARS

184

CHOCOLATE CARMELITA BARS

1¾ cups quick or old fashioned oatmeal
1½ cups all-purpose flour
¾ cup brown sugar, firmly packed
¾ cup butter flavor Crisco, melted
1 Tbsp. water
½ tsp. baking soda
¼ tsp. salt, optional
1 cup chopped nuts
1 cup (6 oz.) semi-sweet chocolate pieces
1 (12½ oz.) jar (1 cup) caramel ice cream topping
¼ cup all-purpose flour

Heat oven to 350°. Grease a 9x13 inch baking pan. Combine first 7 ingredients; mix well. Reserve 1 cup; press remaining onto bottom of prepared pan. Bake 10 to 12 minutes or until light brown; cool 10 minutes. Top with nuts and chocolate pieces. Mix caramel topping and ¼ cup flour until smooth; drizzle over chocolate pieces to within ¼ inch of pan edges. Sprinkle with reserved oat mixture. Bake additional 18 to 22 minutes or until golden brown. Cool completely. Makes 32 bars.

Bonnie Hein, Fergus Falls

CHOCOLATE CHIP BARS

Crust:
½ cup butter
1 cup flour
1 Tbsp. brown sugar

Mix like pie crust. Press into a 9x9 inch pan and bake at 350° for 10 minutes.

Filling:
2 eggs
1½ cups brown sugar
½ tsp. vanilla
¼ cup flour
½ tsp. baking powder
¾ cup coconut
½ cup nutmeats
1 (12 oz.) pkg. chocolate chips

Beat eggs; add remaining ingredients and just stir until mixed. Bake on top of crust.

Fay Gengler, Caledonia

CHOCOLATE TREATS

2 eggs
2 cups powdered sugar
1 sm. pkg. chocolate chips
2 Tbsp. butter
2 cups miniature marshmallows
½ lb. salted peanuts

Beat eggs and add powdered sugar. Melt the chips and add the butter. Cool and add the egg-sugar mixture. Add marshmallows and peanuts. Drop on wax paper and chill. Store in a cool place.

Note: Recipe is submitted from original Catholic Daughters Cookbook "Everybody's Favorite!"

Mrs. Ed Schissel, Lismore

DOUBLE CHOCOLATE COOKIE BARS

2 cups cream filled chocolate sandwich cookies (24), finely crushed
¼ cup butter, melted

2 cups (12 oz.) semi-sweet chocolate chips
1 (14 oz.) can Eagle Brand milk
1 tsp. vanilla
1 cup chopped nuts

Preheat oven to 350°. Combine cookie crumbs and butter. Press firmly on bottom of a 9x13 inch pan. In microwave, melt 1 cup chips, sweetened condensed milk and vanilla. Pour over prepared crust, top with nuts and remaining chips. Bake 20 minutes or until set. Cut into bars, store in tightly covered container. Makes 24 to 36 bars (these freeze well).

Clarice Vik, Crookston

CHOCOLATE GRAHAM REFRIGERATOR BARS

½ cup butter or margarine
¾ cup sugar
2 beaten eggs
2 cups miniature marshmallows

4½ cups honey graham cereal (1½ cups finely crushed)*
1 tsp. vanilla
½ cup milk chocolate chips

*Can also use graham crackers.

In a saucepan, melt butter or margarine over low heat. Remove from heat. Blend in sugar, then beaten eggs. Return to low heat. Cook and stir until bubbly. Be careful, it likes to scorch. Cool. Stir in marshmallows, cereal and vanilla. Spread in a well buttered 9x9x2 inch pan. In saucepan, melt chocolate over low heat, stirring constantly (microwaving is recommended). Drizzle over cereal mixture; cover and chill. Cut into bars and store in refrigerator. Can also double the recipe for an 8x11 inch pan. I use a little milk and margarine to thin the chocolate chips.

Wilma Meyer, Caledonia

CHOCOLATE PIZZA SQUARES

½ cup peanut butter
½ cup white sugar
½ cup brown sugar
½ cup margarine
1 egg

½ tsp. vanilla
1½ cups flour
2 cups miniature marshmallows
Chocolate chips

Mix above ingredients, except marshmallows and chocolate chips, and put in an ungreased jelly roll pan. Bake at 375° for 10 minutes. Put marshmallows on top and bake until light brown, then put chocolate chips on top and bake 3 minutes more.

Laurie L. David, Faribault

COOKIES & BARS

CHOCOLATE MARSHMALLOW BARS

½ cup boiling water	1 egg, beaten
3 Tbsp. cocoa	1 cup white sugar
1½ tsp. baking powder	¼ cup butter or margarine
1 tsp. vanilla	¼ cup sour milk or buttermilk
Pinch of salt	1 cup flour

Mix all ingredients and put in a 9x12 inch cake pan. Bake at 350° for 15 to 20 minutes. Cut **big marshmallows** in half and when bars are just out of the oven, cover the top with marshmallows and return to oven so the marshmallows get soft. Let cool and then frost.

Frosting:

1 cup brown sugar	3 Tbsp. milk
3 Tbsp. butter	½ cup chocolate chips

Boil brown sugar, butter and milk 1 minute and then add chocolate chips. Frost bars. Freezes well.

Martha Schoenborn, Mahnomen

CHOCOLATE MINT BARS

Cake Layer:

1 cup flour	4 eggs
1 cup sugar	1 (16 oz.) can Hershey's syrup
½ cup butter or margarine	

Heat oven to 350°. Grease a 13x9x2 inch pan. In large mixer bowl, combine all ingredients and beat until smooth. Pour into prepared pan. Bake 25 to 30 minutes or until top springs back when lightly touched. Cool completely in pan.

Mint Cream Center:

2 cups powdered sugar	1 Tbsp. water
½ cup butter or margarine, softened	½ to ¾ tsp. mint extract
	3 drops green food color

In small bowl, combine all ingredients and beat until smooth. Spread on the cooled cake layer, cover and chill.

Chocolate Topping:

6 Tbsp. butter or margarine	1 cup chocolate chips

In small saucepan over very low heat (microwaving is recommended), melt margarine and chocolate chips. Remove from heat; stir until smooth. Cool slightly and pour over other chilled mixture. Cover and chill at least 1 hour.

Note: I use about 7 to 8 tablespoons margarine and 1½ to 1¾ cups chocolate chips for a little thicker topping.

Marcella Jeno, Owatonna
District Deputy, 1992-1996

DELUXE CHOCOLATE MARSHMALLOW BARS

Crust:

¾ cup margarine
1½ cups sugar
3 eggs
1 tsp. vanilla
1⅓ cups flour

3 Tbsp. cocoa
½ tsp. baking powder
½ tsp. salt
½ cup chopped nuts, if desired

Mix all ingredients and put in a greased 15x10 inch jelly roll pan. Bake at 350° for 15 to 18 minutes. Sprinkle about **4 cups miniature marshmallows** on crust and put in oven for 2 to 3 minutes, then spread marshmallows with spatula.

Frosting:

3 Tbsp. butter or margarine,
   melted
1 cup peanut butter

1¾ cups chocolate chips
   (I use some butterscotch)
2 cups Rice Krispies

Heat margarine, peanut butter, and chips on low heat to melt. Add Rice Krispies, mix and spread over marshmallows.

Variation: Agnes uses only 1⅓ cups chocolate chips for frosting.

Jeanette Schad, Plainview
Agnes Novak, Fergus Falls

CHOCOLATE REVEL BARS

1 cup butter
2 cups brown sugar
2 eggs
2 tsp. vanilla
2½ cups flour
1 tsp. baking soda
½ tsp. salt

3 cups quick oatmeal
1 (12 oz.) pkg. chocolate chips
1 (15½ oz.) can sweetened
   condensed milk
2 Tbsp. margarine
2 tsp. vanilla
1 cup walnuts

Cream butter and sugar; add eggs and vanilla. Sift flour, soda and salt; add oatmeal. Mix these all together. Put ⅔ mixture in the bottom of a 15x10½ inch pan. Melt chocolate chips, milk and margarine; add vanilla (a microwave is the best place to melt chips and milk). Add nuts. Spread over crust. Add the ⅓ oat mixture. Because it is so thick, it takes some doing to spread it around. Sometimes, I spread it on wax paper and piece it that way. Bake at 350° for about 25 minutes. Cut in about 75 pieces.

Kathy Phipps, Blue Earth

• • • • • • • •

The greatest mistake you can make in life is to be continually fearing that you will make a mistake.
Lucille Miller, Mazeppa

COOKIES & BARS

CHOCOLATE OATMEAL SQUARES

¾ cup flour
½ tsp. salt
½ tsp. soda
½ cup butter
6 Tbsp. white sugar
6 Tbsp. brown sugar

½ tsp. vanilla
½ tsp. water
1 egg
1 cup oatmeal
1 cup chocolate chips

Sift flour, salt and soda. Cream shortening and sugars. Add vanilla, water and egg. Beat well, then add oatmeal. Place in a greased 9x13 inch pan. Sprinkle chocolate chips on top. Bake at 375° for 3 minutes. Remove from oven. Cut through with knife, making a marbleized effect. Return to oven and bake for 12 to 14 minutes.

Note: Recipe is submitted from original Catholic Daughters Cookbook "Everybody's Favorite!"

LaVonne Metz, Lismore

CHOCOLATE AND OAT BARS

1 cup unsifted flour
1 cup quick-cooking oats
¾ cup light brown sugar, firmly packed
½ cup butter, softened

1 (14 oz.) can Eagle Brand sweetened condensed milk
1 cup chopped nuts
1 cup chocolate chips

Preheat oven to 350°. In a bowl, combine flour, oats, brown sugar and butter; mix well, reserving ½ cup. Press remaining oat mixture on bottom of a 9x13 inch pan. Bake 10 minutes. Pour sweetened condensed milk evenly over crust. Sprinkle with nuts and chocolate chips. Top with remaining oat mixture; press down. Bake 25 to 30 minutes. Cool. Store, covered, at room temperature.

Mary Ham, Plainview

CHOCOLATE ZUCCHINI BARS

4 eggs
1½ cups salad oil
2 cups sugar
2 cups flour
2 tsp. baking soda
2 tsp. cinnamon

1 tsp. salt
4 Tbsp. cocoa
1 tsp. vanilla
3 cups grated zucchini
1 cup chopped nuts, optional

Beat eggs, oil and sugar for 2 minutes. Add dry ingredients all at once and mix well by hand until smooth. Stir in vanilla, zucchini and nuts. Pour into a greased 15x10x1 inch jelly roll pan. Bake at 350° for 25 to 30 minutes. Frost with cream cheese frosting.

Cream Cheese Frosting:

1 (3 oz.) pkg. cream cheese, softened
½ cup butter

2 cups confectioner's sugar
2 Tbsp. cocoa
1 tsp. vanilla

Patti Feuerhelm, St. Charles

CLUB CRACKER BARS

Club crackers	1 cup brown sugar
½ cup butter	1 cup coconut
⅓ cup milk	1 cup graham cracker crumbs

Line cookie sheet with the club crackers. Boil butter, milk, brown sugar, coconut and crumbs for 7 minutes, stirring constantly. Pour into lined cookie sheet. Put another layer of crackers over this.

Frosting:

1½ cups sugar	1 cup chocolate or peanut
⅓ cup butter	butter chips (dark chocolate
⅓ cup milk	are best)

Boil the sugar, butter and milk for 1 to 2 minutes. Add the chips. Cool and frost.

Mary Ann Pongratz, Mankato

FUDGE CRACKER LAYER BARS (NO BAKE)

Filling:

2 sticks oleo	2 cups (about 24) graham
½ cup milk	crackers, crushed
½ cup white sugar	1 box Keebler Club soda
1 cup brown sugar	crackers

Mix all ingredients, except soda crackers, and boil 5 minutes on low heat, stirring constantly. Spray a 9x13 inch pan. Line with one layer of whole soda crackers (green box), do not crush. Pour half the filling over crackers. Add another layer of crackers; top with remaining filling. Top with third layer of crackers and frost.

Frosting:

1 cup chocolate chips	⅔ cup peanut butter
1 cup butterscotch chips	

Melt chips and peanut butter and gently spread over top cracker layer. Store in refrigerator. Cut into small bars, like candy.

Lorraine Amazi, Owatonna

MOM'S CORN FLAKE BARS

1 cup white sugar	1 tsp. vanilla
1 cup Karo syrup	6 to 7 cups corn flakes
1 cup peanut butter	

Bring to a boil the sugar and syrup. Add peanut butter and vanilla. Mix corn flakes into mixture. Drop by teaspoon on waxed paper or press into greased 9x13 inch pan.

Shirl Maher, Blue Earth

COCONUT BARS

½ cup oleo or shortening
2 eggs
2 cups brown sugar
1 cup flour
1 tsp. salt

2 tsp. baking powder
1 tsp. vanilla
1½ cups flaked coconut
½ cup nuts

Melt shortening in saucepan over low heat. Remove and add eggs and brown sugar; mix well. Add all dry ingredients, mixing well. Stir in vanilla, coconut and nuts. Spread in a 9x13 inch well greased pan. Bake at 350° for 30 minutes. Cool and cut into bars. Makes 2 dozen.

Mary A. Doffing, Winona

CHEWY COCONUT RAISIN-NUT COOKIES

1 cup brown sugar
½ cup white sugar
½ cup butter or margarine
½ tsp. vanilla
2 eggs

2 cups flour
2 cups raisin-nut bran cereal
1½ cups flaked coconut
1 tsp. soda
¼ tsp. salt

Cream the sugars, butter, vanilla and eggs. Add the remaining ingredients. Shape dough into balls and place on ungreased cookie sheet. Bake until light brown, 8 to 10 minutes. Cool 1 minute before removing from cookie sheet. Makes about 4½ dozen cookies.

Marilyn Rewitzer, New Ulm

"GOOD MAMA" COOKIE BARS

½ cup butter
1¼ cups vanilla wafer crumbs
1 (8½ oz.) can crushed pineapple
1 (6 oz.) pkg. lemon chips
1 cup flaked coconut

¼ cup maraschino cherries, chopped
1 cup chopped pecans
1 can sweetened condensed milk

Melt butter in a 9x13 inch pan. Spread evenly over this the vanilla wafer crumbs. Drain the juice from the crushed pineapple. Get this as dry as possible. Mix the pineapple, lemon chips, flaked coconut, maraschino cherries, and pecans with the sweetened condensed milk. Pour this mixture over the crumb base. Bake at 350° for 30 minutes. Cool and cut into squares.

Vicki Andrejewski, Waseca

COOKIES & BARS

CRESCENT CHEESE BARS

2 pkgs. crescent rolls	1½ cups sugar
2 (8 oz.) pkgs. cream cheese	2 eggs, separated
1 tsp. vanilla	½ cup chopped nuts (almonds)

Unfold and place package of crescent rolls on bottom of greased 9x13 inch pan. Mix cream cheese, vanilla, 1 cup sugar and egg yolks; beat until creamy. Pour on top of layer of rolls in pan. Unfold and place second package of rolls on top of cheese mixture. Beat 1 of the egg whites until frothy and spread on top of rolls, then sprinkle the ½ cup sugar and chopped nuts on top. Bake at 350° for 30 minutes (325° for glass dish). Cut into bars.

Theresa Mollert, St. Peter

CRESCENT ROLL BARS

1 pkg. crescent rolls	⅓ cup sugar
1 (8 oz.) pkg. cream cheese	½ tsp. vanilla
1 egg yolk	Sliced almonds

Use the crescent rolls to line the bottom of a 9x12 inch pan. Mix the remaining ingredients and spread over the first layer. Top with the remaining crescent rolls. Bake at 350° for 20 minutes. Top with glazing and sliced almonds.

Marilyn Rewitzer, New Ulm

DATE BARS

1 cup dates, chopped	1½ cups oatmeal
½ cup sugar	1½ cups flour
½ cup water	1 tsp. soda
1 cup butter, melted and cooled	1 cup chopped walnuts,
1 cup brown sugar, packed	optional

Cook and cool dates, sugar and water. Mix melted and cooled butter with brown sugar, oatmeal, flour, soda and walnuts. Press ⅔ of mixture in a 9x13 inch pan. Spread with cooked filling. Sprinkle remaining ⅔ of crust mixture on top. Bake at 350° until bubbling and light brown, about 20 minutes.

Gerry Kratz, Buffalo City, WI

* * * * * * * *

A true friend is one who knows you as you are, understands where you've been, accepts who you have become, and still gently invites you to grow.   *Abbey Press*
Zonda Befort, Mazeppa

DATE BARS

3 eggs
1 cup sugar
⅓ cup shortening
1 cup flour
¼ tsp. salt

1 tsp. baking powder
1½ cups pitted sliced dates
1 tsp. vanilla
1 cup pecan pieces

Beat eggs and sugar until thick. Add shortening and beat. Sift flour, salt, baking powder and add to above mixture. Add dates, vanilla and pecans. Bake at 350° for 30 minutes. Cut in 1x4 inch bars while warm; roll in confectioner's sugar. Let cool. Makes 2 dozen bars.

Pat Schlink, Winona

DATE STICKS

3 eggs
1 cup brown sugar
2 tsp. hot water
2 tsp. vanilla
1 cup flour, sifted 3 times

2 tsp. baking powder
½ tsp. salt
Grated rind of 1 lemon
1 cup dates
½ cup nuts

Beat eggs; add brown sugar. Add hot water and vanilla. Add dry ingredients; fold in dates and nuts that have been floured. Bake at 350° for 30 minutes or just until done. Cut into strips when a little cooled and roll in powdered sugar.

Rosie Frank, Caledonia

FRUIT CAKE SQUARES

6 Tbsp. butter or margarine
1½ cups graham cracker crumbs
1 cup coconut
2 cups candied fruit, cut up, or
  use green and red candied
  fruit

1 cup dates, halved
1 cup nuts, coarsely chopped
1 (15 oz.) can Eagle Brand
  sweetened condensed milk

Melt butter in a 15½x10½x1 inch pan (note: I like to use just a 9x13 inch pan). Sprinkle on crumbs over melted butter. Sprinkle coconut over butter. Distribute fruit as evenly as possible over coconut. Cut dates into small amount of flour so they don't stick, then put dates over candied fruit. Sprinkle on nuts. Press mixture lightly with hands to level it in pan. Pour condensed milk evenly over the top. Bake at 350° for 25 to 30 minutes. Cool completely before cutting. Remove from pan.

Rosemary Walz, Mahnomen
District Deputy, 1992-1996
State Treasurer, 1996-present

FRUITY FINGER BARS

1 (6 oz.) pkg. dried mixed fruit bites
1 cup prepared apple juice
½ cup chopped walnuts
1 pkg. yellow cake mix
⅓ cup margarine, softened
1 egg

Heat oven to 350°. Grease a 9x13 inch pan. In small saucepan, combine first 3 ingredients. Cook over medium heat until liquids almost absorbed, stirring occasionally; set aside. In large bowl, blend cake mix, margarine and egg until crumbly. Reserve ½ cup crumbs for topping. Press over base. Sprinkle with reserved crumbs. Bake at 350° for 30 to 40 minutes or until light golden brown. Cool completely and cut in bars. Makes 36 bars.

Lucille Buck, Owatonna

GOODIE BARS

First Layer:
½ cup butter
5 Tbsp. cocoa
¼ cup sugar

Melt over hot water. While melting, beat **1 egg** with a fork and add to above when melted. Mix **2 cups crushed graham crackers** and **2 cup flaked coconut**. Spread this mixture in a 9x13 inch pan. Put in refrigerator or freezer to harden.

Second Layer:
2 cups powdered sugar
½ cup soft butter
2 Tbsp. vanilla instant pudding
Scant ¼ cup milk

Mix until stiff enough to spread, then spread over first layer. Cool again.

Third Layer:
1 (6 oz.) pkg. chocolate chips
2 Tbsp. butter

Spread over hardened bars; chill. Cut into bars. These bars must be kept in refrigerator.

Agnes M. Cawley, Waseca

GRANDMA'S BARS

1 cup white sugar
1 cup white syrup
1½ Tbsp. butter
1 (18 oz.) jar chunky peanut butter (2 cups)
2 tsp. vanilla
6 cups corn flakes
1 cup chocolate chips

Cook sugar, syrup and butter until sugar dissolved, only a very small time. Add peanut butter; stir until melted. Add vanilla, then corn flakes; mix well. Put in a 9x12 inch pan. Sprinkle with chocolate chips; when melted, spread as frosting. Cool, cut and enjoy!

Helen Lynch, Plainview

COOKIES & BARS

194

HAWAIIAN BARS

1 cup butter or margarine   1 cup sugar
2 cups flour
    Mix and pat in a 9x13 inch pan. Bake at 350° for 15 minutes. Cool.

2 (8 oz.) pkgs. cream cheese   2 tsp. vanilla
¼ cup sugar   2 cups crushed pineapple,
¼ cup milk   drained
    Mix cream cheese, sugar and milk. Fold in vanilla and pineapple. Spread over base. Mix **2 cups coconut** and **2 tablespoons melted butter**. Sprinkle over top. Bake 15 to 20 minutes. Cool. Refrigerate.

Margaret Murphy, Adrian

HAWAIIAN CHEESE BARS

1 cup flour   2 Tbsp. milk
½ cup sugar   1 egg
½ cup butter   1 tsp. vanilla
1 (8 oz.) pkg. cream cheese,   1 (18 oz.) can crushed
  softened   pineapple
2 Tbsp. butter   1 cup flaked coconut
2 Tbsp. sugar   1 Tbsp. melted butter
    Combine flour, sugar and ½ cup butter; crumble. Pat into greased 9x9 inch pan. Bake at 350° for 14 to 19 minutes. Cool slightly. Mix the cheese with 2 tablespoons butter, milk and egg. Fold in vanilla and pineapple. Spread over crust. Combine coconut and melted butter for topping. Bake at 350° for 15 to 20 minutes.

Adelia Sondag, New Ulm

BANANA CREAM BARS

2 cups flour   1½ cups sugar
1 tsp. soda   2 eggs
1 tsp. salt   ¾ cup sour cream
½ cup butter or margarine   3 to 4 mashed bananas
    Sift dry ingredients. Cream butter and sugar. Add remaining ingredients and beat until mixed. Bake in a 10x15 inch pan at 375° for 25 minutes.

Frosting:
2 cups powdered sugar   3 Tbsp. sour cream
⅓ cup butter   1 tsp. vanilla
    Blend and frost cooled bars.

Florence Walker, Red Lake Falls
Leone Brule, Crookston

TRIPLE GOOD BARS

2 cups raisins
1 (14 oz.) can sweetened condensed milk
1 Tbsp. grated lemon peel
1 Tbsp. lemon juice
1 cup (2 sticks) margarine or butter, softened

1⅓ cups brown sugar
1½ tsp. vanilla
2½ cups quick oatmeal
1 cup flour
1½ cups nuts
½ tsp. baking soda
¼ tsp. salt, optional

Heat oven to 370°. Grease a 9x13 inch pan. In a medium saucepan, combine the first 4 ingredients. Cook over medium heat, stirring constantly, just until mixture begins to bubble. Remove from heat when thickened and let cool. Beat margarine, sugar and vanilla until fluffy; add remaining ingredients. Reserve 2 cups of this mixture; spread remainder on bottom of prepared pan and press. Spread cooled raisin mixture to within ½ inch of edges. Sprinkle with remaining oat mixture; pat lightly. Bake 25 to 30 minutes or until golden brown. Cool completely; cut into 1x2 inch bars. Makes 4 dozen.

Gerie Dobie, International Falls

DESSERT BARS

1 box yellow cake mix
1 cup brown sugar
½ cup butter or margarine
2 eggs

2 tsp. vanilla
1 (6 oz.) pkg. chocolate chips
¼ cup nuts

Mix all ingredients except chips and nuts. Spread out in pan. Sprinkle chips and nuts on top. Bake at 350° for 25 minutes. Don't over bake.

Bonnie Zimmerman, Waseca

DREAM BARS

½ cup margarine
½ cup brown sugar
1 cup flour
1 cup brown sugar
2 eggs
1 tsp. vanilla

2 Tbsp. flour
½ tsp. baking powder
¼ tsp. salt
1½ cups coconut
1 cup walnuts

Mix margarine, ½ cup brown sugar and 1 cup flour until crumbly. Pat into a 6x11 inch pan. Bake at 375° for 10 minutes. Mix 1 cup brown sugar and eggs; add vanilla. Mix 2 tablespoons flour, baking powder and salt. Sift over coconut and walnuts. Add to sugar and egg mixture and pour over baked crust. Bake at 375° for 20 minutes. This can be doubled for a 9x13 inch pan.

Evelyn Pawlowski, Argyle

COOKIES & BARS

196

MILLIE'S BARS

¾ cup margarine	Pinch of salt
1¼ cups sugar	3 heaping Tbsp. cocoa
3 eggs	2 cups coconut
1 cup flour	1 can Eagle Brand milk

Cream margarine and sugar. Beat in eggs, one at a time. Stir in dry ingredients. Grease a 9x13 inch pan. Bake at 325° for 25 minutes. Take out of oven and put mixed coconut and Eagle Brand milk on top of cake. Bake at 325° for 25 minutes.

Frosting:

Boil ½ **stick margarine, 1½ cups sugar** and **6 tablespoons milk;** add ⅔ **cup chocolate chips.** Blend until melted. Pour over bars. Let set.

Delores Vlaisavljevich, Eveleth

OUT OF THIS WORLD BARS

2 cups crushed graham crackers	1 lg. bag coconut
½ cup melted butter	1 (3 oz.) pkg. cream cheese
2 cans sweetened condensed milk	2 cups powdered sugar
	2 Tbsp. butter

Mix crushed graham crackers and melted butter. Pat in a 9x13 inch pan and bake at 350° for 10 minutes. Mix sweetened condensed milk and coconut. Put on top of crust. Bake at 350° for 15 to 20 minutes. Cool. Mix cream cheese, powdered sugar and butter and spread on top.

Vivian Fick, Slayton

BLONDE BROWNIES

1 cup flour	1 cup brown sugar, firmly packed
½ tsp. baking powder	
⅛ tsp. soda	1 Tbsp. hot water
½ tsp. salt	1 slightly beaten egg
½ cup nuts	1 tsp. vanilla
⅓ cup shortening	½ cup chocolate chips

Sift the flour, baking powder, soda and salt; add nuts and set aside. Melt the shortening; remove from heat. Add brown sugar and hot water. Cool slightly. Add the egg and vanilla. Add the flour mixture. Spread in a greased 9x9 inch pan. Sprinkle with chocolate chips over the top. Bake at 350° for 20 to 25 minutes.

Jean Medeck, Rice

COOKIES & BARS

SPICEY BANANA BARS

1 cup flour	¼ tsp. allspice
¾ cup sugar	¼ cup butter or oleo, softened
½ tsp. baking powder	⅓ cup mashed banana
½ tsp. salt	(about 1)
¼ tsp. soda	1 egg
¾ tsp. cinnamon	¼ cup milk
¼ tsp. cloves	⅓ cup nuts

Sift dry ingredients. Cream the butter and bananas; add the egg and beat well. Add the dry ingredients alternately with milk, beginning and ending with dry ingredients. Blend thoroughly after each addition. Stir in nuts. Spread in well greased 9x13 inch pan. Bake at 350° for 22 to 25 minutes. Frost while warm.

Lemon Frosting:

2 Tbsp. melted butter	1 tsp. lemon juice
1 Tbsp. hot water	1 cup powdered sugar, sifted

Combine butter, hot water and lemon juice. Blend in sifted sugar. Thin with additional hot water, a few drops at a time, if necessary.

Marie Hudson, North Mankato
State Secretary, 1976-1980

HERSHEY BROWNIES

1 stick margarine	1 tsp. vanilla
1 cup sugar	1 cup flour
4 eggs	½ bag Heath brickle bits
1 (16 oz.) can Hershey syrup	7 Hershey bars

Cream margarine and sugar; add eggs. Mix in syrup, vanilla and flour and; mix well. Pour into greased jelly roll pan. Sprinkle brickle bits over top; pat down. Bake at 350° for 25 to 30 minutes. While warm, cover with Hershey bars. Spread when melted.

Judy Potter, International Falls

KATHERINE HEPBURN'S BROWNIES

2 sqs. unsweetened chocolate	½ tsp. vanilla
1 stick butter	¼ cup flour
1 cup sugar	1 cup chopped nuts
2 eggs	

Melt chocolate and butter over medium heat. Remove from heat and add sugar, eggs and vanilla and beat. Stir in flour, salt and nuts. Pour ingredients into an 8x8 inch pan and bake at 325° for 40 minutes.

Roberta Tissek, St. Paul

HERSHEY'S DUTCH CHOCOLATE BARS AND FROSTING

1 cup butter	2 tsp. vanilla
2 cups sugar	1 cup flour
½ cup Hershey's Dutch cocoa	1 cup chopped nuts
4 eggs	

Spray a 9x13 inch pan with cooking spray. Melt butter and cool. Mix sugar and cocoa (Dutch cocoa is very important). Mix in the melted butter. Beat in all eggs at once until smooth and glossy. Add vanilla, flour and nuts. Bake at 350° for 30 to 35 minutes.

Frosting:

½ cup heavy cream	1 tsp. vanilla
1⅓ cups chocolate chips	

Scald cream in pan on stove or a bowl in the microwave. Add chocolate chips and stir until smooth. Add vanilla and spread on bars. Chill.

Mavis Wheelock, Waseca

HIP HUGGERS

½ cup butter or margarine	2 cups quick oatmeal
1 cup brown sugar	1 cup semi-sweet chocolate
1 egg	chips
½ tsp. vanilla	1 can sweetened condensed
¾ cup flour	milk
½ tsp. soda	1 tsp. vanilla
½ tsp. salt	½ cup chopped walnuts

Cream butter or margarine and sugar; heat in egg and vanilla. Add flour, soda and salt, sifted together. Stir in oatmeal. Remove ¾ cup of this mixture for topping. Press the rest of this mixture in an 8x11 inch pan. Combine chips and condensed milk over low heat or put in microwave until chips melt, stirring occasionally. Remove from heat and add vanilla and nuts. Mix well and spread over oatmeal layer. Drop the reserved topping over top. Bake at 350° for 25 minutes (no longer). Cool and cut in squares.

LaVonne Slater, Rushmore

* * * * * * * *

Joy and gladness for all who seek you. Psalm 43
Ruth Sawyer, Ellendale

KEEBLER BARS

Layer One:
Line a 9x13 inch pan with **Keebler club crackers.**

Layer Two:

1 cup graham cracker crumbs	⅔ cup white sugar
1 stick margarine	½ cup brown sugar
¼ cup milk	

Mix all ingredients and boil 5 minutes. Pour over crackers and spread.

Layer Three:
Add second layer of **Keebler club crackers.**

Layer Four:

½ cup butterscotch chips	⅔ cup peanut butter
½ cup chocolate chips	

Melt ingredients and frost bars. Refrigerate until frosting is set. (I use all chocolate chips.) Cut into bars.

Catherine Stebbins, St. Peter

LEMON BARS

1 (22 oz.) can lemon pie mix	1 pkg. one step Angel Food cake mix

Stir all ingredients carefully. Spread in greased and floured jelly roll pan (15x10x1). Bake at 350° until light brown and top springs back when lightly touched.

Frosting:

1 (3 oz.) pkg. cream cheese, softened	2 tsp. milk
	2 cups powdered sugar

Cream ingredients and spread on cooled bars.

Elaine Gilmore, Fairmont

LEMON SQUARES

1 cup flour	½ tsp. baking powder
½ cup butter	¼ tsp. salt
¼ cup powdered sugar	1 cup sugar
2 eggs	2 Tbsp. lemon juice

Heat oven to 350°. Blend flour, butter and powdered sugar thoroughly. Press evenly in an 8x8 inch square pan. Bake 20 minutes. Beat remaining ingredients and pour over crust; bake 20 minutes. When cool, sprinkle with powdered sugar (sifted).

Mary Ann Pongratz, Mankato

LITTLE FELLOW LEMON BARS

½ cup butter
2 cups sugar
4 eggs

1 Tbsp. flour
⅓ cup lemon juice

Cream butter and sugar; add eggs, one at a time, blending after each. Add flour and mix well. Add lemon juice. Fill pastry lined muffin tins ⅔ full. Makes 4 dozen small pies. Bake at 350° for 30 minutes or until yellow brown.

Ruth Kobilarcsik, Plainview

LOVE BARS

1 cup flour
½ cup shortening
3 tsp. brown sugar
1½ cups brown sugar
2 well beaten eggs

½ cup nuts
1½ cups coconut
1 tsp. vanilla
4 Tbsp. flour

Mix the first 3 ingredients; place in greased pan and bake at 350° for 10 minutes. Mix the rest of the ingredients and pour on top of crust. Bake at 350° for 30 minutes. Cool and cut into squares.

Cristel Schumacher, Waseca

NIEMAN MARCUS SQUARES

½ cup margarine, melted
1 box yellow cake mix
3 eggs
1 (8 oz.) pkg. cream cheese, softened

1 lb. confectioner's sugar
½ cup flaked coconut
½ cup walnuts or pecans, chopped

Combine margarine, cake mix and 1 egg. Stir until the dry ingredients are moistened. Pat the mixture in a well greased 15x10 inch jelly roll pan. (Use a smaller pan for thicker bars.) Beat the remaining eggs lightly, then beat in the cream cheese and sugar. Stir in coconut and nuts. Pour the mixture in the pan, spreading evenly. Bake at 325° for 45 to 50 minutes, or until golden brown. Cool pan on wire rack to room temperature. Cut into 4 dozen squares when cool.

Amelia Bartkowski, International Falls

FROSTED MOLASSES BARS

¼ cup shortening
½ cup white sugar
1 egg
½ cup molasses
½ cup milk
½ cup raisins, optional

2 cups flour
1½ tsp. baking powder
¼ tsp. soda
¼ tsp. salt
½ tsp. vanilla

Cream shortening and sugar; beat in egg. Add rest of ingredients and mix well. Place in an 11x16 inch deep pan or cookie sheet. Bake at 350° for 15 to 20 minutes. Spread with powdered sugar frosting while warm. Can be served with whipped topping rather than frosting.

Loretta Chisholm, Ada

MAGIC COOKIE BARS

½ cup margarine or butter
1½ cups graham cracker crumbs
1 (14 oz.) can sweetened
    condensed milk

1 (6 oz.) pkg. chocolate chips
1⅓ cups coconut
1 cup nuts

Preheat oven to 350°. In a 9x13 inch baking pan, melt margarine in oven. Sprinkle crumbs over margarine. Mix and press into pan. Pour sweetened condensed milk evenly over crumbs. Top evenly with remaining ingredients. Press down firmly. Bake 25 to 30 minutes or until browned. Cool thoroughly before cutting. Store loosely covered at room temperature.

Sharon Klinkhammer, Mahnomen

NO-BAKE GRANOLA BARS

½ cup firmly packed brown sugar
½ cup light corn syrup
1 cup peanut butter
1 tsp. vanilla
1½ cups quick-cooking rolled
    oatmeal

1½ cups crisp rice cereal
1 cup raisins
½ cup coconut
½ cup sunflower seeds
2 Tbsp. sesame seeds

In a medium saucepan, combine brown sugar and corn syrup. Bring to a boil, stirring constantly. Remove from heat. Stir in peanut butter and vanilla; blend well. Combine remaining ingredients in a large bowl. Add first mixture and mix well. Press into ungreased 9 inch square pan. Cool, then cut into bars. Wrap bars individually and grab one on the way out the door when you're really in a rush.

Beatrice A. Fry, International Falls

NOODLE BARS

½ cup white syrup ¾ cup peanut butter
½ cup white sugar 5 cups Chinese noodles

Bring syrup and sugar to a boil; remove from heat. Add peanut butter and stir until smooth. Add noodles and stir until coated. Put into a 9x13 inch pan.

Frosting:

¾ cup chocolate chips ¼ cup butterscotch chips

Melt chips until smooth and spread over bars.

Joyce Kadlec, Pipestone

MIXED NUT BARS

1½ cups flour ½ cup margarine
¾ cup brown sugar 1 (12 oz.) can mixed nuts
¼ tsp. salt

Mix first 4 ingredients and pat in a 9x13 inch pan. Bake at 350° for 10 minutes. Remove from oven and sprinkle mixed nuts on top.

Topping:

1 (6 oz.) pkg. butterscotch chips 2 Tbsp. margarine
½ cup white syrup

Melt ingredients in microwave. Bake at 350° for 10 minutes.

Variation: Gloria uses 1 tablespoon butter or margarine for the topping.

Clara Hess, Marshall
Gloria Schoenborn, Mahnomen

NUT GOODIE BARS

1 (12 oz.) bag chocolate chips ¼ cup vanilla pudding mix
1 (12 oz.) bag butterscotch chips (not instant)
2 cups peanut butter 2 lbs. powdered sugar
½ cup evaporated milk 1 lb. Spanish peanuts
1 cup margarine

Melt both chips and peanut butter. Spread half on greased jelly roll pan. Bring milk, margarine, and pudding mix just to a boil; add powdered sugar. Spread over the first layer. Add Spanish peanuts to remaining half of first mixture. Spread on top and chill. Makes approximately 8 dozen.

Tina Rein, Moorhead

COOKIES & BARS

203

ORANGE-RHUBARB BARS

Filling:

3 Tbsp. cornstarch	½ cup sugar
¼ cup water	3 cups diced rhubarb
1 cup cut up orange slices	1 tsp. vanilla

Dissolve cornstarch in water; cook all until thick and cool. Add vanilla and set aside. Make ahead and set aside to cool.

Batter:

1 cup brown sugar	¼ tsp. salt
½ cup white sugar	1 tsp. soda
½ cup butter	1½ cups flour
2 eggs	

Mix batter; pour half on bottom of a 9x13 inch pan that has been greased and floured. Spread on filling and top with remaining batter. Bake at 350° for 25 to 35 minutes. Cool and cut into bars. May also be rolled in powdered sugar or frosted with thin powdered sugar icing. For a larger recipe, there is enough filling for 1½ recipes of batter and use an 11x17 inch jelly roll pan. Enjoy.

Mrs. Emil Trnka, St. Peter

PEANUT BUTTER SURPRISE BARS

2 cups peanut butter	1 (12 oz.) pkg. milk chocolate
1 cup sugar	chips
2 eggs	

Stir peanut butter, sugar and eggs by hand until well blended. Press into a 9x13 inch baking pan. Bake at 325° for 20 minutes. Pour chocolate chips over top and let set until melted, about 5 minutes. Spread evenly over the top.

Note: This recipe is correct, there is no flour.

Carol Wencl, Medford

PEANUT BUTTER BARS

2 cups peanut butter	1½ sticks butter
2½ cups powdered sugar	1 lg. Hershey bar
½ tsp. vanilla	1 (6 oz.) pkg. chocolate chips
½ cup melted butter	½ stick wax, cut in small pieces
½ cup brown sugar	

Mix peanut butter, powdered sugar, vanilla, melted butter and brown sugar and spread on cookie sheet or in a 9x13 inch pan. Melt 1½ sticks butter, Hershey bar, chocolate chips and wax in double boiler. When melted, spread over mixture; chill 10 minutes and cut.

Pat Depuydt, St. Peter

COOKIES & BARS

PEANUT BUTTER-RICE KRISPIES

1 cup white sugar
1 cup white syrup
1½ cups peanut butter
6 cups Rice Krispies

Heat the sugar and syrup, but do not boil. Add the peanut butter. Pour over Rice Krispies and spread in a 9x13 inch pan. Can be frosted with melted chocolate chips or butterscotch chips.

Eunice Cole, Argyle

PECAN BARS

1½ cups flour
½ cup butter
¼ cup brown sugar

Mix and press into a greased 9x13 inch pan. Bake at 350° for 15 minutes.

⅔ cup brown sugar
1 cup maple syrup
2 beaten eggs
2 Tbsp. flour
½ tsp. vanilla
1 cup chopped pecans

Mix brown sugar and syrup in pan. Simmer 5 minutes. Pour over beaten eggs, stirring constantly. Stir in rest of ingredients.

Gloria Schoenborn, Mahnomen

PECAN PIE SQUARES

3 cups flour
¼ cup plus 2 Tbsp. sugar
¾ cup margarine or butter, softened
¾ tsp. salt

Heat oven to 350°. Grease a 15½x10½x1 inch jelly roll pan. Beat flour, sugar, margarine and salt in large bowl on medium speed until crumbly (mixture will be dry). Press firmly in pan. Bake until golden brown, about 20 minutes. Prepare filling.

Filling:
4 eggs, slightly beaten
1½ cups Karo light or dark corn syrup
3 Tbsp. margarine or butter, melted
1½ tsp. vanilla
1½ cups sugar
2½ cups chopped pecans

Mix all ingredients, except pecans, until well blended. Stir in pecans. Pour over baked layer; spread evenly. Bake until filling is set, about 25 minutes; cool. Cut into 1½ inch squares.

Ann Kuhn, Mahnomen

COOKIES & BARS

HUNGARIAN POPPY SEED NUT SLICES

1 cup soft butter
1 cup plus 2 Tbsp. white sugar
1 lg. egg
1 tsp. vanilla
1 tsp. cinnamon

1 ½ cups almonds, finely chopped
½ cup poppy seed
2 cups all-purpose flour
¼ tsp. salt
Colored sugar

Beat butter and sugar in mixer bowl until light and fluffy. Add egg, vanilla and cinnamon; beat 2 or 3 minutes. Add nuts and poppy seeds and beat 1 minute more. Gradually stir in flour and salt. Refrigerate until dough is firm, about 2 hours. Shape into two rolls about 2 inches in diameter. Roll in 2 tablespoons sugar. Wrap in wax paper and refrigerate 3 hours. Preheat oven to 325°. Roll logs in colored sugar if desired. Slice dough ¼ inch thick. Place on ungreased cookie sheets. Bake 20 minutes or until edges begin to brown. Cool on wire racks. Makes 6 dozen, 70 calories each.

Note: It is important to have the almonds very finely chopped. A good Christmas cookie.

Fran Janous, Owatonna

PRAYER BARS

¼ lb. butter
4 Tbsp. cocoa
2 tsp. vanilla
1 egg, beaten

2 cups graham crackers, crushed
½ cup coconut, flaked
½ cup powdered sugar
½ cup chopped nuts

Melt butter and cocoa over hot water. Add vanilla and egg. Mix well and add all other ingredients. Press into 9x13 inch pan. Put in refrigerator and let stand awhile.

2nd Layer:
¼ cup butter
1 tsp. vanilla
2 Tbsp. cream
2 or 3 tsp. dry vanilla pudding mix

2 cups powdered sugar
Giant size chocolate Hershey bar

Cook butter, vanilla, cream and pudding mix for 1 minute. Stir in powdered sugar and spread over other layer. Melt giant size Hershey bar over hot water and spread over 2nd layer. Cut into small squares.

Lee Mikolai, Blue Earth

PINEAPPLE BARS

1 (20 oz.) can crushed pineapple, undrained
2 cups flour
1½ cups sugar

2 eggs
2 Tbsp. soda
½ tsp. salt

Beat all ingredients. Bake in jelly roll pan at 350° for 30 minutes.

Frosting:

1 (3 oz.) pkg. cream cheese
¼ cup margarine
1 tsp. vanilla

3 cups powdered sugar
1 Tbsp. cream or milk

Cream the cheese and margarine and add rest of ingredients. Spread on bars and sprinkle ½ **cup chopped nuts** on top.

Variation: Marie adds 2 cups coconut to the bars.

Janet Miller, Owatonna
Marie Kolb, Mentor

PUMPKIN BARS

4 eggs
1 cup sugar
1 cup salad oil
1 (15 oz.) can pumpkin
1 cup flour
1 tsp. soda

2 tsp. cinnamon
½ tsp. cloves
2 tsp. baking powder
½ tsp. salt
½ tsp. ginger
½ tsp. nutmeg

Mix the first 4 ingredients in a large bowl. Sift the dry ingredients and add to pumpkin mixture. Mix well and pour into a greased and floured 12x18x1 inch pan. Bake at 350° for 25 to 30 minutes.

Frosting:

1 (6 oz.) pkg. cream cheese
¾ stick butter
1 tsp. vanilla

1 Tbsp. cream or milk
4 cups powdered sugar

Beat cheese, butter, vanilla and cream or milk until smooth. Add powdered sugar until correct consistency to spread. Cut into 2x3 inch bars. Makes 36 bars. These freeze very well.

Variation: Florence adds 1 cup walnuts.

Joyce Stock, Mahnomen
State Regent, 1986-1990
1st Vice State Regent, 1984-1986
Florence Walker, Red Lake Falls
Mary Dvoracek, West, TX
National Director, 1992-1994
Marsha Cerar, Moorhead
Barb Neilson, Slayton
Mary Nowak, Blue Earth

COOKIES & BARS

PIZZA BARS

1 cup butter
1 cup brown sugar
1½ cups flour
½ tsp. salt
½ tsp. soda
2 cups oatmeal

30 caramels
2 Tbsp. water
1 (12 oz.) pkg. M&M's
1 (12 oz.) pkg. chocolate chips
White almond bark

Cream butter and brown sugar. Add flour, salt and soda. Mix in oatmeal. Spread in jelly roll pan. Bake at 350° for 10 minutes. Melt caramels and water. Spread on crust. Sprinkle with M&M's and chocolate chips. Drizzle melted white almond bark on top.

Vivan Helget, St. James

SOUR CREAM RAISIN BARS

Crust:

1 cup brown sugar
1 cup margarine
1¾ cups oatmeal

1 tsp. baking soda
1¾ cups flour

Mix ingredients and pat half into a 9x13 inch pan. Bake at 350° for 7 minutes.

Filling:

3 egg yolks, beaten
1½ cups sour cream
2½ Tbsp. cornstarch

2 cups raisins, cooked, drained
and cooled
1 tsp. vanilla

In a heavy saucepan, mix egg yolks, sour cream, and cornstarch. Boil until thick. Add raisins and vanilla. Pour into crust and put remaining crumbs on top. Bake at 350° for 30 minutes.

Ottilia Winter, Iron

RAISIN BARS

1 pkg. spice cake mix
1 (20 oz.) can raisin pie filling

2 eggs, beaten

Preheat oven to 350°. Using solid shortening, grease and flour a 15x10 inch jelly roll pan. In a large bowl, combine all ingredients by hand, do not use mixer. Stir until well mixed. Pour into prepared pan. Bake 20 to 30 minutes.

Frosting:

1 (3 oz.) pkg. cream cheese
2 Tbsp. half and half or milk
½ stick soft margarine (4 Tbsp.)

1 tsp. vanilla
2 cups powdered sugar

Mix well and frost. You can use your favorite frosting if desired.

Laurine Somers, Slayton

COOKIES & BARS

REESES PEANUT BARS

2 cups powdered sugar
2½ cups graham crackers, crushed

1 cup butter or margarine, melted
1 cup peanut butter
½ cup chocolate chips

Mix powdered sugar and crushed graham crackers. Add melted butter or margarine; mix well. Add peanut butter and mix. Put in a 9x13 inch pan; spread and pat down. Cover with the chocolate chips. Put in warm oven a few minutes to melt chips, then spread and cool.

Hazel Foyt, International Falls

RESTAURANT BARS

1 cup white sugar
1 cup brown sugar
2 cups creamy peanut butter
3 cups Rice Krispies
2 cups corn flakes

2 sticks margarine
4 cups powdered sugar
7 Tbsp. milk
2 pkgs. instant vanilla pudding

Combine sugars and peanut butter and melt in microwave for 4 minutes. Add Rice Krispies and corn flakes. Spread into a jelly roll pan. Melt margarine; add powdered sugar, milk and instant pudding. Spread on first layer and set aside.

Frosting:

1½ cups chocolate chips

1 stick margarine

Melt margarine and chocolate chips; spread over second layer.

Lorrayne Yutrzenka, Argyle

RHUBARB BARS

2 cups flour
1 cup margarine
3 Tbsp. sugar
4 beaten egg yolks
2 cups sugar

¼ tsp. nutmeg
4 Tbsp. flour
¾ cup canned milk or cream
Dash of salt
6 cups diced rhubarb

Mix first 3 ingredients and pat into an 18x15 inch pan. Bake only until golden brown. Bake at 350° for 10 to 12 minutes. Mix remaining ingredients, adding rhubarb last. Spread over crust and bake at 350° for 45 minutes.

Meringue:

4 egg whites
½ cup sugar

1 tsp. vanilla

Beat egg whites; add sugar and vanilla. When stiff and dry, spread over top of baked bars. Bake at 375° for another 15 minutes.

Cora Jones, Eveleth

COOKIES & BARS

209

RHUBARB BARS

4 cups diced rhubarb	1½ cups sugar
¼ cup water	1 tsp. vanilla
3 Tbsp. cornstarch	

Dice rhubarb; place in saucepan with water. Mix cornstarch and sugar; add to rhubarb and cook until thick. Mix in vanilla. Cool slightly.

Crust:

1½ cups rolled oats	1½ cups flour
1 cup brown sugar	½ tsp. salt
½ cup margarine	½ tsp. soda
½ cup shortening	2 cups coconut

Mix ingredients until crumbly. Put half in a 9x13 inch pan; spread filling on top and sprinkle with remaining crust ingredients. Bake at 350° for 30 minutes or until browned.

Joan Driessen, Owatonna

RHUBARB CREAM SQUARES

Crust:

| 1½ cups flour | ¼ cup chopped nuts |
| ¾ cup butter or margarine | |

Combine and mix like pie crust and press into a 9x13 inch pan. Bake at 300° for 15 minutes.

Filling:

4 cups fresh or frozen rhubarb,	1 cup sugar
cut into small pieces	3 Tbsp. cornstarch
2 Tbsp. water	

Combine ingredients in saucepan and bring to a boil. Simmer 5 minutes until thickened. Spoon over crust and let cool.

Topping:

1 cup miniature marshmallows	1½ cups milk
1 (8 oz.) carton Cool Whip	Coconut
1 (4 oz.) pkg. instant vanilla	
pudding	

Fold marshmallows into Cool Whip and spread over cooled rhubarb. Mix vanilla pudding with milk and pour over the whipped cream layer. Garnish with coconut and refrigerate.

Mary Hansen, Currie

COOKIES & BARS

RHUBARB BARS

1 cup flour	2 cups rhubarb, chopped
1 tsp. baking powder	1 (3 oz.) pkg. strawberry jello
¼ tsp. salt	¼ cup margarine, melted
¼ cup butter, softened	1 cup sugar
1 egg	½ cup flour
1 Tbsp. milk	

In a bowl, combine the 1 cup flour, baking powder and salt. Cut in the ¼ cup butter. Add egg and milk and pat into a greased 9 inch baking pan. Cover with the chopped rhubarb and sprinkle with the dry jello. Mix the ¼ cup melted margarine, sugar and flour. Sprinkle this on top of the rhubarb. Bake at 350° for 45 to 50 minutes. Cool and cut into squares and serve.

Marilyn Petit, Plainview

RICE KRISPIE BARS

1 cup sugar	6 cups Rice Krispies
1 cup white Karo syrup	¾ cup butterscotch chips,
1 cup peanut butter	melted

Cook the sugar and Karo syrup just until you see a few bubbles. Remove from heat. Add peanut butter; mix well. Stir in the Rice Krispies. Put in a 9x13 inch pan. Top with melted butterscotch chips. Cool and cut into bars.

Mary Burns, Janesville

MICROWAVE RICE KRISPIE BARS

1 cup chocolate chips	3 cups Rice Krispies
1 cup marshmallows	½ cup peanut butter

Melt chips and marshmallows in microwave for 1 minute on medium-low. Mix in Rice Krispies; add peanut butter. Press into suitable container.

Linda Willetto, Blue Earth

RICE KRISPIE CARAMEL BARS

1 lb. marshmallows	1 pkg. caramels
1 stick butter	¼ cup butter
6 to 8 cups Rice Krispies	1 can sweetened condensed milk

Make a batch of Rice Krispie bars using the first 3 ingredients. Pour half of the mixture into a buttered pan. Melt or microwave the remaining ingredients and pour over the bars. Add a top layer of Rice Krispie mixture. Press and refrigerate.

Kris Sellner, New Ulm

COOKIES & BARS

SEVEN LAYER BARS

½ cup butter
1½ cups graham cracker crumbs
1 cup Angel Flake coconut
1 cup chocolate chips
1 cup butterscotch chips
1 can sweetened condensed milk
1½ cups chopped walnuts

Melt butter and graham cracker crumbs. Press on bottom of a 9x13 inch cake pan. Sprinkle coconut and both chips evenly on the crumbs. Pour sweetened condensed milk evenly over all and top with walnuts. Bake at 350° for 30 minutes or until light brown.

Margaret Piekarski, Fergus Falls
Cecilia Raleigh, St. Paul

SPANISH PEANUT BARS

1½ cups flour
½ cup butter
¾ cup brown sugar

Mix until crumbly; pat in a 9x13 inch pan. Bake at 375° for 10 minutes.

1 (6 oz.) pkg. butterscotch chips
½ cup white corn syrup
1 Tbsp. water
1 Tbsp. butter
2 cups Spanish peanuts

Melt chips, syrup, water and butter over low heat until smooth; add nuts and pour over crust. Bake at 375° for 8 minutes. Do not over bake. Will be gooey when you take it from oven.

Lorraine Klasfus, North Mankato

SOUR CREAM RAISIN BARS

1¾ cups flour
1 cup brown sugar
1¾ cups minute oatmeal
1 cup butter or oleo
1 tsp. soda

Mix like pie crust. Pat half of mixture in a 9x13 inch pan; save rest for top. Bake at 350° for 15 minutes. Simmer **2 cups raisins** in 1½ **cups water** for about 15 minutes; drain.

Filling:

4 egg yolks, beaten
2 cups sour cream
3 Tbsp. cornstarch
1 cup white sugar
1 tsp. vanilla
½ tsp. cinnamon

Boil until thick, stirring constantly, then mix with drained raisins and spread on first layer. Put rest of crumbs on top and bake about 20 minutes. Do not overbake.

Agnes M. Cawley, Waseca
Helen Cahill, Moorhead
Geneva Fessel, Waterville

COOKIES & BARS

212

SHORTBREAD

1 lb. softened butter   4 cups flour
1 cup sugar

Beat butter, alternating sugar and flour. Bake in a jelly roll pan or a 9x13 inch pan at 300° for 1 hour. Score top and let cool.

Bonnie Zimmerman, Waseca

SWISS CHOCOLATE DESSERT BARS

1½ cups flour   1 cup sugar
¾ cup margarine or butter   ⅛ tsp. salt
¼ cup sugar   2 Tbsp. flour
1 (4 oz.) bar sweet cooking   2 eggs
   chocolate   ¾ cup chopped pecans or
¼ cup butter or margarine   coconut
¾ cup evaporated milk

Mix 1½ cups flour, ¾ cup margarine, and ¼ cup sugar; press into bottom of an ungreased 9x13 inch pan. Bake at 375° for 10 minutes. Meanwhile, melt chocolate, ¼ cup butter and milk over low heat. Stir until smooth. Add 1 cup sugar, salt, 2 tablespoons flour and eggs; beat well. Pour over crust. Sprinkle with chopped pecans or coconut. Bake 25 to 30 minutes.

Monica Stoderl, Iona

TOFFEE BARS

1 cup butter or margarine   1 cup walnuts, chopped
1 cup brown sugar   1 (6 oz.) pkg. (1 cup) semi-sweet
1 tsp. vanilla   chocolate chips
2 cups flour

Cream butter, sugar and vanilla. Add flour and mix well. Add nuts; press mixture into an ungreased 15½x10½x1 inch jelly roll pan. Bake at 350° for 25 minutes. Spread chocolate chips over hot bars; let melt and spread. Cut while warm.

Fay Gengler, Caledonia
Helen Foltz, Detroit Lakes

* * * * * * * *

Someone who sticks his head above
the crowd gets hit by rotten fruit.
Bertha Schmitt, Mazeppa

TURTLE BARS

1 cup oatmeal	¾ cup butter
¾ cup brown sugar	52 caramels
1 tsp. soda	5 Tbsp. milk
1 cup flour	8 to 10 Hershey's almond candy
¼ tsp. salt	bars

Mix all dry ingredients. Melt butter and add to dry ingredients and mix. Save ¼ of the mixture. Press the rest into a 9x13 inch greased pan. Melt caramels in milk. Pour over the oatmeal mixture. Layer candy bars on top of caramels and sprinkle with remaining dry mixture. Bake at 350° until brown, about 15 to 20 minutes.

Zonda Befort, Mazeppa
State Education Chair, 1988-present

ZUCCHINI CRISP

5 cups zucchini, peeled, seeded and sliced	6 Tbsp. butter or margarine
⅓ to ½ cup sugar	1 cup flour
1 tsp. cinnamon	½ cup brown sugar
¼ cup lemon juice	1 tsp. baking powder
¾ cup water	½ tsp. salt

Cook the zucchini with sugar, cinnamon, lemon juice and water for 10 minutes. Place zucchini mixture in a 9 inch pie pan. For topping, mix butter, flour, brown sugar, salt and baking powder until crumbly. Sprinkle this over zucchini. Bake at 350° for 45 minutes. Serves 6 to 8. Tastes like apple pie.

Rose Guillemette, Mankato
State Regent, 1984-1986

* * * * * * * *

HOPE: Be of good courage, and he shall strengthen your heart, all ye that hope in the Lord. Psalm 31:24
Cordelia Lermon, West Concord

* * * * * * * *

Whenever I am lonely or lost in despair,
I call upon my Savior and I find him always there.
Albert Theel
Ester Kaiser, Claremont

COOKIES & BARS

214

✠ QUALITY OF LIFE ✠

"Quality of Life" is directed to the aid and sanctification of individuals and groups including benefits to those in need – such as the elderly and ill. Their lives are more meaningful and pleasant by our personal visits, special parites on holidays and involvement through community and hospice programs. A special program for the ALZHEIMER'S SAFE RETURN coincides with CDA weekend. . the third Sunday in October.

This segment also involves helping persons with special needs who are living in pregnancy care centers, rehabilitation centers for drug and alcohol abuse, homes for abused women and children and nursing homes. Day care centers such as Head Start welcome CDA volunteers.

Supporting those who are underprivileged, bereaved, handicapped, victims of poverty and the forgotten require sharing our time and love.

This segment also emphasizes family values. CDA campaigns against pornography in conjunction with MORALITY IN MEDIA, TURN OFF TV Day and supports neighborhood watch groups preventing gang activities.

Community issues with special emphasis on the following are an important part of quality of life: HABITAT FOR HUMANITY, we provide financial support and participate in building homes. The first home completed, nationally by Catholic Daughters, was in October, 1995, in Oklahoma City, OK. ENVIRONMENTAL preservation by recycling, adopting highways, beaches and rivers. RURAL LIFE providing awareness and informative programs in our areas. PRISON MINISTRIES while assisting spiritual directors/chaplains and participating in REC (Residents Encounter Christ) weekends.

Worldwide issues include PROJECT HANDCLASP where we donate materials such as sewing, medical, school supplies and toys to be transported by US Navy ships and distributed throughout the world at their ports of call. ADOPT A CHILD is supporting a foster child in eastern countries. Cash donations provide food, clothing and education to many. CATHOLIC CHARITIES provide emergency meals, shelter and financial assistance. MISSIONS/PROPAGATION OF THE FAITH where bandages, gowns, medical supplies and monetary donations are supplied to leper colonies. Canceled stamps, greeting cards, religious materials, eye glasses are collected and distributed to many around the world by our members.

"No one is so rich as to need another's help; no one is so poor as not to be useful in some way to his or her neighbor. And the disposition to ask assistance from others with confidence, and to grant it with kindness, is part of our nature."

–Pope Leo XIII
Betty Hager & Eulalia Koll,
past State Quality of Life Co-Chairs

Alzheimer's Safe Return Program

The Alzheimer's Association Safe Return program is a program to help locate and return a lost or missing Alzheimer's patient to safety. Many times people with Alzheimer's disease, confused and disoriented, may set off to find something that's familiar and reassuring to them and become lost. At this wandering stage of the disease, they may no longer be able to speak, so they cannot ask for help. The Alzheimer's Association Safe Return program is a safety net that enables others to help them. The program enrolls Alzheimer victims in a national database and provides them with an identity bracelet, wallet card and clothing labels. When an individual wanders away, family member or care givers can call a toll-free 800 number and a computer network of 17,000 law enforcement agencies can be alerted. When a missing person is found, the bracelet and other identifying materials provide the person's name, identification number and the toll-free number to call so the family can be reunited.

Shirley Seyfried,
past Project Chair

* * DESSERTS * *

AL'S FAVORITE DESSERT
Maple ice cream   **Creme de cocoa (dark)**

Pour a small amount of creme de cocoa (dark) over maple nut ice cream and serve. GOOD!

Alice Miller, Caledonia

ALMOND CLOUD
1 lg. Angel Food cake   **3 egg whites**
½ cup butter   **1½ tsp. almond flavoring**
1½ cups powdered sugar   **1 lg. tub Cool Whip**
3 beaten egg yolks

Cut Angel Food into pieces. Put half of pieces into a 9x13 inch pan. Cream butter, powdered sugar and beaten egg yolks. Fold in beaten egg whites (stiff). Add almond flavoring. Fold in ¾ tub of Cool Whip. Spread over Angel Food and top with other half of Angel Food pieces. Top with remaining Cool Whip. Sprinkle with ½ **cup toasted almonds**. Cover, chill at least 24 hours.

Ann Sturm, St. Peter

ALMOND BARK KRISPIE BARS
1 pkg. vanilla almond bark   **2 cups salted peanuts, chopped**
4 cups Rice Krispies   **fine**

Melt the almond bark in top of double boiler. Add Rice Krispies and peanuts and mix. Pour in a greased 9x13 inch pan. When cool, cut into bars.

Marjorie Forte, Eveleth

PETAL PINK ANGEL CAKE
1 pkg. Angel Food cake mix   **1 tsp. unflavored gelatin**
1⅓ cups water   **¼ cup confectioner's sugar**
¾ tsp. almond extract   **¼ cup sliced natural almonds**
Red food coloring   **Fresh raspberries for garnish**
2 cups whipping cream, chilled

Prepare cake as directed on package. Fold in ½ teaspoon almond extract. Place 3 cups batter in medium bowl. Fold in 3 drops red food coloring. Spoon ⅓ of white batter into an ungreased 10 inch tube pan. Cover with half of the pink batter. Repeat layering with white and pink batters. Bake and cool cake following package directions at 350°. Place whipping cream, gelatin and ¼ teaspoon almond extract in large bowl. Beat at medium speed with mixer. Add confectioner's sugar gradually. Beat at high speed until soft peaks form. Tint with 3 drops of red food coloring. Place cake on serving plate. Frost sides and top with whipped cream mixture. Decorate with almond and raspberries to form flowers. Use almonds as petals and raspberries as center of flowers. Serves 12 to 16.

Mary Pahlen, Crookston

ANGEL FOOD CAKE DESSERT

1 Angel Food cake
2 or 3 frozen Heath bars
1 (8 oz.) carton Cool Whip
2 Tbsp. caramel ice cream topping

Cut cake into 3 layers. Crush Heath bars in plastic bag. Fold into the Cool Whip and add the caramel topping. Fill layers and outside of cake. Refrigerate.

Irene Yutrzenka, Argyle

FRENCH APPLE BREAD PUDDING

3 eggs
1 (14 oz.) can sweetened condensed milk
3 med. apples, peeled, cored and finely chopped
1¾ cups hot water
¼ cup butter, melted
1 tsp. cinnamon
1½ tsp. vanilla
4 cups bread cubes
½ cup raisins

Preheat oven to 350°. In a large bowl, beat eggs; add milk, apples, water, butter, cinnamon and vanilla. Stir in bread and raisins, moistening completely. Turn into a buttered 9 inch square pan. Bake 1 hour or until knife inserted in center comes out clean. Cool, or serve slightly warm with ice cream. Refrigerate leftovers.

Mary Lynn Portz, Pipestone

APPLE CRISP

4 cups apples, cut up
1 cup sugar
1 Tbsp. flour
¾ tsp. cinnamon
¾ cup oatmeal
¾ cup brown sugar
¾ cup flour
½ tsp. soda
½ tsp. baking powder
⅓ cup butter

Mix apples, sugar, 1 tablespoon flour and cinnamon. Put into greased 7x11 inch pan. Top with remaining ingredients that have been blended together. Bake at 350°.

Note: Use 1½ times these amounts for a 9x13 inch pan.

Marjorie Scheidecker, Fergus Falls

APPLE CRISP

6 apples, peeled and sliced
1 cup sugar
¾ cup flour
½ cup butter or margarine
Cinnamon to taste
½ cup water

Place sliced apples in a 7x11 inch pan or a 9 to 10 inch square pan. Mix sugar, flour and butter in bowl until crumbly. Sprinkle over apples. Sprinkle cinnamon and water over everything. Bake at 350° for 1 hour. Watch it as ovens vary.

Alice Buse, Slayton

APPLE CRISP

6 lg. apples	1 cup corn flakes
1 tsp. cinnamon	½ cup flour
1 tsp. salt	1 cup sugar
¼ cup water	⅓ cup butter

Slice apples into an 8 inch greased pan. Sprinkle with cinnamon and salt and pour water over apples. Crush corn flakes. Mix corn flakes, flour and sugar. Add melted butter and mix until crumbly. Spread mixture over apples. Bake at 350° for about 40 minutes.

Vera Walch, Plainview

MICROWAVE APPLE CRISP

Apples to cover bottom of dish	1 cup brown sugar
Sugar and cinnamon	½ cup butter
1 cup flour	1 cup instant oatmeal

Slice apples into your dish; sprinkle with sugar and cinnamon and cook for 5 minutes. Mix remaining ingredients and put over apples. Cook another 10 minutes or until apples are done.

Phyllis Novak, Fergus Falls

APPLE CRISP IN MICROWAVE

4 cups apples, sliced	½ cup margarine, melted
1 cup sugar	½ cup oatmeal
¼ cup flour	1 cup flour
Cinnamon to taste	1 cup brown sugar

Place sliced apples in a 9x9 inch glass pan. Mix sugar, ½ cup flour, and cinnamon and spread over apples. Mix margarine, oatmeal, 1 cup flour and brown sugar. Crumble over top. Bake on high for 5 minutes. Let set 3 minutes; bake 5 more minutes on high. Let set and serve.

Linda Willete, Blue Earth

NUTTY APPLE CRISP

8 to 10 lg. apples, pared and sliced	Ground cinnamon
	1 to 2 tsp. butter or margarine

Mound sliced apples in an 8 inch square baking pan. Sprinkle with cinnamon and dot with butter.

Topping:

¾ cup flour	½ cup chopped walnuts
½ cup brown sugar	1 to 1½ tsp. ground cinnamon
⅓ cup soft butter or margarine	Dash of salt

Combine flour, brown sugar and butter until crumbly. Add nuts, cinnamon and salt. Sprinkle topping over apples. Bake in a preheated 350° oven for 30 to 40 minutes until apples are tender. Serve warm; top with a scoop of ice cream. Makes 9 servings.

Blanche Marcotte, Slayton

APPLE CUSTARD KUCHEN

1 cup flour
2 Tbsp. sugar
¼ tsp. salt
½ tsp. baking powder
¼ cup butter, softened

2 cups sliced apples
¼ cup plus 2 Tbsp. sugar
1 tsp. cinnamon
2 egg yolks
1 cup heavy cream

Heat oven to 400°. Stir flour, 2 tablespoons sugar, salt and baking powder. Work in butter until crumbly. Pat into an 8x8 inch pan and press firmly and half up the sides. Arrange apples in pan. Mix the rest of the sugar with cinnamon. Sprinkle on top. Blend the egg yolks and cream. Pour over all. Bake until custard is set.

Adelia Sontag, New Ulm

APPLE MACAROON

10 lg. tart apples, peeled and
  sliced
½ cup sugar
1 tsp. cinnamon
⅓ cup butter or margarine
2 cups all-purpose flour

2 cups sugar
1½ tsp. salt
4 eggs
2 tsp. vanilla
Whipped cream

Heat oven to 350°. Place apples in buttered 13x9x2 inch pan. In a small bowl, combine ½ cup sugar and cinnamon; sprinkle over apples. Dot with butter. In large bowl, combine flour, 2 cups sugar, salt, eggs and vanilla. Beat until well blended. Spread over apples. Bake 1 hour. Garnish with whipped cream.

Kay Miller, Crookston

APPLE TORTE

1 egg
¾ cup sugar
¾ cup sliced apples
¼ cup walnuts

1 tsp. baking powder
½ cup flour
Dash of salt
¼ tsp. almond extract

Beat eggs; add sugar, apples and nuts. Add remaining ingredient and mix well. Pour into a greased pie tin. Bake at 325° for 45 minutes. Serve with cream or ice cream. Fast and easy. Makes a tasty dessert. The top gets a meringue look.

DeEtte Reitter, New Ulm

* * * * * * * *

Friends, let us love one another because love is from God. I John 4:7
Mary Jane Gray, Blue Earth

BANANA DESSERT

Mix **2 cups graham cracker crumbs** with **1 stick melted butter or margarine** and press in a 9x13 inch pan and refrigerate.

2 eggs	**1 tsp. vanilla**
2 stick butter or margarine	**2 cups powdered sugar**

Mix and beat 15 minutes; spread on crust. Cover with **2 large sliced bananas.** Top with **1 (No. 2) can crushed drained pineapple.** Cover with **1 large carton Cool Whip.** Refrigerate overnight.

Lori Maas, Medford

LAYERED BANANA PINEAPPLE DESSERT

1½ cups graham cracker crumbs	3½ cups cold milk
¼ cup sugar	2 (4 serving size) pkgs. Jell-O
⅓ cup margarine or butter, melted	vanilla instant pudding
	1 (20 oz.) can crushed pine-
3 bananas, sliced	apple, drained
1 (3 oz.) pkg. cream cheese	1 (8 oz.) tub Cool Whip, thawed

Mix graham cracker crumbs, sugar and margarine in a 9x13 inch pan. Press evenly onto bottom of pan. Arrange bananas on crust. Beat cream cheese in large bowl with wire whisk until smooth. Gradually beat in milk. Add pudding mixes. Beat until well blended. Spread evenly over banana slices. Spoon pineapple evenly over pudding mixture; spread whipped topping over pineapple. Refrigerate 3 hours or until ready to serve.

Geri Voit, Moorhead

BANANA-STRAWBERRY DESSERT

1 (12 oz.) box vanilla wafers, crushed	4 bananas
	Fresh strawberries, cut in half
1½ cups powdered sugar	1 pt. cream, whipped
2 eggs	2 Tbsp. powdered sugar
2 tsp. vanilla	

Spread ¾ of crumbs on buttered 9x13 inch pan. Beat powdered sugar, eggs and vanilla with mixer. If too thin, add more powdered sugar. Spread over crumbs with wet knife. Slice bananas lengthwise and arrange alternately with fresh strawberries over powdered sugar layer. Cover with whipped cream sweetened with 2 tablespoons powdered sugar. Sprinkle rest of crushed vanilla wafers on top. Refrigerate overnight.

Florine Driscoll, Moorhead

BANANA SPLIT TORTE

2 cups graham cracker crumbs
²/₃ cup margarine, melted
1 (16 oz.) can crushed pineapple, drained
3 lg. bananas

2 cups powdered sugar
2 eggs
1 cup butter, softened
1 tsp. vanilla
1 (12 oz.) carton Cool Whip

Mix crumbs and margarine; pat in a 9x13 inch cake pan for crust. Drain pineapple juice into shallow bowl, slice bananas into juice; set aside. Beat powdered sugar, eggs, butter and vanilla until firm. Spread on crust. Layer banana slices on top; spread pineapple over bananas. Top with Cool Whip. Garnish with maraschino cherries, nuts or coconut if desired. Refrigerate for 8 hours.

Judy Potter, International Falls
Dee Alt, St. Peter

BANANA SPLIT DESSERT

½ cup graham crackers (approximately 12)
¾ cup sugar
½ cup butter, melted
5 or 6 bananas
Lemon juice

½ gal. strawberry ice cream, softened
1 pt. whipping cream
Maraschino cherries
Nuts

Butter a 9x13 inch pan. Combine graham crackers, sugar and melted butter. Press firmly into pan. Chill. Cut bananas lengthwise, dip in lemon juice and line cake pan. Spread softened ice cream on top of banana layer. Whip whipping cream (adding no sugar); spread on top of ice cream layer. Sprinkle with maraschino cherries and nuts. Freeze. When ready to serve top with hot fudge sauce.

Hot Fudge Sauce:
½ cup butter
1 cup chocolate chips

1½ cups evaporated milk
2 cups powdered sugar

Melt the butter and chocolate chips. Add evaporated milk and powdered sugar. Bring to a boil and boil 8 minutes. May be rewarmed in microwave on low.

Cyrilla Frodl, Waterville

* * * * * * * *

Lord, as in the case of the rich young man, you teach us that we must be "free from" in order to be "free for". Blessed are you poor in spirit! The riches of the kingdom of heaven belong to you.

Sister Mary Charleen Hug SND
Jane Armon, Blue Earth

BLUEBERRY BUCKLE

1¼ cups flour
½ cup sugar
1½ tsp. baking powder
½ cup margarine, softened
⅓ cup milk

1 tsp. grated lemon peel, optional
½ tsp. vanilla
1 egg
1½ cups fresh or frozen blueberries, thawed and drained

Mix first 8 ingredients. Spread batter in an 8x8x2 inch pan. Place blueberries on top, then sprinkle on topping and bake at 350° for 45 to 50 minutes or until golden brown.

Crumb Topping:
½ cup sugar
⅓ cup flour

¼ cup butter, softened
½ tsp. cinnamon

Mix until crumbly.

Marietta Johanneck, Red Lake Falls

BLUEBERRY CAPISTRANO

40 soda crackers, crushed
½ cup butter or margarine, melted
½ cup walnuts, finely chopped
4 egg whites, beaten

1 cup sugar
1 can blueberry or raspberry pie mix (I prefer raspberry)
Cool Whip

Crush soda crackers fine; add melted butter or margarine and nuts. Mix and spread in a 9x13 inch pan. Beat egg whites until stiff; add sugar and beat until stiff peaks form. Spread over crust and bake at 350° for 20 minutes or until lightly browned. Spread pie mix over meringue. Cover with Cool Whip and chill. Better when chilled overnight.

Hazel Foyt, International Falls

BLUEBERRY DESSERT

18 graham crackers, crushed
½ cup sugar
¼ cup melted butter
1 (8 oz.) pkg. cream cheese

½ cup sugar
2 beaten eggs
1 can blueberry pie filling

Combine graham crackers, sugar and butter and pat into bottom of a 9x13 inch pan. Mix cream cheese, sugar and eggs. Spread over crust. Bake at 375° for 20 minutes. Cool and top with blueberry pie filling. Cut into squares to serve.

Irene McNea, Fairmont

BLUEBERRY DELIGHT DESSERT

1 cup graham cracker crumbs	2 eggs, beaten
½ cup butter or margarine	½ cup sugar
½ cup sugar	1 (8 oz.) pkg. cream cheese

Mix graham cracker crumbs, butter or margarine and ½ cup sugar. Press in a 9x13 inch pan. Combine eggs, ½ cup sugar and cream cheese. Pour over crumbs. Bake at 350° for 20 minutes. Cool.

Blueberry Mixture:

4 cups fresh or frozen blueberries	1 Tbsp. lemon juice
1 cup water	2 Tbsp. cornstarch
1 cup sugar	2 Tbsp. minute tapioca

Place blueberries, water, and sugar in a saucepan. Add lemon juice, cornstarch and tapioca. Cook until thick, stirring constantly. Cool and pour over crust. Top with whipped cream. Can use 1 can of blueberry pie filling.

Leah Pagnac, Argyle

EARLY PIONEER BLUEBERRY PUDDING

4 cups blueberries	8 slices white bread, crust
1 cup sugar	removed
½ cup water	

Bring blueberries, sugar and water slowly to a boil and simmer for 10 minutes. Butter the bread and put two slices, butter-side down, in a loaf pan. Cover with portion of hot berry mixture. Layer bread and berries, ending with berries. Let cool and refrigerate until set. Slice and serve with a little whipped topping.

Margaret Ann Erjavoc, Eveleth

BUTTERSCOTCH DESSERT

1 cup flour	1 cup powdered sugar
½ cup chopped nuts	1 (9 oz.) carton whipped topping
1 Tbsp. sugar	2 pkgs. instant butterscotch
1 stick margarine	pudding
1 (8 oz.) pkg. cream cheese, softened	3 cups milk

Mix flour, nuts, sugar and margarine well. Press into a 9x13 inch pan and bake at 350° for 10 to 15 minutes. Cool. Cream the cream cheese and powdered sugar; add half of the whipped topping and spread over crust. Mix the pudding with milk and whip well; spread over creamed layer. Spread the other half of the whipped topping over top. Chill.

Margaret Slinger, Slayton

BUNDT CAKE

1 pkg. yellow cake mix
1 pkg. instant vanilla or lemon
   pudding
1 cup cold water

½ cup oil
4 eggs
¼ cup poppy seeds

Mix all ingredients. Grease and flour bundt pan. Bake at 350° for 40 to 45 minutes. Top will crack and look wet. Test with toothpick.

Terri Ingram, Waseca

CANDY BAR ANGEL DESSERT

1 (12 oz.) Angel Food cake
1 (5 oz.) pkg. instant vanilla
   pudding
1 tsp. vanilla

1 (12 oz.) carton whipped
   topping
3 (1¼ oz.) Heath bars, crushed

In a bowl or pretty baking dish, crumble the cake. Mix the pudding according to directions and add the vanilla. Spoon over the cake. Spread the whipped topping over the pudding. Sprinkle the crushed bars over the topping. (To crush the candy bars, cover them, then tap lightly with a hammer or other heavy object.)

Beulah Scheurer, Mankato

CARAMEL DESSERT STRATA

1 cup brown sugar
½ cup butter
2 Tbsp. corn syrup
About 12 slices bread, crusts
   removed
1½ cups milk

6 eggs
1 tsp. vanilla
¼ tsp. salt
2 cups sweetened whipped
   cream
Mixed berries, such as black-
   berries and raspberries

Combine sugar, butter and corn syrup in a medium heavy saucepan. Stir over medium heat until butter is melted and mixture comes to a boil. Pour into a 9x13 inch baking dish. Arrange 6 pieces of bread to make an even single layer. Cover with a second layer of bread slices. Whisk milk, eggs, vanilla and salt until blended. Pour over bread; cover with plastic and chill over night. Bake at 350° for 40 minutes. Serve with whipped cream and berries.

Mary L. Pagnac, Argyle

223

CHERRY DESSERT

30 or 40 saltine crackers, crushed
½ stick butter or margarine
4 egg whites
1 cup sugar
½ tsp. almond extract
1 can blueberry or cherry pie
  filling

Finely crush crackers and combine with butter or margarine. Put into a 9x13 inch pan. Beat egg whites; add sugar and almond extract. Spread over the cracker crust. Bake at 400° for 10 minutes; cool. Spread pie filling over the baked crust. Sprinkle with nuts. If higher dessert is desired, use a 9x11 inch pan.

Irene Yutrzenka, Argyle

CHERRY DESSERT

Crust:

1½ pkgs. graham crackers
¼ cup soft margarine
¼ cup sugar

Crush graham crackers fine. Blend in margarine and sugar. Press in a 9x13 inch pan. Bake at 375° for 8 minutes. Cool.

Filling:

½ pt. whipping cream
2 cups cold milk
2 (3 oz.) pkgs. instant vanilla
  pudding
1 can cherry pie filling

Whip the cream; add milk and pudding to the whipped cream and beat until thick. Pour over the graham cracker crust. Spread the pie filling evenly over and sprinkle top with ¼ cup graham cracker crumbs reserved from the crust. Refrigerate.

Rose Spaeth, Eveleth

CHERRY DESSERT

Crust:

¼ cup butter
½ cup sugar
1 pkg. (10 or 11) graham
  crackers, crushed

Mix melted butter, sugar and crushed graham crackers. Put in a 9x12 inch pan and then add the cream cheese mixture.

Cream Cheese Mixture:

1 (8 oz.) pkg. cream cheese
½ cup sugar
2 eggs
1 tsp. vanilla
1 can cherry pie filling

Blend cream cheese sugar, eggs and vanilla well. Bake at 350° for 15 minutes or less. When cool, pour pie filling on top. Refrigerate until serving. Blueberry pie filling works well also.

Cathy Bjorklund, Moorhead

CHERRY BERRIES ON A CLOUD

3 egg whites (1/3 to 1/2 cup)
1/4 tsp. cream of tartar
3/4 cup sugar
1 (3 oz.) pkg. cream cheese, softened
1/2 cup sugar
1/2 tsp. vanilla
1 cup chilled whipping cream
1 cup miniature marshmallows

Heat oven to 275°. Cover baking sheet with heavy brown paper. Draw outline of heart that measures 9 inches across greatest width, on the brown paper. Beat egg whites and cream of tartar until foamy. Add 3/4 cup sugar, 1 tablespoon at a time, continuing to beat until stiff and glossy. Do not underbeat. Spoon meringue into outline on paper, building up sides. Bake 1 1/2 hours. Turn oven off, leaving meringue in oven with door closed 1 hour. Remove; finish cooling away from draft. Blend cream cheese 1/2 cup sugar and vanilla. Chill cream in a bowl and beat until stiff. Gently fold whipped cream and marshmallows into cream cheese mixture. Pile into meringue shell. Cover and chill 12 hours.

Cherry-Berry Topping:

1 (21 oz.) can cherry pie filling
1 tsp. lemon juice
2 cups sliced strawberries, or
1 (16 oz.) pkg. frozen strawberries, thawed

Stir all ingredients. Just before serving, cover shell with topping. Cut into wedges, Makes 6 to 8 servings.

G. Babich, Eveleth

CHERRY SUPREME DESSERT

2 cups graham cracker crumbs
3/4 cup chopped nuts, optional
3/4 cup brown sugar, packed
1 1/4 tsp. cinnamon
3/4 cup melted margarine
1 box Cherry Supreme or Cherry Chip cake mix
1 pkg. Cool Whip
1 can cherry pie filling

Mix crumbs, nuts, brown sugar, cinnamon and margarine. Press half of mixture in a 9x13 inch ungreased pan. Prepare cake mix as directed on package. Pour half of batter over crumb mixture in pan. Sprinkle with remaining crumbs and repeat batter over crumbs. Bake at 350° for 50 minutes or less. Cool in pan and chill in refrigerator. Now spread Cool Whip over cake. Lastly, spread pie filling over top. Keep in refrigerator until ready to serve.

Cecilia Spartz, Slayton

CHERRY ICE CREAM DESSERT

1½ cups Rice Krispies
1 cup flake coconut
½ cup chopped nuts
¼ cup brown sugar
¼ cup melted butter
1½ qts. ice cream
1 can cherry pie mix

Mix Rice Krispies, coconut, nuts, brown sugar and butter. Grease a 7x11 inch pan and spread half of mixture in bottom of pan. Spread on soft vanilla ice cream on top of crust; put rest of krispie mixture on top. Freeze. When ready to serve, heat pie mix and put some on each serving. Just warm the cherry pie filling. Serves 6 to 10.

Julia Sullivan, Moorhead

CHEESECAKE

2 Tbsp. graham cracker crumbs
4 (8 oz.) pkgs. cream cheese, softened
1 cup sugar
4 eggs
1 tsp. lemon juice
½ tsp. vanilla
¼ tsp. lemon rind
1 (4¾ oz.) pkg. strawberry Danish junket
1 qt. strawberries

Sprinkle bottom of lightly greased 9 inch springform pan with crumbs. Combine cream cheese and sugar, mixing at medium speed on electric mixer until well blended. Add eggs, one at a time, mixing well after each addition. Blend in juice, vanilla and rind; pour into pan. Bake at 325° for 50 minutes. Loosen cake form rim of pan. Cool before removing rim of pan. Cook junket in saucepan until thick and cool. Add strawberries to junket and put on top of cheesecake. Chill. Serves 10 to 12.

Linda Pansier, Faribault

INDIVIDUAL CHEESE CAKES

24 vanilla wafers
2 (8 oz.) pkgs. cream cheese
1 cup sugar
2 eggs
¼ tsp. salt
1½ tsp. vanilla

Put a vanilla wafer in 24 paper lined muffin tins. Cream rest of ingredients until smooth. Divide among the 24 cups. Bake at 350° for 17 minutes. Cakes will fall when cooled. Divide a can of favorite pie filling among the 24 cakes. My favorite is cherry, but blueberry, strawberry, etc. may be used. Chill several hours or overnight.

Mary Jo Luhman, Goodhue
District Deputy, 1994-present

NO-BAKE CHEESECAKE (LOW CALORIE)

2 env. unflavored gelatin	1 cup milk
¾ cup sugar	2 Tbsp. lemon juice
⅛ tsp. salt	1½ tsp. grated lemon rind
2 egg yolks	1 tsp. vanilla

Mix gelatin, sugar and salt thoroughly in top of double boiler. Beat egg yolks and milk and add to gelatin mixture. Cook over boiling water, stirring constantly until gelatin is dissolved, about 5 minutes. Remove from heat and stir in lemon juice, rind and vanilla. Chill, stirring occasionally, until mixture mounds slightly when dropped from a spoon. While mixture is chilling, prepare topping.

Crumb Topping:

2 Tbsp. melted butter	2 egg whites
1 Tbsp. sugar	¼ cup sugar
½ cup graham cracker crumbs	½ cup non-fat dry milk
¼ tsp. nutmeg	½ cup ice cold water, combined
¼ tsp. cinnamon	with dry milk and whipped
3 cups creamed small curd	
cottage cheese (24 oz.)	

Mix butter, 1 tablespoon sugar, cracker crumbs, cinnamon and nutmeg. Sieve or beat cottage cheese on high speed of electric mixer, about 3 minutes. Stir into gelatin mixture. Beat egg whites until stiff. Beat in remaining ¼ cup sugar. Fold into gelatin mixture. Fold in whipped dry milk. Turn into an 8 inch spring form pan. Sprinkle with crumb mixture and chill until firm. May be made a day in advance.

Celestine Neeser, Lesiston

PETITE CHEESECAKES

3 (8 oz.) pkgs. cream cheese	5 eggs
1 cup sugar	1 tsp. vanilla

Cream the cheese and sugar until fluffy. Add eggs and vanilla. Bake at 325° for 45 minutes in paper lined muffin tins (⅔ full). Remove from oven and allow to "sink in".

Frosting:

2 cups sour cream	½ tsp. vanilla
½ cup sugar	Fresh fruit or pie filling

Mix sour cream, sugar and vanilla. Return to oven for 5 minutes. Cool and freeze (tin and all). When ready to serve, thaw at room temperature for about 30 minutes. Top with fruit or pie filling.

Jane Kemper, Waubun

CHRISTMAS CRANBERRY DESSERT

2 cups cranberries	2 eggs
2 cups unpeeled, chopped apple	1 cup or more sugar
	1 cup flour
½ cup sugar	½ cup melted butter
½ cup walnuts	½ cup shortening

Place cranberries and apples in greased 10 inch pie plate and sprinkle with the sugar and nuts (if doubled, use an 11x15 inch pan). Beat eggs; add sugar and beat thoroughly. Add flour, melted butter and shortening. Pour over fruit. Bake at 350° for 60 minutes until crust is golden. Serve warm with sauce.

Sauce:

1 cup half and half	1 tsp. vanilla
1 cup sugar	1 Tbsp. cornstarch
1 stick butter	2 Tbsp. lemon juice

Cook all ingredients, except lemon juice, about 25 minutes or until it thickens, stirring often. Before serving, add lemon juice.

Josephine Boland, Winona

BAKED CUSTARD (MICROWAVE)

1¾ cups milk	½ tsp. vanilla
¼ tsp. salt	3 eggs
¼ cup sugar	Nutmeg or cinnamon

Combine ingredients and mix well. Pour into 4 (6 oz.) custard cups and sprinkle with nutmeg or cinnamon. Microwave on defrost for 15 minutes or on high for 5 minutes. Check with a table knife until it comes out clean.

Angeline DeWitte, Holland

CHIP DREAM LOG

1 (6 oz.) pkg. chocolate chips	1 (8 oz.) pkg. mixed fruit
1 (6 oz.) pkg. butterscotch chips	2 to 3 cups miniature
1 (8 oz.) pkg. cream cheese	marshmallows
	Coconut

Melt chips in double boiler. Add cream cheese and melt together. Add fruit and marshmallows. Put in refrigerator for ½ hour. Put coconut on wax paper and roll mixture into logs. Refrigerate.

Cleone Flynn, Plainview

CLARA'S CUSTARD

4 eggs
½ cup sugar
¼ tsp. salt

1 tsp. vanilla
1 qt. milk

Beat eggs, sugar, salt and vanilla. Scald milk and add slowly, stirring constantly. Put into greased baking molds. Place in pan of water at 300° for 40 minutes. Knife comes out clean when done.

Bev Bragg, International Falls

CHOCOLATE ECLAIR DESSERT

Graham crackers
2 (3 oz.) pkgs. French vanilla
   instant pudding
3 cups milk
1 (8 oz.) carton Cool Whip
2 sqs. chocolate

3 Tbsp. butter
2 tsp. vanilla
1 tsp. Karo syrup
2 Tbsp. milk
1½ cups powdered sugar

Line bottom of a 9x13 inch pan with whole graham crackers. Mix pudding with milk until thickened. Fold in Cool Whip. Pour half of mixture over graham crackers. Layer and cover pudding with more graham crackers. Pour remaining pudding over second layer of crackers. Add another layer of crackers and refrigerate while making frosting. Melt chocolate squares and butter until smooth. Remove from heat. Add vanilla, Karo syrup and milk. Blend. Add powdered sugar and beat until smooth and creamy. Frost over third layer of crackers. Refrigerate 24 hours before serving.

Andrea Olsen, Waseca

CHOCOLATE PIZZA

1 (12 oz.) pkg. Baker's real
   semi-sweet chocolate chips
1 lb. white almond bark, divided
2 cups Kraft miniature
   marshmallows
1 cup crisp rice cereal
1 cup peanuts

1 (6 oz.) jar red maraschino
   cherries, drained and halved
2 Tbsp. green maraschino
   cherries, drained and
   quartered
⅓ cup Baker's angel flake
   coconut
1 tsp. oil

Melt chocolate chips with 14 ounces of the almond bark in large saucepan over low heat, stirring until smooth; remove from heat. Stir in marshmallows, cereal and peanuts. Pour onto greased 12 inch pizza pan. Top with cherries; sprinkle with coconut. Melt remaining 2 ounces almond bark with oil over low heat, stirring until smooth; drizzle over coconut. Chill until firm; store at room temperature. Preparation time is 15 minutes plus chilling.

Mary Barry, Owatonna
Jill Adolphson, Argyle

CHOCOLATE SAUCE

¼ cup margarine
¾ cup sugar
¼ cup cocoa

⅓ cup cream or milk (I use milk to cut down on fat)
½ tsp. vanilla

Melt margarine in a saucepan. Add sugar, cocoa and cream or milk. Boil 1 minute, stirring to prevent burning. Remove from heat. Add the vanilla. Serve hot or if stored in refrigerator may be reheated in the microwave.

Betty Dahlhoff, Slayton

CHOCOLATE UPSIDE DOWN CAKE

1¼ cups cake flour
¾ cup sugar
2 tsp. baking powder
Pinch of salt

1 sq. unsweetened chocolate
2 Tbsp. butter
½ cup milk
1 tsp. vanilla

Mix dry ingredients in a mixing bowl. Melt chocolate and butter and add milk and vanilla. Stir chocolate mixture into dry ingredients and mix thoroughly. Pour into a greased 9x9 inch pan.

Topping:

2 Tbsp. cocoa
½ cup brown sugar

½ cup white sugar
1½ cups boiling water

Mix cocoa and sugars. Pour over the top of the cake batter. Pour boiling water over the top of all. Bake at 350° for 1 hour.

Father Jack L. Krough, New Richland

COOKIE SALAD

2 cups buttermilk
2 sm. pkgs. instant vanilla
    pudding
1 (12 oz.) carton Cool Whip

2 cups mandarin oranges,
    drained
1 pkg. fudge striped cookies,
    broken up

Mix buttermilk and instant pudding. Fold in Cool Whip; refrigerate. Add mandarin oranges and cookies when ready to serve.

Marjorie Forte, Eveleth

CRANBERRY DESSERT

1½ Tbsp. butter
½ cup white sugar
¼ cup water
¼ cup Carnation milk

1 cup flour
½ tsp. soda
1 cup whole cranberries
½ cup pecans

Mix ingredients and put in a greased layer pan. Bake at 350° for 30 to 35 minutes. Serve the sauce on top of dessert that is warm.

Topping Sauce:

¼ lb. butter
1 cup sugar

½ cup Carnation milk

Bring to a rolling boil for 3 to 40 minutes; add **1 teaspoon vanilla**.

Lauretta Welter, Crookston

COCONUT PUDDING DESSERT

1st Layer:
1 cup flour   ½ cup nuts
1 stick margarine

Mix and press into a 9x13 inch pan. Bake at 350° for about 10 minutes or until lightly brown. Let cool.

2nd Layer:
1 (8 oz.) pkg. cream cheese   1 cup Cool Whip
1 cup powdered sugar

Mix and spread over 1st layer.

3rd Layer:
2 pkgs. instant coconut pudding   2½ cups milk

Mix pudding (any flavor can be used) and milk; spread over 2nd layer. Use 1 cup Cool Whip to frost. Keep refrigerated.

Beverly Jorgensen, Argyle

CREAM PUFFS

½ cup butter   Pinch of salt
1 cup water   4 eggs
1 cup flour   1 tsp. vanilla

Place butter and water in saucepan; bring to a boil. Add flour and salt, beating vigorously until mixture leaves the side of the pan. Remove from heat; add eggs, one at a time, beating thoroughly. Add vanilla. Drop mixture on greased baking sheet or in muffin tins. Bake at 410° for 20 minutes. Reduce heat to 375° and bake another 20 minutes.

Note: Recipe is submitted from original Catholic Daughters Cookbook "Everybody's Favorite!"

Mrs. Wilfred Fritz, Lismore

CREAM PUFF DESSERT

1 cup water   4 cups milk
½ cup margarine   1 (8 oz.) pkg. cream cheese
1 cup flour   1 (8 oz.) carton Cool Whip
4 eggs   Chocolate syrup
2 sm. boxes instant pudding*

*French vanilla or flavor of your choice.

Bring water and margarine to a boil. Remove from heat and stir in flour. Add eggs, one at a time, stirring well after each. Spread in an 11x15 inch pan. Bake at 400° for 25 to 35 minutes. Cool. Mix pudding with milk and cream cheese. Refrigerate 20 minutes. Spread on crust. Top with Cool Whip. Drizzle on chocolate syrup before serving and cut into squares to serve.

Mary Johanning, Adrian
Vera Walch, Plainview

DANISH CUSTARD

3 eggs	2 cups scalded milk
¼ cup sugar	½ cup light brown sugar
⅛ tsp. salt	1 Tbsp. rum flavoring

Beat eggs until light. Add sugar and salt. Stir in milk slowly. Beat custard until well blended. Sift brown sugar and place in bottom of mold or custard cups. Drizzle rum flavoring over sugar. Pour custard on top of brown sugar. Place baking dish in pan of hot water and bake at 350° until custard is firm, about 1 hour. Chill and invert contents onto a platter or dessert plates. Brown sugar forms a caramel sauce. Serves 5.

Sally Lubinski, Plainview

DAVID'S DESSERT

2 (3 oz.) pkgs. Jell-O lime gelatin	½ to ⅔ (8 oz.) carton frozen whipped topping, thawed
2 cups boiling water	
2 cups cold water	8 Oreo cream-filled chocolate sandwich cookies

Dissolve the gelatin in the boiling water. Add cold water and stir. Chill until slightly thickened, about 1½ to 2 hours. Measure 1¾ cups of the thickened gelatin; pour this into a 9x5 inch loaf pan that has been sprayed with nonstick Pam spray. Chill for 5 minutes. Mix remaining gelatin with whipped topping. Crush the cookies into fine crumbs. Carefully spoon ⅓ of the whipped topping mixture atop the gelatin in pan. Sprinkle with half of the cookie crumbs. Again, top with ⅓ of the whipped topping mixture; sprinkle with remaining cookie crumbs. Top with the final ⅓ of the whipped topping mixture. Chill for about 4 hours. Unmold and cut into serving squares. Serves 6 to 8.

Evelyn Ann Cherne, Eveleth

DEEP DARK SECRET

1 lb. dates	½ cup sifted flour
1 cup sugar	1 tsp. baking powder
1 cup nuts	2 tsp. vanilla
4 egg yolks	½ tsp. salt

Mix all ingredients. Fold in **4 egg whites**, beaten stiff. Spread ½ inch thick in a 9x13 inch greased cake pan. Bake at 350° for 30 minutes. When cool, break up into small pieces and place half on bottom of a large glass plate. Over this, cut **3 or 4 bananas, 1 can crushed pineapple** and **2 oranges**; let set 1 hour in refrigerator. Put the rest of broken cake pieces on top of fruit. Just before serving, spread **whipped cream** over top. Garnish with **cherries** and **nuts**. You can use fruit cocktail for fruit mixture if desired.

Mae Haugstad, Caledonia

DANISH APPLE DESSERT

2½ cups flour	1 tsp. salt
1 Tbsp. sugar	1 cup shortening

Mix above like pie crust. Beat **1 egg yolk**. Add **milk** to make ⅔ cup. Add to above a little at a time. Roll out half; put in a 9x12 inch pan. Crush **2 cups corn flakes** on top. Add filling made of **8 to 10 sliced apples, cinnamon** to taste and ½ **cup sugar**. Beat egg white mixture and spread on top. Bake 1 hour. Frost with powdered sugar while hot.

Dolores Wesley, Waterville

DIRT DESSERT

1 (8 oz.) pkg. cream cheese	2 pkgs. instant vanilla pudding
½ stick margarine	1 (12 oz.) carton Cool Whip
1 cup powdered sugar	1 lb. Oreo cookies
1½ cups milk	

Beat first 4 ingredients until well blended. Add instant pudding and Cool Whip. In blender, crumb Oreos. In a flower pot, layer cream mixture and Oreos. Make sure last layer is Oreos. Chill. Before serving, put flowers in pot to look like real plant. HAVE FUN!

Gen Bleess, Blue Earth

PAN ECLAIRS

Whole graham crackers	1 (8 oz.) carton Cool Whip
2 pkgs. vanilla instant pudding	1 can fudge frosting
2½ cups milk	

Line a 9x13 inch pan with whole graham crackers. Combine pudding mix, milk and Cool Whip. Pour half of mixture on top of graham crackers. Add another layer of whole graham crackers, remaining pudding mixture and another layer of graham crackers. Cover all with fudge frosting that has been softened in microwave. Cool until set. Fudge frosting can be powdered sugar frosting rather than prepared frosting.

Nellie Cullen, International Falls

FLORENTINE SUNDAE

1 can pineapple rings, drained	Grated semi-sweet chocolate
1 qt. orange or lemon frozen sherbet	Chopped nuts
	Flaked coconut

Place a pineapple ring in bottom of dessert dishes. Top with scoop or two of sherbet or one each of lemon and orange. Sprinkle grated chocolate, nuts and coconut on top and serve immediately with small cookie or wafer.

Mrs. James Klug, Caledonia

MEXICAN FRIED ICE CREAM

¾ cup butter or margarine   ¾ cup coconut
1½ cups brown sugar   ¾ cup chopped nuts
3¾ cups cornflakes   ½ gal. ice cream

Melt butter or margarine and brown sugar. Add crushed corn flakes, coconut and chopped nuts. Pat half of crumbs in a 9x13 inch pan. Put ice cream on top and then sprinkle the rest of the crumbs on top. Freeze.

Kathleen Riopelle, Argyle

FROZEN DESSERT

1 (16 oz.) box sour cream   2 bananas, sliced
1 (8 oz.) box Cool Whip   1 can pineapple tidbits, drained
½ cup sugar   1 (10 oz.) can cherries, cut up
1 tsp. vanilla   and drained
2 Tbsp. lemon juice   ½ cup nuts

Mix the first 5 ingredients, then fold in pineapple tidbits, cherries, bananas and nuts. Put in a 9x13 inch pan and freeze. Take out 1 hour before serving because it freezes very hard.

Alice Ethier, Argyle

FRUIT COCKTAIL DESSERT

1 cup sugar   ½ tsp. salt
1 cup flour   1 tsp. soda
1 tsp. vanilla   2 well beaten eggs
1 (No. 2½) can fruit cocktail,
    drained

Mix well and put in a 9x12 inch pan and sprinkle with ½ **cup brown sugar** and ½ **cup nuts** on top. Bake at 300° for 1 hour. Serve with whipped cream or ice cream.

Elnora Winter, Mahnomen

FRUIT-FILLED JELLY ROLL

2 Tbsp. melted butter   1 Tbsp. lemon juice
1 can pie filling   ¼ tsp. nutmeg

Combine and spread in flat cookie sheet. Beat **4 egg whites** until thick. Add ⅓ **cup sugar** and beat until stiff. Beat **4 egg yolks** until thick. Add ½ **cup sugar,** ½ **teaspoon vanilla** and ½ **teaspoon salt** and beat well. Stir in ¾ **cup flour** and **1 teaspoon baking powder.** Fold into egg whites and spread over filling pan. Bake at 350° for 20 to 25 minutes. Cool slightly. Spread towel with **powdered sugar.** Turn cake onto it and roll. Use **fresh fruit** or **pie filling.** Slice and serve with whipped cream.

Dorothy Iraci, International Falls

GLAMOUR TORTE

1 box white cake mix	1 cup shredded coconut
½ cup granulated sugar	1 cup chopped nuts
1 Tbsp. cornstarch	¾ cup maraschino cherries,
¼ tsp. salt	drained and chopped
1 (No. 2) can crushed pineapple	1 (8 oz.) carton Cool Whip

Mix and bake white cake mix as per directions in two layers, saving 2 egg yolks. Cool. In saucepan, combine sugar, cornstarch, salt, and egg yolks; mix well. Cook until thick, stirring constantly. Cool. Add pineapple, coconut, nuts and cherries. Split cake, spread mixture between layers. Frost cake with Cool Whip. Refrigerate before serving.

Edna Jane Nolte, Delphos, OH
National Regent, 1990-1994

HAWAIIAN DESSERT

1 pkg. yellow cake mix	4 cups milk
1 Tbsp. oil	1 (8 oz.) pkg. cream cheese,
1 (20 oz.) can crushed pineapple	softened
3 pkgs. instant coconut cream	Cool Whip
pudding	Coconut

Mix cake mix according to directions; add oil. Bake in two 9x13 inch pans. Bake at 350° for 15 minutes. Cool. Drain pineapple. Mix puddings with milk. Blend cream cheese and pineapple into pudding and pour on cakes. Top with Cool Whip. Sprinkle with coconut and place a cherry on each piece. Keep refrigerated or freeze.

Alice Lynch, Winona

HEAVENLY PIE

1 cup diced apples, tart	1 egg yolk
1 cup sugar	1 tsp. baking powder
3 heaping Tbsp. flour	1 egg white, beaten stiff
½ cup walnuts, chopped	

Combine all ingredients, except egg white; mix well. Fold in egg white and place in buttered pie tin. Bake at 350° until well done, 35 to 40 minutes. Will be lightly brown. Serve topped with whipped cream. (Should turn out crisp, yet chewy.)

Note: This recipe was originally devised by my husband for a bake off, but as it didn't use enough flour and shortening, was rejected. How things have changed. This is my husband's favorite pie and has been baked for him every Christmas holiday.

Phyllis Wirries, Moorhead

HOT FUDGE PUDDING

1½ cups Bisquick
½ cup sugar
½ to 1 cup chopped nuts
½ cup milk
½ cup brown sugar, packed
1½ cups boiling water
1 (6 oz.) pkg. semi-sweet pieces

Heat oven to 350°. Mix Bisquick, sugar, nuts and milk. Turn batter into greased 2 quart baking dish. Sprinkle with brown sugar. Pour water over chocolate pieces and let stand 1 or 2 minutes until chocolate melts, then stir until blended. Pour over batter. Bake 40 to 45 minutes. Let stand 5 minutes to cool slightly. During baking, the pudding will rise to the top of the dish and sauce will form at the bottom. Invert servings on plates and dip sauce over each serving. Serve with cream or ice cream. 6 to 8 servings.

Rita Yetzer, Medford

HOT FUDGE SAUCE

In double boiler, melt ½ cup butter and 4 squares unsweetened chocolate. Stir slowly, adding 3 cups sugar, 1 cup at a time until blended. Add ½ teaspoon salt. While stirring, slowly add 1 (13 oz.) can evaporated milk. Cook 8 to 10 minutes. Add 1 teaspoon vanilla. Store in refrigerator. Makes 1 quart.

Cecelia Raleigh, St. Paul

IRISH CREME

1 can Eagle Brand condensed milk
4 eggs
1 cup blended whiskey or brandy
1 Tbsp. chocolate syrup
½ tsp. instant coffee
¼ tsp. coconut extract
¼ tsp. almond extract
1 tsp. vanilla

Put all ingredients in blender and blend for 2 minutes. Put in bottle and store in refrigerator.

Rosemary Walz, Mahnomen
State Treasurer, 1996-present

QUICK LEMON DESSERT

Mix 1 lemon cake mix (yellow cake mix can be used) and bake as directed on package.

Frosting:

1 (20 oz.) can crushed pineapple with juice
1 (3 oz.) box instant lemon pudding mix

Mix pineapple and juice with the pudding mix and top cake when cool. Serve with Cool Whip. Keeps well in refrigerator.

Evelyn Feit, Luverne

LEMON ANGEL DESSERT

5 egg yolks
1½ cups white sugar
⅓ cup lemon juice
½ cup butter or margarine
1 lemon rind, grated

5 egg whites
½ pt. cream, whipped
1 sm. size Angel Food cake (loaf
style or ½ of round)
Nuts

Beat egg yolks until yellow. Add 1 cup sugar and lemon juice. Add butter and rind and cook over very low heat until thick. Cool. Beat egg whites. Add ½ cup sugar, then whipped cream. Combine this with cooled, boiled mixture. Break half of the cake in small pieces in a 9x13 inch pan. Pour half of the lemon mixture over cake pieces and repeat cake and mixture again. Sprinkle with nuts and freeze.

Bernice Boedigheimer, Perham

LEMON BISQUE

24 graham crackers
⅓ cup sugar

8 Tbsp. butter

Roll out graham crackers; mix in sugar and blend in butter. Use half of crumbs on top and half on bottom of an 8x8 inch pan.
Filling:

1½ cups whipping cream
1 sm. can Borden's Eagle Brand
milk

Juice of 3 lemons
Rind of ½ lemon

Whip cream; add milk, lemon juice and rind. Mix by hand well. Pour over crumbs and sprinkle crumbs on top and refrigerate for several hours before serving. Green coloring may be added to filling mixture. This is a good light dessert.

Elsie M. Bateman, Detroit Lakes

LEMON DELIGHT

1 box lemon jello
¾ cup hot water
4 egg yolks
1 cup sugar
Juice of 1 lemon

Rind of 1 orange
4 egg whites
½ pt. cream
½ lb. vanilla wafers

Dissolve jello in hot water. Cool. Combine egg yolks, ½ cup sugar, lemon juice and rind. Cook in double boiler until thick. Cool. When jello begins to thicken, add egg mixture. Beat egg whites until stiff; add ½ cup sugar. Add to above mixture. Whip cream and fold into above mixture. Crush wafers. Put half in bottom of a 9x13 inch pan. Pour in mixture and top with remaining crumbs. Refrigerate.

Edna Hanson, Blue Earth

LEMON TART

Crust:

1 cup flour   ½ cup chopped nuts
½ cup margarine

Combine ingredients and put in bottom of lightly greased 9x13 inch pan. Bake 20 minutes or until lightly browned. Cool.

Topping:

1 (8 oz.) pkg. Philadelphia   1 cup powdered sugar
cream cheese   1 cup Cool Whip

Mix cream cheese with powdered sugar and blend in Cool Whip with mixer. Spread on cooled crust. Top with **lemon pudding** and serve with whipped cream.

Corine Deeny, Waterville

MAULTUSCHEN

5 cups flour   8 baking apples, peeled, cored
1½ tsp. salt   and thinly sliced
1½ cups shortening   4 Tbsp. sugar
¾ cup ice cold water   Cinnamon

Sift flour and salt. Cut in shortening; add water, half at a time. Mix and press with a fork or fingers. Press together, making 4 balls. Chill. Roll out each pastry ball, one at a time, to a large thin round. Spread apples over pastry. Sprinkle one tablespoon sugar over apples and cinnamon to taste. Carefully roll and seal ends with cold water. Fit 4 rolls snuggly in a 9x13 inch pan. Bake at 375° for 30 minutes.

Custard:

4 eggs, slightly beaten   3 cups milk, scalded
⅓ cup sugar   Dash of nutmeg
½ tsp. salt

Beat eggs, sugar and salt. Slowly add scalded milk and vanilla. Continue to beat. Add nutmeg. Pour over hot apple rolls, making certain tops are moist. Bake at 325° for 30 minutes. Cool 20 minutes before serving. Serve 1 inch slices with cheese for a meal. Keeps for several days in refrigerator. Also good cold. Serves 10.

Peggy McConnell, Crookston

* * * * * * * *

One who sows sparingly will reap sparingly, and one who sows bountifully will reap bountifully. I Corinthians 9:6
Vicki Boeckman, Blue Earth

MEXICAN FRUIT CAKE

1 (20 oz.) can crushed pine- apple, undrained	1 cup sugar 2 eggs, beaten
2 tsp. baking powder	1 cup chopped pecans
2 cups flour	1 cup coconut

Pour pineapple into bowl. Add all other ingredients. Bake in a 9x13 inch pan at 350° for 30 to 35 minutes.

Frosting:

¾ box powdered sugar (3 cups)	½ stick butter, softened
1 (8 oz.) pkg. cream cheese	2 tsp. vanilla

Beat ingredients and pour over cooled cake. Sprinkle more chopped pecans over top. Easy, good and keeps well.

Sue Forster, New Ulm

FRUIT PIZZA

1 roll Pillsbury sugar cookie dough	1 tsp. vanilla Fresh fruit
1 (8 oz.) pkg. cream cheese	½ cup apricot preserves
¼ cup powdered sugar	1 tsp. water

Pat dough on a pizza pan. Bake at 350° for 10 minutes. Cool. Mix the cream cheese, powdered sugar and vanilla. Spread on cooled crust. Slice fruit on cream cheese mixture (any fresh fruit you like can be used; strawberries, kiwi, grapes, peaches, etc). Mix the preserves and water. Brush on fruit. Chill.

Genevieve Lanoue, Marshall

FRUIT PIZZA

Crust:

½ cup powdered sugar	1½ cups flour
¾ cup margarine	Chopped nuts, optional

Mix ingredients and pat in a large pan. Bake at 350° for 10 to 15 minutes or until lightly browned on edges. Cool Crust.

Filling:

1 (8 oz.) pkg. cream cheese, softened	½ cup sugar 1 tsp. vanilla

Mix cream ingredients and spread over crust.

Glaze:

2 tsp. cornstarch	½ cup sugar
1 cup fruit juice, pineapple or orange	1 tsp. lemon juice

Heat ingredients. Remove from heat when thickened. Cool. Arrange **assorted fresh or canned fruit** (any fruit you wish) on cream cheese layer. Brush glaze over fruit to cover. Chill.

Dorothy Jones, St. Charles
Mary Jo Luhman, Goodhue
District Deputy, 1994-present

FRUIT PIZZA

1 Jiffy yellow cake mix	½ cup nuts
1 egg	1 (4½ oz.) carton Cool Whip
2 Tbsp. flour	1 (8 oz.) pkg. cream cheese
2 Tbsp. soft butter	1 (11 oz.) can mandarin oranges,
2 Tbsp. brown sugar	well drained

In a well greased and floured 12 inch round pizza pan, combine cake mix, egg, flour, soft butter, brown sugar and nuts. Press into pan with wax paper coming up to edge of pan. Blend Cool Whip with cream cheese. Put on cake when cooled. Get **fruit** (kiwi, sweet berries, grapes, bananas, and oranges) ready while cake is baking. Slice kiwi, clean and prepare fruit. Start edge of cake with mandarin oranges, placed sideways. Make second row of halves of green grapes. Row three bananas, etc. until cake is covered with fruit. Cover with sauce made from **1 medium to large orange,** squeezed to make ½ cup juice and **2 grated orange rinds**. Bring to boil and add **cornstarch** with **water** to thicken. Cool and drizzle over fruit. Set overnight.

Laura Pitha, New Ulm

HOT FUDGE SUNDAE TOPPING FOR MICROWAVE

½ cup sugar	Dash of salt
1½ Tbsp. cornstarch	½ cup water
2 Tbsp. cocoa	

Using a 1 quart microwave measuring pitcher, mix sugar, cornstarch, cocoa and salt well. Add water and stir. Microwave 1 minute. Stir and microwave 1 more minute. Stir and microwave another minute. Add **2 tablespoons margarine** and **1 teaspoon vanilla** when the consistency of hot fudge sauce. Great on ice cream. Enjoy.

Carol Rupp, Adrian

KEEBLER DESSERT

1 (3 oz.) box vanilla instant pudding	2 sm. cans mandarin oranges
	1 (8 oz.) carton Cool Whip
1 cup buttermilk	1 pkg. Keebler Fudge Stripe
½ cup milk	cookies

Beat pudding, buttermilk and milk. Add mandarin oranges. Fold in Cool Whip. Crush cookies, reserving ¾ cup for top. Put the rest of cookie crumbs in a 7½x11½ inch pan. Place the mixed ingredients in pan on top of crumbs. Add the reserved crumbs on top of dessert. Chill.

LaVerne Scully, Slayton

DISAPPEARING MARSHMALLOW BROWNIES

1 (12 oz.) pkg. butterscotch chips 4 tsp. baking powder
1 cup butter   4 eggs
2 tsp. vanilla   3 cups flour
1⅓ cups brown sugar

Melt chips and butter; cool. Add remaining ingredients. Fold in **1 (12 oz.) package chocolate chips** and **40 miniature marshmallows**. Spread in a greased cookie sheet. Bake at 350° for 20 to 25 minutes.

Sue Carpenter, Caledonia

MARSHMALLOW-MINT DESSERT

1 pt. whipping cream   1 (16 oz.) can pineapple tidbits,
¼ cup sugar   drained
¾ pkg. colored marshmallows   2 cups vanilla wafers, crushed
1 pkg. sm. colored after-dinner ¾ Tbsp. butter, melted
  mints

Whip cream and sweeten with sugar; add; colored marshmallows, mints and pineapple. Mix wafer crumbs and melted butter. Line an 8x10 inch pan with ¾ of crumb mixture. Top with marshmallow mixture. Top with remaining crumbs and chill for 24 hours.

Monica Galvin, Currie

MOON CAKE

1 cup water   2 (3 oz.) pkgs. vanilla instant
½ cup margarine   pudding
1 cup flour   1 (8 oz.) carton Cool Whip
4 eggs   Chocolate syrup
1 (8 oz.) pkg. cream cheese   Chopped nuts
3½ cups milk

Bring water and margarine to a boil. Add flour, all at once. Stir until mixture forms a ball. Remove from heat. Cool a few minutes and add eggs one at a time, beating each time with a spoon. Spread into ungreased 11x15 inch jelly roll pan. Bake at 400° for 30 minutes. Do not open oven during baking time. Do not prick bubbles. Blend cream cheese and milk; mix in dry instant pudding. Spread on crust and cool in refrigerator for 20 minutes. Frost with Cool Whip. Drizzle with chocolate syrup and sprinkle with nuts. Very yummy!

Kathy Steiner, St. Peter
Dorothy Diekmann, Owatonna

MANDARIN ORANGE DESSERT

3 egg whites
¼ tsp. cream of tartar
1 cup sugar
1 cup chopped nuts
1 cup crushed Rice Krispies
1 pt. whipping cream
⅓ cup powdered sugar
1 pkg. instant vanilla pudding
¾ cup coconut
2 sm. can mandarin oranges, drained

Beat egg whites and cream of tartar. Gradually add sugar and beat until stiff. Add nuts and Rice Krispies. Spread into a 9x13 inch greased pan. Bake at 350° for 25 minutes; cool. Whip cream and add powdered sugar and pudding; mix well. Add coconut and oranges. Spread over cooled crust. Refrigerate for 12 hours before serving.

Florence Klonecki, Winona

NORWEGIAN TART APPLE ALMOND CAKE

6 apples
1 cup butter
1 cup sugar
1 cup flour
1 cup slivered almonds

Peel apples; cut in half and slice. Layer them in a deep oiled 9x13 inch pan. Cream butter until fluffy; add sugar, then flour. Combine well, then add almonds and pour over apples in pan. Bake at 325° for 35 minutes. Serve warm with heavy cream or ice cream.

Josephine Boland, Winona

TANGY ORANGE DESSERT

1 can sweetened condensed milk
1 (16 oz.) carton Cool Whip
1 (6 oz.) can orange juice, undiluted
2 cans mandarin oranges, drained

Stir sweetened condensed milk vigorously until it thins out somewhat, then stir in or fold in the Cool Whip. Mix in the undiluted, thawed condensed orange juice by hand until blended. Fold in the drained orange segments. Spoon mixture into crumb-lined pan, sprinkle with crumb mixture over the top. Refrigerate until firm and until ready to serve. Cut into squares. (This also freezes well.)

Crumb Base:
60 Ritz crackers, crushed
½ cup sugar
½ cup butter

Blend ingredients. Divide, using about ⅔ of mixture for bottom crust in a 9x12 inch pan. Sprinkle remaining over filling.

Pernilla Ernster, Caledonia

ORANGE TAPIOCA

2¾ cups water
1 pkg. orange gelatin
2 pkgs. vanilla tapioca pudding mix
1 (8 oz.) carton Cool Whip
1 can mandarin oranges, optional

Mix water, gelatin, and tapioca and cook for 4 to 5 minutes. Let cool. Beat mixture and Cool Whip with hand mixer. Add drained mandarin oranges if desired.

Mary Pytleski, Fairmont

FRESH PEACH COBBLER

½ cup butter
1 cup flour
2 tsp. baking powder
1½ cups sugar
¾ cup milk
4 to 5 lg. peaches
½ cup water

Melt butter in baking dish. Mix flour, baking powder, 1 cup sugar and milk; pour into baking dish. Peel and slice peaches and arrange over batter. Sprinkle remaining ½ cup sugar over peaches and then pour water on. Bake in preheated 350° oven for 50 minutes.

Marie Deschene, Argyle

PEANUT BUTTER PARFAIT DESSERT

Crush **1 package Oreo cookies**. Save ¼ cup for top. Top with **1 quart vanilla ice cream** (I used cookies and cream instead of vanilla). Top with **1 cup salted peanuts**. Top with **1 jar chocolate ice cream sauce**. Top with **1 carton Cool Whip**. Top with remaining ¼ cup crushed Oreo cookies. Freeze and enjoy!

Marcella Jeno, Owatonna

PEAR TART

1 tsp. salt
¾ cup sugar
1 tsp. baking powder
2 cubes butter
2 lg. cans pear halves

Mix dry ingredients. Cut in butter until blended. Press lightly in 2 large quiche pans. Bake at 325° for 15 minutes. Remove and place pear halves around pan in circle.

Topping:

1 cup sour cream
½ cup brown sugar
½ tsp. cinnamon
2 egg yolks
½ tsp. vanilla

Spoon topping over pears and bake at 325° for 30 minutes. Sprinkle almonds on top.

MayElla Demaster, Mahnomen

PECAN TASSIES

1 (3 oz.) pkg. cream cheese   **1 cup sifted flour**
½ cup butter

Cook cream cheese and butter at low temperature until soft. Stir in flour; chill. Shape into 24 (1 inch) balls. Place in ungreased small muffin tins. Shape into tart shells.

Filling:

1 egg   **1 tsp. vanilla**
½ cup brown sugar   **Dash of salt**
1 Tbsp. butter   **²/₃ cup pecans**

Combine egg, sugar, butter, vanilla and salt. Chop pecans fine. Place half of nuts into shells, then add egg mixture. Top with remaining nuts. Add 1 large pecan atop each pastry. Bake at 325° for 25 minutes.

Robina Raymond, International Falls

PINEAPPLE-OATMEAL DESSERT

Filling:

4 Tbsp. flour   **¼ cup lemon juice**
1 cup sugar   **3 Tbsp. butter**
1 (No. 2) can crushed pineapple   **¼ tsp. nutmeg**

Mix the flour and sugar in a saucepan. Stir in the pineapple, lemon juice, butter and nutmeg. Cook slowly, stirring constantly until thickened. Set the filling aside.

Crust:

¾ cup soft shortening (part butter)   **½ tsp. soda**
1 cup brown sugar   **1 tsp. salt**
1¾ cups flour   **1½ cups rolled oats**

Mix the shortening and brown sugar in mixing bowl. Add the flour, soda and salt. Add the rolled oats. Mix it in thoroughly, but lightly. Place half of the crumb mixture in a greased and floured 9x13 inch pan. Press lightly and flatten with hands to cover the bottom of pan. Spread with the pineapple mixture. Cover with the remaining crumb mixture, patting lightly. Bake until lightly brown at 400° for 25 to 30 minutes. Best served warm. Add ice cream to make it even better.

Shirley Ettestad, Ranier (International Falls)
State Regent, 1990-1994
State First Vice Regent, 1986-1990

PIEROGI (POLISH)

2 lbs. dry cottage cheese	Dash of nutmeg
4 eggs	Dash of cinnamon
¼ tsp. salt	Butter and bread crumbs
1 cup flour	

Force cheese through strainer. Mix all ingredients except butter and crumbs. Work with hand until smooth. Divide into four equal parts. On floured board, form into a roll about 1½ inch wide. Flatten slightly with knife and cut in bias or diamond shapes. Simmer in boiling salted water for about 5 minutes until they float to the top. Carefully lift out and serve with bread crumbs browned in butter. (Be careful not to burn the butter.) We like to pour a sauce made of **1 cup sour cream, 2 tablespoons sugar** and **½ teaspoon cinnamon**. Can also fill with fruit such as plums or prunes.

Kathy Dibble, Chicago

PLUM PUDDING

2 cups prunes	½ tsp. cinnamon
1 cup raisins	1 box jello (cherry or lemon)
2 cups grape nuts cereal	1 cup boiling water
¼ cup sugar	1 cup prune juice

Cook prunes and raisins until soft; remove seeds. Cool. Add grape nuts, sugar and cinnamon. In separate bowl, mix jello in hot water and prune juice, then mix fruit mixture and jello. Refrigerate until set. Top with whipped cream;

Ann Kulzer, Bejou

PINEAPPLE CAKE DESSERT

2 eggs	¼ tsp. salt
1¼ cups sugar	1 (20 oz.) can crushed
2 cups flour	pineapple
1 tsp. baking soda	

Mix eggs and sugar well. Add flour, baking soda and salt and mix well. Add pineapple; blend well on a very slow speed. Put in a 9x13 inch greased pan.

Topping:

½ cup brown sugar	½ cup nuts

Mix and sprinkle on top of cake. Bake at 350° for 35 to 45 minutes or until done. Melt **1 stick oleo** (½ cup). Add **1 (8½ oz.) package sweetened condensed milk** and **1 teaspoon vanilla**. Prick warm cake all over with fork. Pour above mixture over warm cake. Serve either hot or cold, plain, with ice cream or whipped topping.

Dorothy Osborne, New Ulm

PINEAPPLE SLICE

Crust:

2½ cups graham cracker crumbs   ½ cup margarine

Mix graham cracker crumbs with soft or melted margarine; pat evenly in a greased 8x11 inch pan. Bake at 350° for 10 minutes.

Filling:

½ cup soft margarine   1 (20 oz.) can crushed pine-
1½ cups icing or powdered sugar   apple, well drained
1 unbeaten egg

Mix margarine, powdered sugar and unbeaten egg well and spread evenly over cooled crust. Spread very well drained pineapple over filling, then top with ½ **pint whipping cream** (whipped) or **1 (8 oz.) carton Cool Whip**. Refrigerate. (4 layers.) Cut in squares and serve as a dessert, delicious.

Lea Raymond, International Falls

POPCORN CAKE

½ cup margarine   1 cup M&M's chocolate candies
1 bag lg. marshmallows   1 cup peanuts
4 qts. popped popcorn   1 cup gum drops, optional

Melt margarine and marshmallows in large saucepan. Remove from heat and stir in popped popcorn until coated. After mixture has cooled slightly, mix in M&M's, peanuts and gum drops. Press mixture firmly in tube pan and cool overnight. Turn out and slice.

Variation: With 5 quarts popcorn, add ½ cup oil to the above.

Carolyn Begich, Eveleth
Rose Moran, Crookston

PRETZEL DESSERT

1 cup chopped pretzels   1 (8 oz.) carton Cool Whip
1 stick oleo, melted   1 (16 oz.) can crushed
1¼ cups sugar   pineapple
1 (8 oz.) pkg. cream cheese,   2 Tbsp. cornstarch
softened

Mix pretzels, oleo and ½ cup sugar. Press into an 8x8 inch pan and chill. Mix cream cheese, Cool Whip and ½ cup sugar. Spread over chilled crust. Drain pineapple and save juice. Cook juice, ¼ cup sugar and cornstarch until thickened. Mix in pineapple and spread over filling. Chill well before serving.

Margaret Jeffrey, Winona

POPPY SEED DESSERT

1 cup graham cracker crumbs ½ cup nutmeats, chopped fine
1 cup flour ½ cup melted butter or oleo

Combine crumbs, flour, nuts and butter and press into a 9x13 inch pan. Bake at 325° until lightly browned. Cool. Soak 1½ **tablespoons plain gelatin** in ¼ **cup water.**

Filling:

¼ cup poppy seed 5 egg yolks (reserve whites)
1 cup sugar 2 Tbsp. cornstarch
1½ cups milk ½ tsp. salt

Mix and cook in a double boiler until thickened. Add **1 teaspoon vanilla** and the gelatin mixture to above. Stir and cool.

5 egg whites ½ cup sugar
½ tsp. cream of tartar 1 (8 oz.) carton Cool Whip

Beat egg whites until frothy; add cream of tartar and sugar gradually and beat until stiff. Fold in cooled filling and spread on top of crust. Let set ½ hour or more, then top with Cool Whip and refrigerate until served. ENJOY!

Genevieve Molling, Caledonia

PRUNE DUMPLINGS (Svestkové Knedlíky)
A Czech recipe

2 eggs, slightly beaten 1 tsp. salt
½ cup milk 24 prunes, pitted and cooked
2 to 2½ cups flour, unsifted

Mix all ingredients, except prunes, well. If necessary, mix in a little more flour so dough will not be sticky when handled. Take a teaspoon of dough (about the size of a walnut) and pat into a circle on a floured board. Make large enough to cover one prune, pinching dough tightly around prune. Cook in boiling salted water about 15 minutes. Take one out and cut in half to see if done, if not, cook about 5 minutes longer. To serve, cut dumplings and pour on hot melted butter and sprinkle with cinnamon and sugar. Makes about 2 dozen. Recipe may be cut in half. These are good served with ham or fried chicken and a tossed salad. These can be made with frozen prunes. Wrap dough around fruit while still frozen. Cooking time should be extended 5 to 10 minutes more.

Patricia Deml, Owatonna

* * * * * * * *

A thing of beauty is a joy forever...John Keats
Catherine Mino, Blue Earth

PUDDING N' FRUITS

1 (4 oz.) pkg. vanilla pudding	2 sm. cans mandarin oranges,
1 (8 oz.) carton sour cream	drained
½ cup milk	2 apples, cut up
1 can pineapple chunks, drained	3 bananas, cut up

Blend the first 3 ingredients. Mix pudding and fruit and spoon into dessert dishes. Makes about 8 to 10 servings.

Alma Gagner, Red Lake Falls

PUDDING DESSERT

¼ cup brown sugar	1 cup flour
1 cup coconut	½ cup margarine

Mix and brown in a 375° oven, stirring often to get crisp. After it is brown and crisp, spread ¾ of mixture in bottom of 9x13 inch cake pan. Add **1 large package prepared pudding**; cool, then whip **½ pint of cream** and spread on top. Chill, sprinkle remaining coconut mixture on top and return to refrigerator.

Pauline Bennett, Marshall

PUDDING CAKE DESSERT

Bake **1 package Jiffy yellow cake mix** in a 9x13 inch pan and cool. Beat **1 (8 oz.) package cream cheese, 1 large package instant vanilla pudding** and **2 cups milk** (mixture will be thick). Put over cake. Drain **1 large can pineapple** and spread over pudding mixture. Cover with **Cool Whip**, sprinkle with **toasted coconut** and refrigerate.

Elnora Winter, Mahnomen

PUMPKIN DESSERT

1 (16 oz.) can pumpkin	1 tsp. cinnamon
1 (12 oz.) can evaporated milk	½ tsp. cloves
3 eggs	1 white or yellow cake mix
½ tsp. salt	½ cup chopped walnuts
1 tsp. vanilla	1 cup butter
½ tsp. ginger	

Combine the first 8 ingredients and mix well. Pour into a 9x13 inch cake pan, then sprinkle dry cake mix over top of mixture. Sprinkle walnuts over that. Melt butter and drizzle over all. Bake at 350° for 50 minutes or until golden brown. Serve with whipped cream.

Variation: Jeanette substitutes 4 teaspoons pumpkin spice for those listed and/or use 1 cup chopped pecans.

Irene Neisen, Mahnomen
Jeanette Schad, Plainview

PUMPKIN DESSERT

24 graham crackers, crushed

1/3 cup sugar

1/2 cup margarine

1/8 tsp. butter flavoring

2 eggs

1/2 cup sugar

1 (8 oz.) pkg. cream cheese, softened

2 cups pumpkin

1/2 cup sugar

1 tsp. cinnamon

1/2 tsp. salt

3 egg yolks

1/2 cup milk or half and half

1 tsp. vanilla

1/2 tsp. burnt sugar flavoring

1 env. plain gelatin

1/4 cup cold water

3 egg whites

1/4 cup sugar

1 carton whipped topping

Mix graham cracker crumbs, 1/3 cup sugar, margarine and butter flavoring and press into a 9x13 inch pan. Beat 2 eggs, sugar and cream cheese and add onto the crust. Bake at 350° for 20 minutes. Let cool. Cook pumpkin, sugar, cinnamon, salt, 3 egg yolks, 1/2 cup milk, vanilla and burnt sugar flavoring. Keep cooking until thickened. Add gelatin which has been dissolved in cold water. Take from heat and cool. Add 3 egg whites with 1/4 cup sugar and add to the cooled pumpkin mixture. Put this pumpkin mixture onto the crust and cover with whipped topping. Chill for a while before serving.

Margaret Slinger, Slayton

PUMPKIN PIE DESSERT

1 pkg. yellow cake mix without pudding

1/2 cup butter

1 egg

Save 1 cup dry cake mix for the topping. Mix rest of ingredients and put in well greased 9x13 inch pan.

Filling:

2/3 cup milk

1 (1 lb.) can pumpkin or 3 cups

2 eggs

1 tsp. vanilla

1/2 tsp. ginger

1/8 tsp. cloves

3/4 cup white sugar or 1/2 cup brown sugar

1/2 tsp. salt

1 tsp. cinnamon

Mix all and pour over crust.

Topping:

1 cup dry yellow cake mix

1/4 cup white sugar

1 tsp. cinnamon

1/2 cup butter or margarine, softened

Mix all ingredients and crumble over the pumpkin mixture. Bake at 350° for 45 minutes or until done. When serving, top with Cool Whip or ice cream.

Jean Demmer, Caledonia

PUMPKIN TORTE

1st Layer:
24 graham crackers, crushed   ½ cup oleo or butter
½ cup sugar

Mix ingredients and pat lightly into a 9x13 inch pan.

2nd Layer:
2 eggs   1 (8 oz.) pkg. cream cheese
¾ cup sugar

Beat eggs, sugar and cream cheese. Pour over crust and bake at 350° for 20 minutes. Cool.

3rd Layer:
1 (1 lb.) can pumpkin   1 tsp. cinnamon
¾ cup sugar   1 env. gelatin
½ tsp. salt   1 cup cold water
3 eggs, separated   Cool Whip or whipped cream
½ cup milk

In a saucepan, mix pumpkin, ½ cup sugar, salt, egg yolks, milk and cinnamon. Cook until thick. Remove from heat. Dissolve gelatin in cold water. Add to cooked mixture. Cool mixture well. Beat the egg whites with ¼ cup sugar. Fold in cooled pumpkin mixture. Pour over the baked and cooled crust. Serve with whipped cream or Cool Whip.

Agnes Prairie, Russell

PUNCH BOWL CAKE

1 pineapple or lemon cake mix   5 or 6 bananas, sliced
2 sm. boxes instant vanilla   1 lg. carton Cool Whip
  pudding   A few maraschino cherries
2 cans cherry pie filling   1 cup chopped nutmeats
2 cans crushed pineapple,
  drained

Fix cake mix and pudding mixes (separately) according to their package directions. Using a very large bowl (this will fill a punch bowl), crumble half of the baked cake into the bottom of the bowl. Mix 1 box of pudding and pour over the cake in the bowl. Cover with 1 can of pie filling, 1 can of pineapple and half of sliced bananas. Spread with half of the Cool Whip. Repeat layers of cake, pudding, pie filling, pineapple, bananas and Cool Whip. Top with cut up cherries and sprinkle nutmeats over. This makes a pretty dessert and is excellent for a large crowd. It can be made early in the day and served in the evening.

Lorraine Halbersma, Pipestone

RASPBERRY DESSERT

1 cup raspberry juice with cold water if needed to make 1 cup
1 (3½ oz.) pkg. raspberry jello (sugar free may be used)
½ cup cold water
1 pt. whipping cream, whipped and sweetened
1 Angel Food cake
2 (10 oz.) boxes frozen raspberries, drained (save juice)

Heat 1 cup juice and water mixture; dissolve jello in it. Add cold water. Chill until jiggly stage. Fold in whipped cream. Break cake into small pieces. Add raspberries to cream mixture. Layer the cake pieces and whipped mixture in a 9x13 inch pan. Chill. Keep in the refrigerator.

Jane Hill, St. Peter

RASPBERRY AND CREAM CHEESE STRIPS

1 (3 oz.) pkg. cream cheese
4 Tbsp. butter or margarine
2 cups biscuit mix (Bisquick)
¹/₃ cup milk
½ cup raspberry preserves
1 cup sifted powdered sugar
1 to 2 Tbsp. milk
½ tsp. vanilla

Cut cream cheese and butter or margarine into biscuit mix until crumbly. Blend in the ¹/₃ cup milk. Turn dough onto floured surface; knead 8 to 10 strokes. On waxed paper, roll dough to a 12x8 inch rectangle. Turn onto greased baking sheet; remove paper. Spread raspberry preserves down center ¹/₃ of dough. Make 2½ inch cuts at 1 inch intervals on long sides. Fold strips over filling. Bake at 425° for 12 to 15 minutes. Combine powdered sugar, remaining milk and vanilla; drizzle on top baked strips. Makes 12 joined strips.

Angeline Bonach, Eveleth

RASPBERRY LAYERED DESSERT

1½ cups crushed pretzels
¾ cup melted butter
2 Tbsp. sugar
1 (8 oz.) pkg. cream cheese
1 cup sugar
1 (9 oz.) carton Cool Whip
2 (3 oz.) pkgs. raspberry jello
2 cups hot water
2 (10 oz.) pkgs. frozen raspberries

Mix pretzels, melted butter and sugar. Put in a 9x13 inch pan. Bake at 350° for 10 minutes. Blend cream cheese and sugar. Fold in Cool Whip. Place on top of pretzel crust. Cool. Dissolve jello in hot water. Add partially frozen raspberries. Mix and put on cooled cream cheese mixture. Let stand. Serve with whipped cream. This is a pretty Christmas dessert.

Alana Kuznia, Argyle
Josie Pick, Slayton

RED-WHITE AND BLUEBERRY DESSERT

1½ cups flour
¾ cup brown sugar
¾ cup margarine
¾ cup walnuts, finely chopped
1 pt. fresh blueberries (2 cups)
1 (8 oz.) pkg. cream cheese

1 tsp. vanilla
1 (7 oz.) jar marshmallow creme
1 (8 oz.) carton Cool Whip
1½ pts. fresh raspberries or
strawberries (3 cups)

Mix flour and brown sugar; cut in margarine and add nuts. Press into a 15x10x1 inch pan. Bake at 325° for 10 to 15 minutes. Cool. Sprinkle blueberries over crust. Beat cream cheese and vanilla until fluffy. Add marshmallow creme and beat until combined. Fold in Cool Whip. Spread over blueberries. Refrigerate 1 hour. Sprinkle raspberries or strawberries over top of cheese mixture.

Glaze:

1¼ cups sugar
2 cups water

¼ cup cornstarch

Cook until thick. Remove from heat. Stir in **1 (3 oz.) package raspberry or strawberry jello**. Cook 20 to 30 minutes. Spoon over berries. Refrigerate 1 hour. Serves 25.

Eloise Kettner, Mahnomen

RHUBARB CHEESECAKE SQUARES

Crumb Base:
½ cup butter
1 cup flour
¾ cup oatmeal

½ cup brown sugar
¼ tsp. cinnamon

Blend all the ingredients for the crumb base until they form coarse crumbs. Pat half of crumbs into a greased 9x9 inch pan.

Filling:

1 (8 oz.) pkg. cream cheese,
room temperature
¾ cup sugar
1 egg

⅛ tsp. nutmeg
2 cups rhubarb, cut up
¼ tsp. cinnamon

Combine all ingredients except rhubarb, and blend until smooth. Gently stir in rhubarb. Spread filling over crust. Top with reserved crumbs. Bake at 350° for 40 to 45 minutes. Cool dessert and keep refrigerated.

Beverly Puterbaugh, St. Charles

RHUBARB COBBLER

4 to 5 cups rhubarb, chopped
1½ to 2 cups sugar
Cinnamon to taste
1 Tbsp. butter
1 cup flour
1 Tbsp. sugar
Pinch of salt
1 tsp. baking powder
¼ cup butter
¼ cup milk
1 egg, beaten

Put rhubarb in large casserole dish; mix sugar and cinnamon and put over rhubarb. Dot with butter. Sift dry ingredients; cut in butter, then add milk and egg, which have been mixed. Stir gently; put on top of rhubarb by spoonfuls (dough will be stiff). Bake at 375° for about 40 minutes. Cool, serve with ice cream or whipped cream.

Sylvia Diedrick, Crookston

AMAZING RHUBARB COBBLER

½ cup margarine
1 cup flour
½ cup sugar
2 tsp. baking powder
½ cup milk
3 cups rhubarb, cut up
1 cup sugar
1 cup hot water
Cinnamon and nutmeg to taste

Melt margarine in an 8 inch square pan. Make batter of flour, ½ cup sugar, baking powder and milk. Spoon batter over melted margarine. Place rhubarb which has been cut up fine, over the batter. Stir the 1 cup sugar into hot water until dissolved. Pour over the rhubarb and sprinkle with cinnamon and nutmeg to taste. Bake at 350° for 40 minutes. Makes 4 to 6 servings.

Jeanette Bartelt, Janesville

RHUBARB CRISP

Crust:

1 cup flour
¾ cup oatmeal
1 cup brown sugar
½ cup melted margarine

Mix all ingredients and press half of mixture in a 9 inch square pan. Put **4 cups chopped rhubarb** on top.

Sauce:

1 cup sugar
¼ tsp. salt
2 Tbsp. cornstarch
1 cup water
1 tsp. vanilla

Combine ingredients in a saucepan and cook until thick. Pour the cooked sauce over rhubarb and sprinkle the remaining crumb mixture on top. Bake at 350° for 1 hour. Chill and cut into squares or serve warm with either ice cream or whipped cream.

Patricia Crummy, Argyle

RHUBARB CRUMBLE

3 to 4 cups rhubarb, cut up	1 cup flour
3 eggs, beaten	1½ cups brown sugar
1½ cups sugar	1 tsp. baking soda
2 Tbsp. flour	5 Tbsp. butter or margarine

Grease a 7½x11 inch pan. Put in rhubarb. Mix eggs, sugar and the 2 tablespoons flour. Pour over rhubarb. Crumble 1 cup flour, brown sugar, soda and butter. Sprinkle over top. Bake at 350° for 45 minutes. Serve with Cool Whip or ice cream.

Betty Ericson, International Falls

RHUBARB CRUMBLE

3 cups diced rhubarb	⅓ cup brown sugar
2 Tbsp. orange juice	⅔ cup sifted flour
¾ cup sugar	⅛ tsp. salt
¼ tsp. cinnamon	¼ tsp. soda
1 Tbsp. butter	⅔ cup quick oats
¼ cup melted shortening	

Arrange rhubarb in an 8x8 inch greased pan. Sprinkle with orange juice, sugar and cinnamon. Dot with butter. Combine melted shortening and brown sugar. Sift flour, salt and soda. Mix with oats. Blend with brown sugar mixture and spread over rhubarb. Bake at 375° for 40 minutes. Serve warm with whipping cream.

Annette Audette, Red Lake Falls

RHUBARB CRUNCH

1 cup flour	¼ cup flour
5 Tbsp. powdered sugar	¾ tsp. baking powder
½ cup butter or margarine	Dash of salt
2 eggs	2 cups rhubarb
1½ cups sugar	

Mix flour, powdered sugar and butter. Pat into bottom of an 8 or 9 inch pan. Bake at 350° for 15 minutes. Beat eggs until fluffy. Add sugar, flour, baking powder and salt. Stir and add rhubarb. Pour over crust. Bake at 350° for 35 minutes. Serve with whipped cream or ice cream.

Marge Breneman, Moorhead

EASY RHUBARB CRUNCH

4 cups frozen or fresh rhubarb
½ cup sugar
1 pkg. dry white, yellow or butter brickle cake mix
½ cup melted margarine
1 cup coconut
1 cup chopped nuts

Layer (do not mix) rhubarb, sugar and cake mix in a 9x13 inch pan. Pour margarine over cake. Sprinkle with coconut and chopped nuts. Bake at 350° for 1 hour.

Nancy Andert, Slayton

RHUBARB AND CHERRY DESSERT

Crust:
1 cup oatmeal
1 cup brown sugar
1 cup flour
½ cup soft butter
4 cups diced rhubarb

Mix all ingredients, except rhubarb and put half in bottom of a 9x13 inch pan. Put half of rhubarb on top of crust.

Cherry Mixture:
1 cup water
1 cup sugar
1 Tbsp. cornstarch
Dash of red food coloring
1 tsp. almond extract
1 can cherry pie filling
½ cup nuts, optional

Boil water, sugar and cornstarch until thick; add coloring, extract and pie filling. Pour mixture over crust. Add remaining rhubarb and sprinkle with rest of crust and the nuts. Bake at 350° for 45 minutes.

Dorothy Kratochwill, Waseca

RHUBARB DELIGHT (NO BAKE)

Graham crackers
3 Tbsp. cornstarch
½ cup water
4 cups rhubarb
1 cup sugar
1½ cups Cool Whip
1½ cups miniature marshmallows
1 pkg. instant vanilla pudding
2 cups milk

Crush graham crackers with rolling pin and cover bottom of a 9x13 inch pan for a lower crust. Save 1 cup crumbs for topping. Dissolve cornstarch in water; have ready to add to rhubarb and sugar which has been cooking; thicken. Cool. Combine Cool Whip and marshmallows and use as third layer (following crumbs and rhubarb). For fourth layer, prepare pudding as directed on package and spread on top. Sprinkle crumbs on pudding layer.

Martina Schweisthal, Medford

255

MICROWAVE RHUBARB DESSERT

4 cups rhubarb, cut up	1 cup flour
1 cup sugar	¾ cup rolled oats
¼ cup flour	1 cup brown sugar
½ tsp. cinnamon	½ cup margarine
½ cup water	

Combine the first 5 ingredients and put in an 8x8 inch glass dish. Cover with plastic wrap. Microwave 3 minutes on high. Mix the remaining 4 ingredients and sprinkle over rhubarb mixture. Microwave 8 minutes on high or until rhubarb is tender.

Mary Lou Petit, Plainview

RHUBARB DESSERT

4 to 5 cups rhubarb, cut up	2 to 3 cups miniature
1 cup sugar	marshmallows
1 (3 oz.) pkg. strawberry or	1 white or yellow cake mix
raspberry jello	

Put rhubarb in lightly greased 9x13 inch pan. Sprinkle the sugar over it, then the dry jello, then marshmallows. Prepare the cake mix according to package directions and pour the batter over the other ingredients. Bake for 45 minutes or until it tests done. Let cool completely. Cut and serve with the rhubarb layer up, topped with a spoonful of whipped topping or vanilla ice cream.

Lexie Mancina, Eveleth

RHUBARB DESSERT

Graham Cracker Crust:

1¼ cups graham crackers,	¼ cup sugar
crushed	6 Tbsp. melted butter

Mix graham cracker crumbs and sugar in a pan and pour melted butter over it. Press into pan for crust.

4 cups rhubarb	1 Tbsp. cornstarch
1 cup sugar	1 pkg. instant vanilla pudding
¼ cup water	

Cook rhubarb, sugar, water and cornstarch until thick; cool. Pour on crust. Mix pudding as directed on the package and cool until set.

Topping:

½ cup whipping cream or Cool   1¼ cups miniature marshmallows
Whip

Mix and pour over rhubarb sauce, then add pudding mix on top. Let set in refrigerator for about 2 hours.

Fran Timmers, St. Paul

RHUBARB DESSERT

1 box yellow cake mix
4 cups rhubarb
1 cup sugar
1 cup whipping cream

Mix cake as directed on package. Top cake batter with rhubarb and sprinkle sugar over it. Pour cream over this mixture. Bake at 350° for 35 to 40 minutes or until golden brown. Top with Cool Whip or ice cream. Simply grand tasting just plain and so simple to make.

Comments: The cake rises and the rhubarb, sugar and cream go down to form a pudding.

Helen Pagel, New Ulm
Fran Frodl, Owatonna
Everybody's Favorite Cookbook Chair

RHUBARB DESSERT

Crust:
2 cups flour
1 cup butter
3 Tbsp. sugar

Mix ingredients and put in a 9x13 inch pan. Bake 15 to 20 minutes. Cool.

First Filling:
7 cups rhubarb
1 cup water
2 cups sugar
6 Tbsp. cornstarch

Cook until thick like pudding, about 2 to 3 minutes. Cool, then pour onto cooled crust. Add a layer of Cool Whip.

Second Filling:
1 pkg. instant vanilla pudding
1¾ cups milk
1 (8 oz.) carton Cool Whip

Prepare the instant pudding. Put on top of Cool Whip layer. Add more Cool Whip. Serve.

Ottilia Winter, Iron

RHUBARB DESSERT

1 cup flour
5 Tbsp. powdered sugar
½ cup butter or margarine
4 eggs, well beaten
2½ cups sugar
½ cup flour
1½ tsp. baking powder
½ tsp. salt
4 cups rhubarb, sliced fine

Mix first 3 ingredients and pat in bottom of a 9x13 inch pan. Bake at 350° for 15 minutes. Mix rest of ingredients and pour over crust. Bake 35 minutes more. Cool and serve with whipped cream.

Anne Varner, Zumbrota

RHUBARB DESSERT

4 cups rhubarb, cut ¼ to ½ inch
    pieces
1½ cups sugar
1 cup flour

1 unbeaten egg
1 tsp. baking powder
½ tsp. salt
½ cup butter or margarine

In an oiled 9x13 inch pan, place rhubarb and ½ cup sugar. Mix flour, remaining sugar, egg, baking powder and salt. Melt butter and pour over flour mixture. Mix until moistened. Sprinkle flour over rhubarb. Bake at 350° for 35 minutes.

Anna Akemann, Waseca

RHUBARB DREAM DESSERT

1 cup flour
5 Tbsp. powdered sugar
½ cup butter or oleo, softened
2 beaten eggs

1½ cups sugar
¼ cup flour
½ tsp. salt
2 to 3 cups rhubarb, finely cut

Mix the first 3 ingredients and press into a 7x11 inch pan. Bake at 350° for 15 minutes. Watch closely. Blend eggs, sugar, flour and salt. Add rhubarb and blend. Spoon onto crust. Bake at 350° for 35 minutes. Chill. Serve with whipped cream. Can double recipe for a 9x13 inch pan.

Marie Hudson, North Mankato
State Secretary, 1976-1980
Genevieve Gardner, Caledonia

RHUBARB MERINGUE DESSERT

1 cup flour
2 Tbsp. sugar

½ cup butter or oleo
½ cup nuts

Mix and bake in a 9x13 inch pan at 350° for 15 minutes.

2½ cups diced rhubarb
3 egg yolks
2 Tbsp. flour
½ cup cream

1½ cups sugar
1 tsp. vanilla
Pinch of salt

Mix and place on top of crust and bake for 45 minutes.

3 egg whites
3 Tbsp. water

6 Tbsp. sugar

Beat until stiff. Put on top and bake 10 to 15 minutes.

Dolores Zammert, Euclid

RHUBARB DESSERT

2 cups flour
1 cup butter
2 Tbsp. sugar
1/8 tsp. salt
6 egg yolks
2 cups sugar
4 Tbsp. flour
1 cup cream
1 grated orange rind
5 cups rhubarb, cut up
6 egg whites
6 Tbsp. sugar
1 tsp. vanilla

Mix flour, butter, sugar and salt. Press into a 9x13 inch pan. Bake at 350° for 10 to 15 minutes or until lightly brown. Beat egg yolks, sugar, flour, cream and orange rind. Add rhubarb and spread over crust. Bake at 350° for 40 to 50 minutes or until set. Test with a knife like custard. Beat egg whites until stiff. Add sugar and vanilla. Spread over baked mixture and brown at 350° for about 10 minutes.

Edna Sullivan, Mahnomen

RHUBARB NUT DESSERT

4 cups chopped rhubarb
1 cup sugar
1 (3 oz.) box strawberry jello
1½ cups water
1 white cake mix
1 stick oleo or butter
1 cup nuts

Put rhubarb in a 9x13 inch pan. Sprinkle sugar and jello over rhubarb. Add water. Sprinkle dry cake mix over. Slice oleo or butter on top. Top with nuts. Bake at 350° for 45 minutes or until golden brown. Serve warm or cold with whipped cream.

Bernice Collins, Iona

RHUBARB PUDDING

4 to 6 cups rhubarb
1 to 1½ cups sugar
2 Tbsp. flour
2 Tbsp. butter or oleo
¼ tsp. salt
¼ tsp. cinnamon
1 Tbsp. lemon juice, optional

Mix rhubarb, sugar, flour and butter in a 4 quart casserole or similar pan.

Crust:

1½ cups flour
5 Tbsp. shortening
1 Tbsp. sugar
1/8 tsp. salt
1 tsp. baking powder
½ cup milk

Mix flour and shortening with sugar, salt and baking powder. Add milk. Dough will be sticky. Pat or roll dough to cover top of rhubarb mix. Bake at 350° for 30 to 45 minutes or until crust is brown and rhubarb is juicy.

Rosemary Kramer, Winona

RHUBARB PUDDING CAKE

4 to 5 cups sliced rhubarb	2 cups flour
1/3 cup sugar	2 tsp. baking powder
1 cup sugar	1 cup milk
1/2 cup soft butter	2 cups sugar
1 tsp. salt	2 Tbsp. cornstarch
1 tsp. vanilla	2 cups boiling water

Mix rhubarb with 1/3 cup sugar. Cream 1 cup sugar, butter, salt and vanilla. Sift flour and baking powder and add to creamed mixture, alternately with milk. Batter will be quite thick. Spread this batter over rhubarb. Mix 2 cups sugar and cornstarch. Sprinkle over top of batter, then pour boiling water over all. Bake at 325° for 45 minutes, then at 350° for 10 minutes or until it tests done and has a nice glazed brown top. Serve warm or cold with ice cream or Cool Whip.

Variation: This recipe is also excellent with apples or peaches. If you use these, add an extra 1/3 cup sugar in bottom of pan.

Lucille Taylor, Adrian
State Education Chairman and District Deputy, 1966-1970

RHUBARB-STRAWBERRY COFFEE CAKE

Filling:

3 cups rhubarb, chopped	1/3 cup cornstarch
1 (16 oz.) pkg. frozen strawberries	2 Tbsp. lemon juice
1 cup sugar	

Combine and cook fruit for 5 minutes. Mix sugar and cornstarch and stir in the remaining ingredients. Cook and stir until thick; cool.

Batter:

3 cups flour	1 cup butter
1 cup sugar	1 cup buttermilk
1 tsp. soda	2 eggs
1 tsp. salt	1 tsp. vanilla
1 tsp. baking powder	

Sift dry ingredients in bowl and cut in butter. Quickly stir in buttermilk, eggs and vanilla until moist. Spread half of batter in a 9x13 inch pan; add filling. Dot with remaining batter. Mix 1/2 **cup flour, 3/4 cup sugar, 1/4 cup butter** and 1/2 **teaspoon cinnamon** and sprinkle on top. Bake at 350° for 40 minutes.

Rita Plante, Crookston

RHUBARB ROYAL

1 cup flour
1 cup sugar
¼ tsp. salt
1 tsp. baking powder
¼ cup shortening

1 egg
4 cups rhubarb, cut up
1 cup strawberries, sliced
1 cup sugar
1 tsp. cinnamon

Mix dry first 5 ingredients like pie crust. Beat egg and add to dry mixture until moistened. Mix remaining ingredients. Sprinkle dry ingredients over rhubarb mixture and bake at 350° for 25 to 35 minutes or until brown.

Veronica Hoefer, Red Lake Falls

RHUBARB TAPIOCA DESSERT

¼ cup minute tapioca
1½ cups water
1½ cups sugar
½ tsp. salt, optional

2½ cups diced rhubarb
1 cup canned crushed pineapple with juice

Soak the tapioca in ¾ cup of the water for 5 minutes or until soft. Meanwhile, put the remaining water, sugar, salt (if desired), rhubarb and pineapple in a saucepan and bring to a full boil. Lower the heat until rhubarb is tender but not mushy. Add the tapioca, water mixture and return all to full boil, stirring constantly until tapioca is cooked and clear looking. Cool for 20 minutes; stir and use or it can be stored in the refrigerator for 1 week. Can be served with whipped cream or ice cream. Can also be used as filling for short cake and for topping.

Agnes Habeck, Delavan

RHUBARB TORTE

1 cup flour
Dash of salt
2 Tbsp. powdered sugar
½ cup butter
1¼ cups sugar
2 Tbsp. flour
⅓ cup cream

3 egg yolks
2¼ cups rhubarb, cut fine
3 egg whites
¼ tsp. salt
1 tsp. vanilla
6 Tbsp. sugar

Blend flour, salt, powdered sugar and butter until crumbly. Press into a 9x9 inch pan and bake at 325° for 20 to 25 minutes. Combine sugar, flour, cream and egg yolks in saucepan. Stir well. Add rhubarb. Cook until mixture is thick and rhubarb is tender. Pour over baked crust. Beat egg whites until frothy. Add salt and vanilla and gradually add the sugar. Beat until sugar is dissolved and very stiff. Pour meringue over rhubarb mixture. Brown in moderate oven. Chill before serving.

Bernadine Flynn, Windom

RHUBARB SWIRL

Crust:

1½ stick soft butter   4 Tbsp. brown sugar
2 cups flour

Combine ingredients and press into a 9x13 inch pan. Bake at 350° for 10 minutes; cool.

Filling:

¾ cup sugar   1 (3 oz.) pkg. instant vanilla
3 cups diced rhubarb   pudding
1 (3 oz.) pkg. red jello   1½ cups milk
     1 (8 oz.) carton Cool Whip

Pour sugar over rhubarb and let set for 1 hour. Simmer rhubarb-sugar mixture until tender, about 8 to 10 minutes. Add jello and set aside until syrupy. Mix pudding and milk; fold in Cool Whip and mix well. Pour syrupy rhubarb mixture into pudding mixture and swirl. Pour into cooled crust. Chill several hours or overnight. May use graham cracker crust if desired.

Leona Holland, Owatonna

RHUBARB TART

Crust:

2 cups flour   ½ cup shortening
½ cup butter   2 Tbsp. sugar

Mix ingredients and put into a 9x13 inch pan.

Filling:

6 egg yolks   ½ tsp. salt
2 cups sugar   1 cup cream
4 Tbsp. flour   5 cups rhubarb

Cream all ingredients, except rhubarb; add rhubarb and spread mixture over crust. Bake at 350° for 40 to 45 minutes.

Topping:

6 egg whites   2 tsp. vanilla
8 Tbsp. sugar   ½ cup flake coconut

Beat egg whites well. Add 2 tablespoons sugar at a time, beating after each addition. Beat it until it holds peaks. Add vanilla and put meringue on custard. Sprinkle with coconut and return to oven to brown lightly for about 10 minutes. Serve slightly warm.

Variation: Darlene adds ¼ teaspoon cream of tartar to meringue.

Gertrude Grubish, Waterville
Darlene McGuire, St. Charles

RHUBARB TORTE

1 cup flour	3 Tbsp. flour
2 Tbsp. sugar	½ cup milk
½ cup margarine	3 egg yolks
¼ tsp. salt	3 cups cut rhubarb
1¼ cups sugar	

Mix first 4 ingredients as you would for pie crust. Pat into a 9 inch square pan. Bake at 325° for 20 minutes. While this is baking, mix in a 2 quart saucepan the rest of the ingredients. Cook over medium heat until thick, stirring constantly. Put this mixture over the baked crust.

Meringue:

3 egg whites	¼ cup sugar

Mix and pour over filling. Bake until lightly brown.

Kay Cox, Adrian
District Deputy, 6 years
State Legislature Chairman, 6 years

RICE PUDDING

½ gal. whole milk	1 tsp. vanilla
1½ cups regular rice	5 egg whites
5 egg yolks, beaten	¼ tsp. cream of tartar
¾ cup sugar	½ cup sugar
¼ tsp. salt	

Cook milk and rice over low heat or in double boiler until most of milk is gone, about 1 hour or so. To the beaten egg yolks, add ¾ cup sugar, salt and vanilla. Add some rice mixture to eggs, then add mixture to the rice and cook a couple of minutes, until thickened. Pour into a 9x13 inch glass pan. Sprinkle with cinnamon. Beat egg whites until stiff with the cream of tartar. Gradually add sugar and continue beating until all mixed. Put meringue over the rice and bake at 375° for 10 minutes. Delicious. I like to serve this with main meal rather than dessert. Also an excellent pot luck dish.

Joan Parries, Moorhead

DESSERTS, PIES & PASTRIES

* * * * * * * *

Confucious say: "Man afraid of a new idea is a coward".
Dorthea Hadlick, Blue Earth

RICE PUDDING

2 cups water	1 cup sugar
Pinch of salt	6 eggs
1 cup long grain rice	1 Tbsp. vanilla
8 cups milk	Raisins, optional
1 stick butter	

Bring water and salt to a boil in a large pot. Add rice and boil for about 7 minutes, covered. There should be a little water left. Add milk and butter and bring to a boil again. Turn heat to a low setting and continue cooking for 1 hour, covered. While rice-milk is cooking, beat sugar, eggs and vanilla. Add raisins if desired. Let set until rice is done. Add egg mixture to rice. Stir well. Top with cinnamon.

Angeline DeWitte, Holland

RICE PUDDING

1 cup milk	1 tsp. salt
1½ cups sugar	1 Tbsp. cooking oil
4 cups water	1 cup raisins
2 cups uncooked rice	

Combine milk and sugar; set aside. Combine water, rice, salt and oil in Dutch oven or large saucepan. Bring to a full rolling boil, stirring once or twice. Cover and turn heat down to a simmer. Simmer for 10 minutes. Add milk mixture and raisins to rice. Cover for 5 or more minutes until the raisins soften, absorbing milk. Sprinkle cinnamon on top of each serving.

Lori Mickelson, Waseca

THE NEXT BEST THING TO ROBERT REDFORD

First Layer:

1 cup flour	½ cup chopped nuts
½ cup oleo	

Mix and spread in a 9x13 inch pan. Bake at 350° for 10 minutes.

Second Layer:

½ (8 oz.) carton Cool Whip	1 (8 oz.) pkg. Philadelphia
1 cup powdered sugar	cream cheese

Beat and put on top of baked crust.

Third Layer:

1 lg. box instant chocolate pudding	3 cups milk

Beat and put on second layer. Cover with other ½ **carton Cool Whip**. May put chopped nuts, toasted coconut or slivered chocolate candy bar on top.

Alice Hoehn, Waseca

SHERBERT DESSERT

50 vanilla wafers
½ cup margarine

1 lg. carton whipped topping
3 different colors of sherbet

Crush vanilla wafers and mix with margarine. Press into a 9x13 inch pan, saving ¾ cup for topping. Cool the crust. Spread thin layer of whipped topping over the cooled crust, then put small scoops of different colors of sherbet over the topping. When you have sherbet over whole pan, cover with more topping to filling between and make a thin layer over top. Sprinkle rest of crumbs over top and freeze. Cut in squares to serve.

Mary Ann Janous, Owatonna

SKOR CAKE

1 Duncan Heinz Moist Deluxe yellow cake mix without pudding
2 eggs

1 (6 oz.) box chocolate instant pudding
2 cups water

Beat ingredients with electric beater. Pour into a greased 9x13 inch pan. Bake at 350° for 35 to 40 minutes. Cool.

Topping:
½ cup butter or margarine
2 egg yolks
1 cup powdered sugar

1 (8 oz.) carton whipped topping
3 lg. Skor or Heath bars

Melt butter and cool. Add egg yolks and powdered sugar. Fold in whipped topping. Pour over baked cake. Crush Skor or Heath bars and sprinkle on top of cake. Store in refrigerator.

Leonette Koeplin, Moorhead

SOUR CREAM COFFEE CAKE

⅓ cup packed brown sugar
¼ cup sugar

2 tsp. cinnamon
½ cup chopped pecans

Combine topping ingredients; set aside.

Cake:
½ cup butter or margarine, softened
1 cup sugar
2 eggs
1 (8 oz.) carton sour cream

1 tsp. vanilla
2 cups flour
1 tsp. baking powder
1 tsp. baking soda
¼ tsp. salt

Cream butter and sugar in a bowl. Add eggs, sour cream and vanilla; mix well. Combine flour, baking powder, baking soda and salt. Add to the creamed mixture; beat until combined. Pour half of the batter into a greased 9x13 inch pan. Sprinkle with half the topping. Add remaining batter and topping. Bake at 325° for 40 minutes or until cake tests done. Yield: 12 to 15 servings.

Mary Vuk, Eveleth

DESSERTS, PIES & PASTRIES

SIMPLE DESSERT

1 cup Bisquick 1 egg
¾ cup sugar 1 can pie filling

Mix the Bisquick, sugar and egg. In bottom of an 8x8 inch pan, put pie filling and then pour mixture over. Melt **1 stick margarine** and drizzle over the above. Bake at 350° for 45 minutes.

Mary Ann Simon, Mahnomen

STRAWBERRY CHEESE CAKE

Crust:

¾ cup ground pecans 3 Tbsp. butter or margarine,
¾ cup graham cracker crumbs melted

Combine and press into the bottom of a 10 inch spring form pan; set aside.

Filling:

4 (8 oz.) pkgs. cream cheese, 1¼ cups sugar
softened 1 Tbsp. fresh lemon juice
4 eggs 2 tsp. vanilla extract

Beat the cream cheese in a mixing bowl until smooth. Add eggs, sugar, lemon juice and vanilla; mix thoroughly. Spoon over crust. Bake at 350° for about 50 minutes or until the filling is almost set. Remove from oven and let stand 15 minutes, but leave oven on.

Topping:

2 cups (16 oz.) sour cream 1 tsp. vanilla extract
¼ cup sugar

Combine ingredients and spread over cake; return to oven for 5 minutes. Cool to room temperature. Refrigerate 24 hours. Several hours before serving, prepare glaze.

Strawberry Glaze:

¼ cup water 3 Tbsp. lemon juice
2 Tbsp. cornstarch 1 qt. whole fresh strawberries,
1 jar strawberry jelly hulled
Red food coloring, optional

In a saucepan, combine water and cornstarch; add jelly and cook over medium-high heat, stirring constantly until jelly melts and mixture thickens. Remove from the heat; stir in food coloring if desired and lemon juice. Cool to room temperature. Just before serving, loosen and remove sides of pan. Arrange berries on top, points up. Spoon glaze over berries, allowing some to drip down sides of cake. Yield: 12 servings.

Diane Gauthier, Eveleth

STRAWBERRY DELIGHT

Crust:

½ cup margarine ⟶ 1 cup flour
¼ cup brown sugar ⟶ ½ cup chopped nuts

Mix lightly and put all in a 9x13 inch pan. Bake at 400°. Stir occasionally until golden brown. Press half of mixture in bottom of pan and reserve other half for spreading over top.

Filling:

2 cups sliced strawberries ⟶ 1 cup sugar
or 1 (10 oz.) pkg. frozen ⟶ 1 Tbsp. lemon juice
strawberries, thawed ⟶ 1 tsp. vanilla
2 egg whites ⟶ ½ pt. whipping cream, whipped

Beat strawberries, egg whites, sugar, juice and vanilla for 20 minutes. Fold whipped cream. Pour on crust. Top with reserved crumbs. Freeze overnight.

Variation: Florence suggests that if using frozen berries, use only ⅔ cup sugar, 2 tablespoons lemon juice and 1 cup whipping cream.

Carol Balster, Wilmont
Agnes M. Cawley, Waseca
Florence Magner, Waseca

FROZEN STRAWBERRY DESSERT

1 bite size box Keebler pecan ⟶ 1 Tbsp. lemon juice
sandies ⟶ 1 (10 or 16 oz.) pkg. frozen
3 egg whites ⟶ strawberries
1 cup sugar ⟶ 1 (12 oz.) carton Cool Whip

Crush sandies and line a 9x13 inch pan, reserving some to sprinkle lightly on top of dessert. Beat egg whites for 20 minutes at high speed. Add sugar, lemon juice and strawberries. Fold in Cool Whip. Pour on top of crust. Sprinkle crumbs on top.

Madeline Dufault, Crookston

STRAWBERRY DESSERT

1 Angel Food cake, broken into ⟶ 2 pkgs. strawberry jello
small pieces ⟶ 2 cups hot water
1 lg. pkg. frozen strawberries ⟶ 1 pt. whipping cream

Put cake pieces in a 9x13 inch pan. Partially thaw strawberries. Dissolve jello in boiling water; add berries. When jello begins to thicken, add whipping cream and pour over broken pieces of cake. Refrigerate.

Alice Lynch, Winona
District Deputy, 1988-1990

STRAWBERRY DESSERT

1 (8 oz.) box vanilla wafers, crushed
½ cup soft butter, not oleo
1 cup packed powdered sugar
2 well beaten eggs
Vanilla
½ pt. whipping cream
1 (10 oz..) pkg. frozen strawberries
¾ cup chopped nuts

Put half of crumbs in a 9x11 inch pan. Mix butter, powdered sugar, eggs and vanilla and put on top of crumbs. Mix whipping cream, strawberries and nuts and put on the butter mixture. Top with remaining crumbs. Refrigerate for several hours.

Angie Authier, Plymouth

STRAWBERRY DESSERT

½ cup oleo
1 cup flour
2 Tbsp. sugar
1 (8 oz.) pkg. cream cheese
1 cup powdered sugar
1 sm. carton Cool Whip (2 cups)

Mix oleo, flour and sugar and put in a 9x13 inch pan. Bake at 350° for 10 to 15 minutes. Cool. Beat cream cheese. Mix with powdered sugar and Cool Whip. Put on cooled crust. Top cream cheese layer with **4 cups whole fresh strawberries** (1 quart). Set them on side by side. Cook **1 box Danish strawberry pie glaze** as directed on package. When slightly cool, pour over strawberries. Let set. Top with **Cool Whip**.

Joan Pirkl, Medford

STRAWBERRY SHORTCAKE

2 cups flour
4 tsp. baking powder
1 Tbsp. sugar
½ tsp. salt
6 Tbsp. butter or Crisco
1 egg
½ cup milk
1 qt. berries
1 cup whipping cream, whipped

Sift all the dry ingredients and cut in butter as for pie crust. Beat egg and milk until blended and mix with dry ingredients. Pat out dough into a square or round on a floured board. Bake on a greased sheet in a moderately hot oven for 15 to 20 minutes. Split cake when it has cooled a little. Serve with sweetened strawberries between layers and on top. Garnish with whipped cream.

Note: Recipe is submitted from original Catholic Daughters Cookbook "Everybody's Favorite!"

Mrs. Katheryne Schnieder, Lismore

STRAWBERRY PRETZEL DESSERT

1½ cups crushed pretzels	1 lg. carton Cool Whip
¾ cup sugar	2 (3 oz.) pkgs. strawberry Jell-O
½ cup melted butter	2 cups boiling water
1 cup sugar	2 sm. pkgs. frozen strawberries
1 (8 oz.) pkg. cream cheese	

Blend the first 3 ingredients and pat into a 9x13 inch pan. Bake at 350° for 5 minutes. Beat sugar and cream cheese; add half of Cool Whip and spread over cooled crust. Dissolve Jell-O in water; add slightly thawed berries. When partially set, pour over cream cheese. Add remaining Cool Whip for top. Garnish with fresh strawberries when in season. Let set overnight.

Dorothy Kahle, New Ulm

STRAWBERRY-RHUBARB PUFF

1 (10 oz.) pkg. frozen strawberries, thawed	½ tsp. salt
	⅓ cup salad oil
1 (16 oz.) pkg. rhubarb, thawed	⅔ cup milk
½ cup sugar	Butter
2 cups flour	2 Tbsp. sugar
2 Tbsp. sugar	1 tsp. cinnamon
3 tsp. baking powder	

Heat oven to 425°. In an ungreased 9x9 inch pan, mix strawberries, rhubarb and ½ cup sugar. Place in oven. Measure flour, 2 tablespoons sugar, baking powder and salt into bowl. Combine oil and milk; add all at once to flour mixture. Stir well until mixture forms a ball. Drop dough by spoonfuls into hot fruit. Make indentation in each ball, dot with butter. Mix cinnamon and sugar; sprinkle on biscuits. Bake 20 to 25 minutes.

Variation: May use fresh rhubarb and strawberries. May use cherries or any other fruit; increase sugar to 1½ cups; add ½ cup water.

Mary Warner, Owatonna

STRAWBERRY SQUARES

1 (10 oz.) pkg. frozen strawberries	1 cup cream, whipped
	⅓ of a lg. Angel Food cake
1 (3 oz.) pkg. strawberry jello	

Drain strawberries. Use juice, plus water, to prepare jello as directed on package. When jello starts to congeal, fold in berries and the whipped cream. Break Angel Food cake into bits in a 9 inch square pan and pour jello mixture over. Refrigerate until set up, about 4 to 5 hours.

Coletta Lonneman, Wilmont

BAKED-IN-STRAWBERRY SHORTCAKE

1 cup flour
½ cup sugar
2 tsp. baking powder
½ tsp. salt
½ cup milk
1 egg

2 Tbsp. butter or margarine, melted
1½ cups red, ripe, firm strawberries, sliced
1 recipe Crumble Topper (below)

Sift dry ingredients. Add milk, egg, and melted butter and beat 2 minutes. Turn into an 8x8x2 inch pan. Top with sliced strawberries.

Crumble Topper:

Combine ½ cup flour, ½ cup sugar and cut in ¼ cup butter or margarine until mixture resembles coarse crumbs. Add ¼ cup chopped nuts. Sprinkle over strawberries. Bake at 375° for about 35 minutes. Cut into squares.

Lorraine Kantor, International Falls

GRAHAM STREUSEL CAKE DESSERT

2 cups graham cracker crumbs
¾ cup chopped nuts
¾ cup brown sugar
1¼ tsp. cinnamon
¾ cup butter, melted

1 pkg. yellow cake mix
1 cup water
¾ cup vegetable oil
3 eggs

Mix crumbs, nuts, brown sugar, cinnamon and butter. Reserve. Beat cake mix, water, vegetable oil, and eggs in large mixer bowl on low speed for 30 seconds, then medium speed for 2 minutes. Pour 2⅓ cups batter into greased 9x13 inch pan. Sprinkle with 2 cups crumbs mixture. Pour remaining batter into pan, sprinkle with remaining crumbs mixture. Bake 45 to 50 minutes. Cool. Drizzle with vanilla glaze.

Vanilla Glaze:

1 cup powdered sugar
1 to 2 Tbsp. water
Pinch of salt

1 tsp. butter
½ tsp. vanilla

Eileen Harguth, Waseca

SWEETENED CONDENSED MILK

¾ cup sugar
⅓ cup water

4 Tbsp. butter
1 cup dry milk crystals

In a 2 cup glass measure, add sugar, water and butter. Microwave on high for 1½ to 2 minutes until mixture boils, stirring every 30 seconds. Combine in blender with dry milk; process until smooth. Cover and refrigerate until needed. Makes 1 cup.

Vivian Fick, Slayton

SWEDISH RICE

1 cup Uncle Ben's white rice	¾ cup sugar
4 cups milk	1 tsp. salt
5 eggs, separated	1 tsp. almond extract
3 heaping Tbsp. cornstarch	10 tsp. powdered sugar

Bring 6 cups water to a boil; add rice. Boil until done. Strain and rinse with cold water. Heat milk and add rice. Cook about 5 minutes. Beat egg yolks and add to rice. Mix cornstarch, sugar, salt and almond extract and add to mixture. Bring to boil. Cook until thick (watch carefully). Place in a 9x13 inch pan (I spray with Pam). Beat egg whites with powdered sugar and put meringue on rice and brown.

Karen (Jim) Hammers, Perham

TASTY DESSERT

1 yellow cake mix	½ cup oil
1 can mandarin oranges and juice	4 eggs

Mix cake mix, oranges, oil and eggs. Beat 2 minutes at medium speed. Bake in greased 9x13 inch pan at 350° for 35 to 40 minutes. Cool.

Frosting:

1 (No. 2) can crushed pineapple and juice	1 box instant vanilla pudding
1 cup coconut	1 (12 oz.) pkg. Dream Whip

Stir pineapple and juice, coconut and pudding mix. Fold in Dream Whip and frost cake.

Carla Brady, Medford

THREE LAYER DESSERT

½ cup butter	¾ cup milk
¼ cup sugar	1 cup whipped cream
1 cup flour	Any kind of fruit
Nuts, optional	2 pkgs. any flavor jelly
24 marshmallows	

Mix butter, sugar, flour and nuts. Spread in a 9x13 inch pan. Bake 15 minutes or until golden brown. Cool and crumble in pan. Melt marshmallows in milk. Cool; add whipped cream. Spread on crumbs. Drain fruit and place on marshmallow mixture. Top with layer of jelly dissolved in water. Refrigerate overnight.

Beatrice Caron, Mankato

INSTANT TORTE DESSERT

1 stick oleo	1 cup powdered sugar
½ cup chopped pecans	1 lg. carton Cool Whip
1 cup flour	2 pkgs. instant pudding
1 (8 oz.) pkg. cream cheese	3 cups milk

Mix oleo, pecans, and flour like pie crust and press into a 9x13 inch pan. Whip cream cheese; add powdered sugar. Fold in Cool Whip and pour on cooled crust. Mix pudding and milk and pour over cream cheese filling.

June Ankeny, Blue Earth

TRIFFLE DESSERT

1 box Angel Food cake mix	1 pt. fresh whole strawberries,
1 (3½ oz.) pkg. vanilla or lemon	cut in half
instant pudding and pie filling	1 kiwi fruit, sliced
mix	1 (8 oz.) carton Cool Whip
2 cups milk	

Make Angel Food cake as directed on the box; bake and cool. Cut or break into bite size pieces. Make pudding using milk. Layer cake pieces in a Triffle bowl, pudding, whole strawberries, kiwi fruit and Cool Whip, ending with the strawberries and kiwi. Very pretty and tasty.

Donna Connors, Waseca

A GARDEN OF SPRING TULIPS CAKE

1 pkg. Super Moist lemon cake mix	1 container deluxe lemon frosting
1¼ cups water	20 gumdrop (tulips)
⅓ cup vegetable oil	10 green leaf shaped tulips
3 eggs	20 green toothpicks
1 pkg. lemon pie filling (not instant)	2 sm. assorted colored gumdrops
	¾ cup pie filling

Heat oven to 350°. Generously grease and flour 2 round pans. Beat cake mix (dry), water, oil and eggs on low speed 30 seconds. Beat on medium speed 2 minutes. Pour into pans. Bake 25 to 35 seconds or until cake springs back when touched lightly in center. Cool 10 minute. Remove from pans; cool completely on wire rack. While cake is cooling, prepare lemon pie filling according to package. Fill layer of cake with pie filling place top layer and frost with frosting. Garnish with gumdrop tulips.

Mary Pahlen, Crookston

272

TURTLE SUNDAE DESSERT

1 pkg. German chocolate
  cake mix
1 (14 oz.) pkg. caramels
½ cup evaporated milk

6 Tbsp. butter or margarine
1 cup chopped pecans
1 cups semi-sweet chocolate
  chips

Mix cake according to package directions. Set aside half the batter. Pour remaining batter into greased and floured 9x13 inch pan. Bake at 350° for 18 minutes. In a saucepan over low heat, melt caramels, milk and butter. Add nuts and pour over cake. Sprinkle chocolate chips over caramels. Pour remaining batter over chips. Bake 20 to 25 minutes. Cool. Serve with scoop of ice cream. Makes 20 servings.

Veronica Knoll, Argyle

TWO-TONE DESSERT

1 cup flour
½ cup oleo
½ cup nuts
1 (8 oz.) pkg. Philadelphia
  cream cheese
1 cup powdered sugar
1 (10.8 oz.) carton Cool Whip

1 (3.4 oz.) pkg. instant vanilla
  pudding
1 (3.4 oz.) pkg. instant chocolate
  pudding
2½ cups milk
1 Hershey almond bar

Combine the flour, oleo and nuts. Pat on bottom of a 9x13 inch pan. Bake at 350° for 10 minutes. Cool. Cream the cream cheese and powdered sugar. Fold in Cool Whip. Put on cooled crust. Combine puddings and milk. Beat until thick. Put on top of the second layer. Put rest of Cool Whip on top of that. Grate Hershey bar on the very top. Refrigerate overnight.

Margaret Short, Slayton

VANILLA ICE CREAM

6 eggs
2½ cups sugar
6 cups milk

2 Tbsp. vanilla
4 cups light cream
½ tsp. salt

Beat eggs until light; add sugar. Combine rest of ingredients; add to egg mixture. Freeze in ice cream freezer. Makes 1 gallon.

Marie Nelson, Pipestone

BELGIAN PUDDING

1 (11 oz.) pkg. graham crackers   1 cup raisins
2 qts. cold milk   1 cup milk
½ cup granulated sugar   ½ cup flour
2 cups brown sugar   6 eggs, beaten
¾ cup dark corn syrup

In a large kettle, soak the graham crackers in the 2 quarts cold milk for 10 minutes. Add both sugars, corn syrup and raisins. Bring to a boil over medium heat and cook until the mixture is well blended, stirring constantly. Remove from heat. Put 1 cup milk and flour in a pint jar, cover and shake well. Pour this into a bowl and add some of the hot graham mixture to blend. Pour contents of bowl slowly into first mixture and stir well to prevent curdling. Cook until mixture boils. Remove from heat ana add beaten eggs slowly to kettle mixture. Return to heat and cook 1 minute. Pour into well buttered 4 quart crockery bowl (not glass or metal) and let stand until steam disappears. Bake at 350° for 1 hour. Cool completely. Unmold, slice and serve after it is chilled. Keeps well in refrigerator. 16 to 24 servings.

Lorraine Halbersma, Pipestone

WALNUT STICKS

½ cup butter   Some vanilla
1 cup flour   2 Tbsp. flour
2 eggs   ¼ tsp. baking powder
1½ cups brown sugar   ½ cup chopped walnuts

Rub butter and flour and pat into a 7x11 inch pan. Bake at 350° for 10 to 15 minutes. Beat the eggs; add brown sugar, vanilla, flour, baking powder and walnuts. Pour over the crust and bake 30 minutes.

Frosting:
1½ cups powdered sugar   2 Tbsp. butter
1 tsp. almond extract   2 Tbsp. orange juice or more

Mix ingredients. I always squeeze a fresh orange.

Dorothy Kahle, New Ulm

* * * * * * * *

Do unto others as you want them to do unto you.
Ann Callaghan, Blue Earth

WHIPPED CREAM CAKE

1 cup whipping cream
2 eggs
1 tsp. vanilla
1½ cups flour
2 tsp. baking powder
½ tsp. salt
1 cup sugar

Whip cream until it holds soft peaks; add eggs, one at a time, beating well after each addition. Stir in vanilla. Sift flour, sugar, baking powder and salt. Add to creamed mixture. Stir until blended. Pour into floured 8x8 inch pan. Bake at 350° for 40 minutes or until done. Serve with strawberries.

Martha Matejcek, Medford

YOGURT CREAM WITH FRESH FRUIT

1 (8 oz.) carton strawberry or
    vanilla yogurt
½ cup Kemps cottage cheese
1 Tbsp. honey
1 to 2 drops red food color,
    optional
Assorted fruits

In blender container, combine first 4 ingredients, cover and blend until smooth. Slice or cut fresh fruit into chunks. Dip in lemon juice or fruit fresh to avoid discoloration. Arrange fruit on serving platter; serve with yogurt cream. Makes about 1½ cups dip. Preparation time: 30 minutes.

Loretta Engesser, Blue Earth

YVONNE'S SPECIALTY

1 cup sifted flour
2 tsp. baking powder
¼ tsp. salt
¾ cup sugar
2 Tbsp. cocoa
½ cup milk
2 Tbsp. vegetable oil
1 cup chopped nuts
1 cup brown sugar
¼ cup cocoa
1¾ cups hot water

Preheat oven to 350°. Blend first 5 dry ingredients in a bowl. Stir in the milk, salad oil and nuts. Spread in a 9 inch square pan. In a small bowl, blend the brown sugar and cocoa and sprinkle the mixture over top of the batter. Pour the hot water over all ingredients and bake for 45 minutes. Serve warm or cold with rich milk or cream.

Yvonne Kersting, Mahnomen

ANGEL PIE

Crust:

6 egg whites   1 tsp. vinegar
Pinch of salt   1 tsp. vanilla
1 tsp. cream of tartar   1½ cups sugar

Beat egg whites and salt until foamy; add cream of tartar and beat until fluffy. Add vinegar and vanilla. Gradually add sugar and beat well. Put in an ungreased 9x13 inch pan and bake at 250° for 50 to 60 minutes. Turn upside down, supporting corners on four cups until cool.

Filling:

6 egg yolks   Pinch of salt
½ cup sugar   1 Tbsp. butter
Rind and juice of 1 lg. lemon

Beat egg yolks until light; add sugar, lemon rind and juice, salt and butter. Cook on top of stove until it coats a spoon. Cool to lukewarm; pour over baked meringue. Spread with sweetened whipped cream or Cool Whip. Store in refrigerator. Keeps for days.

Elaine Sable, Owatonna
Marilyn Pelowski, International Falls

APPLE PEAR CRUMB PIE

2 cups apples, peeled and diced   ¼ tsp. cinnamon
3½ cups canned pears, drained   ½ cup raisins
    and sliced   1 Tbsp. lemon juice
⅓ cup sugar   1 unbaked pie crust
2 Tbsp. flour   2 Tbsp. butter
¼ tsp. salt

Combine apples, pears, sugar, flour, salt, cinnamon, raisins and lemon juice; mix well. Turn into the unbaked pie shell. Dot with butter. Sprinkle with crumb topping. Bake at 450° for 10 minutes. Cover with foil and continue baking at 350° for 40 minutes more or until apples are tender.

Crumb Topping:

¼ cup flour   1 (3 oz.) pkg. cream cheese
½ cup brown sugar   ½ cup chopped nuts
¼ tsp. salt

Combine flour, brown sugar and salt. Cut in the cream cheese until crumbly. Stir in nuts. Cover top of pie when warm.

Alice Turk, Eveleth

SWEDISH APPLE PIE

5 to 6 med. apples
1 Tbsp. sugar
1 tsp. cinnamon
½ cup melted butter, or butter
   and margarine combination
1 cup sugar

1 cup flour
1 egg
Pinch of salt
1 tsp. vanilla
½ cup chopped walnuts

Peel, core and slice apples into a 9 or 10 inch pie pan (Pyrex works best). Sprinkle combined sugar and cinnamon evenly over apples. In a small bowl, combine the remaining ingredients; mix well and spread evenly over apples. Bake at 350° for 45 minutes. Serve hot or cold. (There is no bottom crust.)

Helen Cavanaugh, Plainview

BANANA PIE

1½ cups milk
¾ cup sugar
2½ Tbsp. cornstarch
2 egg yolks
1 tsp. vanilla

2 or 3 bananas
1 (9 inch) pie crust, baked and
   cooled
¼ cup coconut, flaked

Into saucepan, put milk, sugar, cornstarch and egg yolks. Mix well and cook until thick. Add vanilla and cool. Meanwhile, cut up 2 to 3 bananas into crust. Pour filling over bananas. Meringue can be put on top, but we like it sprinkled with coconut.

Josephine Befort, Zumbrota

FRESH BLUEBERRY PIE

1 cup sugar
1 qt. blueberries
3 Tbsp. cornstarch
¾ cup water
¼ tsp. cinnamon

¼ tsp. nutmeg
¼ tsp. cloves, optional
1 Tbsp. butter
1 Tbsp. lemon juice
1 baked pie shell

Combine sugar, 1 cup blueberries, cornstarch, water, cinnamon and nutmeg in saucepan. Cook over medium heat until thick and clear; stir often. Remove from heat and add butter and lemon juice; stir until blended. Cool. Fold in remaining 3 cups of fresh berries. Pour into pie shell. Refrigerate. Serve with whipped topping.

Carol Dalton, International Falls

BUTTERSCOTCH PEACH PIE

4 lg. peaches	½ or ⅓ cup white sugar
1 (9 inch) unbaked pie shell	¼ cup butter
½ or ⅓ cup brown sugar	3 Tbsp. flour

Slice peaches in pie shell. Heat sugars, butter and flour in saucepan over low heat or in microwave. Cover peaches with sauce and bake at 350° for 30 minutes. Can use lattice top and bake longer. I always use coconut top.

Coconut Top:

¼ cup white sugar	¾ cup coconut
¼ cup butter	Pinch of salt
½ cup flour	

Put over peaches, return to oven and bake until light brown, about 15 minutes or more.

Marilyn Ellenz, Caledonia

SIMPLE CHEESECAKE

1 pkg. lemon instant pudding	1¾ cups milk
1 (8 oz.) pkg. cream cheese	

Mix pudding according to package and mix in cream cheese and milk.

Crust:

10 to 20 graham crackers, crushed fine	2 Tbsp. melted butter or oleo
	1 Tbsp. brown sugar

Crush graham crackers finely and stir in melted butter or oleo and brown sugar in pie pan. Put pudding and cream cheese mixture in the crust and refrigerate overnight.

Roberta Tissek, St. Paul

EASY CHEESE CAKE**

⅓ cup white sugar	1 tsp. vanilla
1 (8 oz.) pkg. cream cheese, room temperature	1 (8 oz.) carton Cool Whip
	Graham cracker crust
1 (8 oz.) carton sour cream	

Whip sugar, cream cheese, sour cream and vanilla until fluffy. Fold in Cool Whip and pour into crust. Refrigerate overnight. Can top with berries if desired.

Millie Fangmeier, Pipestone

CHERRY PIE

2 (16 oz.) cans sour pitted
cherries
²/₃ cup juice from cherries
2 Tbsp. tapioca
1 cup sugar

¼ tsp. nutmeg
⅛ tsp. salt
Pastry for 2 crust pie
1 Tbsp. butter

Drain cherries. Mix reserved juice, tapioca, sugar, nutmeg and salt. Let stand for 15 minutes. Add cherries and pour into pastry-lined pie pan. Dot with butter and put on top crust. Bake at 425° for about 45 minutes.

Marian O'Brien, International Falls

CHOCOLATE MARBLE CREAM CHEESE PIE

1 (8 oz.) pkg. cream cheese,
softened
½ cup granulated sugar
1 tsp. vanilla extract
2 egg yolks
1 tsp. unflavored gelatin
¼ cup water

1 (4 oz.) pkg. semi-sweet
chocolate, melted
1 cup whipping cream
Cookie crust (below)
Strawberries, optional
Pecan halves, optional

Beat cream cheese, sugar, and vanilla until smooth. Add egg yolks one at a time, until well blended. Combine gelatin and water in small saucepan over low heat. Stir until gelatin is dissolved. Cool slightly. Beat gelatin into batter. Combine ¾ cup batter and melted chocolate. Whip cream until soft peaks form. Fold half of whipped cream into chocolate batter and remaining half into vanilla batter. With large spoon, alternately place spoonfuls of chocolate and vanilla batters into crust until all batter is used. With small spatula or knife, swirl batter to form marble pattern. Chill 3 hours. Garnish with strawberries and pecan halves if desired, or use chocolate swirls or other fruit. You choice. Serves 8 people.

Cookie Crust:

1½ cups chocolate cookie
crumbs

2 Tbsp. granulated sugar
6 Tbsp. melted butter

Press mixture into bottom and sides of a 9 inch pie pan. Bake at 350° for 8 minutes. Cool.

Nancy Palo, Eveleth

* * * * * * * *

*Mary, give me some of your patience
and help me to lead my family to your son.*
Rita Willmert, Blue Earth

CHOCOLATE BANANA PUDDING PIE

4 sqs. semi-sweet chocolate	2¾ cups cold milk
2 Tbsp. milk	2 (4 serving size) pkgs. Jell-O
1 Tbsp. margarine or butter	vanilla or banana cream
1 graham cracker crust	flavor instant pudding*
2 med. bananas, sliced	1½ cups thawed Cool Whip*

*Can use Jell-O vanilla flavored sugar-free reduced calorie instant pudding and Cool Whip lite.

Microwave chocolate, milk and margarine in medium microwaveable bowl on high for 1 to 1½ minutes, stirring every 30 seconds. Stir until completely melted. Spread evenly in crust. Refrigerate 30 minutes or until chocolate is firm. Arrange banana slices over chocolate. Pour milk into large bowl; add pudding mixes. Beat with a wire whisk for 1 minute. Let stand 5 minutes. Spoon over bananas in crust. Spread with whipped topping. Refrigerate 4 hours or until set.

Ann Klinkhammer, Mahnomen

CHOCOLATE PECAN PIE

1 cup pecans	¼ cup butter
1 cup chocolate chips	1 tsp. vanilla
1½ cups white syrup	3 eggs
¼ cup sugar	

Place pecans and chips in a 9 inch pie tin. Dissolve all remaining ingredients on low heat, except eggs. Beat eggs well and add to cooled mixture. Pour over chips and nuts and bake at 375° for 40 minutes.

Loretta Knott, Red Lake Falls

COCONUT PIE (SELF CRUST)

4 eggs, beaten	2 cups milk
¼ cup margarine	1 tsp. vanilla
1½ cups sugar	1½ cups coconut
½ cup flour	

Combine eggs, margarine and sugar. Beat until fluffy. Add remaining ingredients and mix well. Pour into a 10 inch pie pan. Bake at 350° for 45 minutes or until golden brown. The crust will form on the edge and middle will appear soft. Do not over bake.

Bernice Voit, Mahnomen

CREAM PUFF PIE

½ cup water   ½ cup flour
¼ cup butter or margarine   2 eggs
½ tsp. salt

In a large pan, bring water, butter and salt to a boil. Add flour at once and stir until a smooth ball forms. Remove from heat, beat in eggs one at a time; continue stirring until mixture is smooth and shiny. Spread in bottom and half way up sides of a well greased pie pan. Bake at 400° for 35 to 40 minutes. Cool completely and fill with whatever your desire.

Marian Schloegel, Winona

IMPOSSIBLE FRENCH APPLE PIE

6 cups sliced, pared tart apples   ½ cup Bisquick
1¼ tsp. cinnamon   2 eggs
1 tsp. nutmeg   2 Tbsp. margarine or butter,
1 cup sugar   softened
¾ cup milk

Heat oven to 325°. Grease a 10x1½ inch pie plate. Mix apples and spices. Turn into pie plate. Beat remaining ingredients until smooth, 15 seconds in blender on high or 1 minute with hand beater. Pour into plate.

Streusel:
1 cup Bisquick   ⅓ cup packed brown sugar
½ cup chopped nuts   3 Tbsp. firm margarine or butter

Mix until crumbly. Sprinkle on top of pie. Bake until knife inserted in center comes out clean, 55 to 60 minutes.

Catherine Shikonya, Winona

FRENCH SILK PIE

1 cup sugar   3 eggs
¾ cup butter or margarine   1 (8 oz.) carton chocolate Cool
3 sqs. or 3 oz. unsweetened   Whip
    chocolate   1 (9 oz.) baked pie shell
1½ tsp. vanilla

Cream sugar and butter. Melt chocolate and cool. Add to creamed sugar mixture. Add vanilla. Add eggs, one at a time, beating well after each egg, about 2 minutes between each egg. Put in pie shell. Cool overnight, then add chocolate Cool Whip on top of pie.

Marlene Stadler, Medford
Dorothy Klement, New Ulm

DESSERTS, PIES & PASTRIES

HOT FUDGE CHOCOLATE PIE

¼ cup cocoa	2 eggs, well beaten
1 cup sugar	1 stick butter, melted
2 tsp. vanilla	1 (8 inch) unbaked pie shell
2 Tbsp. flour	

Mix all ingredients and pour into pie shell. Bake at 350° for 25 minutes. Serve warm with ice cream.

Inez Johnson, Slayton

HOLIDAY PIE

1 (16 or 17 oz.) can fruit cocktail	1 pt. whipping cream (2 cups)
⅛ tsp. mint extract	3 Tbsp. powdered sugar
1 (3 oz.) pkg. Jell-O strawberry gelatin	1 (9 inch) baked pie crust
	Red food coloring
1 cup boiling water	

Drain fruit cocktail, reserving liquid. Save ⅓ cup of fruit for garnish. Add extract to remaining fruit and mash. Dissolve gelatin in boiling water. Refrigerate until cold to touch. Whip the cream and powdered sugar until stiff. Slowly beat cold gelatin into whipped cream. Continue beating while adding mashed fruit cocktail. Freeze for 15 minutes, stirring twice. Mound this mixture into baked pie crust. Freeze for 1 hour. Refrigerate until served. Boil the reserved liquid from fruit cocktail until ⅛ cup remains. Color with red food coloring. Cool; combine with reserved fruit. Use as garnish when serving the pie. Makes 1 pie; serves 5 or 6.

Dena Bozicevich, Eveleth

LEMON PIE SUPREME

4 eggs, separated	1 cup boiling water
½ cup sugar	1 Tbsp. butter
4 Tbsp. cornstarch	½ cup sugar (for meringue)
1 (6 oz.) can frozen lemonade, thawed	

Beat egg yolks; add ½ cup sugar mixed with cornstarch. Add lemonade. Put water and butter in saucepan and heat to boiling. Over low heat, slowly add the egg yolk mixture, stirring constantly. Cook until thick. Remove from heat. Beat egg whites until frothy. Gradually add ½ cup sugar and beat until stiff. Fold about half the meringue into the lemon mixture. Pour into baked pie shell. Top with remainder of meringue. Brown in oven.

Bernice Bateman, International Falls

FLUFFY LEMON PIE

3 eggs, separated
1 cup sugar
1 lemon and rind

3 Tbsp. boiling water
1 baked pie crust

Beat egg yolks until thick and lemon colored. Gradually add ½ cup sugar. Mix well and add grated rind and juice of lemon. Slowly add boiling water. Cook in double boiler until thin custard stage. Beat egg whites until firm. Gradually add remaining sugar. Fold meringue into custard. Fill a previously baked pie crust. Brown in oven if desired.

Rose Nixon, Winona
State Regent, 1974-1978

SOUR CREAM LEMON PIE

1 cup sugar
3½ Tbsp. cornstarch
1 Tbsp. lemon rind, grated
½ cup fresh lemon juice
3 egg yolks, slightly beaten
1 cup milk
¼ cup butter

1 cup cultured sour cream
1 (9 inch) baked pie shell
1 cup heavy whipping cream,
  whipped
Lemon twists for garnish,
  optional

Combine sugar, cornstarch, lemon rind, juice, egg yolks and milk in heavy saucepan. Cook over medium heat until thick. Stir in butter and cool mixture to room temperature. Stir in sour cream and pour filling into pie shell. Cover with whipping cream or Cool Whip. Store in refrigerator.

Regina Schettler, Wilmont
Marva Taylor, Adrian

MOTHER'S LEMON PIE

5 egg yolks
1½ cups sugar
2⅓ cups water

2 lemons, grated with juice
  squeezed out
½ tsp. salt
2 to 3 Tbsp. cornstarch

Beat egg yolks; add sugar, water, lemon rinds and juice, salt and cornstarch. Beat in double boiler kettle. Let cook until it bubbles. Pour in baked pie shell. Beat egg whites until very stiff; add a little sugar and put over pie and bake at 400° for a few minutes until light brown.

Viola Maehren, St. Paul
State Legislative Chairman, 1992-1994
State Second Vice Regent, 1986-1988

LEMON GELATIN CHIFFON PIE

1 pkg. lemon jello	4 Tbsp. lemon juice
3 egg yolks, slightly beaten	3 tsp. grated lemon rind
½ cup sugar	3 egg whites
1 cup water	Salt

Combine lemon jello, egg yolks and 4 tablespoons sugar in double boiler. Stir well and add water. Cook until mixture coats spoon, stirring constantly. (Do NOT over cook.) Remove from heat; add lemon juice and rind. Chill until thickened. Beat egg whites until foamy; add salt and remaining 4 tablespoons sugar gradually. Beat until stiff. Fold jello mixture into egg whites.

Graham Pie Shell:

12 graham crackers	4 Tbsp. melted butter

Roll graham crackers to fine crumbs. Add melted butter. Press into pie pan. Pour mixture into pie shell and chill until firm.

Celestine Nesser, Lewiston

LEMONADE PIE

2½ cups graham cracker crumbs	1 can Eagle Brand sweetened
½ cup sugar	condensed milk
½ cup butter, melted	1 (20 oz.) can crushed pine-
1 lg. carton Cool Whip	apple, drained well
1 (12 oz.) can frozen lemonade	1 cup nuts, chopped

Mix cracker crumbs, sugar and melted butter and pat in two 8 inch pie pans or one 9x13 inch pan. Place Cool Whip, frozen lemonade and milk in bowl of mixer and whip until very stiff. Fold in pineapple and nuts. Place in shell and refrigerate.

Florence Klonecki, Winona

MERINGUE

2 Tbsp. sugar	$1/8$ tsp. salt
1 Tbsp. cornstarch	1 tsp. vanilla
½ cup water	6 Tbsp. sugar
3 egg whites, room temperature	

In small saucepan, cook 2 tablespoons sugar, cornstarch and water. Cook until clear and cool completely. Beat egg whites, salt, and vanilla until soft peaks form, then add remaining 6 tablespoons sugar and the cooled cornstarch mixture. Beat until stiff. Spread on pie filling, sealing edges well. Bake at 375° for 10 minutes.

Rosella Sogge, Fairmont

PEACH PIE

5 to 6 peaches, sliced
1 cup white sugar
½ cup whipping cream or half
and half

2 Tbsp. flour
Pastry for double crust pie

Combine all ingredients in a bowl and mix well. Put in unbaked pie shell and cover with top crust. Bake at 400° for 15 minutes, then at 375° for 25 to 30 minutes.

Marie Nelson, Pipestone

OUT OF THIS WORLD PEACH PIE

1½ cups oatmeal
⅔ cup almonds, optional
½ cup margarine
½ cup brown sugar

1 pkg. peach jello
1 cup boiling water
2 cups vanilla ice cream
2 cups diced peaches

Toast oatmeal at 350° for 5 minutes; add almonds and toast 5 minutes more. Remove from oven; add melted margarine and brown sugar. Reserve ½ cup for topping. Pat remaining into bottom of an 8x8 inch pan. Mix jello and water; add the ice cream and peaches. Refrigerate until set. Sprinkle crumbs on top. Store in refrigerator. Serves 9.

Vicki Boeckman, Elmore
District Deputy, 1984-1990, 1992-1994
Community Chairperson, 1984-1990
State Treasurer, 1994-1996
State Secretary, 1996-present

ONE CRUST PEACH PIE

½ cup water
1½ Tbsp. cornstarch
1 cup sugar
1 cup fresh peaches
2 Tbsp. butter

½ tsp. salt
¼ tsp. cinnamon
¼ tsp. nutmeg
½ to 1 tsp. rum extract

Combine water, cornstarch, sugar and fresh peaches (peeled and mashed) in saucepan. Cook, stirring constantly, until boiling. Boil 1 minute, stirring. Add butter, salt, cinnamon, nutmeg and rum extract. Cool. Slice **3 cups fresh peaches** into baked pie shell. Pour filling over peaches, carefully covering peaches up to crust sides. Chill. Serve with whipped cream or ice cream.

Helen Cahill, Moorhead

PEANUT BUTTER PIE

1 (3 oz.) pkg. cream cheese
¾ cup powdered sugar
⅓ cup milk
3 heaping Tbsp. chunky peanut
    butter

1 (6 oz.) carton Cool Whip
1 graham cracker crust
Fudge sauce

Cream the cream cheese and sugar with electric mixer until well blended. Add milk and peanut butter; mix well. Fold in Cool Whip. Pour into pie crust and freeze until firm. When ready to serve, heat fudge sauce and drizzle over each slice. Freezes well and keeps for weeks.

Odelia Majerus, Bellechester

PIE

Pie Shell:
2¼ cups flour
¼ tsp. salt
¾ cup vegetable shortening
    or butter

1 tsp. vinegar
2 egg yolks
2 Tbsp. ice water

Make pie shell. Combine dry ingredients. Cut in shortening until crumbs form. Mix vinegar, egg yolks and water in small bowl; add to pie crust mixture. Combine until it forms a ball. Add more water (by teaspoons) if necessary. Wrap and chill for 1 hour or overnight. Roll out for a 9 inch pie pan. Bake at 350° until light brown, about 15 minutes.

Filling:
4 egg whites
½ cup sugar

1 tsp. vanilla

Beat egg whites until stiff. Add sugar and vanilla. Beat until mixture stands in peaks. Pour into baked pie shell. Bake at 325° for 20 minutes, until lightly browned. Remove and cool at room temperature.

Topping:
1 cup whipped cream
¼ cup sugar

1 cup ground pecans

Whip cream. Add sugar and vanilla. Spread evenly over cooled pie. Sprinkle with nuts. Refrigerate for 1 hour.

Idella Miller, Tulsa, OK
National Director, 1992-1996

DESSERTS, PIES & PASTRIES

SOUTHERN PECAN PIE

3 eggs, well beaten
1 cup dark Karo syrup
½ cup sugar
2 Tbsp. butter, melted

1 tsp. vanilla
¼ tsp. salt
1 cup or more pecans
Pastry pie shell

Combine all ingredients and place in an unbaked pastry shell. Bake at 350° for 45 minutes.

Margaret Piekarski, Fergus Falls

PASTRY

5½ cups flour
1 lb. lard
1 tsp. baking powder
1 tsp. salt

3 Tbsp. brown sugar
1 egg
²/₃ cup water
1 tsp. vinegar

Mix the first 5 ingredients. Lightly beat the egg, water and vinegar, then mix with the dry ingredients. Put on a floured board and knead it into a ball. Put in a plastic bag and refrigerate. Cut off what you would need for a pie and roll out like you would any other pastry. You can keep in refrigerator.

Alice Ethier, Argyle

HOT WATER PASTRY

2 cups flour, sifted
½ tsp. baking powder
1 tsp. salt

¹/₃ cup boiling water
²/₃ cup shortening

Sift flour, baking powder and salt. Pour water over shortening and mix with fork until creamy; add flour mixture and mix into a dough. Chill thoroughly and proceed as for plain pastry. Makes 1 (9 inch) double crust pie or 2 (9 inch) shells.

Mary Chevalier, Slayton

PIE CRUST

4 cups flour
1¾ cups shortening (I use lard)
1 Tbsp. sugar
1 tsp. salt

1 tsp. baking powder
1 egg, beaten
1 Tbsp. vinegar
½ cup water

Work flour, shortening, sugar, salt and baking powder; add egg, vinegar and water. Work together. Makes 3 double crust pie crusts. Bake at 400° for 10 minutes per pie shell.

Lucy Pansier, Faribault

PIE CRUST MIX

3 cups flour   1 cup Crisco or shortening
1 tsp. salt   2 Tbsp. butter or margarine
½ tsp. baking powder

Mix all ingredients and keep refrigerated. When pie crust is to be made, take 1 cup of the mix and add **1 teaspoon vinegar** and **⅓ cup water.** Mix and roll out pie crust.

Dena I. Zamani, Fergus Falls

EASY NO ROLL PIE CRUST

1½ cups flour   2 Tbsp. milk
2 Tbsp. sugar   ½ cup cooking oil
½ tsp. salt

Blend all ingredients with fork and press into a 9 inch pie tin. Bake at 400° for about 15 to 20 minutes. DO NOT prick before baking.

Lita Schreier, Currie

NEVER FAIL PIE CRUST

1 cup lard   1 egg, beaten
3 cups flour   1 tsp. vinegar
2 tsp. salt   5 Tbsp. water

Blend the lard, flour and salt. Blend the egg, vinegar and water. Add to flour mixture all at once and stir with a fork. Makes 2 double crusts.

Diane Green, Fulda
Florence St. Germain, Argyle

NEVER FAIL PIE CRUST

2½ cups flour   1 cup lard
1 tsp. baking powder   ½ cup cold water
¼ tsp. salt

Mix dry ingredients with lard using a pastry blender or fork, then add water and mix gently. Will make crust for 2 pies and tops if rolled thin.

Lillian Grenier, Red Lake Falls

PIE CRUST

2 cups flour   ½ cup cooking oil
½ cup cold water

Mix, but don't over mix. Roll between two pieces of waxed paper.

Sandy Amberg, Waubun

DESSERTS, PIES & PASTRIES

PIE CRUST

1 cup flour   1 tsp. salt
1 Tbsp. powdered sugar   ½ cup melted margarine

Mix all ingredients with a fork and press into pie tin. Bake at 350° for 15 minutes; fill with cooked pudding filling.

Agnes Novak, Fergus Falls

PINEAPPLE SOUR CREAM PIE

2 cups sour cream   3 Tbsp. sugar
1 lg. box instant vanilla pudding Whipped cream or Cool Whip
  mix right from the box   1 (9 inch) baked pie crust,
1 (8 oz.) can crushed pineapple,   cooled
  undrained

Pour sour cream, pudding mix, crushed pineapple and sugar in a large bowl; beat with spoon until mixed. Pour into pie shell. Top with whipped cream or Cool Whip. Refrigerate. I don't put cream on until ready to serve. Very good.

Vera Boesch, New Ulm

PUMPKIN PIE

½ cup sugar   ¼ cup flour
1 egg   1 tsp. cinnamon
½ tsp. salt   1 tsp. nutmeg
½ cup half and half cream   ¼ tsp. cloves
1 cup pumpkin   1 (9 inch) pie crust

Beat all ingredients well and put into pie crust and bake at 350° for 45 minutes.

Jean Schindler, Red Lake Falls

IMPOSSIBLE PUMPKIN PIE

1 (16 oz.) can pumpkin   ¾ cup sugar
1 (13 oz.) can evaporated milk ½ cup Bisquick baking mix
2 Tbsp. margarine or butter,   2½ tsp. pumpkin pie spice
  softened   2 tsp. vanilla
2 eggs

Heat oven to 350°. Grease pie plate. Beat all ingredients 1 minute in blender on high or 2 minutes with hand beater. Pour into pie plate. Bake until knife inserted in center comes out clean, 50 to 55 minutes. Cool.

Anita McNulty, Eveleth

289

MOTHER'S PUMPKIN PIE

4 eggs, beaten	$1/3$ tsp. allspice
1½ or 2 cups pumpkin	$1/3$ tsp. cloves
1$1/3$ cups sugar	$1/3$ tsp. nutmeg
¼ tsp. salt	$1/3$ tsp. ginger
1 tsp. cinnamon	½ cup cream or half and half

Beat eggs first, then add pumpkin and beat some more. Add sugar and spices, then add cream or half and half and mix again. If the mixture is too thick, add milk or more half and half. Pour into an **unbaked pie shell** and bake at 400° for about 1 hour.

Viola Maehren, St. Paul
State Legislative Chairman, 1992-1994
State Second Vice Regent, 1986-1988

PUMPKIN CHIFFON PIE

1 env. unflavored gelatin	½ tsp. ground ginger
¼ cup cold water	½ tsp. nutmeg
3 eggs, separated	½ tsp. salt
1¼ cups canned pumpkin	¼ cup sugar
½ cup granulated sugar	Graham cracker crust
½ cup milk	1 (8 oz.) carton Cool Whip
¾ tsp. ground cinnamon	

In cup, soften gelatin in cold water; set aside. In double boiler, beat egg yolks lightly. Add pumpkin, ½ cup sugar, milk, cinnamon, ginger, nutmeg and salt. Cook over hot, NOT BOILING, water for 20 minutes or until mixture is thickened, stirring frequently. Add softened gelatin; continue cooking and stirring until gelatin is completely dissolved. Chill in refrigerator until just cool but not set. In small bowl, with electric mixer at high speed, beat egg whites and ¼ cup sugar just until soft peaks form; fold into chilled pumpkin mixture. Pour into cooled pie crust. Chill until firm. Garnish with Cool Whip.

Clara Gillis, Medford

ROSIE'S PUMPKIN PIE

1¾ cups pumpkin	2 Tbsp. sugar
½ tsp. salt	1½ tsp. cinnamon
1¾ cups milk	½ tsp. ginger
3 eggs	½ tsp. nutmeg
$2/3$ cup brown sugar	¼ tsp. cloves

Mix all ingredients in large bowl or blender. Place in **unbaked pie crust shell**. Bake for 1 hour or until firm.

Rosemary Larson, Crookston

DESSERTS, PIES & PASTRIES

PARTY PUMPKIN PIE

32 lg. marshmallows	½ tsp. cinnamon
1 cup pumpkin	1 cup whipping cream
¼ tsp. ginger	1 (9 inch) baked pie shell

Place marshmallows, pumpkin and spices in top of double boiler. Heat over hot water, stirring almost constantly until marshmallows are melted. Cool completely. Whip the cream and fold into cooled mixture. Spoon into pie shell. Chill at least 1 hour before serving. Can be frozen; then thawed 20 minutes before serving.

Viola Maday, Fairmont

RHUBARB PIE

3 eggs	½ tsp. nutmeg
2 cups sugar	3½ cups diced rhubarb
3 Tbsp. milk	1 Tbsp. butter
¼ cup flour	

Heat oven to 400°. Prepare crust. Beat eggs slightly and add remaining ingredients, except butter. Mix thoroughly. Pour into crust and dot with butter. Cover the edge of pie with 2 inch strips of aluminum foil to prevent excessive browning. Remove foil in the last 15 minutes of baking. Bake for 50 to 60 minutes.

Jane Dick, St. Charles

RHUBARB PIE

Crust:

1 cup flour	2 Tbsp. sugar
½ cup oleo	¼ tsp. salt

Mix and pat in a pie pan. Bake at 350° for 20 minutes.

Filling:

3 eggs, beaten	Vanilla
1¼ cups sugar	2 Tbsp. flour
2¼ cups rhubarb	⅓ cup Carnation milk

In saucepan, combine all ingredients and cook over medium heat until thick. Pour into baked crust and top with meringue.

Note: Recipe submitted from original Catholic Daughters Cookbook "Everybody's Favorite!"

Mrs. Isadore Pick, Lismore

RHUBARB PIE

1 cup sugar	½ cup half and half
2 eggs, separated	2 cups rhubarb, diced

Mix sugar, egg yolks and half and half. Mix well. Add diced rhubarb. Put in pie pan over single crust. Bake at 400° for 10 minutes then reduce heat to 350° until filling is set. Take out of oven and put on meringue.

Meringue:
Beat egg whites until stiff; continue beating and add **3 tablespoons sugar** slowly and last add ½ **teaspoon cream of tartar**. Beat a little longer and put on pie filling. Return to oven and bake at 300° to 350° for 10 to 15 minutes.

Clara Hess, Marshall

RHUBARB CUSTARD PIE**

2½ cups rhubarb, cut in ¼ inch slices	½ cup sugar
	1 (9 inch) unbaked pie crust

Mix rhubarb and sugar. Put in pie crust. Bake at 350° until rhubarb starts to get tender. Remove from oven.

Custard:

3 eggs	¼ cup sugar
1 cup milk	½ tsp. lemon extract

Combine the ingredients; pour over rhubarb. Return to oven and bake until knife comes out clean when inserted in middle of pie.

Karen Wiskow, St. Charles

RHUBARB CUSTARD PIE

For 9 inch Pie:	
4 cups rhubarb	3 eggs
2 cups sugar	3 Tbsp. milk
1/3 cup flour	1 Tbsp. butter
For 8 inch Pie:	
3 cups rhubarb	2 eggs
1½ cups sugar	2 Tbsp. milk
3 Tbsp. flour	2 tsp. butter

Make pie crust for 2 crust pie and line pie plate. Mix rhubarb, sugar and flour and put in pie tin. Beat eggs and milk slightly and pour over rhubarb mixture. Put on top crust or lattice top and dot with butter. Bake at 400° for 50 to 60 minutes or until nicely browned. After 25 minutes, reduce heat to 350°.

Anne Donahue, Currie

ONE CRUST RHUBARB PIE

4 eggs	6 Tbsp. butter or oleo, melted
1½ cups sugar	2 tsp. lemon juice
⅓ cup rich milk	

Beat well in bowl and add ¼ **cup soda cracker crumbs** and **2 cups fresh or frozen rhubarb**, cut up. Pour in **unbaked pie shell**. Bake at 450° for 10 minutes, then at 350° for 30 minutes or until rhubarb is tender.

Variation: For a 9x13 inch pan, make as follows:

Crust:

2 cups flour	1 cup butter or oleo
2 Tbsp. sugar	

Mix like pie crust, put in a 9x13 inch pan and bake at 350° for 10 minutes.

Filling:

6 eggs	6 Tbsp. butter or oleo, melted
3 cups sugar	4 tsp. lemon juice
⅔ cup milk	

Beat well and add ½ **cup soda cracker crumbs** and **5 cups cut up rhubarb**. Pour over crust and bake at 350° for about 60 minutes or until rhubarb is tender. Serve with Cool Whip.

Donna Harguth, Waseca

RHUBARB CUSTARD PIE

2 cups sugar	3 eggs, separated
2 Tbsp. flour, rounded	2 heaping cups rhubarb, cut
1 tsp. cinnamon	in small pieces
2 cups rich milk	1 unbaked pie shell

Mix 1½ cups sugar, flour, cinnamon, milk, and beaten egg yolks. Add to rhubarb. Put mixture in unbaked pie shell. Bake at 325° for 10 minutes, then at 350° for 1 hour. Top with meringue made from the egg whites and ½ cup sugar. Brown at 300° for 10 minutes.

Lucille R. Miller, Waseca

RHUBARB PIE

2 cups rhubarb, cut up	Dash of salt
1 cup sugar	2 beaten egg yolks
2 Tbsp. butter	¼ cup half and half cream
¼ cup sugar	1 baked pie crust
2 level Tbsp. cornstarch	

Mix rhubarb, sugar and butter in pan and cook on top of stove until soft. Mix sugar, cornstarch, salt and egg yolks. Add cream and add mixture to rhubarb. Cook until thick. Put into baked crust and cover with meringue.

Lauretta Welter, Crookston

RHUBARB-ORANGE CREAM PIE

Pastry for 9 inch pie shell
3 eggs, separated
1 ¼ cups sugar
¼ cup soft butter or margarine
3 Tbsp. frozen orange juice
concentrate

¼ cups flour
¼ tsp. salt
2½ cups rhubarb, cut in ½ inch
pieces
⅓ cups chopped pecans

Line a 9 inch pie pan with pastry; make high fluted rim. Beat egg whites until stiff; add ¼ cup sugar gradually, beating well after each addition. Add butter and juice concentrate to egg yolks; beat thoroughly. Add remaining cup sugar, flour and salt; beat well. Add rhubarb to yolk mixture; stir well. Gently fold in meringue. Pour into pastry-lined pan; sprinkle with nuts. Bake on bottom rack at 375° for 15 minutes. Reduce heat to 325° and bake 45 to 50 minutes more.

Mary Chevalier, Slayton

PHYLLIS' RHUBARB RUM-SPICE PIE

1 (9 inch) pastry shell
2 Tbsp. margarine
1 cup sugar
½ cup flour
2 eggs
2 cups chopped rhubarb

1 cup milk
2 Tbsp. dark rum
½ tsp. salt
½ tsp. nutmeg
½ tsp. cinnamon
Whipping cream, optional

Bake pastry shell at 350° for 5 minutes; cool. Cream margarine and sugar; blend in flour. Separate eggs; beat yolks. Add to first mixture. Add rhubarb, milk, rum, salt, nutmeg and cinnamon. Beat egg whites until stiff. Fold into other mixture. Place in shell. Bake at 350° for 45 to 50 minutes. Serve with whipped cream if desired.

Michele Maher Ritter, Winnebago

RAISIN CREAM PIE

3 beaten eggs
1 cup sugar
½ tsp. cinnamon
½ tsp. nutmeg
¼ tsp. salt
2½ Tbsp. lemon juice

2 Tbsp. butter or margarine,
melted
1 cup seedless raisins
½ cup broken California walnuts
1 (8 inch) unbaked pastry shell

Combine eggs, sugar, spices, salt, lemon juice and butter. Stir in raisins and nuts. Pour into pastry shell and bake at 375° for 30 minutes or until set in center. Cool.

Teresa G. O'Leary, Waterville

RAISIN CREAM PIE

1 cup raisins	2 Tbsp. flour
½ cup water	1 tsp. cinnamon
1 cup cream (I use half and half)	Pre-baked pastry shell
¾ cup sugar	3 egg whites
3 egg yolks	6 Tbsp. granulated sugar

Combine raisins and water and simmer 5 minutes. Add next 5 ingredients which have been mixed into a smooth paste. Cook over direct heat, stirring constantly until thick. Pour into pre-baked pastry shell. Beat egg whites with granulated sugar until frothy. Continue to beat until stiff peaks are formed. Top pie filling with meringue and bake at 400° until lightly browned.

Anna Hager, Medford

RICE KRISPY ICE CREAM PIE

⅓ cup peanut butter	2 cups Rice Krispies
⅓ cup corn syrup	1 qt. ice cream, softened

Mix thoroughly the peanut butter and corn syrup. Add Rice Krispies. Put into a buttered 9 inch pie plate to form crust. Chill. Spread softened ice cream over crust. Freeze. Serve with an ice cream sauce, fresh fruit or pie filling.

Delores Seykora, Owatonna

SODA CRACKER PIE

1½ cups sugar	1 tsp. cream of tartar
1 tsp. cinnamon	16 soda crackers
1½ Tbsp. lemon juice	Butter
1½ cups water	2 pie crusts

Combine first 5 ingredients until sugar is dissolved. Butter crackers and break into liquid. Pour into pie crust. Top with pie crust. Bake at 375° for 45 minutes. Mixture is very watery.

Jeanne Heer, Winona

SOUR CREAM PIE

1 cup sour cream	1 Tbsp. cornstarch
½ cup sugar	3 beaten egg yolks
1 tsp. cinnamon	1 cup raisins

Mix first 5 ingredients and cook over low heat until thick. Stir often. Add raisins. Put in baked crust. Beat egg whites (put a little cream of tartar in dish first, about ¼ tsp.) until stiff. Top pie filling. Bake until brown.

Julia Martin, Plainview

MOCK SOUR CREAM RAISIN PIE

1½ cups raisins
¾ to 1 cup sugar
Water
1 Tbsp. butter
1 tsp. vanilla

1 cup milk or 1 sm. can evaporated milk and enough milk to make 1 cup
½ tsp. vinegar
3 eggs, separated
1 tsp. cinnamon
2 Tbsp. cornstarch

Place raisins, sugar and water to cover in a pan and bring to a boil. Simmer 10 minutes. Add butter and vanilla to raisin mix. In a different bowl, combine milk and vinegar; add egg yolks, cinnamon and cornstarch. Add above ingredients to raisin mixture and cook over low heat until thick. Pour into a baked pie shell.

Topping:
3 egg whites   4 Tbsp. powdered sugar

Beat egg whites and powdered sugar and pour on top of raisin mixture. Bake at 325° for 8 to 10 minutes. Watch this carefully as it will brown slightly.

Laura Busch, Slayton

SUGAR FREE APPLE PIE

6 med. apples (1 qt.), cut up
1 (6 oz.) can frozen unsweetened apple juice
1 Tbsp. cornstarch or flour

Cinnamon to taste
2 Tbsp. butter or margarine
2 crust pie shell, unbaked

Peel and slice the apples. Add juice and bring to a boil. Simmer for 5 minutes. Add the cornstarch, mixed with water. Bring to a boil and simmer until apples are soft. Add cinnamon and margarine. Pour into unbaked crust. Put a crust on top and seal. Bake at 350° for 45 minutes. This makes a 9 inch pie.

Carol Bertrand, Wilmont
Margaret Huebsch, Perham

FRESH STRAWBERRY PIE

1 cup flour
1 stick margarine
1 qt. strawberries
1 cup sugar
3 Tbsp. cornstarch

2 Tbsp. white corn syrup
1¼ cups water
4 Tbsp. undiluted strawberry jello
3 to 4 drops red food coloring, optional

Mix flour and shortening and pat into a 9 inch pie tin. Bake at 350° for 15 minutes. Cool. Put strawberries in crust. Mix sugar, cornstarch, syrup and water; boil until thick and clear. Remove from heat and add jello and food coloring. Cool to lukewarm; pour over strawberries and refrigerate.

Cleone Flynn, Plainview

FRESH STRAWBERRY PIE

Crust:

½ cup margarine   1 Tbsp. sugar
1 cup flour

Melt and cool margarine. Add flour and sugar; mix and press in a 9 inch pie pan. Bake at 400° for 12 to 15 minutes.

Filling:

1 cup sugar   ½ (3 oz.) box strawberry jello
2 Tbsp. cornstarch   2 cups fresh strawberries,
1 cup water   quartered

Combine sugar, cornstarch and water in saucepan. Cook until thickened, stirring constantly. Remove from heat and add jello. Stir well and cool. Place fresh strawberries in pie shell. Pour cooled mixture over the strawberries. Refrigerate. Serve topped with Cool Whip.

Marilyn Herrig, Wilmont
Mary Heppelmann, Bellechester

STRAWBERRY CHIFFON STYLE PIE

¼ cup margarine or butter   8 packets Equal or 2½ tsp. Equal
¾ cup graham crackers, finely   measure
   crushed   1 Tbsp. lemon juice
2 packets Equal or ½ tsp. Equal   1 env. unflavored gelatin
   measure   ¼ cup water
3½ to 4 cups fresh or frozen   1 (5 oz.) can evaporated milk,
   strawberries   chilled icy cold

Melt margarine. Stir in crushed graham crackers and 2 packets Equal. Toss. Press mixture evenly in a 9 inch pie plate. Press onto bottom and up sides to form a firm even crust. Chill about 1 hour or until firm. Thaw frozen strawberries and crush in a mixing bowl. Stir in 8 packets Equal and the lemon juice; set aside. In a saucepan, stir gelatin and water; let stand 5 minutes. Cook and stir over low heat until gelatin dissolves. Cool. Stir the cooled gelatin mixture into the strawberry mixture. Chill until the consistency of corn syrup, stirring occasionally. Remove from refrigerator. Beat the chilled evaporated milk in a chilled large mixing bowl until soft peaks form. Gradually beat in strawberry mixture. Spoon into crust. Cover and chill 6 hours. Makes 10 servings.

Lora Mae Haler, St. James

STRAWBERRY YOGURT PIE**

2 (8 oz.) containers strawberry
   yogurt
½ cup mashed strawberries or
   1 box frozen strawberries

1 (8 oz.) carton Cool Whip,
   thawed
1 (8 or 9 inch) graham cracker
   crust

Thoroughly combine yogurt and mashed fruit in a bowl. Fold in Cool Whip, blending well. Spoon into crust and freeze about 4 hours. Remove from freezer; let stand a few minutes before serving. Store leftover pie in freezer.

Catherine Shikonya, Winona

"FAVORITE OLDIES"

RHUBARB CRUNCH DESSERT

1 cup flour
5 Tbsp. powdered sugar
½ cup butter or oleo
2 eggs
1½ cups white sugar

¼ cup flour
¾ tsp. baking powder
2 cups rhubarb, cut up
¼ tsp. nutmeg, optional

Mix flour, powdered sugar and butter and pat into a 9x9 inch pan. Bake at 350° for 12 minutes. Beat eggs until fluffy and add sugar, flour, and baking powder, which have been mixed together. Add rhubarb. Pour over crust. Bake at 350° for 40 minutes. Egg mixture will come to the top and form a meringue.

Note: I double this recipe and add about 6 cups of rhubarb for a 9x13 inch pan.

Mrs. Elmer Schroeder
Mrs. Mike Biren
Lois Manka, International Falls

CAKE MIX PRONTO COOKIES

1 (2 layer size) pkg. yellow cake
   mix with pudding
¼ cup butter or margarine,
   softened
⅓ cup cold strong brewed coffee

1 egg
1 (6 oz.) pkg. semi-sweet
   chocolate pieces (1 cup)
½ cup chopped walnuts

In mixer bowl, combine cake mix, butter or margarine, coffee and egg until smooth. Stir in chocolate pieces and nuts. Drop a well rounded teaspoon onto greased cookie sheet. Bake at 375° for 12 minutes. Let stand a few seconds before removing. Makes 4½ to 5 dozen cookies.

Carol A. Allen, International Falls

✝ LEGISLATIVE ✝

Operation Morning Star

Operation Morning Star is the 6 year-old, issue focused, Catholic Daughters of the Americas Legislative Program, dedicated to Our Blessed Mother. Its purpose is to assist members to become better informed on public issues, and to support church teachings on human life, human rights, justice and peace. This program does not endorse candidates or any political party.

A national telephone network has been formed to urge members to call federal government officials, when an important action is imminent. It was first activated nationwide, on March 7, 1996, to urge President Clinton to sign The Partial Birth Abortion Ban Act. Instead of signing the bill, President Clinton vetoed it.

CDA members are also involved in legislative issues at the state level. They attempt to influence legislation by personal visits with lawmakers, letter writing and telephoning. The Minnesota telephone tree was first activated in February, 1995. Members phoned state lawmakers concerning The Woman's Right to Know Amendment, Minnesota Care Health bill, and the Doe v Gomez Minnesota Supreme Court ruling.

Court Legislative Chairs try to educate members, at meetings, by announcements, information sheet handouts, and by giving talks. They seek to educate non-members through church bulletin announcements and brochure enclosures, and by letters to the editors of local papers.

Although Catholic Daughters do not endorse either candidates or political parties, members are encouraged to become involved, privately, in the party of their choice and to support whatever candidates they wish, as private citizens. Many attend precinct caucuses and party conventions, and most vote in elections.

Frances Crummy, *past* **Legislative Chair**

✠ SPIRITUAL ENHANCEMENT ✠

Spiritual Enhancement refers to activities of local, diocesan, state or national nature which are directed to the sanctification of our members. We are women who are firmly committed to the teaching of Christ and deeply loyal to the teachings of the Church and to our Holy Father. Above all, we are loyal to the practice of our religion. We are called to develop our faith through study and practice of spiritual exercises in a society that has become increasingly secularized.

As Catholic Daughters, we are committed to love others. We must first love ourselves to project our love to others. When we feel good about ourselves, we can give good to others. We can be aware of the positive things we and others do. For each of us, in order to enhance our spirituality, we must review what we were and still are taught by the Catholic Church; to love God above all with our whole heart, soul and mind; to love our neighbor as ourselves for the love of God.

Activities include having Eucharistic Liturgies for CDA Members, before or after meetings, at the reception of new members, at the installation of officers, and other court celebrations such as memorial services for deceased members or court anniversaries, Other activities include participation in Church Ministries, such as lectors, Eucharistic ministers, music ministry, welcoming committee, greeters etc.; participation in or conducting paraliturgical services, such as wake or memorial services, or seasonal prayer services. Spiritual Enhancement also includes participation in or conducting retreats and days of recollection which are in ideal way to increase one's spirituality and personal sanctification; and participation in or conducting other special prayer services such as devotions to our Blessed Mother, our Patroness, by praying the rosary, or by sponsoring novenas, or Bible study groups. Evangelization – bringing the good news of God's love, justice, mercy, salvation from sin and hopelessness through faith, is also part of Spiritual Enhancement, as is participation in or sponsoring interfaith services.

Shirley Seyfried, State Spiritual Enhancement Chair

HOT ASPARAGUS PASTA SALAD

1 (8 oz.) pkg. corkscrew pasta	2 Tbsp. water
1 clove garlic, crushed	¼ lb. fully cooked ham,
½ inch fresh gingerroot, minced	julienned or cubed
(optional)	1 (8 oz.) can sliced water chest-
1 Tbsp. cooking oil	nuts, drained
1 lb. fresh asparagus, cut into	1 cup sliced celery
1½ inch pieces	⅓ cup sliced ripe olives
½ lb. shrimp, peeled and deveined	

Cook pasta according to package directions. Meanwhile, in large skillet, saute garlic and gingerroot (if desired) in oil over medium-high heat for 1 to 2 minutes. Add asparagus, shrimp and water; cook until asparagus is crisp tender and shrimp are cooked, about 8 minutes. Stir in ham, water chestnuts, celery and olives. Remove from heat. Drain pasta and place in a large salad bowl; add asparagus mixture. Cover with foil.

Dressing:

6 Tbsp. vegetable oil	¼ tsp. salt
2 Tbsp. white wine vinegar	¼ tsp. pepper
1 Tbsp. soy sauce	⅛ tsp. dry mustard

Combine ingredients and pour over salad and toss. Serve immediately. Yield: 4 to 6 servings.

Pauline Turnbull, Eveleth

BAKED BEANS

Roaster:

8 lbs. small navy beans	4 Tbsp. salt
7 qts. water (enough to cover)	1½ tsp. dry mustard
1 lb. bacon, diced	2 tsp. paprika
2 lg. onions	2 bottles catsup
4 cups brown sugar	

Crockpot:

2 lbs. beans	1 Tbsp. salt
Water to cover beans	½ tsp. dry mustard
½ lb. bacon, diced	½ tsp. paprika
½ lg. onion	½ bottle catsup
1 cup brown sugar	

Pick over and wash beans thoroughly. Cover with water; soak overnight. Simmer in soaking water with control set at 300° (large roaster) until skins pierce easily. Add bacon and onions. Mix brown sugar, salt, paprika, mustard and catsup. Pour over beans. Mix well. Add more water if necessary. Bake at 300° for 4 to 5 hours.

Hazel Foyt, International Falls

BEAN BAKE

1 cup chopped onion
12 slices bacon, cut into 1 inch pieces
1 (16 oz.) can garbanzo beans, drained
1 (16 oz.) can green lima beans, drained
1 (16 oz.) can pork and beans with tomato sauce
1 (15 oz.) can red kidney beans, drained
1 (15 oz.) can black beans, drained
1 cup packed brown sugar (use less sugar for less sweetness)
1 cup catsup
½ cup vinegar

In skillet, cook onion and bacon until bacon is crisp and onion is tender, but not brown. Drain. Combine all ingredients in 3 quart casserole. Bake, covered, at 375° for 1 hour. Uncover and bake about 10 minutes more or until desired consistency. Yield: 12 servings. You may substitute other kinds of beans in this recipe.

Doris Halvorson, International Falls

BAKED BEANS

½ cup green pepper
1 cup chopped onion
1 (30 oz.) can pork and beans
1/3 cup brown sugar
½ tsp. black pepper
½ tsp. mustard
½ cup ketchup

Mix all ingredients and bake at 350° for 1½ hours.

Marge Stencel, New Richland

BAKED BEANS

2 lbs. navy beans
1 Tbsp. soda
2 Tbsp. salt
1 lb. bacon
1½ cups brown sugar

Soak beans overnight. In the morning, bring to a boil with soda. Boil until skins are loose. Drain well and rinse. Set oven at 325°. Cut bacon into small pieces. Add to beans with salt and the brown sugar. Cover with boiling water. Bake 5 hours (without stirring) or until tender in covered crock. Add boiling water as needed.

Evelyn Jackson, Ottertail

BAKED BEANS (ALA MEXICAO)

1 (1 lb.) can pork and beans
¼ cup light corn syrup
2 Tbsp. pimento
Dash garlic salt
1 (8 oz.) can tomato sauce
1 med. onion, chopped
1 Tbsp. prepared mustard
Bacon, cut

Put in greased 1½ quart casserole and put some cut bacon on top. Bake at 300° for about 45 minutes.

Jeanette Raichle, Meriden

BAKED BEANS

2 cups dried navy or northern beans
Bacon, ham or salt pork
1 med. onion, chopped
4 Tbsp. dark molasses
3 Tbsp. brown sugar
1 cup catsup
1 tsp. dry mustard
Salt to taste
Pepper to taste
2 cups hot water (If I have coffee left I use it instead)

Soak beans overnight. Drain. Precook beans for 30 minutes. Add all ingredients and bake until beans are done. This will be several hours.

Variation: may add ½ teaspoon soda and 1 teaspoon paprika.

Dorothy Kliner, Euclid
District Deputy, 1996-present
Helen Fisch, Caledonia

BEAN CASSEROLE

1 lb. hamburger, browned
1 (13 oz.) can pork and beans
1 (16 oz.) can green beans, drained
1 (8 oz.) can lima beans, drained
1 (8 oz.) can kidney beans, drained
1 onion
1 cup catsup
1 Tbsp. dry mustard
1 Tbsp. Worcestershire sauce
3 Tbsp. vinegar
½ cup brown sugar
8 slices of bacon

Mix hamburger and beans. Mix other ingredients and pour over the top. Top with sliced bacon. Bake at 350° for 1 hour.

Sister Kathryn Schoolmeesters, Fergus Falls
Court Cabrini Chaplain

BEANS FOR EVERYBODY

$^1/_3$ cup butter
½ cup minced onions
1 clove garlic
2 tsp. brown sugar
1 tsp. dry mustard
2 (No. 2) cans kidney beans, drained
1 (No. 2) can lima beans, drained
1 can Boston style baked beans
¼ cup catsup
2 Tbsp. vinegar
1 tsp. salt
¼ tsp. pepper

Heat butter, minced onions and garlic for 5 minutes. Add brown sugar and mustard. Add rest of ingredients and pour into a 2 quart casserole. Bake at 350° for 25 minutes. Makes 8 servings.

Marie Maslowski, Red Wing

301

BAKED BEANS

3 cups navy beans	1 tsp. Worcestershire sauce
1 can tomato soup	1 med. onion
1 can water	1 clove garlic
1 Tbsp. catsup	½ cup brown sugar
1 tsp. mustard	¼ lb. salt pork

Soak beans for 2 hours. Boil until skins leave beans. Add all ingredients. Bake at 350° for several hours. Do not let beans dry out. Add water when necessary.

Doris LaBine, Argyle

BRUNA BONAR (SWEDISH BROWN BEANS)

2 cups brown beans	2 Tbsp. vinegar or lemon juice
2 Tbsp. butter	Salt and pepper to taste
¼ cup brown sugar or syrup	

Wash beans and put on to boil in cold water. Simmer until tender, about 3 hours. When done, add the rest of ingredients. Serve hot. Other types of beans may be used if brown beans are not available. This is a favorite dish among Swedish people. Very often served at the smorgasbord.

Florence St. Germain, Argyle

CALICO BEANS

¼ lb. bacon, diced	1 Tbsp. prepared mustard
1 lb. hamburger	1 tsp. salt
½ cup chopped onion	1 (No. 2) can lima beans
1 cup brown sugar	1 (No. 2) can red kidney beans
½ cup catsup	1 (No. 2) can pork and beans
2 Tbsp. vinegar	

Fry bacon until browned slightly. Add hamburger and cook, stirring until crumbly. Add onion and saute until partially cooked. Add sugar, catsup, vinegar, mustard and salt. Drain juice from lima beans and kidney beans and rinse under cold running water. Combine all beans with meat and stir to blend ingredients. Pour into large casserole and bake at 350° for 1 hour. Can also be done in a crock pot. Serves 8 to 10.

Variation: May add ¼ cup barbecue sauce, 2 tablespoons molasses, and ½ teaspoon chili powder.

Rosie McGinty, Holland
Carol Dalton, International Falls

CALICO BEANS

½ lb. bacon, fried crisp
1 lb. ground beef, browned
   in bacon fat
1 med. onion, sauteed
1 (1 lb.) can pork and beans
1 (15 oz.) can kidney beans,
   drained

¾ cup catsup
1 tsp. salt
¼ cup brown sugar
2 tsp. prepared mustard
2 tsp. vinegar

Mix first 5 ingredients. Mix remaining ingredients together, then combine both mixtures. Bake, uncovered, at 350° for 40 to 50 minutes. Nice in the summer as a side dish.

Helen Foltz, Detroit Lakes

CALICO BEANS

6 slices bacon, cut up and
   fried crisp
1 lb. ground beef
1 lg. onion
1 can butter beans

1 can kidney beans
1 (20 oz.) can pork and beans
¼ cup catsup
½ cup brown sugar
1 Tbsp. yellow mustard

Fry bacon and brown beef and onion together. Oven bake all ingredients at 350° for 1 hour. Or you can use slow cooker and simmer for 2 hours.

Olive Hastad, Tempe, AZ
Vice State Regent, 1962-1966
State Regent, 1966-1970
National Director, 1970-1974

SWEET AND SOUR PINEAPPLE BAKED BEANS

2 buds from 1 clove garlic,
   minced
3 lbs. lean ground beef
Salt and pepper, if desired
½ cup chopped onion, sauteed
   until clear
1 Tbsp. Worcestershire sauce
¼ cup brown sugar, dissolved

1 Tbsp. cider vinegar
1 cup green pepper, chopped
1 (20 oz.) can Boston or Bush's
   baked beans
1 (14 oz.) can peeled tomatoes,
   drained
1 (20 oz.) can pineapple chunks
   or tidbits, drained

In a large frying pan, place the minced garlic and chopped up ground beef; brown. Add salt and pepper if desired. Place the chopped onion in a small pan and saute until clear. Drain excess liquid off of browned ground beef. Add Worcestershire sauce, brown sugar, vinegar, green pepper, baked beans, tomatoes and pineapple. Add sauteed onion. In either a Dutch oven or a 3 quart casserole; bake at 300° for 45 minutes to 1 hour. Serve hot with a salad and dessert. ENJOY!

Joan Shipe, Fergus Falls

3 BEAN CASSEROLE

1 can kidney beans, drained
1 can butter beans, drained
1 can B&M beans
½ lb. bacon, cut up (not cooked)

¼ lb. Velveeta cheese, cut in chunks
⅓ cup brown sugar
½ cup white sugar
¼ cup water

Mix all ingredients and bake at 350° for 2 hours.

Joan Steele, Red Wing

WESTERN BEANS

4 bacon strips, diced
1 lg. onion, chopped
⅓ cup dry lentils
1⅓ cups water
2 Tbsp. ketchup
1 tsp. garlic powder
¾ tsp. chili powder
½ tsp. ground cumin

¼ tsp. dried red pepper flakes
1 bay leaf
1 (16 oz.) can whole tomatoes with liquid, chopped
1 (15 oz.) can pinto beans, drained
1 (16 oz.) can kidney beans, drained

Lightly fry bacon in a heavy 3 quart saucepan. Add onion; cook until transparent. Stir in remaining ingredients. Cook over medium heat for 45 minutes or until lentils are tender, stirring once or twice. Remove bay leaf before serving. Yield: 8 to 10 servings.

Diane Wenieke, Lismore

AUNT STASHA'S TOMATO BEANS

¼ lb. bacon
2 cans green beans, drained
1 (8 oz.) can tomato sauce with 2 Tbsp. water

¼ cup sugar
2 Tbsp. flour
Salt and pepper to taste

Fry bacon. Drain and crumble or cut into pieces prior to frying. Add remaining ingredients and simmer 15 to 20 minutes.

Darla Johnson, Perham

GREEN BEAN CASSEROLE

3 cans French style beans
½ pt. sour cream
24 thin soda crackers, crushed

1 can cream of mushroom soup
1 sm. pkg. Velveeta cheese
½ stick oleo

Drain beans; spread in an 8x13 inch pan or casserole. Sprinkle with garlic salt. Mix soup and sour cream. Pour over green beans. Layer thin slices of cheese over top. Spread crackers over cheese. Slice oleo and lay on crackers. Bake at 325° for 30 to 40 minutes.

Rose Guillemette, Mankato
State Regent, 1984-1986

CHEDDAR CHEESE BEAN BAKE

1 can Cheddar cheese soup
1/3 cup milk
3 cups fresh or frozen green
   beans, cooked and drained

1 (3½ oz.) can French fried
   onion rings

In a 1½ quart casserole, stir soup until smooth; gradually add milk. Mix cooked beans and ½ can onions into soup mixture. Bake at 350° for 20 minutes; sprinkle rest of onion rings over top and bake 6 to 8 minutes longer. Serves 6.

Mary Ann Sullivan, Fairmont

FRENCH GREEN BEANS WITH WATER CHESTNUTS

2 (9 oz.) pkgs. frozen French
   green beans

1 (15 oz.) can water chestnuts,
   drained and sliced

Cook beans according to package. Drain water chestnuts and heat thoroughly at 325° for 30 minutes. Add **1 can cream of mushroom soup** to mixture and season to taste with **ground pepper**.

Dorothy Morgan, Morristown

GARLIC BUTTERED GREEN BEANS

1 lb. fresh or frozen green beans
½ cup sliced fresh mushrooms
6 Tbsp. butter or margarine

2 to 3 tsp. onion powder
1 to 1½ tsp. garlic powder
Salt and pepper to taste

Cook green beans in water to cover until tender. Meanwhile, in skillet, saute mushrooms in butter until tender. Add onion powder and garlic powder. Drain beans; add to skillet and toss. Season with salt and pepper and serve.

Josephine Befort, Zumbrota

GREEN BEANS

4 slices bacon, cut in small
   pieces and fried crisp
¼ cup water
¼ cup vinegar

1 can French style green beans
¼ cup sugar
Salt and pepper to taste
1 onion, chopped

Fry bacon. Add water and vinegar to pan, then beans. Put sugar, salt, pepper and onion on beans. Pour liquid over top. Simmer until heated through. Add chopped **hard boiled egg** for garnish.

Variation: May add 1 tablespoon flour. May delete chopped hard boiled egg.

Isabelle King, Winona
Rose Przybylski, Argyle
Mary Dolensek, Eveleth

BROCCOLI CASSEROLE

1 sm. onion	1 can cream of mushroom soup
1 can mushrooms, drained	1 (8 oz.) jar Cheese Whiz
¾ stick margarine	1 sm. pkg. slivered almonds
3 pkgs. frozen broccoli, thawed	Croutons

Saute onions and mushrooms in margarine. Take onions and mushrooms out of margarine. Put thawed broccoli into 2 quart casserole. Pour soup and cheese mixture, onions, mushrooms and almonds over broccoli. Bake at 325° for 30 minutes, covered. Uncover, stir and add croutons on top. Bake 15 minutes more, uncovered. This can be made ahead of time and is excellent reheated. Serves 6.

Joyce Pribyl, Owatonna

BROCCOLI RICE CASSEROLE

2 cups cooked broccoli	1 cup fresh sliced mushrooms
1 cup Cheddar cheese	1 cup sliced water chestnuts,
1 cup cooked rice	drained
1 can cream of mushroom soup	

Mix ingredients and bake at 350° for 25 minutes.

Lane Magnusson, Fergus Falls

BROCCOLI AND RICE CASSEROLE

2 cups rice	1 can cream of chicken soup
1 or 2 (10 oz.) pkgs. broccoli	½ cup milk
cuts, thawed or fresh broccoli	1 sm. onion
1 (8 oz.) pkg. Velveeta cheese	½ soup can water

Cook rice as directed. Cook broccoli until tender. Mix all ingredients and place in casserole. Bake at 325° for 1 hour, uncovered.

Agnes Cummiskey, Currie

SCOTT'S BROCCOLI SUPREME**

1 (10 oz.) pkg. chopped broccoli	¼ tsp. salt
1 (16 oz.) can creamed corn	Dash of pepper
1 slightly beaten egg	3 Tbsp. butter
1 Tbsp. chopped onion	1 cup herb stuffing mix

Cook broccoli until almost done (about 4 minutes) before adding it to the creamed corn, which has been combined with the egg, onion, salt and pepper. Set aside. Melt butter and toss with stuffing mix to coat. Stir ¾ of stuffing mix into broccoli mixture. Pour into lightly buttered casserole. Top with remaining stuffing. Microwave for 6 to 8 minutes on high.

Catherine Mino, Blue Earth

VEGETABLE HOT DISH

2 (10 oz.) pkgs. frozen broccoli florets or California style mixed vegetables
1 can condensed Cheddar cheese soup
¼ cup milk
¼ cup buttered bread crumbs

Cook and drain vegetables. Place in shallow 10x6x2 inch baking dish. Blend soup and milk; pour over vegetables. Top with crumbs. Bake at 350° for about 30 minutes or until hot and bubbly.

Corine Deeny, Waterville

BAKED HASH BROWNS

3 cups half and half
2 Tbsp. butter
1 tsp. salt
1 box frozen hash brown potatoes, thawed
Parmesan cheese

Warm half and half with butter and salt added. Pour over hash brown potatoes that have been placed in a 9x13 inch pan. Sprinkle generous amount of Parmesan cheese over all and bake at 325° for 1 hour. Serves 8.

Irene Neisen, Mahnomen

DELUXE HASH BROWNS

1 (32 oz.) bag hash brown potatoes
2 Tbsp. dry onion
1 can cream of chicken soup
1 (8 oz.) carton sour cream
½ cup butter or margarine, melted
Salt and pepper
2 cups grated hard cheese

Mix ingredients and put in a 9x13 inch pan. Top with **2 cups crushed corn flakes** and ¼ **cup melted margarine**. Bake at 350° for about 45 minutes.

Josephine Kochmann, Mahnomen

BAKED VEGETABLE OMELET

1 cup shredded Monterey Jack cheese
2 cups shredded Cheddar cheese
1½ cups chopped fresh broccoli or 1 pkg. frozen, thawed and drained
1½ cups chopped tomatoes
1 cup milk
¼ cup flour
2½ Tbsp. omelet and souffle seasoning (Watkins)
¼ tsp. garlic salt
¼ tsp. thyme
3 eggs

In an 8 inch square baking dish, layer cheeses, broccoli, and tomatoes. Beat remaining ingredients until smooth; pour over first mixture, then bake, uncovered, at 350° for 40 to 50 minutes or until egg is set. Let stand 10 minutes before cutting. Makes 6 servings.

Genevieve Knott, Red Lake Falls
District Deputy, 1994-present

CARROT CASSEROLE

1 sm. onion	1 can celery soup
3 Tbsp. butter	1 cup Cheddar cheese,
1 lb. sliced carrots, partially	chopped
cooked	1 cup stuffing mix

Saute onion in butter. Mix onion and carrots with rest of ingredients. Bake 30 minutes.

Variation: Add browned sausage.

Neva Quaday, Blue Earth

CARROT CASSEROLE

2 lbs. carrots, sliced and	1 can cream of mushroom soup
cooked slightly	1 (8 oz.) jar Cheese Whiz
1 can mushroom pieces, drained	1 can French fried onion rings
1 can sliced water chestnuts,	
drained	

Mix and bake all ingredients, except onion rings. Bake at 350° for 45 minutes. Top with onion rings the last 5 minutes.

Joan Guck, Perham

CARROT DISH

1 lb. carrots	¼ cup vinegar
1 med. onion	¼ cup sugar
1 green pepper	1 tsp. Worcestershire sauce
1 can tomato soup, undiluted	1 tsp. prepared mustard
¼ cup salad oil	Salt and pepper to taste

Slice and cook carrots (may want to peel first). Add chopped onion and diced green peppers to the cooked carrots. (Onion and pepper are kept raw.) Mix soup, oil, vinegar, sugar, Worcestershire sauce and mustard. Pour over vegetables. Let stand overnight. This may be served hot or cold. (Heated for vegetable dish; cold to use as a salad dish.)

Marie Reisdorfer, Slayton

GINGER CARROTS (AKA SUNSHINE CARROTS)

5 med. carrots	¼ tsp. ginger
1 Tbsp. sugar	¼ cup orange juice
1 tsp. cornstarch	2 Tbsp. margarine
½ tsp. salt	

Slice carrots on bias, 1 inch thick. Cook, covered, in boiling water until just tender, about 20 minutes; drain. Meanwhile, combine sugar, cornstarch, salt and ginger in small pan. Add orange juice. Cook, stirring constantly until mixture thickens and bubbles. Boil 1 minute. Stir in margarine. Pour over carrots, tossing to coat evenly.

Mayme Grund, Eveleth

CAULIFLOWER AU GRATIN

½ cup grated Velveeta cheese (about 2 oz.)
1 med. head cauliflower, half cooked
1 cup medium hot white sauce (below)
Bread crumbs

Stir cheese into white sauce and pour sauce over cauliflower. Sprinkle with bread crumbs which have been mixed with butter. Bake at 350° for 20 minutes or until cauliflower is done and crumbs are browned.

White Sauce:

Melt **2 tablespoons butter** over low heat; add **2 tablespoons flour**. Gradually add **1 cup milk** while stirring until it thickens.

Helen Kraus, Kellogg

EXOTIC CELERY

4 heaping cups celery, cut up
1 can cream of chicken soup
1 sm. jar pimento, undrained
1 (6 oz.) can water chestnuts, drained
1 cup slivered almonds

Cook celery in boiling water for 8 minutes; drain. Add soup, pimento and water chestnuts. Place in a 2 quart casserole. Saute almonds in a little butter and sprinkle over celery. Bake at 350° for 30 minutes, uncovered.

Rosella Sogge, Fairmont

CORN VEGETABLE MEDLEY

1 can Campbell's new golden corn soup
½ cup milk
1 bag California mix vegetables
½ cup shredded Cheddar cheese

In saucepan, heat soup and milk to boiling, stirring often. Stir in vegetables. Return to boiling. Cover, cook over low heat 20 minutes or until vegetables are tender, stirring often. Stir in cheese. Heat through. Serves 6.

Lilianna St. Aubin, Marshall

CORN SOUFFLE

1 can whole kernel corn, drained
1 can cream style corn
2 beaten eggs
1 stick oleo or butter, melted
1 cup sour cream
1 box Jiffy corn meal muffin mix

Mix all ingredients. Bake in a square buttered casserole at 350° for 45 minutes.

Edna Jane Nolte, Delphos, OH
National Regent, 1990-1994

CORN SUPREME CASSEROLE

1 can cream style corn
1 can whole kernel corn, drained
1 cup grated Cheddar cheese
¼ cup melted margarine
2 Tbsp. sugar
1 cup fine uncooked noodles or angel hair pasta
Salt and pepper to taste

Mix and turn into a greased casserole dish. Bake, uncovered, at 350° for 1 hour. Stir after 30 minutes. Serves 8.

Lila McGill, Winona

SCALLOPED CORN

4 Tbsp. butter
1 onion, chopped (optional)
1 green pepper, chopped (optional)
2 cans cream style corn
1 cup milk
1 cup soda cracker crumbs
4 beaten eggs
Salt and pepper

Melt butter; add onions and green peppers and saute. Add corn, milk, crumbs, eggs and seasonings. Mix and pour into greased casserole dish. Bake at 350° for 1½ hours or until knife inserted in center comes out clean.

Bernice Dout, Mahnomen

POTLUCK VEGETABLE CASSEROLE

1 (15 oz.) can whole kernel corn
1 (15 oz.) can cream style corn
1 (10 oz.) bag frozen broccoli, cooked
1 (10 oz.) bag frozen cauliflower, cooked
1 (4 oz.) can mushrooms
1 can cream of celery soup
2 Tbsp. butter
1½ cups bread crumbs
2 cups shredded Swiss cheese

Combine the ingredients in a large casserole baking dish. Cook at 350° for 1 hour. Serves 12 to 15 people.

Margaret Henry, St. Charles
State Treasurer, 1984-1986

ONION CASSEROLE

4 lb. onion
1 can mushroom soup
½ lb. Velveeta cheese
1 Tbsp. lemon juice
Buttered crumbs

Slice onions about ½ inch thick. Parboil in salt water for 5 minutes; drain. Place in buttered casserole. Add mushroom soup, cheese and top with buttered crackers or bread crumbs. Bake at 350° for 25 minutes.

Eunice Larson, St. Peter

CUCUMBERS AU GRATIN

3 Tbsp. flour	¼ tsp. onion juice
3 Tbsp. butter	1 cup grated sharp cheese
1¼ cups milk	⅓ cup fine dry bread crumbs
1 beef bouillon cube	1½ tsp. butter, melted
Dash of pepper	2 med. cucumbers, peeled

Blend flour and butter well. Gradually add milk and stir constantly over heat until sauce boils and thickens. Stir in bouillon cube, pepper, and onion juice. Remove from heat. Add cheese, stirring until melted. Stir in bread crumbs into melted butter to coat them well. Slice peeled cucumbers about ⅛ inch thick into a 6 cup buttered casserole. Put alternate layers of cucumbers and hot cheese sauce. Top with buttered bread crumbs. Cover and bake at 325° for 30 minutes. Remove cover and continue baking for 10 minutes more or until cucumbers are tender and surface browned.

Marion Kruger, Adrian

GERMAN DISH ("NOODLAH")

¾ cup fine chopped onion	1 tsp. salt
1 tsp. oil	1 tsp. baking powder
1 cup water	4 med. sliced potatoes
1 cup flour	

Saute onions in oil until they are pale yellow. Turn up heat and add water and bring to a boil. Blend flour, salt and baking powder in a bowl. Add just enough water to form a dough. Take small dough segments and roll into cone shapes about 2½ inches in length. Add these to the now boiling water-oil-onion mixture. Spread sliced potatoes on top and cover. When the sound of the onion frying is quite audible about 20 minutes on medium heat. Lift lid and check for browness. If the noodlah is not golden brown, replace lid and cook another 5 minutes.

Note: In our family, this was served with fresh water melon.

Helen Bye, Crookston

MARINATED ONIONS

2 lg. sweet onions, sliced in rings	2 tsp. salt
½ cup white vinegar	½ tsp. dill weed
½ cup sugar	¼ cup water

Combine above ingredients and bring to a boil. Pour over onion rings. Cover and let stand overnight in refrigerator. Ready to use. Will keep for weeks in refrigerator.

Ann Warthesen, Theilman

311

ONION RINGS

2 eggs	1 tsp. salt
½ cup milk	1 tsp. shortening
1 cup flour	1 tsp. baking powder

Mix ingredients for batter. Dip **onion rings** in it and fry in deep fat.

Mary Clark, Dundee

AU GRATIN POTATOES

¼ cup chopped onion	⅛ tsp. pepper
¼ cup butter	2½ cups milk
¼ cup flour	5 cups cooked potatoes,
1 tsp. salt	shredded

To make sauce, cook onion in butter until soft. Stir in flour, salt and pepper; add milk. Cook and stir until thickened and bubbly. Cook and stir 1 to 2 minutes more. Remove from heat. Add to potatoes. Bake, uncovered, at 350° for 30 to 45 minutes.

Pat Jennings, Caledonia

BAR HARBOR AU GRATIN SPUDS

2 Tbsp. butter	3 heaping cups cold shredded
2 Tbsp. flour	baked potatoes or thawed
¼ tsp. salt	hash browns
¼ tsp. pepper	Grated Parmesan cheese
1½ cups warm milk	1 (6 oz.) pkg. shredded sharp
1 can Campbell's Cheddar	Cheddar cheese
cheese soup	Paprika

Melt butter in saucepan, adding flour a bit at a time, mixing well until mixture bubbles. Add salt and pepper. Turn heat to low; add milk slowly, while whisking mixture until creamy. Add soup; bring to a bubble again. Immediately remove from heat. Let cool; add potatoes. Put in an 8x8 inch casserole or individual serving casseroles (leaving room at top for cheese to bubble). Sprinkle liberally with Parmesan. Sprinkle shredded Cheddar over top. Sprinkle lightly with paprika. Bake at 400° until cheese melts and is golden brown. These freeze well and make a handy side dish in a short time.

Rozie Ochry, Detroit Lakes
District Deputy, 1988-1992

* * * * * * * *

The gift of happiness belongs to those who unwrap it.
Lorraine Hassing, Blue Earth

CHEESE POTATO PUFF

12 med. potatoes	1 tsp. salt
6 Tbsp. butter or margarine	2 beaten eggs
2¼ cups grated Cheddar cheese	Paprika
1 to 1¼ cups milk	

Peel potatoes and cook until done. Drain and mash well. Add butter, cheese, milk and salt. Stir until cheese is melted. Fold in beaten eggs and pour into well greased 9x13 inch Pyrex pan. Sprinkle with paprika. Bake at 350° for 30 to 45 minutes or until puffy and golden brown on top. Serves 10.

Suzanne Lonneman, Adrian

POTATO PUFFS

2 eggs, separated	1 tsp. dried minced onion
2 cups mashed potatoes	1/8 tsp. garlic powder
2 Tbsp. grated Parmesan cheese	2 to 3 Tbsp. margarine, melted
1 Tbsp. chives	

Beat egg yolks. Add potatoes, cheese, chives, onions and garlic powder. Mix well. Beat egg whites until stiff. Fold into potato mixture. Brush eight muffin cups with margarine. Add potato mixture into cups. Brush remaining margarine over potatoes. Bake at 375° for 30 to 35 minutes. Serve immediately. Makes 8 puffs.

Joanne Halbur, Iona

COMPANY POTATOES

Potatoes	Parmesan cheese
Flour	

Peel and cut medium potatoes (according to number of people) in 4 chunks. Shake equal parts of flour and Parmesan cheese in ziploc bag. Add potatoes and shake. Bake at 400° for 1 hour in buttered pan. Watch! Turn in 30 minutes. Cover with foil. (Delicious, enjoy!)

Ethel Mae Smith, Crookston

CREAMY POTATOES

2 lbs. frozen hash browns, thawed	1 cup grated Velveeta cheese
1 can cream of chicken soup	1½ cups (12 oz.) sour cream
2 Tbsp. minced onion	½ cup melted butter
1 tsp. salt	

Mix all ingredients and put in a 9x13 inch pan. Sprinkle ½ cup crushed corn flakes mixed with 2 tablespoons butter on top.
Variation: Substitute 1 can cheese soup for Velveeta cheese.

Stephanie Stamarski, International Falls
Lori Maas, Medford

CREAM SCALLOPED POTATOES

2 lbs. potatoes (about 6)	2½ cups milk
3 Tbsp. margarine	1 sm. onion (¼ cup)
3 Tbsp. flour	Ham, optional
1 tsp. salt	1 Tbsp. margarine
½ tsp. pepper	

Peal potatoes and cut into thin slices (about 4 cups). Heat margarine in saucepan over low heat until melted. Blend in flour, salt and pepper. Cook over low heat, stirring constantly until smooth and bubbly. Remove from heat. Stir in milk. Heat to boiling, stirring constantly. Boil and stir 1 minute. Arrange potatoes in greased casserole in 3 layers, alternating with onions and white sauce. Bits of ham can be added. Dot with butter. Cover and bake at 350° for 40 minutes. Uncover and bake 60 to 70 minutes. Let stand before serving.

Variation: Substitute chicken broth for milk. Add 1 cup diced ham.

Gladys Doris, International Falls
Veronica Tramel, Morristown
Eunice Cole, Argyle

JO-JO POTATOES

6 or 7 med. potatoes	¾ tsp. salt
¼ cup flour	⅛ tsp. pepper
¼ cup grated Parmesan cheese	⅓ cup butter or oleo

Scrub and quarter the potatoes. Don't peel. Mix flour, cheese, salt and pepper. Place in plastic or paper bag with potatoes; shake to coat well. Melt butter in a 9x13 inch pan. Add potatoes. Bake at 375° for about 1 hour. Turn potatoes 1 or 2 times to brown evenly.

Leona Chesler, Eveleth

LORI'S GOLDEN POTATO SCONES

4 med. potatoes	4 Tbsp. grated Cheddar cheese
2 to 3 Tbsp. melted butter	1½ Tbsp. Parmesan cheese
2 to 3 Tbsp. herbs of your choice*	1 Tbsp. salt

*Use herbs such as parsley, chives, thyme or sage or others.

Peel potatoes, if skin is tough, otherwise wash and dry. Cut potatoes into thin slices, but not all the way through. Use handle of knife from cutting all the way through. Place potato in microwave safe dish or pan. Sprinkle with butter and chopped parsley, chives or sage. Microwave at high for 10 minutes. Rearrange after 5 minutes. Let rest 5 minutes. Sprinkle with grated cheese and Parmesan cheese. Microwave for another 4 to 6 minutes on high or until cheese is melted. Sprinkle with salt. Serve as a side dish.

Margie Deming, Plainview

HASH BROWN AU GRATIN

1 (2 lb.) pkg. frozen hash browns, thawed	½ cup chopped onion
	1 can cream of chicken soup
1 cup shredded Cheddar cheese	1 cup bread crumbs
1 cup sour cream	¼ cup melted butter

Mix first 5 ingredients and spread evenly on a 9x13 inch pan. Bake at 350° for 45 to 60 minutes. Mix melted butter and bread crumbs; sprinkle on top for last 15 minutes of baking.

Variation: Substitute 1 can potato soup for the chicken soup.

Anne Hoehn, Waseca
Millie Fangmeier, Pipestone

GARLIC AND ROSEMARY POTATOES

1 lb. new potatoes	2 Tbsp. fresh rosemary (2 tsp. if dried)
1 Tbsp. virgin olive oil	
4 cloves garlic, peeled and thickly sliced	$^1/_8$ tsp. salt
	Fresh ground pepper to taste
1 Tbsp. minced shallot, or fresh green onion	

Choose small potatoes. Scrub well. If large, cut into thick slices. Steam potatoes for 7 minutes until they are firm, but slightly tender. Pour oil into casserole dish. Add potatoes, garlic, shallot or onion, rosemary, salt and pepper. Toss to mix well. Bake, uncovered, in a preheated 350° oven for 30 minutes. Stir a couple of times during baking so potatoes cook evenly. Low fat, low calorie side dish. Great with roast chicken. Serves 4.

Doris Kern, Owatonna

PARTY POTATOES

1 (32 oz.) pkg. hash browns, thaw slightly	1 tsp. salt
	½ tsp. pepper
¼ cup chopped onion, optional	2 cups crushed corn flakes
1 can cream of chicken soup	½ cup melted butter
2 cups grated sharp cheese	

Place potatoes in heavily greased large casserole. Combine onions, soup, cheese, and salt and pepper; pour over potatoes and mix. Mix crushed corn flakes with melted butter and sprinkle over potatoes. Bake, uncovered, at 350° for 45 minutes.

Variation: May add 1 cup sour cream.

Joan Hannasch, Bellechester
Alice Buse, Slayton

315

PARMESAN POTATOES

4 lg. Russet potatoes, cut	Salt and pepper
lengthwise into eighths	½ cup freshly grated Parmesan
¼ cup olive oil	cheese
1 tsp. dried crushed red pepper	Chopped fresh basil

Position rack on the lowest of the oven and preheat to 375°. Place potatoes on roasting pan. Add oil and red pepper and toss to coat. Season with salt and pepper. Bake until tender on the inside and crusty on the outside, turning once, about 1 hour. Sprinkle on the Parmesan and basil. Serves 4.

Lorraine Habeman, New Ulm

PARTY MASHED POTATOES

5 lbs. cooked potatoes	1 (6 oz.) pkg. cream cheese
1 cup sour cream	Salt and pepper to taste

Mash potatoes and add the sour cream and cream cheese. Mix well; add salt and pepper. Cool and put in refrigerator. Cover. Next day, dot with butter and bake at 350° for 45 minutes to 1 hour.

Variations: Dorothy substitutes ⅓ cup milk for sour cream. Terry includes garlic salt and parsley flakes, or ½ cup chopped chives. Barb uses 1 cup light cream instead of sour cream, and adds onion salt, 1 (10 oz.) pkg. chopped spinach, cooked and drained (optional). Viola adds ½ teaspoon onion salt. Rosemary adds Cheddar cheese as topping.

Irma Vroman, Marshall
District Deputy, 1992-1996
Dorothy Dickman, Owatonna
Terry Stenberg, International Falls
Barb Springman, Wilmont
Viola Ruffing, Adrian
Rosemary Loosbrock Carlson, Slayton

TWICE BAKED POTATOES

4 lg. baked potatoes	Salt and pepper to taste
1½ cups grated Cheddar cheese	Paprika, optional
½ cup sour cream	½ cup bacon bits
½ stick butter	2 chopped green onions

Cut potatoes in halves lengthwise and scoop out most of potato into mixing bowl. Combine potato, cheese, sour cream and seasonings. Beat with mixer until fluffy. Fill potato skins with mixture and top with remaining cheese, bacon and onion. Bake in oven another 20 to 25 minutes.

Teresa Fuerstenberg, Wilmont

BAKED HASH BROWNS

2 lbs. hash brown potatoes
2 cups shredded cheese

1 pt. whipping cream
½ cup butter or margarine

Season to taste. Line in a 9x13 inch pan. Bake at 325° for 1½ hours.

Martha Erickson, St. Peter

HASH BROWN HOT DISH

2 lbs. frozen hash browns
1 cup sour cream
1 can cream of mushroom, chicken or celery soup

2 cups shredded Cheddar cheese
1 cup grated onion
¼ cup melted margarine, mixed with 2 cups corn flakes

Grease a 9x13 inch pan. Put mixed ingredients in pan. Top with corn flake mixture. Bake at 350° for 45 minutes.

Clara Udelhofen, Mankato

SCALLOPED HASH BROWNS

½ cup butter
⅓ cup onion
2 cans cream of chicken soup

2 cups sour cream
2 lbs. hash browns
2 cups Cheddar cheese

Heat butter and onion; add soup, then add sour cream and mix well. Put hash browns in a 9x13 inch pan that is greased. Spread soup mixture over top; sprinkle with cheese.

Topping:

¼ cup melted butter

2 cups post toasties

Mix ingredients and sprinkle on top. Bake at 350° for 1 hour.

Variations: Marie substitutes crushed potato chips instead of post toasties. Donna substitutes 2 cans potato soup instead of the chicken soup and deletes the sour cream. Lita only uses 1 can cream of chicken soup and adds bacon bits to grated cheese in topping. Sandi substitutes 2 cans cream of celery soup instead of the chicken soup, deletes the sour cream, and adds 1 can cream of potato soup. Marilyn substitutes 1 can cream of celery soup along with ½ cup chopped celery for the chicken soup and substitutes 1 can pearl onions instead for the fresh onion.

Ursula Kellen, Iona
Marie Pelzel, Caledonia
Donna Palacec, Eveleth
Lita Schreler, Currie
Sandi Like, Slayton
Marilyn Pelowski, International Falls

QUICK EASY ONION POTATOES**

5 to 6 cups potatoes, peeled   Butter or margarine
1 env. dry onion soup mix

If you are in a hurry, potatoes do not need to be peeled. Slice potatoes into baking dish. Sprinkle with dry soup mix and toss to coat. Dot the potatoes generously with margarine. Cover with waxed paper and microwave for 15 minutes or until potatoes are tender. Stir once or twice during microwaving.

Margaret Hilleshiem, Kellogg

SWEET POTATOES WITH APPLES

3 to 3½ lbs. sweet potatoes   ¼ cup packed brown sugar
2 tart apples, peeled, cored and ¼ tsp. ground ginger
   cut into ¼ inch rings   ¼ tsp. ground cinnamon
½ cup orange juice   2 Tbsp. butter or margarine

In a large saucepan, cover sweet potatoes with water; bring to a boil. Reduce heat, cover and simmer for 30 minutes or until tender. Drain and cool slightly. Alternate layers of sliced sweet potatoes and apples in a greased 9x13 inch baking pan or casserole. Pour orange juice over top. Mix brown sugar and spices; sprinkle over potatoes and apples. Dot with butter. Bake, uncovered, at 350° for 35 to 45 minutes or until apples are tender. Serves 8.

Leona Holland, Owatonna

WENDY'S POTATOES

2 lbs. shredded hash browns   1 can cream of chicken soup
1 pt. sour cream   2 tsp. minced onion
1 cup shredded Colby cheese   1 tsp. salt
1 cup shredded Monterey Jack   ½ tsp. pepper
   cheese   ½ cup margarine, melted

Mix all ingredients. Put in a greased 9x13 inch pan; set aside. Top with **2 cups crushed corn flakes** and ¼ **cup melted margarine** and bake, uncovered at 350° for 1 hour.

Lilianna St. Aubin, Marshall

YUM, YUM POTATOES

1 (2 lb.) pkg. frozen hash browns, ½ pt. whipping cream,
   slightly thawed   unwhipped
1 can cream of potato soup   1 med. onion, diced
1 can cream of celery soup   Shredded cheese, optional
1 (8 oz.) carton sour cream   Butter

Mix all ingredients. Shredded cheese may be added. Top with butter. Put into a 9x13 inch pan which has been greased. Bake at 300° for 2 hours, uncovered. Sprinkle shredded cheese on top the last 20 to 25 minutes.

Theresa DeBrite, Perham

318

CREAMED SAUERKRAUT

1 qt. sauerkraut
Meaty bacon or pork
2 potatoes

¾ pt. sweet cream
2 Tbsp. flour

Cook sauerkraut at least 3 to 4 hours with some meaty pork; add peeled potatoes which have been grated. Simmer until potatoes are done and not too much juice left on sauerkraut. Remove from heat and remove lid. Let stand while you take sweet cream and flour in shaker and shake well. Add to sauerkraut. You can use more or less flour and cream as needed to make sauerkraut creamed. Can be eaten with cooked potatoes or dumplings.

Eleanor Marti, New Ulm

BAKED BANANA SQUASH

1 (3 lb.) banana squash
½ cup brown sugar

¼ cup butter or margarine, softened
1 tsp. paprika

Cut squash into serving pieces. Remove seeds. Place skin side up in baking dish, pour ⅓ **cup hot water** into dish. Bake at 375° for 20 minutes. Brown sugar, margarine and paprika may be added before serving.

Gen Strubel, Slayton

SQUASH BALLS

1 winter squash, acorn or buttercup
2 to 3 Tbsp. soft butter
½ cup brown sugar

1 bag marshmallows
Pepperidge Farm stuffing mix, crushed

Bake squash; scoop out and mash well, adding butter, brown sugar and a little salt. Make into balls; put marshmallows in middle and form squash around it. Crush stuffing mix. Roll squash balls in crushed stuffing coating well. They can be frozen until ready to use. Bake at 350° for 30 minutes. Test by putting a fork in to see if marshmallow is melted.

Shirley Sundby, Argyle

VEGETABLE CASSEROLE

1 (20 oz.) bag California blend frozen vegetables
1 can water chestnuts, sliced

1 can cream of celery soup
1 cup Cheese Whiz

Put frozen vegetables in a 2 quart casserole. Add chestnuts on top. Add soup and melted Cheese Whiz. Bake at 325° for 1 hour. Add **1 can French fried onion rings**. Bake 10 minutes more.

Marion Plante, Crookston

VEGETABLES & MAIN DISHES

VEGETABLE HOT DISH
1 box frozen broccoli, cooked   1 can green beans
1 box frozen cauliflower, cooked 1 can sliced carrots
   Layer vegetables in casserole. Top with **1 stick margarine, ½ pound cheese**, and **1 can cream of chicken soup** (melted together). Top with **croutons**. Bake, uncovered, at 350° for 30 minutes.

Lucille Kraft, Blue Earth
State Monitor, 1952-1958
District Deputy, 1980-1984

SWISS VEGETABLE MEDLEY
1 bag frozen broccoli, carrots   ⅓ cup sour cream
   and cauliflower combination, ¼ tsp. black pepper
   thawed and drained   1 (4 oz.) jar pimento, drained
1 can cream of mushroom soup   and chopped
1 cup (4 oz.) shredded Swiss   1 can French fried onions
   cheese
   Combine vegetables, soup, ½ cup Swiss cheese, sour cream, pepper, pimento, and ½ can onion rings. Pour into a 1 quart casserole. Bake, covered, at 350° for 30 minutes. Top with remaining cheese and onions. Bake, uncovered, 5 minutes longer until cheese is bubbly. Serves 6.

Alyce Miller, Slayton

VEGETABLE CASSEROLE
1 bunch broccoli   ½ cup butter
1 head cauliflower   ¾ stack Ritz crackers
1 bag carrots   ¼ cup butter
½ lb. Velveeta cheese
   Cook vegetables separately. Arrange in casserole baking dish. Melt cheese and butter (I use the microwave). Pour over vegetables. Mix crumbled crackers and ¼ cup melted butter; spread over the top. Bake at 350° for 30 minutes or longer.

Cecelia Nundahl, Perham

VEGETABLE CASSEROLE
1 (16 to 20 oz.) pkg. frozen   1 stack Ritz crackers (about
   mixed vegetables   ¼ lb.)
3 cups shredded Cheddar cheese 1 stick butter or margarine
   Place frozen vegetables in a 7x11 inch baking dish. Cover with cheese. Crush crackers and place over cheese. Melt butter and pour over all. Bake at 325° for 1 hour or until mixture is cooked through, brown and bubbly.

Carol Haubrich, Pipestone

VEGETABLE PIZZA

2 (8 oz.) cans quick crescent dinner rolls
2 (8 oz.) cartons soft cream cheese
½ env. Lipton or Knorr vegetable soup mix

¾ cup chopped black olives
¾ cup chopped broccoli
¾ cup chopped cauliflower
½ cup chopped green onion
1 (8 oz.) pkg. shredded Mozzarella/Cheddar blend cheese

Spread the crescent rolls on a pizza pan and bake according to package directions. Cool. In small bowl, beat cream cheese and vegetable mix. Spread mixture on crescent rolls evenly and gently. Top with olives, broccoli, cauliflower and green onions. Sprinkle with the cheese. Slice into small pieces, serve and enjoy!

Kay Miller, Crookston

TEXAS FRIED GREEN TOMATOES

3 to 4 lg. green tomatoes
2 cups flour
1 Tbsp. salt
1 Tbsp. pepper

1 Tbsp. Lawry's seasoned salt
2 eggs
2 cups milk
Oil for frying

Cut tomatoes into almost ½ inch thick slices. Mix flour, salt, pepper and seasoned salt in one bowl. Mix eggs and milk in another bowl. Dip each tomato slice into the milk mixture, then into flour, back to the milk and then to flour again, coating well. Heat oil in a deep-fryer to 350°; add battered tomato slices a few at a time and cook for 5 minutes or until golden brown. Also can be cooked in heavy skillet, turning once. Serves 4. Note: Can substitute cracker crumbs or cornmeal for flour, and red tomatoes for green.

Alice Boucher, Crookston

ZUCCHINI CASSEROLE

4 cups shredded zucchini
1 onion, shredded
1½ cups sharp cheese, shredded
½ cup oil

½ tsp. oregano
1¼ cups Bisquick
3 eggs
1 tsp. salt

Mix ingredients and place in 3 quart greased casserole. Bake at 350° for 1 hour.

Monica Novak, Red Lake Falls

STUFFED ZUCCHINI

Cut **1 zucchini** in half lengthwise. Scoop out inside and leave about ½ inch. Mix enough **hamburger** with **onion, mushrooms** and **tomatoes**. Season to taste. Cook all ingredients until hamburger is done. Put into zucchini boats and bake until zucchini is done.

Lillian Patterson, Wabasha

ZUCCHINI AND TOMATOES

1 lb. zucchini	Pinch of oregano
2 Tbsp. margarine or butter	Salt and pepper
½ cup chopped onion	1 lg. can tomatoes or equivalent
2 cloves crushed garlic	in fresh
Pinch of basil	⅓ cup grated Cheddar cheese

Wash and cut the zucchini in ½ inch pieces. In a fry pan, saute the zucchini in butter. Add onion and garlic; cover pan and cook until tender, about 10 minutes. Add the spices and tomatoes. Simmer 15 minutes until the sauce is cooked down. Sprinkle cheese on top; cover pan and let cheese melt before serving.

Donna Polacec, Eveleth

ZUCCHINI CASSEROLE

4 cups zucchini, cut into ¼ inch slices	2 Tbsp. butter
¼ cup water	1 can cream of chicken soup
3 med. carrots, shredded	1 cup sour cream
1 med. onion, chopped	1½ cups seasoned croutons with garlic salt

Cook zucchini squash in water. Add salt to taste. Saute carrots and onion in butter until soft. Add soup, sour cream and ¾ cup croutons. Mix in squash and stir gently. Pour into buttered casserole and spread remaining croutons over top. Bake at 350° for 45 minutes.

Note: May add 1 pound seasoned, browned hamburger or 1 can chunk chicken to the casserole.

Dolores Spreter, North Mankato

* * MAIN DISHES * *

BARBECUE SAUCE

⅓ cup Heinz 57 steak sauce	1 (6 oz.) can frozen orange juice
1¼ cups ketchup	concentrate, undiluted

Mix ingredients and simmer for 5 minutes. Especially good on grilled or broiled pork, chicken and turkey. Also good on beef. Keeps well in the refrigerator for months.

Anita McNulty, Eveleth

BAR-B-CUE RIBS/CHICKEN SAUCE

1 cup 7-Up or Bubble Up   **1 cup catsup**

Pour over desired amount of ribs (chicken can be used). Bake at 325° until ribs or chicken are tender. Can be done in crock-pot also.

Agnes Novak, Fergus Falls

MARINADE FOR BARBECUING BEEF

1 cup white wine   **1 cup crushed pineapple**
1 cup soy sauce   **1 tsp. ginger**

A chuck roast holds together well for barbecuing. Marinate the beef overnight. For basting, mix the marinading mixture with ketchup and baste while grilling. A little honey will make the basting stick. Use hickory chips on the coals.

Father Donald Archer, Argyle
Chaplain Our Lady of the Fields

BEER BATTER FOR FISH**

½ cup flour   **2 egg whites, stiffly beaten**
½ cup beer   **1 Tbsp. salad oil**
Salt and pepper to taste

Mix all items and dip fish into before deep frying.

Phyllis Novak, Fergus Falls

BASIC DOLE GOLDEN SAUCE FOR HAM OR CHICKEN

1 (20 oz.) can Dole pineapple   **⅓ cup yellow mustard**
slices, drained (reserve juice) **2 Tbsp. cornstarch**
½ cup brown sugar   **¼ tsp. ground cloves**

In saucepan, combine juice with sugar, mustard, cornstarch and spice; heat until boils and thickens. Add pineapple slices and heat through. Spoon over ham or chicken.

Spice Variation: 1 teaspoon curry powder, or 3 tablespoons soy sauce, or 1 tablespoon chili powder.

Marietta Johanneck, Red Lake Falls

* * * * * * * *

May the God of hope fill you with all joy and peace in believing, so that by the power of the Holy Spirit, you may abound in hope.
Romans 15:13
Marie Reisdorf, St. Charles

SHAKE AND BAKE MIXTURE

4 cups dry bread crumbs	1 Tbsp. celery salt
½ cup vegetable oil	1 tsp. pepper
1 Tbsp. salt	1 tsp. garlic
1 Tbsp. paprika	1 tsp. onion powder

Roll crumbs fine and put in a deep bowl. Stir in oil with fork; add all seasonings and mix well. Keeps well in a covered fruit jar and store in cool place (not refrigerator because it gets moist). Can be used for chicken, pork or fish.

Jean Demmer, Caledonia

ALL PURPOSE TOMATO SAUCE

6 lbs. (about 40) tomatoes, peeled and cored	2 bay leaves
	1 Tbsp. salt
3 med. onions, chopped	1 tsp. sugar
3 garlic cloves	1 tsp. pepper
3 Tbsp. olive oil	½ tsp. Italian seasoning
½ tsp. oregano	Basil and celery salt

Peel tomatoes and put everything in blender except bay leaves. Add bay leaves and cook slowly for 2 to 3 hours. May be frozen in containers. Very good for chili.

Agnes Prairie, Russell

STIR FRY SAUCE

3 Tbsp. brown sugar	2 tsp. soy sauce
1 Tbsp. cornstarch	Juice from 1 can pineapple
3 Tbsp. white wine vinegar	(¾ cup or use water)
1 Tbsp. catsup	

Put all ingredients in a glass cup and microwave until thick.

Irene Landsteiner, Waseca

WHITE SAUCE

¾ cup flour	1 tsp. salt
1 stick Promise margarine*	1⅓ cups non fat dry milk

*Or any other good brand.

Mix and crumble as for pie crust. Store in freezer. To make white sauce, combine **1 cup water** and ½ cup of mix. Stir; cook until thick.

Kathleen Furrer (Katy), St. Paul

* * * * * * * *

Be near me, Lord Jesus, I ask you to stay,
close by me forever, and love me, I pray.
Barb Kleinschmidt, Winona

APPLE PIZZA

1 loaf frozen bread dough	½ cup flour
1 (15 oz.) jar applesauce	½ tsp. cinnamon
½ cup sugar	½ cup butter

When the bread dough is thawed, press with hands into a 9x12 inch lightly greased cake pan. Spoon on the applesauce. Mix the dry ingredients and cut in the butter. Crumble this mixture over the top and bake at 350° for 30 minutes.

Florence Macho, New Ulm

BREAD DUMPLING (NEAL)

4 slices dry bread	¼ tsp. baking powder
1 cup flour	1 egg
½ tsp. salt	

Cube the 4 slices of bread. White, homestyle bread is best. Mix flour, salt, baking powder and egg and enough cold water to make a stiff dough. Mix in cubed dry bread. Add cold water if needed to hold ingredients together, using wet hands to form dumplings about 2 inches around. Drop into large pan of boiling water. Cook for about 15 minutes. Test with a fork. Done if prick is clean. Serve with roast pork or beef or ham with gravy as potatoes. Eat at once. This is a family recipe brought from Bavaria.

Vivian Pfaffinger, Blue Earth

CHEESE SQUARES

2 pkgs. crescent rolls	1 egg, separated
2 (8 oz.) pkgs. cream cheese	1 tsp. vanilla
¾ cup sugar	1 tsp. lemon juice

Roll out 1 package of crescent rolls to fit an 11x16 inch ungreased pan. Mix cream cheese, sugar, egg yolk, vanilla and lemon juice and spread over dough. Roll second package of crescent rolls same size as pan and lay it on top of the filling. Beat egg white slightly and brush on top. Bake at 350° for 25 minutes. Cut in squares and sprinkle with powdered sugar.

Arlene Peterson, Littlefork

CORNED BEEF NOODLE HOT DISH

1 (8 oz.) pkg. noodles	1 can cream of celery soup
¼ lb. grated American cheese	1 cup milk
1 (12 oz.) can corned beef, diced	½ cup chopped onion
1 can cream of chicken soup	¼ cup buttered bread crumbs

Cook noodles in salted water and drain. Mix all ingredients, except bread crumbs, and place in greased casserole dish. Sprinkle bread crumbs over the top. Bake at 350° for 45 minutes. A package of frozen vegetables can also be added if you desire.

Beverly Jorgensen, Argyle

VEGETABLES & MAIN DISHES

CLAM SAUCE AND SPAGHETTI

2 lg. diced onions	1/8 tsp. pepper
1 or 2 cloves minced garlic	1/4 tsp. crushed red chili peppers
8 Tbsp. olive oil	Salt to taste
1/2 tsp. sweet dried basil	2 (8 oz.) cans minced clams

Saute the onions and garlic in the oil. Add everything but the clams and clam juice. Simmer for about 15 to 20 minutes or until the onions are cooked. Put in drained clams (reserve juice). Cook about 5 minutes. Add clam juice as needed. Serve over a plate of cooked spaghetti.

Ramona L. Johnson, International Falls

ORIENTAL ROCK CORNISH GAME HENS

Cornish game hens	1/3 cup soy sauce
Melted butter or margarine	1/3 tsp. MSG
1/3 cup sugar	1/4 tsp. ginger
1 tsp. cornstarch	

Thaw hens. Heat oven to 350°. Wash hens and pat dry. Place hens, breast side up, in open shallow roasting pan. Brush with melted butter; do not cover. Do not add water. Roast 1 1/2 hours, brushing every 1/2 hour with melted butter. While hens roast, stir the remainder of the ingredients and cook over medium heat, stirring constantly until mixture thickens and boils. Boil and stir 1 minute. Cool. During final 1/2 hour, brush hens several times with soy mixture. Serve on platter with remaining sauce over hens or separate. (Hens are usually done in 1 1/2 hours unless stuffed. Allow an extra 30 minutes for stuffed hens.)

Mary Bartley, Blue Earth

CHICKEN ALA KING

1/2 cup butter or margarine	1 3/4 cups chicken broth
1/2 cup diced green pepper	1 (6 oz.) can sliced mushrooms
1/2 cup flour	(save liquid)
1 tsp. salt	2 cups chicken, diced
1/4 tsp. black pepper	1 (4 oz.) jar pimento, drained
2 cups half and half or light cream	

Melt butter or margarine. Saute green peppers. Add flour, salt, pepper, then light cream, then chicken broth and mushroom liquid. Next, add chicken, mushrooms, and pimentos. Heat until hot but not boiling. Serve over pastry shells, toasted English muffins, toast or baking powder biscuits (your choice).

Rose I. Omersa, Eveleth

ARROZ CON POLLO (CHICKEN WITH RICE) SONARAN STYLE

3 to 4 lb. fryer chicken, cut up
¼ cup cooking oil
½ cup chopped onion
½ cup chopped green pepper
2 cups uncooked rice
1 clove garlic, crushed
2 peeled tomatoes or 1 can
   tomatoes, cut up and drained
4 cups chicken broth
Chopped green chilies, optional
Salt and pepper
½ tsp. Cominos or chili powder,
   optional
Other spices, optional

Brown chicken in oil in heavy pot. Remove chicken and saute onions and green peppers until soft. Add the raw rice to the pot and stir to cover with oil. Add rest of ingredients to pot, and return chicken to pot. Cover and cook until chicken is tender and rice has absorbed liquid. You may add more liquid if rice isn't tender. May be baked in oven at 350° for approximately 1 hour or cooked on top of stove. Serve garnished with asparagus tips or peas, or both.

Margaret E. Bruggeman, International Falls

TURKEY OR CHICKEN ALMOND CASSEROLE

5 cups diced chicken or turkey,
   cooked
2 cups diced celery
3 cups cooked long grain rice
2 cans cream of chicken soup
½ cup sour cream
½ cup mayonnaise
1 (8 oz.) can sliced water
   chestnuts
2 Tbsp. chopped onion
1 cup sliced almonds
2 Tbsp. lemon juice
1 Tbsp. salt
¾ tsp. white pepper

Mix first 3 ingredients in a large bowl. Mix next 6 ingredients; add to first mixture. Add remaining ingredients; mix. Place in a 9x13 or 8x12 inch pan. May add diced green pepper or frozen peas.

Topping:
2 cups corn flake crumbs
½ cup sliced almonds
⅓ cup melted butter

Bake at 350° for 35 to 45 minutes. Makes a large casserole. Serves 10 to 12.

Kathleen Prehn, Waterville

BAKED CHICKEN**

1 cut up chicken
Bisquick or flour
Salt and pepper

Shake chicken in Bisquick or flour and salt and pepper mixture. Place in baking dish and sprinkle diced onion over. Cover for 1 hour and then uncover and bake until done and browned.

Veronica Miller, Waseca

BAKED CHICKEN

8 chicken breast halves
1 tsp. salt
½ tsp. pepper
1 can mushroom soup

1 cup shredded Cheddar
   cheese
½ tsp. sage
½ cup chopped onions

Line a 9x13 inch pan with foil. Salt and pepper chicken and put in pan. Mix remaining ingredients and pour over chicken. Bake at 400° for 1 hour.

Viv Gregoire, Marshall

CHICKEN BAKED DISH

3 chicken breasts (3 cups, cut up)
3 cups celery
1 container pimento
1 cup green pepper
1 cup water chestnuts

1 cup Velveeta cheese
1½ cups mayonnaise
1 pkg. frozen peas, cooked a bit
1 pkg. slivered almonds
1 cup soda crackers, crushed

Mix all ingredients, except almonds and crackers. Place almonds on top of the crushed crackers. Bake at 375° for 20 minutes (I usually bake at least 30 to 40 minutes).

Mary Hanzlicek, Owatonna

CHICKEN BOW CASSEROLE

2 boxes bow macaroni
2 boxes frozen peas and carrots
2 cans deboned chicken or
   boiled chicken

2 cans cream of chicken soup
1 can whole mushrooms
1 can shoestring potatoes

Boil macaroni until partially done; add all ingredients except shoe string potatoes. Mix and top with potatoes. Bake at 350° for 1 hour. Serves 10.

Dayis Begich, Chisholm

CHICKEN BREASTS

6 to 8 chicken breasts
8 Tbsp. butter
1 can mushrooms

$^2/_3$ cup Parmesan cheese
1 cup whipping cream

Wash, dry and flour chicken breasts; season to taste. Melt butter in a 9x13 inch pan. Put seasoned and floured chicken in pan. Cover with the mushrooms and Parmesan cheese and whipping cream. Bake at 350° for 1 hour, covered.

Cora Jones, Eveleth

CHICKEN AND BEEF BAKE

1 (3 oz.) pkg. sliced dried beef   1 can cream of mushroom soup
3 skinless chicken breasts   1 cup sour cream
3 slices bacon

Rinse dried beef with cold water; drain well. Lay in bottom of a 9x13 inch pan. Cut chicken breasts into serving pieces and layer over beef. Lay bacon slices over chicken. Bake at 350° for 30 minutes. Combine soup and sour cream, blend well and pour over meat. Cover with foil and bake at 325° for 30 minutes. Uncover and bake 30 minutes longer.

Jean Strelow, Winona

CHICKEN BREASTS

1 (6 oz.) pkg. corn beef   1 can cream of chicken soup
8 strips bacon, browned   1 can broccoli cheese soup
8 chicken breasts   ¼ cup vinegar or wine
1 pt. sour cream

Layer beef in a 9x13 inch pan. Wrap bacon around each chicken breast. Layer chicken on top of corn beef. Mix sour cream, soups and vinegar. Pour over chicken breasts. Bake, uncovered, at 350° for 1½ hours.

Aggie Johnson, St. James

CHICKEN DELIGHT

1 pkg. or jar dried beef   2 cups lite sour cream
4 chicken breasts, boned   2 cans cream of chicken soup
   and halved   1 cup Swiss cheese, shredded
8 strips bacon, microwaved

Cover bottom of a 9x13 inch pan with dried beef. Wrap each breast with strip of cooked bacon. Place wrapped breasts on dried beef. Mix sour cream and soup and spoon over chicken. Bake, uncovered, at 300° for 1¾ to 2 hours. Serve with rice.

Betty Schoenborn, Mahnomen

CHICKEN BREAST CASSEROLE

6 whole chicken breasts   2 cans cream of chicken soup
Oleo   1 cup white wine
Grated Cheddar cheese   Croutons

Place chicken with oleo in a 9x13 inch greased pan. Sprinkle with grated cheese. Top with soup and wine mixture. Sprinkle with croutons and melt on stick of oleo, which can drizzle on top. Bake, uncovered, at 325° for 1½ hours.

Delores Wesley, Waterville

CHICKEN CASSEROLE**

Cooked chicken, cut up or
shredded
1 can cream of mushroom soup
Grated cheese (sharp Cheddar
is good)
1 pkg. Pepperidge Farm
dressing
1 stick melted margarine

Amounts depend on how many you want to serve as to casserole pan size and chicken amount. First, layer cut up cooked chicken, then pour mushroom soup over. Sprinkle grated cheese over and spread dressing which has been mixed with melted margarine over the top of casserole mixture. Bake at 350° for 45 minutes.

Alice Knutson, Slayton

CHICKEN CASSEROLE

2 Tbsp. butter
1/3 cup chopped onion
1/3 cup chopped green pepper
1 (6 oz.) pkg. noodles
1 cup sour cream
1 can cream of chicken soup
1/3 cup milk
1 1/2 cups diced cooked chicken
1/2 tsp. salt
1/4 tsp. pepper, optional
1/3 cup slivered almonds,
optional

Saute the first 3 ingredients; cook noodles. Mix rest of ingredients and gently fold in noodles. Pour in casserole dish. Bake at 350° for 40 minutes. Serves 6 to 8 people.

Marge Stencel, New Richland

QUICK CHICKEN CASSEROLE

1 lb. fresh, frozen or canned
asparagus
1 1/2 cups cooked, cubed chicken
1 can condensed cream of
chicken soup
1/2 cup water
1/4 cup heavy cream
1/2 cup Parmesan cheese,
grated
1 tsp. butter
1 tsp. paprika
Salt and pepper to taste

Put layers of chicken and asparagus in casserole. Blend rest of ingredients and add. Bake at 400° for about 45 minutes.

Hulda McCarthy, Waseca

CHICKEN BROCCOLI CASSEROLE

1 med. onion
1/3 stick margarine or butter
1 can cream of chicken soup
1/2 cup milk
1 (8 oz.) jar Cheese Whiz
2 cups cooked chicken, diced
2 cups cooked rice
2 (10 oz.) pkgs. broccoli

Saute onion in butter. Stir in chicken soup, milk and Cheese Whiz. Add chicken, rice and broccoli. Bake in a 9x13 inch pan, uncovered, at 350° for 30 minutes.

Viola Ruffing, Adrian

BROCCOLI AND CHICKEN DISH

Stew **5 chicken breasts** until tender (can use thighs also). Cool and debone. Can cut into strips. Cook **2 packages frozen broccoli**; drain. Arrange broccoli in bottom of greased flat baking dish. Lay cooked chicken pieces on top of broccoli.

2 cans cream of chicken soup	1 tsp. lemon juice
1 cup mayonnaise	½ tsp. curry powder

Combine and pour over chicken. Mix **½ cup buttered crumbs** and **½ cup shredded Cheddar cheese**. Sprinkle on top. Bake at 350° for 30 minutes.

June Ankeny, Blue Earth

CHICKEN OR TURKEY BROCCOLI CASSEROLE

2 (10 oz.) pkgs. frozen broccoli spears, cooked and drained	1 tsp. lemon juice
	1 can French fried onion rings
2 or 3 cups chicken or turkey, cooked and cubed	½ cup grated sharp cheese
	½ cup bread crumbs
2 cans cream of chicken soup	1 cup potato chips, crushed
1 cup mayonnaise	1 Tbsp. melted butter

Grease a 9x13 inch pan and arrange frozen broccoli spears. Put a layer of cooked cubed chicken or turkey on top of broccoli. Combine soup, mayonnaise, lemon juice and onion rings. Pour over chicken or turkey. Sprinkle grated cheese over all. Mix bread crumbs and crushed potato chips with melted butter. Pour over top and bake at 350° for about 30 minutes.

Emma Reiter, Slayton

CHICKEN AND BROCCOLI CASSEROLE

4½ to 5 lbs. chicken, cut up	1 cup milk
5 cups water	2 cups chicken broth
1 tsp. salt	1 cup mayonnaise
2 to 3 peppercorns	1 tsp. lemon juice
1 rib celery, cut in half	½ tsp. curry powder or mace
1 carrot	1 bunch fresh broccoli or
1 onion	1 (20 oz.) bag frozen broccoli
½ cup flour	1 to 2 cups buttered crumbs

Combine chicken, water, salt, peppercorns, celery, carrot and onion in large kettle. Simmer until chicken is tender. Remove chicken. Strain broth. Cube meat. Preheat oven to 350°. Make sauce; blend flour and milk until smooth. Add broth and cook until thickened. Remove from heat. Add mayonnaise, lemon juice and curry powder. Cook broccoli until tender. Drain and break into pieces. Place in greased 9x12 inch baking dish. Top with chicken, then sauce and crumbs. Bake about 45 minutes until crumbs are brown. Serves 6 to 8.

Helen Curran, Waseca

CHICKEN AND BROCCOLI BAKE

1 pkg. chicken flavor	1 cup Velveeta cheese
Rice-O-Roni, mixed as	1 (10 oz.) pkg. frozen broccoli
directed on package	1 can cream of mushroom soup
3 to 4 cups cooked chicken	1 stick oleo, divided
1½ cups milk	2 cups crushed corn flakes

Mix all ingredients except ½ stick oleo and corn flakes. Bake at 350° for 40 minutes. Top with melted oleo and corn flake mixture and bake 15 minutes more.

Lorraine Sturm, St. James

TWO STEP CHICKEN BROCCOLI DIVAN

1 lb. fresh broccoli or 1 (10 oz.)	1 can cream of broccoli soup
pkg. broccoli, cooked and	⅓ cup milk
drained	½ cup Cheese Whiz
1½ cups cooked chicken or	1 can French onions
turkey	

In shallow casserole, arrange broccoli. Top with chicken. Combine soup and milk. Pour over chicken. Spread Cheese Whiz on top. Bake at 450° for 15 minutes or until hot. Put French onions on last 1 to 2 minutes.

Judy Wiersma, Medford

CHICKEN BROCCOLI DIVAN

1 lb. fresh broccoli, cut into	½ cup skim milk
spears, cooked and drained	⅛ tsp. pepper
1 cup cubed cooked chicken	4 low salt saltine crackers,
1 (10¾ oz.) can Campbell's	coarsely crushed
Healthy Request condensed	1 Tbsp. grated Parmesan cheese
cream of broccoli soup	½ tsp. paprika

In a 2 quart shallow casserole, arrange broccoli. Top with chicken. Combine soup, milk and pepper; pour over chicken. Combine crushed crackers, cheese and paprika; sprinkle over chicken. Bake at 450° for 20 minutes or until hot and bubbling. Makes 4 servings.

Gen Armon, Blue Earth

CHICKEN AND RICE CASSEROLE

1 can cream of chicken soup	2 cups instant rice
1 can chicken and rice soup	2 cups water

Mix and pour into roaster; put **chicken pieces** on top. Bake at 325° for 1½ to 2 hours.

Sue Carpenter, Caledonia

CHICKEN RICE HOT DISH

2 cups rice	1 can cream of chicken soup
1 cut up chicken	2 soup cans water
1 can cream of mushroom soup	1 env. dry onion soup mix

Put rice in small roaster. Layer chicken pieces on top. Mix the canned soups with the 2 cans water and onion soup; pour over the rice and chicken. Bake at 325° for 2 hours.

Hannah Lambert, Waseca

EASY CHICKEN 'N RICE**

4 chicken breast halves	1 (2.8 oz.) can Durkee French
½ cup bottled Italian salad	fried onions
dressing	1¾ cups chicken broth
⅔ cup regular rice, uncooked	½ tsp. Italian seasoning
1 (16 oz.) bag frozen broccoli,	
carrots, water chestnuts and	
red pepper combination	

Place chicken breasts in an 8x12 inch baking dish. Pour salad dressing over chicken. Bake, uncovered, at 400° for 20 minutes. Place rice, vegetables and half can French fried onions around and under chicken. Combine broth and Italian seasoning. Pour over chicken and vegetables. Bake, uncovered, for 25 minutes. Top with remaining onions. Bake for 2 to 3 minutes longer. Let stand 5 minutes before serving. Preparation time is about 7 minutes. Serves 4.

Phyllis Schettler, Worthington

CRESCENT CHICKEN CASSEROLE

½ cup chopped celery	1 can cream of chicken soup
½ cup chopped onion	1 (4 oz.) can sliced mushrooms,
2 Tbsp. butter	drained
4 cups chicken breast, skinned	⅔ cup mayonnaise
or 3 cups cooked chicken	½ cup commercial sour cream
1 (8 oz.) can water chestnuts,	1 (8 oz.) pkg. crescent rolls
drained	

Saute celery and onion in butter until softened. Heat next 6 items until bubbly, then mix with celery-onion mixture. Put in a 9x13 inch greased pan, then separate crescent rolls into 2 rectangles. Lay over mixture. Top with ½ **cup slivered almonds, 1 cup shredded cheese** and **2 to 3 tablespoons melted butter**. Sprinkle over top. Bake at 350° for 45 minutes.

Leona Rapacz, Argyle

CHICKEN DIJON

1 Tbsp. olive oil	²/₃ cup water
4 skinless, boneless chicken breast halves	1 Tbsp. Dijon style mustard
	½ tsp. pepper
1 (10¾ oz.) can Campbell's cream of celery soup	4 cups hot cooked rice with parsley cooked without salt

In skillet, in hot oil, cook chicken 10 minutes or until browned; remove. Pour off fat. In same skillet, combine soup, water, mustard and pepper. Heat to boiling; return chicken to skillet, cover and cook over low heat for 5 minutes or until chicken is no longer pink, stirring often. Serve with rice.

Frances Kunz, Waseca

CHICKEN DIJON

8 oz. chicken breasts, skinned and boned	Juice of 2 lemons
4 Tbsp. Dijon mustard	¼ tsp. lemon pepper
1 cup chicken broth or water	Diet butter
1 clove garlic, minced or ¼ tsp. garlic blend	Salt to taste

In a nonstick skillet sprayed with Pam, brown chicken on both sides. Mix all ingredients for sauce. Pour sauce over chicken and simmer 20 minutes or until chicken tests done. Yield: 2 servings. Es. = 3½ protein.

Jan McDonald, Owatonna

CHICKEN AND DUMPLINGS

½ cup flour	2 Tbsp. butter or margarine
1 tsp. paprika	1 can cream of mushroom soup
2 lbs. chicken pieces	1 can chicken broth

Place flour and paprika in paper bag. Add 2 or 3 pieces of chicken at a time and shake well. Brown chicken in butter; blend in soup and broth, cover and simmer 45 minutes or until chicken is tender.

Dumplings:

1½ cups flour	¹/₃ cup milk
2½ tsp. baking powder	2 eggs, slightly beaten
1 tsp. salt	

Sift dry ingredients and add milk and egg mix until flour is moistened but not smooth. Drop dumplings into simmering sauce and chicken. Cover and cook 15 minutes longer. Do not lift lid during cooking time. Yield: 6 to 8 servings.

Lydia Maxwell, International Falls

DOUBLE CRISPY CHICKEN

7 cups cereal (corn flakes or
   your choice)
1 egg
1 cup milk
1 cup flour
½ tsp. salt
¼ tsp. pepper
3 lbs. frying chicken, cut in
   pieces
3 Tbsp. margarine or butter,
   melted

Put cereal in plastic bag; crush with rolling pin. Should have 2 cups to use for coating chicken. Prepare batter. Beat egg; add milk and add combined dry ingredients. Dip meat in batter; roll in crushed cereal and place in single layer in shallow pan or cookie sheet. Drizzle with melted butter. Bake at 350° for about 1 hour or until chicken is done. Do not cover or turn pieces.

Marie Arnold, Medford

SOUR CREAM CHICKEN ENCHILADAS

1 (4 oz.) can chopped green
   chilies
1 pt. sour cream
2 (10 oz.) cans cream of chicken
   soup
½ lb. shredded Cheddar cheese
½ lb. shredded Mozzarella
   cheese
3 cans white chicken (tuna size)
1 (12 oz.) pkg. flour tortillas
1 (4 oz.) can chopped black
   olives

Mix chilies, sour cream, soup and half of cheeses; divide in half. In one half, add the chicken and roll in tortillas. Put in a greased 9x13 inch pan. Pour remainder of mixture on top with the rest of cheese. Top with black olives. Bake at 350° for 20 to 30 minutes. Cover for first 15 minutes.

Variation: Can add ½ cup chopped onion.

Rita Plante, Crookston
Colleen Bents, Rushmore

* * * * * * * *

RECIPE FOR A GOOD LIFE

Take a bit of thoughtfulness,
Blend it with a smile
Stir in lots of kindness
As you tread life's weary mile.

Mix encouragement with some sunshine
To dry up someone's tear,
Stirring in a few kind words of sympathy
That are most certainly sincere.

Then your reward will be great in Heaven
Your life will be free from strife
If you will follow this recipe
For a good and useful life.

FRIENDSHIP CASSEROLE

3 whole chicken breasts, cooked and diced
2 cans cream of chicken soup
1 can chop suey vegetables, drained
1 can water chestnuts, sliced
1 can Chinese noodles
1 cup chopped celery
2 Tbsp. onion
½ cup Miracle Whip
1 tsp. lemon juice
½ cup salted cashews

Put first 9 ingredients in casserole; cover with cashews. Bake at 350° until bubbly.

Mary Haley, North Mankato

HOLIDAY CHICKEN

3 to 4 oz. dried beef, torn apart
8 boneless skinless chicken breasts
8 slices bacon, halved and limp fried

Place dried beef on bottom of baking dish. Roll chicken breasts into "pillow-like" bundles; lay on top of beef. Drape 2 pieces bacon on each piece of chicken. Bake, uncovered, at 350° for 30 minutes.

Sauce:
1 can mushrooms soup
1 cup sour cream
2 to 3 Tbsp. milk

Pour sauce over chicken and bake 30 minutes longer. Add 15 minutes if refrigerated first. Serve on a bed of rice.

Kathleen Prehn, Waterville

CHICKEN OR TURKEY HOT DISH

2 cups chopped chicken or turkey
2 cups chopped celery
½ cup toasted almonds or walnuts
½ tsp. salt
½ tsp. powdered accent seasoning
2 Tbsp. grated onion
½ cup American cheese, grated
1 cup mayonnaise

Mix all ingredients in a 4 quart dish. Top with **1 cup crumbled potato chips**. Bake at 450° for 10 minutes or at 350° for ½ hour.

Doris Wissman, Winona

CHICKEN RICE HOT DISH

½ cup wild rice, raw
½ cup plain rice, raw
1 can cream of mushroom or celery soup
1 can milk
1 pkg. dry onion soup mix
Salt and pepper to taste
4 to 6 chicken breasts

Mix all and add pieces of chicken on top. Cover and bake in a 9x13 inch pan for 1½ hours. Put under broiler to brown.

Irene Nowacki, Argyle

336

CHICKEN HOT DISH

¾ cup Minute Rice	1 pkg. dry powdered onion soup
1 can cream of chicken soup	Cut up pieces of chicken
1 cup milk	

Grease a 9x13 inch pan. Put rice in bottom; mix soup and milk and pour over the rice. Sprinkle half of the dry onion soup over this, then put the chicken pieces on top. Put rest of onion soup on top of chicken. Cover with foil. Put holes in foil and bake at 350° for 2 hours.

Phyllis Sheridan, Crookston

HONEY NUT STIR-FRY PORK OR CHICKEN

1 lb. pork steak or loin, or	¼ tsp. ground ginger
1 lb. chicken breast	2 Tbsp. vegetable oil, divided
¾ cup orange juice	2 lg. carrots, sliced diagonally
⅓ cup honey	2 stalks celery, sliced diagonally
3 Tbsp. soy sauce	½ cup cashews or peanuts
1 Tbsp. cornstarch	Hot cooked rice

Cut pork into thin strips and set aside. Combine orange juice, honey, soy sauce, cornstarch and ginger in small bowl and mix well. Heat 1 tablespoon oil in large skillet over medium high heat. Add carrots and celery, and stir-fry about 3 minutes. Remove vegetables and set aside. Pour remaining oil into skillet. Add meat; stir-fry about 3 minutes. Return vegetables to skillet; add sauce mixture and nuts. Stir and cook over medium high heat until sauce comes to a boil and thickens. Serve over rice. Serves 4 to 6.

Doris Kern, Owatonna

HUNGARIAN CHICKEN CASSEROLE

2 oz. Crisco or oil	1 cup sliced mushrooms
2 med. onions, finely chopped	2 Tbsp. tomato pulp
2 tsp. sweet red Hungarian paprika	2 to 3 cups stock
	Sm. new skinned potatoes
2 young chickens, cut up and salted	1 cup sour cream
	2 tsp. chopped parsley

Heat Crisco in heavy fry pan. Fry onions, paprika, and chicken all at once. Do not burn. Stir meat all the time. As soon as chicken is fried, add mushrooms and tomato pulp and stock. Bring to a boil. Transfer to casserole and cover. Place in 350° oven for 1½ hours. Add par-boiled potatoes and cook for 1½ hours more, or until all ingredients are tender. Serve in same dish. A few minutes before serving, stir in sour cream (do not allow cream to boil). Sprinkle with parsley if desired. Serve with salad and fresh bread.

Georgette Maas, Medford

CHICKEN HOT DISH

4 cups croutons	2 cans celery soup
¾ cup margarine	1 can milk
3 cups cut up cooked chicken	1 can mushroom pieces
1 box frozen peas	¼ cup green peppers, cut up
1 sm. can cut up black olives	

Mix croutons with margarine. Put half on bottom of pan, then mix rest of ingredients and put over croutons. Add rest of croutons on top. Bake at 350° for 1 hour. Cover with foil while baking.

Angie Wosick, Moorhead

COUNTRY STYLE CHICKEN KIEV

½ cup fine dry bread crumbs	⅔ cup butter, melted
2 Tbsp. grated Parmesan cheese	¼ cup dry white wine or apple
1 tsp. basil	juice
1 tsp. oregano	¼ cup chopped green onions
½ tsp. garlic salt	¼ cup chopped parsley
2 chicken breasts, boned, skinned and split	

Preheat oven to 375°. Combine bread crumbs, cheese, basil, oregano and garlic salt in plastic bag. Dip chicken in melted butter and shake in bag to coat with bread crumbs. Place chicken in a 9x9 inch baking dish. Bake 50 to 60 minutes or until chicken is golden and tender. Mix wine, green onion and parsley with remaining melted butter. Pour butter mixture over chicken when done. Return to oven for 5 minutes.

Barbara Kleinschmidt, Winona
State Publicity Chair, 1995-1996

EASY OVEN FRIED CHICKEN

½ cup bread crumbs, dried	1 Tbsp. salad oil
1 tsp. paprika	Shake of garlic powder, optional
½ tsp. celery salt	1 fryer chicken or your favorite
1 tsp. or less salt	parts
¼ tsp. pepper	

Combine bread crumbs and seasonings. Add oil and mix until well blended. Rinse chicken pieces with water and coat with the crumb mixture. Place in an ungreased shallow pan and bake at 350° for 1 hour or until browned.

Caroline Hanson, Eveleth

NEW ORLEANS WINE SAUCED CHICKEN

4 chicken breast fillets (1¼ lb.)
6 Tbsp. flour
¾ tsp. salt
¼ tsp. pepper
¼ tsp. paprika
4 Tbsp. butter or margarine
¾ cup white wine or water
1 tsp. chicken bouillon
¼ tsp. poultry seasoning
1 bay leaf
1¾ cups sliced mushrooms
½ cup diced onions
¾ cup diced celery
½ cup grated carrots
½ cup sour cream
Green pepper, diced for garnish
Chopped parsley, for garnish

Rinse chicken and pat dry. Mix flour, salt, pepper and paprika. Dredge chicken breasts in mixture. Melt 2 tablespoons butter in large fry pan. Brown chicken on both sides; set aside. Melt remaining butter; stir in remaining flour mixture until smooth. Add wine or water; stir. Add chicken bouillon, poultry seasoning, bay leaf, mushrooms, onions, carrots and celery. Add chicken breasts; cover and simmer 20 to 25 minutes until chicken is cooked to your liking. Remove chicken to platter. Stir sour cream into drippings and cook just until heated through. Pour this sauce over chicken; garnish with peppers and parsley. Serve with mashed potatoes and rest of dinner.

Nancy Palo, Eveleth

ON-YOUR-OWN CHICKEN NUGGETS

Sauce:

1 (8 oz.) can sliced pineapple in juice
1 Tbsp. cornstarch
¼ cup pineapple orange juice
¼ cup barbecue sauce

Prepare sauce by pouring undrained pineapple into the blender. Secure lid and process until it is a thick puree. Pour pineapple into the saucepan and add cornstarch. Blend. Bring to a boil, then reduce heat and simmer, stirring until sauce thickens, about 3 minutes. Remove from heat and set aside.

Chicken Nuggets:

1 egg
2 Tbsp. milk
3½ cups corn flakes, crushed
1 lb. boneless, skinless chicken breasts, cut into nugget-size pieces

Preheat oven to 400°. Whip egg and milk in a small mixing bowl. Place corn flakes in a plastic bag. Dip chicken pieces in egg mixture, then shake with corn flakes to coat. Put coated chicken on a baking sheet. Carefully place baking pan in oven and bake for 15 minutes. Carefully remove baking pan from oven. Serve nuggets with warm pineapple-orange dipping sauce. Makes 4 servings with 265 calories per serving and 3 g fat.

Laurie Sazama, Perham

ORIENTAL CHICKEN

Marinade:

2 Tbsp. oil	1 clove garlic, finely chopped
¼ cup honey	2 Tbsp. parsley
¾ Tbsp. red wine vinegar	1 tsp. ground ginger
¼ cup reduced sodium soy sauce	½ tsp. pepper

Combine ingredients in large flat glass pan. Add **1 skinned, cut up chicken.** Refrigerate at least 2 hours, turning occasionally. For an oven, put in roaster and bake at 350° until done, approximately 1 hour. If grilling, grill chicken 6 inches above white-hot coals, 30 to 45 minutes, until no longer pink near bone. Brush with marinade, turning frequently. If broiling, arrange chicken on baking sheet. Broil 5 inches from heat, 25 to 30 minutes, until no longer pink near bone. Brush with marinade, turning often.

Ceil Headlee, St. Peter

CHICKEN PAPRIKA

2 (2½ lb.) fryers	½ Tbsp. flour
½ tsp. salt	2 cups stock or bouillon
¼ lb. butter	1 Tbsp. heavy cream
1 lg. onion, diced	1 cup thick sour cream
2 Tbsp. paprika	

Rinse chickens; pat dry. Cut in serving pieces; season with salt. Place in covered bowl in refrigerator for 30 minutes. Heat butter in deep pot until light brown. Add onion and cook until transparent; stir in paprika. Add chicken. Cook slowly until pieces are golden brown, then cover and cook 30 minutes longer, or until tender. Sprinkle with flour; add stock or bouillon and heavy cream and stir. Cover and let boil 15 minutes. Remove chicken to warmed serving dish. Stir sour cream into pot; stir and boil 5 minutes. Pour over chicken. Serves 4 to 6.

Maria E. Loeffler, Albany, OR
National Second Vice Regent, 1994-present

BAKED CHICKEN PARMESAN

2¼ cups bread crumbs	1 tsp. Dijon mustard
⅔ cup grated Parmesan cheese	½ tsp. Worcestershire sauce
3 Tbsp. chopped parsley	1 sm. clove garlic or garlic
1 tsp. salt, optional	powder
¾ cup butter	2 (2½ to 3 lb.) broiler fryers, cut

Mix crumbs, cheese, parsley and salt. Melt butter; beat in mustard, Worcestershire sauce and garlic. Dip chicken pieces in butter; roll in crumbs and bake at 350° for 1 hour in shallow pan. Serves 8.

Mary Dvoracek, West, TX
National Director, 1990-1994

NO-PEEK CHICKEN

1 can cream of chicken soup
1 can cream of celery soup
1 cup raw rice
½ cup water or milk
5 chicken breasts
Seasoned salt
1 pkg. onion soup mix

Line bottom of a 9x13 inch pan with aluminum foil. Mix first 5 ingredients and place in pan. Put chicken on top and sprinkle with seasoned salt and dry onion soup mix. Cover tightly with foil and bake at 350° for 2½ hours. "Don't peek!"

Marsha Cerar, Moorhead
Wanda Bauer, Caledonia

CHICKEN PIE

Favorite pie crust
3½ lbs. chicken, cut up
Minced onion to taste
Salt and pepper to taste
¼ cup butter
½ cup water

Divide pie crust in half. Line a 9x13 inch cake pan with pie crust, making sure to cover sides of pan. Place cut up, raw chicken into pan (do not need to de-bone chicken). Seasoned with minced onion, salt and pepper to taste. Dot with butter and add water. Roll out remaining pie crust and place on top, making sure to seal edges. Cut vent holes in top. Bake at 350° for 1 hour.

Eleanor Pankratz, St. Peter

POPPY SEED CHICKEN

2 lbs. chicken, cooked and
  boned and cut in lg. pieces
1 (8 oz.) carton cultured sour
  cream
2 cans Healthy Request mushroom soup
¼ cup water
1½ cups Ritz cracker crumbs
1 Tbsp. poppy seed
1 stick butter or oleo

Place chicken in shallow baking dish. Mix sour cream, soup and water and pour over chicken. Mix crumbs and poppy seed with melted butter. Sprinkle over top. Bake at 350° for 30 minutes.

Imelda Millard, International Falls

CHICKEN STIR-FRY

1 Tbsp. cornstarch
3 Tbsp. soy sauce
1 cup chicken broth
1 cup cooked chicken
1 Tbsp. brown sugar
$\frac{1}{3}$ tsp. garlic powder
Vegetables

Dissolve cornstarch in soy sauce. Combine all ingredients in a wok. Add vegetables. Stir-fry until vegetables are tender. Serve on rice.

Amy Babler, Perham

CHICKEN-RICE ROGER

1 cut up fryer, or equivalent preferred parts
1½ cups raw rice
Salt and pepper to taste
2 Tbsp. grated onion

1 or 2 sm. cans mushroom pieces
4 chicken bouillon cubes, dissolved in 3½ cups hot water
3 or 4 Tbsp. butter or margarine

Flour and then brown the chicken in a little oil. Lightly grease casserole. Put in rice, salt and pepper, onion and mushrooms, including juice. Arrange chicken on top; pour bouillon over it and dot with butter. Cover and bake at 350° for 1 hour.

Harriet Keenan, Eveleth

CHICKEN SPAGHETTI

4 cups chopped chicken
2 cups chicken broth
1 lb. spaghetti
2 med. onions
1 green pepper

2 cups chopped celery
½ lb. Velveeta cheese
Salt and pepper to taste
1 can mushroom soup
1 tsp. Tabasco sauce

Cook chicken; save broth. Cook spaghetti in broth. Chop chicken and vegetables and saute together. Dice cheese. Mix all ingredients. Bake in a greased baking dish at 350° for about 45 minutes.

Doris Morff, International Falls

CHICKEN-SPINACH NOODLE CASSEROLE

1 cup chopped green pepper
1 cup chopped celery
1 cup chopped onion
½ cup margarine
½ lb. Velveeta process cheese spread, cubed
½ (10 oz.) jar sliced salad Spanish olives

1 (4 oz.) can mushrooms, undrained
1 (4 lb.) chicken, seasoned, cooked and cut up
1 (10 oz.) pkg. spinach noodles
4 cups reserved chicken stock
1 (10¾ oz.) can condensed cream of mushroom soup

Saute green pepper, celery and onion in margarine. Stir in Velveeta, olives, mushrooms and chicken. Cook noodles in 3 cups stock until liquid is absorbed. Add soup. Mix all ingredients. Use remaining 1 cup stock if more is needed. Place in lightly greased casserole. Bake at 350° for 15 to 20 minutes.

Helen Laven, Mankato

SWEET AND SOUR CHICKEN OR PORK

1 can pineapple tidbits
2 Tbsp. oil
1 lb. pork or chicken, cubed
½ cup dark syrup
2 Tbsp. soy sauce
¼ cup vinegar
2 Tbsp. catsup

1 clove garlic
½ to 1 cup onions, chopped or
sliced (optional)
½ cup green peppers, chopped
or sliced (optional)
2 Tbsp. cornstarch
2 Tbsp. water

Do not drain pineapple. Heat oil; brown meat and all ingredients, except cornstarch and water. Bring to a boil. Mix cornstarch and water and add to mixture. Boil 2 minutes or until thick as you prefer. Serve over rice. Makes 4 servings.

Barb Thursdale, Waseca
Go-Pher News Editor, 1978-1982

SWEET AND SOUR CHICKEN

1 cup sugar
2 Tbsp. cornstarch
1 (20 oz.) can pineapple
chunks, drained (reserved)

¾ cup vinegar
1 Tbsp. soy sauce
¼ tsp. ginger
1 Tbsp. chicken bouillon

Brown enough **legs, wings or thighs** to fill a 9x13 inch baking pan. Put in bottom of pan. Put in **1 large red or green pepper**, cut in strips. Combine sugar and cornstarch. Add to pineapple juice and enough water to make 1¼ cups. Add vinegar, soy sauce, ginger and chicken bouillon. Stir and boil 2 minutes. Pour over chicken in pan. May add pea pods and partially cooked carrots if desired.

Clara Udelhofen, Mankato

CHICKEN TREMENDOUS

1 cup rice, uncooked
1 pkg. dry onion soup mix
1 chicken, cut up and browned

1 can cream of mushroom soup
2 cups water

Butter a 9x13 inch pan. Sprinkle rice in pan. Sprinkle dry onion soup over rice. Cover with browned chicken pieces. Pour mushroom soup and water mixed over all. Bake at 350° for 2 hours. Add more water if necessary.

Rose Stoltman, Argyle

TERIYAKI-SESAME CHICKEN

½ cup orange juice (no sugar added)
2 Tbsp. teriyaki sauce
¼ tsp. garlic powder
¼ tsp. ground ginger
2 lbs. chicken breasts, skinned
¼ cup plain dried bread crumbs
1 Tbsp. sesame seed

In large glass or stainless steel mixing bowl, combine juice, teriyaki sauce, garlic powder and ginger; add chicken breasts and turn to coat with marinade. Cover with plastic wrap for at least 2 hours in refrigerator. Preheat oven to 350°. In shallow bowl or plate, combine bread crumbs and sesame seed; remove chicken breasts from marinade and coat skinned side of each with crumb mixture. Spray a 9x13 inch pan (flameproof) with cooking spray; transfer chicken to dish, bone side down, and pour reserved marinade over. Bake 45 minutes. Turn oven to broil and continue to broil until chicken is crisp and lightly browned, about 3 to 5 minutes. Transfer chicken to serving platter and drizzle with pan juices.

Cheri Zattoni, Eveleth

THREE CHEESE CHICKEN BAKE

1 (8 oz.) pkg. wide noodles (lasagna)
½ cup onion, chopped
½ cup chopped green pepper, optional
3 Tbsp. butter
1 (10¾ oz.) can cream of chicken soup
⅓ cup milk
1 (6 oz.) can sliced mushrooms, drained, or 1 cup fresh, sliced
1 cup chopped pimento
½ tsp. basil flakes
3 cups cooked chicken, diced
1½ cups cream style cottage cheese
2 cups shredded American cheese
Parmesan cheese

Cook noodles and drain. Cook onion and pepper in butter, until onion looks transparent. Stir in soup, milk, mushrooms, pimento and basil. Place half of the noodles in a greased casserole dish, cover with half of the sauce. Put a layer of chicken, a layer of cottage cheese, American cheese and Parmesan cheese. Repeat layers. Cover and bake at 350° for 45 minutes, or microwave 15 minutes on high.

Lorrayne Yutrzenka, Argyle

• • • • • • • •

Agree with one another, live in peace and the God of love and peace will be with you. II Corinthians 13:11
Shirley Maher, Blue Earth

344

CHICKEN TORTILLA BAKE

4 whole chicken breast, boned
1 (10 or 12 count) pkg. soft corn
tortillas
1 cup chopped Ortega chilies,
canned
1 med. onion, chopped
1 can cream of mushroom or
celery soup
1 can cream of chicken soup
1 cup milk
½ pt. sour cream
1 lb. grated Cheddar cheese

Bake de-boned chicken breast in foil with butter for 1 hour. Cool and cut or tear into strips. Cut tortillas into fourths. Mix chilies, onion, soups, milk and sour cream. Grease a 9x13 inch pan and place tortilla pieces in to cover the bottom. Put a layer of chicken, sauce and grated cheese. Repeat layers until all is used. Bake with cover at 350° for 45 minutes. Uncover and bake 15 more minutes. Can serve with extra chips and salsa if desired.

Variation: Marian substitutes 1 (8 oz.) can Rotel tomatoes for cream of chicken soup. She also sprinkles garlic salt on chicken.

Marian Martin, Crookston

CHICKEN WAIKIKI

1 (3½ to 4 lb.) chicken, cut up
1 (No. 2) can sliced or chunk
pineapple
½ cup brown sugar
2 Tbsp. cornstarch
½ cup vinegar
2 Tbsp. soy sauce
½ tsp. ginger
1 clove garlic, crushed
1 chicken bouillon cube
Green pepper, optional

Coat chicken in flour, salt and pepper; brown in oil. Put into a shallow baking pan. Drain pineapple. Add water to juice to make 1¼ cups. Combine liquid with remaining ingredients in a saucepan. Bring to a boil. Stir until thickened. Pour over chicken in pan. Bake, uncovered, at 350° for 30 minutes, then cover with pineapple and green pepper. Bake 30 minutes more. Serve with white rice.

Kathryn Perszyk, Perham

CHICKEN WENDY

4 boneless chicken breasts
4 slices Swiss cheese
1 can cream of chicken soup
½ cup sherry
2 cups herb croutons
1 stick (½ cup) butter or
margarine

Place chicken in a shallow pan. Cover each piece with sliced cheese. Dilute soup with the sherry; pour over the chicken and cheese. Top with croutons and drizzle melted butter or margarine over the top of the mixture. Bake at 350° for 1 hour or less. Serves 4.

Marie Supalla, New Richland

CHICKEN STIR-FRY**

1 lb. skinless, boneless chicken breast, cut into strips
1 cup broccoli flowerets
½ cup onion wedges
1 (10¾ oz.) can Campbell's Healthy Request condensed cream of broccoli soup
⅔ cup water
2 tsp. low sodium soy sauce
¼ tsp. ground ginger
4 cups hot cooked rice, cooked without salt

Spray nonstick skillet with vegetable cooking spray. Heat 1 minute. Stir-fry chicken in 2 batches until browned; remove. Remove skillet from heat; spray skillet with cooking spray. Stir-fry vegetables until tender-crisp. Add soup, water, soy sauce and ginger; heat to boiling. Return chicken to skillet. Heat through. Serve over rice. Serves 4. Preparation time: 15 minutes. Cooking time: 15 minutes.

Loretta Engesser, Blue Earth

CHICKEN IN WINE

1 (2½ to 3 lb.) fryer or chicken breasts
¼ cup oil
1 med. onion, chopped
½ lb. sliced mushrooms or 1 (4 oz.) can mushrooms
1 can cream of mushroom soup
½ cup dry sherry wine or sherry cooking wine
1 Tbsp. chopped parsley
1 tsp. salt
Dash of pepper
1 tsp. paprika
1 tsp. lemon juice

Brown chicken slowly in oil; drain. Place chicken in single layer in a 9x13 inch pan. Add mushrooms and onions to oil; cook until tender, not brown. Add soup, sherry, seasonings and lemon juice. Blend thoroughly; pour over chicken. Bake, uncovered, at 350° for 1 hour.

Florine Driscoll, Moorhead

ANY DAY DRESSING

1 med. onion
4 Tbsp. butter
10 slices toasted bread, cubed
1½ tsp. salt
¼ tsp. pepper
1 tsp. sage or poultry seasoning
1 cup chicken rice soup
½ soup can water
½ cup celery, chopped

Brown chopped onion in butter. Add the remaining ingredients. Pour into greased baking dish. Bake, covered, at 325° for 1 hour or more.

Margaret Gaul, Iona

DRESSING

8 cups dry bread cubes
6 Tbsp. onion, chopped
2 tsp. salt
½ tsp. pepper

½ tsp. poultry seasoning
Dash of sage
1 cup butter, melted
Hot water or broth

Combine bread cubes, onion and spices. Stir in butter and water or broth to moisten. Makes 8 cups. Can be stuffed in the bird or baked as a side dish.

Rosalie Grams, Janesville

BAKED EGGS

¼ cup margarine
1 cup milk
1½ dozen eggs
1 cup sour cream

2 tsp. salt
¼ cup chopped onions
2 cups cubed ham
2 cups grated cheese

Melt the margarine; beat in milk, eggs, sour cream and salt until blended. Blend in onion, ham and cheese. Bake in a 9x13 inch pan until set, about 35 minutes.

Martha Erickson, St. Peter

BAKED EGG BREAKFAST

1 lb. pork sausage
9 eggs
3 cups milk
1 tsp. salt

1½ tsp. dry mustard
3 slices bread, cubed
1 cup grated Cheddar cheese

Brown sausage; drain. Set aside. Beat eggs well; add milk, salt, mustard, bread and sausage. Stir in cheese. Pour mixture in a well greased 9x13 inch pan; cover and refrigerate overnight. Bake at 350° for 45 minutes. Let stand 10 minutes before cutting. Serves 12.

Variation: May substitute bacon fried and drained, but cut down on salt, or a 3 ounce bottle Hormel Real bacon pieces and cut salt.

Ceil Abts, Winona

BREAKFAST BRUNCH

8 to 10 sliced bread, cubed
¾ lb. shredded Cheddar cheese
1 lb. ham or pork sizzlers,
  precooked
4 eggs, beaten

2½ cups milk
¾ tsp. dry mustard
1 can golden mushroom soup
½ cup milk
1 sm. can mushrooms, drained

Line a greased 9x13 inch pan with bread cubes; sprinkle on cheese. Cut meat and add to top of cheese. Mix eggs, 2½ cups milk and mustard and pour over all. Refrigerate overnight. Before baking, mix soup and ½ cup milk; pour over casserole Top with mushrooms last half hour of baking. Bake at 325° for 1½ hours. Serve hot.

Paulette Hanson, Red Lake Falls

BREAKFAST PIZZA

1 lb. bulk pork sausage	5 eggs
1 (8 count) pkg. refrigerator crescent rolls	¼ cup milk
	½ tsp. salt
1 cup frozen loose pack hash brown potatoes, thawed	⅛ tsp. pepper
	2 Tbsp. Parmesan cheese
1 cup (4 oz.) sharp Cheddar cheese, shredded	

In a skillet, cook sausage until browned; drain off excess fat. Separate crescent dough into 8 triangles. Place in an ungreased 12 inch pizza pan with points toward the center. Press over bottom and up sides to form a crust; seal perforations. Spoon sausage over crust. Sprinkle with potatoes. Top with Cheddar cheese. In a bowl, beat eggs, milk, salt and pepper. Pour into crust. Sprinkle Parmesan cheese over all. Bake at 375° for 25 to 30 minutes. Serves 6 to 8.

Doris Eisbrener, Thief River Falls

EGG DISH

18 jumbo eggs, beaten	2 tsp. salt
2 heaping cups cubed ham (½ to 1 inch cubes)	5 slices bread, cubed small
	1 (8 oz.) pkg. shredded Cheddar cheese
2 cups milk	

Beat the eggs in a large bowl. Add the other ingredients. This can all be done the night before you bake it. Refrigerate until morning. Pour into greased 9x13 inch cake pan and bake in preheated 350° oven for 50 minutes. Top should be just beginning to brown and toothpick or knife should come out clear. For variety, add 1 large chopped tomato, ½ chopped pepper, and ½ chopped onion before baking. Makes 12 large pieces.

Variation: Jean, Marion, and Ester add ½ cup melted butter, 1 teaspoon salt, and 2 teaspoons dry mustard.

Shirley Seyfried, Fergus Falls
1st Vice State Regent, 1994-present
2nd Vice State Regent, 1990-1994
State Treasurer, 1986-1990
Jean Strelow, Winona
Marion Plante, Crookston
Ester Reger, Waseca

* * * * * * * *

My God will fulfill all your needs in Christ Jesus. Phillippians 4:19
Gen Armon, Blue Earth

348

HASH BROWN OMELET

8 slices bacon, cooked crisp and crumbled
4 cups cooked potatoes, shredded
½ cup onion, chopped
½ cup green pepper, chopped
Salt and pepper to taste
4 eggs
¼ cup milk
1 cup shredded cheese

Heat electric skillet to 350°. Fry bacon until crisp; remove meat, leaving some drippings in pan. Sprinkle potatoes, onions, green pepper and salt and pepper on top. Cook until potatoes are brown on bottom. Beat eggs, milk, salt and pepper until light. Pour over potato mixture. Sprinkle cheese and bacon on top. Cover and cook on low heat for 15 minutes. Cut in squares and serve. Serve with toast or muffin, some fresh fruit and you have a complete brunch.

Mary Christianson, Argyle

BREAKFAST CASSEROLE

6 slices bread
1 lb. browned sausage
¼ lb. grated Cheddar cheese
1 (4 oz.) can mushrooms, drained
4 eggs
2 cups milk
1 tsp. dry mustard
1 tsp. onion powder or chopped onion

Break bread into a greased 9x13 inch glass baking dish. Put the browned, crumbled sausage on top of the bread. Sprinkle the grated cheese and mushrooms on next. Mix the eggs, milk, mustard and onion; pour over the mixture in pan. Let the dish stand overnight, covered with foil in the refrigerator. Bake at 325° for 45 minutes. Remove foil and bake another 15 minutes.

Zonda Befort, Mazeppa
State Education Chair, 1988-present

OMELET DELUXE

4 eggs, separated
¼ cup milk
½ tsp. salt
Dash of pepper
¼ tsp. baking powder
1 Tbsp. butter

In a 1 quart bowl, beat egg whites until stiff peaks form. In a small bowl, beat egg yolks with milk, salt, pepper and baking powder until lemon colored. Gently fold into beaten egg whites. Place butter in a 9 inch pie plate, microwave until butter melts. Pour egg mixture into hot butter and spread evenly in pie plate. Microwave 8 to 10 minutes or until center is almost set. Fill with bacon, green onion, cheese, ham, tomato or any combination you like. Fold in half. Top omelet with any sauces: Hollandaise, Spanish, Newburg.

Rose Moran, Crookston

VEGETABLES & MAIN DISHES

EGG BAKE

1 dozen eggs	1 cup chopped ham
Salt and pepper	1 sm. pkg. stuffing mix
1 cup milk	1½ cups hot water
1 cup grated cheese	¼ cup butter

Beat 1 dozen eggs; add a little salt and pepper, then add milk, grated cheese and ham. In another bowl, mix stuffing mix (chicken or herb) with hot water and butter. Add to egg mixture. Pour into greased 9x13 inch pan. Bake at 350° for 40 to 45 minutes.

Debra McNamee, Mahnomen

BROCCOLI EGG CHEESE BAKE

6 eggs	1 (10 oz.) pkg. chopped broccoli,
1 can cream of mushroom soup,	cooked and drained
undiluted	½ cup grated American cheese

Combine ingredients; put in a greased 9 inch quiche or pie pan. Bake at 375° for 30 to 35 minutes. Let stand 5 minutes before cutting.

Elaine Schlichte, Currie
District Deputy, 1992-1996

OMELET SANDWICH EGG BAKE

1 loaf English muffin bread	3 cups milk
½ lb. shredded Cheddar cheese	½ tsp. dry mustard
1 lb. thin sliced deli ham	½ tsp. salt
½ lb. sliced Swiss cheese	1½ cups corn flakes, crushed
8 eggs	¼ cup melted butter

Grease a 9x13 inch pan. Cover bottom of pan with a layer of buttered bread (butter side up). Cover with layer of Cheddar cheese, then a layer of ham and then Swiss cheese. Cover with another layer of bread (butter side up). Blend eggs, milk, mustard and salt and pour over top. Refrigerate 8 to 10 hours or overnight. Mix corn flakes and melted butter just before baking and sprinkle over top. Bake at 350° for 1 hour or until golden brown.

Sue McRaith, Waseca

WESTERN BREAKFAST

1 (12 oz.) pkg. hash browns	2 cups Cheddar cheese
2 cups cubed ham or sausage,	12 eggs
cooked	2 cups milk
1 sm. onion	Salt and pepper
1 sm. can mushrooms	Paprika

Butter a 9x13 inch pan. Place hash browns in bottom. Cover with meat, onions and mushrooms. Add cheese on top. Beat eggs and milk and pour over. Sprinkle with seasonings to taste. Bake at 350° for 1 hour or until eggs are set.

Tina Rein, Moorhead

SCRAMBLED EGG OMELET

6 eggs
½ cup milk
¾ cup broccoli or asparagus,
cut into 1 inch pieces
1 (4 oz.) can mushrooms, sliced
or cut into pieces
2 Tbsp. chopped onion
½ cup shredded cheese

Beat eggs and milk. Saute vegetables, mushrooms and onion. Add egg mixture. When eggs are half cooked, add cheese of your choice. Stir frequently until eggs are fully cooked. Add salt and pepper to individual taste.

Doris Eisbrener, Thief River Falls

SCALLOPED EGGS AND HAM

¼ cup butter or margarine
¼ cup all-purpose flour
2 cups milk
1½ cups fine dry bread crumbs
2 Tbsp. butter or margarine,
melted
4 hard cooked eggs, chopped
1 cup (5 oz.) cubed ham, fully
cooked
⅓ cup chopped tomato,
optional

In a medium saucepan, melt ¼ cup butter. Stir in flour; add milk all at once. Cook and stir over medium heat until thickened and bubbly. In a small bowl, combine bread crumbs and melted butter. In a 1½ quart casserole, layer half the eggs, half the ham, half the sauce and half the bread crumb mixture. Repeat. Bake, uncovered, at 350° for 25 to 30 minutes or until bubbly. If desired, garnish with chopped tomato. Makes 4 servings. Nutritional analysis (per serving): 511 calories, 977 mg sodium, 29 g fat, 279 mg cholesterol.

Lucille Schmitz, Perham

ELEPHANT STEW

1 med. sized elephant
6 barrels of bourbon
2 rabbits, optional
Salt and pepper

Cut elephant into small, bite-sized pieces. Add enough Bourbon to cover. Cook over a kerosene fire for 5 weeks at 465°.

Note: If unexpected guests arrive, the 2 rabbits may be added. This will serve 3,850 people.

Florence Yutrzenka, Argyle

CORNED BEEF HOTDISH

1 pkg. wide noodle, cooked as
directed
2 cans cream of chicken soup
½ cup chopped onion
1 can corned beef
2 cans milk
⅓ lb. Velveeta cheese

Combine noodles, soup, onion, corned beef and milk. Stir to mix well. Top with cheese. Bake, uncovered, for 45 minutes.

Marcia Peterson, Mahnomen

HAM BALLS

2 lbs. ground ham	¼ tsp. salt
1 cup cracker crumbs	1 lb. hamburger
1 cup milk	2 eggs
1 Tbsp. Worcestershire sauce	

Mix well and form into balls. Put in baking dish.

Sauce:

1 cup vinegar	½ tsp. wet mustard
¼ cup water	2 Tbsp. cornstarch
¾ cup brown sugar	

Mix and cover balls with sauce. Bake at 350° for 1 hour.

Neva Quaday, Blue Earth

HARLEQUIN HAM CASSEROLE

¼ cup margarine	2 cups cooked rice
¼ cup flour	½ cup chopped green peppers
1½ cups milk	½ cup sliced water chestnuts
½ cup mayonnaise	¼ cup shredded Parmesan
½ tsp. salt	cheese
2 cups cubed ham	2 Tbsp. pimento

Make cream sauce with margarine, flour, and milk; stir in mayonnaise and salt. Add rest of ingredients; mix well. Pour into 2 quart greased casserole at 350° for 40 minutes. Serves about 6 people.

Joan Pelzel, Caledonia

CRUNCHY HAM CASSEROLE

1 (2 lb.) pkg. frozen cubed hash browns	1 can cream of mushroom soup
½ cup margarine, melted	1 pt. sour cream
1 tsp. salt	2 cups Cheddar cheese, shredded
¼ tsp. black pepper	1½ cups cooked ham, diced
½ cup onion, chopped	(I use 2 cups)

Mix potatoes, melted margarine, salt, pepper, onion, soup, sour cream, Cheddar cheese (reserve ¼ cup) and ham. Spread mixture into a 9x13x2 inch baking pan prepared with nonstick cooking spray.

Topping:

2 cups corn flakes, crushed	¼ cup margarine, melted

Mix crushed cereal with melted margarine. Sprinkle reserved cheese on top of casserole. Add crushed cereal. Bake at 350° for 45 minutes to 1 hour.

Madeline Dufault, Crookston

HAM HOT DISH

2 lg. onions, cut fine	1 lb. ham, diced
1 lb. bacon, diced and fried	1 can mushroom or celery soup
1 pkg. Creamettes macaroni, cooked	1 can lima beans
1 can niblet corn	1 can tomatoes

Saute onions in the bacon grease. Put all ingredients together and bake for 1 hour.

Helen Pope, St. Peter

HAM HOTDISH

3 stalks celery, chopped	1 sm. jar Cheez Whiz
1 sm. onion, chopped	1 can cream of celery soup
¼ cup butter	1 lg. pkg. broccoli, cooked
1 cup water	2 to 3 cups ham, diced
1½ cups Minute Rice	

Saute celery and onion in butter. Add water and rice. Simmer 5 minutes. Add Cheez Whiz, soup, broccoli and ham. Put in casserole and bake at 350° for 30 minuets or until hot.

Cel Berkner, Mahnomen

HAM MEAT BALLS OR LOAF

1 lb. ground pork	½ cup milk
1 lb. smoked ham, ground	½ cup moist fine bread crumbs
2 eggs	½ tsp. pepper

This can be made into balls or loaf, served on a pineapple ring that has been fried in pineapple juice, or used as a garnish around the meat plate.

Sauce:

1 cup brown sugar	¼ cup water
½ tsp. dry mustard	½ cup vinegar

Mix and pour over loaf or balls. Bake at 350° for 1 hour.

Rita Noel, Caledonia

HAM LOAF

¾ lb. ground ham	1¼ tsp. salt
¾ lb. ground beef	¼ tsp. pepper
¾ cup oats, uncooked	1 cup tomato juice
¼ cup chopped onion	1 egg, beaten

Mix all and bake at 350° for 1 hour and 15 minutes. Let stand a few minutes before slicing.

Oveida Shannon, Blue Earth

VEGETABLES & MAIN DISHES

HAM AND RICE STIR-FRY

½ cup rice, cooked
1 cup sliced green onions
1 cup thin sliced celery
4 Tbsp. cooking oil
1 (4 oz.) can mushrooms

1 cup frozen peas
1½ cups leftover ham
2 eggs, beaten
1 Tbsp. soy sauce

Cook rice. Saute onions and celery in oil until tender. Add mushrooms, peas (I give mine a touch in the microwave) and ham. Cook 3 to 4 minutes. Push aside in pan and scramble eggs. Add drained rice and soy sauce. Toss with ham mixture. Let it stand a few minutes to heat well. Makes about 4 servings.

Arlene Peterson, Littlefork

HAM VIENNESE WITH RICE

3 cups hot cooked rice
12 oz. fully cooked ham
1½ Tbsp. butter or margarine
½ cup chopped onion
2 cups thinly sliced celery
1 (10¾ oz.) can condensed
    cream of chicken soup

1½ tsp. mustard
¼ tsp. dill seed
¾ cup sour cream
⅓ cup chopped pimento,
    optional

While rice is cooking, cut ham into thin strips and saute in butter or margarine, about 2 minutes. Use a large skillet. Add onions and celery, continue cooking until vegetables are tender. Stir in soup, mustard and dill seed. Heat thoroughly. Add sour cream and pimentos. Heat, but do not boil. Serve over bed of rice. Serves 6.

Grace Kaveney, St. Peter

UPSIDE DOWN HAM LOAF

3 Tbsp. butter or margarine
6 Tbsp. brown sugar
½ cup dry bread crumbs
6 slices pineapple
6 cherries
3 cups ground ham

3 eggs, beaten
1½ tsp. dry mustard
½ tsp. salt
½ tsp. pepper
3 tsp. minced onion

Spread the bottom of a large skillet with butter and sugar. Melt and mix. Arrange pineapple slices over this and center with Maraschino cherry. Spread ham mixture over this. Cover tightly and cook over low heat for 30 minutes. Serve upside down in pie shaped pieces. Serves 6.

Audrey Johnston, Detroit Lakes

AMISH YUM-A-SETTA

2 lbs. hamburger
¼ onion, chopped
Salt and pepper to taste
¼ cup brown sugar
1 can tomato soup, undiluted

1 (16 oz.) pkg. egg noodles
1 can cream of chicken soup, undiluted
1 (8 oz.) pkg. mild Cheddar cheese (or use ½ Cheddar and ½ Mozzarella cheese)

Brown hamburger (can use ground turkey, or use half turkey and half hamburger). Add onion and salt and pepper to hamburger while browning. Add brown sugar to tomato soup and add all to hamburger mixture. Cook egg noodles; drain and add cream of chicken soup to noodles. In casserole dish; add hamburger/tomato mixture; top with layer of shredded cheese, then noodle and cream of chicken soup mixture as top layer. Bake at 350° for 30 minutes until heated through. (The cheese should be between the meat/tomato mixture and noodle mixture.)

Elaine Sable, Owatonna

BAKED CHOP SUEY

1 lb. ground beef
2 Tbsp. shortening
1 cup celery, cut fine
2 med. onions, cut fine
1 can cream of chicken soup

1 can mushroom soup
1½ cups warm water
½ cup uncooked rice
¼ cup soy sauce
Salt and pepper to taste

Brown beef in hot fat until crumbly; add remaining ingredients, rinsing the cans of soup with the water. Bake in a 2 quart casserole at 350° for 1 hour. Cover with **chow mein noodles**. Bake 15 minutes more.

Genevieve Jahn, Caledonia

BEAN HOT DISH

1 lb. bacon, diced
1 lb. hamburger
1 sm. onion, diced
2 cans pork and beans
2 cans butter beans, drained

2 cans kidney beans, drained
1 cup ketchup
1 cup brown sugar
2 tsp. dry mustard
2 tsp. salt

Brown bacon, hamburger and onion; pour off half the grease. Put in a large casserole. Add pork and beans, butter beans and kidney beans. Mix the ketchup, brown sugar, dry mustard and salt. Pour over the other ingredients. Bake at 350° for 45 minutes.

Diane Pawlowski, Argyle

BEEF CASHEW CASSEROLE

2 lbs. hamburger	½ lb. American cheese
1 onion, chopped	½ cup sour cream
1 (8 oz.) pkg. lasagna noodles,	2 cans cream of mushroom soup
cooked for 8 minutes	1 cup cashews or chow mein
1 sm. can mushrooms	noodles
1 sm. jar sliced black olives	

Brown hamburger and onions. Cook the lasagna noodles as directed on box. Heat the following ingredients in saucepan. Layer ingredients twice in a 9x13 inch pan in this order: hamburger, noodles and sauce. Bake at 350 for 45 minutes (or 1 hour if refrigerated before baking). Add cashews and/or chow mein noodles on top the last 10 minutes.

Patricia Crummy, Argyle

BEEF PATTIE

Combine **1 pound extra lean ground beef** and **¹/₃ cup Carnation milk**. Prepare **1 package Stove Top dressing for pork** according to package directions. Place one scoop of dressing on each patty; pull and turn over. Place in greased pan.

Sauce:

1 can mushroom soup	2 Tbsp. catsup
2 tsp. Worcestershire sauce	

Combine and pour over patties. Bake at 350° for 45 minutes.

Arzella Jerome, International Falls
Cecelia Raleigh, St. Paul

CABBAGE ROLLS (GOTABKI)

1 head cabbage	½ lb. ground pork
2 Tbsp. vinegar	1 egg
1 tsp. salt	½ cup partially cooked rice
1 onion, chopped fine	¼ tsp. poultry seasoning
3 Tbsp. butter	Salt and pepper
1 lb. ground beef	

Wilt cabbage leaves by scalding in boiling water to which vinegar and salt have been added. Drain, cool in cold water and pat dry. Cut out heavy ribs. Saute onion in butter until transparent. Combine meat, egg, rice and seasoning. Spread each leaf with about 2 tablespoons of the mixture. Fold the two opposite sides and roll, starting with one of open ends. Place in pan; add butter and 1 cup hot water. Simmer slowly 2 hours. Cabbage rolls may be served with mushroom sauce, tomato sauce or sour cream.

Kathy Dibble, Chicago

** Used throughout POTLUCK to identify quick and easy recipes.

BEEF STROGANOFF

1 to 1½ lbs. ground beef
3 slices bacon, diced
¼ to ½ cup chopped onion
1½ Tbsp. flour
¾ tsp. salt
¼ tsp. paprika
Dash of pepper
1 can cream of mushroom soup
1 cup sour cream

Brown ground beef and bacon. Add onion. Cook until tender; drain excess fat. Add flour and seasonings. Stir in soup. Cook for 15 to 20 minutes. Stir in sour cream; heat through. Serve on toasted buns.

Helen Chesney, Owatonna

DELICIOUS BURGERS

1½ lbs. ground beef
3 Tbsp. finely chopped onion
½ tsp. garlic salt
½ tsp. pepper
1 cup (4 oz.) shredded Cheddar cheese
¹/₃ cup canned sliced mushrooms
6 bacon strips, cooked and crumbled
¼ cup mayonnaise
6 hamburger buns, split

In a medium bowl, combine beef, onion, garlic salt, salt and pepper; mix well. Shape into six patties, ¾ inch thick. In a small bowl, combine the cheese, mushrooms, bacon and mayonnaise; refrigerate. Grill burgers over medium heat coals for 10 to 12 minutes, turning once. During the last 3 minutes, spoon ¼ cup of the cheese mixture onto each burger. Serve on buns with lettuce and tomato. Yield: 6 servings.

Sharon Marie Lynn, Adrian

CHEROKEE HOT DISH

¾ cup chopped onion
1 lb. hamburger
1 (10 or 11 oz.) can tomatoes or 2 cups cut up tomatoes
1 can cream of mushroom or chicken soup
¹/₈ tsp. thyme
¹/₈ tsp. oregano
¹/₈ tsp. garlic salt
1 cup Minute Rice
1 cup grated Cheddar cheese
1 cup sliced ripe or green olives

Brown onions and hamburger and drain if fatty. Add tomatoes, soups, spices and rice and cook on top of stove until liquid is absorbed and rice is soft. Place in a 9x13 inch pan. Sprinkle with cheese and put under broiler briefly to melt cheese. Can be topped with olives before serving.

Sylvia Steinert, Red Lake Falls

BEEF IN WINE

1 pkg. stew meat	1 can mushrooms
½ to 1 cup wine	2 cans French onion soup

Mix and place in greased casserole dish. Bake at 250° for 6 hours. Serve over rice or noodles.

Joan Gockel, St. Peter

EASY CABBAGE CASSEROLE

1 med. onion, chopped	¹/₈ tsp. pepper
3 Tbsp. butter	6 cups cabbage, coarsely
½ lb. ground beef	shredded
¾ tsp. salt	1 (10½ oz.) can tomato soup

Saute onion in butter. Add ground beef, salt and pepper, heating through, but don't brown. Spread 3 cups cabbage into a 2 quart baking dish. Cover with meat mixture. Top with 3 cups cabbage. Pour tomato soup over top. Bake at 350° for 1 hour.

Dorothy Losinski, Winona

BEEF AND CABBAGE CASSEROLE

2½ lbs. hamburger	1 (16 oz.) can tomato sauce
Onion	1 (10¾ oz.) can cream of mush-
1 cup rice	room soup
1 med. head cabbage, cut up	1 (10¾ oz.) can water

Brown hamburger, onion and rice. Cook cabbage until limp. Layer cabbage and hamburger mixture. Pour sauce, soup and water mixture over all. Bake at 350° for 1 hour.

Rita Heidelberger, Fergus Falls

CHIN CHIN CHARLIE

2 lbs. ground beef, browned and drained	¼ cup uncooked white rice
	¼ cup soy sauce
1 cup chopped onion	1 (4 oz.) can mushrooms with
3 cups celery, sliced diagonally	juice
1 (10 oz.) can cream of mush-room soup	1 can water chestnuts with liquid
1 (10 oz.) can cream of chicken soup	Chow mein noodles

Mix all ingredients in large casserole and top with chow mein noodles after baking at 350° for 45 to 50 minutes. Return to oven and bake long enough to lightly brown and crisp the noodles.

Gertrude Schroeder, Fairmont

CHILI HOT DISH

1 lb. hamburger	1 (16 oz.) can tomato sauce
1 chopped onion	1 cup water
1 can kidney beans	1 tsp. chili powder
1 (8 oz.) pkg. macaroni,	1 tsp. salt
uncooked	1 cup Cheddar cheese

Brown hamburger and onion; add kidney beans, including juice, and macaroni. Add rest of ingredients and let simmer in electric frying pan for 15 minutes. Cover with cheese; let cheese melt and serve.

Mary Garry, Euclid
District Deputy, 1982-1986

HAMBURGER CHOW MEIN HOT DISH

1 lb. browned hamburger	1 can chicken and rice soup
1 cup chopped celery	1 (15 oz.) can mixed vegetables
1 med. onion, sliced	with liquid
2 Tbsp. soy sauce	¾ cup chow mein noodles
1 can cream of mushroom soup	

Mix first 7 ingredients into a 2 quart casserole and sprinkle with chow mein noodles. Bake, uncovered, at 350° for 1 hour. Yield: approximately 8 servings.

Mary Campbell, Blue Earth

CORN MOUSSAKA

1 (17 oz.) can whole kernel corn,	2 eggs, slightly beaten
drained	1½ cups cream style cottage
1½ lbs. ground beef	cheese with chives, drained
1 Tbsp. flour	¼ cup grated Parmesan cheese
1 (8 oz.) can tomato sauce	1 (4 oz.) pkg. shredded
½ tsp. garlic salt	Mozzarella cheese
¼ tsp. cinnamon	

Spread corn in an ungreased 10x6x2 inch baking dish. In a medium skillet, brown the ground beef; drain off excess fat. Add flour; cook and stir for 1 minute. Stir in tomato sauce, garlic salt and cinnamon. Pour over corn in dish. Bake at 350° for 15 minutes. Meanwhile, combine eggs and cottage cheese; spread over meat mixture. Top with Parmesan and Mozzarella cheese. It may be topped with slivered almonds. Bake 10 to 15 minutes more. Makes 6 servings.

Gwen Johannes, Blue Earth

DIFFERENT HOT DISH

1 (8 oz.) pkg. macaroni,
  cooked as usual
1 lb. hamburger
1 med. onion, chopped
1 sm. bottle stuffed olives, chopped

1 can mushrooms
1 can mushroom soup with
  ½ can milk
½ lb. Velveeta, cubed

Brown hamburger and onion. Mix all ingredients. Bake at 375° for 45 minutes or until bubbly.

Margaret Carr Guerber, Blue Earth

FLEISCH KUECHLE (GERMAN)

3 cups flour
1 tsp. salt
Equal amount of water and
  cream
1 cup ground beef

1 cup ground pork
½ cup water
1 sm. onion, chopped fine
Salt and pepper to taste

Mix flour, salt and water and cream to make soft dough so you can handle it real easy to roll out into small circles. Fill with ground beef, ground pork, water, onion, salt and pepper mixture. Spread some meat mixture on half the circle; bring the other half circle dough up and over the meat. Seal the edge (roll a plate edge over the edge of dough and it will seal). Fry in deep fat, first one side, and then the other, until done and golden color.

Fran Janous, Owatonna

FOUR SOUP HOT DISH

1½ lbs. hamburger
Salt and pepper
Onion
1 can cream of celery soup

1 can chicken with rice soup
1 can cream of chicken soup
1 can cream of mushroom soup
1 (8 oz.) pkg. chow mein noodles

Brown hamburger. Season with salt and pepper and onion. Mix soups, hamburger and chow mein noodles (reserve a few noodles for the top). Bake at 350° for 45 to 60 minutes.

Verdelma Strauss, Red Wing

GOULASH

1½ lbs. hamburger
½ diced onion
2½ cups macaroni

1 can tomato soup
1 can mushroom soup
Garlic salt

Brown hamburger and onion. Cook macaroni until tender. Mix with rest of the ingredients. May add ketchup if you want more of a tomato taste. Bake at 350° for ½ hour.

Father Ken Clinton, Janesville

GRANDMA'S SPECIALTY

1½ lb. hamburger
1 lg. onion
1 cup chopped celery
½ cup rice, uncooked
¼ cup soy sauce
1 can cream of mushroom soup
1 can cream of chicken soup
1 cup water

Brown hamburger and onions before adding all other ingredients. Remove excess fat first. Combine and mix well before transferring into casserole. Bake at 350° for approximately 80 minutes, stirring occasionally during baking to distribute the rice.

Marguerite Larson, Owatonna

HAMBURGER-BROCCOLI CASSEROLE

½ (30 oz.) pkg. frozen potato
rounds (4 cups)
1 lb. ground beef
1 (10 oz.) pkg. frozen chopped
broccoli, thawed
1 can French fried onions
1 can cream of celery soup
$1/3$ cup milk
1 cup (4 oz.) shredded Cheddar
cheese
¼ tsp. garlic powder
$1/8$ tsp. pepper

Line bottom and sides of an 8x12 inch casserole with potatoes. Bake, uncovered, at 400° for 10 minutes. Brown hamburger. Add that and broccoli and ½ can of onions. Combine soup, milk, ½ cup cheese and seasonings and pour over rest. Bake, covered, at 400° for 20 minutes. Top with remaining cheese and onions; put in oven until heated through and cheese is melted. If necessary, it can be left in oven longer on low heat.

Rita Jacobs, Plainview

GROUND BEEF AND POTATO CASSEROLE

1 lb. ground beef
2 cups frozen, cut green beans,
cooked and drained
1 (10 oz.) can condensed
tomato soup
¼ cup water
½ tsp. salt
$1/8$ tsp. pepper
2 cups prepared mashed
potatoes
1 (2.8 oz.) can French fried
onions
½ cup shredded Cheddar
cheese

Brown beef; drain. Combine beef, beans, soup, water, salt and pepper. Pour into a 1½ quart casserole. Combine mashed potatoes and ½ can French fried onions. Spoon potato mixture in a ring around the outer edge of the casserole. Bake, uncovered, at 350° for 25 minutes. Top potatoes with cheese and remaining onions and bake 5 minutes longer. Makes 6 servings.

Lorraine Thillen, Caledonia

HAMBURGER POTATO BAKE

1 lb. hamburger	2 or 3 carrots, peeled and cut up
1 onion, chopped	1 can cream of mushroom soup
4 celery stems, cut up	½ soup can water
1 can French cut beans, drained	1 pkg. hash browns or patties

Brown hamburger until no longer pink. Saute onion and celery in hamburger. Put in cake pan with beans, carrots, mushroom soup and water. Put hash browns or patties on top, covering completely. Bake at 350° for 45 minutes.

Mary Ann Pongratz, Mankato

HAMBURGER HOT DISH

1 lb. raw hamburger	1 sm. sliced onion
5 sliced raw potatoes	1 sm. can vegetable soup
4 sliced raw carrots	1 soup can water

Layer meat and vegetables in casserole and top with soup mixed with water. Bake at 325° for 1½ hours or until potatoes and carrots are done.

Phyllis Cuzek, Red Lake Falls

HAMBURGER-POTATO HOT DISH

1 lb. ground beef	1 cup milk
1 onion, cut up	Pepper
4 cups raw potatoes, cut up	Salt (very little needed because
1 cup minestrone soup	of soup)

Brown ground beef with onion. Pour off fat. Mix all ingredients and bake at 350° for 30 minutes.

Mary K. King, Perham

HAMBURGER CASSEROLE

1 lb. ground beef	1 can tomato soup, undiluted
½ cup onions, chopped	3 oz. cooked noodles
¾ cup celery, chopped	½ cup grated Cheddar cheese
1 can cream of mushroom soup, undiluted	Mushrooms, optional

Brown ground beef, onions and celery. Add soups with meat. Add cooked noodles to mixture and place in a greased 2 quart casserole dish. Top with or sprinkle grated Cheddar cheese over all the mixture. Bake, uncovered, at 350° for 15 minutes or until done.

Josie Pick, Slayton

MEXICAN HOT DISH

1 lb. ground round
1 chopped onion
1 clove minced garlic
1 can tomato sauce
1/3 can tomato juice
1/4 tsp. oregano
2 Tbsp. chili powder

1/4 tsp. cumin
1 can kidney beans with liquid
1 bag of corn chips
Lettuce
Additional chopped onion
Shredded cheese

Brown meat, onions and garlic in oil. Stir in tomato sauce, juice, oregano, chili powder and cumin. Grease casserole and alternate layers of beans, chips and meat, ending with corn chips. Pour tomato juice over all and bake, covered, at 350° for 45 minutes, then uncovered for the last 10 minutes. Place lettuce, chopped onion and grated cheese on top before serving.

Doris LaBine, Argyle
Virginia (Ginger) Duffy, Grand Junction, CO
National Director, 1992-1994

MEXICAN STUFFED SHELLS

1 lb. ground beef
1 jar medium picante sauce
1/2 cup water
1 (8 oz.) can tomato sauce
1 can chopped green chilies, drained

1 cup Monterey Jack cheese, shredded
1 can Durkee onions
12 lg. pasta shells, cooked

Brown ground beef; drain. Combine picante sauce, water and tomato sauce. Stir 1/2 cup into beef with chilies, 1/2 cup cheese and 1/2 can onions; mix. Pour half of remaining sauce on bottom of a 10x13 inch pan. Stuff shells and put in pan. Pour remaining sauce over. Bake, covered, at 350° for 30 minutes. Top with remaining cheese and onions. Bake, uncovered, for 5 minutes.

Doris Cerney, Winona

TOMATO AND PEPPER BEEF

1 lb. lean ground beef or ground turkey
2/3 cup quick or regular oatmeal
1 (14.2 oz.) can stewed tomatoes or tomato sauce or diluted tomato soup

1 or 2 onions, chopped or sliced
2 Tbsp. soy sauce
5 tsp. cornstarch
1 chopped green pepper

Mix meat and oatmeal well and shape into 3/4 inch balls. Microwave 5 minutes. Mix rest of ingredients and pour over meat. Microwave 5 minutes until meat is done. Serve over rice, if desired.

Mary Jane Gray, Blue Earth

ONE DISH MEAL

1 bag French fries	1 can cream of celery soup
1 bag Oriental vegetable mix	1 can cream of mushroom soup
2 lbs. hamburger, browned	2 cans of water

Make two layers each of French fries, Oriental mix and hamburger. Pour soup mixed with water on top. Bake at 350° for 1 hour.

Cecilia Plante, Crookston

HAMBURGER HOT DISH

1 lb. ground beef	1 can cream of celery soup
1 tsp. salt	2 cans water
1 sm. onion, chopped	½ cup uncooked rice (not
1 can cream of mushroom soup	Minute Rice)

Brown ground beef, salt and onion. Add rest of ingredients and bake in casserole dish at 350° for 45 minutes. Stir every 15 minute. Sprinkle with **2½ cups chow mein noodles;** bake 45 minutes.

Delores Cedar, Red Wing

LOU'S BUSY DAY HOT DISH

1 lb. hamburger, browned	1 can tomato soup
1 sm. onion	1 soup can water
4 lg. carrots	Salt and pepper
8 to 10 potatoes	

Brown hamburger with onion. Wash and peel carrots and potatoes; slice thickly. Combine hamburger with vegetables. Add soup and water. Put in crockpot on low for 8 hours (2 hours in oven).

Marie Kvam, St. Charles

SURPRISE MEAT BALLS

1 lb. ground beef	18 sm. stuffed olives
½ cup dry bread crumbs	2 Tbsp. shortening
2 eggs	2 Tbsp. Worcestershire sauce
¼ tsp. pepper	1 cup water
½ tsp. onion salt	2 Tbsp. flour
¼ tsp. garlic salt	¼ cup water

Combine beef, crumbs, eggs, pepper, onion salt, and garlic salt; mix well. Shape about 2 tablespoons of mixture around an olive. Brown the meat balls slowly in the shortening. Pour off drippings. Add Worcestershire sauce and 1 cup water. Cover tightly and simmer 20 minutes. Mix the 2 tablespoons flour with ¼ cup water and add to cooking liquid. Cook until thickened, stirring constantly. Serve over the meat balls.

Merle Gostomczik, Medford
District Deputy, 1988-1992

PIG IN THE BLANKET

2 cups rice
2 cups hamburger
Salt and pepper to taste
1 med. onion
1 head of cabbage
1 lg. can tomatoes

Wash rice and soak 1 hour, then mix rice, hamburger, salt and pepper and onion. Wrap in cabbage leaves which have been boiled about 2 minutes. Put 1 tablespoon of mixture to one leaf. Cover with water and add the can of tomatoes. Cook slowly at 325° for about 2 hours.

Phyllis Sheridan, Crookston

POLISH HOT DISH

1 lb. hamburger
½ lb. pork sausage
1 (15 oz.) can tomatoes
2 cups water
1 lg. onion, chopped
1 cup rice, uncooked
Salt and pepper to taste

Mix all ingredients (do not brown hamburger or pork sausage). Place in a greased 2 quart casserole and bake at 350° for 1 hour.

Marie Kleinvachter, Thief River Falls

POTATO PIZZA SUPREME

1 lb. ground beef
½ cup onions
½ tsp. salt
½ tsp. oregano
¼ tsp. cayenne pepper
½ tsp. sugar
1 (15 oz.) can tomato sauce
1 can Cheddar cheese soup
¼ cup milk
1 Tbsp. margarine
4 cups sliced raw potatoes
8 slices Mozzarella cheese
½ cup Parmesan cheese, optional
Pepperoni, optional

Brown beef and onions; add spices and tomato juice. Combine soup, milk and margarine; add to beef. Place potatoes in baking dish; pour sauce mixture over. Bake, covered, at 350° for 45 minutes. Add Mozzarella cheese. Bake, uncovered, for 15 minutes.

Lil Robertson, Argyle

RICE HOT DISH

1 lb. ground beef
1 med. onion
2 cups celery, chopped
2 Tbsp. soy sauce
2 Tbsp. brown sugar
2 cans mushroom soup or 1 can mushroom soup and 1 can celery soup
1 cup rice, uncooked
3 cups hot water

Brown ground beef and onion. Add remaining ingredients. Pour into baking dish and bake at 350° for 1 hour. Very good served over chow mein noodles.

Anne Donahue, Currie

RIGITONI

Cook **rigitoni noodles** as directed on package. In a skillet, brown **1 package hot sausage** and **1 pound lean hamburger**. Drain well and add:

1 (12 oz.) can tomato paste	1 Tbsp. basil
with 1 can water	2 Tbsp. parsley flakes
1 sm. chopped onion	Salt and pepper
2 cloves minced garlic	A little chili powder
1 can mushroom soup with	
1 can water	

Simmer for 30 minutes. In a 9x13 inch pan, put half the cooked noodles and half the sauce; repeat. Top with **Mozzarella cheese**. Bake at 350° for 30 minutes.

Jane Curran, Medford

SEVEN LAYER DINNER

Slice **potatoes** thin, in 1 inch layer, into a 2 quart casserole dish. Slice **carrots**, in a 1 inch layer, covering potatoes. Slice **onions**, covering carrots. Slice **green peppers**, covering onions. Sprinkle ½ **cup rice** over ingredients. Add a layer of **browned hamburger** (1½ lbs.) Pour **1 (15 oz.) can cut, stewed tomatoes**, or **tomato sauce** over the top. Perforate to the bottom with a knife in several places. Cover and bake at 375° for 1 hour.

Sr. Janet Derner, SSND, Clements

LUMPIA (From the Philippines)

2 lbs. ground beef	1 cup shredded cabbage
1½ lbs. ground pork	3 Tbsp. soy sauce
3 Tbsp. oil	2 beaten eggs
½ cup minced onion	Salt to taste
1½ cups minced carrots	1 pkg. egg roll wrappers
1½ cups minced potatoes	

Brown meat; drain and set aside. Heat oil in a pan; add onions, carrots and potatoes. Fry until tender, stirring often; add cabbage, then soy sauce, eggs and salt to taste. Wrap about a tablespoon or so full of the above mixture in an egg roll wrapper, fry in cooking oil until wrappers turn light brown.

Eunice Ramert, Slayton

SAUERKRAUT HOT DISH

1 lb. hamburger	1 qt. sauerkraut and juice
1 can cream of mushroom or	½ pkg. egg noodles, cooked
cream of celery soup	

In casserole, mix browned hamburger, soup and sauerkraut. Add cooked noodles and mix well. Bake at 350° for 1 hour.

Priscilla DesLauriers, Currie

SAUERKRAUT HOT DISH

1½ lbs. ground beef
1 lg. onion
2 sm. cans mushrooms (save liquid)
1 can cream of chicken soup
1 can water (use liquid from mushrooms)
1 lg. jar sauerkraut
2 cups dry noodles, uncooked
1 Tbsp. sugar, optional

Brown ground beef and onion. Add remaining ingredients and bake at 350° for 45 minutes.

Beverly Johnson, St. Peter
Margaret Domeler, New Ulm

SAUERKRAUT HOT DISH

1½ lbs. hamburger
1 (8 oz.) pkg. wide noodles
1 (14 oz.) can sauerkraut, undrained
2 cans cream of chicken soup, undiluted
1 sm. onion

Brown hamburger. Boil noodles according to package directions. Mix all ingredients. Bake, covered, at 350° for 45 minutes.

Martha Sturm, St. James
District Deputy, 1994-present
Elaine Knoff, Slayton

SLOPPY JOE

2 lbs. hamburger
1 cup celery
1 cup onion
½ cup ketchup
1 (10½ oz.) can Franco American beef gravy

Brown hamburger; saute celery and onions. Combine all ingredients and cook until ready.

Doris Morff, International Falls

STRING PIE

1 lb. ground beef
½ cup chopped onion
¼ cup chopped green pepper
1 (15½ oz.) jar spaghetti sauce
1 (8 oz.) pkg. spaghetti, cooked and drained
⅓ cup grated Parmesan cheese
2 eggs, beaten
2 tsp. butter
1 cup cottage cheese
½ cup shredded Mozzarella cheese

Cook beef, onion and green pepper in large skillet over medium-high heat until meat is brown, stirring to separate meat; drain fat. Stir in spaghetti sauce; mix well. Combine spaghetti, Parmesan cheese, eggs and butter in large bowl; mix well. Place in bottom of a 9x13 inch pan. Spread cottage cheese over top. Pour sauce mixture over cottage cheese. Sprinkle Mozzarella cheese over top. Bake at 350° (preheated) until cheese melts, about 20 minutes.

Loretta Briski, Iron

STUFFED BURGERS

1 lb. lean ground beef	Sliced mushrooms, olives,
¼ cup Parmesan cheese	onions, or green peppers*
	Sliced bacon

*Or any other vegetables that you like.

Mix ground beef with the Parmesan cheese. Shape beef into 8 thin patties. Use 4 patties, top each with your selection of vegetables. Place one of the other patties on top of each filled patty, pressing down on the edges to make it stick. You should have 4 stuffed patties. Wrap one slice of bacon around each patty. Use a toothpick to hold in place. Excellent when grilled!

Lori Mickelson, Waseca

SWEDISH STEAMED POTATO SAUSAGE CASSEROLE

1½ cups ground beef	2 tsp. salt
3 cups raw potatoes, ground	¼ tsp. pepper
or grated	½ tsp. ground allspice
2 tsp. ground onion (or more)	

Mix well, using hands, and place in covered casserole. Place in pan of hot water in oven and let steam at 350° for about 2 hours. The hot water prevents a crust from forming, but we prefer the crust and put the water on a shelf below the casserole. Double the recipe for a 3 quart rectangular baking dish and use foil to cover. Cold leftover slices nicely for sandwiches or reheat in the microwave oven. One of our family favorites!

Mary Dosan, Eveleth

TATOR TOT HOT DISH**

1 (12 oz.) pkg. frozen mixed	2 lbs. hamburger
vegetables	1 lg. can mushroom soup or
1 (2 lb.) bag tator tots	3 regular cans

Thaw vegetables in refrigerator overnight. Microwave in 1½ cups water for 5 minutes (10 minutes if frozen). Cook tator tots in oven according to package directions (at 450° for approximately 15 minutes). Fry, season and drain hamburger. Combine hamburger, vegetables and liquid and soup into a large 5 quart baking dish. Stir ¾ of the tator tots, sprinkling the rest on top. Heat at 350° for 15 minutes (soup can be heated with cooked vegetable in microwave for 2 to 3 minutes to eliminate oven time).

Mary Clausen, Argyle

TATOR TOT HOT DISH

1 lb. hamburger
1 sm. onion, diced
1 can mixed vegetables
1 (16 oz.) pkg. tator tots

1 can Cheddar cheese soup
1 cup milk
Salt and pepper

Brown hamburger with onion; put in casserole and cover with mixed vegetables and tator tots. Mix creamed cheese and milk and pour over tator tots. Bake at 350° for 40 minutes or until tator tots are brown.

Note: frozen mixed vegetables may be used.

Father Ken Clinton, Janesville

TATOR TOT HOT DISH

1½ lbs. ground beef
1 med. onion, chopped
1 can mushroom soup

½ soup can milk or water
1 cup grated Cheddar cheese
1 (16 oz.) pkg. tator tots

Brown ground beef with onion in skillet, stirring frequently; drain using hot water. Layer ground beef mixture, soup and milk or water (mixed), Cheddar cheese and top with tator tots in large baking dish. Bake at 350° for 40 minutes. Yield: 6 servings.

Mary Sorenson, Faribault

TATOR TOT HOT DISH

1 lb. lean ground beef
1 can green beans
1 (16 oz.) pkg. frozen tator tots

1 can golden mushroom soup
½ onion, grated
Salt and pepper to taste

Crumble raw ground beef with hands into a 1½ quart greased casserole dish. Drain liquid from beans and discard. Place beans on top of meat. Grate onion over the beans. Add undiluted soup. Top with tator tots. Bake at 350° for 1 hour. Plain cream of mushroom soup works also.

Neva Appel, Thief River Falls

TATOR TOT HOT DISH

1½ lbs. hamburger
1 onion, sliced
1 cup celery
1 can green beans

1 pkg. frozen mixed vegetables
1 can cream of chicken soup
1 can cream of celery soup
1 pkg. frozen tator tots

Brown hamburger, onion and celery. Put in casserole. Add vegetables and soups. Mix and top with tator tots. Bake at 350° for 1½ hours.

Kay Schleich, Winona

THREE BEAN HAMBURGER HOT DISH

1 lb. hamburger	½ cup cut up bacon, browned
½ cup chopped onion	½ cup catsup
1 can butter beans, drained	½ or ¾ cup sugar
1 can Bush's baked beans	2 tsp. vinegar
1 can red kidney beans	

Brown hamburger and chopped onion. Drain grease. Mix rest of ingredients with hamburger and onion in baking dish. Bake at 350° for 40 minutes.

Anna Akemann, Waseca

HAMBURGERS IN TOMATO SAUCE

1 lb. ground beef	½ tsp. pepper
1 lb. ground pork	5 slices bread crumbs
2 eggs	²/₃ cup milk
2 tsp. salt	

Mix the first 7 ingredients thoroughly. Shape into small patties and brown. Put in casserole.

Sauce:

1½ cups tomato sauce	1 tsp. salt
1 can tomato soup	1 tsp. dry mustard
½ cup vinegar	½ cup chopped onion
½ cup sugar	2 Tbsp. Worcestershire sauce

Mix all ingredients, heat and pour over patties. Bake at 350° for 1 hour.

Delores Seykora, Owatonna

UKRAINIAN CABBAGE ROLLS

10 cabbage leaves	½ cup raw rice
½ lb. hamburger	1 Tbsp. water
Salt and pepper	1 tsp. onion flakes

Steam cabbage leaves in 1 inch of water in covered pan for 3 minutes. Cool. Season hamburger with salt and pepper. Brown hamburger; add raw rice, water and onion. Fill cabbage leaves with mixture and roll each leaf tight beginning at stem end. Fasten with toothpick. Season again with salt and pepper. Cover with hot water; steam for 35 minutes, or until rice is soft. Serves 3 or 4.

Mary Ann Janous, Owatonna

UNCLE BEN'S RICE HOT DISH

1½ lbs. ground beef
½ cup chopped celery
1 sm. onion, chopped
1 (14 oz.) can bean sprouts
1 can water chestnuts, sliced
¼ cup soy sauce

1 can cream of mushroom soup
1 can cream of chicken soup
1½ cups water
1 cup uncooked Uncle Ben's
   mixed rice

Brown ground beef, celery and onion. Add rest of the ingredients and place in greased casserole dish. Bake at 325° for 1 hour.

Leah Pagnac, Argyle

VEGETABLE NOODLE HOT DISH

1 (1 lb.) pkg. noodles
2 lbs. ground beef
1 med. onion

1 can vegetable soup
1 can tomato soup
1 can mushroom soup

Cook the noodles until tender; drain. Add all other ingredients. Brown the ground beef. Dice or chop up the onion. Mix the soups and add to browned ground beef and onion and add the noodles. Heat at 350° for 30 minutes.

Ann Maas, Waseca

ITALIAN PASTA AND BEAN SOUP

¼ cup olive oil
2 cups onion, chopped
2 carrots, sliced
½ cup celery or fennel,
   chopped
4 garlic cloves, minced
¾ tsp. dried red pepper flakes
2 bay leaves
1 cup dried white beans,
   soaked overnight

8 cups chicken stock or canned
   broth
4 oz. bow-tie pasta
1 cup chopped canned
   tomatoes
¼ cup chopped fresh parsley
Salt
Fresh grated Parmesan cheese

Heat oil in heavy large pot over medium heat; add onions, carrots, celery, garlic, pepper flakes and bay leaves. Reduce heat to low; cover and cook until tender, about 15 minutes, stirring occasionally. Add beans and 7 cups of stock. Increase heat and bring to boil. Reduce heat, cover partially and simmer until beans are tender, about 1 hour and 15 minutes. Add pasta and tomatoes to soup. Cover and simmer until beans and pasta are tender, adding another cup of stock. Add parsley and salt. Serve, passing cheese separately.

Karen Riopelle, Argyle

AMERICAN LASAGNA

1 lb. ground beef	½ tsp. oregano
2 cloves garlic, chopped	1 (8 oz.) pkg. lasagna noodles
1 (6 oz.) can tomato paste	1 (8 oz.) pkg. Swiss cheese
1 tsp. salt	1 (12 oz.) carton cottage
¾ tsp. pepper	cheese

Brown ground beef with garlic; add tomato sauce, salt, pepper and oregano. Cover and simmer for 20 minutes. Cook lasagna noodles according to package directions. In a baking dish, alternate layers of noodles, Swiss cheese, cottage cheese and meat sauce. Bake at 350° for 30 minutes. Serve with grated Parmesan cheese.

Mary Pytleski, Fairmont

MEATLESS LASAGNA

½ (16 oz.) box lasagna noodles	¼ tsp. garlic powder
3 (12 oz.) cartons cottage cheese	½ tsp. salt
1 lb. Monterey Jack cheese, grated	2 Tbsp. soft butter or margarine
1 cup Parmesan cheese	3 (10 oz.) pkgs. frozen spinach, chopped, thawed and
3 eggs	moisture squeezed out
1 Tbsp. parsley, chopped (or flakes)	¼ cup Parmesan cheese, grated

Cook noodles according to package directions; drain and pat dry. Combine cheese, eggs, parsley, garlic powder, salt and butter. Layer half of noodles with cheese mixture and spinach in a buttered 9x13 inch pan or glass baking dish. Repeat layers. Sprinkle with Parmesan cheese. Refrigerate until ready to bake. Bake, uncovered, at 350° for 50 to 60 minutes or until bubbly. Let stand 10 minutes before serving. Cut into squares. Serves 10 to 12.

Elizabeth Thayer, Medford

EASY LASAGNA HOT DISH**

3½ cups mini lasagna noodles	1 can Cheddar cheese soup
1 lb. hamburger	1 (15 oz.) jar spaghetti sauce
1 sm. onion	or pizza sauce
Green pepper, optional	2 cups Mozzarella cheese

Cook noodles; brown hamburger with onions and green pepper. Drain grease from hamburger. Mix hamburger, noodles, soup and spaghetti or pizza sauce in a 9x13 inch cake pan. Sprinkle Mozzarella cheese over top. Bake, covered, at 350° for 30 minutes.

Nancy Haala, New Ulm

EASY LASAGNA

Sauce:

1 tsp. salt	½ tsp. pepper
1 tsp. basil	1 qt. spaghetti sauce

Mix and put 1½ cup of mixture in a 9x13 inch pan.

12 lasagna noodles	8 slices American cheese
1 lb. hamburger, uncooked	1 (8 oz.) pkg. grated Mozzarella
½ cup chopped onion	cheese
1 cup cottage cheese or Ricotta	1½ cups hot water
cheese	Parmesan cheese

Layer 6 raw noodles in pan width wise, then add half the hamburger. Add the onion, cottage or Ricotta cheese and 1½ cups sauce again. Add the other 6 noodles, then the American cheese, other half of hamburger, the remainder of the sauce and the Mozzarella cheese. Press down to compress and add the hot water. Sprinkle with the Parmesan cheese. Cover with foil and bake at 350° for 1 hour. Uncover and bake 45 minutes longer. Let set 5 minutes before serving.

Lois Manka, International Falls

GROUND TURKEY LASAGNA

1 lb. ground turkey	1 (4 oz.) pkg. shredded
1 lg. onion	Parmesan cheese
1 (14 oz.) can stewed tomatoes	1 tsp. oregano
1 (6 oz.) can tomato paste	1 Tbsp. parsley flakes
1 tsp. basil	1 (8 oz.) pkg. uncooked lasagna
2 Tbsp. parsley flakes	noodles
1 cup water	1 (8 oz.) pkg. Mozzarella cheese
2⅔ cups cottage cheese	
(24 oz. carton)	

Brown turkey and onion; drain and add stewed tomatoes, tomato paste, basil, parsley flakes and water. Mix cottage cheese, Parmesan cheese, oregano and parsley in a bowl. Layer half of uncooked noodles, half of meat mixture, all of cottage cheese mixture, and half of Mozzarella cheese. Repeat noodles and meat mixture and bake, covered, at 350° for 1 hour. Add remaining Mozzarella cheese and bake, uncovered, for 15 minutes.

Mary Bartley, Blue Earth

* * * * * * * *

Better a dry crust with peace than a house
full of feasting with strife. Proverbs 17:1
Mildred Schmitt, Caledonia

LASAGNA HOT DISH

1 lb. hamburger	1 (15 oz.) jar Ragu spaghetti
1 med. onion, diced	sauce
½ green pepper, diced	1 can Cheddar cheese soup
¾ pkg. egg noodles, cooked	1 cup Mozzarella cheese, shredded

Brown hamburger, onion and pepper. Mix in noodles, sauce and cheese soup. Pour into a 9x13 inch pan. Top with cheese. Bake at 350° for 30 minutes. Cool and cut into squares.

Rosie Deutz, Marshall

OVERNIGHT LASAGNA

2 lbs. ground beef	2 tsp. oregano
1 cup chopped onion	1½ tsp. Worcestershire sauce
1 (15 oz.) can tomato sauce	1½ tsp. sugar
1 qt. tomatoes, pureed in blender	2 cups water
1 tsp. salt	1 (8 oz.) pkg. lasagna noodles, uncooked
1 tsp. garlic salt	1 (8 oz.) pkg. Mozzarella cheese

Brown ground beef and onions; add tomato sauce and pureed tomatoes, spices and water. Simmer for 15 minutes and layer in a 9x13 inch pan, the uncooked noodles and sauce. Use a slotted spoon to get most of the meat between the noodles. Pour sauce over all, it will be very soupy. Top with cheese, cover with wax paper then foil (do not use foil alone). Refrigerate overnight. The next morning, bake at 350° for 1 hour. Serve with garlic toast.

Lorraine Olson, Crookston
District Deputy, 1978-1982
Community State Chair, 1982-1984

LINGUINI WITH WHITE CLAM SAUCE

5 cloves garlic, minced	½ cup parsley, chopped
¼ cup olive oil	1 tsp. basil
3 (6 oz.) cans clams, drained (reserve clam broth)	1 tsp. pepper
	1 to 2 tsp. oregano
½ cup dry white wine	1 (16 oz.) pkg. linguini, cooked

Saute garlic in olive oil until golden. Add drained clams and saute 3 to 4 minutes. Add clam broth and remaining ingredients. Cover and simmer 5 to 10 minutes. Serve over cooked linguini with Parmesan cheese and pepper to taste.

Joanne Eck, Eveleth

LINGUINI WITH CLAM SAUCE

2 (6½ oz.) cans minced clams
1 med. green or sweet red
  pepper, chopped
2 green onions, sliced
¼ tsp. dried basil, crushed
¼ tsp. crushed red pepper
2 cloves garlic, minced
¼ cup dry white wine
4 tsp. cornstarch
2 Tbsp. snipped fresh parsley
4 oz. linguine, cooked and
  drained
2 Tbsp. grated Parmesan
  cheese

Drain clams, reserving liquid. In a saucepan, combine reserved clam liquid, green or sweet red pepper, onions, basil, crushed red pepper and garlic. Bring to boiling; reduce heat. Simmer, uncovered, about 5 minutes or until onions are tender. In a small bowl, stir wine and cornstarch. Stir mixture into saucepan. Cook and stir until thickened and bubbly. Cook and stir for 2 minutes more. Stir in clams and parsley. Heat through. In a large bowl, toss linguine with clam mixture. Sprinkle Parmesan cheese atop each serving.

Cel Berkner, Mahnomen

BEST EVER MEAT BALLS

1½ lbs. hamburger
¾ cup oatmeal (fine)
1½ tsp. salt
¾ tsp. pepper
3 Tbsp. chopped onion
1 cup milk

Mix hamburger, oatmeal, salt, pepper, onion and milk. Form into balls the size of half dollars. Place in baking dish.

Sauce:

1 cup catsup
3 Tbsp. vinegar
2 Tbsp. sugar
½ cup water

Mix the catsup, vinegar, sugar and water and pour over meat balls. Bake at 350° for 1 hour. Cover with foil.

Marianne Minten, Perham

BAR-B-QUED MEAT BALLS

1 cup bread crumbs
½ cup milk
1 lb. lean ground beef
Salt and pepper to taste
1½ tsp. Worcestershire sauce
¼ cup vinegar
3 Tbsp. sugar
½ cup catsup
½ cup water
½ cup chopped onion
½ cup green pepper

Mix bread crumbs, milk and ground beef. Season with salt and pepper. Form into balls and place in casserole. Cook rest of ingredients and pour over meatballs. Bake at 375° for 45 minutes.

Joan Steel, Red Wing

VEGETABLES & MAIN DISHES

BARBECUE MEATBALLS

1 to 1½ lbs. hamburger	½ cup chopped onion

Season meat and form into balls; fry until brown. Fry onions in drippings.

Sauce:

½ cup ketchup	2 Tbsp. brown sugar
½ cup water	2 Tbsp. vinegar
2 Tbsp. Worcestershire sauce	1 tsp. dry mustard
2 Tbsp. lemon juice	Salt and pepper to taste

Add sauce to onions and cook slightly. Return meat balls to sauce and cook until done, about 1 hour. Yield: 6 to 8 servings.

Rosina Lamecker, New Ulm

CHAFING DISH MEATBALLS

2 lbs. ground beef	1 lg. grated onion
1 slightly beaten egg	Salt to taste

Mix and shape into balls.

Sauce:

1 (12 oz.) bottle chili sauce	Juice of 1 lemon
1 (10 oz.) jar grape jelly	

Drop balls into sauce and simmer until brown. Refrigerate or freeze. Reheat in chafing dish and serve. Yield: 50 to 60 meat balls.

Jo Elijah, New Ulm

COCKTAIL MEATBALLS

2 lbs. ground beef	1 Tbsp. parsley
½ cup diced bread crumbs	1 tsp. salt
1/3 cup chopped onion	1/8 tsp. pepper
¼ cup milk	1 tsp. Worcestershire sauce
1 egg, beaten	

Mix ingredients and form into small balls; put on cookie sheet and brown at 350°.

Sauce:

1 cup ketchup	¼ cup vinegar
1 cup chopped onion	¼ tsp. chili powder
¼ cup brown sugar	1 Tbsp. Worcestershire sauce
¼ cup white sugar	

Boil and pour over meatballs, simmer for 30 minutes.

Marian Lager, Caledonia

GLAZED MEATBALLS

3 lbs. ground beef
1 can evaporated milk
1 cup oatmeal
1 cup cracker crumbs
2 eggs

½ cup chopped onions
½ tsp. garlic powder
2 tsp. salt
½ tsp. pepper
2 tsp. chili powder

To make meat balls, combine all ingredients (mixture will be soft) and shape into walnut size balls. Place meat balls in a single layer on wax paper lined cookie sheets; freeze until solid. Store frozen meatballs in freezer bags until ready to cook.

Sauce:

2 cups catsup
1 cup brown sugar
½ tsp. Liquid Smoke or to taste

½ tsp. garlic powder
¼ cup chopped onion

Combine all ingredients and stir over low heat until brown sugar is dissolved. Place frozen meat balls in a 9x13 inch baking pan. Pour on the sauce; bake at 350° for 1 hour. Yield: 80 meatballs. (Use the amount from freezer you need and mix amount of sauce accordingly, ½ or ¼.)

Sandy Penning, Wilmont
Millie Fangmeier, Pipestone

MEATBALLS AND GRAVY

1 med. potato
1 med. onion
3 lbs. lean hamburger
Salt and pepper to taste

¼ tsp. sage
¼ tsp. garlic powder
1 can cream of mushroom soup
1 can cream of chicken soup

Grate the potato and onion and then add to the meat. Season with salt and pepper, sage and garlic powder. Mix well and shape into balls; brown well on all sides. Put in casserole and add the soups, which can be diluted with a little water; pour over the browned meatballs. Bake at 325° for 2 hours or until done. You end up with delicious meatballs and gravy.

Marie Kolb, Mentor

MEAT BALLS

1 lb. hamburger
3 slices dry bread
1 egg
1 med. onion

½ cup milk
Salt and pepper
½ pkg. Sloppy Joe mix
1 can cream of mushroom soup

Shape all ingredients, except mushroom soup, into balls; put in cake pan or similar. Pour soup over top and bake at 350° for 30 minutes.

Susan Miner, St. Peter

EASY MEATBALLS

2 lbs. hamburger	2 eggs
1 can Campbell's onion soup	Salt and pepper
1 cup fine stuffing mix	

Mix all of the above ingredients and make into balls. Bake single depth in large baking pan at 375° for 45 minutes, turning them over once. Put into large casserole or baking dish and cover with **2 cans chicken or mushroom soup** and bake for 1 hour. You may add mushrooms if you wish. I have used brown gravy mix and make the gravy in same pan I browned them in. I also heat the creamed soups in the pan I browned them in. They freeze well and can also be used for spaghetti sauce.

Donna Farrell, Marshall
1st Vice State Regent, 1990-1994
State Regent, 1994-present

GOULASH

1½ lbs. hamburger	1 can tomato soup
½ diced onion	1 can mushroom soup
2½ cups macaroni	Garlic salt

Brown hamburger and onion. Cook macaroni until tender. Mix with rest of the ingredients. May add ketchup if you want a more tomato taste. Bake at 350° for ½ hour.

Father Ken Clinton, Janesville

SAVORY MEATBALL CASSEROLE

1 lb. ground beef	Dash of pepper
¼ lb. pork sausage	1 can cream of celery soup
½ cup cracker crumbs	1 can cream of mushroom soup
2 Tbsp. minced onion	1 cup evaporated milk
1/3 cup evaporated milk	½ cup water
1 Tbsp. chili powder	1 tube Pillsbury biscuits

Mix meats, cracker crumbs, minced onion, evaporated milk, chili powder and pepper. Shape into meatballs and brown. Place meatballs in a large casserole dish. Heat soups, milk and water. Pour over the meatballs. Top with tube of Pillsbury biscuits. Bake at 400° for 20 to 25 minutes.

Margaret Slinger, Slayton

378

PORCUPINE MEAT BALLS

1½ lbs. ground beef
½ cup uncooked rice (not
   Minute Rice)
1 tsp. salt

½ tsp. pepper
1 Tbsp. grated onion
1 (10½ oz.) can tomato soup
½ can water

Combine meat, rice, seasoning and onion. Shape into balls. Heat soup and water and drop meat balls into soup mixture. Cover and cook slowly for 1 hour.

Doris Cote, Slayton

SWEDISH MEAT BALLS

2 Tbsp. chopped onion
1 tsp. butter
½ cup dry bread crumbs
½ cup milk
1 egg
¾ lb. ground beef

½ lb. pork
1 tsp. salt
⅛ tsp. pepper
½ tsp. sage
¼ tsp. nutmeg

Brown onions in butter. Soak crumbs in milk; add beaten egg. Add meat, salt, pepper, sage, nutmeg and onions. Form into balls 1 to 1½ inches. Brown and cook slowly for 20 to 30 minutes.

Jane Dick, St. Charles

SWEDISH MEATBALLS

1 lb. ground beef
¼ cup chopped onion
1 cup bread crumbs
1 egg, slightly beaten
1 tsp. salt
1⅓ cups milk

2 Tbsp. butter or oleo
2 Tbsp. flour
1 beef bouillon cube
1 cup hot water
1 tsp. Worcestershire sauce

Combine beef, onion, bread crumbs, egg, salt and ⅓ cup milk. Mix well and form into balls. Brown balls in butter or oleo; remove from pan. Stir flour into pan drippings; stir until smooth and blended. Dissolve bouillon in hot water. Add 1 cup milk, bouillon and Worcestershire sauce to drippings; stir until smooth and blended. Return meatballs to pan. Cover and simmer for 30 minutes.

Margaret Wera, Winona

* * * * * * * *

As you walk along life's pathways through the night and through the day, you will never loose direction if you let God lead the way.
Barbara Rollins
Dolores Karides, Caledonia

SWEET SOUR MEATBALLS

1½ lbs. ground beef	1 Tbsp. grated onion
1 cup milk	3 Tbsp. brown sugar
¾ cup oatmeal	3 tsp. vinegar
1 tsp. salt	½ cup water
¼ tsp. pepper	1 cup catsup

Combine ground beef, milk, oatmeal, salt, pepper, and grated onion and mix lightly. Form into balls. Pack loosely in a single layer in casserole. Mix brown sugar, vinegar, water and catsup and pour over balls. Bake at 350° for 1 hour or until done.

Beverly Root, Waseca

SWEET AND SOUR MEAT BALLS

1 lb. ground beef	½ tsp. pepper
½ cup bread crumbs	1 egg, beaten
1 tsp. salt	¼ cup milk

Mix ingredients and brown.

Sauce:

½ cup chopped onion	¼ tsp. pepper
8 Tbsp. sugar	2 tsp. Worcestershire sauce
¼ cup catsup	6 Tbsp. vinegar

Combine in separate pan. Simmer until onion is tender and sauce looks clear. Add meatballs and heat.

Rita Arendt, Mazeppa

QUICK AND EASY MEATBALLS

2 lbs. ground beef	2 eggs
1 cup corn flakes	2 Tbsp. flour
½ cup milk	2 Tbsp. chopped onion
2 tsp. salt	1 can cream of mushroom soup

Mix first 7 ingredients and shape into balls. Brown in butter, then add soup. Simmer 15 to 20 minutes. Serves 8. (When making a larger amount, put them in a roaster in oven.)

Vera Boesch, New Ulm

MACARONI AND CHEESE HOT DISH

4 cups elbow macaroni	4 cups boiling water
½ stick butter	1 lb. Cheddar cheese
1 lb. small curd cottage cheese	

Put the macaroni in a 9x13 inch pan. Slice butter over the top. Spread the cottage cheese over the butter and pour boiling water over the top. Cover the top with cheese. Bake at 350° for 45 minutes to 1 hour. Let set 10 minutes to absorb the water. May use half recipe as this makes a good amount.

Eunice Fernholz, Detroit Lakes

BLUE RIBBON MEAT LOAF

1 env. Lipton's onion soup mix	1½ lbs. hamburger
1 cup dairy sour cream	1 cup dry, fine bread crumbs
2 eggs, slightly beaten	

Combine soup and sour cream; add eggs. Mix in hamburger. Sprinkle with the cup of bread crumbs and mix well. Put in loaf pan. Preheat oven to 500°. Put meatloaf in oven and turn heat down to 375°. Bake 1 hour (no longer).

Lila Ballman, New Ulm

RAINBOW MEATLOAF

2 lbs. ground beef	1 tsp. hot sauce
1 cup dry bread crumbs	2 tsp. salt
1 cup milk	2 tsp. onion, minced
2 eggs, slightly beaten	6 slices American cheese
3 tsp. butter, melted	

Combine all ingredients except cheese. Place half of the mixture in a 9x5x3 inch loaf pan. Top with cheese. Cover the remaining meat mixture. Bake at 350° for about 1 hour. Cool and slice. This can be served with slices of rye bread if desired.

Nina Smith, Plainview

MEAT LOAF

2 eggs, slightly beaten	1 Tbsp. prepared horseradish
2 lbs. ground beef	1½ tsp. salt
2 cups soft bread crumbs	½ tsp. dry mustard
1 tsp. minced onion	¼ cup milk

Mix main ingredients and put in greased pan. Mix **6 tablespoons brown sugar** and **½ cup catsup** and pour over the top. Bake at 350° for 40 minutes or until done.

Rosie Kelly, Waseca

MEAT LOAF

2 lbs. ground beef	¾ cup catsup
2 eggs	½ cup warm water
1½ cups bread crumbs	1 pkg. dry onion soup mix

Beat ingredients thoroughly. Put into a loaf pan; cover with **strips of bacon**. Pour **1 (8 oz.) can tomato sauce** over all. Bake at 350° for 1 hour. Makes 6 servings.

Lori Thillen, Caledonia

BEEF LOAF

1 lb. ground beef	1 cup uncooked rolled oats
Salt and pepper	1½ cups tomato soup

Mix ground beef, seasoned with salt and pepper and rolled oats well. Shape into a loaf, roll in a little flour and place into a greased loaf pan. Pour the tomato soup over the loaf and bake at 300° to 325° for 1½ hours. Do not use the home canned tomato soup. Serve 3 to 4 people.

Florence Macho, New Ulm

MEAT LOAF

½ to ¾ cup cracker crumbs	½ cup milk
1 lb. hamburger	Salt and pepper
1 med. onion, chopped	

Mix all ingredients and put in loaf pan. Put catsup on the top and bake at 325° for 1 hour.
Variation: Helen adds 2 small eggs.

Pat Jennings, Caledonia
Helen Houselog, Pipestone

MEAT LOAF

1½ lbs. ground beef	1 cup crushed crackers
½ lb. pork sausage	½ cup milk
2 tsp. salt	½ cup evaporated milk
½ tsp. pepper	1 can cream of chicken soup
1 egg, beaten	

Mix the above ingredients and pour into loaf pans. Bake at 300° for 2 hours or until done.

Inez Johnson, Slayton

MEAT LOAF WITH ZESTY TOPPING

2 lbs. ground pork	1 sm. onion
¾ cup milk	2 eggs, beaten
1½ cups soft bread crumbs	1 carrot, diced
⅛ tsp. pepper	

Mix all ingredients and put in a 9x5 inch loaf pan.
Topping:

¼ cup catsup	2 Tbsp. mustard
3 Tbsp. brown sugar	

Mix and put over top. Bake at 300° for 1½ hours.

Lorraine Balster, Wilmont

SICILIAN MEAT ROLL

1 beaten egg
¾ cup soft bread crumbs
½ cup tomato juice
2 Tbsp. snipped parsley
½ tsp. dried oregano, crushed
¼ tsp. salt
¼ tsp. pepper

1 sm. clove garlic, minced
2 lbs. lean ground beef
8 thin slices boiled ham
1 (6 oz.) pkg. shredded
  Mozzarella cheese (1½ cups)
3 slices Mozzarella cheese,
  halved diagonally

Combine egg, bread crumbs, tomato juice, parsley, oregano, salt, pepper and garlic. Mix well with ground beef. On foil or waxed paper, pat meat to a 12x10 inch rectangle. Arrange ham slices on top, leaving a small 1 inch margin around the edges. Sprinkle shredded cheese over ham. Starting from short end, carefully roll up meat using foil to lift. Seal edges and ends. Place roll seam side down in a 13x9x2 inch baking dish. Bake at 350° for 1¼ hours or until done. Place slices on top and bake 5 minutes more until it melts. Serves 8.

Pat Heirigs, North Mankato

CLASSIC MEATLOAF

1½ lbs. lean ground beef
1 (8 oz.) can tomato sauce
1 cup soft bread crumbs
1 sm. onion, finely chopped
1 egg, slightly beaten
2 tsp. Worcestershire sauce

1 tsp. dried thyme leaves
½ tsp. garlic salt
¼ tsp. pepper
1 Tbsp. packed brown sugar
1 tsp. dry mustard

Heat oven to 350°. Reserve ¼ cup tomato sauce. In a large bowl, combine ground beef, remaining tomato sauce, bread crumbs, onion, egg, Worcestershire sauce, thyme, garlic salt and pepper, mixing lightly but thoroughly. Divide mixture into thirds and shape to form three loaves, each about 1½ inches thick; place on rack in open roasting pan. Combine reserved tomato sauce, brown sugar and mustard; spread over top of loaves. Bake at 350° for 40 to 45 minutes or until no longer pink and juices run clear. To serve, cut each meatloaf into 1 inch thick slices. Makes 6 servings (serving size: ½ loaf.) Total preparation and cooking time: 1 hour.

Note: To make soft bread crumbs, place torn bread slices in food processor, fitted with steel blade, or blender container. Cover; process 30 seconds until fine crumbs. 1½ slices will yield 1 cup soft bread crumbs.

Ruth Driscoll, Blue Earth

MARGIE'S MICROWAVE MEAT LOAF

1 ½ lbs. ground beef or turkey	2 egg whites or 1 egg, beaten
Chopped onion	2 Tbsp. Worcestershire sauce
Green pepper	2 slices bread, crumbled
Garlic	⅓ cup catsup
Ground horseradish, as desired	1 tsp. chili powder, optional
⅓ cup mustard	

Mix ingredients in a 2 quart casserole. Shape into ring. Microwave 10 minutes. Pour off liquid, if necessary. Microwave about 5 minutes more or until done. Top with barbecue sauce, if desired.

Mary Jane Gray, Blue Earth

NOODLES ALFREDO

1 (8 oz.) pkg. wide egg noodles	1 Tbsp. parsley flakes
½ cup butter or oleo	¼ tsp. salt
½ cup light cream (20 oz.)	Dash of pepper
1 cup grated Parmesan cheese	

Cook noodles as directed on package. While noodles cook, heat butter and cream in small saucepan over low heat until butter is melted. Stir in cheese, parsley flakes, salt and pepper. Keep warm over low heat. Return drained noodles to kettle. Pour sauce over noodles, stirring gently until noodles are well coated. Serves 5 to 6.

Pat McClain, Marshall

VERY TASTY, TENDER PHEASANT

1 cleaned pheasant	¼ cup white wine
1 med. onion, diced	1 tsp. salt
1 green pepper, diced	1 tsp. pepper
1 clove garlic, diced	1 tsp. basil
1 (8 oz.) can tomato sauce	1 tsp. paprika
1 (7 oz.) can undrained clams	2 Tbsp. parsley
½ lb. sliced mushrooms	1 (10 oz.) pkg. frozen shrimp

In large pan with 3 cups hot water, simmer pheasant for 35 minutes or put in pressure cooker for 20 minutes. Remove meat from bones. Put into a greased casserole. Lightly saute onion, pepper, and cloves in large skillet. Add everything else except shrimp. Simmer 10 minutes. Pour over pheasant. Cover and bake at 350° for 1 hour. Remove, cover and stir in shrimp. Bake 10 minutes more, uncovered. Serve with rice.

Potluck Polly, Stir City

PINEAPPLE CASSEROLE

1 (20 oz.) can pineapple chunks
½ cup sugar
3 Tbsp. flour
3 Tbsp. juice from pineapple

1 cup shredded Cheddar cheese
¼ cup melted butter
½ cup crushed Ritz crackers

Drain pineapple chunks, reserving the 3 tablespoons juice. Combine sugar and flour; stir in the reserved juice. Add cheese and pineapple. Spoon mixture into a greased 1 quart casserole. Combine melted butter and cracker crumbs. Sprinkle over top of casserole. Bake at 350° for 30 minutes.

Mary Lynn Portz, Pipestone

BURRITOS

Filling:

1 to 1½ lbs. hamburger
1 sm. onion
1 sm. can Parmesan cheese
1 (7 oz.) can Old Elpaso taco sauce

Refried beans to taste
1 scant tsp. cumin powder
1 scant tsp. salt
Flour tortillas
Slices of Cheddar or Colby cheese

Brown hamburger and chopped onion. Add Parmesan cheese and can of taco sauce (save some from gravy). Add refried beans (as desired), the cumin powder, salt and pepper. Cook together. Cool slightly, then place large spoonfuls of filling on flour tortillas and roll up. Place in baking dish.

Gravy:

1 can Campbell's chile-beef soup   ¾ to 1 can water

Mix soup, water and reserved small amount of taco sauce (for zestier flavor) together well or run through blender until gravy-like. Pour over tortillas and cover with Cheddar or Colby cheese. Burritos freeze well. Bake until done.

Geri Voit, Moorhead

MEXICAN HOT DISH

1 lg. pkg. Doritos
2 lbs. hamburger, browned with onion
½ can green chili peppers

1 can cream of mushroom soup
1 can cream of chicken soup
1 can mild enchilada sauce
Cheddar cheese

Crush Doritos in large cake pan. Put hamburger mixture on top. Chop peppers and sprinkle over top. Heat soups and sauce and pour over all. Top with cheese and bake at 325° for 35 minutes.

Sharon Reger, Waseca

MEXICAN CASSEROLE

1 to 2 cups tortilla chips
1 lb. ground beef, precooked
1 (8 oz.) can tomato sauce
1 Tbsp. taco seasoning
1 (15 oz.) can chili beans

1 (4 oz.) can chopped green
 chilies
1 cup sour cream
1 cup grated cheese

In an 8 inch round Pyrex dish, layer ingredients in order listed. Microwave on high for 7 to 8 minutes or until hot.

Margaret Liebranz, Owatonna

MEXICAN CASSEROLE

1 lb. ground beef
1 lg. onion, diced
¼ tsp. salt
1 (1 lb.) can chili with beans

1 can tomato soup
1 med. pkg. Fritos
1 cup grated American cheese
Dash of ketchup

Brown beef in skillet; let simmer until done. Add onion, salt, chili, tomato soup and ketchup. Let simmer and stir well to mix. Mixture should be consistency of gravy. If dry, add small amount of water. Line a large casserole with half of Fritos. Pour in meat mixture and top with rest of Fritos. Sprinkle grated cheese over casserole. Bake at 400° until cheese is melted.

Millie Spindler, Owatonna

DEEP-DISH PIZZA

1 (10 oz.) tube refrigerated
 pizza dough
1 lb. Italian bulk sausage
1 (10 oz.) pkg. frozen spinach,
 thawed

1 cup shredded Mozzarella
 cheese
½ tsp. garlic powder
¾ cup commercial pizza sauce
¼ cup grated Parmesan cheese

Pat dough in bottom and up sides of a 9 inch round cake pan, fitting closely where bottom and sides meet. Trim off excess dough by running a sharp knife around edge. Brown sausage in a large skillet over high heat, stirring after. Meanwhile, thaw spinach by removing from package, placing in a microwave safe bowl, and microwaving on high powder for 2 or 3 minutes. When sausage is done, set aside. Place spinach in a sieve and press out all the moisture. Transfer to a bowl. Place sausage in same sieve and allow to drain. Combine spinach with Mozzarella and garlic powder and mix thoroughly with hands to break up clumps of spinach. Layer over dough in pans. Layer sausage evenly over spinach mixture. Spread sauce over sausage. Bake in preheated 425° oven for 10 minutes. Top with Parmesan cheese and bake 10 minutes longer. Let set about 5 minutes before cutting.

Rita Plante, Crookston

DEEP DISH PIZZA

1 tube crescent rolls	4 Tbsp. green pepper, finely
1 lb. hamburger	chopped
1 (6 oz.) can tomato sauce	1 sm. onion, chopped
2 Tbsp. Parmesan cheese	2 cups Mozzarella cheese,
½ tsp. garlic salt	shredded
1 (8 oz.) can French cut green	1 egg
beans, drained	

Press roll dough into a 9 inch pie dish. Brown hamburger; drain grease and add rest of ingredients, except Mozzarella cheese and egg. Mix 1 cup Mozzarella cheese with the egg. Spread over roll dough. Add hamburger mixture and sprinkle with remaining Mozzarella cheese. Bake at 375° for 30 minutes.

Rosemary Rolph, Pipestone

POUR PIZZA

1 lb. hamburger, browned	1/8 tsp. oregano
Onion and green pepper	2/3 cup milk
1 cup flour	2 eggs
1 tsp. salt	1 can pizza sauce
1 1/3 tsp. pepper	Mozzarella cheese

Brown hamburger with onion and green pepper. Mix flour, salt, pepper, oregano, milk and eggs. Pour into a greased and floured 9x13 inch cake pan. Sprinkle meat mixture over dough and bake at 350° (or less) for 15 to 20 minutes. Remove from oven; spread with pizza sauce and Mozzarella cheese. Return to oven for 15 minutes or until cheese melts.

Violet Denault, Calgary, Alberta

PIZZA HOT DISH

1 (7 oz.) pkg. long spaghetti	1 lb. Mozzarella cheese,
1 egg	shredded
1 cup milk	1 lg. jar Ragu sauce
1 lb. hamburger	1 pkg. pepperoni
Salt, pepper and garlic salt	1 tsp. oregano

Cook spaghetti, then cool. Put in a 9x13 inch deep pan. Whip egg and milk; pour over noodles. Brown hamburger; add salt and pepper and put over noodles. Add ¾ cup cheese in a layer. Pour Ragu sauce over this, then the pepperoni. Bake at 350° for 1 hour. The last 15 minutes, put remainder of cheese on and finish baking. Also, can be made and refrigerated overnight.

Variation: Vivian suggests spiral noodles in place of spaghetti.

Dolores Wesley, Waterville
Veronica Robbie, International Falls
Vivian Helget, St. James

PIZZA CASSEROLE**

2 pkgs. crescent rolls	1 (8 oz.) pkg. shredded Cheddar
1 (15 oz.) jar pizza sauce	cheese
1½ lbs. ground beef, browned	1 (8 oz.) pkg. shredded
	Mozzarella cheese

Spray in a 9x13 inch pan with Pam. Line pan with 1 package crescent rolls. Pinch edges to make crust. Spread with pizza sauce. Add ground beef, then any other things you like on pizza (pepperoni, mushrooms, olives, onions, etc). Put the cheeses over. Put remaining package of crescent rolls on top. Bake at 350° for 30 minutes. Let set 5 minutes before cutting and serving.

Jennifer Anderson, Argyle

PIZZA HOT DISH

Uncooked noodles	Garlic salt and chili powder to
1 lb. hamburger	taste
1 can tomato soup	Mozzarella cheese
1½ soup cans tomato juice	American cheese
	Parmesan cheese

Put a single layer of noodles in a 9x13 inch pan. Brown hamburger and drain well; put over noodles. Mix tomato soup, tomato juice and seasonings together and pour over hamburger and noodles. Put the Mozzarella and American cheese on top. Bake, covered, at 350° for 45 minutes. Let set 20 minutes and sprinkle top with Parmesan cheese.

Clara Fuerstenberg, Wilmont

PIZZA HOT DISH

6 to 8 lasagna noodles	Mushrooms
1 egg	Salt and pepper
½ cup milk	½ tsp. garlic powder
2 lbs. hamburger	1 tsp. chili powder
Onion	1 lg. jar Ragu spaghetti sauce
Green pepper	Mozzarella cheese
Celery	Pepperoni slices

Layer cooked lasagna noodles in a 9x13 inch pan. Beat egg and milk very well and pour on noodles. Brown hamburger, onion, green pepper, celery, mushrooms, salt and pepper, garlic powder and chili powder. Drain off fat and put mixture on noodles. Pour spaghetti sauce on top; add Mozzarella cheese and pepperoni slices. Bake at 350° for 1 hour.

Eleene Gorman, Avoca

PASTA PIZZA SQUARES

1 (8 oz.) pkg. lasagna noodles
1 lb. bulk Italian sausage
2 cups (8 oz.) shredded
   Mozzarella cheese
½ cup grated Parmesan cheese
Fennel Seed
Oregano
1 (8 oz.) can pizza sauce
1 (4 oz.) pkg. sliced pepperoni
1 sm. green pepper, sliced
1 (2½ oz.) jar mushrooms, sliced

Cook lasagna noodles according to package directions. Cook sausage and drain off fat. Arrange half of cooked noodles in bottom of an ungreased 9x13 inch pan and sprinkle ¾ cup Mozzarella cheese, ¼ cup Parmesan cheese, fennel seed, and oregano over noodles. Arrange sausage, pepperoni, sliced green pepper, and mushrooms on top. Add half of sauce and remaining lasagna noodles; pour other half of sauce on top. Bake, uncovered, at 350° for 15 minutes. Sprinkle with remaining Mozzarella and Parmesan cheese. Bake for 15 minutes more or until hot. Cut into squares to serve. Makes 8 servings.

Jeannie Altepeter, Thief River Falls

PIZZA MANICOTTI

1 lb. Italian sausage
1 (28 oz.) can whole tomatoes,
   undrained and cut up
1 (15 oz.) can pizza sauce
2½ cups shredded Mozzarella
   cheese
1 (15 oz.) pkg. Ricotta cheese
½ cup quartered pepperoni slices
½ cup snipped fresh parsley or
   2 Tbsp. dried parsley
1 egg
1 (8 oz.) pkg. manicotti shells,
   uncooked
6 green pepper rings, optional
¼ cup black olives, sliced

Brown sausage until no longer pink; drain. Add tomatoes and pizza sauce; mix well and set aside. In mixing bowl, combine 1½ cups Mozzarella cheese, Ricotta cheese, pepperoni, parsley and egg. Stuff each uncooked manicotti shell evenly with mixture. Arrange stuffed shells in a 9x13 inch baking dish. Spoon tomato mixture over shells. Arrange pepper rings over tomato mixture. Sprinkle evenly with olive slices. Cover with plastic wrap. Refrigerate 12 hours or overnight. Heat oven to 350°. Remove plastic wrap, cover with foil, and bake 50 minutes to 1 hour or until hot and bubbly. Remove foil and sprinkle with remaining 1 cup Mozzarella cheese. Recover for 5 minutes or until cheese is melted. Makes 8 servings.

Dotty Jones, St. Charles
District Deputy, 1994-present

VEGETABLES & MAIN DISHES

EASY MANICOTTI

1 lb. ground beef	¼ cup bread crumbs
1 egg	1 tsp. salt
¼ cup milk	Dash of pepper
¼ tsp. garlic powder	1 sm. onion, chopped
1 (4 oz.) pkg. Mozzarella cheese, cubed	1 box manicotti shells
	1 qt. spaghetti sauce
	2 cups water

Mix first 9 ingredients together. Stuff 14 uncooked shells with mixture. Place 1 cup of the spaghetti sauce in the bottom of a 9x13 inch pan. Place stuffed manicotti in pan and spread remaining sauce on top. Add about 2 cups of water until manicotti are covered. Cover with foil and bake at 350° for 1 hour or until done. Even better when reheated.

Christine Hoel, Eveleth

PIZZA MAC

1 pkg. macaroni and cheese plus milk and margarine	1 lb. hamburger, browned with onions if desired
2 eggs	1 (8 oz.) pkg. Mozzarella cheese
1 (14 oz.) can pizza sauce	

Prepare macaroni and cheese as directed. Mix in slightly beaten eggs. Place in greased 9x13 inch pan and bake at 375° for 10 minutes. Spread on top in layers: first the pizza sauce, then browned hamburger or meat of your choice, and lastly the Mozzarella cheese. Bake at 375° for 10 minutes. This plus a salad makes a quick and tasty meal.

Catherine Hauch, St. Peter
State Regent, 1980-1984
Second Vice Regent, 1978-1980
District Deputy, 7 years

TACO CASSEROLE

2 lbs. ground beef	1 cup shredded Cheddar cheese
1 med. chopped onion	1 cup corn
2 (20 oz.) cans chili beans	1 pkg. taco seasoning
1 (20 oz.) can tomatoes	1 tsp. salt

Brown meat; add onion and saute until tender. Drain grease. Add next 6 ingredients; mix and put in a 9x13 inch pan. Bake at 350° for 45 minutes, stirring 1 or 2 times. Cover meat mixture with **corn chips**. Bake 5 more minutes. Before serving, cover chips with **lettuce** and **black olives**. Serve with **sour cream**.

Mary Knoll, Waseca

HOT TAMALE PIE

²/₃ cup cornmeal
¾ tsp. salt
1²/₃ cups milk
1 Tbsp. butter
¼ cup onions
½ lb. ground beef

½ tsp. salt
Dash of pepper
½ tsp. chili powder
1 cup tomatoes, drained
¹/₃ cup ketchup
¾ cup shredded Cheddar
  cheese

In a saucepan, combine cornmeal and ¾ teaspoon salt. Gradually stir in milk; heat, stirring constantly until it is thick. Line casserole with cornmeal mixture and bake at 350° for 15 minutes. In a saucepan, melt butter; add onions and beef. Saute until onions are tender and beef is browned. Stir in salt, pepper, chili powder, tomatoes and ketchup. Pour over cornmeal in casserole. Top with cheese. Bake for 40 minutes.

Note: Recipe is submitted from original Catholic Daughters Cookbook "Everybody's Favorite!"

Margie Hoffer, Lismore

POTATO PIZZA

2 lbs. ground beef
5 cups potatoes, thinly sliced
1 (11 oz.) can Cheddar cheese
  soup
½ cup milk
1 (15 oz.) can tomato sauce

½ tsp. oregano, crushed
½ tsp. sugar
½ cup Mozzarella cheese,
  shredded
¼ cup Parmesan cheese, grated

Brown the ground beef in a medium skillet; drain the fat. Place the browned ground beef on the bottom of a 9x13 inch baking dish. Layer the potatoes over the meat. Mix the soup, milk, sauce and spices in a small bowl. Pour over the potatoes and meat. Cover the pan with foil. Bake at 375° for 45 minutes. Uncover and sprinkle with the cheeses. Bake an additional 10 minutes.

Patty Durand, Argyle

UPSIDE DOWN PIZZA

2 lbs. ground beef
1 lg. onion
1 pkg. Schillings Thick and Zesty
  spaghetti mix
3 (8 oz.) cans tomato sauce

1 (8 oz.) carton sour cream
2 cups Mozzarella or Swiss
  cheese
1 pkg. crescent rolls

Brown ground beef and onion. Add spaghetti mix and tomato sauce. Cook a few minutes, then pour in a 9x13 inch pan. Spread the sour cream and grated cheese over top. Cover with the rolled out crescent roll. Bake at 350° for 30 minutes.

Adeline G. Timmer, Lakeville

QUICK TACO PIE

1 lb. ground beef
½ cup chopped onion
1 (1¼ oz.) pkg. taco seasoning
  mix
¾ cup Bisquick
1¼ cups milk
3 eggs

Cheese
¼ head Iceberg lettuce,
  shredded
1 tomato, diced
⅓ cup ripe olives, sliced
Sour cream, optional

Cook and stir ground beef and onions in skillet until beef is brown; drain. Stir in seasoning mix; spoon in lightly greased 8 inch square pan; set aside. Beat Bisquick, milk and eggs until almost smooth, about 1 minute. Pour over meat mixture. Bake at 400° for 25 to 30 minutes. Sprinkle with cheese. Bake a couple of minutes longer or until cheese is melted. Cool for 10 minutes. Garnish with lettuce, tomatoes and olives and, if desired, sour cream. Serves 6 to 8.

Ann Rothschadl, Waubun

BISCUITS AND GRAVY

1½ lbs. seasoned or unseasoned
  pork sausage
Morton's sausage and meat
  loaf seasoning
½ cup flour
1½ to 2 cups milk
1 batch homemade biscuits or
  2 tubes Pillsbury biscuits

Brown pork sausage and add some Mortons to your taste. Mix in flour after meat is browned. Add milk; cook slowly to desired thickness. Spoon generous helping over baked biscuits. Enough sauce for 12 to 16 biscuits.

Monica Beauchane, Red Lake Falls

CHOP SUEY

1 lb. lean pork, diced
1 or 2 Tbsp. shortening
2 Tbsp. soy sauce
¼ tsp. salt
1 cup beef bouillon
1 cup chopped onions

1 can chop suey vegetables,
  drained
1 Tbsp. cornstarch
¼ tsp. ground ginger
1 Tbsp. molasses
¼ cup water

Brown meat in shortening. Add soy sauce, salt and bouillon. Cover and cook until meat is tender. Add onions and chop suey vegetables. Cook 10 minutes. Blend cornstarch, ginger, molasses, and water. Add and stir until thickened. Serve over rice or chow mein noodles with additional soy sauce to taste. A basic recipe. Use your judgement to increase various ingredients and add extra chopped celery and a can of drained bean sprouts to "stretch".

Gertrude R. Indihar, Eveleth

CHOP SUEY

1 whole onion	1 cup celery, cut wide
4 lbs. pork, beef, or leftover roast	

Cover with water in pressure cooker. Cook 30 minutes. Turn pressure down. Add **2 tablespoons dark molasses** and **3 tablespoons soy sauce**. If using leftover roast, it would be seasoned. If using fresh meat, salt and pepper meat before cooking. Make thickening using gravy from leftover roast or juice from cooking with a little cornstarch.

Ruth Dornack, Wabasha

BARBECUED RIBS

3 lbs. short ribs	1 cup catsup
1 tsp. paprika	1/3 cup vinegar
Salt to taste	1 cup water
1 lg onion, diced	2 tsp. chili powder

Place ribs in baking dish. Mix all other ingredients and pour over ribs and bake until tender. If ribs start to become dry, add water. Spoon sauce over the ribs several times during baking. Bake, covered, at 325°, testing for doneness.

Dorothy Kliner, Crookston
District Deputy, 1996-present

CHOW MEIN

2 cups pork or diced chicken	1 can mixed Chinese
2 Tbsp. butter	vegetables, drained
2 cups thinly sliced celery	1 (4 oz.) can mushrooms,
1½ cups sliced onion	drained
1/8 tsp. salt	2 Tbsp. cornstarch
2 cups beef broth	2 Tbsp. soy sauce

Brown pork or chicken lightly in butter. Add next 4 ingredients. Cook, covered, for 15 minutes or until just tender. Add Chinese vegetables, mushrooms and cornstarch, mixed with soy sauce. Simmer 2 minutes. May also add pea pods.

Kathleen Zender, St. James

MARINADE FOR GRILLED PORK CHOPS

¾ cup soy sauce	1 Tbsp. brown sugar
¼ cup lemon juice	1 clove garlic, minced
1 Tbsp. chili sauce or catsup	6 pork chops, 1 inch thick

Mix all marinade ingredients. Place chops in single layer in plastic bag with marinade. Seal. Refrigerate for several hours, turning occasionally. Grill chops until done and enjoy.

Lucille Taylor, Adrian
State Education Chairman
District Deputy, 1966-1970

PORK CHOPS WITH APPLE STUFFING

4 pork loin chops, each about 1½ inches thick
Paprika
2 cups dry herb stuffing mix

½ cup apple juice
2 Tbsp. margarine or butter, melted
1 med. unpared all-purpose apple, finely diced

Arrange pork chops, meaty parts to outside edges, in rectangular 11x7x1½ inch dish. Sprinkle with paprika. Mix remaining ingredients. Mound in center of dish. Cover tightly and microwave on medium (50%) for 20 to 23 minutes. Rotate dish a half turn every 7 minutes, until pork is done (170° on meat thermometer). Serves 4, with 405 calories per serving.

Note: A 500 watt microwave is not recommended. For those living alone, wrap tightly and freeze the unused portion.

Agnes Habeck, Delavan

PORK CHOPS AND DRESSING

4 pork chops
3 cups soft bread cubes
2 Tbsp. chopped onion
¼ cup melted oleo
¼ cup water

¼ tsp. poultry seasoning
¼ tsp. sage
1 can cream of celery soup
⅓ cup water

Brown chops on both sides; place in shallow baking dish. Lightly mix bread crumbs, onion, oleo, ¼ cup water and seasonings. Place mound of stuffing on each chop. Blend soup and ⅓ cup water and pour over chops and stuffing. Bake at 350° for 1 hour.

Leona Welsh, New Albin, IA

RIBS OR PORK CHOPS WITH BARBECUE SAUCE

Sauce:

4 Tbsp. minced onion
1 can tomato soup
¾ cup water
3 Tbsp. vinegar
2 Tbsp. Worcestershire sauce
1 tsp. salt

1 tsp. paprika
1 tsp. chili powder
½ tsp. pepper
Dash of cloves
¼ tsp. cinnamon

Combine all ingredients in order listed and heat to boil. Braise **ribs** under broiler until brown. If **4 pork chops** are used, fry until brown. Place meat in roaster and pour on the sauce. Bake at 350° for 1 hour. If more meat is used, double the sauce recipe.

Eva Balaski, International Falls

BAKED PORK CHOPS

Amount of pork chops needed   Ketchup
Salt and pepper to taste   Water to cover chops

Roll pork chops in flour. Place in large pan or casserole and season with salt and pepper. Cover with ketchup, using about 1 tablespoon for each chop. Cover with water and place in 400° oven. Keep pan covered and bake 1½ hours, turning them when nearly done to brown on other side.

Meg Schmidt, Fergus Falls
State Apostolic Chair, 1990-1992
District Deputy, 1992-1996

BARBECUED PORK STEAKS

4 pork shoulder steaks   1 Tbsp. quick cooking tapioca
1 Tbsp. cooking oil   ¹/₃ cup bottled barbecue sauce
1 lg. onion, sliced thin   ¼ cup dry red wine
1 lg. green pepper, sliced thin   ½ tsp. ground cumin
2 tomatoes, sliced

Cut pork steaks in half crosswise; trim off excess fat. In skillet, brown the steaks on both sides in hot oil. Drain steaks on paper toweling. In a 3 or 4 quart slow crockery cooker, arrange onion, green pepper and tomatoes. Sprinkle tapioca over vegetables. Place pork steaks atop vegetables. In a bowl, combine barbecue sauce, wine, and cumin; pour over meat and vegetables in crockery cooker. Cover and cook on low heat, setting for 6 to 8 hours, or until meat and vegetables are tender. Serve on platter.

Note: I start cooker on high until it starts to bubble.

Nellie Cullen, International Falls

PORK CASSEROLE

¾ pkg. seasoned bread stuffing   ¼ cup mayonnaise
1 cup broth or gravy   ½ tsp. salt
3 cups pork roast, cooked and   2 egg yolks
   chopped   1½ cups milk
½ med. onion   2 cans cream of celery soup
½ cup celery, chopped   1 cup grated cheese

Mix seasoned bread with broth or gravy and put ¾ of mixture into a 9x13 inch greased pan or casserole. Mix meat, onion, celery, mayonnaise and salt; spread over bread mixture. Top with remaining ¼ of the bread mixture. Beat eggs and milk and pour evenly over the mixture, cover with foil and refrigerate overnight. Take out 1 hour before baking. Spread soup over top and bake, uncovered, at 325° for 40 minutes. Sprinkle with cheese and return to oven for 10 minutes; cut into squares. Serves 10.

Helen Johnson, Caledonia

BAR-B-Q PORK CHOPS

½ cup catsup	2 Tbsp. brown sugar
½ cup water	1 Tbsp. Worcestershire sauce
1 tsp. dry mustard	1 sm. onion, diced

Mix and pour over **6 browned pork chops**. Simmer 30 minutes. For added zest, add a drop of Tabasco sauce just before done.

Sylvia Jensen, Thief River Falls

PORK CHOP HOT DISH FOR SIX

6 med. pork chops, ¾ inch thick	1 cup raw rice
2½ cups water	Green pepper
1 pkg. onion soup mix	Chili sauce

Brown pork chops well on both sides in a little oil. Remove from skillet to side dish. Simmer in same skillet the water and onion soup mix for 7 minutes. Grease a 9x13 inch pan. Spread raw rice over the bottom of pan. Place pork chops on top of rice. Place one ring of green pepper on each pork chop. Add **1 tablespoon chili sauce** in the middle of each pepper ring. Pour the soup mixture carefully over the chops being sure the rice is completely covered. Cover with tin foil and bake at 350° for 1½ hours. If dry, add a little water.

Ina Deming, Plainview

PORK CHOP POTATO CASSEROLE

4 potatoes, sliced	Salt and pepper
½ med. onion, chopped	1 can cream of mushroom soup
1½ cups sliced carrots	Milk
Flour	4 pork chops

Arrange potatoes, onions and carrots in greased baking dish or roaster. Sprinkle each layer with 1 tablespoon flour, dash of salt and pepper. Mix soup with milk and pour over above ingredients. Place pork chops on top and season well. Cover and bake at 350° for 1 hour or longer until chops are done. Uncover and bake 10 minutes longer to brown chops.

Cecilia Plante, Crookston

PORK AND RICE CASSEROLE

1 cup raw rice	4 Tbsp. soy sauce
2 cups chopped celery	2 cups water
1 cup chopped onion	Salt to taste
1 cup or 1 lg. can mushrooms	5 cups diced and browned pork

Combine all ingredients and put in greased casserole. Bake at 350° until meat is tender. More water may be added if necessary.

Alicia Phelan, Currie

PORK CHOPS AND RICE

6 pork chops
1 Tbsp. fat
1 tsp. salt
Pepper
2 onions
1 clove garlic, minced
2½ cups hot water
1 can condensed tomato soup

¼ cup chopped green onion
  and tops
¼ cup diced celery
¼ green pepper, chopped
2 Tbsp. parsley, flaked
Pinch of thyme
Pinch of marjoram
½ bay leaf, crushed
¾ cup raw rice

Brown chops in fat and season with salt and pepper. Remove chops and drain all but fat. Slice large onions and brown with garlic. Add hot water, soup, green onions and tops, celery, peppers, parsley, thyme, marjoram and bay leaf. Mix in raw rice. Pour all over chops in a baking dish and bake in moderate oven about 1 hour.

Helen Schmitz, Red Lake Falls

PORK CHOP-RICE DISH**

1 (14½ oz.) can beef consomme   1 cup raw rice
1 (11 oz.) can French onion soup   4 or 6 pork chops

Brown the chops. Put soups and rice in baking dish. Lay chops on top. Cover with foil. Bake at 350° for 1 hour or until done.

Fran Janous, Owatonna

SAUCY BAKED PORK CHOPS

6 center cut pork chops
1 med. onion, sliced
1 Tbsp. Worcestershire sauce

1 can cream of chicken soup
3 Tbsp. catsup

Trim fat from pork chops. Heat **2 tablespoons oil** in skillet. Brown chops. Season to taste with salt and pepper. When brown, put into casserole and mix remaining ingredients; pour over chops. Cover and bake at 350° for 50 to 60 minutes or until done.

Ione Gonsorowski, Thief River Falls

POOR MAN'S PIEROGI

4 or 5 slices bacon, diced
½ cup chopped sweet onion

½ med. head cabbage, cut up
1 (12 oz.) pkg. noodles, cooked

In Dutch oven or heavy pan, saute the bacon and onion. Add the cut up cabbage and slow simmer for about 45 minutes (don't scorch). Stir in the cooked noodles. Homemade noodles are the best but a good quality brand will do.

Margaret Ann Erjavec, Eveleth

PORKETTA

Pork butt roast   **1 heaping tsp. fennel seeds**
Salt and pepper   **Parsley flakes**
Garlic salt

Select a pork butt roast evenly balanced with meat and fat. Cut it almost in half lengthwise and open like a book. Generously sprinkle both sides with salt, pepper and garlic salt. Prop fennel seeds sparingly on one side. Sprinkle parsley flakes generously on other cut side, then sprinkle both sides again with garlic salt and pepper. Put the roast together again and tie securely with a heavy string. Generously sprinkle the roast on all sides with salt, pepper, garlic salt and pepper, in that order, using pepper twice. Place in roasting pan and press fennel seeds on the top side and then press a good amount of parsley flakes on top. Cover and bake at 325° for 3 to 4 hours or until the roast will pull apart with a fork. The ingredient amounts are not specific because they depend on the size of the roast and how spicy your family likes it. The meat is pulled apart with forks and usually served as a sandwich with hard rolls. Also good cooked in a crock pot.

Constance Gasperlin, Eveleth

SAUERKRAUT AND DUMPLINGS

Place **1 quart sauerkraut, a little water** and **some pork pieces** together in a roaster. Bake at 350° for approximately 2 hours. Into this mixture, grate **1 potato** and return to oven for 30 minutes.
Dumplings:
2 eggs   **1½ tsp. baking powder**
½ cup milk   **½ tsp. salt**
1½ cups flour

Mix ingredients and then spoon dip this mixture into sauerkraut. Cover tightly and return to oven for 30 minutes. Do not peek!

Rose Nachreiner, New Ulm

EASY FULL MEAL SAUERKRAUT HOT DISH**

1 pork steak   **1½ cups frozen hash brown**
1 onion   **potatoes**
                                       1 pkg. or can sauerkraut

Cut pork steak in about 8 pieces; brown, then add chopped onion, hash browns, and sauerkraut. Bake 1 hour.

Marie Karsnia, International Falls

POLISH REUBEN CASSEROLE

2 (16 oz.) cans sauerkraut
1 med. onion, diced
2 (10½ oz.) cans cream of
  mushroom soup
1⅓ cups milk
1 Tbsp. prepared mustard
1 (8 oz.) pkg. med. width noodles

1½ lbs. Polish sausage, cut in
  ½ inch pieces
2 cups shredded Swiss cheese
¾ cup whole wheat bread
  crumbs
2 Tbsp. melted butter

Preheat oven to 350°. Grease a 9x13 inch baking pan. Rinse sauerkraut in colander with cold water. Press to drain well. Combine onion, soup, milk and mustard in a bowl and blend well. Spread sauerkraut in baking pan. Top with uncooked noodles. Spoon soup mixture evenly over noodles. Top with sausage pieces. Spread cheese over sausage. Combine crumbs and butter. Sprinkle evenly over top of casserole. Cover pan tightly with foil. Bake 1 hour or until noodles are tender. Makes 8 to 10 servings.

Charlene Adank, Medford

SAUERKRAUT HOT DISH

1½ lbs. pork steak, cubed
1 med. onion, chopped
2 celery stalks, chopped
1 (16 oz.) can sauerkraut,
  undrained
1 (8 oz.) pkg. noodles, cooked
  and drained

1 (10¾ oz.) can condensed
  cream of mushroom soup,
  undiluted
1 (4 oz.) can mushrooms,
  drained
Salt and pepper to taste

In a large skillet, brown meat. Add the onions and celery and cook until onions are transparent. Stir in sauerkraut, noodles, soup and mushrooms. Season with salt and pepper. Spoon into a greased 2 quart casserole. Cover and bake at 350° for 1½ hours or until the meat is tender. Stir occasionally. Yield: 6 to 8 servings. (I also use hamburger or ground turkey instead of the pork.)

Marie Tuve, Elysian

FORGOTTEN ROAST

4 lbs. roast (beef or pork)
1 can mushroom soup
2 Tbsp. Worcestershire sauce

1 pkg. dry onion soup mix
Salt and pepper
Tenderizer

Place roast in center of foil. Pour over soup and Worcestershire sauce. Sprinkle over dry soup mix and salt and pepper and tenderizer. Wrap. Place in cake pan and bake at 250° from 7 a.m. to 5 p.m. Makes it's own gravy. Delicious!

Lucile Tyrrell, Eveleth

SAUSAGE AND ASPARAGUS AU GRATIN

1 lb. pork sausage links
1 Tbsp. water
3 Tbsp. butter
3 Tbsp. flour
1½ cups milk
Salt

1 tsp. pepper
¾ cup grated sharp Cheddar
  cheese
1 (10 oz.) pkg. frozen asparagus
  spears or 1 lb. fresh asparagus
6 slices toast

Place sausage links and water in cold frying pan. Cover tightly and cook slowly for 5 minutes. Remove cover and brown links. Melt butter in saucepan; stir in flour. Add milk, stirring constantly, until mixture thickens. Add salt, pepper and grated cheese. Stir until cheese melts. Cook frozen or fresh asparagus spears in boiling water until tender. Season. Arrange sausage links and asparagus spears on toast. Serve with cheese sauce. Serves 6.

Carol Allen, International Falls

SOUTHERN BAKED PORK CHOPS

6 to 8 loin chops
Salt and pepper
1 Tbsp. salad oil
½ cup butter
½ cup chopped onion
½ cup chopped celery

½ cup chopped green pepper
1 (8 oz.) can whole kernel corn,
  undrained
1 pkg. corn bread mix
⅛ tsp. dried thyme
1 egg

Preheat oven to 350°. Lightly grease a 9x9x2 inch pan. Brown chops on both sides in large pan. Remove chops and pour off drippings. Heat butter in pan. Add onion, celery and pepper. Cook until tender, about 5 minutes. Add corn and remove from heat. Add stuffing mix, thyme and egg. Stir until well blended. Turn stuffing into dish arrange chops on top. Cover chops with foil. Bake 1 hour.

Iris Rivers, Winona

SLICED PORK WITH GREEN PEPPERS

1 lb. lean boneless pork
1 Tbsp. soy sauce
3 Tbsp. water
1 Tbsp. cornstarch

2 Tbsp. vegetable oil
3 green onions and tops, cut into
  2 inch lengths
1 green pepper, thinly sliced

Cut pork into thin pieces, about 2 inches long. Mix with soy sauce and 1 tablespoon water and cornstarch. Let stand 15 minutes. Preheat wok on medium heat. Add oil. Stir in onions and pork. Stir-fry for 10 minutes. Add remaining water. Turn heat to low; cover and simmer for 10 minutes. Remove cover and add pepper slices and stir-fry for 2 minutes. Serve with rice.

Jane Rowe, Owatonna

BEEF-STUFFED PORK ROAST

Barbecue Sauce:

1 (14 oz.) bottle catsup	½ cup chili sauce
⅓ cup wine vinegar	¼ cup brown sugar
2 Tbsp. lemon juice	2 Tbsp. Worcestershire sauce
2 Tbsp. prepared mustard	2 Tbsp. cooking oil
3 Tbsp. steak sauce	1 tsp. dry mustard
¼ tsp. salt	¼ tsp. pepper
1 clove garlic, minced	

Combine in a medium saucepan and simmer for 30 minutes.

1 (3 lb.) pork loin	Dash of pepper
Barbecue sauce (above)	1 (6 oz.) can sliced mushrooms,
½ lb. ground beef	drained
¼ cup chopped onion	¼ cup fine dry bread crumbs
1 sm. clove garlic, minced	¼ cup grated Parmesan cheese
¼ tsp. salt	

To butterfly loin, split meat lengthwise, almost all the way through, then spread flat. Pound out to 15x10 inch rectangle, ¾ inch thick. Brush top with ¼ cup of barbecue sauce. Combine ground beef, onion, garlic, salt, pepper and ¼ cup barbecue sauce. Spread evenly over roast. Press mushrooms into ground beef mixture. Sprinkle bread crumbs and Parmesan cheese over meat. Starting from 10 inch side, roll up and tie. Place in shallow pan. Roast, uncovered, at 325° for about 2½ hours. Baste with additional barbecue sauce during last 15 to 20 minutes. Pass remaining sauce. Serves 6 to 8.

Florence Yutrzenka, Argyle

VEGETABLE PORK STIR-FRY

¾ lb. pork tenderloin, cut into strips	1½ cups thinly sliced carrots
1 Tbsp. vegetable oil	1 clove garlic, minced
1½ cups mushrooms (fresh if you have them)	1 cup chicken broth
1 lg. green pepper, cut into strips	2 Tbsp. soy sauce
1 rib celery, diagonally sliced	1 Tbsp. cornstarch
	3 cups hot cooked rice

Brown pork strips in oil in a large skillet or wok over high heat. Push meat to the side and add the vegetables. Stir-fry the vegetables for 3 minutes. Combine the broth, soy sauce, and cornstarch and add to skillet. Cook until thick and clear and serve over rice. Serves 6.

Lorraine Haberman, New Ulm

CINNAMON-ORANGE PORK TENDERLOINS

½ cup corn flake crumbs
1 Tbsp. brown sugar
2 tsp. cinnamon
2 tsp. grated orange rind

2 (½ lb.) pork tenderloins
½ Tbsp. plain nonfat yogurt
1½ Tbsp. orange juice

Combine corn flake crumbs, brown sugar, cinnamon and grated orange rind; set aside. Trim off tenderloins. Combine yogurt and orange juice and brush on tenderloins. Dip tenderloins into cereal mixture. Place on rack in a sprayed roasting pan and bake at 350° for 45 to 50 minutes. Let stand for 10 minutes. Slice into thin slices. Makes 4 servings, at 151.8 calories per serving, 3 g fat, 1 g saturated fat.

Dorothy Morgan, Morristown

SESAME PORK

½ cup soy sauce
3 Tbsp. sugar
3 Tbsp. minced onion
2 cloves garlic, minced

2 tsp. ginger
¾ cup sesame seed
2 Tbsp. oil
1 (5 lb.) pork roast

Combine marinade ingredients in a bowl. Add roast and marinate 3 hours in refrigerator, turning and basting frequently. Drain and save marinade. Preheat oven to 375°. Put pork in oiled roasting pan. Roast until tender. Add marinade last 10 minutes. Serve with juice. Can be grilled also.

Rosemary Rolph, Pipestone

REUBEN CASSEROLE

2 (10¾ oz.) can cream of
  chicken or mushroom soup
1⅓ cups milk
½ cup chopped onion
3 Tbsp. prepared mustard
2 (16 oz.) cans sauerkraut,
  drained
1 (8 oz.) pkg. uncooked, med.
  egg noodles

1 (12 oz.) can corned beef,
  crumbled
2 cups shredded Swiss cheese
  (8 oz.)
¾ cup rye bread crumbs,
  toasted
2 Tbsp. butter or regular
  margarine, melted

In a bowl, mix condensed soup, milk, onion and mustard until blended. In a greased 13x9x2 inch baking dish; spread drained sauerkraut and top with uncooked noodles. Spoon soup mixture evenly over noodles. Sprinkle with corned beef, then cheese. In bowl, stir together rye bread crumbs and melted butter until well blended. Sprinkle over top of cheese. Cover tightly with foil. Bake at 350° for 1 hour or until noodles are tender. Serves 8 to 10.

Jean M. Byron, Waseca

BROWN RICE**

1 cup raw rice
1 can French onion soup
1 can beef broth
¼ cup margarine

Mix and pour into an ungreased casserole. Bake at 350° for 1 hour.

Diane Pawlowski, Argyle

CHEESE-RICE CASSEROLE

1 cup raw rice
1 cup diced celery
1 cup grated American cheese
1 cup hot water
½ cup chopped onion
1 cup mushrooms, sliced
1 cup sliced ripe olives
1 cup chopped stewed
   tomatoes
½ cup sliced pimento olives
½ cup salad oil

Combine all ingredients. Bake in a covered casserole at 350° for 1 hour or until the liquid is absorbed and the rice is tender. Extra liquid may be added if necessary. Wild rice may be substituted for all or part of the rice.

Teresa Lehne, Mahnomen

CHINESE FRIED RICE

2 Tbsp. oil
3 cups cold cooked rice
½ to 1 cup shrimp, chicken,
   turkey, cooked pork or beef
2 stalks celery, diced
1 med. onion, diced
2 or 3 green diced onions,
   optional
2 Tbsp. soy sauce
2 beaten eggs, scrambled and
   cooked before using

Heat oil in wok or teflon pan. Add rice, meat, celery, onion and soy sauce. Stir-fry until hot. Add precooked scrambled eggs. Toss and serve.

Arneta Middendorf, Owatonna

ORIENTAL HOT DISH

1 lb. ground beef
½ cup chopped onions
1 cup diced celery
1 can cream of mushroom soup
1 can cream of chicken soup
2 soup cans water
¼ cup soy sauce
1 can chop suey vegetables or
   1 can chow mein vegetables
1 cup uncooked wild rice

Brown beef and onion. Mix all ingredients and bake at 350° for 1½ hours.

Kathy Janisch, Mahnomen

403

VEGETABLES & MAIN DISHES

GREEN RICE

2 pkgs. (or 1 lb.) frozen chopped broccoli, cooked and drained
2 cups cooked rice
1 can cream of chicken soup
1 can water chestnuts, sliced
½ cup chopped onion, pre-cooked
½ cup chopped celery, pre-cooked
1 can mushrooms, sliced
½ cup milk
2 Tbsp. butter
½ (8 oz.) jar Cheez Whiz
Seasonings
Chunks of chicken, turkey, or ham

Mix, then put into casserole or 9x13 inch pan. Put the other ½ jar of Cheez Whiz on top. Bake at 350° for 45 minutes.

Lucille Tyrrell, Eveleth

SPANISH RICE

½ lb. bacon, diced
1 med. onion, diced (½ cup)
½ green pepper, diced
1 (1 lb.) can tomatoes
1½ cups water
¾ cup uncooked rice
½ cup tomato sauce
1 tsp. salt
⅛ tsp. pepper
1 tsp. sugar
1 tsp. Worcestershire sauce

Fry bacon; remove and use fat to saute onion and pepper until tender. Add remaining ingredients. Cook slowly for 45 minutes, stirring often.

Marian O'Brien, International Falls

SPICY RICE CASSEROLE

1 lb. mild bulk pork sausage
1 tsp. ground cumin
½ tsp. garlic powder
2 med. onions, chopped
2 med. green peppers, chopped
2 beef bouillon cubes
2 cups boiling water
1 to 2 jalapeno peppers, seeded and finely minced
1 (6¼ oz.) pkg. quick-cooking long grain and wild rice mix

In a large skillet, cook sausage, cumin and garlic powder, stirring often. Drain. Add onions and green peppers; saute until crisp tender. Dissolve bouillon in water; add to skillet. Stir in jalapenos, rice and rice seasoning packet; bring to a boil. Reduce heat and simmer, uncovered, 5 to 10 minutes or until the water is absorbed. Yield: 4 to 6 servings.

Mary A. Loosbrock, Lismore

WILD RICE

1 cup wild rice, soaked a few minutes
2 onions, diced
1 to 1½ cups celery, cut in ½ inch pieces
1 to 1½ lg. green peppers, cut up
2 sm. cans mushrooms
1 can water chestnuts, sliced
¾ lb. bacon, cut in 1 inch pieces and browned

Put above ingredients into a small roaster; fill to top with water. (Juice from mushrooms may be used as part of liquid.) Very good served with turkey.

Helen Hurlburt, Moorhead

WILD RICE CASSEROLE

1 cup wild rice
½ cup slivered almonds
1 (8 oz.) can mushrooms, drained
2 Tbsp. minced chives
½ cup butter
3 cups chicken broth

Rinse wild rice in cold water 4 or 5 times. Saute wild rice, almonds, mushrooms and chives in butter in skillet until golden. Pour into a greased casserole dish. Stir in broth. Bake, tightly covered, at 325° for 1 hour. Serves 6.

Becky Flynn, International Falls
Go-Pher News Editor, 1982-1992

WILD RICE HOT DISH

1 lb. ground beef
Salt and pepper to taste
1 bunch celery, chopped
½ cup wild rice
1 cup water
4 Tbsp. chop suey sauce
2 lg. onions, chopped
1 can chicken noodle soup
1 can cream of mushroom soup
1 can peas

Brown ground beef and season with salt and pepper. Mix with rest of ingredients. Put in casserole and bake at 350° for 2 hours.

Loretta Raetz, Red Wing

WILD RICE CASSEROLE

1 (8 oz.) pkg. wild rice, washed
¼ lb. bacon, cut up
1 cup raw onions, chopped
1 cup celery, chopped
1 cup green pepper, chopped
¼ lb. butter
½ tsp. pepper
2 tsp. salt
2 cans chicken rice soup
2 cans mushroom soup
1 (4 oz.) can mushrooms, added with liquid

Pour 3 cups boiling water over rice; bring to boil and let set for 20 minutes. Fry cut up bacon until crisp. Saute cut up onions, celery and green pepper in butter with pepper and salt added. Mix all ingredients in casserole. Bake at 375° for 1 hour.

Maureen O'Connor, St. Peter

WILD RICE AND MUSHROOM STUFFING

½ cup butter	²/₃ cup water
1 lb. fresh mushrooms, sliced	4 cups cooked wild rice
½ cup chopped onions	1½ tsp. salt
½ cup minced parsley	¹/₈ tsp. pepper
1 cup chopped celery	

Melt butter in a heavy skillet. Add mushrooms and cook over low heat for 5 minutes. Remove mushrooms. Add onion, parsley and celery to skillet. Cook until onions turn yellow. Add ¹/₃ cup water along with wild rice and seasonings. Mix well. Add remaining water and the cooked mushrooms. Mix well. Simmer for 15 minutes. Makes 8 servings.

Cecilia Headlee, St. Peter

WILD RICE
(It's the Best)

1 cup wild rice	½ cup slivered almonds,
½ cup onion	browned (optional)
¼ cup butter	2 (4 oz.) cans mushrooms and
1 cup celery	juice
¼ tsp. sage	1 can consomme or chicken
¼ tsp. basil	stock
1 Tbsp. parsley flakes	

Wash rice and soak 3 hours or overnight; drain. Put all together in a 2 quart dish and bake at 350° for 1½ hours. Can't be beat! Warm up; add a little water (don't want it too dry).

Carol Vande, St. Peter

WILD RICE CASSEROLE

1 (8 oz.) pkg. wild rice	Parsley flakes
½ lb. bacon, chopped	2 chicken bouillon cubes
1 cup chopped onion	¹/₃ cup hot water
1 cup chopped celery	1 can sliced water chestnuts
1 can cream of mushroom soup	1 sm. container mushrooms
1 can cream of chicken soup	2 Tbsp. bacon drippings
1½ tsp. Beau seasoning	Small amount garlic, optional

Cook rice until tender. Fry bacon until crisp. Add onions, celery, soups and seasonings to fried bacon. Dissolve bouillon cubes in hot water and add to mix. Combine rice and all other ingredients in casserole. Cook, covered, at 325° for 1½ hours. Remove cover and cook another 15 minutes.

Terry Stenberg, International Falls

WILD RICE CASSEROLE

1 lb. sausage meat	1/8 tsp. oregano
2 med. onions, chopped	1/8 tsp. thyme
2 sm. cans mushrooms	1/8 tsp. marjoram
2 cups washed wild rice	1/8 tsp. pepper
1 Tbsp. salt	1 tsp. Accent
1/4 cup flour	1/2 cup toasted slivered
1/2 cup cream	blanched almonds
2 1/2 cups condensed chicken broth	

Saute sausage meat; drain on paper towels. In that fat, saute onion and mushrooms and the cooked sausage. Meanwhile, cook thoroughly washed wild rice. Boil for 20 minutes; add salt to this and drain. Mix flour with cream and beat until smooth. Add chicken broth and cook until thick; add seasoning to meat mixture and wild rice. Pour into casserole; bake at 350° for 30 minutes and put toasted almonds on when ready to serve.

Carol Walhovd, Brownsville

WILD RICE CASSEROLE

4 cups boiling water	1/4 tsp. celery salt
1 cup uncooked wild rice	1/4 tsp. garlic salt
1 can cream of mushroom soup	Pepper
1 can cream of chicken soup	Onion salt or powder
2 beef bouillon cubes, dissolved in 1 cup hot water (can use 1 cup Campbell beef broth)	Paprika
	3/4 cup chopped celery
	4 Tbsp. chopped onion or more
1 tsp. salt	1 1/2 lbs. ground beef
1 bay leaf, crumbled	2 sm. cans mushrooms, drained

Pour 4 cups boiling water over rice and let stand in this hot water for 15 to 20 minutes. Drain well and put in a large greased casserole. Add the soups, water with bouillon (or broth), and seasonings. Mix gently. Saute celery and chopped onion in butter; put in with rice. Brown ground beef; drain off any fat that may be in it. Stir into rice mixture. Refrigerate overnight until ready to use. Bake at 350° for 2 hours. If dry, cover up. I usually add the whole can of beef broth. Great to make Saturday night for Sunday company.

Leona Rapacz, Argyle

* * * * * * * *

Believe God and he will strengthen you and direct your way.
Trust in him, be reverent to him and grow old in his ways.
Florence Becker, Caledonia

RICE CASSEROLE

6 strips chopped bacon	1 cup wild and white rice
Onion, chopped	combination
½ chopped green pepper	1 can mushroom soup
2 to 3 stalks celery	

In skillet, brown bacon, onion, green pepper and celery. Precook rice until kernels start to open. Put in casserole with mushroom soup. Bake at 350° (or lower) for 1 hour.

Clari Miller, International Falls

EASY SCALLION SALMON

½ cup chicken broth	⅛ tsp. pepper
2 slightly beaten eggs	1 (16 oz.) can salmon, drained,
½ cup milk	skinned, deboned and flaked
2 Tbsp. parsley flakes	2 cups herb-seasoned stuffing
1 Tbsp. instant onion flakes	croutons
½ tsp. dry mustard	1 cup shredded Cheddar cheese
¼ tsp. salt	

Combine chicken broth, eggs, milk, parsley, onion, mustard, salt, and pepper. Stir in salmon, croutons and cheese. Turn into a 9 inch pie plate. Bake, uncovered, at 350° for 35 to 40 minutes.

Vegetable Sauce:

2 Tbsp. melted butter	¼ tsp. salt
2 Tbsp. flour	Dash of pepper

Blend ingredients and add **1 cup milk**; cool until bubbly. Cook 2 minutes more. Stir in **1 cup cooked peas**. Heat thoroughly. Cut salmon dish in pie-shop pieces and serve with hot vegetable sauce over the top. Serves 4 to 6.

Lois Fischer, Blue Earth

SALMON PUFF

4 eggs, slightly beaten	2 cups soft bread cubes
½ cup milk	(about 2½ slices)
1 can cream of mushroom soup	1 Tbsp. parsley
1 can salmon, drained and	1 sm. onion, minced
flaked	2 Tbsp. butter or margarine
	½ tsp. lemon juice

In a large bowl, combine eggs, milk and soup. Stir in remaining ingredients. Pour into a 10x6x2 inch baking dish. Bake at 350° for 50 minutes, or until mixture appears set. Let stand 5 minutes before serving.

Betty Ericson, International Falls

SALMON LOAF WITH MUSHROOM SAUCE

2 (2 lb.) cans salmon, drained
Juice from a half a lemon
½ tsp. grated onion
2 cups bread crumbs

1⅓ cups heated milk
4 eggs
6 Tbsp. melted butter

Reserve liquid from salmon. Flake salmon and remove skin and bones. Add juice of lemon and grated onion; mix well. Add bread crumbs and heated milk. Add well beaten eggs. Bake in well buttered loaf pan, set in dish of water, at 325° to 350° for 1½ hours.

Sauce:

¼ cup butter
2 Tbsp. flour
2 cups milk

1 med. can mushrooms
2 Tbsp. liquid from salmon
2 Tbsp. liquid from mushrooms

Mix butter, flour, milk and mushrooms. Add liquids and heat until thick. Serve warm over slice of salmon loaf.

Ruth Kobilarcsik, Plainview

SALMON LOAF

1 (1 lb.) can red salmon
½ cup bread crumbs
1 tsp. chopped parsley
1 Tbsp. lemon juice
2 egg yolks

½ cup hot milk
2 Tbsp. melted butter
Salt and pepper
2 egg whites, beaten stiff

Mix all and add beaten egg whites. Put in small loaf pan. Bake at 350° for 1 hour.

Mary Powers, Moorhead

SALMON LOAF

1 lg. can red salmon, drained
½ tsp. salt
½ cup fine bread crumbs

½ cup milk
3 egg whites, beaten stiff

Mix, folding egg whites in last.

Sauce:

Juice of salmon
1 Tbsp. flour

½ cup milk
3 egg yolks

Mix and boil ingredients of sauce; spread over when ready to serve.

Betty Burg, Caledonia

* * * * * * * *

To live and die for Christ, extend a welcome to those who are weak in faith. Do not enter into disputes with them. Romans 14:1
Mildred Lee, Caledonia

VEGETABLES & MAIN DISHES

SALMON LOAF

1 lg. can salmon	¾ cup milk
2 eggs, beaten	Salt and pepper to taste
1 cup saltine crackers or bread crumbs	Celery salt to taste
	½ chopped onion

Mix in order given. Place in a well greased baking dish. Bake at 350° for 40 minutes. Turn on platter and serve with salmon loaf sauce or a white sauce. You can also make salmon patties with this recipe.

Bertha M. Wacha, Slayton

SALMON PATTIES

1 egg	¼ cup mayonnaise
1 (14 oz.) can salmon, drained	2 tsp. instant minced onion
½ cup uncooked rolled oats	⅛ tsp. salt
⅓ cup grated carrots	Freshly ground pepper

Mix and shape into 4 patties. Brown in **2 tablespoons cooking oil** until golden brown. May also be topped by a slice of cheese on cooked side of patty, to melt while bottom side cooks and served on toasted buns or English muffin. Tuna may be used in place of salmon (use 6½ to 7 oz.)

Isabelle Rahm, International Falls

HOMEMADE SAUSAGE

2 lbs. hamburger	3 Tbsp. Morton's Tender Quick
¼ tsp. onion salt	½ tsp. whole peppers, cracked
⅛ tsp. garlic salt	¼ tsp. mustard seed
1 cup cold water	

Mix well. Make two rolls and wrap in foil. Twist ends. Let stand in refrigerator for 24 hours. Boil 1 hour or bake at 275° for 2 hours. Cool and wrap. Freeze or keep in refrigerator.

Variation: Use plain salt instead of Morton Tender Quick and cook immediately.

Mary Korpi, Virginia

SHRIMP CURRY

1½ cups celery, sliced fine	Salt and pepper to taste
1 sm. onion, chopped	Curry powder to taste
1 can mushrooms (or use fresh)	½ to 1 lb. small salad shrimp
1 can water chestnuts, sliced	½ pt. sour cream
1 can cream of shrimp soup	

Saute celery and onion. Add mushrooms, water chestnuts and shrimp soup. Season with salt and pepper and curry. Add shrimp. Just before serving, add sour cream. Serve over cooked rice. Yield: 4 to 6 servings.

Vivian (Vi) Larson, Argyle

SLOVENIAN EGG DUMPLINGS

2 eggs
1/3 cup water
1 cup flour
1/2 tsp. baking powder
1/4 tsp. salt
2 qts. salted boiling water or
    light broth

Beat eggs and water. Sift or stir the dry ingredients well. Stir flour mixture into egg and water, adding more flour if necessary to make an almost stiff batter. Drop dumplings from teaspoon into boiling water or broth. Cover and cook 10 minutes. Drain and serve with chicken or beef stews.

Jennie Forte, Eveleth

SLOVENIAN SARMAS

(As demonstrated by Mary Ann Stanich in the ethnic kitchen at IRONWORLD.)

1 good sized head of cabbage
1 1/2 lbs. each (raw) ground beef,
    ground pork, ground ham
1 cup raw rice
1 1/2 tsp. salt
1/4 tsp. pepper
1 Tbsp. onion flakes
1 Tbsp. garlic flakes
2 lbs. sauerkraut
1 (8 oz.) can tomato sauce
1/2 cup vinegar

Freeze cabbage head at least two days before and then thaw and remove core (freezing will allow you to separate the leaves easily). Mix meat, rice, salt, pepper, onion and garlic together. Put spoonful of meat mixture on cabbage leaf and fold up envelope fashion. Layer sauerkraut and stuffed cabbage leaves in Dutch oven. Fill with water to cover. Put tomato sauce over top. Add vinegar and boil at least 1 1/2 hours. Tastes better the longer it cooks or the next day.

Rose Ferroni, Eveleth

ANN'S SPAGHETTI SAUCE

1 lb. Italian sausage
1 lb. extra lean ground beef
1 sm. onion, chopped
2 cloves garlic, minced
1 (30 oz.) jar spaghetti sauce
2 (15 oz.) cans tomato sauce
1 fluid oz. garlic juice
1 Tbsp. Italian seasoning
1 bay leaf
Pepper, optional
1/2 cup Parmesan cheese

Brown meats separately. Drain fat from sausage. Brown ground beef with onions and garlic. Add spaghetti sauce and tomato sauce. Sprinkle in Italian seasoning. Add bay leaf. Simmer 2 hours. It is very important to add Parmesan cheese to sauce 30 minutes before serving. Serve over spaghetti.

Ann Reff, International Falls

AUNTIE'S BAKED SPAGHETTI
(From my childhood in St. Paul)

1 lb. ground beef	1 tsp. rosemary
3 slices lean bacon, chopped	1 tsp. marjoram
½ cup chopped onion	1 tsp. oregano
½ cup chopped green pepper	1 tsp. salt
1 (14 oz.) can tomatoes	½ tsp. pepper
1 (8 oz.) can tomato sauce	12 to 14 whole cloves
1 (6 oz.) can tomato paste	1 (7 oz.) pkg. spaghetti
1 tsp. basil	

Brown the beef to crumbly; set aside. Saute bacon, onion, green pepper, then add sauces and all herbs. Simmer 10 minutes. Add beef to sauces. Break in half, then boil spaghetti; drain and chill in cold water. Mix all ingredients and place in a 9x13 inch casserole. Sprinkle with **Parmesan cheese**. Bake at 350° for 45 minutes to 1 hour. Cut into squares.

Please note: Whole cloves are most important in this recipe! You may cut them in half - all will blend. Do not use ground cloves.

Helen A. Schoen, Medford

SPAGHETTI

3 lbs. hamburger	2 Tbsp. parsley flakes
1 tsp. Worcestershire sauce	1 onion, chopped
2 tsp. salt	1 pepper, chopped
¼ tsp. pepper	1 sm. can tomato paste
1 tsp. basil	1 cup water
¾ tsp. oregano	1 lg. can tomatoes, blended in
1 tsp. garlic salt	blender first
2 tsp. celery salt	1 sm. can tomato sauce
2 Tbsp. sugar	

Brown hamburger either in skillet or microwave and drain grease. Put in large pan and add all the other ingredients. Bring to boil and simmer for about 1 hour. Can be used on top of spaghetti noodles or mix with mostaccioi noodles for a main dish. Makes enough sauce for two pounds of noodles. (If I'm in a hurry, I will mix all the other ingredients in a pan and start them simmering while the hamburger is browning, then just add the hamburger to the sauce.)

Shirley Seyfried, Fergus Falls
1st Vice State Regent, 1994-present
2nd Vice State Regent, 1990-1994
State Treasurer, 1986-1990

FLORENTINE SPAGHETTI

1½ lbs. ground beef, browned
1 (6 oz.) pkg. cooked spaghetti
1 (32 oz.) jar spaghetti sauce
1½ cups cottage cheese
2 (10 oz.) pkgs. frozen spinach
1 (12 oz.) pkg. shredded
    Mozzarella cheese

In a 9x13 inch pan, layer ingredients 2 or 3 times. Sprinkle top with **Parmesan cheese**. Bake at 350° for 30 minutes. Serves 10 to 12.

Rose Dulek, Winona

ITALIAN SPAGHETTI

Approximately ¼ cup olive oil
3 med. onions, chopped
2 cloves garlic
2 (6 oz.) cans tomato sauce
2 (6 oz.) cans tomato paste
Salt and pepper to taste
½ tsp. cumin
½ tsp. paprika
½ tsp. thyme
⅛ tsp. red pepper
¼ tsp. cloves
½ tsp. rosemary
1 Tbsp. brown sugar
1 lb. hamburger

Put olive oil in large skillet. Fry chopped onions and garlic for a few minutes in oil. Add sauce and paste and cook for a few minutes more. Add seasonings and thin down with water to desired thickness. Cook about 3 hours. Add water when necessary. About 1 hour before done, add meatballs lightly browned in a skillet. Serve over **long cooked spaghetti**.

Dolly Meyer, North Mankato

ITALIAN SPAM-SPAGHETTI CASSEROLE

1 sm. onion, minced
1 sm. clove garlic, minced
¼ cup vegetable oil
1 (12 oz.) can Spam luncheon
    meat, diced
¼ cup snipped parsley
1 tsp. salt
Salt to taste
¼ tsp. pepper
½ tsp. oregano leaves
¼ tsp. basil leaves
1 (16 oz.) can stewed tomatoes
½ lb. spaghetti, broken in 2 inch
    lengths
¼ cup grated Parmesan cheese

Saute onion and garlic in the oil until tender, but not browned. Add Spam and saute lightly, then add parsley, 1 teaspoon salt, pepper, oregano, basil, and tomatoes. Bring to boil and simmer, covered, about 15 minutes. Meanwhile, cook spaghetti in boiling salted water until tender. Drain and put in shallow 2 quart baking dish. Top with the sauce and sprinkle with Parmesan cheese. Bake at 375° for about 30 minutes. Makes 6 servings.

Patricia L. Skraba, Eveleth

MICROWAVE SPAGHETTI**

1 Tbsp. butter	1½ cups water
1 cup chopped onion	½ tsp. ground oregano
1 lb. ground beef	½ tsp. basil
1 tsp. salt	¼ lb. spaghetti, uncooked
¼ tsp. pepper	Grated Parmesan cheese
2 (8 oz.) cans tomato sauce	

Place butter and onion in a 2 quart microwave safe casserole. Heat in microwave on high about 3 or 4 minutes. Add beef. Cook on high 3 or 4 minutes or until beef is no longer pink. Stir halfway through cooking time; drain. Add salt, pepper, tomato sauce, water, oregano and basil. Cook, covered, on high for 4 minutes. Break spaghetti and stir into sauce. Cook, covered, on high for 18 to 20 minutes or until spaghetti is tender. Stir twice during cooking time. Sprinkle with Parmesan cheese. Serve.

Geneviev E. Gardner, Caledonia

PASTA SPAGHETTI DINNER

1 sm. pkg. spaghetti	½ tsp. salt
1 Tbsp. vegetable oil or butter	¼ tsp. pepper
1 lb. ground beef	¼ tsp. lemon pepper
1 sm. onion, chopped fine	1 dry pkg. spaghetti sauce mix
1 tsp. garlic powder	1 (6 oz.) can tomato paste
½ tsp. season "All" salt	3 cans water
¼ tsp. basil leaves	

Boil spaghetti for 10 to 12 minutes; drain. Add vegetable oil or butter and toss. Brown hamburger with onion; add all spices, dry spaghetti sauce, tomato paste and water. Pour all sauce mixture over the buttered spaghetti. Gently bring to almost boil, cover and simmer 20 minutes. Stir frequently. May serve with garlic bread or garlic toast.

Note: For thicker sauce, decrease the water to 2 cans.

Renee Kern, Owatonna

* * * * * * * *

Love is a power that transforms the soul,
fills hearts with heaven and gives life its goal.
Loretta Inman
Lorraine Thillen, Caledonia

Sour Cream Sauce:

2 Tbsp. butter

1 pt. sour cream

Cornstarch

1 egg, well beaten

1 cup grated Cheddar cheese

Salt and pepper

Sprinkling paprika

In double boiler, melt butter; add sour cream. Thicken with cornstarch. Cook for 10 minutes; add beaten egg. Cook 10 minutes longer and add cheese; stir until smooth. Use over long spaghetti. I also make in the microwave and it works very well. Excellent when used over a meat, tomato sauce on spaghetti.

Spaghetti Tomato Sauce With Meat:

1 lb. hamburger, browned

1 packet Lawry's spaghetti sauce

1 lg. can tomatoes

Season to taste and simmer until well done. Onion diced is also very good in this sauce.

Dorothy Kliner, Euclid
District Deputy, 1996-present

SPAGHETTI SALSA DI POMODORI PADRE
(To Serve 50 People)

12 to 15 lbs. ground beef

6 cups chopped onion

Salt and pepper to taste

5 tsp. oregano

5 Tbsp. basil

7½ Tbsp. Italian seasoning

5 tsp. garlic powder

2½ tsp. Tabasco sauce

5 tsp. chili powder

2½ tsp. crushed red pepper

1⅔ cups brown sugar

12 (4 oz.) cans mushrooms with liquid

10 sm. cans tomato soup

5 lg. cans tomato juice (this is regulated by volume of pot)

5 (6 oz.) cans tomato paste

4 lg. cans tomato sauce

Dry parsley

20 lbs. spaghetti

Brown meat and onions and season with salt and pepper. Add spices and remaining ingredients except parsley. Simmer for 3 or 4 hours, uncovered, periodically skimming fat. Stir frequently to keep from burning. Just before serving, stir in some dry parsley for coloring. Serve over spaghetti noodles.

Father Robert Herman, Medford
Court St. Anne Chaplin

* * * * * * * *

Oh Lord, our Lord, how glorious is your name over all the earth!
You have exalted your majesty above the heavens. Psalm 8:1
Genevieve Gardner, Caledonia

SPAGHETTI PIE

Crust:

6 oz. spaghetti
1/3 cup grated Parmesan cheese

2 eggs, well beaten

Cook and drain spaghetti. Add Parmesan cheese and eggs. Put into a buttered 10 inch pie plate. Crust will be thick.

Filling:

1 lb. ground beef
1 med. onion, chopped
Oregano
Garlic

Salt
1 qt. jar spaghetti sauce
1 (12 oz.) carton cottage cheese
1/2 cup Mozzarella cheese

Brown ground beef with chopped onion. Add spaghetti sauce. Spread layer of cottage cheese on crust; top with meat and sauce mixture. Bake at 350° for 20 minutes. Sprinkle on Mozzarella cheese and bake 5 minutes more. May be baked in oblong cake tin.

Jean M. Byron, Waseca

SPAGHETTI PIZZA BAKE

1/2 lb. spaghetti
2 beaten eggs
1 cup milk
1 (32 oz.) jar spaghetti sauce
1 lb. ground beef
1 cup chopped onion

1 cup chopped green peppers
Garlic salt
Salt and pepper
1 cup pepperoni slices
1 sm. pkg. Mozzarella cheese

Break spaghetti into small pieces and cook according to package directions. Drain and add eggs and milk. Put in a greased 9x13 inch pan. Pour sauce over spaghetti. Cover with browned and drained ground beef, onion, green pepper and seasonings. Arrange pepperoni slices on top and cover with cheese. Bake at 350° for 35 to 45 minutes. Allow to stand 5 minutes before cutting in squares.

Agnes Prairie, Russell

PEACHY PORK RIBS

1 (7¾ oz.) jar strained peaches
1/3 cup ketchup
1/3 cup vinegar
2 Tbsp. soy sauce

1/2 cup packed brown sugar
2 cloves garlic, minced
1 tsp. ground ginger

Combine all ingredients. Marinate **4 pounds country style pork ribs** in sauce overnight. Bake at 350° for 1 hour.

Amy Tammaro, Eveleth

BARBECUE SPARERIBS

3 to 4 lbs. ribs	½ tsp. paprika
1½ tsp. salt	¼ tsp. red pepper
½ tsp. black pepper	½ tsp. chili powder
2 sliced onions	1 cup catsup
2 Tbsp. vinegar	¾ cup water
2 Tbsp. Worcestershire sauce	

Place ribs in a roaster; sprinkle with salt and pepper and cover with onion. Mix sauce ingredients; pour sauce over ribs, cover and bake at 350° for 1½ hours. Baste occasionally, turning ribs once or twice. Remove cover the last 15 minutes of baking. Replace onions if fallen off and brown ribs.

Patti Feuerhelm, St. Charles

BARBECUED SPARE RIBS

3 lbs. spareribs	1 med. onion, sliced
Water	½ cup bottled barbecue sauce
1 Tbsp. salt	¼ cup dark corn syrup
1 Tbsp. mixed pickling spices	

Cut ribs in serving-sized pieces and place in large kettle. Cover with water; add salt, pickling spices and sliced onion. Heat water to boiling. Lower heat; cover and simmer ribs for 1 hour. Remove from heat and allow ribs to cool in liquid. When ready to broil ribs, remove ribs from water and arrange in single layer on rack in broiler pan. (Put some water on the bottom of pan.) Combine barbecue sauce and syrup in a cup. Brush over ribs. Broil 4 inches from heat, turning and basting often, 20 minutes or until ribs are evenly coated. Serves 6 to 8.

Helen Shaw, Winona

BARBECUE SAUCE FOR RIBS

1 (6 oz.) can tomato paste	¼ tsp. cinnamon
¾ cups water	1 tsp. chili powder
3 Tbsp. vinegar	1 tsp. salt
4 Tbsp. grated onions	½ tsp. pepper
2 Tbsp. Worcestershire sauce	½ cup sugar
1 tsp. paprika	Dash of ground cloves

Simmer until well blended. Pour over ribs that have been brought to a boil, then simmered in salted water for about an hour until nearly tender. Bake at 350° for 20 minutes, basting the sauce over the ribs a few times. Covers 6 large country pork ribs.

Fran Timmers, St. Paul

BARBECUED STEAK

1 cup ketchup	1½ Tbsp. prepared mustard
½ cup water	1 Tbsp. brown sugar
¼ cup vinegar	½ tsp. salt
¼ cup chopped green pepper	⅛ tsp. pepper
¼ cup chopped onion	4 lbs. round steak, cut in pieces

Combine all ingredients, except round steak, in a saucepan. Bring to a boil, then simmer gently 5 minutes over low heat. Keep hot. Cut round steak in serving size pieces. Place in roasting pan. Pour hot barbecue sauce over meat. It is alright to layer meat, but make sure sauce covers all pieces. Cover tightly and bake at 325° for 1½ to 2 hours or until meat is fork tender. Serves 8 to 10.

Myrna Surprenant, Currie

BEEF BRISKET

2 lg. onions	1 cup brown sugar
1 (4 to 6 lb.) fresh beef brisket	1 bottle Bennett's chili sauce

Put one sliced onion in the bottom of roaster. Place brisket on top of onion slices. Season to taste. Add second sliced onion over top of brisket. Mix brown sugar and chili sauce; pour over top. Seal roaster with foil and bake at 300° to 325° for 3 or 4 hours. Use sauce for gravy.

Veronica Robbie, International Falls

CALIFORNIA CASSEROLE

Coat **2 pounds (bite sized) round steak** with ⅓ **cup flour** and 1 **teaspoon paprika**. Brown meat thoroughly in ¼ **cup oil**. Add 1 **cup water**. Simmer 30 minutes until tender. Transfer to large baking dish. Heat **1 can cream of chicken soup in** the pan where you browned the meat. Blend in **2 cups water** gradually. Bring to a boil, stirring constantly, and combine with meat. Add **1 can small onions**, drained.

Butter Crumb Dumplings:

2 cups flour	1 tsp. dry onion flakes
4 tsp. baking powder	1 tsp. poppy seed
½ tsp. salt	¼ cup salad oil
1 tsp. poultry seasoning	1 cup milk
1 tsp. celery seed	

Combine flour, baking powder, salt and poultry seasoning; stir in celery seed, onion flakes and poppy seed. Add salad oil and milk. Stir until moistened. Drop teaspoon size into **cup of melted butter**; roll into **1 cup bread crumbs**. Bake, uncovered at 425° for 20 to 25 minutes.

Cecelia Raleigh, St. Paul

CHILI RELLENO CASSEROLE

1 lb. ground beef round steak	1½ cups grated Cheddar
½ cup chopped onion	cheese
Salt and pepper to taste	1½ cups milk
2 (4 oz.) cans green chilies,	½ cup flour
diced	4 eggs, beaten

Brown meat and onion; drain fat. Season with salt and pepper. Spread half of chilies in a 7x10 inch pan or baking dish. Sprinkle with cheese and top with meat mixture. Combine milk and flour; mix well. Add to beaten eggs and pour over meat. Top with remaining chilies. Bake at 350° for 45 to 50 minutes or until knife inserted comes out clean. May serve with salsa. Serves 8.

Barbara Tomassoni, Eveleth
District Deputy, 1994-present

BEEF AND POTATO SALAD DIJON**

¾ lb. all-purpose potatoes	½ cup coarsely ground onion
¾ lb. cooked lean beef, sliced	2½ Tbsp. chopped fresh parsley
⅛ inch thick and cut into	Mixed salad greens
1 inch wide strips	

Cut potatoes into 1 inch pieces; place in saucepan and cover with cold water. Bring to a boil; cover and simmer 10 to 12 minutes or until tender. Drain potatoes.

Mustard Dressing:

¼ cup coarse-grain or regular	1½ Tbsp. white wine vinegar
Dijon-style mustard	¼ tsp. salt
2 Tbsp. vegetable oil	¼ tsp. pepper

Combine ingredients in a large bowl. Add hot potatoes to dressing; toss gently to coat, then cool. Add beef, onion and parsley to potato mixture, mixing lightly. Serve immediately or cover and refrigerate. To serve, arrange salad greens on serving platter; top with beef mixture. Makes 4 (1½ cup) servings. Total preparation and cooking time is 30 minutes.

Ruth Driscoll, Blue Earth

STEAK BITS AND GRAVY

2 Tbsp. oil	4 cups water
1 (2 lb.) steak, cut into bite size	4 beef bouillon cubes or equal
pieces	amount of other beef soup
1 cup grated carrots	base
1 Tbsp. dehydrated onions	Thickening for gravy

Heat oil and brown steak. Add carrots, onions, water and soup base; simmer 20 to 30 minutes. Thicken liquid for gravy. Serve with potatoes, rice or noodles. Sour cream may be added for flavor.

Dorothy Doll, Perham

PEPPER STEAK

1½ lbs. round steak	2 to 3 Tbsp. soy sauce
1 (10½ oz.) can French onion soup	1 tsp. pepper
	1 Tbsp. cornstarch
1 (14 oz.) can whole tomatoes	¼ cup water
1 green pepper, seeded and cut up	Hot cooked rice or mashed potatoes

Cut round steak into thin strips. In skillet, cook and stir beef strips until no longer pink. Add soup and liquid from tomatoes; simmer 30 minutes. Add green pepper; simmer 15 minutes. Cut tomatoes into quarters; add soy sauce and pepper. In a small bowl, combine cornstarch and water; stir into meat mixture. Heat and stir until mixture boils and thickens. Serve over rice.

Kay Miller, Crookston

PEPPY PEPPER STEAK

1 lb. lean round steak	1 green pepper, cut into strips
¼ cup cooking oil	1 can beef bouillon
½ tsp. salt	3 Tbsp. cornstarch
Dash of pepper	⅔ cup water
¼ cup chopped onion	1 Tbsp. soy sauce
1 cup sliced celery	2 cups cooked converted rice

In large skillet, brown strips of round steaks in cooking oil. Cover and simmer 15 minutes. Add salt, pepper, onion, celery, and green pepper. Cook until tender. Add beef bouillon. Combine cornstarch and water. Add small amount of meat sauce to cornstarch mixture, then add to meat sauce. Add soy sauce. Cover and bake at 350° for 30 minutes. Serve over rice.

Edna Hanson, Blue Earth

SALISBURY STEAK

1 (10¾ oz.) can condensed golden mushroom soup	½ tsp. salt
	⅛ tsp. pepper
1½ lbs. ground beef	1 onion, finely chopped
½ cup dry bread or cracker crumbs	1 egg, slightly beaten
	⅓ cup water

Heat oven to 350°. In medium bowl, combine ¼ of soup with remaining ingredients except water; mix well. Shape into 6 patties; arrange in single layer in a 9x13 inch or an 8x12 inch baking dish. Bake, uncovered, for 30 minutes. Skim off fat. In small bowl, combine remaining soup and water; spoon over patties. Return to oven and bake for 10 minutes. If desired, garnish with mushroom slices. Makes 6 servings.

Jeannette Malterer, Waseca

REST-A-LOT-STEW

2 lbs. beef stew meat, cubed
4 cups thickly cut carrots
4 cups thickly cubed potatoes
1 lg. onion, quartered
1 can cream of mushroom soup
½ cup water
Salt and pepper

Brown meat, if desired, in small amount of oil. Place with remaining ingredients in medium casserole with tight fitting lid. Place in a 275° oven for 4 to 5 hours.

Arleen Borden, International Falls

OVEN BEEF STEW

2 lbs. stewing meat, not browned
2 cups cubed carrots
2 cups cut up potatoes
2 cups celery
4 sm. onions
1 slice bread, torn in pieces
3 Tbsp. minute tapioca
1 Tbsp. sugar
2 cans whole or stewed tomatoes
(med. size), or 1 (12 oz.) can
V-8 juice
1 Tbsp. salt
½ tsp. pepper
⅛ tsp. ginger
¼ tsp. cinnamon

Place all ingredients in a large kettle or roaster. Bake at 250° for 5 hours. Keep covered but stir occasionally.

Lennett (Wegsheid) Savchuk, Wilmar
State Publicity Chair, 1991-1993
Regina Olson, Perham
Mary Lou Petit, Plainview

BEEF STROGANOFF

1 lg. sweet onion, sliced into
¼ inch slices
1 clove garlic, minced
1 lb. mushrooms, sliced thick
1 lb. linguine or noodles
12 oz. lean beef, cut into 1½x1
inch strips
3 Tbsp. flour
1 cup beef bouillon or beef
stock
1 cup nonfat sour cream
Pepper
Parsley

Cook onion, garlic and mushrooms in ½ inch of water in non-stick skillet, adding more water if necessary, over medium heat until partially done, about 4 minutes. Meanwhile, cook pasta until al dente. Add beef strips to vegetables and cook until meat is done to desired degree. Mix flour with beef stock or bouillon. Add to beef mixture and stir until thickens. Add sour cream and stir in until just heated. Serve hot over pasta and sprinkle pepper and parsley on top for garnish.

Andrea Olsen, Waseca

BEEF STEW

2½ lbs. stew meat or 1 (3 lb.) roast
2 Tbsp. tapioca
1 can golden mushroom soup
½ env. dry Lipton onion soup mix
2 potatoes
4 to 5 carrots
4 to 5 sm. whole onions

Place meat in casserole or crock pot. Sprinkle with tapioca. Add the mushroom soup. Sprinkle with dry onion soup mix. Cover casserole and bake at 325° for 3 hours. If using crock pot, cook on low for 6 hours, adding vegetables at start. In oven, add vegetables after 3 hours, baking 1 hour longer.

Veronica Doherty, Adrian

NO NAME HOT DISH

2 lbs. stew meat
1 lg. onion, diced
2 cups celery, sliced
1 can mushroom soup
½ can water
4 Tbsp. soy sauce
1 cup Minute Rice
3 Tbsp. brown sugar
1 can bean sprouts and liquid
1 can mushrooms

Saute meat, onion and celery until meat is brown, then mix with the remaining ingredients in a casserole or baking dish. Bake at 350° for 45 minutes to 1 hour. Can be made the day before.

Rose Guillemette, Mankato
State Regent, 1984-1986

NOODLE STRUDEL

1 (10 oz.) pkg. wide egg noodles
3 eggs, beaten
2 lbs. small curd creamed cottage cheese
1 cup sugar
1 cup sour cream
1½ cups golden raisins
Buttered graham cracker crumbs

Cook and drain noodles; add to well beaten eggs and stir to coat noodles. Combine remaining ingredients, except crumbs, with noodles. Put in greased 9x13 inch pan. Smooth top with spatula and sprinkle with a good amount of buttered graham cracker crumbs. Cover with foil and bake at 350° for 1 hour. Can be served warm or cold. When cold, it cuts nicely into small squares and is a good side dish to bring for pot luck.

Marcella Kilbride, Eveleth

TACOS

1 cup flour
1 cup cornmeal
5 Tbsp. cornstarch
Pinch of salt
2 cups milk
2 eggs

Mix dry ingredients; add milk and eggs. Fry in skillet like pancakes.

Lil Beaumont, St. Peter

CREAMY TUNA RICE

1 cup water	1½ cups uncooked rice
½ cup milk	1 can tuna
¼ tsp. salt	½ tsp. dill weed
6 slices American process cheese	2 Tbsp. parsley, optional

Bring water, milk and salt to a boil. Add cheese slices and stir until melted. Add rest of ingredients and stir. Remove from heat and let stand 15 minutes or until liquid is absorbed. Stir. Serves 4.

Marie Maslowski, Red Wing

QUICK FIXIN TUNA CASSEROLE

½ cup milk	1 (16 oz.) pkg. frozen gemelli pasta
¼ cup water	
2 Tbsp. flour	1 (6½ oz.) can tuna, drained
2 tsp. sliced green onions	Herb seasoning
Frozen peas, carrots and onion	Potato chips, coarsely crushed

In small bowl, combine milk, water and flour; blend well. In a large skillet, combine milk mixture, green onions and frozen vegetables with pasta; bring to a boil and stir in tuna. Cover and cook over low heat 1 minute or until thoroughly heated. Transfer to serving dish. Sprinkle with potato chips. Serve immediately.

Erma Christ, Winona

TUNA-CHEESE CASSEROLE

1 (7¼ oz.) box Flavo-Rite macaroni and cheese with mild white Cheddar cheese	1 (4 oz.) can button mushrooms
	¼ cup chopped celery
	¼ cup chopped onion
1 (10½ oz.) cream of celery soup	1 or 2 Tbsp. cooking oil
1 (6½ oz.) can tuna in water, drained	Buttered bread crumbs or crushed cereal, optional

Cook the macaroni and cheese according to directions on the box. Drain and add the cream of celery soup and drained tuna. Saute the mushrooms, chopped celery and onions in the oil in a small fry pan until tender crisp. Combine the two mixtures in a 1½ or 2 quart casserole and heat in microwave until bubbly. Or the casserole could be topped with the bread crumbs or crushed cereal and heated in a conventional oven at 350° for about 30 minutes until hot, and crumbs are brown.

Dorothea A. Hadlick, Delavan
State Treasurer, 1980-1984
District Deputy, 1972-1978

SURPRISE POTATO TUNA BAKE

2 (7 oz.) cans tuna	1 (10 oz.) can cream of mush-
3 (2¼ oz.) cans shoe string	room soup
potatoes	1 (3 oz.) can mushrooms
1 (14½ oz.) can evaporated	1 (4 oz.) can or jar pimentos
milk	

Don't add any salt as potatoes and soup are seasoned. Mix all ingredients and bake in a well greased 2 quart casserole at 375° for 45 minutes.

Variation: Can substitute 1 (1 lb.) can salmon, if you haven't tuna; or can substitute 2 cups cooked chicken and use 1 can cream of chicken soup instead of mushroom soup.

Lorna Sexton, Waseca

TUNA HOT DISH

1 can cream of mushroom soup	1 green pepper, chopped
1 can cream of chicken soup	1 cup mayonnaise
1 (4 oz.) pkg. noodles	1 sm. jar pimentos
2 cans tuna (I use white albacore)	1 can asparagus
1 sm. can mushrooms	¼ lb. sharp shredded cheese

Mix the soups. Cook noodles according to package directions. Add tuna and cooked noodles to the soup mixture. Place in a greased 9x13 inch pan (this is the bottom layer). Mix mushrooms, green pepper, and mayonnaise; add pimento. Place in layer above soup mixture. Drain asparagus and layer on above mixture in casserole. Top with the shredded cheese. Bake at 350° for 1 hour. Serves 10.

Cleota Platt, Slayton

TURKEY OR CHICKEN CASSEROLE

1 cup diced onion	3 cups turkey or chicken, cut up
¾ cup diced green pepper	1 (4 oz.) can mushrooms
1 cup diced celery	1 can chow mein noodles
½ cup margarine	½ cup sliced almonds
3 cans cream of chicken or	
celery soup, or combination	

Saute onions, green pepper and celery in margarine. Mix the soups with the meat and mushrooms and add to the sauteed vegetables. Line a 9x13 inch pan with noodles. Add meat and vegetable mixture. Sprinkle almonds on top. Bake at 350° for 40 minutes.

Mary Pytleski, Fairmont

TURKEY CROUTON HOT DISH

1½ pkgs. seasoned croutons	½ cup onions
1 cup melted butter	2 eggs
1 cup water	1½ cups milk
4 cups diced turkey or chicken	1 can cream of chicken soup
½ cup celery	Shredded cheese

Mix the croutons, melted butter and water. Add turkey, celery and onions. Beat eggs lightly; add milk. Mix into the crouton mixture and pour into a 9x13 inch pan. Cover with foil and refrigerate overnight. Spread the cream of chicken soup on top and bake, uncovered, for 40 minutes. Sprinkle with cheese and bake 10 minutes more.

Mary L. Pagnac, Argyle

TURKEY NOODLE BAKE

2 cups chopped celery	1 can cream of mushroom soup
1 lg. onion, chopped	1 can chicken broth
¾ cup chopped green pepper	1 tsp. Worcestershire sauce
1 sm. can mushrooms, drained	1 lb. Polish noodles
1 sm. jar pimento, drained	3 to 4 cups cooked chicken or
½ can sliced water chestnuts	turkey
¾ cup oleo or butter	½ lb. grated cheese

Combine first 6 ingredients; cook until slightly crisp. Combine soup with broth; add to vegetables. Add Worcestershire sauce. Cook noodles and rinse. Layer noodles, chicken, vegetable mixture, and cheese in that order in greased casserole Cover and bake at 300° to 325° for 1 to 1½ hours. Uncover last 15 minutes.

Marie M. Fier, New Ulm

TURKEY TETRAZZINI

1 lb. spaghetti, uncooked	2 cups water
½ cup chopped onion	1 lb. shredded cheese
1 clove garlic	2 lbs. diced cooked turkey
1 Tbsp. butter	¼ cup chopped pimento
4 cans mushroom soup	

Cook spaghetti in boiling salted water until just tender, but not soft; drain. Cook onion and garlic in butter until tender. Blend in soup and water; stir until smooth. Add half of cheese. Cook over low heat until cheese is melted, stirring occasionally. Fold in turkey and pimento. Put spaghetti into greased baking pan and pour turkey mixture over it. Sprinkle on remaining cheese. Bake at 450° until sauce bubbles and browns.

Alice Miller, Caledonia

TURKEY CHILI

1 lb. lean ground raw turkey
  breast
1 cup chopped celery
1 (16 oz.) can stewed tomatoes
1 (8 oz.) can tomato sauce
1 (6 oz.) can vegetable juice
  cocktail
2 (16 oz.) cans red kidney
  beans, drained

1 bay leaf
2 Tbsp. dried minced onion
1 tsp. dried basil, crushed
½ tsp. instant beef bouillon
  granules
½ tsp. ground cumin
¼ tsp. garlic powder
¼ tsp. crushed pepper, optional
Toasted pita chips, optional

Spray a cold large skillet with nonstick coating. Add turkey and celery. Cook until turkey is no longer pink, stirring to break up pieces. Stir in tomatoes, tomato sauce, juice cocktail, beans, herbs, seasonings, and ½ **cup water**. Bring to boiling; reduce heat. Simmer, uncovered, for 20 minutes, stirring occasionally. Discard bay leaf. Serve with toasted pita chips if desired. Makes 4 servings, with 380 calories per serving and 4 g fat. Low cholesterol recipe.

Marge Olson, Eveleth

TURKEY SUPREME

1 (8 oz.) pkg. seasoned dressing
1 cup water
1 stick margarine
3 cups turkey or chicken,
  cooked and chopped
½ cup chopped onion
3 green onions, cut

½ cup chopped celery
½ cup mayonnaise
¾ tsp. salt
2 eggs
1½ cups milk
1 can cream of mushroom soup
1 to 1½ cups grated cheese

Mix dressing, water and margarine. Place half in a 9x13 inch pan; pat down firm. Mix meat, onions, celery, mayonnaise and salt. Spread on stuffing. Top with remaining stuffing. Beat eggs; blend with milk and pour over mixture. Cover with foil and refrigerate overnight. Take out of refrigerator 1 hour before baking. Spread with soup. Bake, uncovered, at 325° for 40 minutes. Sprinkle with cheese and bake 10 minutes longer.

Dorothy Iraci, International Falls

HONEY WALLEYE

1 egg
2 tsp. honey
2 cups butter flavored crackers,
  crushed (about 45 to 50)

½ tsp. salt
4 to 6 (1½ to 2 lb.) walleye fillets
⅓ to ½ cup cooking oil
Lemon wedges, optional

In a shallow bowl, beat egg; add honey. In a plastic bag, combine crackers and salt. Dip fish in egg mixture, then shake in bag until coated. In a skillet, cook fillets in oil for 3 to 5 minutes per side or until golden and fish flakes easily with a fork. Serve with lemon wedges if desired. Yield: 4 to 6 servings.

Diane Gauthier, Eveleth

VENISON OR BEEF JERKY

3 lbs. venison or beef, sliced,
  cubed or shaved
Salt and pepper to taste

1 lg. jar Teriyaki sauce
¾ cup soy sauce

Freeze meat. Remove from freezer, thaw half way (meat is easier to cut, slice or cube if it still has some frost within). Prepare meat. After meat is cut up, lay in a marinating pan flat. Make 1 layer of meat, cover with sauce. Make second layer of meat, cover with sauce. Repeat until meat and sauce are all used up. Marinate 24 to 36 hours. Place in refrigerator. Stir your meat or flip your marinating container every 12 hours. Place the meat in a food dehydrator for 24 to 48 hours, depending on the thickness of your meat.

Ruth Ann Block, Waterville

WILD GAME BEAN BAKE

1 lb. venison or moose
  hamburger, browned
1 chopped onion
½ cup chopped celery
½ lb. cut up bacon or side pork,
  browned slightly

1 (28 oz.) can Bush's baked
  beans
1 ring venison or moose bologna
  or Polish sausage

Brown hamburger, onions and celery. Add browned bacon or side pork. Put baked beans in a large baking dish; add hamburger mixture. Next, fold in diagonally sliced sausages. Bake at 350° for about 1 hour or until it gets heated through and thick. Serve with biscuits or fresh bread.

Monica Beauchane, Red Lake Falls

SHELLEY'S TERIYAKI VENISON STIR-FRY

Marinade:
½ cup soy sauce
½ cup beer
1 clove garlic, chopped fine

2 Tbsp. finely chopped onion
1/8 tsp. ground ginger
½ tsp. sugar

Pour marinade over **2 pounds venison steak**, cut into 2x½ inch strips. Cover and let sit for at least 3 hours, or refrigerate overnight. Drain meat; save liquid. Put 1 tablespoons oil in wok or fry pan; heat on high 4 minutes. Put half of meat in pan; stir-fry 2 minutes or until brown. Push to side and do same to remaining meat. Put heat on low; pour ½ cup marinade in pan and simmer, covered, stirring occasionally for 20 to 30 minutes. Add additional marinade as needed.

Norena Guerard, International Falls

"FAVORITE OLDIES"

BEEF STROGANOFF

1 lb. ground beef	½ cup raw rice
1 cup chopped celery	1 can dried chow mein noodles
½ cup onion	1½ cups water
1 can cream of mushroom soup	2 Tbsp. soy sauce
1 can cream of chicken soup	

Brown beef, celery and onions. Add remaining ingredients and pour into a buttered 2 quart casserole. Sprinkle top with crushed potato chips. No salt or pepper, soup will take care of it. Bake at 350° for 1½ hours or cook rice first; shortens baking time. Serves 8.

Ann Reff, International Falls

SAUSAGE AND RICE CASSEROLE

1 lb. bulk sausage or hamburger	1½ cups milk
¾ cup chopped celery	¼ cup chopped green pepper
½ cup chopped onion	3 to 4 Tbsp. soy sauce
½ cup raw rice	Salt and pepper to taste
1 can mushroom soup	

Fry hamburger or sausage until grease can be poured off. Add celery and onion; cook a few minutes. Mix all ingredients. Bake in a casserole at 350° for 1½ hours. Stir occasionally the first 40 minutes. Tuna may be used in place of sausage with equally good results.

Alice Ditsch, International Falls

BAR-B-QUE RIBS

½ cup catsup or tomato paste	1½ tsp. salt
¼ tsp. Tabasco sauce or	⅛ tsp. chili powder
Worcestershire sauce	½ tsp. prepared mustard
1 cup water	2 sliced onions
1 tsp. brown sugar	

Mix all ingredients and pour over ribs; if not moist enough, add more water or make more sauce and pour over ribs. Bake until ribs are done and sauce has boiled down and thick sauce is over ribs. Baste often. Bake, covered, at 375° for 1½ to 2 hours.

Emilee Schultz, International Falls

✞ EDUCATION ✞

Education provides an opportunity for our young people to share their God-given talents and for adults to advance their own education and share their life experiences.

Scholarships may be given by Local and State Courts at the Elementary and High School level. Criteria for awarding scholarships may be based on qualities other than scholastic achievement, such as Christian service, leadership abilities or community service. Scholarships are also available from National CDA for National Graduate, NCEA in Special Education and Youth/JCDA.

Local courts sponsor the Education Contest which is divided into three age groups and four categories. The categories are Art, Poetry, Essay, and Poster. Directions and guidelines for the contest originate with the National CDA Board so all local CDA Courts follow the same criteria. Each contest has two themes which the students may choose between when preparing their entry. First place winners of local contests advance to the State contest, and First place winners at the State level advance to the National Contest. Prizes are awarded at each level.

Religious Education is an area that can involve youth by their participation in and assistance with Catechesis, Field Trips and Retreats. Adults can grow spiritually by leading and participating in Study Groups, Retreats, Marriage Encounters and Formation Programs which would include Encyclicals and Pastoral Letters. Families should be encouraged to visit historical places, Shrines and Museums.

Youth and adults can volunteer to work with local literacy programs, tutoring in school, mentoring younger students, reading to children or becoming a "classroom helper, parent or grandparent".

There are many ways to keep educating ourselves and our families, and to share skills and knowledge with others who can benefit from that sharing.

Zonda Befort, *past* **State Education Chair**

✝ NATIONAL PROJECTS ✝

The projects give each Catholic Daughter the opportunity to demonstrate the love and charity she feels toward the less fortunate in our society and the world at large, it also represents a response to Christ's call to us - His servants.

APOSTLESHIP OF THE SEA provides services (spiritual, physical and psychological) to foreign seamen at US port locations in the Great Lakes, Gulf of Mexico and the Atlantic and Pacific Oceans. Seamen Centers and chaplains provide safe havens after months on the world's waters. In addition to monetary contributions, Christmas boxes filled with personal hygiene items, stationary supplies and holiday goodies are delivered from all parts of the country.

COVENANT HOUSES are located in Alaska, New Jersey, Florida, California, Texas, Louisiana, New York, Washington DC, Ontario, Mexico, Honduras and Guatemala providing a place of safety to our nation's troubled teens. Catholic Daughters support the advocacy rights and welfare of children.

DISASTER FUND at times of natural disasters, such as earthquakes and floods, monetary donations are sent to the Bishops where such disasters occur.

FATHER PEYTON - THE FAMILY ROSARY We have financially assisted this mission to bring the rosary to many individuals through television produced by Father Peyton and the Family Theater Production. Thousands of rosaries have been made by members for distribution all over the world. Father Peyton's motto: *"The family that prays together-stays together"* is demonstrated by CDA families across the country.

HEALTH AND LIFE and Catholic Relief Services is our interntaional project with a goal to remedy medical tragedies that afflict the poorest of the poor.

MOTHER THERESA and her Missionaries of Charity have long been a favorite of CDA members. These women are true examples of life and love 'taking care of the least of His brethren'.

SCHOLARSHIPS FOR TEACHERS OF EXCEPTIONAL CHILDREN is conducted in cooperation with the Special Education Department of the National Education Association where $1,000 scholarships are awarded annually to teachers working with special children.

SOAR (SUPPORT OUR AGING RELIGIOUS) originated in 1986 with a $25,000 contribution in seed money for this organization. Grants for capital improvements are awarded for updating wiring, fire alarms, new furnace systems, other building refurbishing, vans, health equipment to these individuals who have devoted their lives to us.

Through donations to these national projects by our courts across the country, we have even greater impact in demonstrating our motto.. "IN UNITY & CHARITY".   – Lois M. Nelson, 1st Vice State Regent

* * SALADS * *

ACINI DE PEPE SALAD (PASTA)

1 (16 oz.) pkg. Acini de Pepe
1 cup sugar
2 Tbsp. flour
½ tsp. salt
1¾ cups pineapple juice
2 eggs, beaten
1 Tbsp. lemon juice
3 (11 oz.) cans mandarin
  oranges, drained

2 (20 oz.) cans chunk pineapple,
  drained
1 (20 oz.) can crushed pineapple, drained
1 (9 oz.) carton whipped
  topping
1 cup miniature marshmallows,
  optional
1 cup coconut, optional

Cook Acini in 3 quart boiling salted water. Drain, rinse and cool. Combine sugar, flour, salt and gradually stir in pineapple juice and eggs. Cook over medium heat until thick; add lemon juice, and cool to room temperature. Combine cooled mixtures, mix lightly and refrigerate overnight in airtight container. Next morning, add fruits and topping and mix thoroughly. Refrigerate again in air-tight container until well chilled. May stay for as long as a week. Also can freeze, but it changes texture. Serves 25.

Loretta Nemanick, Eveleth

FROZEN APPLE SALAD

1 (9 oz.) can crushed pineapple
2 beaten eggs
½ cup sugar
Dash of salt

3 Tbsp. lemon juice
2 cups unpared apple, finely
  diced
½ cup celery, finely diced
1 cup heavy cream, whipped

Drain pineapple, reserving syrup; add water to syrup to make ½ cup. Combine eggs, sugar, salt, lemon juice and syrup mixture. Cook over low heat, stirring constantly, until thick. Chill. Fold in pineapple, apple, celery and whipped cream. Makes 1 large mold or 2 small molds. Freeze until firm. Keeps 2 or 3 months in freezer.

Mary Powers, Moorhead

SWEDISH APPLE SALAD

2 cups apple, diced
½ cup celery, chopped
2 cups shredded cabbage
¾ cup green grapes

¼ tsp. salt
2 Tbsp. sugar
½ cup plain yogurt

Combine apple, celery, cabbage and grapes. Combine salt, sugar and yogurt. Mix and refrigerate.

Jeanne Reck Sula, Winona

ALMOND SALAD

1 (2¼ oz.) bag sliced almonds   1 can mandarin oranges
½ cup water   ¼ cup green onions, chopped
2 Tbsp. sugar   ¼ cup celery
Head of lettuce

Under low heat, fry almonds in water and sugar. Continue frying until water is almost absorbed, stirring frequently. Toss lettuce, mandarin oranges, green onions, and celery in salad bowl.

Dressing:
¼ cup oil   ½ tsp. salt
2 Tbsp. vinegar   ½ tsp. pepper
2 Tbsp. sugar   2 tsp. parsley

Combine ingredients; add fried almond mixture and stir. Add to salad greens and toss. May be served warm or cool.

Cheri Zattoni, Eveleth

APRICOT FLUFF

2 (3 oz.) boxes apricot jello   2 lg. jars baby food apricots
2 cups hot water   puree
¼ cup sugar   1 (8 oz.) pkg. cream cheese,
1 (16 oz.) can crushed pineapple   softened
    with juice   1 lg. carton Cool Whip

Dissolve jello in hot water; add sugar. Bring mixture to a boil. Add crushed pineapple with juice and baby apricot puree. Cool mixture to room temperature. Whip mixture into softened cream cheese. Blend until smooth. Fold in Cool Whip. Let set in refrigerator for several hours or overnight. You can garnish this in many ways: with mandarin oranges, cherries, mint leaves, etc. To lower sugar and fat, use sugar free jello, lite cheese and Cool Whip.

Variation: Mary skips the baby food and adds 3 tablespoons milk to the cream cheese.

Jean Bierly, Blue Earth
Mary Condon, Medford
Lucille Taylor, Adrian

APRICOT JELLO SALAD

1 (6 oz.) pkg. apricot jello   1 cup plain yogurt
1½ cups boiling water   2 cups Cool Whip
1 can apricots, drained

Dissolve jello in boiling water. Add water to drained apricot juice to make 1 cup; add to jello. Cool jello. Puree apricots; add to cool jello with yogurt and Cool Whip. Let set in refrigerator.

Joyce Kerrigan, Winona

COTTAGE CHEESE APRICOT SALAD

1 pkg. lemon jello	½ cup walnuts, coarsely
1 cup boiling water	chopped
1 cup apricot juice	½ cup maraschino cherries
1 sm. carton cottage cheese	1 cup sliced apricots
1 (12 oz.) carton whipping cream, whipped or Cool Whip	

Dissolve jello in hot water with juice. Chill until partially set. Fold in cottage cheese, whipped cream (or Cool Whip), walnuts, cherries and apricots. Garnish with apricot slices if desired. Serves 8.

Dorothy Kubicek, Owatonna

BACON-CAULIFLOWER SALAD

1 head lettuce	1 onion
½ head cauliflower	1 lb. bacon

Break lettuce and cauliflower in pieces. Section onion into rings. Fry bacon and cut up. Layer in order listed above.

Dressing:

¼ cup sugar	⅓ cup Parmesan cheese
1 cup mayonnaise	Salt and pepper to taste

Mix and spread over the top of salad. Cover tightly for several hours or overnight until ready to serve. Mix well before serving.

Rozie Ochry, Detroit Lakes
District Deputy, 1988-1992

SWEET SOUR BEANS ON LETTUCE

Fresh picked green or yellow beans	1 Tbsp. flour
	1 Tbsp. sugar
2 to 3 slices bacon, cut up	2 Tbsp. vinegar
⅓ cup chopped onion	Pepper
1 Tbsp. chopped green pepper, optional	Leaf lettuce

Cut beans in small pieces and cook in small amount of lightly salted water. (Do not overcook.) Fry bacon pieces until crisp. Remove bacon onto paper towel. Pour off grease, saving ½ tablespoon to saute onion and green pepper. Sprinkle flour and sugar over onions and mix well, stirring steadily while adding bean water and vinegar (adjust amount of pepper and sugar to your taste). Cook until consistency of syrup. Add bacon and beans. Serve over a bed of leaf lettuce. For a full meal dish, add boiled diced potatoes along with beans.

Esther Palubicki, Perham
State Treasurer, 1970-1974
State First Vice Regent, 1976-1978
State Regent, 1978-1980

SALADS, SOUPS & SANDWICHES

431

BEAN SALAD

1 can peas, drained
1 can French cut green beans, drained
1 can wax beans
1 can kidney beans

2 cups diced celery
1 lg. green pepper, diced
1 onion, sliced
2 sm. jars pimento
1 tsp. salt

Mix all ingredients, except salt, then add salt.

Dressing:
1 cup vinegar
1½ cups sugar

½ cup Wesson oil

Shake dressing well. Pour over vegetables and allow to sit overnight. Drain well before serving.

Jeanette Kruger, Plainview
Diana Killian, Iron

GARDEN BEAN SALAD

1 (16 oz.) can cut green beans
2 (17 oz.) cans lima beans
1 (16 oz.) can kidney beans
1 (16 oz.) can wax beans
1 (15 oz.) can garbanzo beans
1 lg. green pepper, chopped
3 celery stalks, chopped

1 (2 oz.) jar sliced pimento, drained
1 bunch green onions, sliced
2 cups vinegar
2 cups sugar
½ cup water
1 tsp. salt

Drain all cans of beans; place in a large bowl. Add green pepper, celery, pimento and green onions; set aside. Bring remaining ingredients to a boil in a heavy saucepan; boil for 5 minutes. Remove from heat and immediately pour over vegetables. Refrigerate several hours or overnight. Serves 12 to 16.

Mary Ann Spieker, Lismore
Gladys Boucher, Crookston

BLUEBERRY SALAD

2 (3 oz.) pkgs. blackberry jello
2 cups boiling water
1 sm. can crushed pineapple

1 can blueberries
1 cup pineapple and blueberry juice, combined
1 env. Dream Whip

Dissolve jello in water. Drain juice from pineapple and blueberries and add to jello mixture. Reserve ½ cup of dissolved jello. Add fruits to remainder of jello; pour into an 8x8 inch pan and let set. Prepare Dream Whip according to package directions. Blend in reserved jello. Spread on top of salad.

Betty Cramer, Pipestone
Edith Wittrock, Waseca
Madelyn Tauer, Plainview

432

BLT IN A BOWL SALAD

1 head Iceberg lettuce	2 hard cooked eggs, sliced
Mustard Dressing (below)	4 slices bacon, halved and
1 cup sliced fresh mushrooms	cooked crisp
½ cup thinly sliced radish	2 sm. tomatoes, cut into wedges
½ cup chopped sweet red onion	

Core, rinse and thoroughly drain lettuce; chill in disposable plastic. Prepare mustard dressing. Shortly before serving, line 4 individual serving bowls with a few outer lettuce leaves. Cut remaining lettuce into bite size chunks to measure 2 quarts. Combine with mushrooms, radish and onion. Divide among the 4 bowls. Top with egg slices and bacon strips. Garnish with tomato wedges. Serve at once with mustard dressing. Makes 4 servings.

Mustard Dressing:

½ cup oil	1 tsp. chopped parsley
¼ cup vinegar	½ tsp. celery salt
1 Tbsp. sugar	¼ tsp. onion powder
1 tsp. prepared mustard	¼ tsp. fresh garlic

Combine all ingredients in a jar. Cover and shake well to blend. Shake again just before serving. Makes ¾ cup dressing.

Agnes Joens, Wilmont
District Deputy, 1974-1978

BROCCOLI SALAD

Dressing:

1 cup mayonnaise	⅓ cup sugar
2 Tbsp. cider vinegar	

Mix and let set overnight or a few hours.

1 bunch broccoli flowerets	½ lb. bacon, fried crisp and cut
½ cup slivered almonds	up fine
1 cup diced celery	1 cup raisins
½ lb. green grapes	1 cup sunflower seeds
½ lb. red grapes	

Mix and add to dressing.

Shirley Ettestad, International Falls
Joyce Clemens, Eyota
Gladys Boucher, Crookston
Helen Laren, Mankato
Lori Maas, Medford
Uraula Kellen, Iona

BROCCOLI SALAD

3 bunches broccoli	1 (2¼ oz.) pkg. sliced almonds
½ onion	1 cup raisins
1 cup celery, chopped	1 Tbsp. real bacon bits
1 cup seedless green grapes	

Break broccoli into small clusters. Chop onion and celery. Slice green grapes and mix all ingredients.

Dressing:

1 cup lite mayonnaise	⅓ cup sugar
1 Tbsp. vinegar	1 tsp. lemon juice

Mix and pour over salad.

Dolores Fath, Wilmont

BROCCOLI SALAD

1 bunch broccoli, chopped fine	¾ cup sunflower kernels
½ med. red onion, chopped fine	1 cup raisins
6 firm Italian tomatoes, chopped fine	1 bunch red grapes
2 stalks celery, chopped fine	½ lb. bacon, cooked crisp, drained and crumbled

Combine all ingredients.

Dressing:

1 cup mayonnaise	¼ to ½ cup lemon juice
½ cup sugar	

Combine and pour over salad. Refrigerate.

Ann Coulombe, International Falls

BROCCOLI SALAD

2 fresh bunches broccoli, chopped	1 purple onion, chopped
2 carrots, peeled and cut up small	½ lb. bacon, cooked and crumbled
	½ lb. Cheddar cheese, grated

Dressing:

1 cup sugar	1 Tbsp. vinegar
1 cup mayonnaise	

Chill vegetables and dressing. Mix in the dressing when ready to serve. Keeps well.

Marietta Johanneck, Red Lake Falls

434

BROCCOLI SALAD

1 bunch broccoli, cut up (6 cups)
1 onion, diced
1 cup raisins
1 cup salted toasted sunflower
   seeds
¾ cup mayonnaise or salad
   dressing
⅓ cup sugar
1½ Tbsp. vinegar
5 strips bacon, fried and diced

Peel any hard stems from broccoli before cutting up. Combine broccoli, onion, raisins and sunflower seeds. Mix mayonnaise, sugar and vinegar and mix with broccoli mixture. Add bacon just before serving.

Leonette Eikens, Caledonia
Dorothy Vito, Eveleth
Eleanor Gessner, Plainview

BUTTER PECAN SALAD

1 (9 oz.) carton Cool Whip
1 (sm.) box butter pecan or
   vanilla instant pudding mix
   (can use sugar free)
1 (20 oz.) can crushed pineapple, undrained
½ cup chopped pecans
1 cup miniature marshmallows

Mix all ingredients, using the pudding dry. Very rich, but delicious.

Agnes Novak, Fergus Falls
Lorraine Kraft, Blue Earth

CABBAGE SALAD

1 med. head cabbage
3 or 4 bananas
1 med. apple
1 can fruit cocktail
1¼ cups salad dressing
1 pt. whipping cream
¼ cup sugar
1 tsp. vanilla
Real cherries

Shred cabbage, slice bananas, dice apple and drain fruit cocktail. Mix in the cabbage. Add mixture to salad dressing. Whip whipping cream until thick. Add vanilla and sugar. Put real cherries on top and refrigerate until ready to serve.

Mary Ellen Garske Spikerman, St. Paul

KRISPIE CABBAGE SALAD

4 cups shredded cabbage
1 cup chopped celery
1 cup chopped cauliflower
   buds

Refrigerate and add dressing just before serving.

Dressing:

1 cup mayonnaise
1 cup sour cream
¼ cup chopped green onion
¼ cup chopped green pepper
1 tsp. salt
2 Tbsp. sugar
1 Tbsp. vinegar
½ cup chopped cucumber

Natalie McCleary, Crookston

435

CASHEW SALAD

½ cup brown sugar
1 Tbsp. lemon juice
1 cup salad dressing
1 (7 oz.) box cooked macaroni
2 cups chopped celery
¼ cup diced onion
2 cups cubed meat (chicken, turkey, crab or ham)
1 cup salted cashews

Mix brown sugar with lemon juice until smooth. Add salad dressing. Stir sauce into noodles and other ingredients. Add cashews just before serving. (I also add a cup of shredded cheese.)

Natalie McCleary, Crookston

CAESAR SALAD

1 clove garlic
6 to 8 anchovy filets, halved
¼ cup olive oil
2 Tbsp. lemon juice
2 Tbsp. Parmesan cheese, grated
1 egg yolk
1½ tsp. Worcestershire sauce
⅛ tsp. freshly ground pepper
1 lg. head Romaine, torn into pieces
1 cup garlic-flavored croutons

Place all ingredients, except Romain and croutons, in a blender. Whirl until anchovies are finely chopped. If dressing is made ahead of serving time, cover and refrigerate. Bring to room temperature before using. For serving, place Romaine in a large salad bowl. Stir dressing and pour over Romaine. Toss until every leaf is glossy. Add croutons and mix gently. Serve immediately! There are approximately 10 fat grams per serving.

Kathryn Walz, Detroit Lakes

CARRIE'S CRUNCHY SALAD

2 cups diced cauliflower
2 cups thinly sliced carrots
2 cups thinly sliced radishes
2 med. tomatoes, diced
1 cup Miracle Whip
¼ cup ketchup
1 tsp. Worcestershire sauce
Garlic salt and pepper to taste

Prepare vegetables. Mix remaining ingredients for dressing and pour over salad. If made more than 1 hour ahead of serving, hold the tomatoes back until just before using.

Suzanne Lonneman, Adrian

CARROT SALAD

10 good sized carrots
Milk
¾ cup salad dressing
1 Tbsp. sugar
1 tsp. vinegar
¾ cup raisins
1 cup seedless green grapes, cut in half

Peel and shred carrots. Add milk to salad dressing to thin. Put in sugar. Mix in a bowl and put in vinegar, raisins and green grapes.

Mary Ellen Garske-Spickerman, St. Paul

CARROT SALAD

2 lbs. cut up carrots	¾ cup vinegar
1 lg. onion, diced	½ cup oil
1 lg. pepper, diced	1 tsp. salt
1 (10 oz.) can tomato soup	½ tsp. pepper
1 cup sugar	1 tsp. dry mustard

Boil carrots in salt water for 5 minutes. Drain and cool. Add onions and peppers. Combine remaining ingredients and pour over carrots. Refrigerate for 24 hours. Serves 12.

Elaine Sylvster, Crookston

CAULIFLOWER SALAD

1 head cauliflower	1 cup Miracle Whip
2 Tbsp. onion	¼ cup honey
1 green pepper	1 cup shredded Cheddar
1 lb. bacon	cheese

Break cauliflower into small pieces. Chop onion and green pepper. Fry bacon until crisp and break into bits. Mix Miracle Whip and honey. Add cheese and Miracle Whip mixture to other ingredients and chill until ready to serve.

Janet St. Germain, Argyle

CABBAGE CAULIFLOWER SALAD

2 cups Miracle Whip	1 head cauliflower, chopped
⅓ cup Parmesan cheese	1 sm. cabbage, chopped
⅓ cup sugar	1 bottle Bacos
Salt and pepper	

Mix first 4 ingredients for dressing. Layer cauliflower on bottom, then half of dressing, ½ bottle of Bacos, chopped cabbage, other half of dressing and other half bottle of Bacos.

Alana Kuznia, Argyle

CHERRY SALAD

2 cans cherry pie filling	1 (8 oz.) carton Cool Whip
1 can crushed drained pineapple	¼ cup lemon juice
1 can sweetened condensed milk	Miniature marshmallows

Mix all ingredients and chill.

Kathleen Zender, St. James

CHERRY VEGETABLE SALAD

1 pkg. cherry jello	1 cup apples, cut up
2 cups hot water	1 cup celery, cut up
¼ cup red hot candies	½ cup walnuts

Dissolve jello in 2 cups hot water. Stir in and dissolve red hots in jello mixture. Let partially set and stir in apples, celery and walnuts.

Kathleen Altobell, Moorhead
State 2nd Vice Regent, 1980-1982

CHICKEN CURRY SALAD

3 cups cubed cooked chicken
1 cup chopped celery
1 (8 oz.) can sliced water chestnuts, well drained
½ tsp. salt
1 cup mayonnaise

2 tsp. curry powder (or less)
2 tsp. lemon juice
2 tsp. soy sauce
1 (16 oz.) can mandarin oranges, drained

In a large bowl, combine chicken, celery, chestnuts and salt; set aside. Mix mayonnaise, curry, lemon juice, and soy sauce. Stir in chicken mixture. Gently stir in oranges, saving 5 segments for garnish. Cover and store. Can be made the day before.

Carla Brady, Medford

OVERNIGHT COLESLAW

12 cups shredded cabbage
(1 med. head)
1 green pepper, chopped
1 med. red onion, chopped
2 carrots, shredded
1 cup sugar

2 tsp. sugar
1 tsp. dry mustard
1 tsp. celery seed
1 tsp. salt
1 cup vinegar
¾ cup vegetable oil

In a large bowl, combine first 4 ingredients. Sprinkle with sugar; set aside. In a saucepan, combine remaining ingredients for dressing; bring to a boil. Remove from the heat and pour over vegetables, stirring to cover evenly. Cover and refrigerate overnight. Stir well before serving. Serves 12 to 16.

Marcella Gengler, Lismore

CABBAGE LEMON SALAD

⅓ cup vinegar
⅓ cup water
1 cup sugar
Dash of salt
1 (3 oz.) box lemon jello
3 (16 oz.) pkgs. cole slaw mix

1 onion, diced
Celery, chopped (as desired)
1 Tbsp. celery seed
1 Tbsp. mustard seed
¾ cup salad oil

In a saucepan, bring first 4 ingredients to a boil; add jello. Stir and cool. Combine cabbage, onion and celery in large pan. Add celery seed and mustard seed. Pour salad oil over vegetables. Pour dressing over vegetables; mix. Juice thickens as it cools. Makes 1 gallon. Keeps 2 to 3 weeks in refrigerator.

Theresa Neigebauer, Waseca

6 WEEK COLE SLAW

1 head cabbage, shredded	1 cup sugar
2 or 3 carrots, shredded	½ cup vinegar
1 green pepper, shredded	½ cup water
1 onion, shredded	

Allow shredded vegetables to soak in salted water for 1 hour. Boil remaining ingredients; cool and pour over drained vegetables. Keeps well for several weeks.

Luanne Haun, Winona

COOKIE SALAD

2 sm. pkgs. instant French vanilla pudding	2 cans mandarin oranges
1 cup buttermilk	1 (16 oz.) pkg. chocolate covered graham crackers
1 (16 oz.) carton Cool Whip	

Mix pudding and buttermilk; let stand for 2 minutes. Mix in Cool Whip; drain mandarin oranges and stir in. Let chill in refrigerator until ready to serve. Just before serving, crush cookies and stir in salad.

Carol Palmer, Owatonna

COOKIE SALAD

2 cups buttermilk	1 pkg. striped fudge cookies
1 pkg. vanilla pudding	1 lg. carton Cool Whip
2 sm. cans mandarin oranges	

Mix buttermilk and vanilla pudding; add mandarin oranges and put in refrigerator and let it set. Before serving, crush the cookies and add the Cool Whip, mixing them in the pudding mixture. You can use grapes or other fruit if you wish.

Viola Maehren, St. Paul
State Legislative Chairman, 1992-1994
Jean Landsteiner, St. James

COTTAGE CHEESE SALAD

1 pkg. lime jello	1 cup crushed pineapple, drained
1½ cups hot water	
½ cup pineapple juice	½ cup celery
¼ tsp. salt	1 cup cottage cheese
¼ cup mayonnaise	

Prepare jello, hot water, pineapple juice and salt. When cooled and partially set, whip until foamy. Add mayonnaise, crushed pineapple, celery and cottage cheese.

Barbara Schreier, Currie

CRAB SALAD

1 (16 oz.) pkg. fettucini noodles, cooked
1 cup onion, diced
1½ cups celery, diced
⅔ cup creamy Italian dressing
2 Tbsp. lemon juice
½ tsp. oregano
2 tsp. celery seed
¼ tsp. pepper
1 tsp. salt
1 pkg. shredded Cheddar cheese
1 green pepper, diced
1 to 2 lbs. mock crab
2 cups mayonnaise

Mix all ingredients and chill overnight. Very good. Serve on lettuce leaf, or as a side dish.

Variation: Katy suggests using 1 large package of frozen vegetables as substitute for those mentioned, and using low-calorie dressing.

G. Babich, Eveleth
Katy Furrer, St. Paul

CRUNCHY 7-UP CRANBERRY MOLD

2 cups cranberries
2 cups 7-Up
½ cup sugar
¼ tsp. salt
1 env. unflavored gelatin
¼ cup cold water
1 cup diced celery
1 cup crushed pineapple, drained

Cook cranberries in 7-Up until skins pop; add sugar and salt. Continue cooking 5 minutes. Sprinkle gelatin over water to soften, then add to mixture and chill. When nearly solid, stir in celery and pineapple. Pour into a 1 quart mold and chill. Makes 6 servings.

Margaret Gaul, Iona

FRESH CRANBERRY SALAD

1 (12 oz.) pkg. cranberries
1½ cups white sugar
3 pkgs. jello (1 each, wild cherry, raspberry and strawberry)
3 cups boiling water
2 cans mandarin oranges, drained and cut in pieces
1 cup chopped nuts
1 (8 oz.) can crushed pineapple, undrained

Grind cranberries in blender; stir in sugar and set aside. Prepare 3 packages of jello with 3 cups boiling water. Cool until thickened. Add mandarin oranges, nuts and pineapple. Stir well; pour into oiled 8 cup mold (or bundt pan). Chill overnight. Can be inverted on plate to serve large group or wedges cut and removed individually. Lasts at least a week!

Dilly Pierce, Owatonna

FROZEN CRANBERRY SALAD

1 (8 oz.) pkg. cream cheese, softened
2 Tbsp. mayonnaise (Hellman's)
¼ cup sugar
1 lg. can crushed pineapple, drained
1 can whole cranberries (cranberry sauce)
¾ cup nuts
1 lg. carton Cool Whip

Beat mayonnaise into cream cheese. Add sugar. Blend in remaining ingredients, folding Cool Whip in last. Put in a 9x12 inch pan. Cover and freeze. Take out of freezer 20 minutes before serving.

Olive Hastad, Tempe, AZ
Vice State Regent, 1962-1966
State Regent, 1966-1970
National Director, 1970-1974

CRANBERRY TOPHATS

1 (16 oz.) can jellied cranberry sauce
3 Tbsp. lemon juice
1 cup heavy cream, whipped
1 (3 oz.) pkg. cream cheese, softened and whipped
¼ cup sifted powdered sugar
¼ cup mayonnaise
1 cup chopped walnuts

Crush cranberry sauce with fork; add lemon juice and mix well, using a rotary beater, if desired. Divide cranberry mixture evenly in 12 paper cups. Combine whipped cream, cream cheese, powdered sugar and mayonnaise. Fold in nuts. Spread over cranberry layer in each cup. Freeze until firm. To serve, remove salads from paper liners and invert so cranberry mixture is on top. Serves 12.

Aurore Bedard, Argyle

CRANBERRY RING SALAD

2 cups cranberries
1½ cups cold water
1 cup sugar
1 Tbsp. unflavored gelatin
Salt
½ cup chopped nuts
¾ cup diced celery
Lettuce
Shrimp
Mayonnaise

Wash cranberries; add 1 cup cold water and cook until tender. Add sugar and cook for 5 minutes. Soften gelatin in ½ cup cold water; stir into hot cranberries; add salt. Chill until mixture begins to thicken. Add nuts and celery; mix thoroughly. Pour into oiled ring mold. Chill until firm. Unmold and place on large salad plate. Place light lettuce around salad, arrange shrimp in center. Garnish with mayonnaise. Serves 8.

Carol A. Allen, International Falls

441

MOM'S CRANBERRY SALAD

1 orange	1 pkg. lemon jello
2 cups cranberries	1½ cups hot water
1 cup sugar	

Grind orange and cranberries. Add sugar; let stand. Mix lemon jello and hot water. When cool, mix the cranberry mixture with jello. When partly set, add chopped nutmeats on the top. Refrigerate. Serves 6 to 8.

Julia Sullivan, Moorhead

CRANBERRY SALAD

1 (6 oz.) pkg. sugar free cherry jello	2 cups light sour cream
2 cups boiling water	⅓ cup chopped celery
1 (16 oz.) can whole cranberry sauce	⅓ cup walnuts

Dissolve jello in boiling water. Add cranberry sauce and chill until partially set. Fold in sour cream, nuts, and celery. Chill until serving time.

Noella Audette, Red Lake Falls

LEONA'S CRANBERRY SALAD

2 cups hot water	1 cup commercial sour cream
2 pkgs. cherry jello	½ cup chopped nuts
1 can whole cranberry sauce	

Cool jello to thicken; add sauce and sour cream. Add nuts last. Put in an 8x8 inch pan. Double recipe for a 9x13 inch pan.

Leona Rapacz, Argyle

CUCUMBER AND GRAPE SALAD

2 (8 inch) cucumbers, peeled and sliced thin	6 Tbsp. sugar
⅛ cup salt	1 Tbsp. dill seed
6 Tbsp. water	A little parsley
6 Tbsp. vinegar	2 cups seedless grapes

Add salt to cucumbers and weigh down for 15 minutes. Drain cucumbers and then weigh down for another 15 minutes. Add water, vinegar, sugar, dill seed and parsley. Add grapes (red for color). Chill for several hours before serving. Sounds strange, but oh so good!

Claudia R. Bosch, Dickinson, ND
National Director, 1992-1996

SALADS, SOUPS & SANDWICHES

442

DELI GARDEN PASTA SALAD

1 (8 oz.) bag curly noodles
½ bunch broccoli, chopped
1 tomato, chopped
¼ cup onion, chopped
½ cup sliced black olives
1 tsp. dill weed
1 tsp. salt
¼ tsp. pepper
¼ tsp. sugar
1 can sliced water chestnuts
1 (16 oz.) pkg. bottle Hidden
Valley Ranch dressing

Cook noodles; cool. Add vegetables. Mix seasonings and dressing; toss. Best if made a day before.

Barb Neilson, Slayton

SALAD ELAINE

Salad:
Red or green leaf Romaine, or
a combination
Red or green seedless grapes,
cut in half
Apple, cut up
½ cup chopped celery
Broken walnuts
Bleu cheese

Assemble salad and serve on individual salad plates.

Cheesy Herb Croutons:
½ (1½ lb.) loaf white bread,
cubed
3 Tbsp. olive oil
1½ tsp. Salad Supreme
½ cup Parmesan or Romano
cheese
Croutons

Spread cubes on cookie sheet; sprinkle them with olive oil. Combine other ingredients and sprinkle over bread. Bake at 350° for 1 hour, stirring occasionally; cool. Store, tightly covered, in refrigerator.

Dressing:
½ cup sugar
2 tsp. celery seed
1 tsp. dry mustard
1 tsp. salt
3 Tbsp. grated onion
⅓ cup white vinegar
1 cup oil

Mix ingredients in order given. Serve over salad with Cheesy Herb Croutons.

Kathleen Riopelle, Argyle

44 CALORIE-A-CUP-SALAD

1 head cauliflower, broken into
bite size pieces
¾ cup celery, cut up
4 shredded carrots
1 sm. onion, chopped
1 sm. pkg. frozen peas, thawed
1 head broccoli, broken in bite
size pieces
1 (8 oz.) bottle diet creamy
cucumber dressing

Put all ingredients in a large bowl. Add dressing and mix well. Cover and refrigerate. Amount depends on the size of the cauliflower and broccoli heads.

Mae Van Overbeke, Marshall

FANTASTIC FRUIT SALAD

1 (20 oz.) can juice packed
   pineapple chunks
1 (16 oz.) can lite mixed fruit
²/₃ cup powdered milk
1 pkg. vanilla instant pudding

1 cup Cool Whip
1 cup plain yogurt
4 sm. apples, diced
3 bananas, sliced

Drain juice from canned fruit into a six-cup bowl. Add powdered milk to juice. Add pudding and whisk. Add Cool Whip and yogurt and combine with fruits. Chill well. Serves 18.

Eloise Kettner, Mahnomen

FROSTED JELLO SALAD

1 (3 oz.) pkg. orange jello
1 (3 oz.) pkg. lemon jello
2 cups boiling water
1½ cups cold water
Juice of 1 lemon

2 bananas, sliced
1 (20 oz.) can crushed pineapple, drained (save juice)
10 lg. marshmallows, quartered
   (10 miniature equals 1 lg.)

Mix orange and lemon jello. Add boiling water; dissolve jello. Add cold water. Pour lemon juice over sliced bananas. Add drained pineapple, bananas and marshmallows to jello mixture. Pour into a 9x13 inch pan and chill until firm.

Frosted Topping:

2 Tbsp. flour
½ cup sugar
1 egg, slightly beaten
1 cup reserved pineapple juice

1 (8 oz.) carton Cool Whip
½ cup shredded sharp Cheddar
   cheese

Mix flour, sugar, egg and pineapple juice; cook until thick. Cool mixture, cover top with wax paper. When cooled, fold in Cool Whip. Spread on top of jello mixture. Sprinkle shredded cheese on top. Keep chilled. Cut into squares to serve. May be made in large shallow bowl.

Beverly Puterbaugh, St. Charles

FRUIT SALAD

1 (20 oz.) can chunk pineapple,
   drained (reserve juice)
1 Tbsp. lemon juice
2 Tbsp. margarine
2 Tbsp. cornstarch
2 Tbsp. water

½ cup plain low fat yogurt
⅓ cup low fat margarine
8 cups diced apple
2 cups green grapes
1 to 2 tsp. poppy seed
1½ cups toasted pecans

Mix pineapple juice with lemon juice and margarine. Heat until boiling. Mix cornstarch with water and stir into hot mixture. Cook until thickened. Cool completely. Add plain low fat yogurt and low fat margarine. Stir into mixture of fruit and nuts.

Virginia Maday, Fairmont

GOLDEN FRUIT SALAD AND DRESSING

1 lg. fresh pineapple	1 cup strawberries, halved
1 sm. mango	1 cup honey dew melon balls

Prepare pineapple by peeling and dice into bite size pieces. Do the same with the mango. Wash, stem and slice strawberries. Prepare melon balls.

Poppy Seed Dressing:

¼ cup orange juice	½ tsp. poppy seed
2 Tbsp. vegetable oil	¼ tsp. grated orange rind
1 Tbsp. honey	⅛ tsp. dry mustard
1 Tbsp. white wine vinegar	

Combine ingredients in a screw top jar. Shake well. Ready to serve on fruit mixture.

Martha Manderfeld, Medford

CHICKEN SALAD OVER SHOESTRINGS

¼ cup cream	1 cup celery, diced
¼ cup salad dressing	1 Tbsp. minced onion
2 cups chicken or turkey, cooked	Salt and pepper to taste
	1 (4 oz.) can shoestring potatoes
1 cup carrots, shredded	Lettuce leaves

Mix cream and salad dressing; add chicken or turkey and vegetables. Add salt and pepper. Add crispy shoestring potatoes and serve on a lettuce leaf.

Delores Von Ruden, Owatonna
Jane Curran, Medford

CHICKEN SALAD

1 cooked stewing chicken, cut up	6 boiled eggs, chopped
1 can peas	1 sm. bottle olives
2 cups celery, diced	1 cup salad dressing, flavored to taste with mustard, pepper
1 onion, diced	and salt

Add **chow mein noodles** just before serving.

Ardith Kohnert, Waseca

CHICKEN SALAD

1 box macaroni shells, cooked	½ pt. salad dressing
1 cup chicken, cubed	½ pt. Cool Whip
1 cup celery, diced	½ lb. cashew nuts (save half
1 (4 oz.) can crushed pineapple	for top)

Mix all ingredients. Chicken broth may be added if too thick.

Esther Echternach, New Richland

TROPICAL CHICKEN SALAD

2 cups cooked chicken, cubed
1 cup chopped celery
1 cup mayonnaise (not salad dressing)
½ to 1 tsp. curry powder
1 (20 oz.) can chunk pineapple, drained
2 lg. firm bananas, sliced
1 (11 oz.) can mandarin oranges, drained
½ cup flaked coconut
Salad greens, optional
¾ cup salted peanuts or cashew halves

Place chicken and celery in a large bowl. Combine mayonnaise and curry powder. Add to chicken mixture and mix well. Cover and chill for at least 30 minutes. Before serving, add the pineapple, bananas, oranges and coconut, toss gently. Serve on salad greens, if desired. Sprinkle with nuts. Serves 4 to 6.

Irene Nowacki, Argyle
Carla Brady, Medford

MANDARIN CHICKEN SALAD

2 cups cooked chicken, chopped
1 Tbsp. minced onion
1 tsp. salt
1 cup green grapes
1 cup diced celery
1 cup mandarin oranges, drained
½ cup slivered almonds
1 cup cooked macaroni rings
1 cup salad dressing
1 cup cream, whipped

Combine chicken, onion and salt; refrigerate several hours. Add grapes, celery, oranges, almonds and macaroni rings. Mix with salad dressing and refrigerate. When ready to serve, fold in whipped cream. Serves 8 to 10.

Donna Kertz, Thief River Falls

CURRIED CHICKEN SALAD

6 chicken breasts, cooked and cubed
2 apples, cubed
1 can pineapple tidbits, drained
½ cup golden raisins
Red or green seedless grapes, optional
½ cup coconut
½ tsp. salt
3 Tbsp. chutney
1 Tbsp. curry powder
2 Tbsp. chicken broth
1 cup mayonnaise

In mixing bowl, combine chicken, apples, pineapple, raisins, grapes and coconut. Sprinkle with salt. Stir in chutney. In small saucepan, simmer curry powder in chicken broth, stirring to a smooth paste. Add curry paste to mayonnaise. Stir into salad mixture. Chill. Serve on crisp lettuce leaves. Serves 6.

Elaine Kroening, Plainview

446

SPECIAL CHICKEN SALAD (100 servings)

2 gal. cut up chicken
1 cup minced onion
Salt and pepper
3 lbs. macaroni rings
3 lbs. seedless green grapes
4 cups diced celery
4 cans mandarin oranges, drained
2 cups slivered almonds
2 qts. salad dressing
3 cups cream

Marinate the chicken, onion and salt and pepper overnight in refrigerator. The next morning, cook the macaroni rings; drain and cool. Slice the grapes; add celery and oranges and combine with above ingredients. Add almonds and salad dressing. Just before serving, whip cream and fold in chicken-fruit-macaroni mixture.

Sherryl Holzer, Perham

HAM AND BARLEY SALAD

¾ cup pearl barley
1 (8 oz.) can water chestnuts, drained and chopped
1 cup celery, chopped
¼ cup green onion and tops, chopped
¼ cup green pepper, chopped
¼ cup red pepper or pimento
1 cup cooked ham, cubed
1 pkg. dry Italian salad dressing mix
1 tsp. sugar (or to taste)
¼ cup salad oil
½ cup cider vinegar
2 Tbsp. fresh parsley
5 cherry tomatoes

Cook barley according to package directions; drain and chill. Combine barley, chestnuts, celery, onion, peppers and ham; mix well. Combine next 4 ingredients; mix. Add salad dressing to barley mixture. Chill several hours. Garnish with parsley and tomatoes.

Marie Hapka, Argyle

EASY FRUIT SALAD**

1 sm. box instant vanilla pudding (can use sugar free)
1 (20 oz.) can pineapple chunks, undrained
2 cups sliced strawberries
1 (11 oz.) can mandarin oranges, drained
2 apples, sliced
2 bananas, sliced
1 lg. kiwi fruit, sliced

Mix pudding with undrained pineapple. Add rest of fruit. Chill. Can use other fruit.

Lorraine Kraft, Blue Earth

JELLO SALAD

1 (3 oz.) pkg. dry orange jello
1 (3½ oz.) pkg. vanilla pudding (not instant)
1½ cups water
1 (8 or 12 oz.) carton Cool Whip
1 can fruit cocktail or other fruit

Mix dry ingredients in a saucepan and add water. Boil for 1 minute. Cool until slightly thickened. Add Cool Whip and fruit.

Lorena Lasha, Thief River Falls

LIME-VEGETABLE MOLDED SALAD

2 pkgs. lime Jell-O, dissolved	²/₃ cup frozen peas, thawed
1 cup hot water	²/₃ cup carrots, grated
½ cup cold water	²/₃ cup celery, finely diced
¹/₃ onion, grated into hot Jell-O	²/₃ cup shredded lettuce
2½ Tbsp. vinegar	²/₃ cup sharp cheese, shredded
White or black pepper	1 sm. jar pimento

Dissolve Jell-O in hot water. Add cold water and onion into hot Jell-O so as to use juice. Add vinegar and pepper. Let mixture cool; add peas, carrots, celery, lettuce and cheese. Fold in pimento. Pour into a lightly greased container and let set.

Marianne Berger, New Ulm

GRAND OLD DAY SALAD

¼ cup sugar	2 Tbsp. vinegar
1 (2 oz.) pkg. sliced almonds	1 pkg. Ramen Oriental soup mix
1 (10 oz.) container sesame seeds	(blue package)
½ cup oil	1 pkg. cole slaw mix
2 Tbsp. sugar	1 bunch green onions, chopped

Bake ¼ cup sugar, almonds and sesame seeds until caramelized at 450°. Watch carefully so it doesn't burn; cool. Mix the oil, sugar and vinegar with the seasoning packet from the Ramen noodles. Mix cole slaw mix, green onions, caramelized mixture and dressing. Break up noodles and add just before serving.

Lorraine Sturm, St. James

FRUIT MACARONI SALAD

2 eggs	1 can mandarin oranges, drained
1 cup sugar	
Dash of salt	1 (16 oz.) can fruit cocktail, drained
2 Tbsp. flour	
1 (16 oz.) can pineapple tidbits	1 pkg. miniature marshmallows
1 (7 oz.) pkg. ring macaroni, cooked	1 pt. whipped cream (Cool Whip), optional

Add eggs, sugar, salt, flour and juice of pineapple in sauce pan. Boil until thick. Pour over cooked macaroni rings and let stand overnight in refrigerator. When ready to serve, add the pineapple, mandarin oranges, fruit cocktail, marshmallows and whipping cream. Add whipped cream last. You can use Cool Whip. Keep in refrigerator until ready to serve.

Bertha M. Wacha, Slayton

LIME CHEESE SALAD

1 sm. pkg. lime jello	½ cup chopped nuts
2 cups boiling water	1 cup cream, whipped
2 cups miniature marshmallows	1 sm. carton cottage cheese
1 sm. can crushed pineapple	

Mix jello in boiling water; add marshmallows. Stir, let melt and cool. Add remaining ingredients. Pour into mold; refrigerate. Makes about 8 large servings. May use sugar-free jello in place of sweetened.

Alice Ditsch, International Falls

GERMAN WILTED LETTUCE

1 head lettuce	Dash of pepper
1 sm. onion, diced	4 slices bacon, diced
3 Tbsp. sugar	¼ cup vinegar
½ tsp. salt	¼ cup water

Tear lettuce coarsely; add onion, sugar, salt and pepper. Fry bacon until golden brown; add vinegar and water. Bring to a boil. Pour over lettuce, mix and serve.

Carrie Palme, Minneapolis

MACARONI (MEAT) SALAD

1 pkg. shell macaroni	1 Tbsp. Western dressing
1 cup whipping cream	(enough for color)
Sugar and vanilla	1 can Spam or other meats
1 cup Miracle Whip	2 or 3 carrots, shredded

Cook macaroni as directed; cool. Whip cream and add sugar and vanilla. Mix with Miracle Whip and Western dressing. Cut Spam into chunks. Mix all ingredients and chill. Celery can also be used. It is also good with chicken, tuna or eggs.

Angeline Kostrzewski, Argyle

MACARONI SALAD

1 pkg. macaroni (size depends on how many you serve)	1 sm. can peas
	1 cup Miracle Whip
1 can Spam, chopped*	1 cup shredded cheese, optional
1 cup chopped celery	
1 sm. onion, diced	1 sm. jar stuffed olives, sliced

*You may substitute leftover ham, or leftover cooked chicken, or canned tuna in place of canned Spam.

Cook macaroni according to directions. Cool and put in large bowl. Add all above ingredients to macaroni.

Variation: Diane adds ½ cups French dressing.

Mary Curtis, Slayton
Diane Pawlowski, Argyle

MACARONI RING SALAD

1½ cups salad dressing (not
mayonnaise)
½ cup milk
2 Tbsp. vinegar
2 Tbsp. lemon juice
2 Tbsp. sugar
2 tsp. Grey Poupon mustard
1 Tbsp. grated onion
¼ tsp. black pepper
¼ tsp. paprika
1 tsp. parsley
⅛ tsp. celery salt
⅛ tsp. garlic powder
Cubed ham, optional
1 (7 oz.) box macaroni rings,
cooked, drained and chilled
1¼ cups diced celery
½ cup cubed American or
Colby cheese
1 (8 oz.) pkg. frozen green peas

Combine the dressing ingredients and pour over macaroni rings, celery, cheese and peas. Mix well and chill. Salad is best when refrigerated overnight. If adding ham to the salad, add more milk.

Marva Taylor, Adrian

PARMESAN VEGETABLE TOSS

4 cups bite size broccoli
4 cups bite size cauliflower
1 lg. sweet onion, thinly sliced
and separated into rings
⅓ cup Parmesan cheese
¼ cup sugar
½ tsp. salt
½ tsp. basil leaves
2 cups mayonnaise or salad
dressing
1 lb. bacon, crisply cooked
and crumbled
1 lg. head lettuce, torn into bite
size pieces
2 cups seasoned croutons
1 (8 oz.) can sliced water
chestnuts

In large bowl, combine broccoli, cauliflower and onion. In small bowl, combine cheese, sugar, salt, basil and mayonnaise; mix well. Add vegetables to dressing; toss gently. Refrigerate several hours. Just before serving, add bacon, lettuce, croutons and water chestnuts; toss lightly. Serves 20 to 24. This salad is just right for large groups, but can be cut in half very easily.

Mary Nell Gust, International Falls

TRIPLE ORANGE AMBROSIA SALAD

2 cups boiling water
1 (6 oz.) pkg. orange jello
1 pt. orange sherbet
1 sm. (11 oz.) can mandarin
oranges, drained

Mix water and jello until dissolved; add sherbet. Stir until smooth; add oranges. Put in an 11x7 inch glass pan; refrigerate until served.

Mae Machulda, St. Paul

SALADS, SOUPS & SANDWICHES

HEAVENLY ORANGE FLUFF

2 (3 oz.) pkgs. orange gelatin
2½ cups boiling water
1 (13½ oz.) can crushed
    pineapple
1 (6 oz.) can frozen orange
    juice concentrate, thawed

2 (11 oz.) cans mandarin
    oranges, drained
1 (3¾ oz.) pkg. instant lemon
    pudding mix
1 cup cold milk
1 cup whipping cream, whipped

Dissolve gelatin in boiling water; add undrained pineapple and concentrate. Chill until partially set. Fold in oranges; pour into a 13x9x2 inch pan. Chill until firm. Beat pudding and milk with rotary beater until smooth. Fold in whipped cream. Spread over gelatin; chill. Makes 12 to 15 servings.

Meg Schmidt, Fergus Falls
District Deputy, 1992-1996
State Apostolic Chair, 1990-1992

ORIENTAL SALAD

1 stalk Napa cabbage, cut fine
5 green table onions and part
    of the greens, cut fine
2 pkgs. Ramen noodles (not
    the seasoning)
¼ cup sesame seed

½ cup butter or oleo
1 sm. pkg. slivered almonds
½ cup vinegar
2 Tbsp. soy sauce
1 cup oil
½ cup sugar

Cut cabbage and onions fine. Toast noodles (break noodles in small pieces so it toasts well), sesame seeds, butter or oleo, and almonds well in fry pan. Mix remaining ingredients to make the sauce a day ahead of time and refrigerate. When it's time to serve the salad, combine all ingredients (be sure and shake sauce before putting it in the other ingredients). Very good salad.

Reda A. Goemer, St. Paul

OVERNIGHT SALAD

½ head lettuce
1 cup celery
½ cup chopped onions
1 cup frozen peas, partially
    cooked
½ cup green peppers
Additional ½ head lettuce

1 pt. real mayonnaise
3 Tbsp. sugar
1 cup shredded Cheddar
    cheese
6 to 8 slices bacon, fried crisp
    and cut, or ¾ cup Bacos

Layer first 6 ingredients in a 9x13 inch pan in order given. Spread the mayonnaise evenly over. Sprinkle sugar over. Spread shredded cheese and bacon over top. Let stand overnight. Don't mix.

Rose Labat, Marshall
Judy Bernard, Mt. Iron

GRANDMA BESSIE'S MAYONNAISE SALAD

6 to 7 good size potatoes
2 cups Miracle Whip
2 Tbsp. yellow mustard
¼ cup milk
Celery powder to taste
Onion powder to taste
Sugar or honey

Cucumber, diced
Onion, diced
Green pepper, diced
Tomato, diced
Celery, diced
Paprika
Eggs, boiled

Cook potatoes with their jackets on. While potatoes are cooking, mix next 5 ingredients; add just enough sugar or honey to sweeten to taste. Should taste tangy with a hint of sweetness to it. Mix vegetables into the dressing mixture. After potatoes have cooled, off, peel and cube them. Add potatoes to dressing mixture. Sprinkle with paprika over top. Slice hard boiled eggs and arrange on top of the salad and serve.

Katy Furrer, St. Paul

ORANGE BUTTERMILK MOLDED SALAD

1 (8½ oz.) can crushed pineapple in syrup
1 (6 oz.) pkg. orange or apricot jello
2 cups buttermilk

1 (8 oz.) carton Cool Whip, thawed
¼ cup chopped pecans, optional

In a large saucepan, bring pineapple and syrup to boil. Remove from heat; stir in jello. Cool to room temperature. Stir in buttermilk and fold in Cool Whip and pecans. Pour into 8 cups mold. Chill 4 hours or overnight.

Ann Rasmussen, International Falls

PASTA SALAD**

1 med. box macaroni shells
1 lg. bottle Zesty Italian dressing
Parmesan cheese (fresh works well)
Green pepper, diced

Black olives, sliced
Tomatoes, optional
Cauliflower, optional
Broccoli, optional
Some type of salami or turkey, optional

Boil macaroni until done. Mix in part of the Italian dressing while shells are still slightly warm (save a small amount of dressing to add to salad right before serving). Add rest of ingredients; chill.

Mae Maas, Faribault
District Deputy, 1996-present

OVERNIGHT SALAD

1 sm. pkg. vanilla pudding	1 can mandarin oranges,
1 sm. pkg. lemon jello	drained
1 scant cup boiling water	1 can pineapple tidbits, drained
¼ pt. whipping cream	1 cup miniature marshmallows

Cook pudding mix. Mix jello with boiling water; cool. Combine jello with pudding. Fold in rest of ingredients. Store overnight in refrigerator. Colored marshmallows are pretty. Can be doubled.

Roberta Tissek, St. Paul

PARTY SALAD

1 (No. 2) can crushed pineapple	1 cup chopped celery
1 pkg. lime jello	1 cup nutmeats, optional
1 (8 oz.) pkg. Philadelphia	1 cup cream, whipped, or
cream cheese	1 (8 oz.) carton Cool Whip

Heat pineapple to boiling. Add jello; cool. Combine cream cheese, celery and nutmeats. Add jello mixture. Fold in whipped cream. Put in mold or dish and chill.

Ellen Vortherms, Adrian

FRUIT SALAD

1 (20 oz.) can lite unsweetened	1 lg. can lite fruit cocktail
chunk pineapple, drained	1 sm. can mandarin oranges
1 Tbsp. cornstarch	Any fresh fruit

Put pineapple syrup in saucepan. Add cornstarch and cook over medium heat, stirring constantly until thickened. Cool. Drain fruit cocktail and mandarin oranges. Put in large bowl with pineapple. Chill. Use any extra fruit. (Do not use fruit cocktail and mandarin juice in recipe as pineapple alone gives it more tang.) Pour chilled sauce over fruit. Mix gently and refrigerate. If using bananas, add just before serving.

Inez Balster, Wilmont

PINEAPPLE CREAM CHEESE SALAD

2 cups crushed pineapple,	1 pkg. unflavored gelatin
undrained	1 (8 oz.) pkg. cream cheese
1 cup sugar	½ pt. cream, whipped, or
Juice of 1 lemon	1 (8 oz.) carton Cool whip

Heat first 3 ingredients. Add gelatin that has been dissolved in ½ cup cold water; stir to dissolve. Cool. Mix grated cream cheese and whipped topping. Add pineapple mixture. Put into bowl; chill until firm. Can add cherries and/or nuts.

Millie Fangmeier, Pipestone
·   Valery Hudson, Moorhead

DREAM SALAD

1 (No. 2) can crushed pineapple, drained
1 sm. pkg. lemon jello
1 (8 oz.) pkg. marshmallows
1 (8 oz.) pkg. cream cheese
1 cup Cool Whip
1 sm. pkg. cherry jello

Add water to pineapple juice to make 2 cups liquid. Bring to a boil; remove from heat and dissolve lemon jello in this. Stir in the marshmallows until almost melted. Chill until it begins to thicken. In a separate bowl, mix cream cheese, pineapple and Cool Whip. Add this to lemon mixture. Pour into a 9x13 inch pan; refrigerate until set. Prepare cherry jello according to package directions. Pour this over top of the cooled jello mixture. Refrigerate until set.

Note: I also occasionally put a layer of green jello on the bottom of the pan to make a 3 layer salad. Serves 12 to 16.

Marie Jones, Owatonna

FRESH FRUIT BOWL

2 or 3 bananas (not overripe)
1 (15½ oz.) can chunk pineapple
3 cups green and/or red seedless grapes
2 apples, pared and diced
2 or 3 oranges, peeled and diced
2 Tbsp. cornstarch
¹/₃ cup sugar
½ cup water
¼ cup lemon juice or Real lemon

Mix all fruit in a bowl (grapes may be halved; may vary amounts of fruit). In a saucepan, combine remaining ingredients to make sauce. Bring to a boil. Boil until thick. Pour over fruit immediately. Keeps for several days in refrigerator.

Delores Schik, Perham

HOT PINEAPPLE SIDE DISH

1 (20 oz.) can pineapple chunks,
  drained (reserve ¼ cup)
½ cup sugar
3 Tbsp. flour
¼ cup butter or margarine, melted
1½ cups Cheddar cheese,
  divided
²/₃ cup coarsely crushed saltine
  crackers (14 quarters)

In a medium bowl, combine sugar and flour. Add butter and 1 cup cheese; mix well. Sprinkle crushed crackers on top; drizzle with reserved pineapple juice. Bake, uncovered, at 350° for 30 to 35 minutes or until bubbly around edges. Remove from oven; sprinkle with remaining cheese. Serves 6.

Elaine Sable, Owatonna

FRUIT SALAD

1 (20 oz.) can pineapple, undrained
1 can mandarin oranges, drained
½ cup raisins
½ cup roasted peanuts
½ cup celery, chopped
1 cup green and/or red grapes
2 apples
4 bananas

Mix ingredients and chill. Drain and add **1 (8 oz.) carton yogurt** (any flavor) and **2 tablespoons honey** just before serving. Cover with **shredded Cheddar cheese**.

Jennifer Anderson, Argyle

GERMAN POTATO SALAD

6 strips bacon
3 Tbsp. flour
½ tsp. salt
½ cup sugar
½ cup vinegar
1 cup water
1 onion, chopped
8 baked potatoes

Fry bacon and cut in small pieces. Stir in flour, salt, sugar, vinegar and water. Bring to boil; add onion. Pour over cut, cooled potatoes. Heat when ready to serve.

Margaret Gengler, Caledonia

GERMAN POTATO SALAD

2 cups water
⅓ cup vinegar
1 Tbsp. salt
3 Tbsp. cornstarch
½ cup diced, cooked bacon
1 qt. cooked red potatoes, diced or sliced
Onions as desired

Place 1½ cups water, vinegar and salt in saucepan; heat to boiling. Mix cornstarch with remaining water. Add to hot mixture; stir. Boil until thickened, stirring constantly. Stir in cooked bacon and drippings. Mix with hot potatoes and onions. Heat all together so flavor mixes with potatoes. A crockpot works well for this.

Marilyn Rewitzee, New Ulm

MOM'S POTATO SALAD

7 lg. potatoes, cooked and diced
6 eggs, boiled, cooled and diced
½ cup celery, diced
1 lg. onion, diced (½ to ¾ cup)
1¼ to 1½ cups salad dressing
1½ Tbsp. dark vinegar
1½ Tbsp. prepared mustard
2 to 3 Tbsp. sugar
Salt and pepper to taste
2 Tbsp. milk

Place potatoes, eggs, celery and onion in a large bowl. Mix remaining ingredients for dressing; add to the vegetables and mix well. Chill well before serving.

Laura Busch, Slayton
Barbara Schreier, Currie

HOT GERMAN POTATO SALAD

6 med. potatoes, boiled in skins
6 slices bacon
¾ cup chopped onion
2 Tbsp. flour
1 to 2 Tbsp. sugar
1½ tsp. salt
½ tsp. celery seed
Dash of pepper
¾ cup water
⅓ cup vinegar

Peel potatoes and slice thin. Fry bacon slowly in skillet, then drain on paper. Saute onion in bacon fat until golden brown. Blend in flour, sugar, salt, celery seed and pepper. Cook over low heat, stirring until smooth and bubbly. Remove from heat. Stir in water and vinegar. Heat to boiling, stirring constantly. Boil 1 minute. Stir in the potatoes and the crumbled bacon bits carefully. Remove from heat, cover and let stand until ready to serve. Serves 6 to 8.

Darlene Hoffman, Owatonna
Charlotte Suedback, Slayton

DELICIOUS POTATO SALAD

4 eggs
1 cup sugar
1 cup white vinegar
1 tsp. prepared mustard
1 tsp. salt
1 qt. salad dressing
10 lbs. red potatoes, cooked
and cubed
12 hard boiled eggs, chopped
2 cups celery, diced
12 green onions
1 tsp. dill weed

Beat eggs slightly. Mix next 4 ingredients; add to eggs and boil on medium heat until slightly thick, stirring constantly. Strain to remove any lumps. Mix with salad dressing. Add remaining ingredients; mix and chill. This dressing will keep for weeks in refrigerator.

Kay Cox, Adrian
District Deputy, 1966-1970
Legislative Chairman, 6 years

QUICK FRUIT SALAD**

1 (21 oz.) can peach pie filling
3 firm bananas, sliced
2 cups strawberries, halved
1 cup chunk pineapple

Combine all ingredients in bowl. Chill overnight or 3 to 4 hours. May substitute 1 cup seedless grapes for the pineapple.

Margaret Stangler, Waterville

RASPBERRY CRANBERRY RELISH MOLD

1 (6 oz.) pkg. raspberry jello
1 cup boiling water
2 cups whole cranberry sauce
¼ cup lemon juice
½ cup horseradish

Mix jello and water. Add rest of ingredients. Chill in mold. Serve with roast, turkey or pork.

Jeanne Heer, Winona

SALADS, SOUPS & SANDWICHES

RASPBERRY PRETZEL SALAD

1½ cups crushed pretzels	1 (8 oz.) carton frozen whipped
¾ cup melted butter or margarine	topping, thawed
2 Tbsp. granulated sugar	2 (3 oz.) pkgs. raspberry gelatin
1 (8 oz.) pkg. cream cheese	2 cups boiling water
1 cup granulated sugar	2 (10 oz.) pkgs. frozen rasp-
	berries, thawed

Mix pretzels, butter or margarine, and 2 tablespoons sugar. Press into a 9x13 inch pan. Bake at 350° for 10 minutes; cool. Beat cream cheese with 1 cup sugar; fold in whipped topping. Spread this mixture over the cooled crust. Dissolve gelatin in boiling water; cool. Add raspberries; mix well. Chill until partially set. Pour over second layer. Chill for several hours before serving.

Patricia L. Skraba, Eveleth

SARAH'S EASY HOLIDAY SALAD**

2 (3 oz.) boxes raspberry jello	2 cups applesauce
2 cups boiling water	1 can cranberry sauce

Dissolve jello in boiling water. Add applesauce and cranberry sauce; mix well. Refrigerate to set. Enjoy!

Variation: Joyce substitutes 2 packages frozen raspberries (thawed) for cranberry sauce. She also adds a topping of 1½ packages miniature marshmallows and 1 pint sour cream, which is refrigerated overnight, then beat together as whipping cream.

Mary Jane Gray, Blue Earth
Joyce Stock, Mahnomen
State Regent, 1986-1990
State First Vice Regent, 1984-1986

RAMEN CABBAGE SALAD

½ head cabbage	2 Tbsp. sugar
4 green onions and tops	½ tsp. pepper
½ cup slivered almonds	Seasoning packet from Ramen
3 Tbsp. sesame seeds	noodles
½ cup corn or sesame oil	1 pkg. chicken flavored Ramen
3 Tbsp. vinegar	noodles
1 scant tsp. salt	

Chop the cabbage along with the green top onions. Use the green and add to cabbage. Brown the almonds and sesame seeds in a little dab of butter until lightly brown. Cool and add to salad. Mix next 6 ingredients for dressing in pint size jar. Shake and mix well. Break the noodles apart form the soup mix packet and add to rest of the salad just before serving. Very good.

Variation: Clara uses 1 whole head cabbage and adds 2 or 3 shredded carrots for color.

Gail Heim, Medford
Julie Schugel, New Ulm
Clara Udelhoffen, Mankato

RHUBARB SWEET SALAD

3 cups rhubarb
1½ cups white sugar
2 Tbsp. water

1 pkg. red jello
1 pkg. miniature marshmallows
Cool Whip

Cook the rhubarb and sugar with the water until tender, then add jello and half of marshmallows until dissolved; mix well. Cool until thick. To serve, add Cool Whip and rest of marshmallows; mix.

Elsie Walz, Mahnomen

SPEZZIELLO SALAD

1¼ cups spezziello macaroni
2 cans mandarin oranges
1 can pineapple tidbits
3 eggs, well beaten
3 Tbsp. flour

1 cup sugar
Juices from drained fruit
1½ cups miniature marshmallows
1 lg. carton Cool Whip

Cook macaroni in salted boiling water; drain (spezziello is small, like tapioca). Drain the fruit and save juices. Combine the cooked spezziello and fruit. Cook the egg, flour, sugar and juices. Add marshmallows and cooked sauce. Cool in refrigerator. Just before serving, add the Cool Whip and stir.

Cecilia Mazour, Mahnomen

PASTA AND SALMON SALAD

1 cup chopped salmon,
  cooked or canned
⅓ cup chopped celery
⅓ cup Italian parsley, chopped
8 to 10 shallots, peeled and
  minced

¼ cup chopped pimento
1 cup cooked pasta (angel
  hair spaghetti)
Optional: chopped olives, green
  peppers, tomatoes, and
  hard boiled eggs

Mix first 5 ingredients in a large bowl; add pasta and toss gently.

Dressing:
2 Tbsp. vegetable oil
Juice of 1 lemon

¼ cup chopped fresh dill or
  ⅛ cup dry
⅓ tsp. dry mustard

Mix and pour over salad.

Ann Callaghan, Blue Earth

ROTINI SALAD

1 cup sugar
2 cups mayonnaise
¾ cup vinegar
1 can condensed milk

Onion
Celery
Shredded carrots
2 cups Rotini noodles

Mix all ingredients, except noodles; let stand. Boil noodles; cool. Add the dressing mixture.

Kathy Felten, Caledonia

SALADS, SOUPS & SANDWICHES

458

SAUERKRAUT SALAD

1 lg. can sauerkraut, well
  drained
1 green pepper, diced
1 lg. onion, diced
  Mix all ingredients.

1 sm. jar pimento, chopped
1 tsp. celery seed
1 cup celery, chopped

Dressing:
¾ cup sugar
½ cup Wesson oil

½ cup sugar

Mix and pour over sauerkraut mixture; mix well. Let stand at least 12 hours in refrigerator before eating. Will keep well for at least 2 weeks.

Lucille Krause, Waterville

SHRIMP SALAD

1 (10 oz.) pkg. frozen salad
  shrimp
1 cup diced stuffed olives
1 cup raw rice, cooked and
  cooled
  Mix all ingredients in order.

½ cup chopped green pepper
½ cup diced celery
1 cup sm. cauliflower buds
Salt and pepper to taste

Dressing:
1 cup mayonnaise
2 Tbsp. salad oil
1 Tbsp. vinegar
2 Tbsp. sugar

1 Tbsp. grated onion
½ Tbsp. mustard
1 Tbsp. lemon juice

Mix ingredients and toss over salad ingredients. Refrigerate for 3 hours or overnight.

Donna Farrell, Marshall
State Regent, 1994-present
State First Vice, 1990-1994

SHRIMP SALAD

1 (8 oz.) pkg. shell macaroni
1¾ cups chopped celery
1 med. onion, chopped
4 hard boiled eggs, chopped
1²/₃ cups salad dressing

⅓ cup French dressing
Salt and pepper to taste
2 sm. cans shrimp, rinsed and
  drained (or 1 frozen bag)

Cook macaroni according to directions on package. Combine macaroni, celery, onion, and eggs. Mix salad dressing, French dressing, and salt and pepper; add to macaroni mixture. Stir in a large bowl. Last, add shrimp to the mixture. Keep refrigerated.

Joan Andrews, Slayton

SALADS, SOUPS & SANDWICHES

SHRIMP SALAD

1 cup chopped celery
1 cup shredded carrots
¼ cup chopped onion
1 cup Miracle Whip
2 cans shrimp
2 cans shoestring potatoes

Mix first 4 ingredients. Add shrimp and shoestrings before serving.

Elsie Kaffine, Eveleth

COOL SNICKERS SALAD**

1 (8 oz.) carton Cool Whip
3 Snickers candy bars
3 to 4 Red Delicious apples

Cut the candy bars into small pieces. Dice, but do not peel the apples. Mix all the ingredients, except apples. Do not add apples until ready to serve. Other bars (Mars, Milky Way, etc.) may be used instead of the Snickers.

Barb Kahle, New Ulm

SNICKER BAR SALAD SUPREME

3 Granny Smith apples
2½ cups Snickers bar, chopped
1 (8 oz.) carton Cool Whip

Cut apples into small pieces. Mix with candy bars; add Cool Whip.

Marie Maslowski, Red Wing

SPAGHETTI SALAD

1 lb. spaghetti, cooked
1 to 2 tomatoes, diced
1 cucumber, diced
1 onion, diced
1 green pepper, diced
1 stalk diced celery (put in as
   much as you like)
1 (8 oz.) bottle Italian dressing
2 to 4 Tbsp. Salad Supreme
   Schilling seasoning

Boil spaghetti; drain. Run water over to cool. Add vegetables. Pour Italian dressing over mixture; add Salad Supreme and seasoning. Chill and serve cold.

Rosalie Doering, Caledonia

FRESH SPINACH SALAD

Dressing:
¹/₃ cup sugar
½ tsp. paprika
1 Tbsp. lemon juice
1 tsp. dried onions
½ tsp. salt
½ tsp. celery seed
1 Tbsp. honey
½ cup salad or olive oil

Heat all ingredients, except oil, until sugar melts; add oil. Pour into container. Add **1 small can drained mandarin oranges**; chill.

1 bag fresh spinach
6 to 8 slices bacon, fried and
   crumbled
1 med. red onion, sliced
1 sm. pkg. almond slivers,
   browned

Wash spinach. Take off stems; drain. When ready to serve, layer spinach, bacon, onions and almonds. Pour dressing over; toss.

Jeanne Schuetzle, Cary, IL

SPINACH FRUIT SALAD

1 lb. spinach leaves
1 avocado, diced
1 pt. strawberries, sliced
2 bananas, sliced
2 green onions, chopped

Mix ingredients in a large salad bowl.

Poppy Seed Dressing:

½ to ¾ cups sugar
⅓ cup wine vinegar
1 Tbsp. onion
1 tsp. salt
1 cup oil
1 to 2 Tbsp. poppy seeds

Combine all ingredients and shake well to mix. Pour over salad just before serving.

Mary Lynn Portz, Pipestone

STRAWBERRY SALAD

1 pt. strawberries, washed
  and sliced
1 med. red onion, sliced
1 bunch leaf lettuce

Mix in a large bowl.

Dressing:

¾ cup Miracle Whip
¼ cup milk
1 tsp. poppy seed
2 Tbsp. white wine vinegar
⅓ cup sugar

Mix all ingredients in a small bowL. Whip until smooth. Pour dressing over salad and toss gently. Quick, easy and very good!

Mary Nell Gust, International Falls

STRAWBERRY SALAD

2 pkgs. vanilla tapioca pudding
3 cups boiling water
1 (3 oz.) pkg. strawberry jello
1 (9 oz.) carton Cool Whip
1 (10 oz.) pkg. strawberries

Blend pudding and water and bring to a rolling boil. Add jello and cool to room temperature. Add Cool Whip and strawberries and refrigerate.

Elaine Salentiny, Euclid

STRAWBERRY JELLO SALAD

1 pkg. strawberry jello
¾ cup boiling water
1 pkg. frozen strawberries
1 (8 oz.) pkg. cream cheese
1 cup whipped cream
1 cup miniature marshmallows
1 cup nuts, optional

Dissolve jello in boiling water. Add strawberries and cream cheese. Beat with beater (may do cream cheese only if you like the strawberries in larger pieces). Add whipped cream, marshmallows and nuts. Refrigerate. Is also very good with raspberries.

Bernadette Brandt, Marshall

461

SUMMER SALAD

1 lg. can chunk pineapple	1 Tbsp. lemon juice
3 or 4 oranges, peeled and	2 Tbsp. cornstarch
cut into chunks	2 sliced bananas

Drain pineapple. Mix oranges and pineapple. Combine pineapple juice, lemon juice and cornstarch. Cook until clear and thick; let cool. Pour over bananas so they will not darken. Combine with rest of fruit. Decorate with cherries. Other fruits may also be used.

Agnes Schwanz, Frazee

MARINATED SUMMER SALAD

1 bunch broccoli	1 cup grated Cheddar cheese
1 onion, diced	1 pkg. Italian dressing mix,
1 lg. tomato, diced	prepared

Cut broccoli, only using top stalk. Cut in small pieces all remaining ingredients. Marinate overnight.

Pat Szarke, Perham

SUNFLOWER SEED SALAD

1 pkg. Bow Tie macaroni	1 cup onion, chopped
¼ cup oil	1 cup sunflower seeds
1 cup bacon bits	1 jar Parmesan dressing (about
1 cup celery	14 oz. size)

Cook macaroni according to package directions. Add rest of ingredients to cooked pasta (drained). Toss with dressing. Let stand overnight in refrigerator. Super salad!

Jean Peterson, Eveleth

SURPRISE WALDORF SALAD

2 cups unpeeled apples, diced	1 cup celery, cut in 1 inch pieces
1 Tbsp. sugar	½ cup pecan pieces
½ tsp. lemon juice	¼ cup mayonnaise
Dash of salt	½ cup cream, whipped

Sprinkle apples with sugar, lemon juice and salt. Add celery and nuts. Mix mayonnaise and whipped cream, then put on fruit mixture.

Variation: Can add ½ cup chopped dates and miniature marshmallows (I do)! Reduce celery to ½ cup these things are added.

Mary Lou Fenske, New Ulm

TUNA SALAD

1 (6 oz.) can tuna, drained
1 cup shredded cabbage
1 grated carrot
1 chopped green onion
2 tomatoes, chopped
1 tsp. mayonnaise
2 Tbsp. plain yogurt
1 Tbsp. lemon juice
Lemon pepper and salt to taste

In a bowl, combine tuna, cabbage, carrot, onion and tomatoes. Blend mayonnaise with yogurt, lemon juice, pepper and salt. Mix with tuna mixture. Chill.

Armella Willaert, North Mankato

TURKEY 'N APPLE PASTA SALAD

¾ cup mayonnaise
1 Tbsp. lemon juice
1 Tbsp. French mustard
2 cups spiral pasta, cooked
and drained
¾ lb. (3 cups) turkey breast,
julienne cut
2 apples, chopped
1 cup sliced celery, chopped
Iceburg lettuce leaves

In a large bowl, combine first 3 ingredients for dressing. Stir in remaining ingredients, except flavors. Serve salad on lettuce-lined plates. Preparation time: 30 minutes. Serve this recipe with crusty bread and fresh fruit. Makes 7 cups.

Tip: To make a delicious tuna salad, substitute 2 (6.12 oz.) cans drained flaked Geisha tuna for the turkey.

Loretta Engesser, Blue Earth

TURKEY SALAD

8 cups turkey, cooked and
cut into bite size pieces
4 cups chopped celery
5 hard boiled eggs, cut into
pieces
2 cups white grapes, halved
1 sm. can pineapple tidbits,
well drained
Salt and pepper to taste
2 cups Miracle Whip
¼ cup French dressing
½ cup half and half cream
¼ cup milk
½ tsp. white pepper

Mix first 6 ingredients. Mix last 5 ingredients and add to salad.

Lila Ballman, New Ulm

RAW VEGETABLE SALAD

1 bunch broccoli
1 head cauliflower
6 stalks celery
1 lg. onion, chopped
1 pkg. frozen peas
1 cup sour cream
2 cups mayonnaise

Wash everything well and combine with last 2 ingredients. May also use Miracle Whip.

Genevieve Lanoue, Marshall

RAW SALAD

2 cups raw cauliflower, cut small
2 cups raw broccoli, cut small
1 cup chopped onion
1 cup chopped celery
1 cup frozen peas, uncooked
1 cup sour cream

1 cup mayonnaise
2 Tbsp. vinegar
2 Tbsp. sugar
3 drops Tabasco sauce
Salt to taste

Mix first 5 ingredients well. Mix remaining ingredients and pour over salad. Serve.

Evelyn Meese, Owatonna

VEGETABLE SALAD

4 to 5 slices fried bacon
1 pkg. slivered almonds
1 cup mayonnaise or Miracle Whip
1/3 cup sugar

2 Tbsp. white vinegar
1 bunch broccoli, cut up
1 cluster purple grapes, cut in half
1 1/2 stalks celery, cut up

Fry bacon; cool and crumble. Toast almonds or fry with a little margarine; cool. Mix next 3 ingredients for dressing; add to the rest of the ingredients. Sounds strange, but it is delish!

Roseanne Barnard, Waterville

VEGETABLE SALAD

2 cans peas, drained
2 cans French style seasoned beans

1 onion, chopped
1 green pepper, chopped
4 stalks celery, chopped

Mix all ingredients.

Dressing:
1/2 cup vegetable oil
1 cup sugar
1/2 cup vinegar

2 Tbsp. water
Salt and pepper

Mix ingredients and add to salad. Chill and serve.

Nell Cook, Plainview

VEGETABLE SALAD

1 head cauliflower
1 bunch broccoli
1 cup celery
1 cup cucumber

1 green pepper
1 cup water chestnuts
1 cup black olives
Some cherry tomatoes

Mix all vegetables, except tomatoes; set aside.

Dressing:
1 pkg. dry Italian dressing
1 bottle creamy Italian dressing

Mix ingredients and add to salad mixture. Let stand overnight. Turn bowl occasionally if you have a tight lid on it. Add tomatoes just before serving.

Jeanie Sinclair, St. James

SALADS, SOUPS & SANDWICHES

VERMICELLI SALAD

1 lb. vermicelli or angel hair spaghetti
2 cucumbers, peeled, seeded and chopped
1 green pepper, chopped
2 med. tomatoes, chopped
1 bottle Schilling Salad Supreme spice mix
1 (8 oz.) bottle Zesty Italian dressing

Break spaghetti into small pieces; cook, drain and rinse. Mix all other ingredients. Add spices and dressing. Make a day ahead and let marinate. Makes a big batch and keeps well.

Jean Arvison (Edna Sullivan), Pine Island

VEGGIE SALAD

1 bunch broccoli
1 head cauliflower
3 sticks celery
1 pkg. frozen peas
1 bunch green onions
1 cup mayonnaise
1 (8 oz.) carton sour cream
1 sm. pkg. Original Hidden Valley Ranch dressing
Garlic salt
1 tsp. dill weed

Slice or chop all vegetables very small. Mix all remaining ingredients and pour over the vegetables. Refrigerate 3 to 4 hours. Serves 15 to 20.

Clari Miller, International Falls

NINE VEGETABLE SALAD

1 cup celery, cut fine
1 cup carrots, cut fine
1 cup green pepper, cut fine
1 cup onion, cut fine
1 cup cauliflower, cut fine
1 cup tomato, cut fine
1 cup cucumber, cut fine
1 cup broccoli, cut fine
1 cup black ripe olives, cut fine (optional)

Mix all ingredients.

Dressing:
1 bottle Italian dressing
1 pkg. dry Italian cream dressing

Mix dressings; pour over salad. Keeps 7 to 10 days in refrigerator.

Mary O'Brien, Currie

WATERGATE SALAD

1 box pistachio instant pudding
1 (16 oz.) can pineapple
1 (12 oz.) carton Cool Whip
Nuts
1 cup miniature marshmallows

Stir pudding and pineapple. Let stand 30 minutes; stir in Cool Whip, nuts and marshmallows.

Esther Echternach, New Richland

SIX VEGETABLE SALAD

1 lg. can peas, drained
½ cup sliced green onions and tops
½ cup sliced red radishes
1 cup sliced celery
1 cup shredded carrots
1 cup fresh cauliflower florets

Put prepared vegetables in large bowl.

Dressing:
⅓ cup salad oil
⅔ cup vinegar
1 cup sugar
2 tsp. salt
⅛ tsp. pepper

Mix ingredients, stirring until sugar dissolves. Pour desired amount over vegetables. Cover and marinate in the refrigerator 24 hours or longer. Drain before serving. Makes about 5 cups of salad.

Pat McClain, Marshall

VEGETABLE SALAD

1 head cabbage, shredded
1 head cauliflower, cut in small pieces
1 bunch broccoli, cut in small pieces
1 (10 oz.) bag frozen peas
1 bunch green onions, cut small
1 lb. bacon, fried and crumbled
1 cup sunflower seeds
Shredded carrots, optional
Green peppers, optional
Celery, optional

Mix all ingredients; set aside.

Dressing:
2 cups salad dressing
¼ cup sugar
⅓ cup grated Parmesan cheese

Mix and pour over vegetables. Makes a very large batch.

Mary Barry, Owatonna

WALLA WALLA SALAD

1 lg. head Romaine lettuce
½ med. Walla Walla, Maui, or other sweet onion
½ cup diced red or yellow bell pepper
⅓ cup crumbled Bleu cheese
2 Tbsp. spoon balsamic vinegar
1 (2 oz.) can anchovy fillets
1 to 3 cloves garlic, minced

Rinse, drain and crisp Romaine leaves. Cut leaves into 1 inch wide strips. Coarsely chop onion. In salad bowl, combine lettuce, onion, bell pepper, cheese, vinegar and oil from anchovies. Chop anchovies and add to salad along with garlic to taste; mix well. Serves 8 to 10.

Maria E. Loeffler, Albany, OR
National Director, 1988-1992
3rd Vice National Regent, 1992-1994
2nd Vice National Regent, 1994-present

SALADS, SOUPS & SANDWICHES

466

CHICKEN WILD RICE SALAD

2/3 cup mayonnaise
1/3 cup milk
2 Tbsp. lemon juice
1/4 tsp. dried tarragon, crumbled
3 cups cooked chicken, cubed
3 cups cooked wild rice
1/3 cup sliced green onions
1 (8 oz.) can sliced water chestnuts, drained
1/2 tsp. salt
1/8 tsp. pepper
1/2 lb. seedless green grapes, halved
1 cup salted cashews

Blend mayonnaise, milk, lemon juice and tarragon; set aside. In large bowl, combine chicken, wild rice, green onions, water chestnuts, salt and pepper. Stir in mayonnaise mixture until blended. Refrigerate, covered, 2 to 3 hours. Just before serving, fold in grapes and cashews. Garnish with grape clusters. Makes 8 (1 cup) servings.

Avis Weydert, St. Peter

WILD RICE CHICKEN SALAD

2/3 cup wild rice, cooked and chilled
3 cups diced cooked chicken
1 1/2 tsp. seasoned salt
1 cup mayonnaise
1 cup toasted almonds, slivered
1 1/2 cups green grapes, halved
1 can water chestnuts, sliced

Mix cooked rice, chicken, salt and mayonnaise. Chill overnight. Add almonds, grapes and water chestnuts and chill until serving. May use white rice or a mixture of white and wild rice if preferred.

Sharon Stevens, Fergus Falls

WILD RICE SALAD

1 cup wild rice, uncooked
3 cups diced, cooked chicken
1 cup sliced celery
Green onions, diced (to taste)
1 (6 oz.) pkg. slivered almonds
1/4 cup salad dressing
1 cup sour cream

Mix all ingredients. Cover and refrigerate overnight.

Marge Eiden, Fairmont

WILD RICE SALAD (LOW SALT)

1 cup uncooked wild rice
Seasoned salt, optional
2 cups diced, cooked chicken
1 1/2 cups halved green grapes
1/3 cup sliced water chestnuts, drained
3/4 cup light mayonnaise
1 cup cashews, optional
Lettuce leaves

Cook rice according to package directions, omitting salt or substituting seasoned salt, if desired; drain well. Cool to room temperature. Spoon chicken, grapes, water chestnuts and mayonnaise into large bowl. Toss gently with a fork; cover and chill. Just before serving, add cashews, if desired. Serve on lettuce leaves or line a bowl with lettuce leaves and fill with salad.

Teresa Willitte, Blue Earth

WILD RICE SALAD

1 cup wild rice	2 Tbsp. soy sauce
3½ cups water	2 Tbsp. white vinegar
½ tsp. salt	1 tsp. sugar
½ carrot, peeled	½ tsp. ground ginger
½ onion	2 cups fresh spinach, chopped
1 stick celery	2 tomatoes, chopped
2 cloves garlic	1 cup green onion, chopped
¼ cup oil	¾ cup bacon, crumbled

Cook wild rice in water with salt. Add the carrot, onion, celery and garlic. Bring to boil; reduce heat to a simmer and cook until rice is tender. Remove the vegetables from the rice and cool slightly. In a separate bowl, combine oil, soy sauce, vinegar, sugar and ginger. Add to warm rice. Cover and refrigerate until well chilled. Just before serving, mix in the remaining ingredients.

Phyllis J. Conway, St. James

WILD RICE SALAD

2 cups blanched broccoli, cut into bite size pieces	10 lg. ripe olives, sliced (or more if you like)
2 cups cauliflower, cut into bite size pieces	10 artificial crab legs, cut up
2 cups cooked wild rice	Seven Seas Creamy Italian dressing

Mix all ingredients and add enough dressing to make very moist. Can be made the day before using.

Sue Forster, New Ulm

* * SOUPS * *

CHICKEN DUMPLING SOUP

5 cups cooked chicken (about 2¾ lb. uncooked)	¾ lb. frozen sliced carrots
	1 chopped onion
3 qts. chicken broth	Salt and pepper to taste
¾ lb. frozen peas	

Combine chicken, broth and vegetables. Simmer for 10 minutes.

Dumplings:

1 egg	1 cup flour
⅓ cup milk	Dash of salt

Combine and drop tiny balls of dough into the boiling soup from the end of spoon. Cook about 5 minutes. Dumplings will rise to the surface when done.

Patty Durand, Argyle

CHICKEN VEGETABLE SOUP AND DUMPLINGS

2 qts. cold water
2 tsp. salt
¼ tsp. pepper
1 Tbsp. chicken flavored soup
  base
1 onion, chopped
3 stalks celery, cut up

2 lg. carrots, sliced
3 potatoes, diced
¼ cup regular rice or ½ cup
  instant
1 cup cut up cabbage or
  broccoli
1 cup cut up chicken

Combine ingredients and cook until done, approximately 20 minutes. Simmer.

Dumplings:

2 eggs
¾ cup plus 1 Tbsp. flour

Salt and pepper

Mix ingredients well. Drop a little at a time into soup. Simmer 5 to 10 minutes.

Josephine Befort, Zumbrota

LITTLE SOUP DUMPLINGS

1 egg
4 Tbsp. flour

Pinch of salt
1 tsp. vegetable oil

Mix eggs with flour, salt and oil. Spoon the mixture, ¼ teaspoon at a time, into boiling soup and cook 2 to 3 minutes. The dumplings are the last ingredient added to the soup. Can be used in chicken, beef or potato soup.

Mary Ernster, Caledonia

BEEF-BARLEY SOUP

²/₃ cup med. Quaker barley
1 lb. lean ground beef
1 (1 lb.) can Bush's baked beans
  or kidney beans
1 (46 oz.) can V-8 vegetable
  juice
1 qt. water
1 (10½ oz.) can cream of
  mushroom soup
1 (10½ oz.) can cream of celery
  soup

½ tsp. garlic powder
½ tsp. onion salt
½ tsp. paprika
½ tsp. salt
½ tsp. pepper
1 (9 oz.) pkg. frozen mixed
  vegetables
¾ cup Velveeta cheese, cut in
  small pieces
1 cup milk

Boil 4 cups water in a 6 quart saucepan. Stir in barley and boil at medium heat for about 15 minutes. Drain water from the barley and rinse barley once more with water. Brown beef in frying pan for 5 minutes, stirring constantly. Add all the ingredients into large saucepan; boil on low heat for 20 minutes, stirring occasionally. Makes 20 (1 cup) servings.

Rosemary Walz, Mahnomen
District Deputy, 1992-1996
State Treasurer, 1996-present

CREAM SOUP BASE

2 cups powdered milk	2 Tbsp. dried onion flakes
¾ cup cornstarch	1 tsp. basil
⅓ cup chicken bouillon	

Combine all ingredients. Use ⅓ cup of mixture to 1½ cups water. Cook until thickens. Use as base for cream soups or as white sauce for hot dishes or vegetables.

Andrea Olsen, Waseca

CREAM OF ASPARAGUS SOUP

1 cup asparagus, chopped and cooked (reserve ½ cup liquid)	2 Tbsp. flour
	Pepper to taste
1 sm. onion, chopped	1 cup skim milk
2 Tbsp. margarine	

Mash cooked asparagus and onion. Melt margarine in saucepan. Add flour and pepper. Cook and mix well. Gradually add milk, stirring constantly. Add reserved vegetable liquid. Cook over medium heat, stirring until slightly thickened. Add asparagus; heat thoroughly. Sprinkle with paprika when served. Makes 3 servings.

Kate Huneke, Bellechester

MOM'S NAVY BEAN SOUP

2 cups navy beans	3 ribs of celery, chopped
2 qts. water	1 cup tomato juice
1½ lbs. ham or shank	2 tsp. salt, optional (taste first)
1 lg. onion, chopped	¼ tsp. pepper
3 carrots, diced	1 clove, optional (I omit)

Wash beans and soak overnight. Place beans, water, meat and onion in pan; bring to boil, reduce heat and cook gently until beans are tender. Add carrot, celery, tomato juice, salt, pepper and clove, if preferred. Cover and cook until vegetables are tender.

Rita Schiller, Owatonna

POLISH SAUSAGE BEAN SOUP

1 med. potato, diced	1 can bean with bacon soup plus 1 can water
2 med. carrots, diced	
1 med. onion, diced	1 ring (or less) skinned, sliced Polish sausage
2 stalks celery, diced	
3 cups water	Salt and pepper to taste

Simmer all ingredients until done. Serve with crust bread.

Margaret Welander, Fergus Falls

BEEF MEDLEY

1 lb. ground beef	3 carrots, sliced
2 or 3 sliced onions	2 potatoes, cubed
2 tsp. salt	1 (No. 2) can tomatoes
2 tsp. pepper	1 sm. can tomato sauce
1/3 cup pearl barley	2 tsp. A-1 steak sauce
6 cups water	

Cook beef for 2 or 3 minutes in a large kettle with cover. Add onions, salt and pepper. Next, add pearl barley and water. Simmer, covered, for 1 hour, then add remaining ingredients. Simmer, covered, for 1 more hour. Makes a delicious, nutritious meal.

Veronica Robbie, International Falls

BROCCOLI CHEESE SOUP

1 cup water	2 cups milk
1 chicken bouillon cube	1 lb. Velveeta cheese, cubed
1 (10 oz.) pkg. frozen chopped broccoli	1 can cream of chicken soup, undiluted
1 med. carrot	1 Tbsp. minced onion flakes
2 to 3 Tbsp. butter or margarine	1 Tbsp. Worcestershire sauce
3 Tbsp. flour	Pepper to taste

Heat water and bouillon cube to boiling. Add broccoli and carrot. Cook 5 minutes or until tender. Remove from heat, but do not drain. In separate saucepan, melt butter. Add flour slowly. Gradually add milk and cook until thickened. Stir in cheese, soup, onion, Worcestershire sauce and pepper. Add broccoli-carrot mixture. Heat thoroughly and serve. Serves 10 to 12.

Dotty Jones, St. Charles
District Deputy, 1994-present
Lucille Rassier, Littlefork
Gretta Short, Slayton

CHICKEN BARLEY SOUP

1 (2 to 3 lb.) broiler-fryer chicken, cut up	1 chicken bouillon cube, optional
2 qts. water	1 tsp. salt, optional
1½ cups diced carrots	1 bay leaf
1 cup diced celery	½ tsp. poultry seasoning
½ cup barley	½ tsp. pepper
½ cup chopped onion	½ tsp. dried sage

In large kettle, cook chicken in water until tender. Cool broth and skim off fat. Bone chicken and cut into bite size pieces; return to kettle along with remaining ingredients. Simmer, covered, at least 1 hour or until vegetables and barley are tender. Remove bay leaf. Serves 5. One serving has 259 calories. Diabetic exchanges: one serving (prepared without bouillon and salt) equals 2½ lean meat, 1 starch, 1 vegetable.

Rita Rotta, Perham

471

CHILI

1 to 2 lbs. ground beef	1 (6 oz.) can tomato paste
1 med. onion	1 (1 lb.) can cooked tomatoes
1 (1 lb.) can chili beans	1 (4 oz.) can mushrooms
1 lg. can tomato juice	1 to 2 tsp. salt
1 (8 oz.) can tomato sauce	1 to 2 Tbsp. chili powder

Brown meat and onion. Combine all other ingredients. Start with about ⅔ can of tomato juice and add more as it thickens and cooks. Simmer for about 1½ to 3 hours. The secret is to let it cook and simmer for a long time.

Dolly Meyer, North Mankato

EXCELLENT CHILI

3 qts. canned tomatoes	1 lg. green pepper, chopped in
2 lg. cans regular chili beans	small pieces
1 sm. can (or more) hot chili	2 to 3 tsp. salt
beans	2 level tsp. pepper
2 to 3 lg. chopped onions	1 tsp. paprika (or more)
2 lbs. ground beef, browned	3 tsp. regular chili powder (or
1 lg. red pepper, chopped in	more)
small pieces	2 tsp. "hot" chili powder

Mix all ingredients real good; put into large kettle. Bring to a boil, stirring often. Lower heat; simmer for 1 hour or more. It thickens as it cooks, so stir often, so it doesn't burn down to your kettle.

Note: If you don't have any red peppers on hand, you can use 2 green peppers,. Can freeze leftovers, as this makes a large batch. Serve with white crackers.

Marguerite Salzle, Waseca
Mary La Bine, Argyle

GRANDPA'S CHILI

1½ lbs. ground beef	6 weiners, cut in ¼ inch slices
1 med. onion, chopped	3 med. carrots, sliced
1 (14 oz.) can kidney beans	1 (10 oz.) can tomato soup
and juice	1 tsp. salt
1 (10 oz.) can mushrooms and	¼ tsp. pepper
juice	1 tsp. chili powder

Brown beef; remove and put in large saucepan. Add remaining ingredients. Stir and bring to a boil. Cover and simmer for 1 hour. Add more water if it gets too dry. Can add more chili powder to suit taste.

Robina Raymond, International Falls

NOW THAT'S CHILI

1 lb. lean ground beef
1 clove garlic, minced (about
   1 tsp.)
1 lg. onion, finely chopped
   (1 cup)
1 med. green pepper, finely
   chopped
2 Tbsp. chili powder
¼ tsp. allspice

¼ tsp. coriander
1 tsp. cumin
½ tsp. salt or to taste
1 Tbsp. sugar, optional
½ cup water
2 cups (16 oz.) canned crushed
   tomatoes
1 (16 oz.) can red kidney beans
   with liquid

Cook beef, garlic, onion and green pepper in a heavy skillet over medium-high heat, stirring frequently to break up meat. Cook until onion is soft and meat has lost it's pink color. Add remaining ingredients and bring to a boil. Cover and reduce heat. Simmer the chili for 45 minutes, stirring frequently.

Variation: Isabelle adds bay leaves.

Garnet Ames, Inernational Falls
Isabelle Tomczak, International Falls

CHRISTMAS EVE CHOWDER

2 cups cubed potatoes
½ cup sliced carrots
½ cup diced celery
¼ cup diced onion
½ tsp. salt
½ tsp. pepper
2 cups boiling water

¼ cup butter or margarine
¼ cup flour
2 cups milk
1 can cream corn
¼ cup American cheese
½ to 1 cup diced ham

Cook vegetables in water for 10 minutes. Melt butter; add flour and gradually stir in milk. Cook until thickened; add to vegetables. Add cream corn, cheese and ham.

Margaret Tibodeau, Blue Earth

CLAM CHOWDER

6 potatoes, peeled and cut
   into bite size pieces
2 carrots, coarsely grated
3 or 4 chicken bouillon cubes
¼ cup butter
5 cups water
¼ tsp. pepper
2 onions, chopped fine

1 stalk celery, cut fine
1 Tbsp. parsley flakes
1 tsp. salt
1 can cream of celery soup
1 can mushroom stems and
   pieces, drained
1 (13 oz.) can evaporated milk
2 sm. cans clams with liquid

Combine first 10 ingredients; simmer until vegetables are tender. Add soup, mushroom stems and pieces, evaporated milk and clams with liquid. Simmer 10 to 15 minutes and serve.

Eleanor Klavetter, Plainview

CLAM CHOWDER

1 (6½ oz.) can minced clams
¼ cup chopped onion
2 Tbsp. butter
1½ cups diced potatoes
2 Tbsp. water

2 cups milk
⅛ tsp. celery salt
⅛ tsp. onion salt
⅛ tsp. pepper
Additional salt to taste

Drain clams. Cook onion in butter; add potatoes, clam juice and water. Cook until tender. Add clams, milk and seasonings. Heat, but do not boil.

Joan Barkovic, International Falls
State Treasurer, 1980-1982

NEW ENGLAND CLAM CHOWDER

3 slices bacon
1 lg. potato, peeled and cubed
1 med. stalk celery, chopped
1 sm. onion, chopped
¾ tsp. salt
⅛ tsp. pepper

⅛ tsp. thyme
2 (6½ oz.) cans minced clams, drained (reserve liquid)
¼ cup flour
3 cups milk

In large saucepan, fry bacon until crisp; drain on paper towel. To drippings, add potato, celery, onion, salt, pepper, thyme and liquid from clams. Heat to boiling and cook covered, about 10 minutes or until vegetables are tender. Combine flour and milk; add to vegetable mixture. Heat over medium heat until mixture thickens, stirring occasionally. Stir in clams. Heat through, but do not boil. Garnish with crumbled bacon. Serves 5 to 6.

Jeannette Malterer, Waseca

HAMBURGER SOUP

1 lb. ground beef
2 Tbsp. butter or margarine
1 tsp. salt
½ cup chopped onion
1 cup diced carrots
1 cup diced potatoes

1 cup diced celery
1 cup chopped cabbage
1 cup tomatoes, green beans or corn
2 Tbsp. rice

Brown beef in butter. Put in crock pot with salt, onions, carrots, potatoes and celery; cook until vegetables are almost done. Add rest of ingredients and finish cooking.

Margaret Tibodeau, Blue Earth
Margaret Welander, Fergus Falls
Janice Thraen, Iona

HEARTY HAMBURGER VEGETABLE SOUP

1 lb. hamburger
1 med. onion, chopped
1 med. green pepper (1 cup)
2 big ribs celery, or more
½ cup carrots
1 (16 oz.) can tomatoes or
   stewed tomatoes
¼ cup barley
Seasoned salt and pepper to
   taste
1 can beef broth
6 cups water
1 env. Lipton instant vegetable
   soup mix

Brown meat in Dutch oven, breaking up lumps with fork. Pour off all but 2 tablespoons of drippings. Add onions, green pepper, and celery; saute for 5 minutes. Add carrots, tomatoes, barley, seasoned salt and pepper. Add broth and water; bring to a boil. Lower heat, cover and simmer 1 hour or until barley is tender. Add soup mix and cook 30 minutes longer.

Ann Rasmussen, International Falls

SPLIT PEA SOUP

2 qts. water
Ham bone and 1 or 2 cups
   ham, diced
1 onion, diced
½ cup diced potatoes
Salt and pepper to taste
1 lb. or 2 cups yellow split dried
   peas
5 peppercorns
⅓ cup sliced carrots

Simmer all for 2 hours.

Joyann Espeseth, Mahnomen

HEARTY SPLIT PEA SOUP

2 lbs. dried green peas
2 qts. water
1 ham bone and 3 lbs. ham meat
2 cups chopped celery
2 cups onion, chopped
2 cups carrots, cut fine
Little parsley, pepper and salt
½ tsp. thyme
½ tsp. rosemary
1 bay leaf

Place peas in large pan with the water; cover and boil 2 minutes. Remove from heat and let stand 1 hour. Add remaining ingredients and let simmer for 2 hours.

Patrica Gavin, Caledonia

SOUP STOCK

12½ lbs. tomatoes
5 lg. carrots, cut fine
5 lg. onions, cut fine
1 bunch celery, cut fine
1 green pepper, cut fine
Salt

Cook for 1 hour. Makes about 6 quarts. Also good to use with spaghetti for hot dish.

Ann Klinkhammer, Mahnomen

GERMAN POTATO SOUP

6 cups cubed potatoes	½ tsp. salt
1¼ cups chopped celery	¹/₈ tsp. pepper
½ cup onion	4 slices bacon, fried
5 cups water	Little chopped parsley

Combine first 6 ingredients; boil slowly for 1 hour. With a potato masher, mash all ingredients. Add fried bacon and parsley.

Dumplings:

1 egg	½ tsp. salt
¹/₃ cup water	¾ cup flour

Stir ingredients until smooth and stiff. Drop by teaspoon into the boiling soup. Simmer for 10 minutes after dumplings are added.

Mary White, Brownsville

POTATO SOUP

6 cups potatoes, sliced thin	½ tsp. salt
2 cups carrots, sliced thin	¼ tsp. pepper
6 slices bacon	1 cup milk
1 cup chopped onion	1 cup beer
1 cup diced celery	2 cups light cream

In a 4 quart cooker, cook potatoes and carrots in boiling salted water until tender; drain. Saute bacon until crisp; drain and crumble. Saute onions and celery in 2 tablespoons of grease from bacon until onions are transparent. Combine all ingredients and simmer approximately 30 minutes. DO NOT BOIL. Serve with shredded cheese and garnish with parsley. Makes 2 quarts.

Genevieve Fairbanks

POTATO SOUP

2 stalks celery, chopped	Dash of pepper
1 cup onion, chopped	Dash of garlic powder
5 med. potatoes, cubed	2 cups milk
2 carrots, sliced	1 cup cubed cheese
5 chicken bouillon cubes	

Add celery, onion, potatoes, carrots, bouillon, pepper and garlic powder and cook until tender. Add milk and cheese; heat through. Serves 6.

Kathy Riopelle, Argyle
Gladys Wimmer, Littlefork

476

SALMON CHOWDER

1 (1 lb.) can salmon, drained	1 (1 lb.) can tomatoes
¾ cup chopped onion	1 (8 oz.) can whole kernel corn
½ cup chopped green pepper	½ tsp. salt
¼ cup butter or margarine	¼ tsp. thyme
1 cup boiling water	Dash of pepper
⅓ cup salmon liquid	1 bay leaf

Break salmon into large pieces. Cook onion and green pepper in butter or margarine until tender. Combine all ingredients and cook for 15 minutes or until vegetables are tender. Remove bay leaf. Serves 6.

Marge Breneman, Moorhead

ZALNOKA (SAUERKRAUT SOUP)

½ cup sauerkraut	¼ cup flour
1 cup water	6 eggs
1 cup milk	

Boil sauerkraut and water 10 minutes. Thicken milk with flour; add to sauerkraut over low heat, stirring until smooth and consistency of medium gravy. If too thick, add a little milk. When thickened, add eggs, one at a time; do not stir. Let cook slowly about 1 hour, or until eggs are done. Serve over cooked potatoes. Add a vegetable and some cheese, and you have a complete meal. Czeck origin. For gravy consistency, may need to add more milk.

Patricia Deml, Owatonna

SPINACH SOUP

4 cups water	2 eggs
4 chicken bouillon cubes or	¼ tsp. oregano
4 tsp. granules	¼ cup Parmesan cheese
½ pkg. frozen spinach or	
½ (16 oz.) can	

Boil water and bouillon for 5 minutes. Add spinach and simmer until done. Beat eggs, oregano and cheese. Pour slowly into spinach soup so it threads, stirring constantly. Serve with crackers and fresh vegetable salad.

Kathy Wilcke (Edna Sullivan), Battle Creek, IA

* * * * * * * *

I will give thanks to you, O Lord, with all my heart.
I will declare all your wondrous deeds. Psalm 9:2
Lorraine Schmidt, Caledonia

TOMATO SOUP

8 qts. whole tomatoes
5 to 6 med. onions
½ cup sugar
¾ cup flour
½ cup butter
¼ cup salt

Do not peel tomatoes. Grind onions in blender. Boil tomatoes and onions until cooked. Strain in food press. Mix remaining ingredients and then with some of tomato mixture. Combine all ingredients. Bring to a boil and hot pack. Process 20 minutes in hot water bath.

Debra McNamee, Mahnomen

CURSILLO HOMEMADE TOMATO SOUP

2 lg. (gal. size) cans tomatoes
1½ Tbsp. soda
½ lb. butter
¼ to ½ cup dry onion flakes
3 to 4 Tbsp. parsley flakes
1 Tbsp. pepper
2 Tbsp. salt
1½ gal. whole milk

Boil and mash tomatoes; add soda (will foam up; stir down). Add butter. Add onion, parsley, pepper and salt. Do not boil. Taste and adjust salt and pepper. I like to thicken with Wondra flour. Delicious. Serves 35 to 40.

Mary Jahoda, Moorhead

TUNA CHOWDER**

1 (10½ oz.) can split pea soup
3 tsp. instant minced onion
1½ cups cold water
1 cup whole milk
⅓ cup Minute Rice, uncooked
1 (9¼ oz.) can water packed
   tuna, drained
½ tsp. salt
Dash of pepper
1 tsp. prepared mustard

In saucepan, combine soup, onion, water and milk; bring to a boil. Add remaining ingredients and simmer 6 to 8 minutes, stirring occasionally.

Edna Hanson, Blue Earth

TURKEY SOUP

1 turkey carcass
2 carrots, peeled and sliced
2 bay leaves
½ cup barley or brown rice
   (can use wild rice)
1 lg. onion
3 to 4 stalks celery, including
   leaves
½ tsp. salt or to taste

Cover with 2 or 3 quarts water. Skim foam if necessary. Simmer 2 to 3 hours. Remove carcass.

Joyann Espeseth, Mahnomen

TURKEY CHOWDER

½ cup med. chopped onion
2 stalks celery, diced
3 Tbsp. butter
2 Tbsp. flour
½ tsp. salt
1/8 tsp. pepper
2 cups broth
2 lg. carrots, sliced thin

1 (10 oz.) pkg. frozen vegetables
3 cups milk
1 (8 oz.) pkg. diced American cheese
1 cup diced cooked turkey (or more)
1 Tbsp. parsley

Saute first 3 ingredients; tenderize, then add next 4 ingredients. Blend until thickened, then add carrots and vegetables. Cook for 30 minutes, then add remaining ingredients. Heat until cheese is melted but don't boil. Serves 6.

Margaret Welander, Fergus Falls

CREAMY VEGETABLE MEDLEY SOUP

2 Tbsp. chopped onion
6 Tbsp. butter or low fat margarine
5 Tbsp. flour
1 cup chicken broth*
2 cups skim milk
½ cup diced celery

1 cup chopped broccoli
1 cup sliced carrots
1 cup chopped cauliflower
Dash of nutmeg and pepper
½ to 1 cup shredded or cubed cheese**

*I use 2 teaspoons chicken bouillon granules or 2 cubes dissolved in 1 cup hot water..

**I've used Velveeta, or can use low fat cheese.

Saute onion in melted butter or margarine over medium heat. Blend in flour. Remove from heat and gradually stir in broth to make smooth paste. Add remaining broth and milk, stirring until smooth. Heat 7 to 9 minutes over medium heat until slightly thickened, stirring occasionally. As liquid heats, microwave vegetables just until tender. Add vegetables to thickening soup. If desired, stir in shredded or cubed cheese. Heat soup about 15 minutes on medium until it reaches serving temperature. Serve with bread sticks, crackers or cheese for a delicious meal. I usually double this recipe so I'm sure to have leftovers! Adjust amounts of vegetables as desired.

Cathy Nelson, Owatonna
Phyllis Wirries, Moorhead

* * * * * * * *

There is an appointed time for everything and a time for every affair under the heavens. Ecclesiastes 3:1
Caryl Ryan, Caledonia

EASY VEGETABLE SOUP

1 lb. ground beef	2 (16 oz.) cans stewed tomatoes
1 cup chopped onion	3½ cups water
1 clove garlic, minced	4 beef bouillon cubes
1 cup sliced carrots	1 Tbsp. parsley flakes
1 cup sliced celery	¼ tsp. dried basil leaves
1 cup frozen green beans	1 tsp. salt
¼ cup regular rice	⅛ tsp. pepper

Cook ground beef, onion and garlic in Dutch oven until beef is browned, about 10 minutes; drain off fat. Add remaining ingredients; bring to boiling. Reduce heat and simmer, covered, for 50 minutes or until vegetables are tender. Makes about 2¾ quarts. May not need the salt as the bouillon cubes are quite salty.

Lillian Walske, Winona

LO-CAL CREAM OF VEGETABLE SOUP

2 cups chicken broth	1 cup cooked rice
3 cups cut up vegetables	2 cups skim milk

In a 3 quart saucepan over high heat, heat broth and cut up vegetables to boiling. Reduce heat to low; cover and simmer until vegetables are just tender (5 to 25 minutes, depending upon vegetables), stirring often. Spoon half of the broth, half of vegetables and cooked rice into blender; cover (with center part of blender cover removed) and blend at low speed until smooth. Pour mixture into bowl. Repeat with remaining broth and vegetables. Return blended mixture to saucepan. Stir in milk; heat through. Makes about 6 servings.

Amy Tammaro, Eveleth

WILD RICE SOUP

1 lb. ground beef	¼ tsp. pepper
1 tsp. salt	4 ribs chopped celery
1 Tbsp. Italian seasoning	2 lg. onions, chopped
1 cup uncooked wild rice	3 cans cream of mushroom
1 cup water	soup
3 Tbsp. Tabasco sauce	2 soup cans water or ½ water
2 tsp. bouillon cubes	and ½ wine

Brown beef with salt and seasoning. Add wild rice and water, Tabasco sauce, bouillon, pepper, celery and onions. Simmer, covered, 30 minutes. Stir, then add mushroom soup and liquid. Cover and simmer 30 minutes. If too thick, add water.

Variation: A substitute for Italian seasoning is ¼ teaspoon each basil, oregano, and a dash of cayenne pepper. I soak the wild rice before adding the soup.

Phyllis Umhoefer, Mankato

WILD RICE

½ cup raw wild rice
1 sm. onion, chopped
2 Tbsp. margarine
2 cups water
1 can cream of celery soup

1 can cream of chicken soup
4 cups milk
1 lb. Velveeta cheese
Turkey, ham, chicken or hamburger (amount as desired)

Cook rice until tender, 50 to 60 minutes. Fry onion in margarine. Add water, soup and milk; heat and add cheese. Stir until fully heated and cheese is melted. Add rice and meat.

Rosemary Larson, Crookston

WILD RICE SOUP

1 (4 oz.) pkg. bacon, chopped
into small bits
¾ cup chopped onion
¾ cup chopped celery
⅓ cup chopped green pepper
1 can water

3 sm. cans Campbell's cream of
mushroom soup
1 can chicken broth
½ cup wild rice (3 cups cooked)
Sherry wine to taste
(about 1 Tbsp.)

Caution: If you use canned chicken broth, check for saltiness. Brown bacon bits until very crisp. Add onions, celery and green pepper. Saute until onions are clear. Add water and simmer until vegetables are tender. In another kettle, put the canned mushroom soup and chicken broth; whip with wire whip until very smooth. Add cooked wild rice and vegetable-bacon mix. If too thick, add water. Soup should be creamy. Bring to boil and last of all, add about 1 tablespoon dry sherry wine. Be careful with the sherry. Add only enough to subtly flavor the soup. Too much is worse than not enough.

Angeline Brascugli, International Falls
Monica Ahern, Mankato

WILD RICE SOUP

6 Tbsp. butter
1 Tbsp. minced onion
½ cup flour
3 cups chicken broth
2 cups cooked wild rice
⅓ cup minced ham

½ cup finely grated carrots
3 Tbsp. slivered almonds,
chopped
½ tsp. salt
1 cup half and half
2 Tbsp. dry sherry, optional

Melt butter in saucepan; saute onion until tender. Blend in flour; gradually add broth. Cook, stirring constantly until mixture comes to a boil and boil 1 minute. Stir in rice, ham, carrots, almonds and salt; simmer about 5 minutes. Blend in half and half and sherry; heat to serving temperature. Garnish with snipped parsley or chives. Makes 6 cups.

Dorothy Losinski, Winona
Arlys Fells, Waseca

HOT CHICKEN FOR SANDWICHES

1 cup diced chicken, cooked	½ cup broth
1 Tbsp. diced onion	½ tsp. Lawry's salt
2 Tbsp. tapioca	1 bouillon cube

Put all in crock pot and cook until thickened.

Margaret Tibodeau, Blue Earth

BARBECUE FOR A CROWD

2 cups water	4 Tbsp. vinegar
2 cups dehydrated onions	4 Tbsp. reconstituted lemon
12 lbs. ground beef	juice
4 tsp. salt	4 Tbsp. Worcestershire sauce
2 tsp. pepper	4 cans condensed tomato soup
4 Tbsp. sugar	4 cups catsup
2 tsp. dry mustard	4 cups celery, chopped fine

Add the water to the dehydrated onions; set aside. Brown the ground beef; remove fat. Add the onions, salt, pepper, sugar, mustard, vinegar, lemon juice and Worcestershire sauce. Add the tomato soup and catsup. Stir in the celery; simmer on top of the stove for 45 minutes. Add more catsup it if needs more moisture. Makes 7½ quarts. This recipe freezes well. (Can be cut in fourth for everyday.)

Pat Rivard, Argyle

BEEF AND BREW SANDWICHES

1 (5 to 6 lb.) rolled roast	½ tsp. salt
¼ to ½ tsp. garlic salt	½ tsp. pepper
¼ to ½ tsp. thyme	1 tsp. minced onions
¼ to ½ tsp. celery salt	1 stick oleo or butter
¼ to ½ tsp. oregano	6 lg. green peppers

Preheat oven to 350°. Season roast on one side with half of all seasonings. Add butter and a little water. Cover and bake 1½ hours, then turn over and season with rest of seasonings. Add the green pepper strips to roaster and add enough water to cover peppers. Bake another 1½ hours. When done, remove and cut into thin strips. Return to roaster and reheat in juices. Serve on hard rolls.

Loretta Briski, Eveleth

15-MINUTE BEEF BARBECUE

1 lb. beef round tip steaks, cut	3/4 cup prepared barbecue
1/8 to 1/4 inch thick	sauce
2 tsp. vegetable oil	4 crusty rolls, split
1 med. onion, cut into thin wedges	

Stack beef steaks; cut lengthwise in half and then crosswise into 1 inch wide strips; set aside. In large nonstick skillet, heat oil over medium-high heat until hot. Add onion; cook and stir 3 minutes or until lightly browned. Remove from skillet; keep warm. In same skillet, add beef (half at a time) and stir-fry 1 minute or until outside surface is no longer pink. (Do not overcook.) Stir in onion and barbecue sauce; heat through, stirring occasionally. Spoon equal amount of beef mixture on bottom half of each roll; close with top half of roll. Makes 4 servings (serving size: 1 sandwich). Total preparation and cooking time: 15 minutes.

Ruth Driscoll, Blue Earth

CHOW MEIN BURGERS

1 lb. ground beef	1/3 cup cold water
1/2 cup chopped onion	3 Tbsp. soy sauce
3/4 tsp. salt	2 Tbsp. cornstarch
1 (16 oz.) can Lachoy Chop	8 hamburger buns
Suey vegetables, drained	1 (3 oz.) can chow mein noodles

Combine ground beef with onion; cook until meat is browned and onion is tender. Add salt and chop suey vegetables. Stir water, soy sauce and cornstarch; stir into beef mixture. Cook 1 to 2 minutes until thick and bubbly, stirring to coat vegetables and meat. Split, toast and butter hamburger buns; spoon mixture on bottom halves. Crumble chow mein noodles over sandwiches; cover with top halves of buns or serve mixture between untoasted hamburger buns.

Catherine Illg, Currie

PIGS IN A BLANKET**

1 can tube biscuits	Cheese slices
Wieners, slit each one	

Shape biscuit dough oblong. Put cheese into slit in weiner. Wrap biscuit dough around weiner. Seal edges. Rub biscuit with a little oil. Place on cookie sheet. Bake at 400° for 15 to 20 minutes. Quick sandwich.

Mary Phillips, Owatonna

SALADS, SOUPS & SANDWICHES

SHREDDED BEEF ON A BUN

1 (5 to 6 lb.) chuck beef roast
1 cup chopped onion
1 cup chopped celery
Garlic powder to taste
Salt and pepper to taste
½ cup red wine vinegar
Kaiser rolls (or your choice)

Cut roast into chunks; brown in electric fry pan. Add onion, celery, garlic powder, salt and pepper. With two forks, break meat apart while it is cooking. Add wine vinegar after about an hour of cooking. Cook on low heat all day. Serve on Kaiser rolls. Can also be cooked in a crock pot on low heat for 11 to 12 hours. Serve with barbecue sauce, horseradish or mustard, or others.

Alice Turk, Eveleth

HOT DOG SANDWICH SAUCE

4 cans Hormel chili without
  beans
4 cans tomato soup
1 cup sugar
3 cans water

Boil all ingredients; put in crock pot. Serve on hot dogs for crowd.

Mary Ann Schmitz, Caledonia

HOT HAM AND CHEESE BUNS

½ cup butter
¼ cup mustard
¼ cup chopped onion
Buns
Ham
Swiss cheese

Mix first 3 ingredients and spread on buns. Add ham and cheese. Heat in oven or microwave.

Marilyn Rewitzer, New Ulm

PEANUT BUTTER AND BANANA SANDWICH

2 slices white bread
Butter, not margarine
Peanut butter (Skippy is best)
1 banana, sliced in ³/₈ inch slices

Fold open bread as you would your Bible. On one slice, spread generously with butter. On the other slice, spread more generously with peanut butter. Place 9 banana slices on peanut butter side of each sandwich. (If you place the bananas on the buttered side, it will taste different and it would have to be called banana butter sandwich...Yuk!) Place buttered slice face down on peanut butter banana half. With both hands, grasp sandwich firmly to keep banana slices from escaping...and enjoy! P.S. A glass of milk is also a must. Note: Anything more complicated in the kitchen, I can't handle.

Father Gerald Meidl, Marshall
State Chaplain, 1994-present

SISTER JANE'S SLOPPY JOES

1 lb. ground beef
1½ cups chopped onions
1½ cups chopped celery
1 can tomato soup
2 Tbsp. vinegar
1 Tbsp. prepared mustard
1½ tsp. salt
Chili powder
1 Tbsp. catsup
1 Tbsp. BBQ sauce, optional

Simmer 30 minutes or bake in slow oven for 1 hour.

Rosie Kelly, Waseca

SOME OF THAT STUFF

1 can tuna, drained
3 hard boiled eggs, chopped
½ cup grated Cheddar cheese
1 stalk celery, chopped
Small bit of onion
1 or 2 Tbsp. Miracle Whip
6 to 8 hamburger buns

Mix tuna and other ingredients; spoon onto buns. Place on cookie sheet and cover with foil. Heat through at 350° for 20 minutes.

Louise Kees, Red Lake Falls

TOOTSA'S FILLED BUNS

1 lb. ground beef
Salt and pepper
Chopped onion
2 cups raw grated cabbage
1 loaf frozen white bread dough, thawed

Brown the ground beef; add salt, pepper and chopped onion to your taste. Add the grated cabbage and simmer for 15 minutes. Divide the bread dough into 12 pieces. Roll piece of dough on floured surface into a 5 inch circle and put $1/12$ of the mixture (slightly cooled) on center of circle. Bring up edges and pinch together to seal well. Place sealed side down on lightly greased cookie sheet and bake at 325° for about 30 minutes. Freeze well and can be reheated in microwave or regular oven. Also good made with packaged coleslaw mixture chopped a little finer. Make a double batch and have some for the freezer.

Margaret Ann Erjavec, Eveleth

TURKEY SALAD SANDWICH

12 oz. diced turkey
½ cup chopped water chestnuts
3 Tbsp. minced red onion
1 cup seedless grapes, halved
2 Tbsp. rice or apple cider vinegar
2 Tbsp. lite mayonnaise
2 Tbsp. Dijon mustard
1 Tbsp. thawed apple juice concentrate
12 slices reduced calorie bread

In a medium bowl, combine first 4 ingredients. In a separate bowl, whisk next 4 ingredients until thoroughly combined. Combine dressing with turkey mixture. Divide mixture into 6 sandwiches. Makes 6 sandwiches. 2 oz. protein, 1 tsp. oil, 1 starch per diet center.

Jan McDonald, Owatonna

485

MOLDED CHICKEN SALAD

1½ cups chopped chicken, cooked
1 cup diced celery
1 tsp. minced onion
1 cup mayonnaise
2 hard boiled eggs, chopped

1 pkg. Knox gelatin, dissolved in ½ cup cold water, then ½ cup hot water and cooled
1 pkg. lemon jello
¾ cup hot water
½ cup orange juice
1 can cranberry sauce

Mix first 5 ingredients. Fold gelatin into chicken mixture. Dissolve lemon jelly in hot water. Add orange juice and cool. Add cranberry sauce that has been whipped. Place half of cranberry mixture in bottom of a 9 inch square pan; let set. Add salad mixture, let set and add rest of cranberry mixture; refrigerate.

Beatrice A. Fry, International Falls

WILL POWER TONIC

1 qt. determination
1 cup desire
1 Tbsp. common sense

1 Tbsp. foresight
1 Tbsp. energy
1 Tbsp. stick-to-it-tiveness

Bring determination to a boil and slowly stir in other ingredients, starting with the cup of desire. Without this basic ingredient, the time will be flat and have no effect. The last ingredient to go into the tonic is the stick-to-it-tiveness. Let steep for 1 hour. You will be a stronger, better person and on the way to a real success.

Margaret Zimmerman, Waseca
State Secretary
State Vice Regent

✝ MARY...OUR PATRONESS ✝

The Magnificat

My Soul magnifies the Lord
and my spirit rejoices in God my Savior
For he has regarded the lowliness of His handmaid;
Behold, henceforth, all generations shall call me blessed;
For He who is Mighty has done great things for me,
and Holy is His Name;
His mercy is from generation to generation
on those who fear Him.
He has shown might with His arm,
He has scattered the proud in the deceit of their heart.
He has put down the mighty from their thrones,
and has exalted the lowly.
He has filled the hungry with good things,
and the rich He has sent away empty.
He has given help to Israel, His servant,
Mindful of His mercy,
even as He spoke to our fathers,
To Abraham and his descendants forever.

Luke 1:46-55

"Rejoice...O Daughter of Jerusalem...the Lord, your God is in your midst." Zeph. 3:14, 17a. Mary, in whom the Lord, our God, has made his dwelling, is the daughter of Zion in person, the ark of the covenant, the place where the glory of the Lord found joy.

Blessed among all women is Mary because she believed in the fulfillment of the Lord's word. She stands out among the poor and humble and gave her consent to be and do all that God asked of her with her response, "Behold, I am the handmaid of the Lord; let it be done to me according to your word." Filled with the Holy Spirit, she made the Word visible to the poor and the lowly in the humility of his flesh. At the birth of the Christ Child Mary provided the vital link in the whole mystery of the Incarnation. At the presentation of Jesus in the temple, Simeon spoke words that revealed to her that she would have to live her obedience in faith by suffering at the side of the suffering Savior and that her motherhood would be mysterious and sorrowful and yet she did not waver.

Mary's faith sustained her as she called upon her son to provide help at a wedding at which the wine had run out, that found her at the foot of the cross, and with the apostles in the upper room when the Holy Spirit came upon them. It is through Mary that the Holy Spirit begins to bring men, the objects of God's merciful love, into communion with Christ.

The Mother of God shared in the fullness of Jesus' redemption from the moment of her conception to the completion of her earthly pilgrimage. Ever since then, her motherhood has extended to the brothers and sisters of her son who still journey on earth surrounded by danger and difficulties.

We imitate Mary who kept her heart and her eyes on Jesus from the manger in Bethlehem to the streets of Nazareth and Jerusalem, from the foot of the cross on Calvary, to His glorious resurrection and ascension.

Pope Pius XII declared Mary to be the patroness of the Americas under the title of "Our Lady of Guadalupe" in 1954. Our lady had appeared to an Aztec farmer, Juan Diego, there in the year 1531, and instructed him to ask the bishop to build a church in that place. The bishop's request for a sign from the Lady was fulfilled when Juan brought him a bouquet of roses from the snow covered mountain. Juan Diego opened his cloak to present the flowers and to everyone's amazement there appeared the image of Our Lady. The cloak, with the image on it, is still viewed today inside the Basilica of our Lady of Guadalupe, near Mexico City, by pilgrims from around the world.

Shirley Ettestad, National Director

APPLE PIE FOR DIABETICS

1 Tbsp. cornstarch	1 tsp. apple pie spice
1 (12 oz.) can apple juice concentrate	1 unbaked pie shell
	Second crust for top
4 cups sliced apples	

Mix cornstarch and apple juice concentrate. Cook, stirring until it begins to clear. Stir in sliced apples and spice. Pour into unbaked crust and top with second crust. Bake at 350° for 35 to 40 minutes. Mix filling ingredients and spread on cooled crust. Top with your favorite fruits (grapes, pears, apples, kiwi, blueberries, strawberries, raspberries, peaches, bananas, etc.)

Agnes Wencl, Medford

EASY APPLE PIE (DIABETIC)

2 whole graham crackers, crushed	1 pkg. sugar free lemon gelatin
5 med. apples, peeled and sliced	1 pkg. sugar free vanilla pudding mix (cook and serve variety)
2 cups water	2 Tbsp. water
½ tsp. cinnamon	½ cup vanilla flavored low fat yogurt
¼ tsp. nutmeg	

Spray 9 inch pie pan with cooking spray. Sprinkle with graham cracker crumbs, reserving 1 tablespoon for garnish. Bring apples, 2 cups water and spices to boil in large saucepan. Reduce heat to low; simmer 5 minutes, stirring frequently. Stir in gelatin. Mix pudding with about 2 tablespoons water and stir into apple mixture until well blended. Bring to full boil on high heat. Remove from heat and let stand for 5 minutes. Spoon into pie plate. Sprinkle with reserved crumbs. Refrigerate for 3 hours or until set. Garnish each serving with 1 tablespoon yogurt. Serves 8. Per serving: 90 calories, 1 g fat, 0 mg cholesterol, 135 mg sodium, 19 mg carbohydrates, 2 g dietary fiber, 2 g protein. Exchanges: 1 fruit, ½ starch.

Dolores Goraczkowski, Fairmont

BANANA MUFFINS

2 eggs	⅔ cup dry milk
½ tsp. baking soda	1 tsp. vanilla
4 slices bread, cubed	2 med. bananas (very ripe)

Combine all ingredients in bowl; beat with electric mixer until smooth. Pour into 12 muffin cups (sprayed with no-stick spray). Bake at 375° for 12 minutes. They are NOT high and fluffy muffins. They look like they have fallen, but they are delicious! Exchanges: 3 muffins equals ½ meat, 1 bread, 1 fruit, ½ milk. Serves 4.

Jule Erjavec, Eveleth

BANANA-NUT BREAD

1 cup mashed very ripe
   banana (about 3 small)
½ cup sugar
½ cup plain nonfat yogurt
¼ cup margarine, melted
1 tsp. vanilla extract
1 egg

1 egg white
2 cups all-purpose flour
1 tsp. baking powder
½ tsp. baking soda
¼ tsp. salt
¼ cup chopped pecans, toasted
Baking spray with flour

Combine first 7 ingredients in a large bowl; beat at medium speed of an electric mixer until well blended. Combine next 4 ingredients; stir in pecans. Add flour mixture to banana mixture, stirring just until moistened. Spoon batter into an 8½x4½x3 inch loaf pan coated with spray. Bake at 350° for 1 hour and 5 minutes or until a wooden pick inserted in center comes out clean. Cool 10 minutes in pan on a wire rack; remove from pan and cool completely on a wire rack. Serves 4. Serving size: 1 slice.

Betty Hager, Owatonna
State Quality of Life Co-Chair, 1996-present
State Membership Chair, 1992-1996
State Secretary, 1988-1992

BANANA BRAN MUFFINS (NO SUGAR)

1 cup flour, sifted
2½ tsp. baking powder
⅛ tsp. salt
1 cup whole bran cereal
1 med. egg, beaten

2 sm. ripe bananas, mashed
½ cup currants
¼ cup skim milk
2 Tbsp. cooking oil

Mix flour, baking powder, salt and bran. Combine remaining ingredients. Make a well in center of dry ingredients; add liquids all at once. Stir just to moistened; fill well greased muffin pan ⅔ full. Bake at 400° for 15 minutes or until done. Serve at once or warm later.

Armella Tembruell, Owatonna

LOW FAT BRAN MUFFINS

1 cup flour
2 tsp. baking powder
½ tsp. baking soda
½ tsp. cinnamon
2 cups 100% Bran cereal
1¼ cups skim milk

⅓ cup brown sugar, firmly
   packed
1 egg
½ cup applesauce
Raisins, optional

Heat oven to 400°. Mix dry ingredients in large bowl. Mix cereal, milk and sugar in another bowl. Let stand 5 minutes. Stir in egg and applesauce. Add to flour mixture; stir just until moistened (batter will be lumpy). Spoon batter into muffin pan sprayed with nonstick cooking spray, filling each cup ⅔ full. Bake for 18 to 20 minutes or until golden brown. Serve warm. Makes 12 small or 6 large.

Cathy Bjorklund, Moorhead

SPECIAL DIET

LO-CAL BROCCOLI SALAD

1/3 cup plus 2 tsp. mayonnaise
1 Tbsp. vinegar
2 Tbsp. sugar
1/4 cup plain yogurt
1 bunch broccoli, cut into bites
1 1/2 cups chopped celery

1 bunch green onions
1 cup raisins (plump in water)
1 1/2 cups green grapes, drained
   and cut in half
4 Tbsp. bacon bits

Mix first 4 ingredients for dressing. Mix remaining ingredients for salad. Pour dressing over salad and chill.

Odelia Majerus, Bellechester

SAVORY BROWN RICE

1 cup brown rice
2 green onions with tops,
   chopped
1 Tbsp. vegetable oil

1 tsp. caraway seeds
1 cinnamon stick
1 cup chicken stock
1 1/2 cups water

Rinse rice in several changes of water. Saute onion in oil with seeds and cinnamon stick for 3 minutes. Stir in rice and saute 1 minute. Add stock and water. Cook 30 to 40 minutes. Simmer until rice is tender and liquid absorbed. Fluff rice with fork. Remove cinnamon stick. Serve immediately.

Armella Willaert, North Mankato

BROWNIES (NO FAT) LOW CHOLESTEROL

1/2 cup plus 2 Tbsp. natural
   applesauce
1 1/2 cups sugar (less if sauce
   is sweetened)
1 tsp. vanilla

1/2 cup cocoa
3/4 cup flour
1 tsp. baking powder
1/4 tsp. salt
2 egg whites

Mix applesauce, sugar and vanilla in bowl. Sift dry ingredients; add to first mixture gradually while mixing. If you wish, beat the egg whites and add to above or add 2 unbeaten egg whites. Pour into square (or round) 9x9 inch baking pan. Bake at 350° for 35 to 40 minutes.

Frosting (low fat):
1 cup sugar
3 Tbsp. cornstarch
3 Tbsp. cocoa
1 cup hot water

Dash of salt
1 Tbsp. butter or oleo
1 tsp. milk

Boil first 5 ingredients until it thickens, stirring constantly. When thickened, add butter and vanilla. Spread on cake while hot.

Alice Panos, Medford

COCOA BROWNIES (LOW FAT, NO CHOLESTEROL)

½ cup boiling water
½ cup unsweetened cocoa
   powder
1½ cups sugar
⅓ cup corn oil

1 tsp. vanilla
4 egg whites (room temp.)
1¼ cups flour
1 tsp. baking powder
¼ tsp. salt

Preheat oven to 350°. Combine water and cocoa; mix with whisk until well blended and smooth. Add remaining ingredients; mix well. Pour in a 9x13 inch pan sprayed with cooking oil. Bake 25 minutes. Makes 32 bars.

Ruth Nelson, Detroit Lakes
Lillian Walske, Winona

FAT FREE CARROT MUFFINS

½ cup sugar
2¼ cups flour
1 tsp. cinnamon
1 tsp. salt
1 tsp. baking soda
½ tsp. baking powder
¼ tsp. ginger
3 med. carrots, finely shredded
   (1½ cups)

1 (8 oz.) container vanilla nonfat yogurt
½ cup thawed frozen non-fat
   no cholesterol egg substitute
½ cup unsweetened applesauce
½ cup dark raisins
⅓ cup brown sugar
1 tsp. vanilla
1 tsp. confectioner sugar

In medium bowl, combine first 7 ingredients. In a large bowl with wire whisk or fork, mix next 7 ingredients until well blended. With spoon, stir flour mixture into carrot mixture just until flour is moistened. Spoon batter into large muffin pans. Bake 30 minutes or until toothpick inserted in center comes out clean. Sprinkle with confectioners sugar.

Evelyn Brady, Medford

DIABETIC DESSERT

1 (20 oz.) can unsweetened
   pineapple with juice
1 sm. pkg. sugar free strawberry
   jello

½ cup cold water
1 (8 oz.) carton Cool Whip
1 baked Angel Food cake

Bring pineapple and juice to boil in saucepan. Dissolve jello in cold water, then add to pineapple. Let stand until firm. Stir in Cool Whip and mix with broken up cake. Store in a lightly sprayed 9x13 inch pan and refrigerate.

Lorraine Halbersma, Pipestone

NO FAT OR SUGAR CHEESECAKE

2 whole graham crackers, crushed
1 pkg. sugar free lemon gelatin
¼ cup boiling water
2 cups nonfat small curd cottage cheese
2 Tbsp. lemon juice
1 (8 oz.) carton lite frozen whipped topping

Sprinkle graham cracker crumbs in bottom of a 9x9 inch pan, sprayed with nonstick cooking spray. Dissolve gelatin in boiling water. Put 1 cup cottage cheese, lemon juice and dissolved gelatin in container of blender. Process on liquify until smooth; add remaining cottage cheese and process until smooth. Pour into large bowl and fold in whipped topping. Pour over crumbs and chill until firm, about 10 minutes. Cut into squares to serve. Garnish with a few graham cracker crumbs or lite cherry pie filling. Serves 9.

Dolores Goraczkowski, Fairmont

NO EGGS CHOCOLATE CAKE

3 cups flour
2 tsp. soda
½ tsp. salt
2 cups sugar
6 Tbsp. cocoa
¾ cups vegetable oil
3 Tbsp. vinegar
2 cups cold water

Mix all dry ingredients; make a well then add oil, vinegar and water and mix well. Bake at 350° in a 9x13 inch pan for 30 minutes.

Variation: Can use applesauce in place of cocoa and vanilla. Mix 2½ teaspoon allspice in flour mixture. Decrease water to 1 cup and stir in 1 cup unsweetened applesauce. For oatmeal molasses cake, omit cocoa and vanilla. Mix 1 cup quick cooking oats, ¾ cup raisins and 1½ teaspoons allspice to flour mixture. Mix 4 tablespoons dark molasses with the water.

Dolores Zammert, Euclid

ZERO CALORIE DRESSING

½ cup unsalted tomato juice
½ cup unsalted catsup
¼ tsp. vinegar
Dash of dry mustard
Dash of pepper
Dash of oregano
¹/₈ tsp. celery seed

Combine all ingredients in tightly covered jar. Shake well until mustard and oregano have dissolved. Refrigerate at least 4 hours before serving. Makes 1 cup.

Le Johnson, Owatonna

EGG SUBSTITUTE

6 egg whites
¼ cup nonfat dry milk
1 Tbsp. vegetable oil
2 drops yellow food coloring

Combine in mixing bowl; blend until smooth. Store up to 1 week in refrigerator. ¼ cup equals 1 egg.

Paulette Hanson, Red Lake Falls

491

GRANDMA'S CHICKEN SOUP (LOW SODIUM)

1 (2½ to 3 lb.) chicken, cut up
3 qts. water
1 Tbsp. margarine
Onion, as desired

1 med. carrot, halved
2 celery ribs, halved
8 to 10 peppercorns
Bouquet Garni (below)

In a large Dutch oven or stock pot, bring chicken and water to a boil. Simmer, covered, for 1 hour. Cool and remove chicken pieces and bones. Refrigerate stock until fat congeals on top. Skim fat and discard. Meanwhile, in small skillet, melt margarine; add onion, carrot and celery. Saute 5 to 10 minutes. Add vegetables, shredded chicken and dried bouquet to chicken stock. Heat thoroughly.

Bouquet Garni:

1 Tbsp. parsley flakes
¼ tsp. dried marjoram
¼ tsp. dried basil

¼ tsp. dried thyme
¼ tsp. tarragon
1 bay leaf

Agnes Kotewa, Fairmont

EASY TO BAKE FISH FILLETS

¾ cup chopped celery
6 Tbsp. chopped onion
4 Tbsp. chopped fresh parsley
¼ cup low sodium corn oil or
   melted margarine

1 lb. fish fillets
¹/₈ tsp. pepper
Paprika

Preheat oven to 450°. Mix celery, parsley and margarine. Place mixture on top of fillets in a shallow baking dish. Season with pepper and paprika. Cover and bake 20 minutes or until fish flakes easily with a fork. 1 serving exchange equals 3 meats, 1 fat. Recommended for diabetic-living heart.

Donna Bertrand, Wilmont

DIABETIC CAKE

2 cups raisins
2 cups water
1 cup unsweetened applesauce
2 eggs
2 Tbsp. liquid sweetener
¾ cup cooking oil

1 tsp. baking soda
2 cups flour
1¼ tsp. cinnamon
½ tsp. nutmeg
1 tsp. vanilla
½ tsp. salt

Cook raisins in the water; drain off remaining water. Add applesauce, eggs, sweetener and cooking oil; mix well. Blend in baking soda, flour, cinnamon, nutmeg, salt and vanilla; mix well. Bake in a 9x13 inch pan at 350° until toothpick inserted in center comes out clean.

Leona Holland, Owatonna

DIABETIC FRUIT BARS

1 cup chopped dates	1 cup flour
½ cup chopped prunes	1 tsp. soda
½ cup raisins	1 tsp. vanilla
1 cup water	½ cup walnuts
1 stick butter or margarine	¼ tsp. salt, optional
2 eggs	

Cook dates, prunes, raisins and water for 5 minutes. Add butter or margarine; let cool. Beat eggs and add to fruit. Mix in flour and soda. Add vanilla and nuts to cooled fruit mixture. Pour into a 9x13 inch greased pan. Bake at 350° for 25 minutes.

Variation: Evelyn divides recipe into greased mini-muffin pans using regular cupcake papers. Bake at 350° for 15 minutes.

Agnes Pfaffinger, Blue Earth
Dolores Fath, Wilmot
Evelyn A. Mees, Owatonna

FROZEN FRUIT CUP**

3 mashed bananas	1 (12 oz.) can frozen orange
1 (20 oz.) can crushed pineapple	juice
with juice	1 can diet 7-Up or Sprite

Mix all ingredients and divide into 5 or 6 ounce plastic cups. Freeze until firm. Garnish with fresh strawberries.

Virginia Maday, Fairmont

FRESH FRUIT SALAD

1 cup strawberries	¼ cup plain low fat yogurt
1 cup blueberries	¾ tsp. cornstarch
2 cups honeydew melon, cubed	½ tsp. cinnamon
¼ cup nonfat sour cream	½ tsp. vanilla

Mix fruits in large bowl. Combine rest of ingredients and pour over fruit mix.

Marilyn Benson, Adrian

LOWFAT GRANOLA

4 cups rolled oats	1 cup whole almonds
1 cup rolled rye	1 cup sunflower seeds
1 cup rolled barley	½ cup real maple syrup
½ cup Millet	

Mix all ingredients in a large pan. Roast at 300° for 1 hour, turning about every 10 minutes. Add ½ cups raisins after roasting.

Evelyn Rountree, International Falls

SPECIAL DIET

LOW CAL HOT DISH**

1 sm. head cabbage	1 can tomato soup
1 lb. hamburger	

Cook cut up cabbage; drain. Brown hamburger; put in strainer to drain grease. Pour boiling water over the meat to take out as much grease as possible. In a casserole, put cabbage first, then meat and then pour the tomato juice over. Bake at 350° for 30 minutes or can use your microwave. Reheats well.

Tess Korth, Wilmont

MOLASSES DROP COOKIES (DIABETIC)

¾ cup shortening or Wesson oil	1½ tsp. cinnamon
¾ cup molasses	½ tsp. soda
2 eggs	½ cup milk
2¼ cups sifted flour	½ cup seedless raisins
4 tsp. baking powder	½ cup chopped nuts
½ tsp. salt	

Slowly melt shortening or oil. Cool. Add molasses and eggs; beat well. Sift flour, baking powder, salt, cinnamon and soda. Add alternately with milk to first mixture. Add raisins and nuts. Drop by teaspoon on greased baking sheet. Bake at 425° for 8 to 10 minutes.

Evelyn A. Mees, Owatonna

OLD FASHION RAISIN BARS

1 cup raisins	1¾ cups flour
1 cup water	1 tsp. cinnamon
½ cup salad oil	½ tsp. allspice
1 egg	½ tsp. cloves
¼ tsp. salt	½ cup nuts
¼ tsp. soda	

Bring raisins and water to a boil in saucepan; set aside to cool. Mix remaining ingredients in order; fold in raisins. Bake in a 9x13 inch greased pan at 350° for 30 minutes. Cool and frost if desired.

Louise Kees, Red Lake Falls

RHUBARB DESSERT

7 cups cut rhubarb	½ pkg. strawberry jello
¼ to ⅓ cup sugar	½ stick margarine
½ pkg. cake mix	

Put rhubarb in a 9x13 inch pan; sprinkle with sugar. Mix the cake mix with the jello and sprinkle on top. Melt the margarine and pour over all. Bake at 350° for 40 minutes. Non fat frozen yogurt or Cool Whip may be used as a topping.

Myrna Murphy Ventrucci, Eveleth

CHOLESTEROL FREE OAT-CRUNCH COOKIES

1 cup packed brown sugar
½ cup light corn oil spread
(1 stick)
½ cup white sugar
¼ cup egg substitute
2 tsp. vanilla

1½ cups flour
1½ tsp. baking soda
¾ tsp. salt
2 cups oatmeal
½ cup crunchy nutlike cereal

Preheat oven to 350°. Beat brown sugar, margarine, white sugar, egg substitute and vanilla. Beat in flour, baking soda and salt. Stir in oats and cereal. Roll in balls. Place on greased cookie sheet. Bake 8 minutes. Store in airtight container. Makes 4 dozen cookies. 1 gram fat, 0 mg cholesterol.

Jan Nordin, Slayton

SUGARLESS APPLESAUCE COOKIES

1 tsp. soda
1 cup sugarless applesauce
1 cup chopped nuts
1 cup raisins or dates
2 cups plus 1 Tbsp. flour
½ tsp. salt

½ tsp. cinnamon
½ tsp. nutmeg
½ tsp. cloves
½ cup margarine
1 Tbsp. plus 1 tsp. artificial
sweetener

Mix all ingredients. Bake on greased cookie sheet at 350° for 15 minutes.

Marian Martin, Crookston

HEALTHY PANCAKES

1 cup flour
2 tsp. baking powder
2 egg whites

1 cup skim milk
1 Tbsp. margarine, melted

Mix dry ingredients into bowl. Beat egg whites; add milk. Pour egg-milk mixture into dry ingredients; mix well. Add melted margarine. Drop spoonfuls on a hot nonstick griddle. When pancakes are puffed and full of bubbles, turn and cook on other side.

Sugarless Pancake Syrup:

1 Tbsp. cornstarch
2 Tbsp. cold water
1 cup boiling water
2 tsp. margarine

¼ tsp. vanilla
¾ tsp. maple flavoring
Sugar substitute equal to
½ cup sugar

Blend cornstarch with cold water. Add boiling water and boil 5 minutes, stirring constantly until smooth. Remove from heat; add remaining ingredients. Store in refrigerator. Warm before serving. Serve with pancakes. Makes 7 large pancakes (93 calories each). Syrup has 3 calories per tablespoon.

Mary Ann Haines, Winona

OVEN FRIED POTATOES WITH OREGANO (LOW FAT)

3 med. baking potatoes	1 tsp. oregano
1 Tbsp. olive oil	2 Tbsp. cider vinegar
½ tsp. black pepper	

Preheat oven to 400°. Scrub potatoes and cut lengthwise into quarters. Place in bowl and cover with water. Let stand for 30 minutes; drain and pat dry. Place potatoes and oil in a bowl and toss to coat evenly. Place on baking sheet. Sprinkle with pepper and oregano. Bake 45 to 50 minutes or until tender. Remove from oven and sprinkle with vinegar. 88 calories per serving, 2 g fat.

Diane Sammon, Morristown

PUMPKIN MUFFINS

1 cup pumpkin	3½ Tbsp. sugar, optional
6 slices bread, cubed	1 tsp. vanilla
2 eggs	²/₃ cup dry milk
1½ tsp. cinnamon	½ cup raisins
½ tsp. baking soda	

Blend everything but the raisins using an electric mixer; add raisins. Pour into 12 sprayed muffin cups. Bake at 350° for 30 minutes. These are not high puffy muffins, they look like they have "fallen", but they are delicious. Makes 4 servings. Exchanges: 3 muffins equals 1 bread, 1 vegetable, ½ milk, ½ meat, 1 fruit.

Jule Erjavec, Eveleth

RASPBERRY STREUSEL MUFFINS

¼ cup plain nonfat yogurt	1 cup skim milk
1¹/₃ cups sugar	1½ tsp. vanilla
1 egg	1½ cups red raspberries
2¹/₃ cups flour	¼ cup sugar
1 Tbsp. plus 1 tsp. baking powder	2 tsp. cinnamon
½ tsp. salt	¼ cup flour
	1 Tbsp. margarine

Cream yogurt and 1¹/₃ cups sugar; beat at medium speed until light and fluffy. Add egg, beating well. Combine the flour, baking powder and salt. Add to creamed mixture alternately with milk; stir well after each addition. Stir in vanilla and fold in raspberries. Spoon batter into greased muffin pan, filling ²/₃ full. Combine remaining ingredients until crumbly. Sprinkle on top of muffin batter. Bake at 375° for 25 to 30 minutes or until golden brown. Remove from pans immediately; cool on wire rack. Makes 6 large muffins.

Lucretia Heer, Winona
District Deputy, 1990-1994

REESE'S PEANUT BUTTER PIE

8 graham cracker squares,
crushed
4 tsp. diet margarine, melted
2 cups skim milk
1 sm. box Jell-O sugar free
pudding (not instant)
6 Tbsp. peanut butter

Mix crumbs and margarine. Press into an 8 inch pie pan. Mix milk with pudding mix and cook; stir in peanut butter while HOT. Pour this into crumb crust. Chill at least 3 hours. Makes 4 servings. This is a very rich pie. Cut into 8 pieces. Exchanges: ¼ pie equals 1½ meats, 2½ fat, 1 bread, 1 milk.

Jule Erjavec, Eveleth

DIABETIC REFRIGERATOR CAKE

1 pkg. graham crackers,
crushed
1 stick margarine, melted
2 (3 oz.) boxes orange sugar
free jello
1 cup water
1 (20 oz.) can crushed pineapple, drained
2 cups lite whipped topping
1 can mandarin oranges, rinsed

Mix graham cracker crumbs and margarine; reserve about 1 cup. Pat remainder in a 9x13 inch pan. Mix gelatin with water and 1 cup pineapple juice; let set until syrupy. Beat gelatin until fluffy; fold in whipped topping. Add pineapple and oranges. Pour over crust; sprinkle with reserved crumbs. Chill and cut in squares to serve.

Dolores Goraczkowski, Fairmont

SUGAR-FREE PUMPKIN PIE

1½ cups pumpkin
¼ cup Sugar Twin
¾ tsp. ginger
1 tsp. cinnamon
½ tsp. nutmeg
½ tsp. salt
2 eggs
1 cup undiluted condensed milk

Mix all ingredients; pour into unbaked 8 inch pie shell. Bake at 375° for 45 minutes.

Alice Ditsch, International Falls

BAKED RHUBARB DESSERT

4 to 5 cups rhubarb
6 tsp. Sugar Twin (can use up to
9 tsp.)
¼ cup tapioca
1 sm. pkg. sugar free strawberry
jello
1½ cups boiling water

Put all ingredients in casserole; mix. Put casserole in pan of water and bake at 350° for 1 hour.

Evelyn A. Mees, Owatonna

RAISIN-DATE OATMEAL COOKIES

1/3 cup safflower oil	1/2 tsp. baking powder
2 egg whites	1 tsp. salt sense
1 cup brown sugar	1 tsp. cinnamon
1/2 cup skim milk	2 cups quick oatmeal
1 tsp. vanilla	1/2 cup raisins
1 cup flour	1/2 cup dates, cut up

Blend all ingredients in food processor, or you can mix or blend your usual way. Stir in the raisins and dates at the end. Bake at 375° for 12 minutes. Makes 3 dozen. Each cookie has 70 calories, trace of fat, 0 cholesterol. .

Florence Hamele, Waterville

SALT SUBSTITUTE

5 Tbsp. onion powder	1 tsp. thyme
1 Tbsp. garlic powder	1/2 tsp. white pepper
1 Tbsp. dry mustard	1/2 tsp. celery seed

Mix well. Store in shaker-type jar.

Helen Lynch, Plainview

SCALLOPED POTATOES

4 cups potatoes, peeled and thinly sliced	Salt and pepper to taste
	1 1/2 cups skim milk
3 Tbsp. flour	3 Tbsp. margarine
1 Tbsp. curry powder	1 Tbsp. chopped parsley,
1 onion, peeled and sliced thin	optional

In a lightly oiled casserole, place a layer of potatoes. Sprinkle with flour and curry powder, then place a layer of onions. Sprinkling each layer with flour and curry powder, alternate potatoes and onions until all are used. Season with salt and pepper. Heat the milk and margarine; pour over potatoes. Cover and bake at 350° for 1 hour. Remove cover and bake another 30 minutes to brown. Makes 6 servings, approximately 150 calories per serving.

Theresa Neigebauer, Waseca

DIET SOUP

1 head cabbage, cut up	1 lg. green pepper
1 whole stalk celery	Some tomatoes
6 onions	

Cut all above ingredients up in bite size pieces. Cook in large kettle of water. DO NOT add salt. Add **1 package onion soup mix**. You can eat as many bowls of this as you wish.

Barbara Tomassoni, Eveleth
District Deputy, 1994-present

SEAFOOD PASTA

1 cup medium white sauce	1 cup frozen peas
½ lb. spaghetti	¼ cup pimento
1 green pepper, diced	½ lb. farmer cheese, cubed
6 oz. crab or lobster	¼ cup onion, diced
8 oz. cooked shrimp	Salt and pepper to taste
1 cup sliced fresh mushrooms	

Make white sauce. Cook spaghetti; drain and rinse. Combine all ingredients, except white sauce. Turn into casserole and pour white sauce over mixture. Cover and bake at 350° for 30 minutes. Remove cover and bake an additional 15 minutes.

Note: I use the imitation crab or lobster. May also substitute macaroni for spaghetti. This is a low fat recipe.

Cathy Hackett, Morristown

LOW FAT-LOW SODIUM CASSEROLE SAUCE MIX

2 cups nonfat dry milk powder	2 Tbsp. dried onion flakes or
¾ cup cornstarch	1 tsp. onion powder
¼ cup unsalted instant chicken	1 tsp. dried basil
bouillon	1 tsp. dried thyme
	½ tsp. pepper

Blend all ingredients. When ready to use, combine $1/3$ cup mix with 1¼ cups water to equal 1 can soup.

Jane Brady, Medford

DIABETIC SPICE RAISIN COOKIES

1¼ cups water	1 tsp. vanilla
2 cups raisins	1 Tbsp. Sweet 10
$1/3$ cup margarine	1 tsp. soda
½ tsp. cinnamon	1 tsp. baking powder
2 eggs	2 cups flour

Boil water, raisins, margarine and cinnamon for 3 minutes; cool. Beat eggs well and add to raisin mixture; add vanilla and Sweet 10. Dissolve soda in ¼ cup hot water and pour into mixture. Blend baking powder in flour and stir until well mixed. Drop by teaspoon on ungreased cookie sheet; bake at 350° for 10 to 12 minutes. Makes approximately 3 dozen cookies.

Wanda Smith, Owatonna

SUGAR FREE STRAWBERRY PIE

1 baked 9 inch pie shell*
4 cups sliced strawberries
1 sm. box sugar free vanilla
  pudding (cooking kind)

1 sm. box sugar free strawberry
  jello
2½ cups cold water

*Or make graham cracker shell using 1¼ cups crushed graham crackers and 1⅓ cups soft margarine.

Bake shell; cool. Put sliced strawberries (washed and hulled) in pie shell. Make glaze of pudding, jello and cold water. Cook to a boil and cool. Pour cooled and slightly thickened glaze over all. Refrigerate until firm (set). Serve with whipped cream.

Rita Jacobs, Plainview

SUGARLESS COOKIES

1 cup raisins
½ cup dates, ground up
½ cup chopped apples
¾ cup nuts
1 cup water
½ cup Crisco

2 beaten eggs
3 tsp. Sweet 10
1 tsp. vanilla
1 tsp. soda
1 cup flour

Boil raisins, dates, apples, nuts and water for 3 minutes. Add Crisco to melt in fruit mixture. Add remaining ingredients; mix well. Bake at 350° for 10 to 12 minutes.

Armilla Tembruell, Owatonna

BEEF OR TURKEY TACOS (LOW CALORIE)

1 lb. lean ground beef or turkey
1 tsp. seasoning
10 taco shells
2 cups shredded lettuce

1 lg. tomato, diced
1 med. onion
Taco sauce

Brown meat in nonstick skillet or microwave. Place meat in paper towel-lined colander and press out remaining fat with back of spoon. Use plate underneath colander to catch fat. Place meat in bowl and add taco seasonings; mix well. Place taco shells in 250° oven for 5 minutes or microwave according to directions. Fill each heated shell with 2 tablespoons meat mixture. Top with shredded lettuce, diced tomato and onion. Serve immediately. Use taco sauce as desired. Makes 5 servings. 2 tacos equals 237 calories.

Mary Ann Haines, Winona

SPECIAL DIET

QUICK TURKEY ORIENTAL

1 lg. onion, thinly sliced	3 Tbsp. cornstarch
2 Tbsp. vegetable oil	1 tsp. salt
2 cups bias cut celery	1 cup cooked rice
1 cup frozen peas	½ cup sliced cooked turkey
1⅓ cups chicken broth (1 can)	Mushrooms, sliced

Saute onion in oil until crisp tender. Stir in celery; cook 1 minute. Stir in peas; cook 5 minutes. Combine broth, cornstarch and salt; cook over medium heat. Put rice in greased casserole; add cooked vegetables, turkey, and cover with sauce. Slice fresh mushrooms over the top of casserole. Bake at 350° for 30 minutes.

Pamela Kay, Medford
Go-Pher News Editor, 1992-present
State Publicity Chairperson, 1994-1995

HURRY UP VEGETABLE SALAD
(No fat, no cholesterol, low sodium)

⅔ cup sugar	1 med. onion, finely chopped
⅓ cup vinegar	1 (16 oz.) bag frozen mixed
2 tsp. flour	vegetables, thawed and
2 tsp. prepared mustard	drained
1 cup very finely chopped celery	

Combine sugar, vinegar, flour and mustard in small pan. Bring to a boil and boil for 1 minute; cool. Combine celery, onion, and drained vegetables in a 2 quart bowl. Pour sugar-vinegar mixture over vegetables. Chill several hours or overnight. Serve. Salad keeps well in refrigerator for 1 week.

Audrey Kellen, Adrian

WEIGHT WATCHERS SALAD

1 cup crushed pineapple	1 cup lowfat yogurt
1 sm. pkg. lowfat pistachio pudding	2⅓ cups lowfat cottage cheese
	½ cup Cool Whip

Combine all ingredients; mix well. Keep in refrigerator. Serves 8.

Leona Welsh, New Albin, IA

* * * * * * * *

He that loveth correction loveth knowledge;
but he that hateth reproof is foolish. Proverbs 12:1
Vernice Klug, Caledonia

SPECIAL DIET

INDEX

** *Identify quick and easy recipes*

CAKES, CANDIES & FROSTINGS

Cakes

505

DESSERTS, PIES & PASTRIES

Desserts

509

511

512

Sandwiches

SPECIAL DIET

Additional copies of POTLUCK are available from any local court member or can be ordered from:

POTLUCK
Box 161
Medford, Minnesota 55049

Please enclose a check or money order for $17.00 plus $3.00 for postage and handling, made payable to MN State CDA.

- -

Please send me _____ copies POTLUCK. My check/money order is enclosed for _____ , to cover the costs. Please ship to:

Name _____

Street _____

City _____ State _____ Zip _____

- -

Please send me _____ copies POTLUCK. My check/money order is enclosed for _____ , to cover the costs. Please ship to:

Name _____

Street _____

City _____ State _____ Zip _____

- -

Please send me _____ copies POTLUCK. My check/money order is enclosed for _____ , to cover the costs. Please ship to:

Name _____

Street _____

City _____ State _____ Zip _____

- -

Thank You

Crescent Publishing
Telephone (605) 594-3429 • Garretson, SD 57030

We will help your organization with a
Money Raising Project

This book has been printed by Crescent Publishing of Garretson, South Dakota. We specialize in printing cookbooks for all types of organizations, which enables these organizations to raise money for their worthwhile projects.

If your organization is interested in raising money, just fill out this form and mail it to us, and we'll be happy to send you information which gives you complete details about prices, covers, etc.

Send for free information today!

Crescent Publishing
508 Main Street, PO Box 160
Garretson, SD 57030

Please send free information on compiling a cookbook. The name of our organization is:

_____

_____

Please send information to:

Name _____

Address _____

City _____ State _____

Telephone _____ Zip _____

I understand that requesting this information
does not obligate me in any way.